JUAN FELIPE HERRERA

# JUAN FELIPE HERRERA

## MIGRANT, ACTIVIST, POET LAUREATE

Edited by
Francisco A. Lomelí and Osiris Aníbal Gómez

THE UNIVERSITY OF
ARIZONA PRESS
TUCSON

The University of Arizona Press
www.uapress.arizona.edu

We respectfully acknowledge the University of Arizona is on the land and territories of Indigenous peoples. Today, Arizona is home to twenty-two federally recognized tribes, with Tucson being home to the O'odham and the Yaqui. Committed to diversity and inclusion, the University strives to build sustainable relationships with sovereign Native Nations and Indigenous communities through education offerings, partnerships, and community service.

© 2023 by The Arizona Board of Regents
All rights reserved. Published 2023

ISBN-13: 978-0-8165-4975-7 (hardcover)
ISBN-13: 978-0-8165-4974-0 (paperback)
ISBN-13: 978-0-8165-4976-4 (ebook)

Cover design by Leigh McDonald
Cover photograph by Ted Catanzaro
Typeset by Sara Thaxton in 10/14 Warnock Pro with Iva WF and Good Headline Pro

Publication of this book is made possible in part by the proceeds of a permanent endowment created with the assistance of a Challenge Grant from the National Endowment for the Humanities, a federal agency.

Library of Congress Cataloging-in-Publication Data
Names: Lomelí, Francisco A., editor. | Gómez, Osiris Aníbal, editor.
Title: Juan Felipe Herrera : migrant, activist, poet laureate / edited by Francisco A. Lomelí and
    Osiris Aníbal Gómez.
Description: Tucson : University of Arizona Press, 2023. | Includes bibliographical references
    and index.
Identifiers: LCCN 2022051875 (print) | LCCN 2022051876 (ebook) | ISBN 9780816549757
    (hardcover) | ISBN 9780816549740 (paperback) | ISBN 9780816549764 (ebook)
Subjects: LCSH: Herrera, Juan Felipe—Criticism and interpretation. | American literature—
    Mexican American authors—History and criticsm.
Classification: LCC PS3558.E74 J83 2023 (print) | LCC PS3558.E74 (ebook) | DDC
    358.3568—dc24/eng/20221118
LC record available at https://lccn.loc.gov/2022051875
LC ebook record available at https://lccn.loc.gov/2022051876

Printed in the United States of America
♾ This paper meets the requirements of ANSI/NISO Z39.48-1992 (Permanence of Paper).

*In Memoriam*

*Rudolfo A. Anaya (1937–2020)*
*Gary D. Keller (1943–2020)*
*Rolando Hinojosa (1929–2022)*
*Cecile Pineda (1932–2022)*

# CONTENTS

*Acknowledgments*      *xi*

Introduction. Juan Felipe Herrera: A Maverick Alchemist
of Chicano Poetics      3
FRANCISCO A. LOMELÍ

## Part I. Critical Perspectives on Juan Felipe Herrera's Poetics

1. The Chicano Cultural Poetics of Juan Felipe Herrera:
   The Artist as Shaman and Showman      25
   RAFAEL PÉREZ-TORRES

2. "Tender Chaos": Hospitality in Juan Felipe Herrera's Poetics      46
   MARIA ANTÒNIA OLIVER-ROTGER

3. From Fowler to El Salvador: Juan Felipe Herrera's Global "We"      69
   MICHAEL DOWDY

4. "To Go into America as I Go into Myself": Chicana/o
   Indigeneity, the Indigenous Other, and the Ethnographic
   Gaze in Juan Felipe Herrera's *Mayan Drifter*      92
   MARZIA MILAZZO

5. Poetic Language, Indigenous Heritage, the Environmental
   Imaginary, and Social Justice in Juan Felipe Herrera's
   *Rebozos of Love / We Have Woven / Sudor de Pueblos /
   On Our Back*      117
   MARÍA HERRERA-SOBEK

6. Afterlives of Antropoesía: Juan Felipe Herrera and the
   Poetics of (Un)Documentation      136
   WHITNEY DEVOS

viii Contents

7. Juan Felipe Herrera's Voice in Spanish: Local and
Global Pan-Ethnic Relations and Resistance　　162
MANUEL DE JESÚS HERNÁNDEZ-G.

## Part II. On Camaraderie and Poetics: Other Authors Reflect on Juan Felipe Herrera's Impact on Chicano Literature

8. A Rascuache Prayer: Reflections on Juan Felipe Herrera,
My Homeboy Laureate　　187
LUIS ALBERTO URREA

9. Gravy Donuts, 24/7: A Personal Reading of Juan
Felipe Herrera　　195
TOM LUTZ

10. Weaving, Drifting, Assembling: Memoria(s) from
a Migrant's Notebook of Travel　　213
SANTIAGO VAQUERA-VÁSQUEZ

## Part III. The Child-Poet Within Me: Toward an Analysis of Juan Felipe Herrera's Children and Young Adult Literary Production

11. Juan Felipe Herrera's Illustrated Books for Young
Readers: Chicano Children's Literature con Cilantro　　241
MANUEL MARTÍN-RODRÍGUEZ

12. Girlhood and Writing as Sustenance in Juan Felipe Herrera's
*Cinnamon Girl: Letters Found Inside a Cereal Box*　　269
TREVOR BOFFONE AND CRISTINA HERRERA

13. Juan Felipe Herrera's Children's Picture Books: An
Affirmation of Chicano/a Identity through Visual
Literacy and Bilingualism　　289
MARINA BERNARDO-FLÓREZ AND
CARMEN GONZÁLEZ RAMOS

## Part IV. Mapping the Sojourn of a Maverick

14. The Poet, the Playwright, and the Citizen: An Interview
with U.S. Poet Laureate Juan Felipe Herrera　　319
FRANCISCO A. LOMELÍ AND OSIRIS ANÍBAL GÓMEZ

Contents    ix

15. Juan Felipe Herrera: Notes on the Formation of an Artist    363
    RENATO ROSALDO

16. Bibliography by and on Juan Felipe Herrera 2022    368
    DONALDO W. URIOSTE

    *Contributors*    *439*
    *Index*    *445*

# ACKNOWLEDGMENTS

The editors would like to express their heartfelt gratitude to the contributors whose ideas and research illuminate this long overdue critical volume. Their insightful and innovative perspectives give testimony to the wealth and uniqueness of Juan Felipe Herrera's vast oeuvre. We of course attempt here to provide a critical examination into the wide range of his production but, in the process, we cannot help to also present a homage to his exceptionality as a tireless innovator, experimentalist and unrepentant eclectic.

The book's visual component is also the result of a collective effort among artists, and family and friends of the author who generously shared with us intimate and public photographs that depict the trajectory and evolution of the maverick poet. We wish to express our sincerest appreciation for the subventions received from two key sources from the University of California at Santa Barbara to offset publication costs, including color prints, the title page and permissions: Professor Ben Olguín as holder of the Robert and Liisa Erickson Presidential Chair in English and Director of the Global Latinidades Project; and Professor Aída Hurtado as the Luis Leal Endowed Chair in Chicana/o Studies. In addition, we would like to recognize the Department of Special Collections at Stanford University Libraries for providing us documents that will see light for the first time, namely a corpus of visual, epistolary, and literary materials on and about Herrera. Then there are a number of people and entities worth noting for giving us permission to reproduce either photographs, illustrations, or documents: Nicholas Herrera, Sean Miller, Alma Herrera, Natasha Lomelí-Kauka and Jerren Kauka, the Smithsonian American Art Museum, Poetry Foundation, Lee & Low Publishers, Candlewick Press, Children's Book Press, and City Lights Books. Juan Felipe Herrera was also instrumental in lending us family photos and a personal drawing, while assisting us in obtaining certain permissions. We would like to express our sincere gratitude to the author himself for opening his mind, heart, and personal anecdotal archive to us during the extensive interview and the long process of logistics and organization surrounding the manuscript during the past two years. We also want to acknowledge Professor Donaldo W. Urioste for compiling and documenting the most complete bibliography on, about, and by Herrera, which was an extremely helpful tool for the editors as well as the contributors to better capture the breadth, genius, and richness of Herrera's prolific and multidisciplinary life and work. We sincerely appreciate the support we received from the editors and staff at the University of Arizona Press for their commitment and expertise to properly capture the magnanimous qualities of Herrera's writing career. Finally, we wish to thank our respective families who supported us unconditionally while we dealt with the many facets and components of our long-term project on Herrera: Sonia Zúñiga-Lomelí and three children (Natasha G. Lomelí-Kauka, Yazmín S. Lomelí-Gallup and Carlos F. Lomelí); and Lupita Gómez and two sons (Osiris and Octavio Gómez).

JUAN FELIPE HERRERA

"Brownie on a Brownie"—Self-portrait, B&W. 11th & "C" Street, San Diego, Calif. 1964 Courtesy of Juan Felipe Herrera.

# INTRODUCTION

# Juan Felipe Herrera

## A Maverick Alchemist of Chicano Poetics

FRANCISCO A. LOMELÍ

"Chile con karma served on a bed of race."

—*NOTEBOOKS OF A CHILE VERDE SMUGGLER*

"Think of the crossroads [Herrera] is suspended in: linguistically, Spanish and English. [. . .] His mind is constantly translating back and forth between two world languages and we are all the more enriched by his method of synthesis."

—VÍCTOR HERNÁNDEZ CRUZ, INTRODUCTION TO *FACEGAMES*

At the outset it might seem rather odd, or perhaps peculiar, to claim that this is the **first** critical collection on the Chicano poet and writer, Juan Felipe Herrera, especially in light of his long and illustrious career of half a century since 1971. One could easily expect and predict a bountiful surplus of analytical studies, only to find a relatively limited number of scattered approximations on his work that have oftentimes gone unnoticed. It is perhaps more surprising and shocking because, after all, we are dealing with the twenty-first U.S. poet laureate and not some obscure regional author who was a one-hit wonder. One would presumably assume the existence of a multitude of monographic studies or edited volumes on his writings beyond sporadic interviews or critical essays. In fact, one would anticipate finding a robust catalogue of dissertations and an endless list of analytical articles that closely examine or decode meanings in his literature. Truth be told, no booklength or critical collection has been produced, which makes his oeuvre that much more intriguing. The circumstance is so dramatic precisely because he has to his credit a vast and varied literary production that covers the gamut of poetic experimentations, thematic introspections, linguistic rendezvous, clever intertextualities, even fringe soirees of unconventional explorations, and many examples of genre intersectionality that either bridge or obliterate discursive borders. His writings seem to have no limits or boundaries, and often indulge in the quotidian as well as the larger overarching topics of his era at different periods of his personal biography. For certain, he is far from being one dimensional, but instead, quite the opposite: eclectic, broad in approaching his subjects, incessantly diverse, often transnational, of course unorthodox, and most of all, a distinctive maverick in terms of challenging, straddling, and fostering the widest-spanning aesthetics possible. Reading Herrera is an act of having to rearrange your perceptions about things, events, historical or intra-historical happenings, and people. He tends to lead the reader down the path of self-enlightenment regarding preconceived notions of place, history, society, and identity. He is the type of writer we all relish reading again as a pied piper of both the written and spoken word.

In approaching the multidimensional aspects of Juan Felipe Herrera, we have organized this collection into four distinct sections: (a) seven critical treatments on the author's poetics; (b) three interpretive personal readings of Herrera by other established authors; (c) three specialized treatments of his children's and young adult literature; (d) an extensive interview with the writer conducted by the coeditors Lomelí and Gómez; a detailed biography; plus, the most complete bibliography on his entire career, prepared by Donaldo Urioste.

Among the seven critical studies in the first section, Rafael Pérez-Torres offers a detailed account of the various components that comprise the author's poetics and inspiration in "The Chicano Poetics of Juan Felipe Herrera: The Artist as Shaman and Showman." In "'To Go into America as I Go into Myself': Chicana/o Indigenism, the Indigenous Other, and the Ethnographic Gaze in Juan Felipe Herrera's *Mayan Drifter*," Marzia Milazzo examines the writer's grappling with indigenism and its possible trappings by outsiders. Michael Dowdy concentrates on how the Chicano writer makes strategic transitions to encompass a "global we" in his essay "From Fowler to El Salvador: Juan Felipe Herrera's Global 'We.'" Maria Antònia Oliver-Rotger, on the other hand, looks at the concept of hospitality poetics in "'Tender Chaos': Hospitality in Juan Felipe Herrera's Poetics" as a viable method to explain fundamental features of some of his books. In addition, Whitney DeVos, in "Afterlives of Antropoesía: Juan Felipe Herrera and the Poetics of (un)Documentation," looks at the unique writing referred to as "antropoesía" (anthropoetry) which blurs the boundaries between anthropology and poetry plus other distinctions between photo-poems and documentation/undocumentation. María Herrera-Sobek focuses on the four key topics on Herrera's first book, which appears as "Poetic Language, Indigenous Heritage, the Environmental Imaginary, and Social Justice in Juan Felipe Herrera's *Rebozos of Love / We Have Woven / Sudor de Pueblos / On Our Back.*" Manuel de Jesús Hernández-G., in "Juan Felipe Herrera's Voice in Spanish: Local and Global Pan-Ethnic Relations," proposes a close reading of Herrera's works in Spanish to set forth the thesis that they portend to promote a unity of purpose and discursive ideology.

The second section encompasses personal readings, thoughts, explications, and musings by other well-recognized authors who either find inspiration, commonalities or affinities in Herrera's literature, thus presenting rare insights into the inner workings of his aesthetics. For example, in "A Rascuache Prayer: Reflections on Juan Felipe Herrera, My Homeboy Laureate," Luis Alberto Urrea explains how Herrera's poetics can be viewed from a particular point of view of the Chicano "rasquache" sensibility and its unique qualities.[1] Tom Lutz, in "Gravy Donuts, 24/7: A Personal Reading of Juan Felipe Herrera," delves into the origins of the Chicano author's writings. To close the second section, Santiago Vaquera-Vásquez, in "Weaving, Drifting, Assembling: Memoria(s) from a Migrant's Notebook of Travel," constructs a theoretical matrix to understand Herrera's writings as basic products of movement.

The third section entails a close examination into the value and configurations of Herrera's children's and young adult books. Manuel Martín-Rodríguez, for instance, provides the broad context of the major tenets of the subject in "Juan Felipe Herrera's Illustrated Books for Young Readers: Chicano Children's Literature con Cilantro." Trevor Boffone and Cristina Herrera concentrate on one of the author's iconic books of the genre in "Girlhood and Writing as Sustenance in Juan Felipe Herrera's *Cinnamon Girl: Letters Found Inside a Cereal Box.*" The third section is closed by Marina Bernardo Flórez and Carmen González Ramos who analyze and expound on "Juan Felipe Herrera's Children's Picture Books: An Affirmation of Chicano/a Identity Through Visual Literacy and Bilingualism." In addition to an extensive interview with the writer conducted by the coeditors Lomelí and Gómez, the fourth section includes an intimate biography of Juan Felipe

Herrera by the acclaimed writer and anthropologist Renato Rosaldo, a piece that, in many ways, supplements the various anecdotes and meditations explored by Luis Alberto Urrea, Tom Lutz, and Santiago Vaquera-Vásquez.

Herrera's trajectory reflects a long and arduous journey from ragtag poverty to the halls of academe, and from there to the corridors of elite cultural institutions via state, national, and other leading cultural-artistic entities that have bestowed him with numerous literary awards, distinctions, and recognitions. His background stems from starkly humble origins, following his migrant parents from the harvest of one crop after another throughout California in the San Joaquín Valley, the Salinas Valley, and Southern California. Born on December 27, 1948, in the small town of Fowler, California, the constantly moving and unsettled nature of their daily life clearly impacted and shaped young Juan Felipe. His social environment instilled in him an acute appreciation for basic, elementary, even underlying elements of his surroundings, both natural and socially constructed. Initially monolingual in Spanish in elementary school, he developed an ear for sounds, rhythms, tonalities, and modalities aside from the patterns of speech and filtered vocabulary. Therefore, his selection as U.S. Poet Laureate twice, from 2015 to 2016 and 2016 to 2017, catapulted him into an exclusive status by reaching the apex of the literary world, thus marking an unlikely pinnacle of achievement of grandiose proportions, certainly unprecedented for a Chicano writer. However, that is only the tip of the iceberg because, prior to this coveted national award, he had already cemented himself as an outstanding contributor to and innovative architect of Chicano poetry, mixed genres, and children's and young adult literatures. Besides, we must not forget that he had been also appointed California's poet laureate from 2012 to 2014 and served as a member of the prestigious Board of Chancellors in the Academy of American Poets. The list of prizes and accolades almost seems endless: recipient of PEN/Beyond Margins Award, winner of the National Book Critics Circle Award, the Ezra Jack Keats Award, two Latino Hall of Fame Poetry awards, the John Simon Guggenheim Memorial Foundation Poetry Fellowship, the American Book Award from the Before Columbus Foundation, America's Award for Children's and Young Adult's Literature, the Hungry Mind Award of Distinction, the Tomás Rivera Mexican American Children's Book Award, the reputable Ruth Lilly Award, and countless others. As a winner of over fifty awards, including numerous book awards, nominations, fellowships and honorable mentions, he has also been recognized with four honorary doctorate degrees. Quietly and unassumingly, he has amassed an unprecedented production of poetry, original essays, and other richly hybridized writings of mixed media, all contributing to a unique literary construction.

Herrera's humble upbringing is neither contrived nor should it be undervalued. Defining his very fabric and soul, it represents the bedrock of his background and his worldview and, much like his migrant background, it never leaves him because his material privileges were minimal, yet his willful perseverance as a polyglot word master is primarily self-made. From his journeys and meanderings, he has gathered experiences, traveled broadly, become a keen observer, given testimony, witnessed others' condition, pled for justice, denounced unfairness and disparities, and, above all, he has dedicated himself to lifting others by rendering them agency and representation. He indeed partakes in giving voice to the voiceless, and dignity to the unfortunate and downtrodden. He is in great part a people's poet who tries to mirror inequalities as systemic structures of domination that deserve closer examination and an unyielding scrutiny.

One must establish Herrera's origins as a person who developed great intimacy with both the written and spoken word. In large part, it was due to his parents, who constantly delighted him with stories about their Mexican past and their migrant meanderings in California. With a passion for oral tradition, his mother often recited poems, songs, and *corridos* (ballads) to young Juan Felipe along with legendary tales about Mexican folklore, history, and culture: "My imagination comes from my mother, Lucha's daily storytelling, ideas, proverbs, riddles and songs from the Mexican Revolution during the years [she] spent in an orphanage in Mexico City" (Lomelí & Gómez Interview, December 20, 2020). No doubt this sharpened his sense of expression as a medium of endless possibilities, influenced as well by Lucha's penchant for performance. His father died when he was in the tenth grade, but he nonetheless left an indelible mark on Juan Felipe as a keen observer of details in people and the migrant way of life. While riding along with his father in a 1940s Army truck, he acquired a sharp eye and a wide-lens view of his surroundings, including the ebb and flow of nature and characters within a Chicano *Grapes of Wrath*-like setting.

Herrera has come full circle more than once, often returning to his roots and origins, but more frequently reinventing himself, as is clearly evident in many of his books. In that regard, it is virtually impossible to pigeonhole him in terms of a single consistent theme or style (although he nearly exhausts the ruminations of anaphora and incantations),[2] for he stands out as essentially versatile, eclectic, and resourceful as a poet of multiple dimensions and talents.

His proclivity for exploring new topics through innovative modes of experimentation is infinite, much like a food connoisseur who relishes new tastes and flavors in order to create original dishes; sometimes, he even offers recipes. In fact, it is not by chance that he constantly refers to foods— especially herbs—in his writings and lectures; he sees poetry, and even prose, to possess innately sensorial qualities. In the poem "How to Make World Unity Salsa," he proposes a recipe for soul food in *Notebooks of a Chile Verde Smuggler* (Herrera 2002), and this is accentuated in the back cover: "Chile con karma served on a bed of race." For him, you should be able to taste, mix, touch, and smell literature because in his view, it should be palpable as an activity of all the senses (i.e. "Aztec sushi")—usually with hints of signifying more than just food. Cilantro is one of his favorite herbs for its aroma and its peculiar flavor that enhances the taste buds, while he also often refers to different kinds of chile, which tend to challenge sensorial limits or boundaries. In this way, Herrera challenges pure abstraction with materiality and materiality with accessible ingredients for signification.

The poet stands out as an extraordinary writer of multiple talents and susceptibilities. He can be lofty and pointed about subjects of global transcendence, but he can also comfortably manifest himself as down-to-earth. His personal background, as he tells it, is fundamentally diverse and varied, having been "a dishwasher, photographer, arts director, teatrista [theatre enthusiast], antropoetista ('anthropoet'), Aztec dancer, graphic artist, cartoonist, salsa sauce specialist, actor, video artist, and stand-up comedian" (*Notebooks of a Chile Verde Smuggler*, 191), in addition to being an unrepentant migrant or border crosser, a multimedia and plastic arts expert,[3] a director of the Centro Cultural de la Raza in San Diego, a coeditor of various journals (*Citybender, El Tecolote Literario, Metamorfosis*, and others), founder of Teatro Chichimeca and later El Teatro Tolteca, plus Teatro Zapata, a Free Tibet advocate, a teacher, a pundit of creative writing, an apprentice of poet Alurista and mystic-shaman anthropologist Carlos Castaneda, originally a faithful disciple and later a critic of cultural nationalism, a devotee of children's and young adult stories, a composer of undelivered letters to friends, a muralist, a script writer, an Indian rights activist (within the U.S. and Latin America), a barrio homie militant, a guru of Chicano vernacular, a polyglot of intra- and inter-cultural codes, a feminist, a gay rights supporter, a letter correspondent of unsettled sentiments, a chronicler and documentary buff of poor people's and (im)migrants' plight, a frequent Floricanto Festivals attendee, a cultural warrior, an intimate collaborator within the arts scene in the Mission District of San Francisco, an admirer of the Latino Culture Clash comedy troupe, a meticulous student of decolonialism and subaltern studies, firstly a pupil of Hare Krishna and neo-indigenism, an obsessive chronicler of the Chicano movement and movement itself, a memorialist of the horrors of war in Darfur and Senegal, a hesitant dabbler in theory, a yoga addict, an incense burner, a participant in poetry brigades and word troupes, a quixotic dreamer beyond pyramids who ponders the illimited boundaries of utopias, a fan of ethno-biographies and quasi-biographies, a speaker of border jive and Caló (Chicano slang), a founder of percussion and jazz ensembles, a part-time practitioner of Islamic Sufi mysticism and Zen Buddhism, a fanatic of human dignity, a voice against exploitation, marginalization, and disenfranchisement, and many other roles and achievements that speak to his diversity, multiplicity, and range.

As we can appreciate, Herrera also sallies into other worlds, namely Indigenous communities in Mexico, Central American backwoods, isolated African villages, Islamic cultures, border(ing) enclaves, and the vexing complexities and contradictions of modernity. Much of his verve is due to his street smarts and bohemian disposition along with his affinity for rasquache aesthetics, that is, a uniquely Chicano sensibility of practicing the arts via a resourcefulness that can shape minimally available humdrum material sources or even what might be considered "low class" and "bad taste" objects into legitimate works of art. According to Tomás Ybarra-Frausto, "to be rasquache is to posit a bawdy, spunky consciousness, to seek to subvert and turn ruling paradigms [of taste] upside down. It is a witty, irreverent and impertinent posture that recodes and moves outside the established boundaries" (155). "Rasquache, then, definitely encompasses a funky, underdog or outcast attitude towards those who deny their existence" (Lomelí 2004, 112). In other words, "rasquachismo is affirmation and a search for an alternative esthetics by making the most with the least" (Ybarra-Frausto and Mesa-Bains cited by Barnet-Sánchez, 2). Luis Alberto Urrea, in his essay in this collection, "A Rascuache Prayer: Reflections on Juan Felipe Herrera, My Homeboy Laureate," develops further this concept by delving into its many complexities as an attitude toward art production.

Herrera's artistic trajectory embodies a one-person vanguard in constant motion due to his engagement in most of the major literary movements of the twentieth and twenty-first centuries while embracing a nucleus of trends and tendencies along with his own particular style of mixing and blending what originated within a grassroots Chicano poetics that at times hinges between hallucinogenic and surreal techniques. This brings into the forefront his predisposition toward what might be termed a literary alchemy whereby he mixes and matches an array of styles and elements of signification—often creating neologisms in the process—or what Santiago Vaquera-Vásquez emphasizes as "assemblage" in his essay, "Weaving, Drifting, Assembling: Memoria(s) from a Migrant's Notebook of Travel." His originality and evolution showcase many moments in his work of extreme experimentations with language, form, discourse, storytelling, the use of polysemy and plurivalence as central components of wordplay, including poetic voices that exemplify people beyond his own personal experience, as in *Senegal Taxi* (2013), where he establishes a distance—as a kind of chronicler-witness—with a series of sketches of voices that unleash their existential predicaments in the midst of war and violence. If that were not enough, Herrera creates partial poetic portraits of people via "mud drawings" in the herein mentioned work, rendering the voices an earthy visual effect. Again, he generates hybrid depictions by crafting various mediums with poetic representations, demonstrating a clear knack for what Ana Castillo has called "genre jumping" or "genre leaping"[4]—which can be seen as a consolidation or amalgamation of modalities—sometimes shifting from one genre to another register in an instant: that is, he is constantly in a permanent flux of transitoriness. The result is a mélange or, perhaps more accurately, an alchemy of distinctive literary forms (poetry, prose, journalism, drama, essay, lyricism) mixed in with abstractions, manifestos, testimonies, comedy, irony, satire, parody, spoofs, jive, plus playful and mischievous portrayals. He possesses a flair for the understatement with a sharpened intellectual wit (e.g. "Because our organ donor got lost in a Bingo game" in *187 Reasons Mexicanos Can't Cross the Border: Undocuments, 1971–2007*, 30) in order to extract greater meaning, but he can also be contrastive ("infernodise" vs. "paradise" in *Notebooks of a Chile Verde Smuggler*, 44, and "anarchic spiders with bow ties and briefcases" in *Night Train to Tuxtla*, 144), subtle ("rock roses" and "barbed butterflies," *Notebooks of a Chile Verde Smuggler*, 75); or outright political ("spawn[ing] a new generation of 'melting pot' ventriloquists" in *Notebooks of a Chile Verde*

*Smuggler*, 105). In sum, he operates much like a literary synthesizer with an infinite range and breadth, offering insights into people's thought processes, the construction of word glyphs, and understanding otherness. His curiosity is so boundless that the reader can only ask: what's next? What new horizons can he embrace and create? What new forms and literary expressions will he metamorphose into? The possibilities seem infinite.

He is many things at once while defying any facile categorization, label, or tag: a social poet, a dedicated poetic calligrapher, a keen observer and analyst of (im)migration issues and the human condition, a canvas artist of ignored stories, a self-designated "Post-Chicano Beatnik" (*Notebooks of a Chile Verde Smuggler*, 128) or perhaps a "post-Beatnik Chicano," an understudy of hardcore barrio life (sometimes represented as barrio-centric) from Logan Heights in San Diego, sometimes a trickster, at times part-mystic, a performing artist, someone perfecting the Southwest shuffle, a musician, a Carlos Santana and Che Guevara wannabe with a bandanna, a meta-poet, a multimedia fanatic, consistently a maverick and nonconformist, an unabashed believer in quixotism, an itinerant peddler of new stylistic amalgamations, a commentator on racial relations and politics, an errant troubadour, a restless and tireless poetic voice, a minimalist who reminds us of larger struggles, a master of paradox, an architect of rapid-fire verses, an unrelenting and ingenious experimenter of alchemy beyond conventional confines and practices and boundaries of poetry (e.g., form, language, perspective, etc.), a conscience for the epic stories of untold chronicles, a common tourist of the incongruous donkeys painted as zebras (or fantasy zonkeys) on Calle Revolución in downtown Tijuana, a performer of orality, a gypsy in disguise, an expert of homages to departed dear friends or personalities who contributed quietly to the arts or social movements without fanfare, a diligent philosopher and provocateur of fairmindedness and justice, a nostalgia seeker intent on reviving the pachuco (a stylized Chicano youth from the 1930s and 1940s), a student of meditation, and, finally, a shaman and showman and "quicksilver poet," as Rafael Pérez-Torres points out in his essay in this volume, "The Chicano Cultural Poetics of Juan Felipe Herrera: The Artist as Shaman and Showman."

As a voracious reader and a world-class writer of thirty-four books, Herrera expresses the world he experiences through his own particular lens, as if it were a Rubik's cube to take apart and put together again. He stands out as a visionary of reason who readily confronts, dissects, and deconstructs ambiguities as well as contradictions, thus unfolding the inner mechanics of their unwieldy nature.

He opts to expose incongruities with the shared goal of extracting meaning while shedding light on subjects that are either thorny or too complicated to easily comprehend. In other words, he appears to relish placing himself within the hyphen or the liminal spaces that require decipherment, thus illustrating the infinite capabilities of language as an intermediary of meaning. He is a sophisticated presence in current American literature as he blazes new uncharted trails in poetics with cutting-edge treatment of subjects and topics. He has been an epicenter of productivity with an infinite capacity for innovation as well as a curious experimentalist with a boundless eye for creating constant and consistent permutations of newness. His writings are rooted in human experience as they move and meander through a variety of social contexts: beginning with indigenist explorations into identity, a definite affinity with migrant farmworkers and immigrants, social marginalization (either barrio minorities, Indigenous peoples or others who are left behind), and in particular, a focus on the phenomenon of different kinds of movement or being in motion (physical, as in marches; transnational, as in migrations; mental, as in transformations; psychological, as in acquiring a new conscience; experiential, as in pilgrimages; poetic, as in adjusting the word to new kinds of writings). With his travels to faraway destinations or local pubs, Herrera populates his pages with characters and subjects to showcase their dignity, humanity, and authenticity, capturing their soul in a special way. And, of course, he has become a leading voice in the development of relevant children's and young adult literature in order to highlight the universality of growing up in a pluralistic society.

Notwithstanding, Herrera knows full well that he does not stand alone as a writer, seeing himself more as a descendant or inheritor of an intellectual community that has taught, led, inspired, or influenced him, either directly or with artful subtlety. He is a limitless receptor of nuanced linguistic registers, a cunning analyst on the role of power and hegemony on disenfranchised peoples, a boundless sympathizer with the underdog, a sophisticated and skillful generator of new ideas and thoughts, but most of all, a creator of original poetic constructions that dazzle the reader with innovative approaches to time-worn concepts—almost always exceeding expectations in the use of genres. In many ways, he is a people's poet because he implants the immediate semantics with cognitive structures of meaning by invoking authors of great distinction, reverence, and respect. He admits being a composite of all who have left an indelible mark in his creative mind, echoing a long list of:

**Writers:** the lyrical existentialism of Pablo Neruda, the rural-themed rawness of Federico García Lorca, the neologisms and *creacionismo* of Vicente Huidobro, the flower and song aesthetics of Nahua poet Nezahualcóyotl, the economical and unpretentious style of ee cummings, the border consciousness of Gloria Anzaldúa, the Spanglish and play on words of Alurista and José Antonio Burciaga, the surrealism of Antonin Artaud, the free spirits of Jack Kerouac and Oscar Zeta Acosta, the anarchism of the Beat Generation, the anti-bourgeois and laconic existentialism of Jean-Paul Sartre and Albert Camus, the farmworker Teatro Campesino of Luis Valdez, the earthy populism of John Steinbeck;

**Philosophers:** the haiku master Matsuo Bashō, the back-to-basics lifestyle of the hippie cultural movement, the ecumenical teachings and sense of liberation of Dalai Lama, the ideological determination of Malcolm X;

**Labor Leaders:** the spiritualism and non-violence of César Chávez, the conviction and commitment to ecology and women of Dolores Huerta;

**Artists:** the cubism and longevity of Pablo Picasso, the iconic pictorial metaphors of Allen Ginsberg, the symbolic autobiography of Frida Kahlo, the artistic versatility and unique surrealism of Salvador Dalí, the definition and praxis of Mexican muralism of Diego Rivera, the Latino/a muralists of the Mission District in San Francisco;

**Performers and Actors:** the tawdry Chaplinesque humor of Cantinflas, the satire of the Latino performance troupe Culture Clash;

**Musicians:** the fusions and crossovers between American pop and Latin American tropical jazz such as Carlos Santana; and

**Family Members and Friends:** his parents Lucha and Felipe, Margarita Luna Robles, Francisco X. Alarcón, Víctor Hernández Cruz, Renato Rosaldo, Ernesto Padilla, and of course many others.

However, his salient hallmark and signature rest on his ability to blend, meld, re-signify and mix (even remix) languages and variant codes, literary forms and styles while revolutionizing content: rasquache and stylized discourse combine seamlessly into a coherent whole while breaking down walls of literary pedigrees. In other words, he makes literary alchemy work in creative ways, thanks in great part to his encoded Spanglish dexterity as a tool, a strategy, and an objective. He aspires to communicate pathos while interjecting awe in the reading experience, always reaching out to a complacent reader who might not acknowledge the pure transformative qualities of reading whilst indulging in the rich space of imagination. Herrera takes his alchemist strategies and techniques seriously: "A true Renaissance individual, [he] is the inimitable synthesizer, a factory of hybridity, and a maelstrom of nonconforming productiveness" (Lomelí 2008, xvi). He is indeed a prodigious presence in the field of Chicano/a literature, clearly displaying compound inspirations and goals

> [. . .] ranging from the highly philosophical to the rasquache political, from the irreverent to the socially engaged, or from the subliminal lyricist to the stubbornly quixotic. Essentially a fertile rhapsodist of passion and conviction, his works tend to be exercises in experimentation in form and nuance, that is, into stretching imagery and concepts, or minimalist minutiae, into free-flowing fragments that gain coherence through the magic of his poetry. (Lomelí 2008, xx)

Herrera's first book, *Rebozos of Love / We Have Woven / Sudor de Pueblos / On Our Back* (1974), written as a series of chants, emerged from within Chicano literary circles when cultural nationalism and Amerindian spirituality were much in vogue as a way of recovering either a lost or forgotten literary legacy, as well as a social identity. For this reason, he wrote it mainly in Spanish with some English words combined with Spanglish or code-switching and what María Herrera-Sobek calls in this volume, "linguistic agglutinations" with Nahuatl, bringing to mind again his alchemist hand. From here he did not produce his next book until 1983, titled *Exiles of Desire*, in which he continued the trend of composing in Spanish, except his subject matter deviated considerably, covering the sense of being exiled in the metropolis. It represents quite a departure by abandoning the utopic renderings of an idealized Indigenous world and thus facing the harsh realities of hardcore barrios and living with the challenges of being an ethnic minority. Here he experiments with transgeneric forms by mixing photography and poetry to provide insight into the Chicano Moratorium of 1970. Through the 1980s, Herrera initiates a spiraling series of highly innovative works that become intense experiments thematically and stylistically by using testimonies and haikus in such works as *A Night in Tunisia: Newtexts* (1985), *Facegames* (1987), *Zenjose: Scenarios* (1988) and this culminates in his tour de force collection *Akrílica* (1989), which epitomizes his venturing into decidedly formalized experimentations with the limits of what poetry can address and represent. Newness and originality become a driving obsession; by breaking new ground with every publication, Herrera expanded the contours of Chicano poetics, while influencing mainstream poetic tradition. Succinctly put, by the time Herrera became a leading Chicano poet of hybrid verses, he also gained notoriety and distinction as a bona fide American writer. He became a major figure due to his dexterity with craft, word games, including formal and semantical innovations. Every new text was a sensation filled with surprises, intrigue and novelty, essentially reinventing himself at every turn. As Víctor Hernández Cruz observes in his "Entroverción"[5]—in the place of a preface or forward—in *Facegames* (1987, ii), "Herrera is as close as we come to a total expression mechanism. His senses are not just multicultural; they are coming through a variety of artistic forms."

Perhaps his first major watershed work at this juncture is the bilingual collection titled *Akrílica* (1989), consisting of numerous expressionistic sketches and fanciful explorations in a wide variety of techniques, often resembling an art exhibit. His poetics, as discussed amply in various essays in this volume, explodes with relevance on the issues of the modern world: the crisis in Central America, genres as straightjackets, further fusion of the plastic arts (e.g., watercolors, acrylic paints) and writing and textures. As Ishmael Reed notes in the back cover in *Akrílica*, "He writes in the language of 21st century America," but this was barely 1989. There is something prophetic about that statement as he traversed into the twenty-first century as a Prometheus of neo-vanguard tendencies, using Chicano poetry for its hybridity and admixtures as a torch. He continued the insatiable trend to revolutionize the space between poetry and other genres and forms of art in such works as *Memoria(s) from an Exile's Notebook of the Future* (1993), *The Root of a Thousand Embraces: Dialogues* (1994) and *Night Train to Tuxtla* (1994). These are contemplative collections about distinct dilemmas and quandaries of existing in different parts of the globe: the second work delves into Frida Kahlo's psyche through one-way dialogues and the third presents symbolic— and sometimes noir—incursions into his personal history. The latter offers an emblematic quest into his past, or as he states in the introduction, "This is in a way, my own Southwest shuffle, a zoom-zoom train of travels into myself, my soul languages, and into the communities which I have visited" (*Night Train*, xiii). In addition, he closes out the twentieth century with a series of immediate literature, such as *187 Reasons Why Mexicanos Can't Cross the Border: An Emergency Poem* (1995), which spoofs the anti-immigrant sentiment in California that reached a climax with Proposition 187, a blatant attempt to curtail medical and educational services to immigrants. Here we find an engaged and passionate voice in the defense of basic human rights. He closed out the twentieth century with four distinctive works: *Love After the Riots* (1996), which structures each poem with a progressive timeline to indicate that it is time to act; *Border-Crosser with a Lamborghini Dream* (1999), which is at times a hilarious look at issues surrounding migration and resorts to a "punk half panther" voice to question twisted reason; *Lotería Cards and Fortune Poems: A Book of Lives* (1999), which represents an in-depth poetic reinterpretation of the popular Mexican game of *lotería*, a kind of cultural bingo with archetypical figures in play; and the multi-genre nonfiction work, *Mayan Drifter: Chicano Poet in the Lowlands of America* (1997), which encases a search into the Indigenous world and its nostalgic lure while also expressing a degree of disenchantment with the process.

Near the end of the twentieth century, an additional form of literary contribution emerged with Herrera's incursion into writing children's and young adult literature, such as *Calling the Doves/El canto de las palomas* (1995) and *CrashBoomLove: A Novel in Verse* (1999), respectively. Much of the subject matter surrounds growing up, gaining a sense of identity, belonging, and acculturating—themes Herrera knows intimately. With *Crash-BoomLove* and *Cinnamon Girl: Letters Found inside a Cereal Box* (2005)—both a certain form of anti-novels—he embarks on a blended mix of genres by writing a narrative in verse, thus expanding the possibilities for that kind of literary format. Quickly, he becomes a prominent fixture from this time forward with ten other works. Three chapters in this volume (Manuel Martín-Rodríguez, Trevor Boffone with Cristina Herrera, and Marina Bernardo Flórez with Carmen González Ramos) examine and analyze a wide assortment of topics related to this genre of literature that too often is relegated to a back seat. Herrera, in fact, considers that such a literary tradition is central and key to children's and young adults' formative years in terms of laying out a hopeful world view, thereby leading such readers to relate more readily to the experiences and images proffered by the author. He has continued to publish a sizeable roster of works in the twenty-first century in this area that have undeniably contributed to his diversification, expansion, and stature.

A series of milestones appeared between 2000 and 2010 that mark further turning points in Herrera's development and evolution. More than ever, craft takes center stage as he explores new subjects at the same time he also offers updated anthologies—including some remixes—such as *187 Reasons Mexicanos Can't Cross the Border: Undocuments, 1971–2007* (2007) and *Half the World in Light: New and Selected Poems* (2008). Both received rave reviews due to their overarching thematic topics inextricably tied to an aesthetics that shows maturity via successfully revitalized texts. Although most of the poems contained within the two collections are selections from past books, together they gain new significance because Herrera ultimately exhibits a career of prolific writings that otherwise might have been seen as isolated cases. These books, along with *Notebooks of a Chile Verde Smuggler* (2002), demonstrate incantatory qualities through the techniques of anaphora and other alliterations for which he is renowned. In the newer version of the satirical poem, "187 Reasons Mexicanos Can't Cross the Border," in 2007, he deletes the word "why" from the title of the first version in 1995. This emblematic poem is suggestive in so many ways: the 187 verses capture with incisively biting wit a mood of resignation and quiet protest that does not question "why" Mexicanos **can't** cross, but rather, the opposite; it outlines and underscores through a series of ingenious verses why they **do** and **can** cross. The poem is replete with understatement, sardonic commentaries, hyperbole, enjambment, subtle and cathartic tongue-in-cheek humor, philosophical riddles and syllogisms, and cleverly concocted and unforgettable images:

> Because someone made our IDs out of corn
> Because our border thirst is insatiable
>
> . . . . . . . . . . . . . . . . . . . . . .
> Because what will the Hispanik MBAs do
>
> . . . . . . . . . . . . . . . . . . . . . .
> Because the North is really South
>
> . . . . . . . . . . . . . . . . . .
> Because we are still running from the Migra [border agents]
>
> . . . . . . . . . . . . . . . . . . . . . . . . . . . .
> Because a Spy in Spanish sounds too much like "Es Pie" in English
>
> . . . . . . . . . . . . . . . . . . . . . . . . . . . . . . . . . .

Because 125 millions Mexicans can be wrong

. . . . . . . . . . . . . . . . . . . . . . . .

Because 125 million Mexicanos are potential Chicanos

. . . . . . . . . . . . . . . . . . . . . . . . . . . . .

Because 2000 miles of *maquiladoras* [assembly plants] want to promote us . . .

("187 Reasons Mexicans Can't Cross the Border," *187 Reasons*, 29–34)

After 2010 Herrera has continued with a body of new innovations in an attempt to create a new poetics, including *Senegal Taxi* (2013), which is locationally uncharacteristic but consistent with his capacity to capture people's lives with an inordinate sense of sympathy and compassion in the midst of poverty and genocide in Darfur. He deftly negotiates both sides of the conflict by allowing the overall climate of violence and danger to speak for itself. It could be argued that he becomes more confident, and even adamant, about what subjects he chooses instead of skirting difficult situations and circumstances. His commitment to the underprivileged never falls prey to dogmatism or facile discourse. After being appointed California Poet Laureate in 2012–2014, he gained a broader platform, and even more so when he was named the first Latino U.S. poet laureate twice between 2015 and 2017. His production during this period has been remarkable with *Notes on the Assemblage* (2015), *Jabberwalking* (2018), *Borderbus* (2019), *Every Day We Get More Illegal* (2020), and various works of children's and young adult literature. Such works deftly comment on what writing is (for example, "Let Me Tell You What a Poem Brings" in *Half of the World in Light: New and Selected Poems*), its nature, its point of inspiration, its effect, and its overall purpose. Herrera's sophisticated versifications show that he is a poet who slices through the muck of abstraction and mystification on how to write, such as in *Jabberwalking* (the term, referring more to multi-tasking, is based on Lewis Carroll's "jabberwocky"[6] which implies dexterity and mental agility in learning how to write while doing other activities).

In *Notes on the Assemblage, Borderbus,* and *Every Day We Get More Illegal*, Herrera delves with greater determination than ever into the subject of (im)migration and its widespread effects on vulnerable people, while also humanizing them. The sense of urgency becomes apparent during this period because of the many moving parts of the sensitive subject and how (im)migrants tend to be left behind, if not ignored altogether. The concept of "*lo transfronterizo*" (transborder movement) becomes a central issue here. When we asked Herrera why (im)migration had reemerged as a core issue for him after 2015 in his recent works *Borderbus* and *Every Day We Get More Illegal*, he bluntly provided the following answer:

> I have sharpened my view on subject matter—los migrantes, the ones that suffer. It is an increasing condition of violence. I have experimented with poetry, teatro and art for decades. I have changed the text into a more conversational and direct form and a first-person voice. In this way the reader inhabits the person, the people rarely seen face to face. To this day, migrants are the most brutalized, quietly, viciously. I must speak, I must write. Otherwise, I am merely a jester of terms and symbols. (See "The Poet, the Playwright, the Citizen: An Interview with Juan Felipe Herrera" in this volume by Francisco A. Lomelí and Osiris A. Gómez)

For example, in the first book of this grouping, *Notes on the Assemblage*, "assemblage" is synonymous with alchemy as a source of creation. The central thrust of the work denotes conditions of manual labor and violence, while providing artful insights into what it takes to write. The second book, *Borderbus*, in the form of a single poem and exquisitely designed by Felicia Rice, captures an encoded dialogue between two sisters who are being transported on a bus to a detention center. The third book, *Every Day We Get More Illegal*, stands out as a magnum opus for its pointed yet terse and subtle depictions of (im)migrants on a journey of continual shifts and dangers. The motifs of travel and economic refugees are couched in terms of the hushed voices of "seekers" and "wanderers" in constant movement, that is, as meandering souls, walking, limping, crisscrossing under the radar and in the dark, not here and not there, but mesmerized by their travel north:

> The marrow of the collection comes into full view into the title poem "Every Day We Get More Illegal" in which a chorus of people ('spirit exiles') emerges from the shadows to find work and a sense of self. The message is clear: such people struggle to defy illegality as a human condition, and despite their many efforts, illegality hangs over them like Damocles' sword. (Lomelí 2020)

Juan Felipe Herrera's long trajectory in Chicano poetics is well chronicled, given his vast body of work that exhibits a wide-ranging expression of styles, technical experimentations, incursions into linguistic cadences, a broad array of themes and colorful characters, and particularly his penchant for merging and mixing traditional genres with multimedia into new codes of meaning. His overall production reveals a tireless writer whose relentless originality is manifested at every twist and turn, constantly fusing his maverick spirit with an eye for alchemy with the objective of defying time-worn messages. That makes his literature seductive, innovative, ultra-modern, and rich with social commentary. His particular affection for promoting children's and young adult literature is clear evidence of his desire to expand his readership by making his works more experiential objects of accessibility and personal transformation. His uncanny compassion for the vulnerable and disenfranchised is legendary and together forms an epic of the conscience for modern times. Herrera's sensibilities and postmodern impulses are well couched within Chicano poetics, but they also transcend them in his incessant yearning to reinvent himself as the genius of hybridity and as a steadfast source of unbridled literary expression.

## Notes

1. Rasquache or rascuache—often pronounced "rasquachi or rascuachi" (or rasquachismo and rascuachismo)—are two variants in spelling of the same thing, except we generally use "rasquache" after the art critic Tomás Ybarra-Frausto popularized this spelling in his landmark study, "Rasquachismo: A Chicano Sensibility," in *CARA: Chicano Art: Resistance and Affirmation, 1965–1985*, eds. Richard Griswold del Castillo, Teresa McKenna, and Yolanda Yarbro-Bejarano, Wight Art Gallery, 155–162.
2. It is fascinating to note that Herrera indulges frequently in these two modalities in most of his books; more in some than others. However, the book that stands out for the brilliant use of the anaphora is *187 Reasons Mexicanos Can't Cross the Border: Undocuments, 1971–2007* (2007), especially the poems "187 Reasons Mexicanos Can't Cross the Border (Remix)" and "Don't Worry, Baby"; for the incantations, see the entire book by Herrera, *Rebozos of Love / We Have Woven / Sudor de Pueblos / On Our Back* (1974).
3. It is worth noting that Herrera runs what he calls a Laureate Lab Visual Wordist Studio at California State University at Fresno.
4. See "Ana Castillo: An Evening with the Writer. Public Talk at the University of California at Santa Barbara." May 6, 2004. Retrieved from https://www.ciis.edu /ciis-news-and-events/campus-calendar/evening-with-ana-castillo.
5. This is a fabricated word play that connotes the notion of connecting disparate things by suggesting "version" and "introducción" (or introduction).
6. See Lewis Carroll's book *Jabberwocky*, Solmentes Press, 2020.

# Works Cited

Barnet-Sánchez, Holly. "Tomás Ybarra-Frausto and Amalia Mesa-Bains: A Critical Discourse from Within." *Art Journal*, 64.4 (Winter 2005): 91–93. https://doi.org/10.2307/20068425.

Carroll, Lewis. *Jabberwocky*. Decora, Iowa: Solmentes Press, 2020.

Castillo, Ana. "Ana Castillo: An Evening with the Writer. Public Talk at the University of California at Santa Barbara." May 6, 2004. Retrieved from https://www.ciis.edu/ciis-news-and-events/campus-calendar/evening-with-ana-castillo.

Hernández Cruz, Víctor. "Entroverción." In *Facegames*, by Juan Felipe Herrera, i–ii. San Francisco, Calif.: As Is/So & So Press, 1987.

Herrera, Juan Felipe. *187 Reasons Why Mexicanos Can't Cross the Border: An Emergency Poem*. Fresno, Calif.: Borderwolf Press, 1995.

Herrera, Juan Felipe. *187 Reasons Mexicanos Can't Cross the Border: Undocuments, 1971–2007*. San Francisco, Calif.: City Lights, 2007.

Herrera, Juan Felipe. *Akrílica*. Santa Cruz, Calif.: Alcatraz Editions, 1989.

Herrera, Juan Felipe. *Borderbus*. Santa Cruz, Calif.: Moving Parts Press, 2019.

Herrera, Juan Felipe. *Border-Crosser with a Lamborghini Dream*. Tucson: University of Arizona Press, 1999.

Herrera, Juan Felipe. *Calling the Doves/El canto de las palomas*. San Francisco, Calif.: Children's Book Press, 1995.

Herrera, Juan Felipe. *CrashBoomLove: A Novel in Verse*. Albuquerque: University of New Mexico Press, 1999.

Herrera, Juan Felipe. *Every Day We Get More Illegal*. San Francisco, Calif.: City Lights, 2020.

Herrera, Juan Felipe. *Exiles of Desire*. Fresno, Calif.: Lalo Press Publications, 1983.

Herrera, Juan Felipe. *Half of the World in Light: New and Selected Poems*. Camino del Sol Series. Tucson: University of Arizona Press, 2008.

Herrera, Juan Felipe. *Jabberwalking*. Somerville, Mass.: Candlewick Press, 2018.

Herrera, Juan Felipe. *Lotería Cards and Fortune Poems: A Book of Lives*. San Francisco, Calif.: City Lights, 1999.

Herrera, Juan Felipe. *Love After the Riots*. Willimantic, Conn.: Curbstone Press, 1996.

Herrera, Juan Felipe. *Mayan Drifter: Chicano Poet in the Lowlands of America*. Philadelphia: Temple University Press, 1997.

Herrera, Juan Felipe. *Night Train to Tuxtla*. Camino del Sol Series. Tucson: University of Arizona Press, 1994.

Herrera, Juan Felipe. *Notebooks of a Chile Verde Smuggler*. Tucson: University of Arizona Press, 2002.

Herrera, Juan Felipe. *Notes on the Assemblage*. San Francisco, Calif.: City Lights, 2015.

Herrera, Juan Felipe. *Rebozos of Love / We Have Woven / Sudor de Pueblos / On Our Back*. San Diego: Toltecas en Aztlán, 1974.

Herrera, Juan Felipe. *Senegal Taxi*. Camino del Sol Series. Tucson: University of Arizona Press, 2013.

Lomelí, Francisco A. "Juan Felipe Herrera: A Poet in Movement." *Los Angeles Review of Books*, November 14, 2020. https://lareviewofbooks.org/article/juan-felipe-herrera-a-poet-in-movement.

Lomelí, Francisco A. "Juan Felipe Herrera: Trajectory and Metamorphosis of a Chicano Poet Laureate." In *Half of the World in Light: New and Selected Poems*, by Juan Felipe Herrera, xiv–xxiv. Tucson: University of Arizona Press, 2008.

Lomelí, Francisco A. "Origins and Evolution of Homies as Hip Rasquache Cultural Artifacts: Taking the Homies Out of the Barrio or the Barrio Out of the Homies." In *International Perspectives on Chicana/o Studies: "This World Is My Place,"* edited by Catherine Leen and Niamh Thornton, 109–128. New York: Routledge, Taylor, and Francis Group, 2004.

Lomelí, Francisco A. and Osiris Aníbal Gómez. "The Poet, the Playwright, and the Citizen: An Interview with US Poet Laureate Juan Felipe Herrera [December 20, 2020; August 8, 2021; December 20, 2021]." In *Juan Felipe Herrera: Migrant, Activist, Poet Laureate*, edited by Francisco A. Lomelí and Osiris Aníbal Gómez, 319–362. Tucson: University of Arizona Press, 2023.

Reed, Ishmael. "Blurb." In *Akrílica*, by Juan Felipe Herrera, n.p. Santa Cruz, Calif.: Alcatraz Editions, 1989.

Urrea, Luis Alberto. "A Rascuache Prayer: Reflections on Juan Felipe Herrera, My Homeboy Laureate." *Poetry Foundation*. September 14, 2020. https://www.poetryfoundation.org/articles/154196/a-rascuache-prayer.

Ybarra-Frausto, Tomás. "Rasquachismo: A Chicano Sensibility." In *CARA: Chicano Art: Resistance and Affirmation, 1965–1985*, edited by Richard Griswold del Castillo, Teresa McKenna, and Yolanda Yarbro-Bejarano, 155–162. Los Angeles: Wight Art Gallery, 1991.

# PART I

*Critical Perspectives on
Juan Felipe Herrera's Poetics*

## CHAPTER 1

# The Chicano Cultural Poetics of Juan Felipe Herrera

## The Artist as Shaman and Showman

RAFAEL PÉREZ-TORRES

> I write in my notebook with the intention of stimulating good conversation, hoping that will also be of use to some fellow traveler. But perhaps my notes are merely drunken chatter, the incoherent babbling of a dreamer. If so, read them as such.
>
> — MATSUO BASHŌ, *NARROW ROAD TO THE INTERIOR*

Juan Felipe Herrera spins out a whirlwind of creativity and expression. A writer with a voracious curiosity, an absurdist humor, and a showman's flare for style, he is also an artist who uses his craft to inspire deep human emotion as a pathway toward greater insight and understanding—what in some spiritual and philosophical contexts is called illumination. His poetry moves in multiple modes and directions. These movements may have contributed to a notable dearth of critical study addressing the critical and cultural significance of the broad aesthetic palette—incantatory, comical, improvisatory, anecdotal, hallucinatory, theatrical, minimalist, parodic, cosmic—that Herrera employs. His profusion of styles may confound critics who seek to capture the qualities of this quicksilver poet in a circumscribed way. Much of his work appears spontaneous or extemporized, and this may add to the difficulties in developing an effective critical approach to his work. A broader critical focus may afford a perspective on his poetry and how it often relies on affective responses in order to achieve both aesthetic surprise and pleasure—aspects of a showman's brio—and suggest a transformative moment that invites reflection on the spiritual dimensions of human impermanence—a shaman's transformative incantation.

His dynamic poetry restlessly seeks to delight and transport the reader as it generates a Chicano performative cultural poetics. Improvisational and even elusively experimental, Herrera's artistry comes into sharper focus if we consider how it generates a performative cultural poetics. This term is one Herrera employs to describe the work of Latina/o writers and thinkers who for decades have sought to shape new cultural formations. Their work draws from devalued bodies of knowledge to help generate a decolonial consciousness.[1] Herrera recognizes those artists and activists who through their artistry and performances have given us "long lost and abandoned ancestral concepts that we can envision and apply in one way or another, along with a Mexica performative cultural poetics that we have been attempting to build in the U.S.-Mexico borderlands since the indigenista cultural revolution of the first half of the twentieth century" ("Foreword to the New Edition," xiv). Herrera identifies (and identifies with) a Mexicano/Chicano/Latino cultural performativity as a component of decolonial cultural activism. It is this sense of transformative performance that informs and drives his own restless artistic creation, a creation that echoes and evokes and conjures other forms of knowledge.

The present discussion considers the double role of Herrera as a poet who is at once a showman, playing aesthetic sleights of hand, and a shaman, using language for spiritual and emotional transport and transformation. The poetry employs linguistic and poetic forms as part of a performance meant primarily to generate an awareness of shared human suffering and, consequently, connection. Poetry makes evident that this suffering often results from long colonial legacies and continuing inequities related to state power, patriarchy, and nationalism. As such, it demonstrates a decolonial impetus as it aspires—often employing experimental aesthetic forms—to enact a type of cultural, spiritual, and emotional shift. His vast, eclectic, and restless poetic output generates a performative cultural poetics premised on three central compositional elements: (1) acknowledging and honoring a sense of origin; (2) recognizing the social and even physical materiality of language; and (3) pursuing and encouraging a growth of consciousness. His poetic concerns thus resonate with a reclamation of suppressed knowledges and repressed languages (often associated with Maya, Mexican, Huichol, and other Mesoamerican Indigenous practices), experimentation with dialogue and dramatic reenactments (an association with his early involvement in theater) and invocation of language as a medium for incantatory powers. They serve together to generate an enveloping performativity. Throughout, Herrera serves as a kind of postmodern conjurer. The emphasis on play and performance, on the poet as protean creative force and sideshow entertainer, undergirds much of Herrera's poetry and asserts his commitment to a Chicano performative cultural poetics.

His poems at times suggest a literal script—indicating setting, actors, and audience—that draws the reader into becoming a creative participant in a poetic enactment generated through the language on the page.[2] The "Map of Figures" that precedes his poem "Giraffe on Fire"—a long listing of the poem's dramatis personae and settings—offers a good example of how his poetry stages itself theatrically. As his poetry crosses aesthetic and national and philosophical borders in a variety of ways, it performs a decolonial crossing of signification and positionality—an enactment of a performative cultural poetics—in order to resituate the role of reader in relation to the poem. The poet acts through language to create the poems and, simultaneously, to prompt his readers to conjure themselves into an awareness of greater social, ethical, and emotional interconnectedness.

## Content and Context

To concretize these observations, this discussion turns to the textual details drawn from a number of poems spanning two decades, most centrally from the 1999 co-produced book *Lotería Cards and Fortune Poems: A Book of Lives* as well as his 2020 collection *Every Day We Get More Illegal*. Before this turn to the textual, however, I would like to contextualize the formation of Herrera's poetic journey in order to consider somewhat the contours of his aesthetic vocabulary. His achievements and sense of care and compassion expressed so beautifully through words are remarkable, given his recollections of harsh punishments for speaking Spanish instead of English as a child at school. One might say that this pain of being silenced, ignored, or discounted motivated Herrera to speak in multiple registers. Language from the first has embodied a measure of social constraint for the poet. Recalling how his friend, novelist Arturo Islas, once noted in an interview that Chicano and Chicana writers have not been blacklisted, they have been entirely *unlisted*, Herrera writes:

This reminds me of my blurting out a question in Spanish in Escondido elementary school in the mid-fifties and being slapped and warned never to speak in Spanish again. I kept this to myself, didn't tell my parents about it; it went deep inside of me. Then little by little I pulled the words out of my mouth, I brought them back out into the open air, the way my parents sang stories out of their experience, the way my mother caressed poems in the air. ("Train Notes," in *Night Train to Tuxtla*, xiii).

The young poet keeps silent about this traumatic abuse over language, but over time he brings words back into being inspired by the example of his parents who sang stories and caressed poems from their own fleeting and painful experiences. Despite this memory, the school setting was not always one of pain.

Herrera has recalled on several occasions the time he was coaxed by his third-grade teacher, Mrs. Sampson, to stand up in front of the classroom and sing a song. To the surprise of the young boy, his teacher told him, "You have a beautiful voice." He has been using that voice to sing his songs ever since.[3] These experiences mark the manner that his words speak with both an unsettled rebellious spirit and a generous healing heart. The poet uses words to evoke and contest moments of persistent injustice, ignorance, and cruelty and, through their aesthetic rendering, make from them moments of transformative beauty and inspiration. These embryonic sparks have led to a burning creativity—chronicled in over forty books of poems, stories, essays, observations, and visual images—grounded in the poverty and repression of modern social reality and striving to achieve a sense of artistic flight.

The multiple facets of his artistic creativity—crafting not just poetry woven of words but of stories, visual art, *teatro*, mixed media performance, and music—have been noted by those critics seriously examining his work. Literary analyst Francisco Lomelí calls Herrera a most innovative alchemist of metaphoric language and compares his poetic style to the work of e e cummings, Francisco de Quevedo, José Antonio Burciaga, Ricardo Sánchez, and Gloria Anzaldúa to explain its aesthetic range from modernist minimalism to baroque excess (Lomelí 2008, xvi). The comparisons one could draw between the shape of Herrera's ever-shifting poetic style and other poets—as well as musicians, composers, visual and performance artists—would stretch beyond any anticipated national or historical cultural horizon. Because a poem may exhibit various styles and tones that can run in turn from the surreal to the satirical to the silly, poet Stephen Kessler finds his writings "charged with theatrical and athletic energies, with the excitement and extemporaneous performance, spontaneous intervention and rebellion, the claiming of physical and psychic territory, the thrill of discovering natural reserves of resilience and creativity—the resources to live, as Emerson called them—powers of insurgent improvisation" (Kessler 2007, 17). Kessler points to the theatricality and insurgency in his work, the radically creative act of self-formation and discovery the poem as performance engenders. In an online opinion piece, he notes of Herrera: "While he is clearly in the modernist tradition and experimental in his radical poetics—he has been called 'a rock 'n' roll surrealist'—he is also a people's poet, a populist, an entertainer and a joker. He is indeed a bard without borders" ("Opinion: America's New 'Bard Without Borders,'" *Santa Cruz Sentinel* [June 19, 2015], September 11, 2018). Kessler's observations underscore the kaleidoscopic influences that Lomelí's literary analysis likewise suggests: Herrera's poetics are protean, restless, and difficult to characterize compactly.

Their restlessness reflects something of the long artistic and intellectual path the poet has taken from Southern California cultural hipster to San Francisco tropicalist guerrilla poet to Iowa Writer's Workshop craftsman to UC professor-mentor-activist-enchanter to a very public stage as U.S. poet laureate. Herrera himself writes that he has been, "a dishwasher, photographer, arts director, teatrista, antropoetista, Aztec dancer, graphic artist, cartoonist, salsa sauce specialist, actor, video artist, and stand-up comedian" (2002, 191). The description suggests something of the restless, ever emerging, and transformative creativity that is a hallmark of his work. It draws from numerous inspirations and influences that flourish through his poetry: the spontaneity of improvisational jazz and performance art, the vibrant juxtaposition of modernist painting, the Beat poets speaking a jive street patois that ruminates on ultimate reality, the electric charge of wailing guitars played by Carlos Santana and Jimi Hendrix, and the introspective chant and whisper that invokes the spiritual practices of Islamic Sufi mysticism and Zen Buddhism. All these influences help generate the poetic smoke and mirrors of aesthetic enchantment as Herrera bends to the labor of changing minds, hearts, and spirits through his complex, experimental, decolonizing, multisensorial, poetic language. These influences forge three primary elements that guide Herrera's performative cultural poetics. The first element centers on a sense of origin, the memories of family and childhood that serve as a root source for his poetic quest. The second engages a fascination for the materiality of language as an object of experimentation, a material that can meld with other forms of visual expression like drawing, photography, and collage. And the third element concerns a growth of consciousness that results from his exploration and articulation of self-discovery as a Chicano artist in congruence with the large sociopolitical world of Latin America and, more broadly, the Global South.[4] These three elements undergird the various aesthetic forms and stylings upon which his performative cultural poetics relies. They lend a thematic and formal consistency to the social, cultural, political, historical, and aesthetic concerns evoked by his poetry.

## A Sense of Origins

Memories of Herrera's childhood and adolescence trace a strong motif through much of his work, memories that serve as a fountainhead of inspiration. These memories the poet particularly associates with his mother—who "managed to show me the magic of her inner words and worlds"—and his father—who "loved *cuentos* [stories]" and held "the quixotic belief that moving changed one's body cells and kept the world fresh" ("Train Notes," ix). These creative figures in the poet's life create a wellspring of imagination that allows for an entry into making worlds through words—the world-making power of storytelling—and entering the world through the bodily movement that is the inevitable condition of modernity. The movement of the body—as pilgrim or migrant or refugee—regenerates and makes anew the world. Herrera locates his source of inspiration in those who gave him the tools and voice to use his imagination not just to express but to find himself. Their example reveals to the poet, an "awareness of the golden smile that lives inside language" ("Train Notes," x), an awareness that Herrera spends his career attempting to make present for his readership.[5] The possibilities for language as revelation—a lesson learned from the example of his parents' own use of story and song—runs on a parallel track to a veneration for movement that he draws from his father.

Whether it be the transformative movement of dance, the ritualized movement of religious procession, or the disruptive movement of migration and exile, movement for the poet signals change. Even the titles he invents to name his books reflect a fascination with embodied movement: *Night Train to Tuxtla* (1994), *187 Reasons Mexicanos Can't Cross the Border* (1995/2007),

*Mayan Drifter* (1997), *Border-Crosser with a Lamborghini Dream* (1999), *Notebooks of a Chile Verde Smuggler* (2002), *Senegal Taxi* (2013), *Jabberwalking* (2018), and *Borderbus* (2019). While movement for Herrera can offer a potentially cleansing or purifying dimension, it exemplifies a transformative one whether one's movement is due to religious pilgrimage, forced migration, or restless curiosity. Just as with the peregrinations of his family when he was a child moving from work site to work site around the fields and cities of California, movement in his poetry suggests a sense of potential change and growth. Herrera learns from his parents the capacity for transformation and revelation made possible through story and travel.

Explicit in Herrera's later poetry is a focus on the experience of the migrant seeking entry into the United States through the U.S.-Mexico border as a political, social, and sometimes metaphysical journey. The notable collection *Lotería Cards and Fortune Poems* (1999)—explored more fully in a moment—includes a poem titled "El Mojado (The Wetback)." This poem explicitly evokes the undocumented transnational border-crosser as a figure of transformative movement. In the voice of the migrant without papers crossing from one nation to another, the poem notes the things the traveler knows: "The sour races, the time-quilted feet, / the horse-man with a badge on his nose" (92). This expressly material familiarity with the journey north manifests itself next into a reconfigured identity of a grafted geography: "Call them Matamoros—New York / Call them Agua Prieta—Seattle / Call them Tecate—West Liberty, Iowa / Call them Aguililla—San Quintín" (92). Their new names suture together cities and towns in Mexico and the United States. In the end, the poem concludes with a question voiced by the "wetback." It is worth noting that the Spanish language term "mojado" in quotidian use does not carry the pejorative power that "wetback" in American English conveys. This again indicates how Herrera's poetic use of language points to the social values implicated in linguistic expression. In the poem, the "mojado" counts shadows—suggesting perhaps the traveling souls who came before him that did not survive the crossing—and follows them: "They adjust their little mirrors, they guide me, / you want to run with me, esta noche [tonight]?" (92). Invoking perhaps a journey guided by illuminating spirits or shadows, the speaker turns quite literally to the reader and asks if they too will become a part of this nocturnal journey. The poem turns rhetorically from the poem to offer the transformative possibilities of travel as pilgrimage to the audience, breaking down the barrier between audience and performative language.

If the body in motion proves a fascination for Herrera that we may trace to the influence of his father, the constraints against that traveling body prove equally evident and formidable. This awareness of the power for change implicit in movement meets in his poetry moments of constraint, limitation, and closure that are often repressive and violent. The U.S.-Mexico border becomes one of many types of forced exclusions and containment. His bilingual, 2015 poem "Borderbus" (in *Notes on the Assemblage*, 59–63), as one example, focuses on the whispered conversation between two women whose bus is boarded by officials in California after the women have escaped brutality in Honduras and endured the forty-five-day trek to the United States border. Surrounded by anti-immigrant protestors clamoring that the bus be sent back to the border, surveilled by the guards who have boarded the bus, fearing to speak in Spanish with one another so as not to appear suspicious, one of the women reflects on the how her mother told her the most important things in life are freedom, kindness, and good actions towards others:

Freedom comes from deep inside
all the pain of the world lives there
the second we cleanse that pain from our guts

we shall be free and in that moment we have to

fill ourselves up with all the pain of all beings

to free them—all of them.

(Notes, 62–63)

Linking language to power, movement to constraint, freedom to empathy, the poem encapsulates the mechanisms of repression that the border both embodies and represents as a means and symbol of exclusion. These repressive mechanisms provoke the women in the poem to consider the nature of empathy and freedom and how a comprehension and sharing of suffering can be a path for a shared liberation. Characteristically, the appeal to relations between people represents a means to forge generative connections in the face of grinding repression.

Herrera returns to recognize many times over his family as a primary and foundational relationship in his life. Twenty years after the publication of *Lotería*, he dedicates his book, *Every Day We Get More Illegal* (2020), to

"Mama Lucha and Papa Felipe, pioneers, givers of life," a ritual recognition of their gifts. A less evident reference resides in the structure of the collection as a whole. In his review, "Juan Felipe Herrera: A Poet in Movement" (*L.A. Review of Books*, November 14, 2020), Francisco Lomelí takes note of its striking formal structure: "Organized into six sections, each titled 'Address Book for the Firefly on the Road North' and numbered 1–6, including a subsection called 'Interruptions' within section 2, and a final segment titled 'Come with Me,' the book offers a collection of 32 free-flowing fragments." The evocation of the address book as an organizing mechanism is a formal remnant from an earlier iteration of this collection, of which there were over thirty different versions over time. By the time the collection got published in this particular form, it had gone through not only multiple formations, but it was also subject to the editor at City Lights Books, Elaine Katzenberger, who sliced forty pages from the manuscript to create what Herrera calls its "tight, cohesive feeling" (Nilsen, *On The Seawall*, November 3, 2020). In a personal exchange, Herrera explains how one of the earlier versions of the collection—whose working title was for a time "America We Talk About It"—included several found objects (Pérez-Torres, telephone interview with Herrera, January 20, 2021). Among these objects were the contents of a little pocket address book that had belonged to his mother, and which served, he realized, more as a diary where she noted details of her daily life rather than as a directory. He developed a version of this poetic collection using passages from his mother's address book as a framing device for the poetry, but the experience proved too painful for him. The scaffolding of that earlier version did, nevertheless, provide the structure for the collection in its present form with entries framed by the address book for the firefly—that fragile but illuminating creature the poetry associates with the migrant traveler.

In the published collection, each entry of the poetic address book includes a thought or meditation presenting the path on the road north as a journey, as a migration, or as a pilgrimage. This evocation of a journey forms a major reference in the poetic structure, as Herrera had in mind the travels recounted by the 17th-century haiku master Bashō in *The Narrow Road to the Deep North*. The Japanese poet tells of his journey to the northerly interior seeking to renew his art. As he follows the trail, he meets with old friends and famously considers how "every day is a journey, and the journey itself is home" (37). As he undertakes his travels, Bashō recognizes the perils of his trip and how from one moment to the next one could simply freeze to death in the mountains and become nothing but exposed bone. This awareness of mortality at the center of a limited existence undergirds the Zen Buddhist vision evoked by Herrera's meditations in the address book. The first entry reads: "Your consciousness / is ever expanding / onto infinity" (Herrera, *Illegal*, 1). The second entry continues: "we are merely / seekers wanderers / moving alongside / the mountains" (11). And the third notes: "when we reach / the family shrine / made of twigs bitten cloth / shrubs & dirt // we bow" (17). These meditative passages echo the spiritual and physical journey undertaken by Bashō, here invoking both the physical danger and the spiritually inspirational dimensions of difficult journeys. The poem references the return to the family shrine, the location of origin, memory, and source of sustenance for Herrera's work. His poetry in multiple ways returns to home, which itself Herrera recognizes as the original wellspring for his journey through poetry and life.

## The Materiality of Language

The emphasis upon embodied movement through migration or pilgrimage leads to a second significant poetic element: a strong focus on the physicality and materiality of language. This element is often manifest through expressive poetic experimentation. Herrera considers the construction of his poetry when explaining the form of his poems in *Night Train to Tuxtla*:

> It is difficult to speak of my writing experiments since they are mostly unprocessed and in motion, still cooking. One of the directions in this collection is to allow flavors and textures to speak louder than words, to let the environment locate the senses; what is taking place, what is real; to play more with color, motion, taste buds, style, and the various contours of place, voice, landscape, and people; to let phrase, dialogue, language shards, storytelling take charge. In some cases to let the tables turn, just a bit. ("Train Notes," xi)

His turning of tables allows for the form and flavors of the poetic composition to come to the forefront, to stand in for thematic or symbolic development. The 2001 poem "Giraffe on Fire," as an example, opens by including the lines: "I live in a split sky. Yellowish without a sun, yet the sun / envelops the firmament. The bottom is blue, the convex with a woman at / the center. Mexico. Cortez. Malinche. East Los Angeles. San Francisco. El / Paso, yes, the gate of all Mexican dreams—the soft animal, jagged with / ragged dots behind its back that leads to a holy shrine" (50). His poetic experiments unleash multiple currents of linguistic motion and stylistic alchemical melding, the experiments drawing on multiple sensory stimulations that form the material shape of his serious aesthetic play.

The journey through language becomes an engagement with varying degrees of significance that suggest a profound questioning of contemporary social and political formations. In "The PEN Ten: An Interview with Juan Felipe Herrera," Herrera suggests that the relationship between protest and poetry—an ever-present tension between the artistic and political dimensions of *engagée* art—forms part and parcel of a singular impulse: "A poet is always protesting—with her previous conceptions of self, family, nature, forced identity, history, the social constructions of cultural value systems and language itself, time itself—she seeks an entire radical new galaxy" (Jenn Dees, *PEN America*, Sept. 24, 2020). The poet as wonderer and wanderer becomes the driving force where the very form of poetic expression embodies itself as a subject of inquiry. With his more aesthetically experimental poetry, Herrera explains, "I wanted to get in between the image and the projector; to eavesdrop on the past, present, and the future; to find a mirror written under language itself and float through the greenish underside of stanza, icon, syntax; to bend content against pleasure, history against desire, form against flow—to flow trackless" ("Train Notes," xi). Provocatively, the poet explains his aesthetic experimentation in highly physical and sensuous terms, bringing to the fore aesthetic language as itself materially pungent and verdant.

Herrera explores the relation of language and materiality quite provocatively in an explosion of joint creativity. Working collaboratively with the visual artist Artemio Rodríguez, the poet composed over a hundred brief individual poems. The 1999 collection *Lotería Cards and Fortune Poems: A Book of Lives* brings together Rodríguez's linoleum-cut images that reinterpret the symbols—the sun, the cactus, the arrow, the moon—drawn from *la lotería*, a popular Mexican game of chance—a kind of bingo—and Herrera's wildly creative poems that offer a seemingly extemporaneous interpretation, response, and recasting of Rodríguez's prints. The poems and prints face each other in the book, formally foregrounding the relationship between word and image. Since Rodríguez produced the prints first, as scholar and artist Rupert García notes in his introduction to the collection, "the artist's work of imagination and visual representation [conveyed through the materiality of the finished print] preceded and encouraged the ideas and words of the poet [. . . . T]hey have—for the moment and for our edification—allowed their respective experiences and visions to meet in the creation of what is indeed a singular union" (*Lotería*, x–xi). In a very real sense, the poet's words serve to rematerialize the visual artistic image that themselves are materialized on the printed paper. With every turn of the page, the reader is presented with another moment of aesthetic interpretation and reinterpretation. To illustrate: the poem and print titled "La Santa Niña" suggests the image of the Santo Niño de Atocha, in Mexican Catholicism a popular and widely venerated miraculous incarnation of the baby Jesus. Transposed by Rodríguez into a female figure, Herrera's poem uses the imperative voice to address the reader: "Go to her, / from the mercado, your knees dipped / in onion, in charcoal floors. Whisper the desires / the cures, the forgotten knots wrapped secretly / inside your boots" (*Lotería*, 24). The direct address serves to foreground the social function of language: the reader is ordered to obey the commands of the poet's language. By foregrounding this social aspect of language—the imperative voice that commands action—the poetry reveals a connection between language and power, language as a tool of social action, language as a force that is material in and through its social function.

The language and poetry as a social function is suggested by the evocation of the *la lotería* game all together, which is culturally and socially significant. García notes in his introduction that the game in its present form is based on the ancient Indigenous game *patolli*, played in Mexico in the pre-colonial era, and the colonial Spanish game *la lotería* brought to Mexico in the eighteenth century and played still—by Mexicans and people of Mexican descent alike—today. The game thus invokes multiple traditions and nodes of cultural identification, a touchstone of recognition for *Mexicanos* and Chicanos alike. Both artists generate art that weds political and social engagements with a deeply resonant sense of historical and cultural context. Both artists draw aesthetic material from the tortured legacies of Spanish (and then later U.S.) invasion, conquest, and colonization. This is one reason the *Lotería* collection is significant: it playfully links aesthetic performance with its historical source. In a rendering titled "El Aguila," Rodríguez employs Aztec visual imagery to offer an interpretation of the Mexican foundation story of the eagle and the serpent in a battle to the death entwined on a nopal cactus. The print, a stylized version of the image that adorns the center of the Mexican national flag, evokes a sense of deep historical time in its pre-European visual references to Lake Texcoco, the Aztec citizenry at the margin of the print, and the serpent pictured as a version of the Aztec god Quetzalcóatl. The images provide the poet the opportunity to declaim: "Come all ye warriors, all ye poets of El Norte" (*Lotería*, 200). Using an antiquated form of address that stylizes the opening line ("Come all ye warriors"), the imperative voice, which appears repeatedly in these poems, once again foregrounds language as a social tool, as a force that functions in the world beyond language. In this poem, the command is followed by a series of questions that suggest the *longue durée* behind this creation ("Will you trek for three hundred years, follow / your war gods," *Lotería*, 200) and conclude by foregrounding again the idea of transformation ("will you be the eagle, the cacti or the hiss?," *Lotería*, 200). This last question forms a kind of challenge to "all ye poets of El Norte," a reference to the Chicano and Chicana poets who form Herrera's compatriots and among whom he numbers. The poem seeks to enmesh the nationalistic imagery with a sense of deep historical time and the sustained connection between pre-European Indigenous culture and mythology and the politically and socially conscious artistry developed by the "poets of El Norte."

While language helps materialize the long and pained history of the Americas, Herrera also expresses the materiality of poetic language in terms of food and pleasure. The back cover description of his collection *Notebooks of a Chile Verde Smuggler* calls it "a crucible of flavorful language meant to be rolled lazily on the mind's tongue—and then swallowed whole to let its hot and savory sweetness fill your soul." This delightful materialization of language as nutritious and pleasurable codifies the power of linguistic artistry. Herrera explains that experimentation in poetic form is but one way to reach a reader: "We can understand poetry in a billion styles: experiment, tradition, combination, spice, meter, image. It's all there for the poet and for the listener and for all of us. That's what it's all about" (Brown, "Juan Felipe Herrera's Winding Path to Poetry," *PBS News Hour*, June 10, 2015). The enumeration of objects casts his artistry as an experimental combination of various "things" meant to generate a connection to the reader or audience. *Senegal Taxi* (Herrera, 2013) stands as a good case. This collection, addressing the war in Darfur between militia and government-backed forces, is composed largely of a numbered series of what the poet calls "Mud Drawings." *Senegal Taxi* is notable for a number of reasons—its focus on the violent struggles in an international context, its use of a mundane taxi as a line of flight that represents escape from repression, the staging of various voices, including that of a Kalashnikov AK-47, who become the players in this aesthetic performance. The poems as mud drawings connect viscerally to the materiality of the earth (from which the struggle in Darfur springs, over which the military and rebels battle, into which the slain combatants and victims are lain) yet foreground the aesthetic transformation of this material into drawings. This rendering through words suggests the act of representation in the very moment of aesthetic engagement. The poems at once evince a material connection to the physical universe and foreground the manner in which they are illusion, artifice, a reference to something else absent.

## Growth of Consciousness

The physical presence of artistic words generates an impact in the world, underscoring a sense of connection and movement that the poet assumes when taking on the role of bard. Using aestheticized language as a tool for change, Herrera draws on his experiences as an engaged artist, activist, and community member in developing a third critical element in his artistic work: the quest, through artistry, to change perception, to alter consciousness. In particular, he often locates his poetry at the nexus of a Chicano artistry engaged deeply with the greater cultural, social, and political worlds of Mexico, Latin America, and the Global South. The Chicano movement and its inspirations fired the imagination of the young Herrera and formed a basis for the political and aesthetic awareness he developed as a young man. After moving to the Bay Area in the 1970's to attend a master's program at Stanford University, he entered what literary critic Tony Ruiz terms a tropicalist period when the poet lived and worked amid the creative and political fervor centered in the Mission district that drew energies from the fiery wellspring of revolutionary and counter-revolutionary thought and action in Central and Latin America. The lasting influence of his experiences amid these revolutionary spirits developed into what Herrera calls one of his "key concerns as a writer: to unearth the stories about the Chicano and Latin American experience" ("Train Notes," xii). The melding of art to express a position about the deployment and abuse of power—particularly authoritarian forms of state power—flowed out of Herrera's aesthetic and political engagements with the Chicano movement and flourished amid the broader internationalist perspectives brought by political and economic exiles to the streets of south San Francisco. This experience gave the poet profound insight into the lives of people subject to unjust and abusive forms of power, helping to deepen the empathetic and emotional reach of his poetics.

He is drawn to the allure of hybrid collectivity implicit in the conjoining of the Chicano movement as a sociopolitical project and the internationalist dynamics of the Mission community generated by lives in exile. Writing about this period in Herrera's career, Tony Ruiz in "Juan Felipe Herrera: 'Visión Tropical' in San Francisco's Mission District" notes that, because they were historically excluded from the formation of a hegemonic American cultural aesthetic,

> Chicano/a artists during the 1960s confronted exclusionary practices with collective or community-based practices. Herrera was part of a second wave of these writers and artists, and he joined those who turned away from the vehement political stance of earlier movement literature. More specifically, whereas much Chicano/a literature of 1980s continued to affirm cultural origins—often through the autobiography of self and location—Herrera's poetry departed from these rhetorical aims in order to explore new mappings of a broader Latino experience, especially in terms of evolving social and cultural perspectives in California. (129)

Ever curious and by intention driven toward expansive and transformative perspectives, Herrera incorporated the energies of an emergent tropicalist aesthetic with the sociopolitical arts activism of the Chicano movement. In particular, the dedication to social, political, and aesthetic experimentations of the Pocho-Ché Collective drew his attention. In a highly informative memoir piece, "Riffs on Mission District *Raza* Writers," Herrera describes the impetus behind the collective: "They wanted to fuse two disparate realms of political and cultural turmoil and potential collective power: Latin America and the Chicano territories of the United States and Mexico" (217). He goes on to explain that "pocho" is a pejorative term signifying the half-breed Chicano caught in a fractured identity and Ché represents the revolutionary possibility of Latin America itself, evoking the thinker provocateur who died trying to export the Cuban Revolution to other countries, Ché Guevara. The Pocho-Ché collective manifested the artistic and activist spirit of the Mission District, a close-knit, working-class community cut by international liberation politics. The writers of the collective thought of their audience as being from the Third World, the Global South. They thus coupled the revolutionary spirit of the Chicano movement—with its emphasis on nationalism and strong identification with Indigenous fetishism—and the decolonial energies of Third World revolution. The group eventually expanded to incorporate Latina and Latino and other Bay Area writers, critics, and scholars, from Fernando Alegría and José Antonio Burciaga to Ntozake Shange and Jessica Hagedorn. This transnational and collective sensibility inspired by a tropicalist revolutionary fervor spurred the establishment of the Mission Cultural Center in 1977, a Latino arts center that Herrera helped to establish and that continues to be a dynamic center of local culture.

Herrera was one of a growing number of artists and activists responding to the expansionist military policies that characterized a growing and repressive neoconservatism in the U.S. as the 1970s turned into the Reagan era. The struggles for civil rights and social justice articulated through the Chicano movement melded with an increased global awareness of repression at home and abroad under the Reagan administration. In response, Herrera sought to bring together the green tropicalist character of the Bay Area cultural movement with what he calls, "the new hot language of a primordial Aztec Amerindia: the Red Nation" that reinterpreted "the Aztec sunstone as a cultural and historical wheel of social change, prophecy, and as a literary epicenter that could still be applied symbolically to our current social conditions" ("Riffs," 220–221). The urgency of his political energies, grounded in deep historical cultural connection, found resonance and amplification in this fluidly international environment affected by the militaristic and repressive foreign policies of a rising U.S. conservatism.

The experience clearly marks the poet's sense of development, providing a model for embracing and braiding a radical political and poetic project. A rich sense of being between influences engenders a reflection on the function of the artist that, for Herrera, is as creator-destroyer. The artist undoes a sense of mechanistic time in order to assemble some new possibility, a new montage of potentiality. This creative/destructive role of the poet informs Herrera's understanding of his poetic project. Hererra closes his meditation on the Mission District by addressing a letter to his friend, poet Víctor Martínez, considering what motivated the Mission artists:

> Maybe we wanted to simply acknowledge and conjure a crazy realignment with peoples and places cast out into a fabricated arena of temporal loss and jinxed distances, maybe we are at heart time killers, we want an exploded time, of things, ideas and knowledge that we can feel at our side, inside of us, a complex chrono-fission, as though refracted in our mother's tiny liv-

ing rooms, our ringed hands, in thunderous accelerations, potholes, street signs, *ranchero* hats, Frida Rigoberta fists, tawdry publications and voices in Maya, rendings, *rendijas* [openings], all sewn together, really, at random. We are rebel marauder Tiempo [Time] Pilots pillaging the day-to-day linear progression of Western time, of linear history that desires nothing more than to leave us all behind, accompanied only by its own guilt-processing time-keeping units strapped to our 'Modern' psyche [. . . .] How can our writing unlock time, snap us all into a plenum of actual realities? ("Riffs," 228).

The passage envisions the artists as time killers, a punning image evoking art as a leisurely pastime that kills time and also a means to destroy the mechanistic implementation of time that is the beating heart of standardization in modern mechanized society. Herrera crystalizes—through a fantastic confabulation of images ("potholes, street signs, *ranchero* hats, Frida Rigoberta fists, tawdry publications and voices in Maya, rendings, *rendijas*, all sewn together, really, at random")—his artistic quest for change through aesthetic experience, a transformation of self and other to perceive beyond the cruel constraints: of time that is lost, of place that keeps loved ones distant. In place of this constricting reality, the poet imagines and offers a "complex chrono-fission" that the artist as "time killer" can enact, exploding time to free ideas and things and knowledge so they can be more intimately at one's side, inside one. The linear progression of Western time that is a driving component of the modern world becomes the object of pillage for Chicano artists who become marauding rebel "time pilots." They swoop and steal from the dusty museums guarding the cultural treasures of Western Civilization, then buzz the streets of Mexico City to reclaim imagery and idols of the Aztecs and the Maya villages of the Lacandón for stories of massacres and nobility, climbing back through to the dives and beat bars of North Beach to sweep up some be-bop jazz and poetry and hipster rock 'n' roll sensibilities to add to the aesthetic mix. The writer acts as a marauder, stealing from the histories and mechanisms of Western civilization as well as the civilizations and cultures of people, places, and communities left shattered in the wake of a brutal and relentless global capitalist expansion.

## The World in Grain of Sand

By weaving worlds through revelatory words, Herrera's poetry—in the face of broad brutality and repression—seeks to disrupt the logic of control and consumption enacted through the forms of power that organize the modern age: exploitation and repression. A time pilot flying imaginatively through the shopworn objects of history and culture: this is Juan Felipe Herrera, the poet scouring the weary world to gather his material. His journey begins out of silence, out of the demand that he not speak in particular ways. Yet the poet finds in the loving furrow of his family the enchantment and power of language to reveal beauty and to change the heart. The use of language in new and creative ways offers to the poet a means to move beyond the word written on the page and explore how language can be made material in the world. The embodiment of language forms one drive behind the performative cultural poetics developed in his work: the use of language to affirm and enact social change. The effect, finally, is to generate change in the consciousness of the auditor and reader, to bring forward a new awareness and consequently a renewed engagement with the wonder and suffering present in the world beyond the page.

Herrera's artistry creates for his audience a showman's performance that suggests the wonderous illusion of enchantment and transformation. His is a staged show that invites the reader on a journey that may turn into a migration, into an exile, into a pilgrimage, or into a shamanistic journey. His poetry—as well as the broad array of his artistic expression and performance—generates an experience conveyed through that encumbered means of language. The performative cultural poetics he invokes develops out of an expanded awareness of suffering and survival as a result of his journey as a Chicano poet through the world. This awareness—along with his sense of language as material form and as sustenance, and the loving recollections of his family origins—form the thematic and formal elements constitutive of his particular poetics. With his poetry, Herrera provides us an unfolding and evolving series of alchemical performances that seek to make present for his auditors and readers an expanded reality—the plentitude, the potential connection that love engenders, the power of plain but never ordinary people—that modern forms of linear thought ignore.

# Notes

1.  Since the 1990s, the literary critic Stephen Greenblatt has used the term "cultural poetics" in place of "new historicism" to describe his methodology (see Brannigan, "Cultural Poetics: After the New Historicism?," in *New Historicism and Cultural Materialism*, 83–93.) Its usage in the present context is quite

distinct. Herrera views performative cultural poetics as a cultural reclamation of pre-European Indigenous art and thought as a decolonial practice. He recognizes the efforts by many pioneering figures who have struggled to recuperate Nahuatl thought and culture: scholar Angel María Garibay-Kintana, painter Frida Kahlo, professor Miguel León-Portilla, poet Alurista, maestro Andrés Segura, writer Ysidro Macías, activist Tupak Enrique, dancer Florencio Yescas, teacher Renato Rosaldo, scholar Jorge Klor de Alva, and writer Gloria Anzaldúa.

2. The formal quality of poetic language and the social engagement of performative language are often understood to represent contrasting uses of language. In his essay "Poetry and Culture: Performativity and Critique," E. Warwick Slinn explains how performativity has become "a complex accretion" ("Poetry and Culture," 60) that has developed from speech act theory beginning with J. L. Austin through to the theories of embodiment by Judith Butler and of performance by Eve Kosofsky Sedgwick. My discussion relies on Slinn's genealogy and description of the performative. I am struck particularly by a passing observation he makes about Russian linguist Valintine N. Valoshinov that helps explain how the poetic and political dimensions of language are not antithetical but in fact interrelated. In 1927, Valoshinov observed that—since meaning through language always involves a social action—it is a contradiction in terms to think of "an individual speech act" (*Marxism and the Philosophy of Language*, 98). This position disrupts the strong tendencies of language theory to split into opposing camps: one that views language as a form of external instrumentality (language carries messages and names objects) and the other that views language as arising from internal expressiveness (language makes meaning and shapes perception). Viewing language as always a performative social act explains the double movement of the utterance. As Slinn explains in a dense but illuminating passage: "A performative [utterance] engages the real through the double process of performing its own meaning while reaching outside its linguistic content into context or the process of production, engaging and constituting an audience, a witness, a cultural ideology, through the matrices of reiterated practices. In this process, discourse and materiality, or the sense in which materiality is culturally intelligible, become inseparable" (Slinn, 61). Since language is always socially performative (as Valoshinov reminds us), language both produces meaning within its own logical structure of meaning-production as well as "reaching outside" to social production: the reiterated practices that constitute an audience and a witness to the articulation of a cultural ideology. This social dimension of language is what makes discourse material; or, put another way, it is what makes materiality intelligible and nameable through discourse. I argue that Herrera's poetry helps construct and disrupt the socially material aspect of language in his formation of a performative cultural poetics, in part by foregrounding the historically grounded and decolonial dimensions of his poetic language.

3. In the acknowledgments to his collection *187 Reasons Mexicanos Can't Cross the Border: Undocuments, 1971–2007*, Herrera offers "gracias del corazón [heartfelt thanks] to Mrs. Lucille Sampson from third grade, Logan Heights, San Diego, for shocking me by saying I had a beautiful voice."
4. In "The Geopolitics of Knowledge and the Colonial Difference," Walter Mignolo reminds us that the Global South is not a simple geographic location, "but a metaphor for human suffering under global capitalism" (66). Mignolo draws this quote from Boaventura de Sousa Santos in *Toward a New Common Sense: Law, Science, and Politics in the Paradigmatic Transition*, 516.
5. By contrast, Herrera observes about the lack of language in an interview that, "Without language, we lose ourselves and drift away to a partial and frozen sense of identity and an archipelago of abandonment and invisibility" (Dees, n.p.). Language, he insists, helps create a sense both of connection and, subsequently, presence.

## Works Cited

Bashō, Matsuo. *Narrow Road to the Interior and Other Writings*. Translated by Sam Hamill. Boston: Shambhala, 2012.

Brannigan, J. "Cultural Poetics: After the New Historicism?" In *New Historicism and Cultural Materialism*, 83–93. London: Palgrave, 1998.

Brown, Jeffrey. "Juan Felipe Herrera's Winding Path to Poetry." *PBS News Hour*, June 10, 2015. https://www.youtube.com/watch?v=iykpWev3NLY.

Dees, Jenn. "The PEN Ten: An Interview with Juan Felipe Herrera." *The PEN Ten* (blog). *PEN America*, Sept. 24, 2020. https://pen.org/the-pen-ten-juan-felipe -herrera/.

Herrera, Juan Felipe. *187 Reasons Mexicanos Can't Cross the Border: Undocuments, 1971–2007*. San Francisco, Calif.: City Lights, 2007.

Herrera, Juan Felipe. "About the Author." In *Border-Crosser with a Lamborghini Dream*, n.p. Camino del Sol Series. Tucson: University of Arizona Press, 1999.

Herrera, Juan Felipe. "Borderbus." In *Notes on the Assemblage*, 59–63. San Francisco, Calif.: City Lights, 2015.

Herrera, Juan Felipe. *Every Day We Get More Illegal*. San Francisco, Calif.: City Lights, 2020.

Herrera, Juan Felipe. "Foreword to the New Edition: Life in Motion." In *Snake Poems: An Aztec Invocation*, edited by Odilia Galván Rodríguez, David Bowles and Xánath Caraza, xi-xvi. University of Arizona Press, 2019.

Herrera, Juan Felipe. *Notebooks of a Chile Verde Smuggler*. Tucson: The University of Arizona Press, 2002.

Herrera, Juan Felipe. "Riffs on Mission District *Raza* Writers." In *Reclaiming San Francisco: History, Politics, Culture*, edited by James Brook, Chris Carlsson, and Nancy J. Peters, 217–230. San Francisco, Calif.: City Lights, 1998.

Herrera, Juan Felipe. *Senegal Taxi*. Tucson: University of Arizona Press, 2013.

Herrera, Juan Felipe. "Train Notes." In *Night Train to Tuxtla*, ix-xiv. Camino del Sol Series. Tucson: University of Arizona Press, 1994.

Herrera, Juan Felipe and Artemio Rodríguez. *Lotería Cards and Fortune Poems: A Book of Lives*. Introduction by Rupert García. San Francisco, Calif.: City Lights, 1999.

Kessler, Stephen. "Aviso: Forewarned." In *187 Reasons Mexicanos Can't Cross the Border: Undocuments, 1971–2007*, 17–19. San Francisco, Calif.: City Lights, 2007.

Kessler, Stephen. "Opinion: America's New 'Bard Without Borders.'" *Santa Cruz Sentinel*. [June 19, 2015] September 11, 2018. https://www.santacruzsentinel.com/2015/06/19/stephen-kessler-americas-new-bard-without-borders/.

Lomelí, Francisco. "Foreword / Juan Felipe Herrera: Trajectory and Metamorphosis of a Chicano Poet Laureate." *Half of the World in Light: New and Selected Poems* by Juan Felipe Herrera, xv-xxiv. Camino del Sol Series. Tucson: University of Arizona Press, 2008.

Lomelí, Francisco. "Juan Felipe Herrera: A Poet in Movement." In *L.A. [Los Angeles] Review of Books*. November 14, 2020. https://lareviewofbooks.org/article/juan-felipe-herrera-a-poet-in-movement.

Mignolo, Walter D. "The Geopolitics of Knowledge and the Colonial Difference." *South Atlantic Quarterly*, 101.1 (2002): 57–96.

Nilsen, David. "A Conversation with Juan Felipe Herrera." *On The Seawall*, Nov. 3, 2020. https://www.ronslate.com/a-conversation-with-juan-felipe-herrera/.

Pérez-Torres, Rafael. Telephone interview with Juan Felipe Herrera. January 20, 2021.

Ruiz, Tony. "Juan Felipe Herrera: 'Visión Tropical' in San Francisco's Mission District." *The CEA Critic*. 75.2 (2013): 129–141.

Sedgwick, Eve Kosofsky. *Epistemology of the Closet*. University of California Press, 1990.

Slinn, E. Warwick. "Poetry and Culture: Performativity and Critique." *New Literary History*, 30.1 (1999): 57–74.

Soldofsky, Alan. "A Border-Crosser's Heteroglosssia: Interview with Juan Felipe Herrera, Twenty-First Poet Laureate of the United States." *MELUS*, 43:2 (2018): 196–226.

Voloshinov, Valintine N. *Marxism and the Philosophy of Language*. 1929. Translated by Ladislav Matejka and I. R. Titunik. Reprinted by Harvard University Press, 1986.

## CHAPTER 2

# "Tender Chaos"

## Hospitality in Juan Felipe Herrera's Poetics

MARIA ANTÒNIA OLIVER-ROTGER

"I am a daughter of an immigrant . . . but we are a country of laws."

—MELANIA TRUMP

Get loose
after the day-glow artery of a fix.
Power outages propel us into cosmos definition, another forty-million-New-Dollar-Plantation Basilica or is it tender chaos?

—JUAN FELIPE HERRERA, "PUNK HALF-PANTHER"

In its expressive, far-reaching multiplicity, Juan Felipe Herrera's poetry conveys the individual yet communal voice of an ailing, yet vibrant, America. Grounded upon the Mexican American/Chicano/a experience, his work has progressively broadened its scope to a wide range of interrelated fragments of expression and existence: the effects of global capitalism upon Indigenous lives and environment, social and economic displacement, state violence and revolutionary protest, urban culture, the brutalization of Black people and their demands for justice, and, more recently, the effects of "zero tolerance" immigration polices upon Latino/a families and children. Assimilation, he has stated, is not his focus: "It is more like a transformation: multiple ethnic, situational and national identities in flux" (Green 2014). Herrera's diction and poetics are indebted to Chicano/a, socially committed, ritualistic *floricanto*,[1] Pablo Neruda's collective denunciation, Walt Whitman's all-embracing appeal, and Allen Ginsberg's rapid "simultaneities" (Burt 2008). As a "poet chief" of *floricanto*, Herrera is, like Neruda and Whitman, "a namer, singer, word-conjuror, storyteller, spirit-guardian, tribal-unifier, healer,

Papá Felipe Emelio Herrera, right. With friend, José Barrera on left side. October 24, 1904, Denver, Colorado. B&W studio photo.

and psychic voyager: the individual apart who represents the whole" (Nolan, 62). Francisco X. Alarcón contends that his tone is "shamanic" in its ties to antiestablishment, avant-garde movements, spoken word, performance, and popular vernacular (Alarcón 2009). But the Chicano poet often relies on the re-signifying possibilities of language play, accumulation, inventiveness, and double meaning to simultaneously generate semantic confusion, disruption, and transgression. It is hence also appropriate to think of Herrera as a "trickster," a figure who occupies "a shimmering always changing zone of multifaceted contact within which every utterance is challenged and interrogated, all referents put into question. [. . .] [A]ppropriation, inversion and abrogation of authority are always trickster strategies" (Owens, 24).

The epithet "tender chaos" is used to qualify Herrera's poetics as a quasi-oxymoron that brings together the two facets of the poet and echoes the transgression, conflict, and compassion conveyed by his "aesthetics of chaos" (Lomelí, xv). "Tender chaos" qualifies Herrera's poetics as displaying a fundamental concern with confusion, otherness, and the related problems of hospitality and ethical involvement. His poems stage surprising encounters at the level of signification and the performative, teasing readers' expectations through ambivalence and the collision and interplay of multiple discourses, and through a "triangulated address" that enunciates and challenges the emotional, physical borders between individuals (Culler, 8). My discussion of Herrera's poetry deals, first, with the ways in which one of his most famous choral poems "187 Reasons Why Mexicanos Can't Cross the Border" demands a re-signifying, "meta-ideologizing" activity by causing readers to move in through and out of ideologies to generate irony and expose the silencing, stereotyping effects of hegemonic discourses (Sandoval, 111), all of which lead to a dialogue with the "colonizer's own terms" and to autoethnographic knowledge (Pratt, 7). I will also examine the conflation between constative and performative meanings in the meditative, stream-of-consciousness poem, "And If the Man with the Choke-hold," through which Herrera highlights the impossible reconciliation between the realm of ethics or justice and the realm of so-called politics and the law.[2] Finally, I will consider several poems of address from his latest volume *Every Day We Get More Illegal* (2020) as examples of the poet's engagement with otherness and hospitality through the iteration of the simultaneous distance and encounter between two sides of a divided America. Considered together, these poems enunciate and make memorable the muted aspects of an existence to an apostrophized "you" in potentially hospitable yet irresoluble encounters.

## "What a Poem Brings": Poetics and Hospitality

Before you go further,
let me tell you what a poem brings,
first, you must know the secret, there is no poem

to speak of it is a way to attain a life without boundaries, yes, it is that easy, a
poem, imagine me telling you this, instead of going day by day against the
razors, well,
the judgments, all the tick-tock bronze, a leather jacket sizing you up, the
fashion mall, for example, from
the outside you think you are being entertained,
when you enter, things change, you get caught by surprise, your mouth goes
sour, you get thirsty, your legs grow cold standing still in the middle of a
storm, a poem, of course, is always open for business too, except, as you
can see,
it isn't exactly business that pulls your spirit into
the alarming waters, there you can bathe, you can play, you can even join in
on the gossip—the mist, that is,
the mist becomes central to your existence.

(Herrera, "Let Me Tell You What a Poem Brings,"
*Half of the World in Light*, 301)

A critical framework to engage with Herrera's poetics should contemplate his own proclamations about poetic creation expressed in "Let Me Tell You What a Poem Brings." The poem's dedication to Charles Fishman contains a statement about the partiality of our judgment and the hidden truths behind any assertion. The reader may identify Charles Fishman as the widely acclaimed business journalist, author of *The Wal-Mart Effect* (2006), among other national best-sellers, or as the less-known, award-winning poet of the same name, author of *Country of Memory* (2004) and of several poetry volumes. The poem spells out an *ars poetica* through a conversation in which the poet's alter ego interrupts an interlocutor's line of reasoning and goes on to express a counterargument. If we assume that all arguments contain their refutation, we infer that what is at stake in this dialogue is the value or purpose of poetry. The anonymous voice first reveals a secret: "There is no poem to speak of" (*Half of the World*, 301). He thereby suggests that poems may go beyond the established boundaries of what they should presumably look like. The emphasis is not so much on poetry as a literary form as on poetry "bringing" something as if arriving with a gift. The explanation of "what a poem brings" provides analogies that underscore the opposition between the poetic and the non-poetic as distinct dispositions or attitudes embodied by the speaker and his listener/interlocutor, respectively. Herrera's speaker adopts abstract language and urban slang, metaphorical and referential meanings to entreat the listener to abandon a self-protective attitude, which involves rigidity, biases, and stiffness: "going day by day against the razors," "the judgments," "the tick-tock bronze," "a leather jacket / sizing you up" (301). This defensive attitude is pitted against an openness to novelty and surprise, which may even occur in as predictable a place as the "fashion mall" (301). While it promises entertainment, once inside one may be "caught by surprise," feel discomfort, and find oneself "in the middle of a storm" (301). The speaker says the poem is, like the mall, "open for business too," though not for lucrative purposes; its "business" is to pull the reader's spirit into the "alarming waters" and the "mist" of a storm (301).

To describe the poetic as the sudden advent of a storm and its "alarming waters" and as the reveling or playing "in the mist" suggests that it brings an experience that is all at once unpleasant, confusing, but also dynamic and even enjoyable. "Playing around in the mist" may apply to the creative act, the poet's blurring of the contours of signification through ambiguity, ambivalence and even distorting or occluding perception. It may also refer to the interpretive act, the reader's meaning-making process, which involves learning to inhabit the fluid, trying, imprecise realm of poetic language. Entering this misty, alien environment entails both uneasiness and the possibility of freely "bathing" and joining "in on the gossip." Besides conflict, distress, vulnerability, uncertainty, and surprise, the experience also entails pleasure and connection. "Join in on the gossip" conjures the idea of conversation and the collective component of performance and connection with audiences.

Herrera's description of the poetic as "change" and "get[ting] caught by surprise," and "in the middle of a storm," echoes Jacques Derrida's understanding that there is "[n]o poem without accident, no poem that does not open itself like a wound, no poem that is not also just as wounding" in "Che cos'è la poesia [What is poetry?]" (233). In this enigmatic text, Derrida evades the definition of poetry as a literary genre or a modality of writing and states he prefers the terms "poetic" or "poematic" instead of "poetry" or "poem," which is analogous to Herrera's speaker assertion that "there's no poem to speak of" (301). He also expresses the significance of the poem in terms of "arrival" and "gift"—"falling to me, a benediction coming from (of) the other" (233)—and, like Herrera, underscores the entrance into the poetic in terms of change and upheaval:

> [N]othing to be done (*poiein*), neither "pure poetry," nor pure rhetoric, nor *reine Sprache*, nor "setting-forth-of-truth-in-the-work." Just this contamination, and this crossroads, this accident here. This turn, the turning around of *this* catastrophe. The gift of the poem cites nothing, it has no title, histrionics are over, it comes along without your expecting it, cutting short the breath, cutting all ties with discursive and especially literary poetry. (Derrida, 235)

Both authors suggest that what the poetic "brings" is the sudden entrance into an alien environment, the surprise and foreignness of a startling encounter.

Herrera's and Derrida's respective visions of the poetic recall the notion of hospitality. For Herrera, the poetic is "a way to attain a life without boundaries" (301), while for the philosopher, an "act of hospitality can only be poetic," for, like the poetic, hospitality requires an attitude of unconditional openness (Derrida and Dofourmantelle, 2). Derrida states that an act of absolute "unconditional hospitality" is related to the poetic because both entail the constant questioning of the limits that they depend on to take place. "Unconditional hospitality" entails welcoming the foreigner without previous definition or specific criteria for doing so (Derrida and Dofourmantelle, 2).

Derrida states that there is within hospitality itself a paradox, "antinomy," or "aporia," since to allow the entrance to a foreigner one must first be an owner and a host, that is, to have the power to receive and have some control within the law of civil society and the state (Derrida and Dofourmantelle, 77). Derrida finds the unconditional "yes" to a foreigner, an immigrant, an unexpected visitor, an animal, a citizen from another country to be in conflict with the law understood as rights and duties "that are always conditioned and conditional, as they are defined by the Greco-Roman tradition and even the Judeo-Christian one, by all of law and all philosophy of law up to Kant and Hegel in particular, across the family, civil society, and the State" (Derrida and Dofourmantelle, 77). The difference between conditional and absolute hospitality resembles the difference between law and justice: "[Absolute hospitality] is as strangely heterogeneous to [hospitality by rights] as justice is heterogeneous to the law to which it is yet so close, from which in truth it is indissociable" (Derrida and Dofourmantelle, 26). Hospitality entails a constant questioning of the limits of the laws, decisions, theories, and procedures through which one seeks to attain universal consensus about who has the "right" to enter a home, a country, a territory. Herrera's evocative description of the poetic recalls Derrida's "unconditional hospitality" in that it makes evident the impossibility of reconciling the realm of rules, categories, and distinctions, and "the life without boundaries" of poetic creativity. As suggested by the metaphor of the mist, the poetic experience is fluid, blurs limits, and creates uncertainty. As "bathe," "play," "join in the gossip" suggest (301), besides absolute hospitality, for Herrera the poetic requires a spontaneous, carefree attitude within a collective conversation, which ties in with his role as trickster and juggler with multiple American registers.

Hillis Miller's ethical approach to narrative explained in the interview "On Literature and Ethics" sheds further light on the similarity between hospitality and the poetic as "attitudes" or approaches to otherness discussed so far. Miller states that the non-congruence between "following the law" and "doing what is just" in Derrida's thought is analogous to the rift between applying given meanings or preconceptions to a literary text and reading it in its own terms as performative (24): "The interpretation of a literary work, which presumably says something about the specific text in question, looks like it ought to be constative, that is, a statement of fact, but it always has a performative aspect" (25). Comparably to Derrida's description of the poetic and hospitality, Miller describes the interpretive, meaning-making exercise of a text in terms of relinquishing authority, regulations, and control: "The fissure between the constative and the performative, matches the disjunction between law and justice. [. . .] Good reading is defined by the encounter of something in the text that does not match the theory you have" (25). In light of Miller's theories of reading, Herrera's description of the poetic experience as abandoning "judgments," getting "caught by surprise," and entering "change" may be read as an inducement to surrender one's theories and presumptions to welcome unexpected possibilities of signification.

My readings of Herrera's poems "187 Reasons Why Mexicanos Can't Cross the Border," "And If the Man with the Choke-hold," and selected poems of address in *Every Day We Get More Illegal* draw attention to the textual encounters with otherness and the transgression of the limits of signification in Herrera's poetry as invitations to suspend judgment and show hospitality. Otherness, as we will see, is made present through the coalescence of discourse genres whose meanings may complement and/or cancel each other depending on readers' playfulness, their ideological stance, and/or their identification as the poems' addressees. In "187 Reasons" such discourse types include the law, celebrity stories and popular hearsay, politics and politicians, consumer culture and economic relations, history and myth. On the other hand, the testimonial poem "And If the Man with the Choke-hold" conflates subjective perception and beliefs, objective facts and authorized knowledge, and moral and ethical principles. The lyrical poems of address in *Every Day We Get More Illegal* are built on the dehumanizing, dividing, desensitizing rhetoric and gestures of a "you," and a language of a collective speaker that calls for human proximity and mutual recognition. The chosen works call for an "attitude" or "disposition" of welcoming unexpected associations, a willingness to reassign meanings and suspend judgments, and an inclination to shift the power relations between individuals in the process. Those who want to "play" in the "mi(d)st" of these poems will be actively engaged in signifying challenges that pose ethical questions on justice and absolute hospitality.

## Meta-ideological Deconstruction and Re-signification in the Choral Poem

Herrera has stated that "one of the functions of a poem — if indeed we can say that a poem has a function at all — is to turn things on their head or on their side: inside out or concave is the ideal" (*Mayan Drifter* 6). A poem is "a mobius-shaped trek backward and forward" and "an unsettled mestizaje that at every turn aims to subvert itself" (6). This subversion from within oftentimes leads to clever, playful irony, yet its effects are not always straightforward, as it relies on the juxtaposition and intermingling of popular, learned, and authoritative knowledges that interact with each other. The choral poem "187 Reasons Why Mexicanos Can't Cross the Border," for example, incorporates the reference number of an infamous legal proposition from California in 1994 (Proposition 187),[3] whose legal terms and devastating implications are known by most American audiences. The poem provides the title to Herrera's 2007 collection, whose subtitle *Undocuments 1971–2007* playfully brings together the language of the law and creative poetic language. The title of the poem seems to allude to voters' reasons for supporting the proposition and to the desired effect it would have in deterring Mexican immigrants' crossing the border. The poet has often involved audiences in his public readings of "187 Reasons" by inviting them to recite the unifying anaphoric first word of each line ("because"). Listeners join in the making of a list of reasons why Mexicans can't cross the border, but Herrera's signifying ambivalence turns these "reasons" into possible statements about the devastating implications of the law, or about the reasons Mexicans want to cross the border but can't. Under the appearance of a multivocal catalog of possible disincentives to Mexican immigration, the lines in the choral poem suggest that the reasons behind immigrants' crossing of the border are colonial and neocolonial relations and the imbalanced economic relations between Mexico and the U.S. Many of these alternative explanations point to the exclusion or "symbolic deportation" of clandestine workers and their families from the society and the nation they work for, often below the minimum wage (Perea, 965), and to the historical grievances against Mexicans whose lives have been affected by the colonial/imperialist designs of the U.S. upon Mexico and to the latter's economic dependency on the U.S.

The title, epigraph, and first line of the poem introduce the notions of prohibition, regulation, authority, and subjugation within conflicting idioms or registers: the number of the legal proposition, the declarative/indicative "Mexicanos can't cross," the regulatory rebuke in Latin *"Abutebaris modo subjunctive denuo"* (You've been misusing the subjunctive again), and the word "subjunctive" (etymologically related to "subjugate" and indicating a degree of dependence). The formality of the admonishment in Latin about the misuse of the subjunctive in the epigraph, contrasts with the jokiness of the title, and is echoed humorously again in the first of the list of reasons provided by the poem: "Because Lou Dobbs has been misusing the subjunctive again" (29). Herrera's wit relies on audiences' linking the allusion to the legal prohibition in the title with former CNN and current Fox reporter and political commentator Lou Dobbs, an undocumented immigration firebrand. The playful discursive juxtaposition and deconstructive, meta-ideological puzzle points to the historical presence of Mexicans in the United States, to their exclusion from the national body of citizenship and rights, and to the role of U.S. media in the propagation of anti-immigrant discourse: through the double meaning of "subjunctive," the authoritative language and abstract principles of hegemonic laws and discourses are offset against the declarative statement about Dobbs's constant misuse of the subjunctive mood in Spanish, a misuse that suggests both the disrespect for the language spoken by U.S. peoples of Mexican descent and the bigotry of Dobbs' agitating language.[4]

Once and again Herrera highlights the limits of discourse and the displacement of meaning through textual relations that underscore not only the transformative process of identity but also, and most importantly, the obscure side of any statement, what it leaves out and silences, its alternative meaning. His strategy is the "shifting from margin to margin" within a heteroglossia that depends to a great extent on readers' collaboration. In *Chicano Poetics: Heterotexts and Hybridities*, Alfred Arteaga explains that "for him, each poem is a site of play and conflict, an unfinalized process where the reader must participate" (153–154). Audiences are invited to participate in the poem's "gossip" by reciting, making sense of, and relishing in the playful, interactive contrasts of its lines. "187 Reasons" abounds ironically on the elasticity of the U.S.-Mexico border, which makes itself felt in what Aldama calls "forced liminalities" or "margins" (15), whether it is in the discursive and material violence of European colonization and U.S. expansionism, in racial, gender and sexual discrimination in the U.S., or in Mexican migrants' unescapable entanglement in U.S.-Mexico economic relations. Each "reason" in the aggregate list has the potential of being different or "other" to itself by virtue of its disparate meanings, which in turn interact with the differential meanings of other lines in a re-signifying game that may lead to autoethnographic and meta-ideological critique.

Some of the "reasons" in the list provide metonymical images of U.S. consumer culture and of the commercial ties between Mexico and the United States, thus figuring as explanations why Mexicans *do cross* the geopolitical border, not as reasons why they *can't cross it*, while others exploit the double meaning of physical and sexual transborder crossings to highlight the overlapping of sexual and ethnic discrimination: "Because our suitcases are made with maguey biodegradable fibers"; "Because someone made our IDs out of corn"; "Because we're on peyote & Coca-Cola & Banamex"; "Because Latin American petrochemical juice flows first" (Herrera, *187 Reasons*, 29); "Because our huaraches are made with Goodyear and Uniroyal" (31); "Because Mexican queers crossed already" (33). Other "reasons" ambivalently highlight the dependence of U.S. wealth and prosperity on Mexican labor, Mexico's dependence on "El Norte" (a term loaded with the weight of a long history of guestworker programs and agreements), discretional revolving door immigration policies, and U.S. hegemonic anti-immigrant discourse: "Because multiplication is our favorite sport / Because we'll dig a tunnel to Seattle" (29); "Because what would we do in El Norte" (29); "Because the President has a Mexican maid / Because the Vice President has a Mexican maid" (32). The statement "Because we still resemble La Malinche" (29) brings together the ineludible racial mixing or *mestizaje* resulting from colonization—colonization resulting in Mexicans' crossing the border literally and in their being a "racial" and cultural "cross"—the fear of miscegenation and racism in the U.S., and the national stereotype of Mexicans as treacherous—all of which would be "reasons" Mexicans "can't cross." Other explanations invoke ethnic stereotypes used to justify exploitation or to abhor Mexican character, and the also abhorrent yet "desirable" presence of Mexican sexual workers south of the border: "Because of this Aztec reflex to sacrifice ourselves" (30); "Because the Navy, Army, Marines like us topless in Tijuana" (35). Both statements may be turned on their head if they are read respectively as an ironic remark on the exploitation of Mexican labor as a critical commentary on the crossing of U.S. military units south of the border for cheap sexual entertainment. Other lines include statements that read either as descriptions of the interdependence of two nations brought about by the colonial, empire-building enterprise, or as objections to its consequences: "Because we have been doing it for 500 years already" (29); "Because the Mayan concept of zero means 'US out of Mexico'"; "Because Alamo is really pronounced 'Alamadre'" (31).

Still others read as either natural, predictable results or as tragic outcomes of colonialism and/or imperialism, depending on the ideology of the speaker: "Because it's Indian land stolen from our mothers" (29). They are supplemented by hyperbolic cultural stereotypes that may also be read against the grain as declarations on the importance of immigrants' revenues for Mexican families, or on their tenacious resistance to Western imperialist values: "Because we're too emotional when it comes to our mothers" (29); "Because we're locked into Magical Realism" (32).

As we read "187 Reasons" we are invited to "bathe" in the "alarming waters" of the "heteroglot interzone" in each line (Arteaga, 105), which, like a border, invites us into deconstruction and resignification before we move on to the next one. The heteroglot interzone or signifying border extends beyond the very geographical, geopolitical line as part of the Mexican American and Chicano/a multivalent experience of hybridization, exclusion, and discrimination (Aldama, 15). The poem engages us in a crossbreeding of putative antagonistic arguments about Mexican immigrants' legitimate presence in the United States, a "hybrid overlapping" of "the competing discourses of nation" (Arteaga, 105), those in which U.S. national identity is essentially white, Christian, and European, and those which see it as inextricably tied to the expansionist history of the U.S. and its consequences. As we move through, in and out of several discourses set against each other within the same line or across the lines in the poem, we are involved in the re-signifying effects of their encounters and in the possible ethical import within a poetics of hospitality. Herrera's ultimate objective is to lead us to a meta-ideological subversion of the laws of conditional hospitality—the hegemonic legal, cultural, and economic discourses applied to Mexican immigrants—by breaking their boundaries and opening them to the otherness they hide, to the multiple ways in which Mexican lives and work are entwined with U.S. economic interests, with a colonialist past, and with power imbalances and inequalities.

## The Witness's Impossible Assemblage

Herrera's lyrical persona is oftentimes an anonymous testimonial eye/I who observes, makes sense, takes stock, and "assembles" lost or silenced pieces of language and existence by blending and relating them to one other. "Y si el hombre con el choke-hold"/ "And If the Man with the Choke-hold," included in the bilingual collection *Notes on the Assemblage* (2015), is a stream-of-consciousness monologue structured as a chain of related run-on questions, all of which are introduced by a conditional sentence "and if," followed by "why" (19). The poem conveys the inner confusion of a somewhat naïve witness/speaker who attempts to deduce the logical relationship between the premises he holds true and what he observes, perceives, and feels. The ritualistic character of lyric enunciation, accentuated by the simple present, parallelism, and anaphoric repetition (Culler, 289), draws attention to the ever-going, habitual state of the actions described.

In the first two lines, the speaker seems to apply a simple logic to make sense of reality that relies on a correlation between verticalness or standing up and life and lying out flat and death. What he sees challenges his assumptions: "And if the man with the choke-hold pulls the standing man down / why does he live" (*Assemblage*, 19). However, the readers' assumptions are also challenged, as we are faced with the ambivalence of the referent of the subject pronoun, "he." Is the speaker wondering why the man with the "choke-hold" "live[s]" or is he wondering why "the standing man" lives? (19). Similar correlated concepts ("rise," "swagger") appear in the second line, and in the sixth and seventh lines in relation to their opposites ("dead," "prone"): "[I]f the dead man is gone why does he rise," if "it was a teen with / a swagger why is he still prone" (19). In the first case, what the speaker perceives challenges empirical laws based on factual perception; in the second case, the opposition up/down calls attention again to the difference and contradiction between the physical positions. It is up to the readers indirectly involved in the speaker's inner questioning to figure out the "laws" and logic that cause the change in the man and the teen's condition. The third line in the prosaic poem shows an anomalous correlation of events and facts (the "clicking sound" is the sound of the soul "when it leaves," 19), but the soul leaving is rather a perception, something that only the speaker seems to be aware of ("even though no one knows," 19). The next line refers again to the sense of hearing: the woman "stays" and yet she is "the crucible" and "the fire;" The woman is "the voice . . . never heard" and yet the speaker states this "resound[s] for 9 generations" (19). The antagonism between "never heard" and "resound" expose the absence of women's voices because they go unnoticed by an unknown passive agent; yet this does not prevent them from having an echo across generations.

The implicit secondary assumptions behind the speaker's deductive reasoning are at times those of rationality, empiricism, and objectivity, but at other times, these assumptions are the laws of Christian morality and U.S. civic society. In lines seven and eight, what the speaker sees and perceives also deviates from these assumptions: the police are "right," the court "agrees," and the governor speaks "humble," yet "they" "are still lost in the infinite desert" (19). The speaker is baffled by the discordance between the attitude of the representatives of rightfulness—the apparent fairness, frankness, and legitimacy of state authorities who represent the law—and the fact that "they" should be "lost in the infinite desert." Again, the text's meaning depends on the readers' presumption of who "they" are, and on their interpretation of "lost in the infinite desert" literally or metaphorically as a biblical allusion to sin or lack of Christian faith. The ambivalence in some of the premises questioned by the "if/then why" structure points at the rift between the constative (what is apparently moral, right, verifiable, and visible) and the performative (the meaning of human actions and gestures within their unique circumstances) (Miller, 26).

"Scorched with thirst," mentioned later in the poem, resounds with "lost in the infinite desert," which is a possible literal allusion to immigrants or "looters" breaking walls and crossing borders. It also echoes the biblical allegory of African Americans' exile from the American nation.[5] "[B]roke the wall" and "split / the wine" (*Assemblage*, 19) are structurally parallel to "the police were right," "the court was in agreement," "the governor spoke humble;" they occupy the same position in the logical reasoning of the speaker. Looters being "scorched with thirst" is at odds with the previous proposition: "If looters broke the wall and split / the wine why are they still scorched with thirst." Like *Here, take my water* (19), placed in italics to simulate a recognizable allusion, "split the wine" resonates with biblical symbols of God's blessing, Christian righteousness and the joy of communion, hospitality, and generosity (19). While this generosity exists among "looters [who] broke the wall," "protesters marching" are not offered water. The poem features the disparate consequences of the application of Christian morality in the situations observed by the "I" in the poem: how consistent the behavior of looters is with those whose well-meaning pronouncements are "right"; how inconsistent it is that that authorities should mean well, yet "they" should be "lost"; how inconsistent it is that looters should split the wine yet they should be "scorched with thirst"; how heterogeneous the laws of civic participation and equality are to a divided street that does not offer water to protestors marching. Likewise, the conditional "if laws are Freedom for you and me" (19), refers to the theoretical premises of democracy, but "why do we / not speak" is the reality the speaker observes that is contrary to the self-governing principle that laws echo people's will (19). Here, the divergence in the parallelism between morality and the law and between justice and ethics (Miller, 25) is also the schism at the core of the disjunction between absolute hospitality and conditional hospitality.

But the poem contains an alternative discourse, one that draws on subjective experience, perception, and testimony to counteract what is muted and ignored in the application of hegemonic law, morality, and objectivity. This counter-discourse is suggested by the challenge the speaker's secret knowledge poses to rational, fact-based assumptions: the man is dead but he rises; the clicking sound, which suggests the clicking of a trigger, is, for him, the "sound the soul makes when it leaves / even though no one knows" (*Assemblage*, 19); the woman "stays," her voice is "never heard," but it "resound[s] for nine generations" (19). The dead man who rises, the soul that leaves, and the unheard woman who stays and whose voice resounds are paradoxical or contradictory from a "logical" point of view, but suggest an unacknowledged power, spirituality, and resistance, which the speaker is receptive to.

The poem's final appeal to a "you" clearly involves readers as potential addressees of the ambivalent concluding questions, and as participants in the reality described: "That tree" that "stands behind you green with its last two / limbs up / swollen with blood" that does not "suffer," a clear reference to the lynching of and hanging of Black people in the hands of white supremacist groups like Ku Klux Klan, collapses hopeful fertility and resistance, on the one hand, and violence and indifference, on the other (19). The final broken lines detached from the main narrative ("why / does it / blossom torches") provide an uncertain objective correlative to the "theoretical preconceptions" applied to reality and the "fresh judgements" the poem demands us to make as we face the questions the speaker has posed, and the events and knowledge he has recounted. "Blossom torches" conjures up both freedom and destruction. In the light of the previous irresoluble reasoning, the poem's final question brings home the impossibility of reconciling the theoretical premises of the law and an ethics of hospitality.

## Visual and Tactile Encounters in the Poems of Address

The collection *Every Day We Get More Illegal* (2020) was published three years after the termination of Juan Felipe Herrera's term as "Poet Laureate Consultant in Poetry" (2015–2017) and during the last year of Donald Trump's mandate. The "zero tolerance" immigration policies enforced between 2017 and 2021, and the ensuing massive deportations, family separations and the detention of unaccompanied minors in Border and Custom Protection Centers left their mark on the discursive production of illegality. In line with the poet's signifying playfulness, the provocative title works as a mobius strip, a two-fold interpellation to a divided America: from the viewpoint of "we the people" who imagines itself as racially, culturally, and sexually homogeneous (ie. white, Anglo-Saxon, heterosexual, and male-dominated), it voices the hegemonic rhetoric referring to multiple others designated as "illegal." "We" stands for the America that asks to wall off its borders. Alternatively, "we" refers to those whose status is ever more subject to the laws of conditional hospitality. From the viewpoint of migrants, undocumented workers and all those excluded and symbolically deported from the monochromous "we the people," "we" signifies those Herrera describes in terms of "abjection" in his apostrophic poem "You Just Don't Talk About It": "the pushed out the stopped out the forced out / the starved out the fenced out the shot down the cut back the / asphalted out on the other side of the track the suicided the hanged w/o a bedsheet or nothing in the cell" (*Illegal*, 6).

The urgent poetics of address in the poems included in this collection may be viewed as the poet's response to America's ideological division caused by a rhetoric legitimating violence and anger against the most vulnerable, among other circumstances: by the loyalty towards one single person rather than towards the principles of civic society, by the feeling of security and omnipotence around such loyalty, and by the "big lie" that white America was being threatened and abused (Zaretsky). The apostrophic poems underscore the split between an unheard collective "I/we" who speaks to the power-wielding "you," which creates the paradoxical simultaneity of "an addressable and potentially responsive universe" and the "skepticism about the efficacy of lyric discourse" (Culler, 8). This skepticism is even more stressed in these poems by the fact that the interlocutor does not "lissen [sic]," "talk about," "care about," or "notice" what the collective "I/we" is describing. The urgency and persistence of the speaker in "You Just Don't Talk about It," "Don't Push the Button," and "Touch the Earth" cast a doubt upon the possibility of communication with "you," suggesting it is very unlikely that "you" acknowledges "I/we"'s appeal. The poems create the possibility of a conversation yet highlight the unsurmountable distance between the speaker and the addressee. At the same time, through the "indirection" of "triangulated address" the lyrical voice also speaks to "the audience of readers by addressing or pretending to address someone or something else" (Culler, 8).

In poems such as "You Just Don't Talk about It" and "Touch the Earth" there is a steadfast commitment to deixis ("here," "this") and to referential language that designates and makes visible the factual, the embodied, and the material of the lives described. The encounters enunciated underscore what Sara Ahmed, in *Stranger Encounters: Embodied Others in Post-Coloniality*, calls the "economy of touch" and the "visual economy of recognition" (23) that shape the boundaries between "you" and "I/we." An encounter does not occur as an isolated face-to-face meeting but within historical and spatial processes of exclusion and inclusion, which in turn affect the emotions felt towards the bodies of communities and individuals, their visibility or invisibility, including their physical and emotional proximity or distance (6–7). Any encounter at any given time and place presupposes other bodily or face-to-face encounters that have taken place at other times and other places, which in turn shape the asymmetries of power of those involved in it (24). In "You Just Don't" the hypothetical antagonistic meeting in the present brings to the foreground "the prior histories of encounter that violate and fix others in regimes of difference" (8–9). Such "traces" of past actions inflicted on anonymous individuals are expressively recounted through repetition and accumulation (9): "You just don't talk about the rape . . . the lacerations . . . the self-whipping . . . the addictions . . . you do not care about the land you stole . . ." (6–7). The endless lists persistently humanize and make visible the past encounters with "you" of those who are civically inexistent and in turn expose the reasons why they are viewed or perceived as untouchable, outside home, inhabiting the abject "unliveable" and "uninhabitable" zones of social life (53).

These "others" are individuals whose lands have been stolen, who risk their lives to arrive, work and serve, who are stalked, imprisoned, deported, violated, separated from each other, and who face an uncertain, tragic destiny. In their ritualized iteration through the reproachful speaker, the items in the list are at once a denunciation of injustice and an exposé of the indifference of an emotionally detached "you." This "you" has constructed itself as subject at the expense of the expulsion, invisibility and negative emotions towards bodies that are recognized as "stranger than others and come to be livable as unlivable, as the impossible object that both establishes and confounds the border" (Ahmed, 52).

The philosophical poem of address "Listen to Elias Canetti" provides the key to the visual and tactile economy in the poems. The poem alludes to the Bulgarian thinker's anthropological essay on the management of crowds and fear, *Crowds and Power* (1960). One of Canetti's most powerful assertions focuses on the question of the fear of otherness: "There is nothing that man fears more than the touch of the unknown" (15). Crowds grow together as a response to the fear of the touch of the other and to respond together to the violence committed through touch. The unity of the crowd is symbolized with hand gestures and symbols that at once control it and define it as a homogeneous entity in which members are equal in their fear to the touch of others outside its walls. Gesticulation retains the primeval force of the hand, whose significance has come to surpass the rest of the body. The fear of touch materializes in instruments that replace the hand and the face in the exercise of power. Thus, the pristine mechanical impulse to destroy with the hands has "now grown to a complex system of technology, which, whenever it is linked with a real intention to kill, supplies the automatic element of the resulting process, that empty mindlessness which is so particularly disquieting" (218). Canetti opposes this mechanical impulse to the "hardening exercises" of the hands, to the "patience of the hand," "the quiet, prolonged activities of the hand which have created the only world in which we care to live" (213). "The finger signs of monkeys" preceding creativity and writing and "the agreeable sensation that the individual fingers receive from the skin," is, for Canetti, what turns the hand into a "delicate instrument" (213). Echoing *Crowds and Power*, Herrera's "Listen to Elias Canetti" establishes a correspondence between the use of symbols, technology, people's domestication, and the emotional detachment from others. The anonymous speaker in the poem addresses a "you" through questions about their brutal use of force and related political slogans ("are you a hunting pack," "are you the follower of *the killers are always the powerful*" [italics in original], "the Force-eater," *Illegal*, 8), their mechanical behavior (half-machine, half-skin production), their promotion of mindlessness, indifference, and emotional aloofness ("are you a domestication plasma," "a punishment-love hypnosis," "the Symbol-maker of detachment," "the remoteness that is all we know now"), about his aggressive "command of the hand" ("are you the finger exercises taught to monkeys"), and their use of technology for dehumanizing purposes, disembodiment and division ("are you a Segmenter without eyes or heart or blood," "barcode of humans at so many gates," 8).

Also resonating with Canetti's words, another of Herrera's poems of address, "Don't Push the Button," draws on the opposition between the mechanical, defensive hand gesture of "pushing the button" and the creative gesture of poetry and performance. The poem is an obvious allusion to Donald Trump's threat to North Korean leader Kim Jong-Un in August 2017 and to his later tweet in January 2018 in which he boasted his nuclear button was "much bigger and more powerful" than his Korean counterpart's. The voice in the poem laments that those activities resulting from "the patience of the hand" (art, performance, poetry, and music) have lost their function before the expeditive, automatic motion the addressee threatens to make, and the speaker desperately tries to prevent:

art is not enough

performance is not enough
something is missing don't push it to fill the vacuum
. . . . . . . . . . . . . . . . . . . . . . . . . . . . . . . .
it provides an ounce of two of arousal
similar to the walls of Patrols

. . . . . . . . . . . . . . . . . . . .
do not push it I am nervous something is off-kilter
it is beyond words beyond poetry beyond Milton and Sappho
it is beyond Paz and Ko Un [*sic*] it is beyond all the African
drummers it is closer to the ashes of South Sudan and
the green skulls of a Mexican State I cannot mention and
the massacres the massacres so many massacres in plain sight

do not push it . . .

(*Illegal*, 9)

As in "Don't Push the Button," "You Just Don't Talk about It," "Listen to Elias Canetti" and "Touch the Earth Again," the lyrical voice uses imperatives to beseech "you" to become "soft" and hospitable, to see, "notice," "lissen [sic]" "care for," "talk about," "get near," "enter" (6–7) and "come here" (10). In stark contrast with the sudden, precise gesture of "pushing the button" to keep away those the "you" fears, these verbs signify the openness of "we" to alterity through proximity and the demand for visual recognition. In "Touch the Earth (Once Again)," the speaker recites the habitual, reiterative activities "we" do with working fingers and hands:

This is what we do:

this is what the truck-driver does:
this is what the tobacco leaf roller does:
this is what the washer-woman & the laundry worker does:
. . . . . . . . . . . . . . . . . . . . . . . . . . . . . . . . . . . . . .
not to mention the cucumber workers—
not to mention the spinach & beet workers
not to mention the poultry woman workers . . .

(*Illegal*, 10)

The catalogue of jobs mentioned implies the endless production of agribusiness, yet the voice does not focus on collective's mechanical gestures but on the abstract "what we do" (10). The speaker makes "we" visible and closer in their humanity to "you"/the reader through a "visible economy of recognition" that allows "you" to *see* "we" against forms of "misrecognition" (Ahmed, 23). The speaker brings attention to actions such as "bend in the fires no one sees," "stand in that small-town desert sundries store," "walk out they do & stall for a moment they do / underneath this colossal tree with its condor-wings / shedding solace for a second or two," to "their ecstatic colors & their knotted shirts," and to the place they cash "their tiny & wrinkled checks and pay stubs" (*Illegal*, 20).

In the concluding lines of these three poems, it is "we"—those the "you" in the poem does not talk about, care about or listen to—who have "the patience of the hand" and welcome "you" with unconditional hospitality: they "wanted to touch you to meet you against all odds" (7), invite "you" to "come here where we sit / in the annex between walls of a nondescript house" (10) and they "touch the earth—for you" (20). Derrida wonders whether to offer hospitality is necessary "to start from the certain existence of a dwelling," or whether the authenticity of hospitality may not open up "starting from the dislocation of the shelterless, the homeless" (Dufourmantelle in Derrida and Dufourmantelle, 56). In Herrera's lyrical poems of address the speaker's invitation to proximity does not depend on the existence of a singular home in which "we" may welcome "you." Herrera revises the laws of conditional hospitality by enunciating the collective's welcome of "you" from an uncertain place that is not "our" land or "our" territory but a place that does not belong "to neither host or guest but to the gesture by which one of them welcomes the other even and above all if he is himself without a dwelling from which this welcome could be conceived" (Derrida and Dufourmantelle, 62). This revision draws attention to the unconditional hospitable gestures of those the "you" has ignored and expelled from the boundaries of his existence. Herrera's poems of address in *Every Day We Become More Illegal* bring forth the very borders and distance between two sides of America, but they also challenge them as (im)possible places for them to touch and meet.

# Conclusion

The analysis of selected poems reveals the ways in which "tender chaos," or "hospitality," is manifested in Juan Felipe Herrera's poetics through the textual mechanisms developed within several poetic modalities. These modalities—"the choral poem," "the testimonial poem," and the "poem of address"—do not represent the multiple, sometimes-overlapping styles Herrera has cultivated, which include visual poems and calligrams, narrative poems, and poetic dialogues. In the instances represented by the chosen poems, I have looked at hospitality in terms of the surprise and loss of authority created by conflicting meanings, the juxtaposition and interplay between the expectations and associations generated by discourse genres, and the demands made to the reader through the "triangulated address" (Culler, 8) to welcome the abject others who are essential for the addressee's self-constitution. The poet's vision opens the artistic path towards an alternative view of the political and the social through language play, deconstruction, meta-ideologizing, and the re-signifying inventive possibilities engendered by and within encounters with difference, be it at the level of meaning or at the visual, emotional and/or interpersonal level. Herrera's poetics generates encounters that concurrently expose and blur the borders of dominant cultural, social, economic discourses on Mexican migrants, U.S. and Mexican national imaginaries, the borders between the discourse of the law and the discourse of justice, and the borders between individuals created by a "visual economy" and an "economy of touch" that relegates certain individuals to the margins (Ahmed, 23). In all of them the poetic brings to the foreground the incompatibility between the political and ethical dimension of hospitality, an incompatibility that places the reader in an ethical conundrum. The ultimate effect of these multiple encounters upon the readers, the audience, and/or the participants is to suggest what can only be inferred through poetry: the breakdown of social divisions, social and identity categories, geopolitical barriers, and social boundaries. Through poetic chaos, understood as an encounter and a form of border-dissolving hospitality, we enter the ethical terrain of compassion and tenderness.

## Notes

1. The generation of the 1960s and '70s *movimiento chicano*, or Chicano Renaissance, was characterized by strong cultural nationalism. Poets such as Alurista, José Antonio Burciaga, Lorna Dee Cervantes, Margarita Cota-Cárdenas, Juan Felipe Herrera, Carmen Tafolla, Tino Villanueva, and Bernice Zamora were strongly inspired by the Aztec understanding of poetry as "flower and song." The concept referred to the transcendence of the every-day and mortality through symbols that expressed the soul of the community. The *movimiento* adapted this concept to their commitment to oral tradition, a sense of identity and belonging, and radical social transformation.
2. I am relying here on the distinction Jacques Derrida establishes between "the political," which is what he tries to rethink in many of his writings, and "politics."

The latter would include political theory, politology, and even a "programme, an agenda, or even the name of a regime," whereas the former has to do with a personal experience at a certain moment, a "concrete and personal commitment," a "performative commitment" (Bennington and Derrida, 2).

3. Proposition 187, also known as SOS (Save Our State initiative), was passed by California voters in 1994. The law, which prevented immigrants from receiving non-emergency health care and public education, was deemed unconstitutional in 1997. In 2014 California passed a bill making some of its aspects unenforceable and, particularly, unconstitutional.

4. For readers familiar with Dobbs's private life, Herrera's irony will be amplified by his being married to Debi Lee Roth-Segura, a self-identified Mexican American from New Mexico.

5. This allegory was often used by African American Christian liberationist thought to establish a parallelism between African Americans' struggle and Hebrew slaves' journey through the desert. Reverend Martin Luther King Jr's "I Have a Dream" speech is one of the best-known examples of the use of this allusion.

## Works Cited

Ahmed, Sara. *Stranger Encounters: Embodied Others in Post-Coloniality*. New York: Routledge, 2000.

Alarcón, Francisco X. "Los vampiros de Whittier Boulevard o la metapoética chicana comprometida des-mistificadora de Juan Felipe Herrera." *Letras Latinas Blog*, December 2009. http://letraslatinasblog.blogspot.com/2009/12/francisco-x-alarcon-on-juan-felipe.html.

Aldama, Alberto J. "Millennial Anxieties: Borders, Violence, and the Struggle for Chicana and Chicano Subjectivity." In *Decolonial Voices: Chicana and Chicano Cultural Studies in the 21st Century*. Edited by Alberto J. Aldama and Naomi Helena Quiñónez, 11–29. Indiana University Press, 2002.

Arteaga, Alfred. *Chicano Poetics: Heterotexts and Hybridities*. Cambridge University Press, 1997.

Bennington, Geoffrey, and Jacques Derrida. *Politics and Friendship: A Discussion with Jacques Derrida*. Centre for Modern French Thought, University of Sussex, December 1, 1997.

Burt, Stephanie. "Punk Half-Panther." *The New York Times*, August 10, 2008. https://www.nytimes.com/2008/08/10/books/review/Burt2-t.html.

Canetti, Elias. *Crowds and Power*. Translated by Carol Stewart. New York: Continuum, 1960.

Culler, Jonathan. *Theory of the Lyric*. Cambridge, Mass.: Harvard University Press, 2015.

Derrida, Jacques. "Che cos'è la poesia?" Bilingual in French and English. Translated by Peggy Kamouf. In *A Derrida Reader: Between the Blinds*, 221–37. New York: Columbia University Press, 1991.

Derrida, Jacques, and Anne Dufourmantelle. *Of Hospitality*. Stanford University Press, 2000.

Fishman, Charles. *The Wal-Mart Effect: How the World's Most Powerful Company Really Works—and How It's Transforming the American Economy*. New York: Penguin Press, 2006.

Green, Timothy. "From a Conversation with Juan Felipe Herrera." *Rattle*, December 5, 2014. https://www.rattle.com/from-a-conversation-with-juan-felipe-herrera.

Herrera, Juan Felipe. *187 Reasons Mexicanos Can't Cross the Border: Undocuments, 1971–2007*. San Francisco, Calif.: City Lights Books, 2007.

Herrera, Juan Felipe. *Every Day We Get More Illegal*. San Francisco, Calif.: City Lights Books, 2020.

Herrera, Juan Felipe. *Half of the World in Light: New and Selected Poems*. Camino del Sol Series. Tucson: University of Arizona Press, 2008.

Herrera, Juan Felipe. *Mayan Drifter: Chicano Poet in the Lowlands of America*. Philadelphia: Temple University Press, 1997.

Herrera, Juan Felipe. *Notes on the Assemblage*. San Francisco, Calif.: City Lights Books, 2015.

Lomelí, Francisco. "Foreword; Juan Felipe Herrera: Trajectory and Metamorphosis of a Chicano Poet Laureate." In *Half of the World in Light*, by Juan Felipe Herrera, xv-xxiv. University of Arizona Press: 2008.

Miller, Hillis, et al. "On Literature and Ethics: An Interview with Hillis Miller." *The European English Messenger*, 15, no. 1 (2006): 23–34.

Nolan, James. *Poet-Chief: The Native American Poetics of Walt Whitman and Pablo Neruda*. University of New Mexico Press, 1994.

Owens, Louis. *Mixedblood Messages: Literature, Film, Family, Place*. University of Oklahoma Press, 1998.

Perea, Juan. "Los Olvidados: On the Making of the Invisible People." *New York University Law Review* 70 (1995): 965–911.

Pratt, Mary Louise. *Imperial Eyes: Travel Writing and Transculturation*. New York: Routledge, 1992.

Sandoval, Chela. *Methodology of the Oppressed*. University of Minnesota Press, 2000.

Zaretsky, Eli. "The Big Lie." *London Review of Books Blog*, February 15, 2021. https://www.lrb.co.uk/blog/2021/february/the-big-lie.

# CHAPTER 3

# From Fowler to El Salvador

## Juan Felipe Herrera's Global "We"

MICHAEL DOWDY

A defining feature of Juan Felipe Herrera's uncategorizable writings remains undertheorized, perhaps because this characteristic initially appears to be of secondary importance to the poet's more explicit investigations of subjectivity, sociality, history, labor, spirituality, and aesthetics. In so many of Herrera's writings, pronouns jump abruptly and often unpredictably from line to line and from sentence to sentence. I have long puzzled over these dramatic shifts among first, second, and third person viewpoints. In recent years, particularly during and after his back-to-back terms as Poet Laureate of California and of the United States, I have begun to understand these pronominal movements as preliminary, improvisational, and occasionally ecstatic sketches for a poetics of the "global we." In these pages, I will trace the development of Herrera's conceptions of a "global we" through his archives, published texts, and public performances.

Paying special attention to the complex relationships between the places his poems touch down and the pronouns that descend upon and emerge from the social encounters staged there underscores the poet's sustained, and sometimes audacious, attempt to envision and conjure into being a collective, global "we."

Consider, by way of introduction, the exemplary but usually passed-over poem "Fuselage Installation." The poem, which first appeared in the January/

February 1991 issue of *The American Poetry Review*, dramatically expands the expressive and topical ranges that have often guided the public's limited expectations for Chicano/a and Latino/a cultural productions. Printed as the magazine's back cover feature (figure 3.1), the poem begins with a parenthetical stanza, as if citing, in an aside, an absent antecedent:

(My loved ones drift into nothingness
—with little red gifts still
in their anxious arms. Little shirts.)

(Herrera, "Fuselage Installation," 48)

The next quatrain explodes the seemingly self-contained brackets with a startling jump cut announcing that this is a poem of disaster, or its aftermath, of uncertain provenance:

Blaze, the missile shards; your fuselage glitter, stuttered over the wild crazed
mountains; a blast at the exact interval when coffee was being served; on
the last plate,
a frayed napkin casts a claw shadow.

(48)

This stanza's series of four fragments, joined conspicuously by semicolons, is heavy on the poetic devices of parataxis and metonymy and silent on the contextual questions of where, when, how, and why this disaster unfolded. "Fuselage Installation" was reprinted in 1994 in *Night Train to Tuxtla* where it is unchanged from its initial publication in *APR*. Then, in 2008, the poem was included in *Half of the World in Light: New and Selected Poems* where it comes with a new, and helpful, dedication: *"for Scotland"* (original emphasis).

The Lockerbie bombing happened on December 21, 1988, three years before "Fuselage Installation" made *APR*'s back cover. Absent the dedication, it's difficult to discern that Herrera's poem is about, or even addresses, Lockerbie. Letters from the editors of *APR* archived in the Juan Felipe Herrera Papers at Stanford University's Special Collections do not hint at this historical context either—neither the letter accepting the poem for publication from co-editor Arthur Vogelsang, nor the letter of payment from co-editor David Bonnano. Their understanding of the poem's "aboutness"

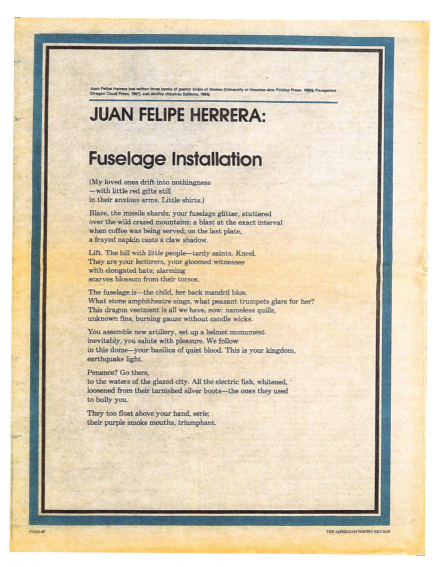

FIGURE 3.1 The American Poetry Review 20, no. 1 (1991). Juan Felipe Herrera back cover feature. Box 6, folder 23 (164). Courtesy of the Department of Special Collections, Stanford University Libraries.

remains unknown. Another poet might have strategically placed contextual details, facts, dates, or place-names to dramatize this specific conjunction in history. Yet another might have dedicated the poem to the 270 people who died in the crash of Pan Am Flight 103. Even the dedication Herrera adds for the third publication date, twenty years after Lockerbie, pins the poem's intervention to the scale of the nation-state. With notable exceptions, such as "Letter to the Hungry Students of Berlin," also from *Night Train to Tuxtla*, Herrera's default geographical metric has been the state. In these ways, saying that this poem is "about" Lockerbie can be a stretch. Yet this is so obviously an Herrera poem that it is as difficult to mistake "Fuselage Installation" for another poet's as it is to attribute the poem's meditations to a general rumination on disaster rather than a specific response to the Lockerbie bombing.

Herrera's fingerprints cover the poem's diction, images, figures, scenes, and modes of address. So much appears here of Herrera's signature style honed in the 1980s and 1990s: from the title's multisyllabic phrase laden with institutional critique, echoing earlier and later "assemblages" of language such as "module metropolis" and "literary asylums," to speculative, sci-fi inflected phrases such as "fuselage glitter" and "claw shadow." But it's the poem's shifty pronouns that constitute the signature of what I am calling Herrera's public "we" poems. Consider how first- and second-person plural pronouns guide the second half of the poem:

This dragon vestment is all **we** have, now: nameless quills,
unknown fins, burning gauze without candlewicks.

**You** assemble new artillery, set up a helmet monument inevitably, **you** salute
with pleasure. **We** follow
in this dome—**your** basilica of quiet blood. This is **your** kingdom, earth-
quake light.
Penance? Go there,

to the waters of the glazed city. All the electric fish, whitened, loosened from
their tarnished sliver boots—the ones **they** used to bully **you**.

They too float above **your** hand, eerie;
their purple smoke mouths, triumphant.

("Fuselage Installation," 48; my emphasis)

The dynamic, unsettling triangulation of "we," "you," and "they" will come to define Herrera's public "we" poems in the 2010s, most prominently during and after his roles as Poet Laureate of California (2012–2014) and then Poet Laureate of the U.S. (2015–2017). There are few, if any, poets in the U.S. whose poems so frequently use the first-person plural "we," and in such a varied, unpredictable, and uncompromising range of ways. The power of Herrera's "we" usually does not derive from a representational poetics wherein the poet speaks for his community, as in the Whitmanian poetics ("voice for the voiceless") taken up by Langston Hughes, Martín Espada, and others. Rather, Herrera's "we" destabilizes hierarchies, angling with ever more abandon into a simultaneously material and mystical global collective that is always in play, always becoming, and ever emergent in fields and streets the world over.

In *Chicano Poetics: Heterotexts and Hybridities* (1997), Alfred Arteaga identified how the epistemological and ontological underpinnings of Herrera's poems can disentangle form from content: "Even when the content of a particular poem may not be noticeably Chicano and the language may be English, there is always a dynamic sense that a sense of self is at stake in the articulation" (154).[1] "Fuselage Installation" dramatizes this "dynamic sense" in instructive ways. The "self at stake" is not limited to a singular, lyric "I" that serves as a stand-in for the poet, nor to a Chicana/o or Latina/o collective. Instead, as is the case across so many of his texts, Herrera's "we" is global, already ready to emerge wherever it is needed.

As depicted in "Fuselage Installation," the Lockerbie bombing becomes just one of the many origin sites for Herrera's public "we" poems. From Scotland to poems of the El Mozote massacre in El Salvador, the riots in Los Angeles, and the Pulse nightclub shooting in Orlando, Herrera has unflinchingly written about the disasters and crises of the late twentieth and early twenty-first centuries. This poetics culminates in his 2015 collection *Notes on the Assemblage*, and his 2020 volume *Every Day We Get More Illegal*. *Notes on the Assemblage* includes poems addressing the disappearance of the forty-three normal school students of Ayotzinapa, Mexico ("Ayotzinapa" / "Ayotzinapa"); the NYPD murder of Eric Garner on Staten Island ("Y si el hombre con el choke-hold" / "And If the Man with the Choke-hold") and the white supremacist murder of nine Black parishioners at Mother Emanuel Church in Charleston, South Carolina ("Poema por poema" / "Poem by Poem"). These poems create "assemblages" of singular and plural pronouns and of Spanish and English, as these three poems appear in versions of each. These assemblages combine Herrera's idiosyncratic poetic vision with potential collective formations against state and white supremacist violence, exhorting into being what the critic Walt Hunter, in *Forms of a World: Contemporary Poetry and the Making of Globalization* (2019), calls a latent "global 'we'" (75). Such poems of public mourning prophecy a "sprung open incandescence," as Herrera puts it in "Ayotzinapa," where individuals merge into an unpredictable, anarchic, collective spirit in the streets.

## "We" in the Archives

At the end of 1982, before his first full-length book *Exiles of Desire* was published the next year, Herrera had already begun conceptualizing his poetic practice within the expansive parameters that would define the public poems of his Poet Laureate years three decades later. On December 2nd, in advance of his appearance on campus that evening, the student newspaper of California State University Fresno (where he would later chair the Department of Chicano and Latin American Studies) ran an advertisement for Herrera's performance (figure 3.2).

This ad in the *Daily Collegian* is a historically significant piece of ephemera because it presents Herrera's signature moves in chrysalis form. Titled "From Fowler to El Salvador," it is perhaps the first extant announcement for a Juan Felipe Herrera solo reading, at least the earliest one housed in the extensive Juan Felipe Herrera Papers at Stanford University's Special Collections.

The ad's features presage Herrera's distinctive style of public self-presentation in his mature writings as well as the many visual productions accompanying his later literary performances. The poet's collages, paintings, sketches, and photographs appear inside many of his thirty-five books and on their covers. First, the title geolocates Herrera's hemispheric poetics, coordinating the U.S. to Latin America, the north to the south, and most specifically, it pinpoints the then most current instance of U.S. American imperialism in Central America, El Salvador. In addition, the alliteration of *Fowl-* and *Sal-* and *-er* and *-or* produces the translingual echoes so essential to the sonic landscapes of many of Herrera's poems. Second, the ad describes Herrera's appearance in the University Lecture Series as a "reading" from his two forthcoming books. This was no typical "lecture," for a conventional lecturer does not bring a band. Not only would Herrera read, he would also

From Fowler to El Salvador 75

FIGURE 3.2 Juan Felipe Herrera reading "From Fowler to El Salvador." Box 56, folder 24 Daily Collegian, CSU-Fresno. Courtesy of the Department of Special Collections, Stanford University Libraries.

be "performing" "sound, image and word collages." The ad thus brings into conjunction Herrera's longstanding commitment to the dynamic intersections of page and stage, print and performance. So, too, the ad's construction with handmade cut-outs highlights Herrera's improvisational poetics and the collages and sketches of cover art on *Notes on the Assemblage* and *Every Day We Get More Illegal*. Note the pasted uppercase "M" in the "pM" and "AdMission" as well as the visible seams along his photo's jagged border. These characteristics amount to a prototype of the poet's attempt to bring multiple media forms into energetic conjunction. Finally, to this "lecture" the poet brings a crew of fellow artists, the TROCA Rhythm and Sign Ensemble, along with "projectionist" Víctor Martínez.

In sum, the ad shows the poet's "we" materializing on the stage of California State University Fresno as a loud, unruly, multisensory collective. Like

## 76  Michael Dowdy

many of Herrera's poems of the 1990s and early 2000s, the ad is maximalist, a bit messy, seemingly unfinished,[2] and it coordinates the migrant labor camps and fields of Fowler, his birthplace, to the hot spots of U.S. imperialism and global conflict. Notably, these communal and aesthetic formations cannot be separated from the material contexts of their emergence. Like any good collage, the ad's juxtaposition startles observers into new knowledge. The ad for "Ski Vail" highlights the contradictions of the U.S. that would later be paramount in the appointment of an anti-imperialist Chicano poet to the post of Poet Laureate during an era of extreme inequality and anti-(im) migrant politics. That's not to mention what I've cropped from the page: a political cartoon on Reaganomics and a letter to the editor addressing the dangers of the United States' Cold War postures.

While this ephemera shows an early instance of Herrera performing a public "we," a private letter from the poet, critic, and labor activist Mark Nowak offers some clues about how such a "we" would be received in its print forms. Nowak wrote to Herrera in his role as editor of *XCP: Cross Cultural Poetics*. Dated June 23, 1997, Nowak includes the first issue of the influential, groundbreaking journal, urges the poet to send him work, and praises Herrera effusively (Figure 3.3).[3]

In his critical study *Social Poetics* (2020), Nowak identifies how a "social poetics"—he borrows the term from Langston Hughes—combines the "forces of the plural and the singular," which "not only coexist, but amplify each other" (177). Nowak's history of leading working-class writers' workshops rhymes with Herrera's long history of leading community workshops, for children and students, in particular, but it is Nowak's theorization of a first-person plural poetics that interests me here. I cite at length from the introduction to his chapter on this collective poetics:

> Pronouns pose and enclose possibilities. *Us* broadens the world of *me*, *we* opens spaces of solidarity for *I*, and *they* broadens the binary. The plural is a collective with an innate potential to embrace, augment, and amplify our imaginings in ways impossible for the singular. If capitalism, neoliberalism, and empire place their sole emphasis on *my* and *mine*, the social (within any socialism and any social poetics) must insist on shifting emphasis in the direction of the pronouns of the first-person plural, toward *we* and *us* and *they*, toward *our, ours, ourselves*. The result of this social shift will be that my burden becomes our burden, my precarity becomes our precarity, [. . .] my

23. June. 97

Dear Prof. Juan Felipe Herrera —

We'd like you to have this copy of the inaugural issue of Xcp: Cross-Cultural Poetics in hope that you might like what you see + send us work for our next issue. We're ardent admirers of your work (I just got your new book, Mayan Drifter, at the bookstore last night) and would consider it an honor to have some of your work in a forthcoming issue of Xcp. If possible, we like to look at larger samplings (10-15 pgs, or more if longer pieces are included) and promise a quick response to any work sent. Please, if you can, think of Xcp for your unpublished work that needs a home!

Blessings, + hoping to hear from you —

Mark Nowak, editor.

**FIGURE 3.3** Letter from Mark Nowak, editor of XCP. June 23, 1997. Box 5, folder 52. Courtesy of the Department of Special Collections, Stanford University Libraries.

future becomes our future, my joy becomes our joy. But how can this be accomplished while maintaining the essential necessity of self-determination within the first-person singular? How can these forces of the plural and the singular, in other words, not only coexist, but amplify each other? (177; original emphasis)

Over the course of his long career, across his many books of poems and uncategorizable writings, Herrera has posed answers to Nowak's rhetorical

# 78  Michael Dowdy

questions. Herrera's first-person plurals open spaces to shift from *my* to *our*, often by imagining the sharing of burdens and joys, griefs and exaltations. For him, when the "forces of the plural and the singular" merge and "amplify each other" they can envision political collectives that are endowed with an organic life force ultimately uncontainable by literary institutions and state violence alike. As I show in the following sections, such amplifications grow more prominent and forceful as Herrera's public profile expands, from the 1980s through the 2010s.

## "We" from the Eighties to the Aughts

When the poem "Exiles" appeared in *Exiles of Desire* in 1983, it marked one of the first occasions in Herrera's writings where such pronouns facilitate propulsive encounters between disparate groups. At one level, the poem represents the gulf between U.S.-based South American exiles from the Southern Cone countries, where they fled U.S.-backed military dictatorships—Herrera names Argentina, Chile, and Uruguay—and U.S.-born Chicanos. The former are described as "They [who] are not there in the homeland," while the latter, who are unnamed but implied, are depicted as "we the ones from here, not there or across, / only here" (*Half of the World*, 23). As suggested by its epigraph from the diary of the painter Edvard Munch—"and I heard an unending scream piercing nature"—this ekphrastic poem addresses Munch's iconic painting *The Scream* (1893). Herrera uses Munch's bridge to unfold an extended metaphor of exile. Like Munch's screaming figure crossing the bridge, the poem's exiles are suspended in time, continually crossing the bridge between south and north, there and here:

> They are in exile: a slow scream across a yellow bridge
> the jaws stretched, widening, the eyes multiplied into blood
>
> orbits, torn, whirling, spilling between two slopes; the sea, black,
>
> swallowing all prayers, shadeless.
>
> ("Exiles," *Half of the World*, 23)

The heavily punctuated nine-line stanza, populated with colons (two), commas (twelve), semicolons (one), and periods (three), draws out its "slow scream" through frequent pauses and parataxis, in order to "hover over" the disappeared in Argentina, Chile, and Uruguay. If South American exiles inhabit the ghostly bridge, Chicanos are "without the bridge, without the arms as blue liquid / quenching the secret thirst of unmarked graves, without / our flesh journeying refuge or pilgrimage" (23). Notably, the singular figure in "The Scream," who is trailed by two ominous figures haunting the background, becomes in Herrera's rendering a collective "they." Exile, in this conception, is a disjointed communal purgatory of persistent, if spectral, pain, rather than an individual condition, as it is often understood.

In the most immediate sense, this poem constitutes a prescient meditation on the incommensurate dimensions of Latinidad and the differences of origin and trajectory subsumed under the identity *Latino*, years before the term really started gaining traction.[4] But the broader conceptual insight of "Exiles" is more capacious. The poem asks readers to reckon with how to live proximate to a suffering, pain, and grief that is very real but that remains ineffable and unable to be shared. In this sense, Herrera's ruminations run through Munch, the Southern Cone, and Chicano history to arrive at echoes of Maurice Blanchot's thinking about the asymmetrical burdens of responsibility and pain in *The Writing of the Disaster* (1995) while also anticipating critiques of literary witness, such as those made by the poet Cathy Park Hong's in her essay "Against Witness" in *Poetry Magazine* (May 1, 2015). But when the attention is placed directly on pronouns, as I believe it should be, "Exiles" can be read through the lens of the Mexican writer Cristina Rivera Garza's reckonings with the social dimensions of grief. "It is impossible to grieve in the first-person singular," Rivera Garza insists. "We always grieve for someone and with someone" (2020, 8). From the beginning, Herrera's poems have grasped this idea intuitively as a cornerstone of individuated art and communal life. Rivera Garza writes:

> There, where suffering lies, so, too, does the political imperative to say, You pain me, I suffer with you, I grieve myself with you. We mourn us. Yours is my story, and my story is yours, because from the start, from the singular—yet generalized—perspective of we who suffer, you are my country, my countries. (7)

In "Exiles," Herrera attempts to join two stories ("Yours is my story, and my story is yours"), but the concept of exile seems to prevent their union. The poem ends with two rhetorical questions posed from "We that look out

80  Michael Dowdy

from / our miniature vestibules . . . / Where is our exile? / Who has taken it?" (*Half of the World*, 24). The reader is left to ponder what is so alluring and impenetrable about exile.

In his memoir of the prehistories and aftermaths of the Pinochet coup on September 11, 1973, *Heading South, Looking North: A Bilingual Journey* (1998), the Chilean American writer Ariel Dorfman describes the symbolic appeal of *exile* over terms such as *refugee*, despite the term's limited practical value:

> The term had no legal significance, no international or technical meaning, no guarantees, no protection. I chose it automatically because I wanted to see my emigration as part of another tradition—a more literary one, perhaps. There was something Byronic, defiant and challenging, about being an exile, something vastly more romantic and Promethean than the fate embodied in that recently coined word *refugee* that the twentieth century had been forced to officialize as a result of so much mass murder and wandering. I was, of course, just as much a victim, just as doomed, as the blurred constellation of anonymous beings who had preceded me, but by rejecting the passive term and opting for the more active, sophisticated, elegant one, I was projecting my odyssey as something that originated in myself and not in the historical forces seething outside my grasp. (236–237)

In contrast to Dorfman, Dorfman's fellow Chilean Roberto Bolaño concludes in his extensive writings on exile, "I don't believe in exile, especially not when the word sits next to the word *literature*" (38; original emphasis). For Bolaño, part of the problem with the concept is "the refrain of the suffering of exiles" (41), which he calls

> a music composed of complaints and lamentations and a baffling nostalgia. Can one feel nostalgia for the land where one nearly died? Can one feel nostalgia for poverty, intolerance, arrogance, injustice? The refrain, intoned by Latin Americans and also by writers from other impoverished or traumatized regions, insists on nostalgia, on the return to the native land, and to me this refrain has always sounded like a lie. (41–42)

Both Dorfman and Bolaño escaped Pinochet's Chile, and each ultimately sees "exile" as a literary construct. For Bolaño, moreover, "exile" is simply a bad fiction. Herrera's poem, on the other hand, imagines the suspended animation of those human beings who do not have recourse to their status as artists. Dorfman calls them "the blurred constellation of anonymous beings" (237) who, Bolaño bluntly insists, lack a safe "bridge" (237) of return to their origin countries. In these ways, Herrera's poem can be read as a recognition of his own (U.S.) Americanness. Once that unsettling origin is established, Herrera can experiment further with ways to join *they* and *we, you* and *I,* individuals and collectives, across the boundaries of states, geographies, and histories. These ways are grounded in Latino/a languages, cultures, and formations but, as in "Fuselage Installation," they often far exceed them.

The process of conjoining guides the drama of "Norteamérica, I Am Your Scar," the intrepid poem that follows "Fuselage Installation" in *Night Train to Tuxtla* (in *Half of the World in Light,* the order is reversed). Because I have argued elsewhere that "Norteamérica, I Am Your Scar" is one of the most powerful, enduring examples of a hemispheric Latino/a poetics,[5] I want to emphasize here the leading role of the poem's pronouns. The ninety-five-line poem includes a whopping eighty-seven pronouns: sixteen first-person singular (*I* and *my*), thirty-one first-person plural (*we, us,* and *our*), and forty second-person (*you* and *your*). The number of second-person pronouns is especially notable because the first one does not come until the twenty-sixth line. Beginning with the title's direct address to the United States, here conceived through a simultaneous geographic enlargement and rhetorical diminishment, the poem triangulates these three pronominal positions into a latent collective formation.

To merge the singular and plural, the poem imagines individual reconciliation to U.S. empire mapping on to collective resistance to it. It also moves from the "I" of the title and the "my friends" and the "I" of the opening couplet to the first-person plural perspective of collective knowledge: "We see how you polish your claws" (*Half of the World,* 132). This close doubling of *you* and *yours,* so common in the poem's latter half, dramatizes the omnipresence of state and corporate power that constricts Chicano/a and Latino/a life choices. As such, the singular possessive *my* attaches to affective states ("anguish" and "resentments") rather than material possessions. The plural possessive *our* is similarly diminished to disposable, metonymic parts: "undershirts," "dishrag," "fender," "hind leg," and "almond eyed typewriter ribbon." ("Roofs" may be an exception, though they are splattered with blood and bile.) In contrast, *your* "industry" and "spirit of bank flowers and helicopter prowls" (132) connotes wealth, power, and menace. After toggling between *I* and *we* to warn and teach this imperial *you*, the poem ends with a transformed "we" coming to life in "the age of the half-men / and the half-women":

> I say to you, now, I celebrate
> when we shall walk with two legs once again
> and when our hands shall burst from your hands.
>
>         ("Norteamérica, I Am Your Scar," *Half of the World*, 133)

Among the poem's onslaught of pronouns, a conspicuous absence illuminates Herrera's world-making. Not a single "they" appears in the poem. The poet sidesteps *us* versus *them* oppositions in favor of *us* with *you* relationalities. This approach not only makes encounters with state power more personal, embodied, and intimate, it positions a multiracial working-class *we* as the fundamental part of *you*, the state.

The concluding lines of "187 Reasons Mexicanos Can't Cross the Border," the standout list poem from 2007's eponymous collection, bring Herrera's pre-laureate "we" full circle from the opening line of "Exiles." As the poet and critic Stephanie Burt notes, "No poet alive, perhaps, uses anaphora better; none relies on it more" than Herrera (92). This especially potent example of the literary device features 187 "Because" clauses, the number of lines parodying California's Proposition 187 (1994), which would have banned undocumented persons from accessing a range of public services. The poem's shape-shifting "we" spans time and space, rejects the claims and allures of juridical citizenship (thus anticipating the raft of recent critiques of citizenship discourses in Latino/a studies), and joins Mexicanos (and even non-Mexicanos) in an alliance of antic resistance against the rhetorics of nativism and xenophobia. Among other categories, the self-contained lines include histories, both broad and specific ("Because we've been doing it for over five hundred years already," 29, and "Because Operation Wetback took care of us in the '50s," 35); taunts ("Because we'll dig a tunnel to Seattle," 29); self-deprecations ("Because we have visions instead of televisions," 31); parodies of stereotypes ("Because multiplication is our favorite sport," 29); antiracist critiques ("Because we can read about it in an ethnic prison," 30); and absurd propositions collapsing distinctions between singular and plural ("Because we never finished our PhD in Total United Service," 31—it's impossible to earn a collective PhD, after all). The overwhelming force and variety of these repetitions conjure a "we" encompassing all Mexicanos (Chicanos, Mexican-Americans, and Mexicans, those "potential Chicanos"), other Latina/o groups ("Because we're in touch with our Boricua camaradas," 34), and, in Herrera's performances, anyone who shows up and participates in the call-and-response, joining him in a raucous chorus of laughter, gesticulation, hesitation, and out-of-order revision.[6] By the time "we" reach the poem's end, experiencing a combination of levity, bleariness, energy, and rage, Herrera has returned to the vehicle of collective movement in the opening phrase of "Exiles": "At the greyhound bus stations" (23). On this mobile terrain, "187 Reasons Mexicanos Can't Cross the Border" ends with a defiant quantification of collective might that will define his Laureate-era "we" poems: "Because you can't deport 12 million migrantes in a Greyhound bus" (35). Because this rapacious poem uses "we" constantly, sometimes toggling to an oppositional "they," this last-second, second-person "you"—one of only three across 187 lines—lands as a defining provocation, a repudiation of the anti-immigrant, fascist dream of banishment as a stupid delusion.

## "We" in the Laureate Years

Herrera's "we" poems during his U.S. poet laureate years became even more focused on recent, specific historical events. Unlike the initial publication of "Fuselage Installation," these poems often come with explicit datelines and dedications. Consequently, in *Notes on the Assemblage*, the global "we" comes into sharp relief in poems addressing the Ayotzinapa disappearances, the police killings of Black men, and the mass shooting of Black parishioners in Charleston. Yet these more disciplined, occasional poems were not, in my view, guaranteed. A public poet is often asked to produce ceremonial poems of measured gravity, calm, and order. Was this a difficult charge for Herrera, whose poems have often been messy, improvisational, maximalist, fevered, just plain *difficult*, as Arteaga explained in 1997 (153)? Yet, Herrera's global "we" had been in play since the outset of his publishing and performing careers. It is precisely from this first-person plural viewpoint that Herrera's Laureate-era poems find their deepest resonances.

In *Forms of a World*, Walt Hunter describes how the poetry of Sean Bonney and Myung Mi Kim "desperately conjures a globalized 'we,' a crowd to come" (66). Using hortatory modes, these English and Korean American poets "enact on the level of poetic form the jostling, prickling, energizing sensations of proximity to heterogeneous others" (Hunter, 70). Hunter concludes that the global "we" has the capacity to envision a "proleptic or anticipatory commons" (73).

While his words apply to Herrera's long poem of the May 1, 2006, pro-immigrant march in Los Angeles, "A Day Without a Mexican" (in *187 Reasons*), they highlight more expansively the ways in which the global "we" stitches together "Ayotzinapa," "And If the Man with the Choke-hold," and "Poem by Poem." Together, their three complementary "we" forms substantiate Herrera's sustained vision of the welling ground force of decentralized people power *as* the "crowd to come" (Hunter, 66).

The necessity and possibility of collective agency underlies Herrera's first-person plural poems. "Poem by Poem" concludes *Notes on the Assemblage* with this very warrant. After a dedication to the nine Black men and women (each named in full) who were murdered by a white supremacist in Mother Emanuel AME Church in June 2015, the poem begins: "poem by poem / we can end the violence (Herrera, 96)." Herrera immediately implies that by "poem by poem" he also means *day by day* ("every day" "after / every other day," 96). This substitution of *poems* for *days* is followed by a shift from the first- to the second-person and further modification of the equation of art and temporality: "you have a poem to offer" (96), he implores gently, "it is made of action" (96). Here, Nowak's "forces of the singular and the plural" "amplify" each other, but with a twist. Rather than beginning from the individual and moving to the collective, "Poem by Poem" begins with "we" as the foundation on which "you" must create your action-poems. From this gruesome event, Herrera calls into action a broad-based American "we." Most prominently, this "we" asks those whose blood is *not* being shed to join what Hunter calls "the crowd to come" (66).

"Ayotzinapa" is more ambitious in scale and bolder in its willingness to speak *for* and *as* the dead rather than in their memory. The poem's dedication—*"for the students, for Mexico, for the world"* (original emphasis)—moves from the forty-three disappeared students who were studying to be rural elementary school teachers at the Raúl Isidro Burgos Rural Teachers College in Ayotzinapa, Guerrero, to the nation-state, and finally to the globe. The students were attacked by the police on September 26, 2014, and the subsequent cover-up enraged Mexicans across sectors and classes. "To this day," John Gibler wrote in 2017 in *I Couldn't Even Imagine That They Would Kill Us*, his meticulously reported oral history of the attacks, "the Mexican federal government continues to disappear the 43 students" (257).[7] Unsurprising to a long-time reader of Herrera is how he pins the hopes of *the world* on students. Since the activism of his *movimiento* days in the late sixties, the poet has usually seen students (from elementary schoolers to university students) as the base of social and political action. (This viewpoint distinguishes him from Nowak, for whom workers are always the base.) But something more unusual and unsettling unfolds in "Ayotzinapa," where the base is students who are no longer living. In the first half of the poem, the "we" is the forty-three disappeared students themselves, who orate collectively from beyond the grave, revivified in Herrera's long, unpunctuated, prose lines. "From Ayotzinapa," the poem begins, "we were headed to Iguala to say to the mayor that we wanted funds for our rural school for teachers" (*Assemblage*, 17). After the poem introduces the very real specter of state terror ("they burned us they dismembered us in trash bags," 17), it builds outward toward living students the world over:

> [. . .] they threw us into the river yet we continue yet we march from here from the bowels of Mexico this river that floods all the schools and all the universities and all the floors of the emperors' palaces we continue at twenty-four years of age we make way through the massacre here from where we were born and from where we died toward all the cities in the world toward all the students and teachers in the world demonstrating on all the streets sprung open incandescent. (17)

The surreal image *a la Herrera* that concludes the poem's main stanza, "streets sprung open / incandescent" (17), transforms the plainspoken language preceding it, where the biblical-scale floods gather the dead and the living into an unstoppable force. Although Herrera may have been unaware of the etymology of the place-name Ayotzinapa, and his depiction of the students' burned bodies being dropped in a nearby river was eventually disproven as part of the Mexican state's gaslighting, the river metaphor is profoundly apposite. Ayotzinapa, Gibler reports, is a Nahuatl word meaning "place of turtles" (219). Inside their hard, durable shells, turtles are able swimmers who move between rivers and land. Imagining "all the students" in the world as turtles slowly discovering their collective precarity *and* potential power underlines how Herrera's river metaphor joins Ayotzinapa—place of turtles—to the world at large.

Apart from this context, one key historical detail missing from Herrera's poem distinguishes the poet's approach to the attacks from Gibler's journalistic practice. The students had been for many years taking over buses for their transportation (because their lack of resources precluded access to other forms of transport), generally with the tacit agreement of bus companies and drivers. The historical irony is that on the occasion of their disappearance the students "were trying to commandeer those buses to attend the annual protest of one of the worst student massacres in history" (Gibler, 223). That massacre was, of course, the state murder of over 300 students in Tlatelolco plaza in Mexico City on October 2, 1968, just days before the start of the 1968 Summer Olympics. In fact, Gibler's oral history (with a foreword by the aforementioned Ariel Dorfman) follows the form of Elena Poniatowska's iconic book of oral testimonies, *La noche de Tlatelolco* (1971). While *Notes on the Assemblage* and *I Couldn't Even Imagine That They Would Kill* were each published by City Lights Books, their approaches to Ayotzinapa diverge. Whereas Herrera uses a global first-person plural, Gibler decides to listen to, and record, students thus:

> Before the police attacks in Iguala, inspired by the Zapatista idea of "to lead by obeying" or "*mandar obedeciendo*" and reflecting upon years of reporting on social struggles and state violence, I had begun to ask myself questions like these: What would it mean to write by listening, to *escribir escuchando*? What form would a writing that listens take? (20)

Herrera's poem does not evince much interest in this sort of listening practice. Rather than listen to the disappeared students' classmates and families, Herrera attempts to bring the dead to life through his river of words. And he aims to bring attention to Ayotzinapa in the U.S.; while the attack and its aftermath enraged Mexicans and galvanized a massive, sustained response, in the U.S. there was relatively little reporting. Nonetheless, Herrera's "we," with its congregation of students and teachers the world over, follows the conception of disparate "we" formations that Gibler spots on a banner during a march in Mexico City following the attacks: "We do not know each other, but we need each other" (231).

The riverine power of marching and demonstrating that propels "Ayotzinapa" flows into the book's following poem, "And If the Man with the Chokehold." Because the title serves as the poem's first line, its initial conjunction ("and") extends the river metaphor. This conjunction connects resistance to state violence in Mexico to state violence in the U.S., in this case anti-Black police brutality. Although the title and first part of the poem seem to allude to the killing of Eric Garner by the NYPD on Staten Island in July 2014, the poem places this one murder in a seemingly unending series of extrajudicial killings. The poem's series of "and" clauses eventually leads onto an interrogative clause, where the first-person plural "we" is called into question, casting some doubt on the collective agency on which the book's final poem, "Poem by Poem," will insist: "And if we march," he asks, "why does the street divide as we pass" (*Assemblage*, 19).

Given that it ends with an image of a bloody tree "blossom[ing] torches," "And if the man with the choke-hold" (19) hauntingly foreshadows the tiki torches at the Unite the Right rally in Charlottesville in August 2017, where the antifascist counter-protester Heather Heyer would be murdered by a white nationalist from Ohio who drove his car into that day's potent materialization of the "crowd to come."

## "We" after the Laureate Years

Soon after I began writing this essay during the midst of a deadly global pandemic, Herrera released another book of poems, *Every Day We Get More Illegal* (2020). The collection's title foregrounds the first-person plural "we" I had been meditating on throughout the summer of COVID, George Floyd, and Kenosha. The title echoes the "every day" action of poem making from "Poem by Poem" and insists that citizenship is no shield for Latinos against the state and its surveillance, imprisonment, and deportation arms. The book includes the standout poem "Touch the Earth (Once Again)," which was initially published in *Poetry Daily* on September 16, 2020, Mexican Independence Day, and which serves here as an apt conclusion to the pronominal dimensions of Herrera's "global we" poetics. The poem begins with a simple collective declaration followed by a colon: "This is what we do." It then proceeds to catalog in cascading anaphora ("this is . . .") what workers from "the cotton truck driver" to the "artichoke worker" "do" before transitioning to a second anaphoric repetition: "not to mention." Then, using the rhetorical technique of paralipsis Herrera does in fact mention a range of *piscadores* (harvesters), from "cucumber workers" to "almost-magical watermelon" workers.

Resounding with the tensile anaphora of "Blood on the Wheel," from *Border-Crosser with a Lamborghini Dream* (1999), "Touch the Earth (Once Again)" clearly presents a more focused range of images than the riotous surrealism of that earlier piece. But the poem moves from a working-class, migrant, and Latina/o *we* that seems to include the poet, to an autonomous *they* that "bend[s] in the fires no one sees" (*Illegal*, 20), then to an unspecified *you* that appears to count the millions of the beneficiaries of *their* labor. This movement hinges on another anaphoric shift from "not to mention" to "notice." The repetition of "notice" at the beginning of lines serves as warnings tacked to all of our glowing screens and devices. It can also be read as conjoining two words (*not* and *ice*) to create a compound of condemnation and resistance to the deportation regime. When viewed as "not ICE" lines such as "notice: how they bend in the fires no one sees" distribute readerly attention between deeply personal seeing practices and state surveillance practices. As a counterpart to Gibler's listening practice, Herrera's plea to *notice*, that is, to *see*, emphasizes how alienated labor (especially agricultural) is erased in all of its wondrous and backbreaking specificities, from "winery workers" to "melon workers." Put simply, the poem celebrates these lives and the acts ("what we do") by endowing them with an agency that is at least partly constituted as a gift "for you," the poem's conspicuous final words calling out all readers of the poem.

Such resonant figures of migrant laborers are an apt place to end this discussion of Herrera's poetics of the "global we." In writing on the book *Lotería Cards and Fortune Poems: A Book of Lives* (1999), Herrera's characteristically uncategorizable collaboration with the visual artist Artemio Rodríguez, the poet and scholar Edgar García argues that the book's representations of migrants reconfigure perceptions of migrant temporality and agency. "Rather than unredeemed victims or mere demographical units," García writes, "the migrant characters in this collection of 104 linocuts paired with poems are (as the title of their book suggests) potent anticipations of a future that refuses to be determined by past conditions" (253). In "Touch the Earth (Once Again)," Herrera presents "potent anticipations of a future that refuses to be determined by past conditions" (*Illegal*, xv) of alienation, dispossession, exploitation, and invisibility. For this future to emerge, "you" have to lead with gratitude and enter the river of "we." As ever, Herrera attends to material conditions while simultaneously reaching toward a numinous unity. *Every Day We Become More Illegal* concludes with the words of the Dalai Lama: "We must develop a sense of oneness of 7 billion human beings" (20). Balancing material and mystical dimensions have guided Herrera's public "we" poetics from "From Fowler to El Salvador" to "Fuselage Installation" to this tender, sensuous poem in yet another year of global upheaval for the world's 7 billion human inhabitants.

## Notes

1. For more on this dynamic, see Carmen Giménez Smith and John Chávez's introduction to *Angels of the Americlypse* and Ralph Rodríguez's introduction to *Latinx Literature Unbound* which describes the burden of representation on Latino/a writers: "Much pressure is imposed either from external or internal forces requiring that writers with Latinx surnames produce work that is recognizably Latinx" (Rodríguez, 2).
2. This open-endedness aligns with Arteaga's notion that Herrera's Chicano subjectivity "is not a state of being but rather an act" in which infinitives—"to play, to conflict"—"work out dialogically unfinalized versions of self" (155).
3. The two pieces that Herrera would submit to Nowak opened the special issue "History/In/Heritance" of *XCP: Cross Cultural Poetics 2*. "Cilantroman: A Performance Cocina" and "Canto for Chan Ki'n Viejo, Last To'o'hil of Najá, Selva Lacandona, Chiapas, Mexico, December, 1997" are now available online at the Open Door Archive, which includes all of the issues of *XCP*.
4. On the relationships between South and North American Latino/a cultural formations, see Juanita Heredia's volume of interviews with Latino/a writers of South American descent, *Mapping South American Latina/o Literature in the United States*.
5. For further discussion of Herrera's hemispheric poetics, see the chapter "Molotovs and Subtleties: Juan Felipe Herrera's Post-Movement *Norteamérica*" in *Broken Souths*.
6. For example, watch Herrera's performance at Los Angeles' Ruskin Art Club on November 20, 2007.
7. In addition to Gibler's oral history, the two-part Netflix documentary, *The 43*, directed by Matías Gueilburt and narrated by the Mexican writer Paco Ignacio Taibo II, offers useful background on the attacks, investigations, and protests.

## Works Cited

Arteaga, Alfred. *Chicano Poetics: Heterotexts and Hybridities*. Cambridge: Cambridge University Press, 1997.

Blanchot, Maurice. *The Writing of the Disaster*. Translated by Ann Smock. Lincoln: University of Nebraska Press, 1995.

Bolaño, Roberto. "Literature and Exile." *Between Parentheses: Essays, Articles, and Speeches, 1998–2003*. Translated by Natasha Wimmer. New York: New Directions, 2011.

## 90 Michael Dowdy

Burt, Stephanie. "Juan Felipe Herrera: Undocumentary." *Close Calls with Nonsense: Reading New Poetry*, 91–94. Saint Paul, Minn.: Graywolf, 2009.

Dorfman, Ariel. *Heading South, Looking North: A Bilingual Journey*. New York: Farrar, Straus, and Giroux, 1998.

Dowdy, Michael. *Broken Souths: Latina/o Poetic Responses to Neoliberalism and Globalization*. Tucson: University of Arizona Press, 2013.

García, Edgar. "A Migrant's *Lotería*: Risk, Fortune, Fate, and Probability in the Borderlands of Juan Felipe Herrera and Artemio Rodríguez's *Lotería Cards and Fortune Poems*." *Modern Philology* 118, no. 2 (2020): 252–76.

Gibler, John. *I Couldn't Even Imagine That They Would Kill Us: An Oral History of the Attacks Against the Students of Ayotzinapa*. Foreword by Ariel Dorfman. San Francisco, Calif.: City Lights, 2017.

Giménez Smith, Carmen, and John Chávez, eds. *Angels of the Americlypse: An Anthology of New Latin@ Writing*. Denver: Counterpath Press, 2014.

Gueilburt, Matías, dir. *The 43*. Netflix docuseries. 2019.

Heredia, Juanita. *Mapping South American Latina/o Literature in the United States: Interviews with Contemporary Writers*. Edited by Norma E. Cantú. Cham., Switzerland: Palgrave, 2018.

Herrera, Juan Felipe. *187 Reasons Mexicanos Can't Cross the Border: Undocuments, 1971–2007*. San Francisco, Calif.: City Lights, 2007.

Herrera, Juan Felipe. "Bonnano, David. Letter. Payment for poetry in American Poetry Review. 12/90." Juan Felipe Herrera Papers. M1043. Department of Special Collections, Stanford University Libraries, Stanford, CA.

Herrera, Juan Felipe. "Cilantroman: A Performance Cocina" and "Canto for Chan Ki'n Viejo, Last To'o'hil of Najá, Selva Lacandona, Chiapas, Mexico, December, 1997." *XCP: Cross Cultural Poetics 2* (1998): 7–25. Open Door Archive, Northwestern University. http://opendoor.northwestern.edu/archive/items/show/479.

Herrera, Juan Felipe. "Daily Collegian, CSU-Fresno, 12/2/82: JFH reading 'From Fowler to El Salvador.'" Juan Felipe Herrera Papers. M1043. Department of Special Collections, Stanford University Libraries, Stanford, CA.

Herrera, Juan Felipe. *Every Day We Get More Illegal*. San Francisco, Calif.: City Lights, 2020.

Herrera, Juan Felipe. "Fuselage Installation." *American Poetry Review* 20, no. 1 (January/February 1991): 48.

Herrera, Juan Felipe. *Half of the World in Light: New and Selected Poems*. Tucson: University of Arizona Press, 2008.

Herrera, Juan Felipe. *Lotería Cards and Fortune Poems: A Book of Lives*. Linocuts by Artemio Rodríguez. San Francisco, Calif.: City Lights, 1999.

Herrera, Juan Felipe. *Night Train to Tuxtla*. Tucson: University of Arizona Press, 1994.

Herrera, Juan Felipe. *Notes on the Assemblage*. San Francisco, Calif.: City Lights, 2015.

Herrera, Juan Felipe. "Nowak, Mark. Letter from Mark Nowak, editor of XCP. 6/23/97." Juan Felipe Herrera Papers. M1043. Department of Special Collections, Stanford University Libraries, Stanford, CA.

Herrera, Juan Felipe. "Poetry at the Ruskin." Reading of "187 Reasons Mexicanos Can't Cross the Border." Ruskin Art Club. November 20, 2007. https://youtu.be /W8Ben-1n5zQ.

Herrera, Juan Felipe. "The American Poetry Review. Vol. 20/No. 1. 1991. JFH back cover feature." Juan Felipe Herrera Papers. M1043. Department of Special Collections, Stanford University Libraries, Stanford, CA.

Herrera, Juan Felipe. "Vogelsang, Arthur. Poetry acceptance letter from Arthur Vogelsang poet and editor, *American Poetry Review*. 11/20/90." Juan Felipe Herrera Papers. M1043. Department of Special Collections, Stanford University Libraries, Stanford, CA.

Hong, Cathy Park. "Against Witness." *Poetry Magazine*. May 1, 2015. https://www .poetryfoundation.org/poetrymagazine/articles/70218/against-witness.

Hunter, Walt. *Forms of a World: Contemporary Poetry and the Making of Globalization*. New York: Fordham University Press, 2019.

Nowak, Mark. *Social Poetics*. Minneapolis: Coffee House Press, 2020.

Poniatowska, Elena. *Massacre in Mexico (La noche de Tlatelolco)*. Translated by Helen R. Lane. Columbia: University of Missouri Press, 1975.

Rivera Garza, Cristina. *Grieving: Dispatches from a Wounded Country*. Translated by Sarah Booker. New York: Feminist Press, 2020.

Rodríguez, Ralph. *Latinx Literature Unbound: Undoing Ethnic Expectation*. New York: Fordham University Press, 2018.

CHAPTER 4

# "To Go into America as I Go into Myself"

Chicana/o Indigeneity, the Indigenous Other, and the Ethnographic Gaze in Juan Felipe Herrera's *Mayan Drifter*

MARZIA MILAZZO

In *Mayan Drifter: Chicano Poet in the Lowlands of America* (1997), Juan Felipe Herrera relates his 1992 journey into Chiapas in search of K'ayum Ma'ax, a Lacandón elder whom he had previously met in 1970, when he was an anthropology student at UCLA. A twenty-one-year-old Herrera had then embarked onto his first trip to Chiapas and headed to Lacanjá Chan Sayab, one of the two largest Lacandón villages, to learn about artistic practices of the present-day Maya (Herrera 1997, 68). Herrera's involvement with the Chicano movement had sparked his interest in Mexico's Indigenous cultures. Unsatisfied with having merely a book knowledge of Indigenous peoples, Herrera wanted a real-life connection. "Rather than talking about them and writing about them," Herrera said in a 2018 interview, "I want[ed] to hang out with them, and sit down and break bread, and film and record and interview, and bring back some of the things that they are making; some art, some stories—as much as possible" (Soldofsky, 208). In 1992, Herrera returns to Chiapas once again equipped with a tape recorder and notebook—the quintessential tools of the anthropologist. However, soon after arriving in the Lacandón village of Nahá in search of K'ayum Ma'ax, Herrera chooses to give away his tape recorder and, in his own words, "let go of my 'ethnographic intentions'" (*Mayan Drifter*, 112). Instead of an ethnographic project, Herrera envisions *Mayan Drifter* as "a personal poem, a manifesto from the heart" (xi). Yet, Herrera does not abandon the ethnographic project altogether, nor does he leave indigenism behind. Even as *Mayan Drifter* moves away from the representation of a mythical Indigenous subject confined to the past that shaped Chicano movement literature in favor of a personal encounter with living Indigenous peoples, it remains indebted to both ethnography and indigenism. The *indígena* remains an instrument of self-discovery and path to ancestral affiliation for the Chicano/a subject in *Mayan Drifter*, which reveals how the literary encounter between the Chicano/a Self and the Mexican Indigenous Other is often structured in inequality. The irony, of course, is that neither can I, a white European woman writing about a Chicano author, disentangle myself, and this writing, from inequality.

Spanning a multitude of themes and genres that have evolved over time, Herrera's literary production is extraordinarily varied, to the extent that, as Francisco A. Lomelí has argued, Herrera "embodies a one-person vanguard in constant movement" (Lomelí, xv). Within this vast and heterogeneous opus, Indigenous Mexico represents Herrera's most longevous concern, having been the source of creative energy from the inception of his long and prolific literary career. *Rebozos of Love / We Have Woven / Sudor de Pueblo / On Our Back* (1974), Herrera's first book, displays the influence of the indigenism and cultural nationalism that shaped the cultural production of the Chicano movement and its aftermath. Here, playful verses combining English, Spanish, and Caló ("quetzalcóatl fruit bro' / sister / simón! / feed on sweet tropical jugo") as well as neologisms appear alongside meditative verses that aim to include the Chicano/a subject within a larger collective of Indigenous pueblos of the Americas ("a m e r i n d i a / en el plan / de la humanidad").[1] Herrera's focus in these poems is not centrally on the Indigenous Other, but on constructing the Chicano/a Self *as* Indigenous primarily through references to *lo indígena* — things and elements that are Indigenous. An expression of the Chicano Renaissance and animated by a utopic impulse, these poems are "spiritualist and cosmological in content" (Lomelí, xvii). They are chants that strive to emulate Indigenous oral forms of expression (Flores, 140). In the poem that opens the collection, the speaker announces that these are ". . . cantos / que cargamos cada dia" (. . . songs / that we carry every day); they are offerings that seek to actualize a "renacimiento revival / de nuestra sangre en nuestras venas" (renaissance revival / of our blood in our veins; n.p.). The speaker here embodies the collective voice of the Chicano/a community that has come to understand itself as a pueblo.

While in *Rebozos of Love* Herrera adopts Aztec and Maya myths, images, and symbols to poetically forge a collective Chicana/o identity, the publication of *Thunderweavers/Tejedoras de Rayos* (2000) marks a distinct moment within Herrera's artistic production. This is the only poetry volume in which Herrera fully directs his gaze towards the struggles of the present-day Maya. In this bilingual collection, the Chicano/a subject withdraws into the background as Herrera becomes the carrier of other peoples' stories. The speaker takes on the voices of four Maya women who survived the 1997 Acteal massacre, in which paramilitary members of the then ruling Partido Revolucionario Institucional (Revolutionary Institutional Party or PRI) killed forty-five innocent Tzotziles, including twenty-one women and fifteen children, while they were praying in a church in Acteal, Chiapas. In one of the poems, the speaker laments:

Why am I Tzotzil?
Why was I born in this land of so many storms?
I plant corn and yet I reap gunpowder
I plant coffee and yet I reap mad spirits
I plant my house and yet I reap the viscera
of this fallen earth

(Thunderweavers/Tejedoras de Rayos, 43)

The tone here is tragic, elegiac, with intermittent glimmers of hope. There is no room for the idealization of an Indigenous way of life, nor space for cosmological references to Aztec deities that centrally informed Herrera's early poetry and, even more prominently, Alurista's *Floricanto en Aztlán* (1971) or Luis Valdez's *Pensamiento serpentino* (1973). Herrera's concern in *Thunderweavers/Tejedoras de Rayos* is no longer with *lo indígena*, but with *la indígena*—the living Indigenous subject, and specifically Tzotzil women, whose experiences are not incorporated into a Chicano/a subjectivity, but are considered on their own terms.

Situated between the politics of *Rebozos of Love* and *Thunderweavers* is *Mayan Drifter*, a work as unique within the Chicano/a canon and U.S. American literature at large as it is complex and paradoxical. Herrera in *Mayan Drifter* constantly questions his own literary project, aware that it threatens to unravel under the racialized weight of history. Herrera rejects the idealization of an Aztec and Maya past that animated Chicano *movimiento* literature and his own literary production at the beginning of his career. "I do not want to add another tired volume to the racks of Chicano movement literature," Herrera writes in *Mayan Drifter*, "the roots stuff of the sixties and also of minority nationalist narratives that tunnel through history in search of an ethnic essence to be conjured in a self-induced Ouija spell" (5). At the same time, Herrera is preoccupied with much more than Chicano nationalism. He is a Chicano, yes, but he is also a writer and traveler who threads uneasily the path of European colonizers and anthropologists who have journeyed through the Mexican lowlands before him. Herrera writes, "It was an odd maneuver to be a Chicano, a person of color, en route to a 'native' topography" (15). Herrera's desire to connect with Indigenous peoples is marked by discomfort.

In order to grapple with the significance of this discomfort, it is useful to consider some of the critical debates that have long surrounded Chicano/a indigenism and Indigeneity.[2] The revival of Indigenous myths and symbols that followed the drafting of *El Plan Espiritual de Aztlán* (1967) was subjected to scrutiny early on.[3] Already before 1980, poet Ricardo Sánchez harshly criticized what he perceived to be Chicano/a writers' estrangement from living Indigenous peoples and their struggles.[4] A more enduring critique of Chicano movement indigenism has come from Chicana feminist writers. In the pivotal essay "Queer Aztlán: The Re-formation of the Chicano Tribe" (1993), Cherríe Moraga famously denounced Chicano nationalists for relying on "a kind of 'selective memory,' drawing exclusively from those aspects of Mexican and Native cultures that served the interests of male heterosexuals" (242). Moraga laments that Chicanos "took the worst of Mexican machismo and Aztec warrior bravado combined it with some of the most oppressive male-conceived idealizations of 'traditional' Mexican womanhood and called that cultural integrity" (242). While Moraga critiques the purpose to which Chicano writers put Indigenous myths and stories, she does not question the adoption of Aztec mythology per se. Rather, following the path that Gloria Anzaldúa opened in *Borderlands/ La Frontera: The New Mestiza* (1987), Moraga's work has often reinterpreted Aztec and Maya mythology in a feminist light.

Interrogating Chicano/a writers' reliance on the mythic, Sheila Marie Contreras in *Blood Lines: Myth, Indigenism, and Chicana/o Literature* (2008) reveals the entanglement of Chicano/a indigenism with imperial circuits of power and its indebtedness to Western forms of knowledge. Contreras writes:

> Chicana/o indigenism draws from a wealth of source material, directly and indirectly, acknowledged and unacknowledged, creating cultural narratives that rely prominently on mythic accounts drawn from anthropology and archeology. Even as Chicana/o indigenist discourse puts forth its critiques of racial domination, colonial violence, and land removal, it remains embedded within the very 'circuits' of knowledge and power that have advanced imperial agendas. (8)

The influence of anthropology and archeology is visible in Anzaldúa's and Moraga's works, in which Mexico's Indigenous people enter largely through archives and museums, rather than through a personal relationship with living Nahua and Maya people. Anzaldúa, for example, first saw the statue of Coatlicue, which in *Borderlands/La Frontera* she describes as a powerful archetype "that inhabits my psyche," in the Museum of Natural History in New York City (1987, 69). Similarly, Moraga first saw the Cihuateteo statues, which become the chorus in her play *The Hungry Woman: A Mexican Medea* (2001), at the National Anthropology Museum in Mexico City (Oliver-Rotger 2005, n.p.). Through a reliance on mythology, Chicana indigenism de-historicizes the relationship between Chicano/as and Indigenous people (Contreras 2008, 117).

Anzaldúa herself affirmed in an interview, "I hate that a lot of us Chicanas/os have Eurocentric assumptions about Indigenous traditions. We do to Indian cultures what museums do—impose western attitudes, categories, and terms by decontextualizing objects and symbols" (2009, 288). Taking Anzaldúa's work to task for confining Indigenous people to a mythological past, María Josephina Saldaña Portillo argues that "the indígena . . . demands new representational models that include her among the living" (2001, 420).[5] Since its representation of Indigenous people is grounded in a real-life encounter with Maya people, *Mayan Drifter* offers precisely one such new representational model. Nonetheless, *Mayan Drifter*, too, remains centrally indebted to anthropology and entangled in the circuits of colonial power that have informed Chicano/a literature's complex relationship with the Indigenous Other from the inception.[6]

Anthropology and Mexico's Indigenous people are intimately tied in Herrera's biography. Having begun his undergraduate studies at UCLA in social work, Herrera ultimately graduated with a degree in social anthropology in 1972 (Soldofsky, 198, 208). In an interview conducted in 2018,

Herrera explains his reasons for studying anthropology as follows: "I said to myself, 'Everyone is talking about culture.' But I really wanted to know about it. Actually, I want[ed] to go to indigenous regions in Mexico and be face to face with the indigenous realities of our culture" (Soldofsky, 208). By the time Herrera enrolls in a master's program in anthropology at Stanford University, he is no longer interested in conducting research in Mexico. Under the mentorship of Renato Rosaldo, Herrera directs his investigative efforts towards Latino writers in the Bay Area (Soldofsky, 208). To a young Herrera who struggles to focus on his research, Rosaldo recommends engaging in ethnopoetics: "'Just write your thesis the way you write your poetry!'" (Soldofsky, 210). After completing his degree at Stanford, Herrera will go on to become one of the leading writers of the Latino/a and Chicano/a literary vanguard emerging in San Francisco's Mission District (Soldofsky, 199). Herrera thus leaves ethnography behind—at least, until he writes *Mayan Drifter*.

*Mayan Drifter* is as much a reflection on the socio-political conditions that have shaped the struggles of the Maya people in Chiapas as it is a meta-reflection on a literary object that strives to engage ethically with its subjects. Juggling between the two is the author and character of Juan Felipe Herrera drifting at the center of the work—painfully aware of the writer's complicity with colonialism, yet unable to avoid a collision with colonial power. Maria Antònia Oliver-Rotger writes that "*Mayan Drifter* inscribes colonialism while it also resists an entirely colonial vision through a self-reflective narrative voice aware of his dual fragmented heritage from the colonizer and the colonized" (2009, 173). Herrera is aware of the tensions that lie at the heart of his project. He concedes, "Colonial consciousness assaults my personal writing project" (*Mayan Drifter*, 4). *Mayan Drifter* thus turns the critical lens onto the author himself, displaying an internalization of Gayatri Spivak's argument that "to confront [subaltern subjects] is not to represent (*vertreten*) them but to learn to represent ourselves (*darstellen*)" (289). Present from the very inception, autocritical reflections reappear in *Mayan Drifter* as Herrera recounts his journey from San Cristóbal de las Casas to the Lacandón village of Nahá, and beyond.

The recurrence of such self-referential and autocritical moments motivates Oliver-Rotger's definition of *Mayan Drifter* as an "autoethnography" (175). In *Imperial Eyes: Travel Writing and Transculturation* (1992), Mary Pratt defines an autoethnography as instances in which colonized subjects undertake to represent themselves in ways that engage with the colonizer's own terms. If ethnographic texts are a means by which Europeans represent to themselves their (usually subjugated) others, autoethnographic texts are those the others construct in response to or in dialogue with those metropolitan representations. (7)

Pratt considers *New Chronicle*, Guaman Poma de Ayala's work on Inca history and customs, as the prototypical autoethnography. However, even as Herrera in *Mayan Drifter* constantly blurs the boundaries between himself and the Maya, he remains an outsider, while Poma is Inca himself. Describing *Mayan Drifter* as an autoethnography, as Oliver-Rotger does, further risks obscuring Herrera's positionality vis-à-vis the Indigenous subjects he writes about.

Nonetheless, the self-reflexivity that characterizes *Mayan Drifter* should not be taken for granted. Herrera constantly critiques colonialism, ethnography, and his own writing project. If ever there was a creative work that puts the positionality of the Chicano/a writer vis-à-vis living Indigenous people under painstaking scrutiny, it is *Mayan Drifter*. And yet, the work also exhibits a problematic relationship with Indigenous peoples, one that Herrera's self-reflexivity does not manage to overcome.

*Mayan Drifter* opens with the following epigraphs:

*I crossed the border full of dignity.*
*My satchel flourishes with so many things*
*from the rainy earth.*

—Rigoberta Menchú

*You'll have to listen to the sounds.*
*You should hear the song of the sky crickets,*
*the passing of the sky, the abandonment of the earth.*

—Viejo Chan K'in Nahá, Lacandón jungle, Chiapas, Mexico

*It will be born out of the clash between the two winds, it will arrive in its own time, the coals on the hearth of history are stoked up and ready to burn. Now the wind from above rules, but the one from below is coming, the storm rises . . . so it will be.*

—Subcomandante Marcos, EZLN Lacandón jungle, Chiapas (n.p.)

In the first epigraph, Herrera begins to construct a symbolic affinity with Rigoberta Menchú that will become further established in the first chapter. Herrera immediately wants us to know that Menchú, like Herrera, is a border crosser. Herrera's choice to open *Mayan Drifter* with an epigraph by Menchú, then, is of utmost significance. In "To América with Love," the opening chapter, Herrera argues that a main task of *Mayan Drifter* "is to disassemble the reading of America and Mexico, to revolt against the lexicon of European Indianism—Gauguin-like escapes into a tropical scrim of berry-eaters and long-haired, silent, punk Quetzalcóatl incarnates" (8). This agenda is not a new one, Herrera writes, as it has preoccupied many writers before him. Among them, Herrera places Miguel Angel Asturias, José María Arguedas, and other indigenist writers who have written about "the displaced *indígena* and campesino wastelands" (9). However, rather than to these male writers, Herrera "feel[s] closest" to Rosario Castellanos (9). Herrera writes that Castellanos rejected the label "indigenist writer," arguing that she wrote about Indigenous people not because she found them mysterious, but because "they live in atrocious poverty" (8). While this statement resounds with Herrera, it is Menchú, not Castellanos, whom Herrera more explicitly cites as a model. Herrera is unequivocal: "Rigoberta's work inspires this text" (9). Herrera's placing of *Mayan Drifter* alongside Menchú's testimonio *I, Rigoberta Menchú: An Indian Woman in Guatemala* (1983) suggests that he views both works as being engaged in similar politics and doing similar work. This is one of many instances in *Mayan Drifter*, to cite Gabriele Pisarz-Ramírez, in which "Herrera's desire for kinship overrides his awareness of the differences between him, the Chicano traveler, and the Maya" (282). This move, in fact, obscures how the Menchú's and Herrera's relationship to the Maya people they represent is fundamentally different. Yet, the blurring of boundaries between the Chicano Self and the Indigenous Other in *Maya Drifter* begins already from the title, which suggests that the "Mayan drifter" is the "Chicano poet" himself.

In calling Menchú by her first name, Herrera suggests an intimacy, a familiarity with the author that further silences how inequality structures Herrera's relationship with the Maya. Herrera continues to draw Menchú closer to him, searching for similarities, rather than highlighting differences, as he argues that Menchú in her autobiography "also outlines, indirectly, the role of the poet and the writer's enterprise" (9). Herrera's addition of "indirectly" suggests that he is aware that in *I, Rigoberta Menchú* these are marginal concerns, while they are prominent in *Mayan Drifter*. Herrera does not simply contend that Menchú is preoccupied with the role of the poet, but argues that she *is a poet*. Menchú is "a model for the poet of the twenty-first century" (9). Those who argue otherwise, Herrera notes, "must speak louder" (9). This way, Herrera further places himself in symbolic proximity to Menchú: both are poets, and their role as poets is what's most important about them. Significantly, right after he has established that Menchú is a poet, Herrera announces that he enters *Mayan Drifter* as a poet, a fact to which I shall return.

The second epigraph also features the voice of an Indigenous person, as it reproduces words spoken by Chan K'in, a Lacandón elder whom Herrera first met in 1970, during his first trip to the Lacandón jungle, and who reappears throughout the work. Chan K'in here invites someone, perhaps Herrera himself, to "*listen to those sounds*" (italics in the original) and direct their senses towards the sky. The specification "Nahá, Lacandón jungle, Chiapas, Mexico" signals the importance of place in *Mayan Drifter*, a work that immerses readers into a landscape likely unknown to most of them and describes people who are different from the English-speaking U.S. audience for whom the book is intended. Chan K'in's words place him in the position of the sage who blesses the foreigner with local wisdom and insider knowledge. The epigraph evokes the Indigenous as spiritual guide, teller of stories, and *giver*. Later in *Mayan Drifter*, Herrera describes his second encounter with Viejo Chan K'in. Addressing the changes made to prepare for his encounter with the elder, Herrera writes: "the house was being rearranged for my visit; each element was being positioned, intricately, yet with great care and ease" (166). Herrera is the guest of honor. The house is "rearranged" for Herrera—not for the arrival of Viejo Chan K'in. Herrera is also the spectator, the one who looks at Viejo Chan K'in and describes him in this way:

> At the center Viejo Chan K'in was lying deep in his hammock, on his side, facing me. His curled legs were covered by an old tunic, and his arms fell across his body like water. His hands were dark, hard, large, and crooked. I noticed something odd about his hands: They seemed to be frozen, and the fingers were pulled forward, fixed as if clutching an invisible weight, an eternal machete. His face was small and round, brown with eyes that glimmered; his gaze was gentle. (166)

Chan K'in's appears passively lying on a hammock, wrapped in the traditional tunic that signals his ethnic affiliation. The language Herrera uses to describe Viejo Chan K'in is both poetic and objectifying: first, Viejo Chan K'in's arms evoke a waterfall; then, the arms end with hands that are "dark, hard, large and crooked." Herrera immediately calls attention to the color of Viejo Chan K'in's skin. This is not the only time that Herrera mentions the skin color of the Lacandón people that he describes. Earlier in the work, he describes Antonio, K'ayum Ma'ax's father-in-law, as "ashen colored—almost as if he was made of something other than flesh and tunic, some other substance like vine meshed with stony minerals" (157). Is Antonio human at all? He does not even seem made of flesh but "some other substance." The mention of the tunic alongside the flesh seals Antonio as irrevocably Other: he is *made of* tunic; his body and his tunic have become one. The fetishization of the Lacandones' skin color recurs throughout the work. In "In a Field of Arrows," Herrera writes that "K'ayum Ma'ax leaned over his light-skinned son and smelled his breath" (109). The specification "light-skinned" is irrelevant to the interaction between father and son; it does not help us better understand the significance of the interaction. The fact that it is nonetheless included in the text says more about Herrera than it says about K'ayum Ma'ax's son, signaling the ethnographic, racializing gaze inscribed in *Mayan Drifter*'s representation of Indigenous people.

Returning to the scene of Herrera's encounter with Viejo Chan K'in, the adjectives "dark, hard, large, and crooked," used to describe Chan K'in's hands, make them appear monstrous, too large for his body. They almost do not appear real: "They seemed to be frozen." They are not just passively there, however. They appear to be holding a menacing weapon, "an eternal machete." In the picture that Herrera paints of him, Viejo Chan K'in appears, literally, frozen in time. But his invisible weapon need not worry us: Chan K'in's gaze, Herrera reassures readers, "was gentle." Viejo Chan K'in's passive pose and gentle gaze contrast with the description of his hands, and especially his fingers, which appear almost animalistic, evoking claws. The concurrent idealization and objectification of Chan K'in as both sage and savage shows how the representation of Lacandón people in *Mayan Drifter* reproduces colonial ways of knowing.

The third epigraph takes us again to the Lacandón jungle. This time the speaker is Marcos, former subcomandante of the Ejército Zapatista de Liberación Nacional (Zapatista National Liberation Army or EZLN), who in

"Chiapas: The Southeast in Two Winds, and a Storm and a Prophecy" (1992), announces the arrival of a "wind from below" (296), suggesting the impeding rise of a revolution. The epigraph prefigures the Zapatista uprising. A little more than one year after the journey that Herrera describes in *Mayan Drifter*, the Maya would lead an uprising on January 1, 1994, which deliberately coincided with the North Atlantic Free Trade Agreement (NAFTA).[7] In *Mayan Drifter*, Herrera appears ambivalent about the Zapatista movement, almost incredulous about its existence (Dowdy, 76). Nothing in the text suggests that, during his journey, Herrera realized that a revolution would be imminent. What is more, the Maya that Herrera describes appear passive and defenseless (Pisarz-Ramírez, 284). In Herrera's view, they are "huddled Indian seekers of survival" (*Mayan Drifter*, 121). Powerlessness is what defines them as people. Notice how Herrera describes his trip to the archeological site of Toniná as him moving "down the window slopes and rings of powerlessness with sixty to seventy Tzotzil-Tzeltal Indians and campesinos" (87). Herrera routinely reminds the reader that the Maya are helpless in the face of the Mexican state, U.S. imperialism, transnational corporations, and the intrusive gaze of anthropologists.

Phrases such as "dark-skinned powerlessness" (14) and "tribal powerlessness" (125) permeate *Mayan Drifter*. Herrera wonders: "Would a day arrive when the Lacandones would fight back again?" (140). Herrera seems irritated by what he perceives to be the Lacandones' utter lack of action. In the letter addressed to K'ayum Ma'ax that closes the book, Herrera feels entitled to exhort K'ayum Ma'ax to fight back: "Am I supposed to tell you to take up arms, to turn back to Nahá?" (250). Herrera continues: "Why are you in Palenque? . . . Was it because you had left yourself behind, because you had grown accustomed to the Ladino bank account given to you for caoba timber and Mayan artifact?" (252). According to Herrera, the Lacandones are both unwilling and unable to liberate themselves: they need (foreign) help.

It is thus also in its paternalism and inability to envision resistance on the part of the Indigenous people it represents that *Mayan Drifter* reveals itself as a work more indebted to Latin American indigenismo, and even indianismo, than Herrera admits. Following a traditional indigenist agenda, Herrera is the mestizo writer whose work focusses on Indigenous people with the goal of denouncing the conditions in which they are forced to live and presenting their stories to a foreign audience. Herrera's writing is meant to *help*. Herrera describes *Mayan Drifter* as "my own contribution to the cause of Indian and campesino justice and social change" (5). In the letter that closes the book, Herrera also presents *Mayan Drifter* as a gift to K'ayum Ma'ax, no matter that K'ayum Ma'ax likely does not speak English and that Herrera had just lambasted him for being a coward and potentially corrupt. In the epigraphs, it is telling that the mestizo, embodied by Subcomandante Marcos, is the vanguard announcing an impending revolution, while the Maya, represented by Rigoberta Menchú and Viejo Chan K'in, appear full of dignity, but far from being revolutionary agents of history.

From the inception, the desire to write an ethical text nonetheless imposes upon Herrera an incessant process of self-questioning which will become a leitmotiv throughout the work. In the opening essay, Herrera describes *Mayan Drifter* as his "offering as a poet to Mexico's Indian peoples and to all those who want to think about and reimagine America" (3). *Mayan Drifter* immediately casts an inquisitive lens onto the position of the author and the act of writing itself. Herrera asks, "How do I go about this telling? What position do I occupy?" (4). Engaging in the vexed task of speaking about the Other, the work suggests, requires that the writer should learn to represent himself and continuously question the task that they are about to undertake. Herrera writes:

> Writing tests my faith and responsibility: as a writer, I must attack a formidable cadre of adversaries: language, historical consciousness, traditional and obsolete patronal versions of the *indio*; I must challenge the very idea of "Social Inquiry of the Native"—the canonical ethnographic S.I.N. of the social sciences. To fall back on a stolid "minority poetics" is also another possible folly—that is, to call for a universal and automatic bond among Mexican, Chicano, Latino and Indian peoples. The text wants to negate itself, yet I must keep on; a way to speak is possible and significant. (5)

Self-reflexive moments such as these, and more explicitly autobiographical ones in which Herrera delves into his family history, are not extraneous to ethnographic writing. In fact, as Pratt writes, "personal narrative is a conventional component of ethnographies" (1986, 31).

Autobiographical information, as is the case in *Mayan Drifter*, almost always appears in opening chapters and introductions. These narratives serve to position the subjects of the ethnographic endeavor: "the ethnographer, the native, and the reader" (Pratt 1986, 31–32). This personal narrative, Pratt writes, "persists alongside objectifying description in ethnographic writing because it mediates a contradiction within the discipline between personal and scientific authority" (1986, 32). In *Mayan Drifter*, candid self-critique and the inclusion of personal narrative might appear to threaten Herrera's credibility as a writer. In reality, they reinscribe narratorial authority as Herrera presents himself as a writer who is thoroughly aware of the pitfalls of ethnography and has, ultimately, managed to avoid them.

Herrera, in fact, does not spare ethnography from scrutiny. *Mayan Drifter* can itself be read as a product of the "crisis of representation" that shook anthropology as a discipline in the 1980s and beyond.[8] Anthropology and the figure of the anthropologist are the object of sharp critique throughout *Mayan Drifter*. If Herrera turns the critical lens onto himself, he turns an even sharper lens onto the anthropologists that he encounters during his journey, whether these are Frans and Gertrude Blom or the Mexican anthropology students collecting data for their research projects that Herrera meets at Na Bolom and in the Lacandón jungle. Na Bolom, a museum and research center about the Lacandones turned hotel in San Cristóbal de las Casas, Herrera writes, "was a paradox: what was pronounced and featured for open display was simultaneously erased—el indio, la india [the Indian man, the Indian woman]. Was Na Bolom a tourist trap disguised by a politically correct Indianism and facile environmental platitudes?" (*Mayan Drifter*, 54). The founder of Na Bolom, alongside her anthropologist partner Frans Blom, Gertrude Duby Blom was one of the first Europeans to systematically investigate the "way of life" of the Lacandones, who have been in the crosshairs of anthropologists for more than a century (Palau, 11). An amateur anthropologist and photographer, Gertrude Blom lived in San Cristóbal de las Casas from 1950 until her death in 1993 (Blom 1999, 86). The governor of Chiapas, under the auspices of the Instituto Nacional Indigenista (INI), sponsored her first expedition into the Lacandón jungle in 1943 (Blom 1974, 8).

In *Mayan Drifter*, Herrera exposes the profound contradictions that characterize the museum, about which Gertrude Blom said, "The real monument for Frans Blom is not his grave but Na Bolom" (Blom 1999, 86; my translation). Herrera describes how Na Bolom exoticizes the Maya, effectively rendering them museum pieces, while Maya people exist at its margins, as exploited maids and as objects of desire paraded for foreign tourists. Na Bolom, Herrera writes, "opposed deep changes for the Maya. If it favored *la revolución*, it was only in the same manner as the PRI did—that is, in its rhetoric and gestures in the name of the indigenous peoples of Chiapas" (*Mayan Drifter*, 54). At Na Bolom, the Indigenous subject is displayed, objectified and "preserved" in thousands of images for the cultural enhancements of tourists and researchers. And yet, Herrera himself begins his journey at Na Bolom. The irony of this fact is not lost on him. Herrera writes: "Irony and subterfuge gnaw at the center of this text: How can I speak of and for America if my entry is through the Na Bolom center in San Cristóbal de las Casas, a museum for research on the Lacandón Maya that has profited in many ways by the Othering of these people for almost half of a century?" (4). As a response to this conundrum, Herrera places Na Bolom under investigation, denouncing the exploitation of Indigenous peoples that the museum fosters.

Herrera's critique of anthropology and its damaging relationship to Indigenous peoples does not stop at Na Bolom. When he arrives at K'ayum Ma'ax's home in Nahá, Herrera finds three anthropology students from the Universidad Nacional Autónoma de México (UNAM) "doing what good anthropology students must do" (115). As the students are going over their notes and interviews, Herrera remembers his own previous endeavors in the Lacandón jungle: "It was as if I was looking at myself twenty-three years ago in Lacanjá with canvas bags of appropriate ethnographic paraphernalia" (115). Herrera frequently casts a critical lens onto the intrusive questions that the students ask K'ayum Ma'ax and his family members. In order to extract information, the UNAM students interrupt conversations and take up unwarranted space. In one occasion, Herrera recounts how Luz asks Angélica "an ethnographic question" about the moon and women's relationship to it (126). The question is a good one, Herrera comments, sarcastically. He could imagine the English anthropologist E. E. Evans-Pritchard or the French anthropologist Claude Lévi-Strauss asking a similar question. Making his critique unequivocal, Herrera describes Luz's question as "an arrow-shaped incision into the native" (127). Angélica refuses to answer. Maybe she will do so, Herrera comments, when the question is no longer formulated in Spanish and has "left behind its predator shaped voice" (127). The language that Herrera uses to describe this interaction denounces the work of the anthropologist among Indigenous peoples as violent and predatory.

It is therefore puzzling that Herrera includes some of the ethnographic information that the students so violently extract from the Lacandones into his own book. Herrera might not be the one who asks the questions, but he nonetheless takes the answers and, thereby, participates in the "language thefts for the sake of an enlightened Europe and 'High' America" (105). Herrera does not shun away from including intrusive conversations about sexual practices among the Lacandones. The chapter "El Hombre de la Selva" (The Man of the Jungle), opens as follows:

> The next day, in the kitchen again, Carlos asked K'ayum Ma'ax to clarify something. "How many days did you say you could last with the tejón, the badger?"
>
> "Five days," K'ayum responded with a ball of laughter and maize in his mouth.
>
> "Five days?"
>
> "That's right. You hunt the badger, strip the meat. Then you take the penis bone. [. . .]
>
> Then you better have many lovers to give you sex because you won't be able to stop. Five days, five nights. You will be raw." (143)

The conversation between Carlos and K'ayum, which stretches across an entire page, is reported without commentary. For a work that spends entire paragraphs decrying the coloniality of anthropology, it is strange that it includes such an interaction in the first place. Certainly, Herrera wants us to read the interaction with a critical eye. Nonetheless, it is one of several scenes that document the "way of life" of the Lacandones in a text that announces its departure from ethnography. Here, Herrera appears as a silent observer, the proverbial fly on the wall. He is reporting a conversation in which he is not involved, and for which he is presumably not responsible. He would, after all, never ask such outrageous questions.

Offering insights that are useful for reading this scene, Pete Sigal, Zeb Tortorici, and Neil Whitehead argue in the introduction to *Ethnopornography: Sexuality, Colonialism, and Archival Knowledge* (2020) that ethnography and pornography represent comparable forms of knowledge production. In both cases, they write, "the setup either hides the position of the observer or alternatively places great weight on the ritual of self-reflection" (2). Several scenes involving Lacandón subjects that Herrera describes alternate between these two modes. They also speak to how "all ethnography relates to a deep-seated desire to penetrate the other" (2). This desire enters *Mayan Drifter* under various guises, including through a sexualizing, objectifying gaze. Herrera in this scene engages in a double-theft: he appropriates both the knowledge that the Lacandones impart about their own culture and the anthropology students' work.

The anthropologists in *Mayan Drifter* become the characters onto whom Herrera projects anxieties over his own project. As he observes and scrutinizes the students in their interactions with the Lacandones in Nahá or critiques Gertrude Blom and the Na Bolom "museum machine," Herrera can convince himself that the anthropologist is *out there*—it is not him. Ironically, Gertrude Blom expressed sentiments about anthropologists that were similar to Herrera's. Blom rejected formal ethnography and disparaged anthropologists as "antropolocos," a play on the Spanish words *antropólogo* (anthropologist) and *loco* (crazy) (Palau, 12). Like Herrera, Blom described anthropologists in their interactions with the Lacandones using a critical, even sarcastic tone, calling attention to how they "echa[n] miradas curiosas al interior de sus adoratorios y les asombra[n] con preguntas tontas sobre su 'organización social'" (look into the interiors of their homes with curiosity and surprise them with dumb questions about their "social organization") (Palau, 12; my translation). Nonetheless, as Karina Ruth-Esther Palau writes, "many of her journals read like fieldnotes" (12). Indeed, Gertrude Blom remains one of the anthropologists most closely associated with the Lacandones, having taken more than 55,000 pictures that depicts Lacandones in "their environment" (Blom 1999, 89). Many of these pictures hang on the walls of Na Bolom, while numerous others remain in boxes, undeveloped.

Not unlike Blom, Herrera is convinced that anthropology is something that others do. After all, part of the story that Herrera tells in *Mayan Drifter* is how he "let go of [his] 'ethnographic intentions'" (112). When he arrives in Nahá, Herrera catches himself "acting out an old colonial gesture, following the hardened tradition of anthropologists, archeologists, and 'native seekers'" (105). He has to actively stop himself from "asking / the native questions" (105).

Soon, something changes:

No more questions.
No more cameras.
No more film.
No more recordings or picking up the latest net bag from the shelf. I sickened myself with my own grand quests. I caught myself in my own seeker thirst and seeker suction. . . .

After twenty-three years of going over my memory notes on Nahá, I dropped my nylon bag of intentions. I dropped the archaic grammar of conquest. There was nothing to translate, nothing to take back. How could I take back what Chan K'in José has given me? (106)

From this moment on, Herrera no longer sufficiently questions whether his role among the Lacandones resembles that of an anthropologist. He has decided that it does not. When he places his name at the bottom of a long list of men who have passed through the same region, from the Franciscan monk Fray Diego de Landa to the U.S. anthropologist Roberto Bruce, Herrera describes himself as "the Chicano poet with the funny face" (107). Herrera arrived to Nahá with his tape recorder. "But in a matter of a few hours," he writes, "Nahá had changed all this. . . . I gave the little self-activated machine to K'ayum Ma'ax; the voice box from the States was his now. I let go of my 'ethnographic intentions'" (112). This way, *Mayan Drifter* conceives ethnography as a method that can be easily left behind and as a genre that can be circumvented by writing "an unfinished poem of a desire" (6). This narrow conception of ethnography as something that can be abandoned merely by relinquishing a tape recorder and filed notes sidelines the fact that ethnography is "a key method in maintaining discourses of power, truth, and control" (Miller-Young, 43). In *Mayan Drifter*, ethnography exceeds the methods of data collection.

Disidentifying with the figure of the anthropologist, Herrera announces that he enters "into the text and battle as a poet. This book, then, is a poem" (*Mayan Drifter*, 9). Distilling the multiple genres and mediums that comprise *Mayan Drifter*—which include, among others, travelogue, memoir, ethnography, journalism, drama, poetry and photography—into "a poem" represents yet another disavowal of the work's indebtedness to anthropology. Poetry in *Mayan Drifter* is not theorized as having the potential to carry ethnographic information, but is rather conceived as a tool that can sidestep ethnography. By contrast, Renato Rosaldo shows in *The Day of Shelly's Death: The Poetry and Ethnography of Grief* (2014) that the poet and the ethnographer need not be two separate people. "Like an ethnographer," Rosaldo writes, "the antropoeta looks and looks, listens and listens, until she sees or hears what she did not apprehend at first" (107). Rosaldo conceptualizes the crossing between ethnography and anthropology as "antropoesía or anthropoetry," which he defines as "poetry that situates itself in a social and cultural world; poetry that is centrally about the human condition" (101). Instead, Herrera envisions poetry as intrinsically separate from anthropology. A poem, in Herrera's understanding, is fundamentally subversive: "One of the functions of a poem—if, indeed we can say that a poem has a function at all—is to turn things on their head or on their side: inside out or concave in the ideal. This characteristic is central to my explorations and reflections in this book as a literary project as much as a spiritual quest and cultural investigation" (*Mayan Drifter*, 6). As it endows poetry with the power to overcome ethnography, *Mayan Drifter* positions itself as always already having left ethnography behind. Poetry, in turn, is imagined as innocent, as extricated from the fangs of empire.

Herrera's positioning as a traveler and tourist also disallows, rather than makes visible, a critical engagement with ethnography's intimate relationship with travel writing. Unlike the label of ethnographer, Herrera does not reject the label of traveler. In the process, he fails to investigate how travel writing and ethnography are intimately connected.[9] Herrera is, to some extent, in an ideal position to write an ethnographic work because he does not arrive at his site, the home of K'ayum Ma'ax, as an anthropologist, but as a friend. He is thus able to engage in more intimate conversations and to experience "what a visitor (not an anthropologist) would experience" (Pratt 1986, 43). Herrera does not hesitate to call K'ayum Ma'ax, whom he has not seen since he was twenty-one-years old, "an old friend" (*Mayan Drifter*, 3). But are they really friends?

Herrera's arrival to Nahá is marred with embarrassment. In the village, Herrera meets a man called K'ayum Ma'ax, believing him to be his old acquaintance. But when Herrera shows him an old picture, a moment of misrecognition ensues: "'This is not me,' he says, examining the photo. 'This K'ayum is from Lacanjá Chan Sayab'" (110). Herrera is both in the wrong village and with the wrong K'ayum Ma'ax. Yet, one K'ayum Ma'ax is the same as another, *Mayan Drifter* suggests. Just as Herrera is almost ready to go stay at one of Gertrude Blom's camps, K'ayum Ma'ax, perhaps noticing Herrera's embarrassment, tells him not to worry: "You can stay here, with us" (111). Thanks to K'ayum Ma'ax's hospitality and generosity, Herrera's day is saved.

This hospitality and generosity, however, are not K'ayum Ma'ax's alone. These characteristics are inscribed within a dominant mode of Western literary representation, having informed European descriptions of Indigenous people since the inception of colonial conquest. In Herrera's portraits of the Lacandones, we hear the echoes of Christopher Columbus, who in his 1493 letter to Ferdinand of Spain said of the Taíno, the Indigenous people who lived on the island he called Hispaniola:

> Ellos son tanto sin engaño y tan liberales de lo que tienen, que no lo creería sino el que lo viese. Ellos de cosa que tengan, pidiéndosela, jamás dizen de no; antes, convidan la persona con ello, y muestran tanto amor que darían los corazón[es].

> They are so guileless and so generous with all they possess, that no one would believe it who has not seen it. They never refuse anything which they possess, if it be asked of them; on the contrary, they invite anyone to share it, and display as much love as if they would give their hearts. (Columbus and Jane, 7–9; my translation)

Columbus' portrayal of the Taínos as generous, as freely giving their possessions away, was deliberately crafted to hide the fact that white people violently seized land, possessions, and life itself from Indigenous peoples, and that Indigenous people resisted such dispossession (Milazzo 2022, 39). Columbus's colonial depiction of Indigenous peoples continues to inform self-critical works like *Mayan Drifter*.

Herrera also represents the Lacandones as passively accepting both colonial dispossession and the presence of Herrera himself. Particularly revealing in this regard is a chapter of *Mayan Drifter* titled "Nothing is Taken That Is Not Given: Ode to the Traveling Men." Having announced that he has abandoned his ethnographic paraphernalia, he writes: "I had dropped the archaic grammar of conquest. There was nothing to translate, nothing to take back. How could I take back what Chan K'in José has given me?" (106). Herrera wants the reader to know that he is not taking from the Lacandones; they are freely giving to him. The impossibility of theft returns in the concluding lines of the chapter:

> Could the Lacandones, the ones we quickly see as the 'silent subjects' of Mesoamerican research, also be the "speaking subjects"? Speaking for themselves—across cultural boundaries in time and space? And the 999,500 non-Lacandón Maya of Chiapas?
> Nothing can be taken, only given.
> Nothing was taken that was not given. (108)

The last sentence renders the impossibility of theft categorical. Appearing in a chapter in which Herrera announces that he has "dropped the archaic language of conquest" (106), these statements enact epistemic violence as they erase colonial conquest from the diegetic sphere. The Lacandones, Herrera previously suggested, cannot speak for themselves. They can only be spoken about. The gift, then, is Herrera's. He has not taken from the Lacandones but has given to them the gift of his own voice.

The act of giving constantly repeats itself in Herrera's interactions with K'ayum Ma'ax and the members of his family. It becomes almost a ritual, a leitmotiv: over and over, Herrera gives. When an Indigenous woman asks Herrera for two thousand pesos to buy tortillas, he gives her three thousand (*Mayan Drifter*, 39). When Manuel and Maruch, two young Zinacantecos, invite Herrera into their house—which he introduces as a "their mud and pine home" (50)—Herrera gives them "the customary two liters of pox" as well as "bags of calabaza, aguacate, panela, chilis, cebollas, and a couple of kilos of tortillas" (50). He offers cigarettes to seemingly everybody, including the boys that he meets when he first arrives at K'ayum Ma'ax's home: "I didn't think of the boys' ages or whether they smoked" (103), Herrera candidly concedes. Herrera gives away even his tape recorder. Viejo Chan K'in at first refuses to accept it, but Herrera insists (111). As the generous gestures become a litany, we learn that the act of giving does not come easy to Herrera. It is marred with guilt. Before leaving Nahá, Herrera gives K'ayum Ma'ax a fifty-dollar bill: "I knew I had forced the money on him; it was another one of my awkward gestures; I knew that I could be feeding into something that I didn't believe it, but it wasn't the money, it was simply giving as much as I could" (163). Herrera is tormented by the act of giving. Immediately after he announces the abandonment of his "'ethnographic intentions,'" Herrera writes: "Still, I managed to fall into an old colonial relationship; I was one more visitor dumping guilt and technology, proffering an exchange between the Modern and the Savage" (112). What Herrera laments is not the Lacandones' poverty, but their exposure to technology, revealing how *Mayan Drifter* longs for a Lacandón culture existing in an unchanging past (Pisarz-Ramírez, 282–283). When he arrives in Nahá, Herrera cannot believe that he is in a Lacandón village (98). The satellite dish surprises him, the blasting music bothers him. This is not the Indian utopia he had signed up for. Even as Herrera is aware of the pitfalls of "imperialist nostalgia" (17), he cannot avoid reproducing this nostalgia in his work.

This nostalgia is also inscribed in the ethnographic photographs included in *Mayan Drifter* for, while Herrera abandons his tape recorder, he keeps his camera close. The romantic image of the Lacandón drifting in the water in traditional tunic and a vessel gracing the cover is only one of several images portraying the Lacandones included in the book. As much as Herrera is critical of his tape recorder, he hardly questions the camera. At some point, he even announces that he has given up the camera, even as the camera is still there (*Mayan Drifter*, 106). However, Herrera dismisses its significance: "The camera was a habit more than a project" (162). In his uncritical relationship to the camera and photography itself, Herrera resembles Adriana Mora, the protagonist of Graciela Limón's novel *Erased Faces* (2001), an Afro-Chicana photographer from Los Angeles who travels to the Lacandón jungle to craft a photographic essay of Maya people. Adriana does not question her camera, and neither do the Indigenous people she photographs (Milazzo 2022, 233). Instead, they "trusted her enough to allow her to take photographs of them as they toiled in the jungle or fished in the river" (Limón, 13). Adriana Mora and Herrera both appear oblivious to the fact that photography, as Mireille Miller-Young writes, "did not arise on the margins of empire but was at its core" (43). Even as Herrera criticizes the ways that Na Bolom turns the Maya into objects for the gaze of tourists and anthropologists, so does Herrera.

Herrera shares much more with Adriana Mora than a passion for photography and an uncritical relationship to it. *Mayan Drifter* and *Erased Faces* are two of the few Chicano/a literary works that represent the Maya "among the living" (Saldaña Portillo 2001, 420). In the process, they nonetheless reproduce dominant narratives of travel, spiritual enlightenment, and white saviorism. A central goal of his project, Herrera writes, is "to go into America as I go into myself" (*Mayan Drifter*, 10). The closer Herrera gets to the jungle, the further he enters "into the strange figure and assemblage of myself" (5). As with Adriana Mora, and the colonizers and explorers that precede her, Herrera's journey into the jungle is ultimately inward. Unlike in white narratives of self-discovery in foreign lands, however, the Lacandón jungle is always already home to the Chicano/a, who has "a particular historical and psychic possibility" (10). The Indigenous in this process remains both an ancestor and the locus of love, knowledge, and acceptance for the Chicano/a subject. From *Rebozos of Love* to *Mayan Drifter*, as from *Borderlands/La Frontera* to *Erased Faces*, the Indigenous is invariably available to the Chicano/a for connection and consumption—the Other is, after all, merely part of the Self. Herrera might not have found K'ayum Ma'ax, but in the Lacandón jungle he was bound to find himself.

# Notes

1. Notice that Herrera does not include page numbers in *Rebozos of Love*.
2. According to Guisela Latorre, the term *indigenism* "refers to the act of consciously adopting an Indigenous identity—which may otherwise not be fully self-evident—for a political or strategic purpose" (2). Instead, *Indigeneity* indicates "the organic expressions that emerge from the Indigenous communities themselves, which may or may not have anything to do with the official Indigenism often espoused by nation-states" (3). Chicano/a identity, Latorre argues, exists at the intersection of indigenism and Indigeneity (2–3). While my understanding of indigenism is indebted to Latorre, it also differs from hers. With the term indigenism here I mean an esthetic and discursive formation within Chicano/a literature and theory in which Indigenous people, stories, traditions, symbols, and myths figure centrally.
3. For the text of *El Plan Espiritual de Aztlán* and seminal essays on the document, as well as the idea of Aztlán and its centrality for Chicano/a cultural production more broadly, see: Anaya, Lomelí, and Lamadrid, *Aztlán*.
4. In an interview published in 1980, Sánchez affirmed: "If we are part Indian, then let us affirm all nuances of our Indian-ness, not just pollyanna Indian-ness which never existed. . . . if [U]rista [Alurista] was really so hot on indigenismo, he should have attended the s.w. [Southwest] poets' conference on the [N]avajo reservation/nation . . . he was sent tickets to attend and he didn't . . . maybe he feared coming into contact with Indians who live because they were born of blood and fetal flesh, eat, defecate, piss . . . and die . . . they also drink, fight, and are not angelic nor prissy. No, there are no pyramids nor fancy ideas at the [N] avajo [N]ation, just as our barrios are not beautiful nor edifying . . ." (Bruce-Novoa, *Chicano Authors: Inquiry by Interview*, 233).
5. On Gloria Anzaldúa's work and Indigenismo, see also, Contreras, *Blood Lines*; Saldaña-Portillo, *The Revolutionary Imagination in the Americas and the Age of Development*; and Domino Pérez, "New Tribalism and Chicana/o Indigeneity in the work of Gloria Anzaldúa."
6. I examine the racial politics of *Across the Wire: Life and Hard Times on the Mexican Border* in "Speaking for the Refugee Other: Missioneering, White Saviourism, and the Politics of Ethnographic Representation in Luis Alberto Urrea's *Across the Wire*."
7. On the Zapatistas see, Marcos, *Our World is Our Weapon*.
8. On the "crisis of representation" in anthropology see, for example, Clifford and Marcus, *Writing Culture*; Rosaldo, *Culture and Truth*; and Marcus and Fisher, *Anthropology as Cultural Critique*.

9. On travel writing and ethnography, see Pratt, *Imperial Eyes* and "Fieldwork in Common Places."

## Works Cited

Alurista. *Floricanto en Aztlán*. Illustrated by Judithe Hernández. Seattle: University of Washington Press, 2012.

Anaya, Rudolfo, Francisco A. Lomelí, and Enrique R. Lamadrid. *Aztlán: Essays on the Chicano Homeland; Revised and Expanded Edition*. Albuquerque: University of New Mexico Press, 2017.

Anzaldúa, Gloria. *Borderlands/La Frontera: The New Mestiza*. San Francisco: Aunt Lute Books, 1987.

Anzaldúa, Gloria. "Speaking Across the Divide." *The Gloria Anzaldúa Reader*, edited by AnaLouise Keating. Durham, N.C.: Duke University Press, 2009.

Blom, Gertrude Duby. *¿Hay razas inferiores?* Colección Metropolitana. Mexico City: Secretaría de Obras y Servicios, 1974.

Blom, Gertrude Duby. *Imágenes Lacandonas*. Tuxtla Gutiérrez, Chiapas: Tezontle, 1999.

Bruce-Novoa, Juan. *Chicano Authors: Inquiry by Interview*. Austin: University of Texas Press, 1980.

Clifford, James, and George E. Marcus, eds. *Writing Culture: The Poetics and Politics of Ethnography*. 2nd ed. University of California Press, 2010.

Columbus, Christopher, and Lionel C. Jane. *The Four Voyages of Columbus: A History in Eight Documents, Including Five by Christopher Columbus, in the Original Spanish, with English Translations*. New York: Dover Publications, 1988.

Contreras, Sheila M. *Blood Lines: Myth, Indigenism, and Chicana/o Literature*. Austin: University of Texas Press, 2008.

Dowdy, Michael. "Molotovs and Subtleties: Juan Felipe Herrera's Post-Movement Norteamérica." In *Broken Souths: Latina/o Poetic Responses to Neoliberalism and Globalization*, 61–90. Tucson: University of Arizona Press, 2013.

Flores, Lauro H. "Juan Felipe Herrera (December 27, 1948–)." In *Chicano Writers; Second Series*, 137–145. Vol. 122 of *Dictionary of Literary Biography*, edited by Francisco A. Lomelí and Carl R. Shirley. Detroit: Gale Research, 1992.

Herrera, Juan Felipe. *Mayan Drifter: Chicano Poet in the Lowlands of America*. Philadelphia: Temple University Press, 1997.

Herrera, Juan Felipe. *Rebozos of Love / We Have Woven / Sudor de Pueblos / On Our Back*. San Diego, Calif.: Toltecas en Aztlán, 1974.

Herrera, Juan Felipe. *Thunderweavers/Tejedoras de rayos*. Camino del Sol Series. Tucson: University of Arizona Press, 2000.

Latorre, Guisela. *Walls of Empowerment: Chicana/o Indigenist Murals of California*. Austin: University of Texas Press, 2008.

Limón, Graciela. *Erased Faces*. Houston: Arte Público Press, 2001.

Lomelí, Francisco A. "Foreword / Juan Felipe Herrera: Trajectory and Metamorphosis of a Chicano Poet Laureate." In *Half of the World in Light: New and Selected Poems* by Juan Felipe Herrera, xv-xxiv. Tucson: University of Arizona Press, 2008.

Marcos, Subcomandante. "Chiapas: The Southeast in Two Winds, and a Storm and a Prophecy." In *The Geopolitics Reader*, edited by Gearóid Ó Tuathail, Simon Dalby, and Paul Routledge, 294–198. London: Routledge, 1998.

Marcos, Subcomandante. *Our Word is Our Weapon: Selected Writings*, edited by Juana Ponce de León. New York: Seven Stories Press, 2011.

Milazzo, Marzia. *Colorblind Tools: Global Technologies of Racial Power.* Evanston, Ill.: Northwestern University Press, 2022.

Milazzo, Marzia. "Speaking for the Refugee Other: Missioneering, White Saviourism, and the Politics of Ethnographic Representation in Luis Alberto Urrea's *Across the Wire.*" *Scrutiny2* 24, no. 1 (January 2019): 58–72.

Miller-Young, Mireille. "Exotic/Erotic/Ethnopornographic: Black Women, Desire, and Labor in the Photographic Archive." In *Ethnopornography: Sexuality, Colonialism, and Archival Knowledge*, edited by Pete Sigal, Zeb Tortorici, and Neil L. Whitehead, 41–66. Durham, N.C.: Duke University Press, 2020.

Moraga, Cherríe. "Queer Aztlán: The Re-Formation of the Chicano Tribe." In *Re-Emerging Native Women of the Americas: Native Chicana Latina Women's Studies*, edited by Yolanda Broyles-González, 236–253. Dubuque, Iowa: Kendall/Hunt Publishing Co., 2001.

Moraga, Cherríe. *The Hungry Woman: A Mexican Medea.* Albuquerque, N.M.: West End Press, 2001.

Oliver-Rotger, María Antònia. "An Interview with Cherríe Moraga." *Soundings: Voices from the Gap*, January 2005. http://voices.cla.umn.edu./newsite/soundings/ROTGERmaria-moraga.htm.

Oliver-Rotger, Maria Antònia. "Travel, Autoethnography, and Oppositional Consciousness in Juan Felipe Herrera's *Mayan Drifter.*" In *Imagined Transnationalism in U.S. Latino/a Literature, Culture, and Identity*, edited by Kevin Concannon, Francisco A. Lomelí, and Marc Priewe, 171–199. New York: Palgrave Macmillan, 2009.

Palau, Karina Ruth-Ester. *Ethnography Otherwise: Interventions in Writing, Photography, and Sound in Mexico and Brazil.* PhD diss., University of California Berkeley, 2013.

Pérez, Domino R. "New Tribalism and Chicana/o Indigeneity in the work of Gloria Anzaldúa." In *Routledge Handbook of Chicana/o Studies*, edited by Francisco A. Lomelí, Denise A. Segura, and Elyette Benjamin-Labarthe, 242–254. London: Routledge, 2018.

Pisarz-Ramírez, Gabriele. "Reimagining America: Postnational Perspectives in Chicano Border Discourses." *E Pluribus Unum? National and Transnational Identities in the Americas/Identidades nacionales y transnacionales en las Américas*, edited by Sebastian Thies and Josef Raab, 277–290. Tempe, Ariz.: Bilingual Press/Editorial Bilingüe, 2008.

Pratt, Louise Mary. *Imperial Eyes: Travel Writing and Transculturation*. London: Routledge, 1992.

Pratt, Louise Mary. "Fieldwork in Common Places." In *Writing Culture: The Poetics and Politics of Ethnography*, edited by James Clifford and George E. Marcus, 27–50. University of California Press, 1986.

Rosaldo, Renato. *Culture and Truth: The Remaking of Social Analysis*. Boston: Beacon Press, 1993.

Rosaldo, Renato. *The Day of Shelly's Death: The Poetry and Ethnography of Grief*. Durham, N.C.: Duke University Press, 2014.

Saldaña-Portillo, María Josefina. "Who is the Indian in Aztlán? Re-Writing Mestizaje, Indianism, and Chicanismo from the Lacandón." *The Latin American Subaltern Reader*, edited by Ileana Rodríguez, 402–422. Durham: Duke University Press, 2001.

Saldaña-Portillo, María Josefina. *The Revolutionary Imagination in the Americas and the Age of Development*. Durham, N.C.: Duke University Press, 2003.

Sigal, Pete, Zeb Tortorici, and Neil L. Whitehead, "Introduction: Ethnopornography as Methodology and Critique: Merging the Ethno-, the Porno-, and the -Graphos." *Ethnopornography: Sexuality, Colonialism, and Archival Knowledge*, edited by Pete Sigal, Zeb Tortorici, and Neil L. Whitehead, 1–37. Durham, N.C.: Duke University Press, 2020.

Soldofsky, Alan. "A Border-Crosser's Heteroglossia: Interview with Juan Felipe Herrera, Twenty-First Poet Laureate of the United States." *MELUS*, 43, No. 3 (Summer 2018): 196–226.

Spivak, Gayatri Chakravorty. "Can the Subaltern Speak?" In *Marxism and the Interpretation of Culture*, edited by Cary Nelson and Lawrence Grossberg, 271–313. Champaign: University of Illinois Press, 1988.

Urrea, Luis Alberto. *Across the Wire: Life and Hard Times on the Mexican Border*. New York: Anchor Books, 1993.

Valdez, Luis. *Pensamiento serpentino: A Chicano Approach to the Theatre of Reality*. Centro Campesino Cultural. N.p.: Cucaracha Publications, 1973.

CHAPTER 5

# Poetic Language, Indigenous Heritage, the Environmental Imaginary, and Social Justice in Juan Felipe Herrera's *Rebozos of Love / We Have Woven / Sudor de Pueblos / On Our Back*

MARÍA HERRERA-SOBEK

> ... dedicated to human truth (spiritual, social, economic, political, historical and ecological) and xicano harmony which in our vision can only be practiced through mutual self-respect, self-determination in our endeavors and the self-sacrifice of our individual differences for the sake of a centro cultural de la raza where our indigenous ancestral spirit of brotherhood and sisterhood, amor, justice and peace can flourish in contemporary xicano art forms ...
>
> —JUAN FELIPE HERRERA, DEDICATION, *REBOZOS OF LOVE*

The first book of poetry by U.S. Poet Laureate Juan Felipe Herrera, *Rebozos of Love / We Have Woven / Sudor de Pueblos / on our Back*,[1] was published in 1974 by a small press, Toltecas en Aztlán, located in San Diego, California. This poetry collection is essential in comprehending Herrera's subsequent large literary corpus since its contents encapsulate philosophical and political positions and discussions that become a hallmark of his later writings. In this essay, I focus on the most salient elements that characterize this small but foundational collection of poems since the style of writing and subject matter is reiterated in his extensive creative production spanning some fifty years and over thirty-four books. The four important areas of analysis in this study are: (1) new contributions in poetic language constructions—creativity and originality; (2) Indigenous heritage of Chicanos/as and cultural elements inherited from these ancestors; (3) the environmental imaginary that embraces not only the earth but the cosmos as a whole; and (4) a central interest in promoting and advocating social justice. Herrera highlights these four areas in his dedication, quoted above in the introductory epigraph. In addition, social justice and harmony between human beings and all the entities in the universe are the two important strands that, woven together throughout the poems, contribute in unifying the collection as a whole. These two elements weave a cohesive narrative that is powerful and convincing in the delivery of his unequivocal message of peace, unity, harmony and love.

The overall encompassing theme permeating almost every single poem is the concern for social justice for the beleaguered Chicano/a/Latino/a people and by extension all the downtrodden, oppressed and exploited people of the world. These include the working class, the immigrant, the undocumented worker, the refugee, the Indigenous populations and all peoples who suffer from poverty, hunger, humiliations, homelessness, violence, and even death. Disregarded by many is the biblical exhortation to feed the hungry and to heed the golden rule to "do unto others, as you would want others to do unto you." Herrera underscores a return to humanistic values through humor, satire, needling, witticisms, as well as other poetic strategies examined in this study.

The volume, *Rebozos of Love*, contains forty-six of what Herrera denominates as *cantos*, chants or poems, encompassed within ninety-five pages, thus emphasizing the incantatory aspect with its ritualized recitations that generally enthrall the reader. Some poems are short comprised of four lines while others are as long as twenty-two pages. The poet does not adhere to grammar rules of capitalization, spelling, or to one language, but instead follows his poetic muse. For example, the poems are not titled nor are the pages in the volume numbered. I have titled the poems by using the first line of each poem as the title. I have numbered the poems as well as provided page numbers to aid the reader in finding the poems discussed (see index).

## Graphic Artwork

The graphic artwork designed by Gloria Amalia Flores included in the volume is an important feature of the creative endeavor by Herrera that adds to the significance of the *cantos*. Many of the poems are integrated within the graphic lines of the designs, with the *cantos* and the artwork in conversation

Poetic Language, Indigenous Heritage, the Environmental Imaginary, and Social Justice **119**

with each other. The front and back cover of the book displays graphic artwork that conveys the pre-Hispanic architecture typical of the New Mexico Indigenous population, the Pueblo Indians. The design is abstract but one can discern schematic lines that indicate stacked, multilevel adobe housing with windows and doors much like those still present in Taos, New Mexico. The graphic artwork of the cover offers a preview of the importance Indigenous thought and culture will have on the poems within.

The short, succinct artwork interprets the poems evocatively. For example, on page three, the poem begins with the line "GREEN DESERT SPI-RALS," and the graphic art displays a curved trunk and two cactus arms such as those that grow on saguaro (also "sahuaro"—*carnegiea gigantea*) desert cacti. In the background is a drawing that conveys the path of the sun or perhaps a rainbow. The *canto* includes the words rain and sun. On page eighteen, the *canto* articulates a brief philosophical thought regarding the sun and its place within the cosmos. The canto states:

| EL | THE |
|----|-----|
| SOL | SUN |
| TIENE | HAS |
| DOS | TWO |
| BRAZOS | ARMS |
| UNIDAD | UNITY |
| Y | AND |
| VIDA | LIFE |
| ABRAZALO | EMBRACE IT |
| SI | IF |
| TIENES | YOU ARE |
| FRIO | COLD |

(18; my translation)

The graphic artwork offers a circle at the center and a larger circle outside the inner circle. Within the outer and inner circle is a semicircle with extending arms toward the viewer as if inviting the viewer to embrace it.

Herrera consistently articulates his central concern, the suffering of his *pueblo* or people in *Rebozos of Love*. From their inception his *cantos* introduce the iconic word "rebozos," representing Mexicans at large and the Mexican culture. The "rebozo" is a shawl but the word in Spanish encompasses a more magnified circle of meanings. These semiotic meanings include:

(1) The hardy figure of the *soldaderas* or Mexican women soldiers wearing their black or gray cotton rebozos of the Mexican Revolution (1910–1917);

(2) An Indigenous or mestizo woman's tender love for her child as she holds or protects them while carrying the child on her back wrapped in the rebozo;

(3) A utilitarian garment that serves to carry groceries or clothing, and so forth.

From the book's title, the rebozo is linked closely with love. It implicitly connotes a deep affection for people. Furthermore, the title incorporates issues of hard-working, resilient, but highly-exploited workers. The third and fourth lines ("sudor de pueblos / on our back") evoke a stooped labor workforce in the agricultural fields picking cotton, fruits, and vegetables, or the maquiladora sweatshops of men and women hunched over sewing machines or industrial workers bent on assembly lines or meat-packing plants. "Sudor" or sweat is a metonym for the workers' exploitation and pain. Love is the saving element in this terrible situation. Love, in spite of a difficult life of backbreaking work, aids the people in their survival. Love and beauty are exemplified once again by the rebozo, a garment that can serve numerous utilitarian functions as well as one of incredible beauty.

# Poetic Language

Herrera exhibits an amazing linguistic dexterity in structuring his poetic universe. As a bilingual person fluent in Spanish and English and, in fact, a trilingual person if we take into consideration the Caló, or the spoken variety of Spanish and English found in Chicano barrio neighborhoods, his poetry displays all these linguistic variants as detailed in the following pages. Both Spanish and English are evident in Herrera's stanzas, although Spanish is the dominant language in the collection and serves as the main structural support for the other languages introduced. For example, there are numerous poems written entirely in Spanish (see pages: 22, 79, 80, 81, 82, 85, 86, 87, 88, 90, 91, 92–95). In most of the other poems code-switching is a major characteristic.

Herrera avails himself of numerous poetic techniques to increase the power and message inscribed in his work. There are multiple strategies, both traditional and original, available to the poet with which he can create his cantos. These techniques include alliteration, assonance, metonyms, imag-

Poetic Language, Indigenous Heritage, the Environmental Imaginary, and Social Justice  **121**

ery, figures of speech, such as similes, metaphors, synecdoche, personification, as well as some of the non-traditional strategies expounded in this essay such as the use of Caló.

Sprinkled throughout the volume are other Indigenous languages such as Nahuatl (the language the Mexica—the Aztecs—spoke). A few words of Huichol—another Indigenous group from Central-West Mexico—plus words from the American Southwest, as well as one Maya phrase are also present.

## Code-switching

One of the salient strategies in Herrera's poetic arsenal is code-switching or the switching of linguistic registers, in this case from Spanish to English and vice versa. This is common where two languages are in contact, such as Spanish and English in the United States, due to their continual connections and coexistence in which they mutually influence the other at a semantic and syntactic level. The poet is particularly skilled in integrating code-switching in his poems. This code-switching characteristic is frequently found in early Chicano movement poetry, such as in Alurista's poetry collection, *Floricanto* (1971), as well as in Ana Castillo's collection, *My Father Was a Toltec* (1988), and Alma Villanueva's collection, *Bloodroot* (1982). Code-switching emerged as a new creative style of writing that reflected the spoken language of the Mexican American people. This type of language expression was highly criticized by both Mexicans in Mexico and Euro-Americans in the United States. Mexicans perceived it as a corruption of the Spanish language. On the other hand, it was difficult for mainstream Euro-Americans to understand and appreciate this specific manner of speaking in both English and Spanish since most of these critics were not fluent in Spanish and could not evaluate the originality and creativity involved in code-switching. The introductory poem heading the collection, *Rebozos of Love*, illustrates numerous instances of code-switching (1). For example, the second line reads, "with sunluz grains abriendo los cantos;" the word "sunluz" is an agglutination of two words: one English (sun) and one Spanish luz (light). "Sunluz" is an instance of code-switching within a single word. The poetic voice next switches to English ("grains"), followed by the Spanish phrase, "abriendo los cantos" (opening the songs/chants). The poem continues on page two, stating: "let us offer our hearts a saludar our águila rising / freedom" (let us offer our hearts to greet our eagle rising / freedom). The poem is a prayer, an incantation making an *ofrenda* (offering) to "our eagle." The eagle is a sacred bird within the Aztec culture and respected in the Mexican culture, appearing in the center of the contemporary Mexican flag. It belongs to the foundational historical moment of the founding of the Mexica (Aztec) settlement of their city, Tenochtitlan, present-day Mexico City. According to myth and legend, in 1325 the Aztec god Huitzilopochtli instructed the migrating Aztecs to settle in the land where they saw an eagle posed on top of a cactus devouring a serpent.

Herrera combines code-switching with alliteration to enhance the poetic rhythm, such as in the poem, "ándelen our joyous heart!" (*Rebozos*, 11). In line five he writes: "brillando sonando sing" where the repetitions of the "s" consonants provide a rhythmic sound and the use of Spanish verb endings "ando" add to the rhyme of the poem.

# Caló

A unique poetic language strategy in Herrera's cantos is the repeated use of Caló. Rachel Valentina González defines Caló in her essay titled "*Caló* (Folk Speech)" as "a type of modified Spanish with specialized vocabulary that is used alongside traditional Spanish grammar to produce a hybrid speech register that was popularized among Mexican American urban youth, or *pachucos* in the southwestern United States in the 1930s and 1940s" (197–198). It became highly appreciated and used in Chicano/a literary production at the inception of the Chicano movement in the 1960s in such works as Luis Valdez's farmworkers' theater (*Teatro Campesino*), and in Chicano/a poetry and narrative. It continues to be popular in the present century in this ethnic group's literary renderings. As Rachel V. González underscores, Caló as a "hybrid cultural product and linguistic esthetic is valorized by Chicanos as a marker of cultural nationalism that is rooted in embracing barrio culture, recognizing the strength and value of language within a quest for self-determined cultural roles" (198). Caló is associated with the numerous referential codes related to vernacular Spanish such as Chicano Spanish, Spanglish, *pochismos*, Hispanicized English, Anglicized Spanish, and so forth (197).

For poets, novelists, and playwrights of the early Chicano movement of the 1960s and 1970s, the integration of Caló in their literary works implied a sense of affirmation, group identification, and pride in the perceived genius of cultural creativity in oral expression. In poetry, novels, and plays, Caló imparts humor and a sense of being unique, different, original, and very clever.

Caló displays linguistic characteristics that are specific to its development. Below are some major categories.

1.  English verbs are constructed as Spanish verbs:
    It is possible to convert almost any English verb into a Spanish verb by taking the English infinitive and adding the suffix "-ar" derived from Spanish verbs ending in "-ar" such as "hablar." By adding the suffix "-ar" to the infinitive English verb, it becomes a "Spanish" verb and can be conjugated as such. For example, by adding to the English verb "watch" the suffix "-ar" it becomes the Spanish verb "watchar" and can be conjugated as a Spanish verb. For example, "watcha carnal" (41) and "WATCHA THE EAST SOL" (45).

2.  Spanish words are given a non-traditional meaning:

| | Traditional meaning | Caló meaning |
|---|---|---|
| ese/esa | "that one" | he/she and also "dude" or "chick" |
| Simón (40) | masculine name | yes, sí |
| trucha (61) | trout | clever, sharp such as in "ponte trucha" |
| estufas (14) | stoves | enough, as in "ya estuvo" |
| calcos (86) | tracings | shoes, zapatos |
| chante (9) | casa | house, casa |
| knifas (15) | (none) | knives (English spelling) |

The poet incorporates the above vocabulary to inject a strong sense of community solidarity; of strong identification with his *pueblo*, or people, and of humor for the in-group who is conversant with Caló.

# Popular Spanish (formerly designated as "non-standard Spanish")

In a similar manner to the incorporation of Caló within Herrera's poetry, the bard utilizes popular Spanish to bring the voice of the people into his poetic universe. This inclusive strategy attempts to amplify the voice of the people.

It is a device that provides a platform for the working-class Mexican American community to express themselves in their own language and manner of speaking. In the very long poem that begins on page sixty-nine and ends on page ninety-one, the voice of a *campesino* or farmworker is integrated starting on page seventy-nine and ending on page eighty. It reads as a lament for the passing of time and the transformation of the world that, in his view, has taken a turn for the worse. What used to be his land is now a place where the farmworker and working poor are exploited more than ever:

| | |
|---|---|
| fíjese señor que antes era como | listen, mister, in the past it was as if |
| si fueramo' | we were |
| bendecidos por dios | blessed by God |
| se te caía una semilla y crecía | a seed would fall and a flower would |
| una flor | bloom |
| los indios y nojotro' teniamo' | the Indians and us would have |
| fiesta juntos | fiestas together |
| bajabamo' al río y cojíamo' | we would go down to the river and |
| pescao' | catch fish |

(*Rebozos*, 79; my translation)

The farmworker's voice continues to explain how in years past there was harmony, food was plentiful, and the Indigenous groups and Mexicans lived in peaceful coexistence. With the arrival of the Anglo Americans after the Mexican-American War of 1846–1848, the landscape changed drastically for the worse, according to the farmworker's viewpoint. The *campesino's* voice captures the linguistic characteristics common in popular Spanish. These characteristics include apocope (the dropping of a consonant or syllable at the end of a word) and elision (the omission of one or more sounds within a word or phrase):

| | | |
|---|---|---|
| Fuéramo' | [fuéramos] | apocope, the final "s" is dropped. |
| Teníamo' | [teníamos] | apocope, the final "s" is dropped. |
| Bajábamo' | [bajábamos] | apocope, the final "s" is dropped. |
| Cojiamo' | [cojíamos] | apocope, the final "s" is dropped. |
| Nojotro' | [nosotros] | apocope, the final "s" is dropped and the first "s" is aspirated and pronounced like a "j" ("h" in English) |
| Pescao' | [pescado] | elision, the "d" is dropped |

Other instances of apocope appear such as in the word "pa'" for "para" (for/to). Additionally, archaisms are also introduced such as "mesma" for "misma" (own); "ansina" for "así" (thus) and "muncho" for "mucho" (much) (see pages 80, 81, and 84). By integrating popular Spanish with formal Spanish the flavor of the *campesino* is made evident. The poetic voice and the *campesino's* voice converge, becoming one, and reimagine a better world for all, especially the Chicana/o and Indigenous groups living in the Southwest. These groups are specifically named in the poem: Pima, Xicano, Pápago, Apache, Hopi, Navajo (81, 84).

## Agglutination

*Funk & Wagnalls Standard Desk Dictionary* (1979) defines the word "agglutination" as: adhesion of distinct parts, (2) Ling. A combining of words into compounds in which the constituent elements retain their characteristic forms. The linguistic feature of agglutinating words is a salient attribute of the Nahuatl language. Patrick Johansson Keraudren highlights in his excellent article, "El español y el náhuatl: primeros encuentros" (2020, 18), and informs us of this distinctive trait of Nahuatl.

El náhuatl es una lengua polisintética que permite la composición de bloques verbales compactos, donde los adjetivos, los adverbios y los complementos se funden con los radicales sustantivos o verbales en una masa sonora, unidad expresiva reacia en separar lo circunstancial de lo esencial [. . . .]

La ausencia de bisagras preposicionales en la lengua náhuatl da mucha movilidad al sentido y permite que se forme en el texto un verdadero espectro adjetival, nominal o verbal que obliga al receptor a pasar a una dimensión sensible "impresionista" para poder percibir el mensaje con todos sus matices. En efecto, las unidades lingüísticas que se "aglutinan" en un compuesto verbal, además de calificar o modificar un radical determinado, se funden en una palabra compleja.

The Nahuatl language is polysynthetic that permits the structuring of compact verbal blocks where the adjectives, the adverbs and their complements are fused with the roots of the nouns or verbs producing a single unity. This expressive unity aids in separating the circumstantial from the essential [. . . .]

The absence of prepositional hinges in the Nahuatl language provides a great flexibility to the meaning of words and allows the formation in the text of a truly phantom adjectival, nominal or verbal entity forcing the receptor to access another dimension, both sensible and "impressionistic," thus able to perceive the message in all its possible meanings. In fact, the linguistic units that are "agglutinated" in a verbal unit, in addition to qualifying or modifying a specific root of a word, are fused together to structure a complete word. (18; my translation)

While Herrera does not write his poetry in Nahuatl, he incorporates the structures of Nahuatl word structures and composition in what is called "agglutination," which can be in any language (in English, examples include, "workforce," "payday," "weekend," and so forth).

The second dictionary definition cited above is more pertinent to our present study. Herrera is a master at agglutinating words in his poetry collection analyzed here. There are four types of agglutinations evident in this collection:

1. two Spanish words joined as one (brazosoles; 23),
2. a Spanish and an English word (pancorn; 13),
3. a Spanish and an Indigenous word (maiztlan; 2),
4. two English words (selftorn; 26).

Below is a list of agglutinations and examples of the above categories. See the Spanish and Indigenous words—the Indigenous words all have Nahuatl connections.

| Two Spanish Words | Spanish and English Words | Spanish and Indigenous Words | Two English Words |
|---|---|---|---|
| brazosoles | sunluz | maiztlan | selftorn |
| calaveralmas | pancorn | panaztlan | everyou |
| dulcesón | sunbeso | quetzalmar | everwe |
| ricosón | selfmilpas | vidacóatl | everflowing |
| tuyamía | razarise | kupurisol | songrise |
| tuyomío | solraingotas | divinacóatl | herenow |
| uncorazón | soupraza | | nationhoop |
| rayoscuerpos | souprazarising | | nationdawn |
| ahorasol | | | |

amerindiasol

corazol

razaraiz

amerindia

razamilpa

milparaza

rosaluz

razaluz

rebozoles

The Chicano poet's incorporation of the linguistic process of agglutination is not by happenstance. The blending and uniting of different words in his poems is in keeping with his worldview and ideology of bringing two or more different cultural universes together in harmony. He is underscoring the coming together in a peaceful and creative coexistence of different entities via this linguistic process.

## Repetition

Another strategy that Herrera incorporates in his poetry collection is repetition. Herrera's use of repetition is unique in *Rebozos of Love* because it is often bilingual: Herrera may use a word in Spanish and then repeat it in English or vice versa. This poetic technique affords Herrera the opportunity to highlight and emphasize a rhyme structure as well as an important word. It also demonstrates the similarity between English and Spanish, and in this manner emphasizes the similarities between two cultures. For example, the stanza on page one, line five reads: "para regalar y dar feliz perlas pearls" (in order to gift and give happy pearls pearls; 1). The rhythmic repetition of the consonants and vowels "p," "e," "r," "l," and "s" reinforces the central idea. The Spanish and English word perlas/pearls share linguistic phonetic sounds, creating sonic as well as visual echoes. Below are other examples of Herrera's unique use of repetition.

| Spanish Words | Spanish/ English Words | English/ Spanish Words | Spanish Syllables |
| --- | --- | --- | --- |
| chante/casa (9) | sí/yes (11) | always/siempre (9) | Vicente/vientre (11) |
| | feliz/happy (26) | bright/brillos (26) | Mares/amares (22) |

|                      |                 |                      |
|----------------------|-----------------|----------------------|
| nacer/burning/ born (26) | river/río (30) | Lagos/logos (28) |
| ciclos/cycles (41)   | rejoys/ríos (30) | Mar/amar/collar (44) |
|                      |                 | rosa/mariposa (50)   |
|                      |                 | verdadera/vereda (51) |
|                      |                 | rebozo/regoso (30)   |

# Indigenous Thought and Influence

The Chicano movement of the 1960s experienced enormous influence from Indigenous cultures, including philosophical, cultural, religious, cosmological, sociological, and ecological belief systems. There are two Indigenous groups highlighted in Herrera's *Rebozos of Love* that are analyzed in this study: the Mexica (or Aztecs) and the Huichols. Other Indigenous cultures appear in different poems throughout the collection but the most consistent groups cited are the two named above. In fact *Rebozos of Love* was published by Toltecas in Aztlán Publications located in San Diego, California. The publishers cite the state location as Califaztlán, an agglutination of Calif + Aztlán. Citing this location is a political statement in and of itself. Many Chicanos/as believe that the mythical land of Aztlán was located in what is now the U.S. Southwest and was the original homeland of the Aztecs. Aztlán means "the place of the herons."

The Toltecs were an Indigenous group located in Mexico's central highlands in the present state of Hidalgo where they founded their capital, Tula, in 80 A.D. (Román Piña Chan 1969, 85). They believed their god Quetzalcóatl had prophesied that he would leave them, travel east toward the Gulf of Mexico and eventually return, coincidentally, on the year of the Spanish incursion into Mexico in 1519. The Toltecs eventually declined and Tula fell to the invading Chichimecas (the Indigenous group that later became the Aztecs) in 1200 A.D. (Piña Chan, 87). Herrera's poetry collection is liberally sprinkled with the name Quetzalcóatl. The Toltec god figure was a significant influence in Chicano/a art, literature, political thought and ideology during the period of the Chicano movement. The Aztecs, who called themselves Mexica, are a strong presence in Herrera's poetry as evoked by the use of the word Aztlán, as well as its individual word parts, *az* (Aztec) and *tlan* (land, area): *panaztlan* (13, 14); *maiztlan* (37, 60); *in tloque in nahuaque* (60, 69, 71, 72); *tzalcoatl* (17); *quetzalmar* (25, 65); *quetzal* (25, 35, 40, 47, 65); *quetzals* (37); *quetzalcóatl* (40, 47, 70, 71, 72, 86); *vidacóatl* (65).

The Mexica influence evident in *Rebozos of Love* is not only articulated via key words such as those cited above. Aztec thought and culture permeates the lyrics of the cantos. Aztec religious influence in Herrera's cantos manifests itself in concepts such as those related to the duality of the deity: Señor y Señora, "la creadora y el creador" (female and male creators; 23) of the universe. In conceptualizing the creator of the universe as both male and female, he does not privilege a masculine concept of God. Herrera also incorporates the concept of the "cinco soles" (five suns). Aztec religious teachings conceptualized four previous worlds (under four distinct suns) that had been destroyed. The era in which they were living was the era of the Fifth Sun (see Herrera, 72). Anthropologist Brian M. Fagan writes in his book, *The Aztecs* (1984), that "the Stone of the Sun" symbolized the Aztec cosmos. The Stone of the Sun depicts the perpetual struggle between the forces of good and evil that caused the creation and destruction of these worlds (Fagan, 32–33).

Herrera's concept of "renacer" or renewal stems from this basic Aztec belief in world constructions and destructions. Throughout his poems he advocates for a new world order—"una nueva orden terrenal" (a new earthly order; *Rebozos*, 70)—that will be more just. Renewal of the present world is not limited to the planet earth. His belief of renewal encompasses the whole cosmos beginning with the earth, the planets, the sun, the stars, the galaxies (59), the constellations (53, 70), and the entire cosmos (61, 63, 67, 72). For example, on page six, the canto states: "casa de pechos abiertos / we must die / to ayer soles de huesos" (home of open chests / we must die / to yesterday suns of bones). The canto continues: "nourishing mundos nuevos [new worlds] so prophesized" (6). The cycle of birth—a renewal—and death is repeated throughout the cantos, not in a pessimistic manner but in a joyous, positive view of the possibility of a new world order.

Herrera also includes other Uto-Aztecan tribes such as the Huichols. The Huichols, or Wixáarika, are another Indigenous group cited about seven times throughout Herrera's poetry collection (see pages 15, 33, 85). They are a group of Indians numbering around forty thousand in present-day Mexico and Southwestern United States. In Mexico, they reside mainly in the states of Jalisco, Nayarit, Zacatecas and San Luis Potosí. Known for their artistic sensibilities expressed in their yarn paintings and objects, they are a part of the Aztec peoples and their language forms part of the Uto-Aztecan community.

The Huichols' significant influence on Herrera poetic work relates to his philosophical and religious expression regarding humanity's interconnections with the universe, such as their relationship to plants and animals and the entire cosmos. The concepts of unity and harmony are key components expressed consistently throughout the poet's artistic production. Repeatedly emphasized throughout the stanzas in *Rebozos of Love* is the concept of living a harmonious existence in tune with the cosmos. The poetic voice identifies with the Huichol Indigenous community. He says,

| | |
|---|---|
| hace muchos años huichol | it has been many years ago, Huichol |
| Huichol montañas ground maizitos red | Huichol mountains ground little red corn |
| plumas wrapped en bronce aquí | feathers wrapped here in bronze |
| aquí yo nací | here I was born |
| para siembras y cantar | to plant and to sing |

(33; my translation)

The four-page poem, "Hace muchos años huichol" (Many Years Ago Huichol) (#19, 33–36) enumerates the Huichols' connectedness and unity with the different ecological earth's systems: mountains (representing earth), corn (a metonym for food), feathers (a metonym for birds) and bronze (representing minerals). All of these ecological systems are conjoined to bring meaning to an existence from which humanity derives its meaning through the labor of planting food (body) and singing (soul). The poem reiterates the themes articulated in these first five lines and found within it are flower and song (lira or lyre), the musical instrument, "tambora" or drum made with deerskin. The deer is a highly respected mythological animal among the Huichol and appears in their ritual and religious ceremonies such as the deer dance. The sun, a religious and most significant cosmic entity, is repeatedly invoked in this long poem (*Rebozos*, 33–36).

The animal kingdom is also evoked, such as the iconic serpent (33); the *chapulines* (grasshoppers, 34), *águilas* (eagles, 33, 34); *mariposas* (butterflies, 35) *quetzales* (birds, 35); the rainbow (34); and plants such as corn, *matas* (brush), *milpas* (corn fields), *frutas* (fruits), *hojas* (leaves), and trees. Other geographical and cosmic entities such as oceans, *llanos* (plains), *cielo* (sky), *luz* (light), and *rayos* (rays), also appear. Finally, even God or dios (35) is present in these poems.

Indigenous religious concepts cited (some in Nahuatl) in Herrera's poetry collection are

- Tloqueh Nahuaqueh, or *In tloque; in nahuaque* (71), "referring to the universal and all pervading deity" (Karttunen 309).[2]
- "quetzalcóatl plumed heart of struggle" (70), also known as Quetzalcóatl, "plumed serpent," the god of culture and creation.
- *Ipal Nemohuani* (raíz de la vida or root of life; 73).[3]
- *IN LAK 'ECH*: (TU ERES MI OTRO YO; You are my other me; 95).[4]
- Tonantzin (Aztec for "Our Mother"; 91)
- Aztlán (the Aztec's mythic homeland; 91)
- DADOR DE LA VIDA (Giver of Life; 92).[5]
- Tauyepa (Padre Sol; 32)
- SEÑOR-SEÑORA DE LA UNIDAD SIN FIN (Master and Mistress of the Infinite Unity; 92)

# Environmental Imaginary

Although Chicanos/as are not perceived as environmentally conscious nor viewed as deeply concerned with environmental issues, both nationally and internationally, this could not be further from the truth. In fact, the Chicano/a Movement had its roots in environmental issues. César Chávez was working with the farm workers in the 1950s in an effort to unionize them and achieve social and economic justice. Early in his career as a farm worker leader, Chávez made significant advances and incursions into environmental issues with his focus on heavy and indiscriminate use of insecticides and pesticides in the agricultural fields of California. In some previous publications, such as "Writing the Toxic Environment: Ecocriticism and the Chicana Literary Imagination" (2013), I propose Chávez as the "father of the environmental movement in the United States." He was much aware of the chemical poisoning and damage to the health of the farm working population that both men and women suffered. The Chicano literary renaissance explored these issues in poetry, the novel, and theater productions. Chicano playwright, Luis Valdez, explored these concerns in his early play, *The Shrunken Head of Pancho Villa* (1964) and Cherríe Moraga similarly focused on the environment in her play, *Heroes and Saints* (1994). Helena María Viramontes centered her novel, *Under the Feet of Jesus* (1990) precisely on pesticide poisoning in the fields of California. Poets such as Alurista, Naomi Quiñónez and others highlighted environmental poisoning in their poetry.

Herrera's environmental imaginary focuses on a cosmic sense of unity. The cosmos is conceptualized as a harmonious unit. Harmony between all beings, sentient and non-sentient (minerals, rocks, water, atoms, and so forth) is necessary for survival. The first poem in the collection commences with the invocatory line: "let us gather in a flourishing way" (1) and encompasses the overall philosophical and religious conceptualizations of the poet's universalist vision, that of the interconnections between the cosmos and its life-giving force. The poetic voice continues expanding in the second line of the poem: "with sunluz grains abriendo los cantos" (1). Here sunluz (sunlight) is perceived and privileged as the giver of life and the sunlight's cosmic force is able to "open" not only the "grains" or seeds of food-producing plants but also the "cantos" or songs. The grains function as a synecdoche for life.

The poem reiterates the line "let us gather in a flourishing way" and throughout the poem metaphors for life are encapsulated in words. These include but are not limited to: *pasto* (grassland), *perlas* (pearls), corn, *árboles* (trees), *ríos* (rivers), rainbows, *carne* (meat or flesh), blossoms, rain, *estrella* (star), *cielo* (sky, heaven), garden, *águila* (eagle) branches, *piedras* (rocks), *nopales* (cacti), *plumas* (feathers), figs, *aguacates* (avocados), *mariposas* (butterflies), *mares* (oceans), seeds, and maiztlan (combination of *maiz* or corn and Aztlán, the Aztec mythic homeland). The poem ends with the line "en las manos de nuestro amor" (in the hands of our love; 2) thus uniting in harmony all the cosmic forces enumerated above (plus others) with the all-encompassing vital force of love: spiritual, human, cosmic, heavenly, and so forth. Love, therefore, is essential in acquiring the harmony needed for the survival of the universe and all that is in it.

## Social Justice

The concern for social justice that permeates Herrera's literary production is evident in his first poem heading *Rebozos of Love*. The first line of the poem, "let us gather in a flourishing way" (1), anchors the poet's ideological commitment regarding social justice that will be repeatedly invoked in this poem and subsequent poems in the collection. It is important to note, however, that Herrera does not express his commitment for social justice in a violent way. He does not promote violence; that is not his style or manner of being. His revolutionary call for social justice and social change is expressed through a call for harmony, unity, coming together, peace, and love. These concepts were popular in the transformative decade of the 1960s, particularly with the counter-culture advocates, the anti-Vietnam War generation, the feminist movement, the African American civil rights movement and other political and social movements followed especially by young people under the age of thirty. However, Herrera does not include in his poetry "hippie" counterculture. He anchors his philosophical and religious thought in Indigenous cultures. His urgent message of peace and harmony encompasses the totality of the earth, the cosmos and the entire universe.

The images regarding the environment, sentient and non-sentient beings, and everything existing on earth merge with images of human life co-existing in a harmonious manner and not in an exploitative mode. The poetic voice exhorts the world to come together. The *pasto* or grassland merges with "nuestro cuerpo" (our body; 1). The harmonious interaction yields "feliz perlas" (happy pearls; 1) and the poetic voice continues in with an invitation to "celebrar woven brazos branches ramas," (celebrate woven arms branches branches; 2). The continued merging of humans and plant life is underscored in this first poem and it ends by invoking love to be the creative life force for this amazing harmonious universe: "en las manos de nuestro amor" (in the hands of our love; 2).

## Conclusion

Juan Felipe Herrera's poetry collection, *Rebozos of Love*, examined in this study, provides us with a rich kaleidoscopic tapestry of language articulating his philosophical concepts of peace and love. His desire and vision of seeing a harmonious, unified continent is best expressed in the poem "a m e r i n d i a":

| | |
|---|---|
| a m e r i n d i a | a m e r i n d i a |
| one heart | one heart |
| una tierra | one land |
| pueblos sin fronteras | people without borders |
| tierra sin cadenas | land without chains |
| caras sin correas | faces without leather bindings |

(65; my translation)

Juan Felipe Herrera's poetry more than ever continues to speak to us playfully, eloquently, and insistently and evidences a deep love for humanity.

# Note

1. The translation of parts of the title are thus: shawls of love / we have woven / sweat of our people / on our back. All translations are mine unless otherwise noted.
2. *Tloque Nahuaque* is normally spelled without an "h." Frances Karttunen's book, *An Analytical Dictionary of Nahuatl*, 1992, provides this variant spelling and definition. Also another meaning given is "dueño del cerca y del junto" (owner of close and far).
3. "He Through Whom One Lives," or that which, or by means of which people live, Giver of Life; a deity that is part of the Ometeotl Complex, primordial parents of deities and human creation; also came to be used to refer to the Christian God. See Wauchope and Manning, *Handbook of Middle American Indians*, and Wood, *Online Nahuatl Dictionary*.
4. Mayan in origin.
5. The Nahuatl translation given for the Spanish phrase, "Dador de la vida" is Ipalnemoani (also spelled Ipalnemohuani). The word is found in the 15th century Aztec poet Nezahualcóyotl' writings. See also Wood, *Online Nahuatl Dictionary*.

# Works Cited

Fagan, Brian M. *The Aztecs*. New York: W.H. Freeman, 1984.

González, Rachel Valentina. "Caló (Folk Speech)." In *Celebrating Latino Folklore: An Encyclopedia of Cultural Traditions*, vol. 1, edited by María Herrera-Sobek, 19798. Santa Barbara, Calif.: ABC-CLIO, 2012.

Herrera, Juan Felipe. *187 Reasons Mexicanos Can't Cross the Border: Undocuments, 1971–2007*. San Francisco, Calif.: City Lights Press, 2007.

Herrera, Juan Felipe. *Border-Crosser with a Lamborghini Dream*. Tucson: University of Arizona Press, 1999.

Herrera, Juan Felipe. *Cinnamon Girl: Letters Found Inside a Cereal Box*. New York: Joanna Cotler Books, 2005.

Herrera, Juan Felipe. *CrashBoomLove: A Novel in Verse*. Albuquerque: University of New Mexico Press, 1999.

Herrera, Juan Felipe. *Every Day We Get More Illegal*. San Francisco, Calif.: City Lights Books, 2020.

Herrera, Juan Felipe. *Exiles of Desire*. Houston, Texas: Arte Público Press, 1985.

Herrera, Juan Felipe. *Giraffe on Fire*. Tucson: University of Arizona Press, 2001.

Herrera, Juan Felipe. *Half of the World in Light: New and Selected Poems*. Tucson: University of Arizona Press, 2008.

Herrera, Juan Felipe. *Notebooks of a Chile Verde Smuggler*. Tucson: University of Arizona Press, 2002.

Herrera, Juan Felipe. *Rebozos of Love / We Have Woven / Sudor de Pueblos / On Our Back*. San Diego, Calif.: Toltecas en Aztlán Publications, 1974.

Herrera, Juan Felipe. *The Roots of a Thousand Embraces: Dialogues*. San Francisco, Calif.: Manic D Press, 1994.

Herrera-Sobek, María, "Writing the Toxic Environment: Ecocriticism and the Chicana Literary Imagination." In *A Contested West: New Readings of Place in Western American Literature*. London: Portal Editions, 2012.

Johansson Keraudren, Patrick. "El español y el náhuatl: primeros encuentros." In *Caleidoscopio verbal: lenguas y literaturas originarias*, edited by Osiris Aníbal Gómez, Sara Poot Herrera and Francisco A. Lomelí. Mexico City: Oro de la Noche Ediciones, 2020.

Karttunen, Frances. *An Analytical Dictionary of Nahuatl*. Austin: University of Texas Press, 1983.

Moraga, Cherríe. *Heroes and Saints and Other Plays*. Albuquerque, N.M.: West End Press, 1994.

Piña Chan, Román. *A Guide to Mexican Archaeology*. Mexico City: Editorial Minutiae, 1970.

Quiñónez, Naomi. *Sueño de Colibrí/Hummingbird Dream*. Los Angeles, Calif.: West End Press, 1985.

Valdez, Luis. *The Shrunken Head of Pancho Villa*. Berkeley, Calif.: El Teatro Campesino, 1964.

Villanueva, Alma. *Bloodroot*. Austin, Texas: Place of Herons Press, 1982.

Viramontes, Helena María. *Under the Feet of Jesus*. New York: Dutton Press, 1995.

Wauchope, Robert and Nash Manning, eds. *Handbook of Middle American Indians*, vol. 6: Social Anthropology. Austin: University of Texas Press, 1967.

Wikipedia. "Huichols." https://en.wikipedia.org/wiki/Huichol.

Wood, Stephanie, ed. *Online Nahuatl Dictionary*. Eugene, Ore.: Wired Humanities Projects, College of Education, University of Oregon. https://nahuatl.wired -humanities.org/.

# CHAPTER 6

# Afterlives of *Antropoesía*
## Juan Felipe Herrera and the Poetics of (Un)Documentation

WHITNEY DEVOS

From the earliest beginnings of his career, Juan Felipe Herrera has taken on the role of documentarian. When, in March 1968, Los Angeles erupted as students at Garfield High walked out of class and began the Chicano/a walk-outs (the East Los Angeles high school blowouts), Herrera, then an undergraduate at UCLA, filmed one of the protests on a reel of 8mm film. In 1970, with funding from UCLA's Mexican American Center, he traveled to Chiapas to study Indigenous theatrical expression, a trip which he self-consciously documented in photographs and, later, in the lyric memoir *Mayan Drifter: Chicano Poet in the Lowlands of America* (1997). In 1971, Herrera turned to 8mm once again, taking "footage of United Farm Worker speeches, martial arts demonstrations and practice, the Brown Berets, protests at the California State Capitol in Sacramento, police response to protests, and more" documenting what was likely the Marcha de la Reconquista ("Marcha de la," n.p.). These forays into documentation, filmic and photographic, are evinced in Herrera's earliest poetry, which was itself deeply intertwined with the poet's ongoing studies in anthropology—after graduating from UCLA in 1972 with a major in social anthropology, he went on to receive a master's degree in anthropology at Stanford. His first collection, the bilingual/Spanglish *Rebozos of Love / We Have Woven / Sudor de Pueblos / On Our Back* (1974), connected his poetry to Indigenous forms of oral and visual meaning-making by "revering languages as codices of meaning" (Lomelí, xvii). In *Exiles of Desire* (1983), Herrera's second collection, the poet continues to develop a complex theory of linguistic imaging, most notably in "Photo-Poem of the Chicano Moratorium 1980 / L.A." where the invented genre of the "photo-poem" frames tableau-like prose poems about the Chicano/a uprising as photographic stills.

*Mayan Drifter: Chicano Poet in the Lowlands of America* (1997) attempts to make sense of the poet's travels to Chiapas (1970; 1992–1993) while also recognizing that he must do so in such a way as to "challenge the very idea of 'Social Inquiry of the Native'—the canonical ethnographic S.I.N. of the social sciences" (5). These are just a few examples of the numerous works in which Herrera simultaneously records contemporary events and realities, while also engaging in a reflection on the politics of documentation.

Herrera has resisted describing his work as documentary, likely because of the genre's entangled origins with colonial ethnography. One of the earliest uses of the term "documentary," as it is often pointed out, appears in a review of Robert Flaherty's 1926 *Moana*, a film which "casted" locals in "roles" which they "performed" by staging anachronistic ancestral practices in accordance with the director's whims—and his colonial gaze. The author of this review, filmmaker John Grierson, known as the "father of documentary," was a staunch cultural nationalist whose career included equally troubling, quasi-ethnographic films such as *Of Japanese Descent: An Interim Report* (1945), which portrayed forcibly interned Japanese Canadians as a "problem" in need of solving through assimilation into postwar Anglo-Canadian life. The films of Grierson and Flaherty exist as part of a long tradition in which white ethnographers "documenting" non-white communities constructed their ethnographic subjects as backwards, barbaric, and in need of civilizing, all of which came under increasing scrutiny in the 1970s as a generation of scholars of color, of which Herrera was a part, contested the racist and xenophobic underpinnings of academic anthropology, and its related methods of ethnography and documentary filmmaking. In an interview with Alan Sodofsky, Herrera sketches his work in such a way as to at once reference and complicate the anthropological enterprise:

> I believe in having the widest lens possible while at the same time talking about what I see taking place in the Latina/Latino community. But it's not necessarily in a documentary approach or a "culturalist" approach. It's more

about flashes of insight that I gained at a particular moment, and then [I] include [that] in a poem as opposed to a complete story or a complete investigation—which is closer to anthropology, or "anthropoetics," as Renato Rosaldo says in his magnificent, *The Day of Shelly's Death: The Poetry and Ethnography of Grief* (2013) anthropoetry collection. (217)

Distancing himself from documentary and culturalism, Herrera instead turns toward the innovative work of ethnographer and poet Renato Rosaldo, his former advisor at Stanford. In doing so, Herrera situates himself within an alternative, anti-colonial line of cultural anthropology that contested the white anthropologic gaze by demonstrating how Indigenous epistemologies exceeded Western conceptions of thought and meaning-making. In Herrera's own words, a central scholarly contribution by Rosaldo was to contest "the prevalent notions in the field of anthropology and on the rest of the island of Luzon—the common view that Ilongot peoples lacked a history—by setting out on a trek to uncover and cover Ilongot accounts of the changes they had witnessed through generations" ("Anthropoetry," n.p.). Equally relevant to Herrera, however, were the ways Rosaldo came to challenge the boundaries of enthnography and creative writing: *The Day of Shelly's Death: The Poetry and Ethnography of Grief* responds to the death of his wife and research partner Shelly Rosaldo who fell from a cliff in an Ilongot village of the Northern Philippines on October 11, 1981, through a combination of images, writings, and notes and ephemera related to their ethnographic research. In the book's afterword, "Notes on Poetry and Ethnography," Rosaldo lays out a poetics he calls "antropoesía," theorized as "a process of discovery more than a confirmation of the already known" (106), one comparable to "thick description in ethnography where [. . .] details inspire theory rather than illustrate already formulated theory" (106). Herrera describes the book as "revolutionary; it presents another way, a new way of making poetry matter," a "poem-walk" in which the "images are more like body imprints of a place, space, partner, self; of sheared flesh and of a coming together of two bodies, Renato and Shelly, or four, Renato, Shelly, and their children, Sam and Manny, who were present, or five, with the Ilongot, or six with Luzon, itself" ("Anthropoetry," n.p.). Importantly, Rosaldo's "tracings" of what he calls the "eruption" the event of his wife's untimely death (101) interpellate their ethnographic subjects not as objects but as "witnesses" who appear, for Herrera "with dignity, unfinished, yet whole" ("Anthropoetry" n.p.); through *antropoesía* their comments are transformed from research-related evidence into a window back on to the widowed ethnographer and his wife.

Herrera's preference for "flashes of insight [. . .] gained at a particular moment" ("Anthropoetry" n.p.) in opposition to "a complete story or a complete investigation" ("Anthropoetry" n.p.) characterizes his own diverse iterations of poetic historiography, each of which seek to contest traditional narrative forms of knowledge production. Indeed, as a lifelong student of radical anthropology, he is acutely aware that the conquest of the Americas relied upon delegitimizing of Indigenous epistemic and mnemonic systems of thought. Ever-conscious during his own fieldwork of the ways documentation and its recording mechanisms have justified and sustained colonial power structures, "he knew [. . .] that [. . .] he must disrupt the terms, figures, and images of colonialism if he dared search for the way into America, a path leading back home" (*Mayan Drifter*, 15). History and its archives are countered in Herrera's work by a poetic stewarding of what Diana Taylor in *The Archive and the Repertoire: Performing Cultural Memory in the Americas* has named "the repertoire": those forms which enact embodied memory through "performances, gestures, orality, movement, dance, singing [. . .] acts usually thought of as ephemeral nonreproducible knowledge" (20). The repertoire is intimately bound up with performance and presence, two aspects that mark Herrera's career-long efforts to memorialize the gestures that, in aggregate, make up—and inspire—varied forms of ongoing transnational anti-imperial struggle the state seeks to surveil and, ultimately, extinguish.

## *Exiles of Desire*: The Advent of the Photo-Poem

*Exiles of Desire*'s "Photo-Poem of the Chicano Moratorium 1980 / L.A." marks the ten-year anniversary of the 1970 Chicano Moratorium, a demonstration organized by a broad coalition of Chicano/a activists in East Los Angeles that drew thirty thousand people in opposition to the Vietnam War. The largest antiwar protest organized by people of color in U.S. history, the Moratorium was a peaceful protest to which LAPD responded with helicopters and tear gas; it ended in rioting.

As the Chicano poet Alurista is said to have put it: "The police called it a people's riot; the people called it a police riot" (qtd. In Alfredo Gutiérrez, 10). The day concluded, tragically, with one hundred fifty arrests and the deaths of four demonstrators, including Rubén Salazar, an award-winning journalist known for his reporting on Chicano/a civil rights. Because Salazar was a leading community voice against police brutality, and because he had shared concerns that he was being followed by police in the days leading up to the Moratorium, many viewed his killing as an assassination: Deputy Thomas Wilson of the Los Angeles County Sheriff's Department had fired a tear gas canister into the Silver Dollar Café at point blank range, an act inexplicable in terms of public safety and for which Wilson was never held accountable. Interestingly, however, *Exiles* does not seek to commemorate the events surrounding the 1970 Moratorium, nor unravel the many competing narratives surrounding Salazar's death, but rather it takes as its subject a vigil held ten years later in memory of Salazar and the Moratorium itself.

"Photo-Poem," like many of Herrera's writings from the early 1980s, explores not only what political work Chicano revolt made possible, but that which was thwarted in the wake of the Moratorium: for many, the symbolic end of *el movimiento*. In all that remains unfinished, however, lies the possibility of distinct cultural and political formations in the process of becoming: "It's not a Movement anymore, carnal," Herrera writes four years later in *Facegames*, "Nor really a street fair either. / It's something else" (29).[1] This "something else" is the topic of "Photo-Poem": a series of six prose poems, each titled after a numbered, unpictured "photo," that work together to portray several images drawn from the ten-year commemorative march down Whittier Boulevard held to honor Salazar's memory. The first section, "Photo 1," frames the progression as a "pilgrimage," repurposing Catholic symbols as cultural talismans engaged in contemporary Chicano/a struggle: Salazar is a saint martyred by the Los Angeles Police Department, the Virgin Mary an amulet against tear gas. Entreating futures yet to come, these invented, historically specific icons invoke paradise as an "open street" beyond the reach of horned, devil-like SWAT teams. Together, the images accumulate into an ominous rhythm of a community's search for freedom, a place beyond surveillance and state violence:

> . . . who tattooed the santo-man on our forehead? Rubén Salazar . . . gone forever. Beneath the moon-gray numbers of L.A.P.D. August 29 1970. Running. Searching for a piece. Of open street. *Paraíso negro*. Pleading to the tear gas virgins. Appearing over the helmet horns of the swat men. Iridescent. We walk. Floating . . .
>
> (*Exiles of Desire*, 43)

As the "tattooing" of Salazar suggests, the photo poem explores how unresolved community concerns are incorporated within and onto the body—and the larger body politic ("our forehead")—by means of painful processes. "Photo 4. Anna María Nieto-Gómez / On Stage / Alone" depicts "issues" transposed on the body, "etched" by "knives" as lasting scars:

> . . . the issues that ten years. Knives. Ago were etched. Written hard through our lips. The issues have remained on silent funeral ground. Fading. Into chambers. Briefcases. Pockets. Notebooks. By the off & on bedroom light switch inside the fiber of pillows. That men clutch. At night. Crying. Binding female mate . . .
> . . . is this nightmare. Anna maria? Or. Is *La Familia* loved in chains only? The issues remain & the wind howls.

> (*Exiles of Desire*, 46)

In disjunctive prose, Herrera underscores how Moratorium-related "issues" imposed from the outside come to inhabit all of domestic space. Even as "the issues" once "written hard on our lips" begin to pale under the pressure of quotidian life under capital, fading "into chambers. Brief cases. Pockets. Notebooks," the "issues" take form in the body as self-surveilling "mind-blades" that constantly "cut out. A jagged distance . . . between man and woman" (46), altering community-based gender relations. Recalling helicopters from the Moratorium, the helicopter and "the issues" its blades index torments the collective "we" as much as its "funeral ground" in such a way as to render familial intimacy as a form of bondage. The title's framing of the poem as a "performance" "On Stage / Alone" of Chicana journalist Anna María Nieto-Gómez—founder of *Hijas de Cuauhtémoc*, a student Chicana feminist newspaper, and the feminist journal *Encuentro Femenil*—suggests Herrera takes seriously her "repertoire of embodied practices as an important system of knowing and transmitting knowledge" (Taylor, 26), in particular the transmission of traumatic memory grounded in affective experience. By foregrounding Anna María as a figure who calls out the ways patriarchal state violence is reified in intimate relations that render men "crying" and women "bound" to their sadness, Herrera counters the hyper-masculinist machismo that marked much of the early Chicano movement. Though it ends without resolution, "Photo 4" importantly redirects past-oriented mourning of a martyred Salazar to herald the advent of Chicana-led media and, thus, feminist modes of public memory.

In this spirit, "Photo 5. Sunset" takes up the related task of community history. Participants of the commemorative 1980 march, hailing from across the Central Valley, East Los Angeles, and Colorado, are united by the ubiquitousness of their impulse to record:

> People leave. Slowly. Taking their cameras. Back to Stockton. Colorado. Back
> to Fetterly Street . . .
> . . . we. Leave slowly with a few extra rolls of negatives. Black & white
> who got the viejito in his wheelchair? Or the Varrios Unidos group with the
> placas? Shouting *what do you want?* Answering (the vato with the hoarse
> voice) *justice! When do you want it? Now!*
>
> (Exiles of Desire, 47)

If the first question ("who got the viejito [little old man] in his wheelchair?") seems to suggest the sensationalizing aspects of documenting a protest, the presence of the viejito (who first appears in "Photo 1. Pilgrimage") indexes the multi-generational community involved in the long and ongoing struggle for justice, the emphasis of the second question. Here, the poet includes a chant which cannot be captured by a photographic image, reminding us of all that is lost when we encounter a particular event through the visual alone. In transcribing the famous social justice call and response within his "Photo-Poem," Herrera appeals to the auditory to bring the reader-viewer into the present tense of the scene. This heteroglossic interruption of the lyric voice is one of several visual and linguistic fragments jolts us out of aesthetic contemplation to instead impart a "flash of insight" about an event which at once sought to memorialize the Chicano Moratorium and emphasize the broad community of people—however ephemeral—Salazar's death brought together. From here, the poem suddenly changes scenes as "the stage spins" and we confront a scene of police brutality that might read at first as almost pure documentation, but can be alternately interpreted as a mural imaginatively brought to life:

> . . . la mujer. Con un rifle. Together
> with a man. Marching out of the plywood Emmanuel Montoya painted.
> Jumping high. Into wet grass. Doing steps of being shot. Suddenly.
> Opened up. By the torque of bullets. A gas cartridge pierces

the belly of the woman. Her imaginary rifle disappears the police lifts his
  wooden pipe. Strikes one. 2. Three
4. five 6. Seven. 8. Nine. Ten. Times. On her back. She falls falls. Falls. Bleed-
  ing. Her lips screaming through the tempest *don't leave.*

(Exiles of Desire, 47)

Realizing the scene is fictional brings little comfort, however: the image painted by Bay Area painter and educator Emmanuel Montoya is a depiction of contemporary Chicano struggles against police violence. Yet, perhaps this artistic meditation—a poem about a painting about "real life"—renders Herrera's work all the more powerful: again, a static image of a woman being beaten by the police is made more dynamic and visual as it is pulled in our own imaginations through the duration of the incessant striking of her back, counted out from one through ten.[2] That the woman herself was playfully imagining being shot before "the torque of bullets" adds yet another dimension to the already complex scene. Her predictive movement, merged with the onset of the attack, becomes a kind of choreographing suggestive of the ongoing cycle of structural violence: an aspect so often left out of short-form journalistic articles and archival documents pertaining to singular events which always result from and are embedded in larger networks of local, interpersonal, and geopolitical relations. The poet's drastic switch from East L.A. to San Francisco, the site of murals by Montoya, for example, emphasizes the shared cultural identity of Chicanos/as across Northern and Southern California. The final section, "Poem 6. Night / Aftermath / The Mime at Figueroa St. / Tri-X" travels across national borders to include Latin American peoples brought together by a shared condition of being "beneath *the patrón*. The military. *La Junta*" (48), pointing to the devastating transnational forces of capital (the *patrón*) and interconnected state-sanctioned brutality in Latin America enabled by the U.S. ("the military. *La Junta*"). At the same time, Herrera celebrates the artistic signs which counter repetitive, uncreative quotidian impositions of harm across the hemisphere. As the title suggests, once again dance-like movement serves as a means of knowledge transmission: the mime "teaches us political ballet step. By. Step" (48).

As Urayoán Noel points out in "Bodies That Antimatter: Locating U.S. Latino/a Poetry, 2000–2009," in "Photo-Poem," "the documentary writing dissolves, the hieratic moon survives, tattooed, written on the flesh of the never fully documentable city" (862). The poem's impetus is not so much to attempt to fully document any one city, or even the commemorative march, but to "trace" the "eruption" of Salazar's death and, by extension, the symbolic death of *el movimiento*: the way August 29, 1970, continues to reverberate throughout the Chicano community, as both a day of brutal state oppression and one of organized resistance to a violent colonial militarized state. Most of all, "Photo-Poem" asks us *to* remember and to remember *how* to remember, that there are various modes of remembering, not all of which take linguistic form: murals, mimed gestures, dance, felt trauma. Whether floating, miming, dancing, or photographing, victims of state violence are importantly never cast as passive objects to which things happen but are consistently invested with the creative abilities to communicate myriad— and feminist—ways of being, knowing, and resisting. Herrera approaches the remembering of collective actions as aesthetic experience: a relational, communal process transmitted in multiple ways. The series of images he provides suggest the impacts of one traumatic event index larger, interconnected geopolitical forces across the hemisphere: from San Francisco to El Salvador, "the yearning chests multiply. Into honeycombed spilled / muscles. Flayed. Floating" (48). His synecdoche of chests "honeycombed" and muscles "flayed" evokes dismemberment and torture associated with the right-wing dictatorships brought to power by United States-backed campaigns of political repression and state terror. Yet that they "multiply" also provides a second possible reading, in which the chests become united in the collective struggle of a street movement: "floating," as we shall see, is the verb to which Herrera returns in "un-documenting" Latino/a protests decades later.

## *Mayan Drifter*: The Search for Authentic "American" Descriptions

In December 1992, Herrera set out into the Selva Lacandona in search of K'ayum Ma'ax, a member of the Lacandón Maya whom the poet met in 1970 while doing field work in Chiapas as a graduate student. *Mayan Drifter* chronicles these two cycles of travels through southern Mexico, in a book of five sections which give form to Herrera's multi-directional memory in different genres brought together as "an unfinished poem of desire; a return to America—in the present: a möbius-shaped trek backward and forward to a shattered realm of Indian and campesino villages and bodies, to an unsettled mestizaje that at every turn aims to subvert itself" (6). If 1970 represented a key turning point in the Chicano/a movement, events in Mexico in the early 1990s signaled a shift toward other modes of collective action against the consolidation of neoliberalism. Writing in the wake of the Zapatista uprising, Herrera proposes 1994 as a major epistemological break after which the categories and language through which we think "America" must be reconceptualized: "What subterranean campesino stratum rumbles across the entire continent," he asks, "from Mayas digging through famine to undocumented farm workers dodging armored helicopters in the Southwest?" (4). The reasons the poet found himself "unaware of the groundswell of an impending revolution" (3) during his 1992–1993 return to Chiapas slowly become less opaque over the course of the book as Herrera's *antropoesía* unravels the intricate roots of historic, land-based conflict between the Lacandón Maya and the EZLN (Ejército Zapatista de Liberación Nacional) as a product of the Mexican state. While "Photo-Poem" endeavors to trace the afterlives of the Chicano Moratorium, *Mayan Drifter* attempts to identify not only the impacts of "el levantamiento Zapatista" but its antecedents all the while eschewing "the scholar's or anthropologist's systematic, putatively detached methodology" (Dowdy, *Broken Souths*, 77).

Instead, Herrera retraces his movements through southern Mexico, applying *antropoesía* to retroactively make sense of how certain events he witnessed portended January 1, 1994. A protest in San Cristóbal is illustrative of this introspection: "Was this march an ongoing drum of rebellion about to explode [. . .] ?" he asks, "[. . .] [C]ould it be heard by the Ladino, by the United States, was the Mayan and campesino edge about to break off" (*Mayan Drifter*, 72)? Prefiguring, in many ways, *The Day of Shelly's Death*, *Mayan Drifter* brings material ephemera into his writing, reproducing in full, for example, two flyers from the protest. The first, from the Tzotzil in Ch'enalho, demands the immediate release of community members unjustly incarcerated "por problemas de la tierra que las autoridades y reforma agraria no han querido resolver" (due to problems related to the land that the authorities and the agrarian reform program have not wanted to resolve; Herrera's translation; 70). The second, from the Fray Bartolomé de las Casas Human Rights Office, provides further context of police corruption and anti-gay violence, in English (71). In attempting to interpret the documents, and their distinct rhetorical aims, the poet continually casts doubt upon his ability to do so, in large part due to his positioning as a data collector removed from the community at large: "What about us I thought: / the onlookers, the note takers, the accountants, bookkeepers, and anthropological shadows? What did we know?" (74) This self-conscious questioning reaches a climax when the narrator gives his audio recording device to K'ayum Ma'ax, drawing rhythmic connections between the recorder ("voice taker") and corporate agriculture ("slime makers"):

> The tape recorder was supposed to be my memory maker, my voice taker, my history recorder. I could have recorded stories, myths and tellings, family histories and tales of the village, of the mahogany cutters and slime makers dressed in their corporate-owned bulldozers. But in a matter of a few hours, Nahá had changed all this [. . .] I gave the little self-activated machine to K'ayum Ma'ax, the voice box from the States was his now. I let go of my "ethnographic intentions." (112)

Even as Herrera chides himself for falling into colonial traps ("I was one more visitor dumping guilt and technology, proffering an exchange between the Modern and the Savage," 112), the exchange is complicated by the way it induces him to also shift his relationship to memory. Upon letting go of his "ethnographic intentions" and the various acts of recording they imply, the narrator turns to accessing embodied memory instead: in so doing, he is able to reconstruct the specifics of a photograph image he thought he had forgotten, meeting a young boy in the 1970s (112). Images, as Herrera said of Rosaldo, are the coming together of two bodies and their culturally distinct ways of encoding meaning and historiography. Rather than simply exchanging the archive for the repertoire, the moment encourages the development of a methodology that mediates between them. Herrera records in writing the embodied knowledge of the elder Viejo Chan K'in, for example, as told to him secondhand (118–119). As the narrator transcribes the repertoire, to the extent it's possible, while also letting go of the totalizing impulse to archive, he finds shared, albeit distinct, experiences of life under capitalism and impending ecological destruction imprinted within. Yet the impetus is not to scaffold Chicano identity through the essentialized assimilation of the images of *campesino* life so much as unpacking the relation framed therein, to, as the poet says, "re-collect myself as a member of a disinherited Indian and American family, the Maya of the Lowlands, to reassign myself into a

Afterlives of *Antropoesia* **147**

new, contradictory, fictive kinship system" (7). At times, the feeling is mutual: at one point, the narrator is referred to as a "Hach Wink," the term Lacandón Maya use to refer to member of their own community (113).

*Mayan Drifter* challenges indigenist narratives of Chicano/a cultural nationalism which "tunnel through history in search of an ethnic essence to be conjured in a self-induced Ouija spell" (5), as well as indigenist tendencies in hemispheric American literature that frame Indigenous cultural production as relics of the past whose chief asset lies in posing alternative intellectual genealogies to Western European canons. By venturing to instead "contemplate the Indian and campesino on their own ground" (5), *Mayan Drifter* moves beyond earlier instantiations of research-based documentary poetry such as Neruda's *Alturas de Macchu Picchu* (1946) and Ernesto Cardenal's *Los ovnis de oro: poemas indios* (1988) by arguing that Indigenous world-making practices in fact offer future oriented tactics of an ongoing revolt "ancient, cyclical, and at times hemispheric" (8). For Herrera, Rigoberta Menchú, is a "model for the poet of the twenty-first century" (9), in the way she teaches us to

> stare back at chaos, disaster, and death, be fearless in the face of relentless oppression, learn the languages of the marginalized as well as of the oppressor, remember to assist in organizing exploited communities, remember to break through assigned borders, always fight and forgive—remember the secrets. (8)

Herrera's endorsement of Menchú came just two years before the Maya Ki'che' activist's 1989 *testimonio* came under fire in one of the touchstone debates of the culture wars.[3] If, as Thomas McEnaney writes, the so-called Rigoberta Menchú controversy is inseparable from various processes of *"entextualization,"* by which "an object (a cassette tape, a rock, a personal letter with the remains of a grasshopper) becomes a specific type of text" (394), the third through fifth sections of *Mayan Drifter* presciently anticipates such problematics by reversing these processes. Transforming and translating "the archive" of his journeys into alternate, performance-based genres of the "repertoire," Herrera's prose travel writings are followed by a two-act play, *Jaguar Hotel*, "an unfinished and tattered enterprise" (177) which at once dramatizes the vignettes which come before it and disavows its basis in reality by asserting "All characters are fictive" (178). By including this theatrical work, along with idiosyncratic stage instructions, Herrera encourages readers to experience his journey through a series of embodied movements staged according to the specific conditions of performance: "It is up to the troupe and audience to determine the direction, style, and tempo of the acts and scenes," he writes, "to color and materialize the sets. Key question: can the puzzle of capitalism versus spirit versus magic versus revolution versus genocide versus stage versus writing be solved?" (177). Following the play is the poem "Anahuak Vortex: Mexico City 1995," just over eight pages, which, among many other things, repeatedly indicts Ernesto Zedillo, the Mexican economist and President (1994–2000) associated with the right-wing Institutional Revolutionary Party (PRI). Finally, *Mayan Drifter* closes with its titular section, in many ways the volume's most trenchant critique: a letter to K'ayum Ma'ax, one of Herrera's principal interlocutors in Chiapas. This letter retraces the interrelated events of 1994: the assassination of Luis Donaldo Colosio, NAFTA, the Zapatista rebellion. These generic variations on Herrera's vignettes encourage forms of memory transmission, which, as Menchú exemplifies, exceed the colonial anthropological enterprise. If Herrera's first two sections self-consciously archive the repertoire, his play, poem, and one-sided epistolary transmission also record "acts usually thought of as ephemeral nonreproducible knowledge" (Taylor, 20) but, by giving them a script, conceive of a mobile method of encoding memory meant to be performed or read aloud.

## Indocumentos/Undocuments

Herrera's selected *187 Reasons Mexicanos Can't Cross the Border: Undocuments, 1971–2007*, a survey of 36 years of work, theorizes such creative acts of oppositional epistemology in relationship to national belonging using the invented category in the book's subtitle: "undocuments."[4] Detouring the adjectival immigration status of "indocumentados" or "undocumented" into an invented noun, Herrera shifts the grammatical focus away from people who are or are not "documented" by official papers granting them full or partial citizenship and on to the texts, narratives, and discourses—both official and unofficial—that constitute our social and political identities. In the book's "subtitle" piece, Herrera outlines the classification (fig. 6.1).

His first four bullet points draw attention to the ways in which the state seeks to control, manufacture, authorize, and verify identity and, by extension, subjectivity, through the various and unequal designations of national

# Indocumentos (een-doh-koo-mehn-tohs) / Undocuments / noun:

AZTLÁN CHRONICLES, VOL. 9, NO. 9

- *Multi-vocal passage-ware lacking authorized verifications regarding entry and/or social identity.*
- *Texts utilized by non-state-actors for mobile existence in-between officialized national entities.*
- *A system of undocumented signification of & for the people.*
- *The spoken subject within the context of exile, illegal ID status and/or "alien" assignations.*
- *Transgressive acts of perception and interpretation within a shifting borderlands territory.*
- *Flux moments in-between being & non-being.*

**FIGURE 6.1** "Indocumentos" in *187 Reasons Mexicanos Can't Cross the Border: Undocuments 1971–2007.* Courtesy of City Lights Books.

belonging it applies to residents. Implicitly referencing an Anzaldúan tradition, he reframes civically disempowered Latino/a actors as highly diverse, highly mobile entities utilizing "multi-vocal passage-ware" (201) to move "within a shifting borderlands territory" (201) between both "officialized national entities" (201) in the wry, dual existential status of "being & non-being." Indeed, Michael Dowdy in "Reinventing Ecopoetics: Chicano Poetry's Undocumentary Turn" identifies the contradictory impulses in the undocuments: "Herrera evacuates agency and obscures subjectivity" and at the same time, his phrasing "links hunger, speech, and mobility to the production of 'undocuments'" (28). In the penultimate bullet point in particular, the holders and creators of undocuments occupy a privileged, transgressive discursive position. Herrera's mock-technocratic language satirizes a system of signification upheld by the racial hegemony of the ruling class.

An emphasis on performance and remix, as well as a constant transgression of linguistic, formal, and generic expectations characterizes Herrera's "tribute to the Floricanto movement" (22): *alabanzas* (chants of praise) and *corridos* (ballads) appear alongside and within anaphoric poems, prose narrative, travelogue, manifestos, incantations, Mexica theology, free verse, as well as photo-poems and captioned photographs. Excerpted are both *Exiles of Desire*, including a full reprint of "Photo-Poem of the Chicano Moratorium 1980 / L.A." (275–278), and four excerpts from *Mayan Drifter* appearing in a revised form under the title "One Year Before the Zapatista Rebellion" (174–199). Such "texts utilized by non-state-actors for mobile existence in-between officialized national entities" (201), Herrera argues, represents an artistic strategy that applies to all Latinos/as, all of whom, regardless of citizenship status, are pigeonholed into the category of "illegals" through various processes of racialization, be they legal, political, or cultural. He notes:

> Mexican@s & Latin@s have been historically cast in one way or another as "illegals," & 'undocumented' entities [. . .] through "soft" cultural border-patrol work such as most official media narratives & the "footing" of most political & electoral platforms of the "hard" classifications of foreign & international policy, structured force & military surveillance, then the words & texts of such actors, regardless of their citizenship must become "undocumented" as well [. . . .] (201)

By framing the texts of all Latino/a writers as "undocuments," the poet suggests all the ways in which the process of racialization frames one's relationship to the state and, importantly, the extent to which the state fulfills its national promise. It is through both "hard" and "soft" forms of policing, Herrera suggests, that citizens are distinguished within a racial order that demands assenting to and assimilating within a norm standardized by whiteness, although race is not referenced explicitly in this excerpt. Indeed, recent scholarship corroborates such a claim.[5] Another consequence of this racialization in the United States, however, as Herrera presciently suggests, has been a consolidation of Latinidad: "rising anti-immigrant sentiment, repressive immigration and border enforcement, and the public portrayal of Latino immigrants as criminals, invaders, and terrorists' has reinforced the emergence of a panethnic Latino identity" (Massey and Sánchez, 212),[6] though one that has increasingly come under scrutiny for its frequent elision of Black, Indigenous, and Asian life.[7]

## "A Day Without a Mexican: *Video Clip*"

One such "undocument," "A Day Without a Mexican: *Video Clip*" (2006), found in *187 Reasons Mexicanos Can't Cross the Border; Undocuments, 1971–2007*, is a twenty-page documentary poem celebrating and demanding remembrance of Latino/a activism. The poem takes its name from "A Day Without a Mexican," a day-long international boycott against the Border Protection, Antiterrorism, and Illegal Immigration Control Act of 2005 (H.R. 4437), popularly known as the "Sensenbrenner Bill,"[8] as well as Sergio Arau's film of the same name. Herrera's decision to title—and thus "frame"—this poem by means of Arau's mocumentary situates the work as both in relation to documentary and antagonistic to its conventional form, much in the same way his acknowledgement of Rosaldo distances him from colonial ethnography. Yet Herrera's work, unlike Arau's, is by no means a comedy; instead, as an "undocument," it takes aim at "'soft' cultural border-patrol work such as most official media narratives & the 'footing' of most political & electoral platforms" (201) that characterized Latinos/as as existing largely outside the sphere of U.S. politics, a pervasive mainstream narrative resoundingly refuted by the massive mobilization of Latino/a communities on May Day, 2006.

Herrera's poem labors to situate the protest as part of a much longer, hemispheric history of revolt:

> At the edges frayed the march
> from Mexico City Plaza Tlatelolco Plaza Zócalo conchero danzante
> still in rebellion against            Spanish rule . . .
> . . . . . . . . . . . . . . . . . . . . . . . . . . . . .
>        Centro Cultural de la Raza
> occupied water tank summer of '73
>
> (*187 Reasons*, 54)

Here, el Zócalo and Plaza Tlatelolco, emblematic sites of social unrest and state-sanctioned violence in Mexico City, are brought into relation with the Centro Cultural de la Raza, created after public occupations in which Los

Toltecas en Aztlán, a group of San Diego and Tijuana-based Chicano artists, demanded the city grant the Chicano/a borderlands community rights to a public cultural space. Herrera's frequent and non-chronological references to prior protests in "A Day Without a Mexican" weave the present moment of the 2006 rally into larger historical contexts of violent and non-violent collective political action in the Americas. What unites the protesters in San Diego, East L.A., and Mexico City, and the speaker of the poem—who, throughout, references his own involvement in various social struggles taking place over the course of several decades—is their resistance not only to "Spanish rule" (*187 Reasons*, 54), but the centuries of colonial violence that has followed—and the racial logic it relies upon: "'We know it is racial' another banner" (*187 Reasons*, 62). Individual protests cannot be approached as isolated phenomena, Herrera suggests, but rely and build upon a transnational, multi-generational efforts to resist imperialism and white supremacy. Nativism and nativist legislation, he suggests, may be cyclical, but so, then, are solidarity and resistance. Putting historical moments into relation, Herrera's undocument frames the long and circuitous temporality of the ongoing struggle to end political and economic oppression in the Americas as both past- and future-oriented.

"A Day Without a Mexican: *Video Clip*" indexes the formal conceit of *187 Reasons* more broadly, a collection in which the pieces are laid out by the author "as if they were speaking in their community-moment in time, when their gestation was in motion, and in most cases when their environments and/or narratives were formed" (22). This volume's organizational structure extends Herrera's synchronic approach of recording "flashes of insight . . . gained at a particular moment" so that *187 Reasons* becomes a diachronic archive of punctuated "community-moments in time," each selection a kind of tableau-like cross-section of historically specific Chicano/a cultural narratives. The poem's subtitle "*Video Clip*" reinforces such anthropoetics at work; in contrast to *A Day Without a Mexican*, a full-length feature, Herrera's poem aspires to a series of images that document aspects of the 2006 protest which itself was named after Arau's film, "as opposed to a complete story or a complete investigation" (Soldofsky. 217).

If, as Evren Savci recently explained, "what ethnography allows for is an ability to capture *narratives in practice*, in all their complexity as much as possible while understanding what these practices *mean* to subjects who engage in them" (74), "A Day Without a Mexican: *Video Clip*" takes on a particular ethnographic function in preserving protest signs, banners, and t-shirts. These provide an opportunity for the speaker to reflect upon different—and often competing—claims to citizenship, national belonging, and the privileges afforded therein. The sign "'Yo nací en América soy Americano ok'" (I was born in América I am American ok; 62) articulates a hemispheric claim to citizenship for all people born in the Americas. Here, the nationalistic thrust of *el movimiento* is preserved even as the speaker modifies the concept of a Latinidad nation so as to be constructed outside normative, territorial terms: "everyone is her / between exile and homeland / and exile without a name or a territory / a homeland that does not exist" (49). Other claims, "'Todos contra el muro'" (All against the border wall; 56) and "The world can't wait to drive out the Bush / regime—amnistía general" (57), articulate specific policy demands. During the march, mainstream immigrant rights groups were known to pull signs such as these from protesters and replace them with signs with the more politically palatable, media friendly slogan, "we are americans." Preserving the wide range of political claims, the poem serves to document the diverse political positions held within the Latino/a community.

An important, if unremarked upon, aspect of "A Day Without a Mexican: *Video Clip*" is that its documentary materials highlight the death of a young Chicano activist. The poem opens with two photographs captioned "Continue the Struggle in Anthony's Name. L.A. City Hall, May 1st 2006." Anthony, a fourteen-year-old middle school student, helped organize a student walkout in support of immigrant rights on March 28, 2006 at De Anza Middle School in Ontario, Calif. On the school day immediately following the March 25th protest in LA, nearly forty thousand students across LA, San Diego, Riverside, San Bernardino, Orange, and Ventura counties were involved in walkouts and protests, with participation eclipsing similar actions against Proposition 187 in 1994 and in support of Chicano rights in 1968. Anthony Soltero's walkout, one of several in the Ontario area that took place on the day after, was thus part of a larger, loosely coordinated effort inspired by student protests at other Southern California schools on March 27th. Anthony and three other protesters left DeAnza for Ontario High, where they had planned to join other protesters, but by the time they arrived the campus was already on lockdown (Corrales vs. Bennett, 6460). Two days later, Anthony and the other participating students were called into Vice Principal Gene Bennett's office for disciplinary questioning regarding the truancy. Anthony's mother, Louise Corrales, said she spoke to her son via telephone about the conversation that afternoon. She said Anthony, who was upset, had told her he was suspended and had been told by Bennett that he was going to jail, as the truancy had violated a probation agreement. When Corrales returned home shortly thereafter, she found Anthony with his stepfather's firearm and a self-inflicted gunshot wound, one that proved fatal.

Rather than address or correct the competing narratives surrounding Soltero's death, Herrera's piece instead elects to "undocument" the march in which Anthony's memory—and struggle—were honored by select attendees. Yet by repeatedly returning to Anthony without telling his story directly, the poem provides a stay, however provisional, against Anthony's efforts toward social justice falling into obscurity. Like all elegies, "A Day Without a Mexican: *Video Clip*" addresses the living more urgently than the dead, determined that, if even on a purely symbolic level, Anthony Soltero not be forgotten. First, Anthony's death is acknowledged: "Anthony Soltero now gone / to the skywaves" (59). Then, through ritualized speech, the speaker puts Anthony to rest and offers the poem, indistinguishable from the march, as a dedication: "Anthony may you rest in peace / this is for you / this / is for you" (59); "next to Anthony's mother Anthony looks this way / white T blue backdrop he gazes alive / almost he / Here Now" (59). The ambiguity of the enjambment of "almost" works to presence Anthony, in the form of a protest sign, as gazing "alive," even as it simultaneously acknowledges the poem's failure to bring back the dead. Just as religious iconography influenced "Photo-Poem," spiritual tropes of reincarnation and resurrection play an important role in "A Day Without a Mexican: *Video Clip*." Another suggestive reference describing one of the protestors uses the subjunctive mood to evoke Anthony's spirit in a move that seeks to place him in the highest level of the Mexica (Aztec) afterlife: "marching dissolving Chicano 14-yr-old / across the treetops where he climbs as if / he found a ladder to the 13 heavens of Omeyocán" (63). He is, it turns out, a protestor cited at the beginning of the discussion of this poem:

> Che Guevara T red & black he peers out
> into the multitude for the first time 800,000, 600,000, 500,000
> he meditates from there he stops . . .

. . . . . . . . . . . . . . . . . . .
affirmed

unknown unclassifiable vortex of soul spirit family clan mi-grante

nation crossers nation makers. . . .

("A Day Without a Mexican: Video Clip," 187 Reasons, 63)

By transfiguring Anthony into one of the marchers who is continuing the struggle "in Anthony's name," Anthony "ascends" to a place of high honor, even as his earthly presence proliferates on the ground. Just as Herrera connects May 1, 2006 to previous uprisings, he writes Soltero into the centuries-long struggle Americans have faced in political environments wherein the conditions for democratic possibility have been shaped by neoliberal capitalism and a racial order. In preserving Anthony's name and history, the poem is a repository for tactics of anti-colonial resistance which inform political struggle in the present: "the past becomes the present where we march," Herrera writes, "& the future appears in beige glimpse snaps" (58).[9] Interpreting the poem as working to "convert [. . .] commodified revolutionary signs to tools of collective struggle," Dowdy classifies "A Day Without a Mexican: *Video Clip*" as a pinnacle of Herrera's "poetics of reconciliation" (*Broken Souths*, 66). Yet rather than a commodified revolutionary sign, we might understand the image of Soltero that opens the poem as a "trace" indexing a young Chicano whose political organizing came up against the disciplinary regime of white public school administrators. If one reads "A Day Without a Mexican: *Video Clip*" as underscoring "the failings of documentary poetics," as Noel does, surely it follows that "Even when the poet is/was on the front lines, the poem itself always arrives too late" (861). However, if we follow in Renato Rosaldo's footsteps, "too late"—that is, everything subsequent to the "event"—is in fact the moment where the political work of remembering begins.[10] Interestingly, even as Noel points out that, in the 2000s, "the socially engaged poet will have to write his way around the media pundits and camera crews and bloggers to get to the real story, the undocumented one" (861), both he and Dowdy focus on the big "story" of the poem, the protest—Soltero goes unmentioned. Surely if there is an undocumented "story" of "A Day Without a Mexican: *Video Clip*," it belongs to Anthony, to whom the poem is dedicated and whose absence the title implicitly registers. If the 2006 protests covered on mainstream outlets and studied by academics are the archive, embodied gestures like "walking out" are part of the repertoire, much more difficult to capture, fix, or document. Their strength instead lies in their iterative power to be re-performed. Herrera's "poem-walk" asks us to place Anthony's final act in relation not only to "A Day Without a Mexican: *Video Clip*"—that "struggle" continued "in Anthony's name"—but to the 1980 Chicano Moratorium whose opening lines "A Day Without A Mexican: *Video Clip*" repeats: "This march is holy" (49). Perhaps one of the most radical things a reader can do, Herrera suggests, is to continue to transmit, contextualize, (re)interpret, and reenact these kinds of community histories which exceed dominant forms of knowledge production.

## *The Afterlives of* Antropoesía

The metaphor of "depth of field," as Jean Franco writes in her introduction to *The Day of Shelly's Death*, is what allowed Herrera's one-time adviser to conceive of a kind of "mourning poetry in which his grief does not occur in isolation but ripples outward and is witnessed" (Rosaldo, xvi). Himself believing in "having the widest lens possible" (Soldofsky, 217), Herrera has labored to extend Rosaldo's ethnographic approach to poetry such that personal mourning and the mourning of persons—Rubén Salazar, Colosio, Anthony Soltero—"ripples outward and is witnessed" (Rosaldo, xvi) in such a way as to initiate a process of commemorative discovery as to the enduring resonances of individual lives situated within local, cultural, national, and transnational forms of ongoing revolt. For decades, his work has used poetry as a form to reveal the ways that historical narratives, particularly as they pertain to national tragedies, are not geopolitically neutral: constructed by the state and the status quo, they circulate via that strain of cultural nationalism that begins with Flaherty, Grierson, and the birth of documentary film and finds its current instantiations in mainstream media, the neoliberal academy, and corrupt legislative systems that have outlawed the teaching of race and U.S. history. Constructing a constantly shifting, hemispheric language that acknowledges the aftereffects and rejects the constrictive categories of colonialism and capitalism, Herrera's work makes struggle inextricable from collective embodiment, that is, together they "gather together in a flourishing way" (*Half the World in Light*, 11).

# Notes

1. In this way, *Exiles of Desire* marks a deft transition from Herrera's early poetry, steeped as it was in Chicano cultural or ethnic nationalism, to what Ellie D. Hernández has theorized as "post-movement" poetics (3–5).

2. Throughout the poem, the emphasis on the repertoire has the effect of inducing a desire to supplement with the archive. Perhaps the most powerful example is the mention in "Photo 1. Pilgrimage": if a reader does not know who Rubén Salazar was, or what his ongoing contribution to the Chicano/a community has been, they may look up the name. Depending on how far into the research they get, they may come to understand "the thirty-two year old mother with three. children. / no husband. by the fire hydrant" (43) is a reference to Sally Salazar and her daughters, Lisa and Stephanie, and son, John. Herrera reminds readers that Salazar was not only a martyr for the Chicano/a movement, but a father and husband whose state-induced absence is a daily reality.

3. David Stoll, also trained as a cultural anthropologist also trained at Stanford, challenged the veracity of Mechú's claims by means of conventional forms of ethnography and archival research in state archives. For an array of responses to Stoll's work, see *The Rigoberta Menchú Controversy* (2001), edited by his principal detractor, Arturo Arias. Rosaldo, unsurprisingly, defended Menchú. For more on his position, and the "culture wars" more generally, see Pratt in Arias and Stoll's volume. For a more recent overview of the controversy, see Grandin.

4. Herrera's title is taken from a previous chapbook, *187 Reasons Why Mexicanos Can't Cross the Border: An Emergency Poem* (1994), an activist list poem published in response to Proposition 187, a self-citation underscoring the persistence of anti-immigrant sentiment as well as the ways instances of nativism are repetitive and cyclical.

5. Zepeda-Millán gives an excellent summary of this data (16–17).

6. Indeed, Herrera's undocuments, which include countries from El Salvador to Haiti (*187 Reasons*, 260), assert a cultural heritage of Latinidad elided, erased, and, still, shaped by a dialectical relation to the dominant Anglo culture and its canons—even if throughout *187 Reasons* Herrera's polyvocal, formally promiscuous voice also refuses to serve as synecdoche for a stable, unified "Latinx identity" representing the "Latinx experience." Often playing on the figure of the trickster (181), Herrera achieves this voice in part by remixing a variety of Latino/a and Anglo literary forms. Yet Herrera's understanding of Latinidad is not limited to Latin America: "Juan was well aware that when he talked of Mexico, he was actually talking about Latin America . . . and soon enough he would end up referring to Malaysia or the Philippines . . . Third World border seemed to be illusory . . . superimposed throughout various zones of exploitation throughout the globe" (*Mayan Drifter*, 176).

7.  For a contemporary overview of the limitations of Latinidad, see Tatiana Flores.

8.  The proposed legislation, approved by the House of Representatives on December 16, 2005, made the status of being an undocumented immigrant in the United States—previously a civil violation—into a federal felony offense. Further, the bill sought to punish any individual who "assists, encourages, directs, or induces a person to reside in or remain in the United States," whether "knowing or in reckless disregard of" that person's status as "an alien who lacks lawful authority to reside in or remain in the United States" (Section 202). Such a statute would have subjected countless citizens and civil workers, such as teachers, family members, social workers, lawyers, and all who interact with undocumented people on a daily basis, to fines and/or incarceration. Additionally, H.R. 4437 compelled government officials to detain undocumented individuals and mandated that employers confirm employees' immigration status by conducting background checks. The building of up to seven hundred miles of double-layer fencing along the U.S.-Mexico border at points with the highest number of border crossings was also required.

9.  In 2007, Anthony's parents and one of the students filed suit against Bennett, the De Anza principal, and the Ontario-Montclair School District, alleging violations of the students' and parents' civil rights under 42 U.S.C. § 1983; violations of California's Unruh Act; intentional infliction of emotional distress, and negligently causing Anthony's suicide. U.S. District Judge Stephen G. Larson dismissed the suit. The following year, U.S. 9th Circuit Court of Appeals reviewed the case: a three-judge panel, consisting of two Reagan appointees and one Carter appointee, sided unequivocally with school administrators. The appeals decision, published in 2009, noted that "accounts of the meeting between Bennett and the students differ substantially" (Corales vs. Bennett, 6462).

    However, Bennett and Annette Prieto, a student who testified on behalf of Anthony, agreed upon one key point: during the students' disciplining, the student walkouts and immigration protests were never discussed. While the Sensenbrenner Bill sought to compel educators to enforce violent, anti-immigrant state policy, the interaction is indicative of how quotidian this already is. Bennett's unnecessarily aggressive, threatening behavior reminds us that police are not the only agents of state discipline. Whether or not it included a threat of incarceration, Bennet's "stern" warning, which the court characterized as "perhaps unduly harsh" but not "extreme and outrageous" (6482), missed an opportunity to discuss with four Latino/a students who missed class on a conspicuous day, some of the basic tenets—and failings—of democracy in the United States. Instead, Bennett's behavior bears out Angela Davis's argument that, "When children attend schools that place a greater value on discipline and security than on knowledge and intellectual development, they are attending prep schools for prison" (39).

10. In this way, gauging the "success" of Herrera's poem presents a challenge not unlike assessing the success of the 2006 protests more broadly. The effective-

ness of the 2006 protests depends on how one frames the desired outcome. The Sensenbrenner Bill was ultimately not passed; however, neither was any of the comprehensive immigration reform legislation that had been in the works for years. Numbers in deportations and workplace raids substantially increased, along with anti-immigrant backlash and hate crimes, during and subsequent to the demonstrations. Yet the 2006 protests also help bring California to its current Democratic supermajority: a record number of Latino/a citizens registered to vote in the wake of the Sensenbrenner threat and, while by no means a homogenous voting block, have by and large supported democratic candidates. In the 2021 election to recall Gavin Newsom, an estimated 78.1% percent of Latinos voted no. A recent study on this election found that Latino voters had "increased by nearly 150 percent since the last recall election in 2003, while [. . .] the growth of white voters over the past two decades was only 5 percent. As of the 2020 General Election, Latinos composed 27.9 percent of all registered voters in California" (Galdámez et al.). Taking the long view, as Herrera does, the outcome appears more favorable.

# Works Cited

Arau, Sergio, director. *A Day without a Mexican*. Xenon Pictures, 2004.

Arias, Arturo and David Stoll. *The Rigoberta Menchú Controversy*. Minneapolis: University of Minnesota Press, 2001.

Cardenal, Ernesto. *Los Ovnis De Oro: Poemas Indios*. Madrid: Siglo XXI de España Editores, 1988.

Corales vs. Bennett. U.S. Court of Appeals Ninth Circuit, 6455–6485. 2009. https://law.justia.com/cases/federal/appellate-courts/ca9/07-55892/07-55892-2011-02-25.html. Accessed 17 October 2017.

Davis, Angela Y. *Are Prisons Obsolete?* N.p.: Seven Stories Press, 2011.

Dowdy, Michael. *Broken Souths: Latina/o Poetic Responses to Neoliberalism and Globalization*. Tucson: University of Arizona Press, 2013.

Dowdy, Michael. "Reinventing Ecopoetics: Chicano Poetry's Undocumentary Turn." *Aztlán: A Journal of Chicano Studies*, 41, no. 1 (Spring 2016): 21–53.

Flaherty, Robert, director. *Moana*. Kino Classics, 1926.

Flores, Tatiana. "'Latinidad Is Cancelled' Confronting an Anti-Black Construct." *Latin American and Latinx Visual Culture*, 3, no. 3 (2021): 58–79.

Franco, Jean. Foreword to *The Day of Shelly's Death: The Poetry and Ethnography of Grief*, by Renato Rosaldo, xv-xvi. Duke University Press, 2014.

Galdámez, Misael, et al. "Latino Voters in the 2021 Recall Election." UCLA Latino Policy and Politics Initiative, October 21, 2022. https://latino.ucla.edu/research/latino-voters-in-the-2021-recall-election/.

Grandin, Greg. *Who Is Rigoberta Menchú?* London: Verso Books, 2011.

Grierson, John, director. *Of Japanese Descent: An Interim Report*. Canadian Film Board, 1945.

160 Whitney DeVos

Grierson, John. "Flaherty's Poetic *Moana*." 1926. Reprinted in *The Documentary Tradition*, edited by Jacob Lewis, 25–26. 2nd ed. New York: W.W. Norton, 1979.

Gutiérrez, Alfredo. *To Sin Against Hope: How America Has Failed Its Immigrants: A Personal History*. London: Verso Books, 2013.

Gutiérrez, David G. "Migration, Emergent Ethnicity, and the 'Third Space': The Shifting Politics of Nationalism in Greater Mexico." *The Journal of American History*, 86, no. 2 (Sept., 1999): 481–517.

Hernández, Ellie D. *Postnationalism in Chicana/o Literature and Culture*. Austin: University of Texas Press, 2010.

Herrera, Juan Felipe. "Anthropoetry." *Los Angeles Review of Books*. March 7, 2014. https://lareviewofbooks.org/article/anthropoetry/.

Herrera, Juan Felipe. *Half of the World in Light: New and Selected Poems*. Tucson: University of Arizona Press, 2008.

Herrera, Juan Felipe. *187 Reasons Mexicanos Can't Cross the Border: Undocuments 1971–2007*. San Francisco, Calif.: City Lights, 2007.

Herrera, Juan Felipe. *Mayan Drifter: Chicano Poet in the Lowlands of America*. Philadelphia: Temple University Press, 1997.

Herrera, Juan Felipe. *Facegames*. San Francisco, Calif.: As Is/So & So Press, 1987.

Herrera, Juan Felipe. *Exiles of Desire*. Fresno, Calif.: Lalo Press, 1983.

Herrera, Juan Felipe. "Marcha de la" (1971) [finding aid]. *Juan Felipe Herrera Papers, 1974–2017*. Stanford Library: Special Collections. https://searchworks.stanford.edu/view/pb071kz9723.

H.R.4437. Border Protection, Antiterrorism, and Illegal Immigration Control Act of 2005. 109th Congress. 2005–2006. https://www.congress.gov/109/bills/hr4437/BILLS-109hr4437rfs.pdf.

Lomelí, Francisco A. "Forward / Juan Felipe Herrera: Trajectory and Metamorphosis of a Chicano Poet." In Juan Felipe Herrera, *Half of the World in Light: New and Selected Poems*, xv–xxiv. Tucson: University of Arizona Press, 2008.

Massey, Douglas S. and Magaly Sánchez. *Brokered Boundaries: Immigrant Identity in Anti-Immigrant Times*. New York: Russell Sage Foundation, 2010.

McEnaney, Tom. "'Rigoberta's Listener': The Significance of Sound in Testimonio." *PMLA*, 135, no. 2 (March 2020): 393–400.

Neruda, Pablo. "Alturas de Macchu Picchu." *Revista Nacional de Cultura*, no. 57–58 (1946).

Noel, Urayoán. "Bodies That Antimatter: Locating Us Latino/a Poetry, 2000–2009." *Contemporary Literature*, 52, no. 4 (2011): 852–882.

Pratt, Mary Louise. "*I, Rigoberta Menchú* and the 'Culture Wars.'" In *The Rigoberta Menchú Controversy*, edited by Arturo Arias, 29–48. Minneapolis: University of Minnesota Press, 2001.

Rosaldo, Renato. *The Day of Shelly's Death: The Poetry and Ethnography of Grief*. Durham, N.C.: Duke University Press, 2014.

Rosaldo, Renato. "Notes on Poetry and Ethnography." In *The Day of Shelly's Death: The Poetry and Ethnography of Grief*, 101–113. Duke University Press, 2014.

Savci, Evren. "Ethnography and Queer Translation." In *Queering Translation, Translating the Queer*, edited by Brian James Baer and Klaus Kaindl, 72–83. London: Routledge, 2017.

Soldofsky, Alan. "A Border-Crosser's Heteroglosssia: Interview with Juan Felipe Herrera, Twenty-First Poet Laureate of the United States." *MELUS: Multi-Ethnic Literature of the United States*, 43, no. 2 (Summer 2018): 196–226.

Taylor, Diana. *The Archive and the Repertoire: Performing Cultural Memory in the Americas*. Durham: Duke University Press, 2003.

Zepeda-Millán, Chris. *Latino Mass Mobilization: Immigration, Racialization, and Activism*. Cambridge: Cambridge University Press, 2017.

## CHAPTER 7

# Juan Felipe Herrera's Voice in Spanish

## Local and Global Pan-Ethnic Relations and Resistance

MANUEL DE JESÚS HERNÁNDEZ-G.

> I think it is a matter of communicating. I think it is a matter of joining, of *aligning ourselves with writers from outside of the Chicano condition*. And once we do that, at a large scale, then we will understand ourselves much better, and not only honor each other, but work together.
>
> —JUAN FELIPE HERRERA, [1981] 1985

## The Poetic Evolution of the Poet Juan Felipe Herrera

To trace and understand Juan Felipe Herrera's worldview, we need to consider the three important interviews that offer the critic key biographical elements. These are "Juan Felipe Herrera: San Francisco, California, October 6, 1981" (1985), by Wolfgang Binder; "[Interview:] Juan Felipe Herrera" (2006), by Frederick Luis Aldama; and "A Border Crosser's Heteroglossia: Interview with Juan Felipe Herrera, Twenty-First Poet Laureate of the United States" (2018), by Alan Soldofsky. In Binder's interview, Herrera says that he was born in a small town named Fowler in Fresno County, California. His father and mother were migrant farmworkers who repeatedly traveled between Fresno and San Diego in search of temporary farmhand employment. In this manner, Herrera's grounding in a local site of relations and resistance begins. As part of that migrant flow, in 1953 a five-year-old Juan Felipe began elementary school in Escondido, California. However, his parents continued to migrate in search of work and the child Juan Felipe needed to follow them, enrolling in school after school—including an elementary school in San Francisco. From 1963 to 1967, the family resided in San Diego, however, a teenaged Juan Felipe, 14 to 18 years of age, attended a high school in the barrio.[1] Then, from fall 1967 to 1972, he attended the University of California at Los Angeles where he earned a bachelor of arts in anthropology. During his studies at UCLA, he joined the Chicano movement, continued collaborating with Alurista in cultural and literary projects, studied under various Chicano/a studies professors such as Juan Gómez-Quiñones, and organized the group Teatro Tolteca in 1971. Herrera's poetry from the beginning reveals that it is synonymous with his activist lifestyle, while he carried out several cultural projects.[2] After earning his bachelor's degree, Herrera returned to San Diego to he live and work in 1973. He secured employment at the Centro Cultural de la Raza Toltecas en Aztlán where he eventually was promoted to director. This same center published Herrera's first poetry book: *Rebozos of Love / We Have Woven / Sudor de Pueblos / On Our Back* (1974).

In 1977, Herrera enrolled at Stanford University where he pursued a master of arts in anthropology. But instead of living in the college dormitories or in apartments in Palo Alto, an upper-middle-class neighborhood near the university, he and the young poet Francisco X. Alarcón found housing in the centuries-old neighborhood named La Misión, or the Mission District, a part of the San Francisco area.[3] Unlike the Chicano-Mexicano barrio in San Diego with which Herrera was familiar when he attended high school, the Mission District had a population in the 1970s that was seventy-five percent Latino/a—mainly Nicaraguan and Salvadoran immigrants. That is, in La Misión, Chicanos and Mexicanos were a minority. Residents of this barrio shared with San Diego had low levels of educational attainment (ninety percent of the Mission District residents did not have a high school diploma) and high unemployment.

With the goal of continuing his burgeoning vocation to poetry, he sought a cultural and literary environment by joining the Chicano/a writers' circuit in La Misión. Soon thereafter, he and other Chicano/a aspiring writers began to intermingle and collaborate with other established Latino writers and American writers, among them, the Nicaraguan American Roberto Vargas and the Neorican Víctor Hernández Cruz. Additionally, in the late 1970s the Pocho-Ché Collective, whose members were U.S. Latino/a and Chicano/a writers, was still active in San Francisco, and exiled Chilean writers had moved into the Mission District. Herrera collaborated with them, including the novelist Fernando Alegría, in several projects.[4] Herrera read literary works by these exiles as well as classic texts from El Boom Latinoamericano being read by his roommate Francisco Alarcón, who was enrolled in the Spanish doctoral program at Stanford University. Thus, Herrera began to globalize his world view. It was at the time he was finishing the manuscript in Spanish that would become the book *Akrílica* in 1989. Concurrently, Herrera participated in literary projects headed by Afro-American writers such as Ishmael Reed as well as some led by Anglo-American writers, including Jack Hirschman.

Finding himself in the middle of the La Misión's bustling cultural and literary milieu, Herrera became aware that Chicana/o writers sometimes felt marginalized, ignored, and unpopular. Although always an optimist explorer of cultures, he did not see the new condition of Chicano/a writers as a problem, but as an opportunity to forge friendships and establish collaborative cultural and literary projects inside and outside the United States. His global worldview continued to develop and evolve. When he was interviewed by the German scholar Wolfgang Binder, in "Juan Felipe Herrera: San Francisco, California, October 6, 1981," he brought up the benefits of living in a barrio populated by U.S. Latino/a, Chicano/as, and Mexicanos during the early 1980s:

> One of the things we're doing here, that I am doing here in San Francisco is working preferably with writers, Chicano and Latino writers. We are attempting to organize ourselves into a body that will not only write poetry together, not only publish poetry together, because this is what we have been doing in limited ways for a number of years in small press publications, etc., but to add dimensions to our writing, to our form of expression [. . . .] We're also trying to establish linkages with other communities in other countries and eventually create alliances with them, given that they are progressive and willing to come together, and visit, and actually create an international bond. (Binder, 107)

These Latino/a collaborative literary projects led Herrera to also consider the role of publishers and cultural centers associated with the American mainstream. Although some collaborators favored working with and supporting small publishers associated with their own community, Herrera saw the need and benefits of partnerships with mainstream institutions. He suggested that they needed to think beyond fearing labor exploitation or the appropriation of their art for profit, and, in its place, they should consider as beneficial opportunities that come from working with Anglo-American publishers and cultural centers. Without dismissing the concerns held by Latino/a writers, he summarizes his arguments to Binder:

> I do not see established circles, and publishing houses, and networks as being THE enemy. I think that we have to confront them, and I think that we have to display our work, and challenge them with our work, because when we do that, we are adding a new factor to the thinking of what literature is in the larger framework. And when we do that, then we are actually capable of creating change. (Binder 103)

In hindsight, the 1985 interview by Binder offers a profound understanding of Herrera's poetic evolution: namely the local and global pan-ethnic world view. The biographical notes, details of the collaboration with Alurista, Herrera's vision of Chicano/a literature in the early 1980s, and a look into the Chicano poet's personal rebirth in the Mission District all foretell subsequent developments in his writing career. From the interview, one can see unfold in great detail the rest of his poetry production, including the Chicano poet's achievements within institutions associated with the American mainstream.

Informatively rich at various levels, the Soldofsky interview, "A Border Crosser's Heteroglossia: Interview with Juan Felipe Herrera, Twenty-First Poet Laureate of the United States," features several other elements in Herrera's long career as a poet. Among them, he claims there are cultural connections between San Francisco's Beat poets and early Chicano/a literature from the 1960s, reinforcing various influences on his own development and works: the Beats, the Fresno Poets, Alurista, Luis Valdez, Víctor Hernández Cruz, Ishmael Reed, Lorna Dee Cervantes, and Central American immigrant poets.[5] In fact, he calls the reader's attention to Walt Whitman's influence on multiple American poets, indirectly acknowledging his own debt with the author of *Leaves of Grass*. As an example, Herrera has edited three anthologies featuring poems from his previously published books, and the new configuration shows that, like Whitman, the Chicano poet is constantly remaking himself: changing, developing, and evolving.

# Six Books in Spanish: Herrera's World View Crosses Language

In addition to highlighting Herrera's evolving worldview from an idealized neo-indigenism[6] as part of a local movement of cultural nationalism to a global pan-ethnic view, including an element of political resistance, Soldofsky's interview clearly points to the fact that the Chicano poet first published primarily in Spanish. He began writing poetry in this language in the first grade, around 1965/66, in his Spanish III class taught by a teacher named Nietzel. As homework, Herrera had to write some short pieces in the style of Boris Pasternak: short poem and short verse (Soldofsky, 208). At the height of the Chicano movement in 1974, eighty percent of Herrera's first published collection, *Rebozos of Love*, was composed in Spanish. It was a period in which the Spanish language had been reinforced and highly valued as part of the resurgent Chicano literary renaissance (Acosta, n.p.). Moreover, Herrera initiated his career as a poet who wrote with a specific audience in mind. Typically, he first shared orally his poems in a Chicano-Mexicano community meeting or cultural event, and then he published them via newspapers or literary journals for Chicanos/Mexicanos in San Diego as well as for all Mexican Americans in the Southwest. Also relevant is the fact that bilingualism became a common and preferred practice along the San Diego-Tijuana border with its extensive bilingual media: radio, television, newspapers, bookstores, bars, restaurants, and live entertainment. But, clearly he was also influenced by Afro-American jazz and different kinds of music, such as American pop and Mexican and Latin American sounds.

### *Rebozos of Love / We Have Woven / Sudor de Pueblos / On Our Back*: Dominant Cosmic and Bucolic World View

Regarding its content, the poetry collection *Rebozos of Love* (1974) emerged after Herrera's first pilgrimage from the Chicano/a Southwest—specifically Los Angeles—into Mayan lands in Chiapas and Veracruz, Mexico. The pilgrimage took place in 1970 during a time when Herrera belonged to the Indigenous group, *Servidores del Árbol de la Vida* or Servers of the Tree of Life. He was deeply committed to practicing an Indigenous way of life. The poetic voice quickly recognizes resistance against colonization on the part of many Native peoples of the Americas (Taos, Pimas, Picurís, Navajos, Hopis, Huicholes, Tarascos). However, the pilgrimage unfolds under a cosmic duality based on Aztec and Mayan religions and along a bucolic setting (*mares, aguas, ríos, milpas, árbol, montaña, mariposas, pastos,* or oceans, waters, rivers, corn fields, tree, mountain, butterflies, pastures). Unfortunately, few allusions are made about Indigenous peoples' condition of oppression or their own language or dialect. In this collection, the Chicano poet's personal spiritual search is dominant.

Throughout *Rebozos of Love,* deities like Quetzalcóatl and Tonatiuh ("SEÑOR-SEÑORA DE LA CREACIÓN" or Lord-Lord of Creation) code a mystical dimension. In fact, the closing poem, "DADOR DE LA VIDA" (Giver of Life) foregrounds a cosmic universe via verses written all in capital letters and the phrase "IN LAK 'ECH" (you are my other I). This last phrase associates the book's world view with the Mayans: Cartesian-like, *in lak 'ech* references a relationship within which the *I* may get to know the *other.* All these elements (myths, landscape, phrases) code a romanticized or idealized neo-indigenism shared by Chicano/a writers in the 1960s and the 1970s. All images, techniques, and language experimentation, as well as the book having no title nor a beginning or end, symbolize, one could argue, an unending infinite universe.[7]

*Rebozos of Love* includes two contrasting poems: "Quetzalcóatl" and "Arizon." "Quetzalcóatl," a three-page poem previously published before *Rebozos,* concentrates on an Indigenous Amerindia or the Indigenous Americas; "Arizon," a two-page poem that takes place in the Chicano Southwest, refers to the topic of exploitation. "Quetzalcóatl," like most of the poems in the collection, offers a cosmic vision grounded in "Amerindia," as seen in the following images and metaphors:

| | |
|---|---|
| pulmones punzando | lungs throbbing |
| frentes alzando | foreheads rising |
| corazones laborando | hearts laboring |
| quetzalcóatl | Quetzalcóatl |
| rising spiral árbol | rising spiral tree |
| tule de vida | reed of life |
| ramas de luz | branches of light |
| fruto de raza | fruit of our people |
| dulzura in tloque in nahuaque | sweetness in the lord of the near and far |
| señor-señora | lord-lady |
| dador de la vida. | giver of life |

(*Rebozos,* 71; my translation)

In contrast to such an idealized world view where there is little reference to material conditions and social relations experienced by Native peoples, "Arizon" does offer glimpses into references to labor exploitation and pinpoints class conflict:

| | |
|---|---|
| arizon | arizon (origins of "Arizona") |
| campesinos levantando algodón | farmworkers picking cotton |
| estrellas de oro blanco pa'l ranchero | stars of white gold for the rancher |
| nubes de sal | clouds of salt |
| sellos de sueldo pa'l que hace labor | salary stamps for those who work |
| cuerpos rojos | red bodies |
| climbing cotton flowers | climbing cotton flowers |
| to the dawn weaving una risa sin | to the dawn weaving a painless |
| dolor. | smile |

(Rebozos, 81; my translation)

Similar rural images appear in the two-page poem "los chapulines verdes vuelan" (the green grasshoppers fly; no capital letters in original title) that features exploited farmworkers in Texas, thus coding oppression on both sides of the United States-Mexico border.

Both narrative poems, Michael Dowdy argues in his study "Molotovs and Subtleties: Juan Felipe Herrera's Post-Movement Norteamérica" (61–63), use metonyms to foreground rural struggles by native peoples. Notwithstanding, in *Rebozos of Love* urban labor exploitation receives little or no mention, which is a particularly notable absence in a historical period in which Chicanos/as are already at least eighty percent urbanized. Regarding Herrera's search for a poetic language with which to write *Rebozos of Love*, its imaginary focuses on Aztec and Mayan cosmology and a bucolic setting through which he, Dowdy would suggest, accommodates his voice within a dominant neo-indigenism found in Chicano/a poetry at the time.

## *Akrílica* (1989): From Chicano Neo-Indigenism to Latino/a and Central American Struggles

*Akrílica* (1989) is Herrera's his second book of poetry written in Spanish. Each poem is accompanied by its translation into English,[8] and the thirty-nine poems are strategically placed on 165 pages within six sections. Two of them focus on the Southwest: "Galería" and "Eras." The other four—"Terciopelo," "Amarillo," "America," and "Kosmetik"—link the Mission District and the Southwest with Nicaragua, El Salvador, Guatemala, Latin America in general, Tijuana, and the world. Via these six sections, especially the three Central American countries, Herrera expressly manifests his world view from a local and global pan-ethnic lens. That is, he sees a parallel process: a hegemonic metropolis grounded in the barrio and a military encroachment into Central America.

In considering the marked linguistic experimentations in *Rebozos of Love*, the collection *Akrílica* represents another major effort in carrying out a language search by which to semantically frame his new poems. From a newly discovered poetic language, Herrera constructs his writings in conjunction with art works in a gallery.[9] With section titles marked by visual linguistic registers, the exhibited poems offer multiple portraits: those that feature urban scenes in the Mission District; streets and jail cells in Nicaragua; houses, plantations, and volcanos in El Salvador; invading troops in Guatemala; and other links to the world (Argentina, Chile, South Africa).[10] Specifically, the book's sections identify subtitles via registers taken from the plastic arts: "Exhibitions," "Galleries," "Velvet," "Yellow" and "Kosmetik." In turn, the visual linguistic register, *akrílica* or acrylic, codes the overall book as an exhibit or art gallery. Plastic works are painted via words and verses, figures and scenes, lines and images, and art terms and references. The only two section subtitles not taken from linguistic art registers, "Eras" and "América," place La Misión in specific historical periods and a particular continental space— the Americas (from Tierra del Fuego to Alaska).

Most of these poems exhibit plastic and geographical contexts that first take place in the Southwest, but they also quickly bilocate into Nicaragua, El Salvador and Guatemala with a more international flavor. Four poems feature a Nicaraguan character named Quentino, an imprisoned eighteen-year-old guerrilla fighter. In order of appearance in *Akrílica*, they are: "Quentino," "El diario de Quentino: fragmentos," "Sobre el anti-teatro de *El Diario de Quentino*," and "Párrafos de *El Diario de Quentino*."[11] Five other poems depict El Salvador while "Minerales en las piernas" deals with the rich minerals found in that country.[12] The poem "Plan M-14," in using the *mosca* or fly metaphor, focuses on invading troops in Guatemala and El Salvador. The social acts present in these ten poems, as metonyms, foreground invading troops from the metropolis and oppositional guerrilla struggles. Herrera here is deploying Dowdy's concept of molotovs for global resistance and thereby dissenting from a neoliberal citizenship that seeks hegemony and the submission of Central American countries (61–63).

From such a gallery, the scenes and figures unfold sociocultural elements found in a Latino/a neighborhood. They include the famous Mexican actress Lupe Vélez and a diner named Jesús MacDonald, who is buying from a local fast food restaurant. Metonyms or social acts found in *Akrílica*—rooted in the surreal poetry of Federico García Lorca—vary: eerie streets, consumerism, a marginalized barrio, omniscient flies, a distant mayor, a dead-end future, loneliness, an invaded space, several dubious leaders, a fixed destiny, and an injured Emiliano Zapata. Except for the last one, the images are, Dowdy argues, metonyms that narrate marginalization, exploitation, failed leaders, and an unpredictable future (61–65). Only the Chicano poet, via his art, can escape such an oppressive and surreal world. Chicano neo-indigenism is not present in the pages of *Akrílica*; indeed, such world view is notably absent. Herrera has clearly overcome Alurista's influence, including the Chicano cosmic and bucolic neo-indigenism of *Rebozos of Love*. Instead, the reader witnesses a human urban odyssey whose participants travel circularly into and from Central America as well as into other parts of the world.

## *Tejedoras de rayos* (2000): The Limits of Neoliberal Indigenism

Apart from some poems in Spanish sprinkled in the pages of eight poetry collections published in English from 1989 to 1999,[13] Herrera did not again publish a book in Spanish until 2000: *Tejedoras de rayos/Thunderweavers*, published as a bilingual edition. The massacre of Indigenous people in the town Acteal, which took place under Mexican President Ernesto Zedillo, inspired it as a form of global solidarity with a specific Mexican Indigenous resistance. Its imagery of carnage recalls the repression of a rebellious Native American rag-tag army—the Ejército Zapatista de Liberación Nacional (Zapatista Army of National Liberation or EZLN)—whose uprising became the first militant act against the entry of neoliberalism into Mexico when the North American Free Trade Agreement (NAFTA, 1994–2020) was established.

Rooted in a matrilineal world view, *Tejedoras de rayos* dramatizes the effects of the massacre in Chiapas through the experiences of four female protagonists: Maruch, a grandmother; Pascuala, a mother; Xunka, a lost daughter; and Makal, a newborn baby girl. From their own respective section, each protagonist narrates the personal effects of the massacre on her person and on other members of the town Acteal. In the order of appearance, each section reads: "Xunka: la hija perdida" (Xunka: The Lost Daughter); "Pascuala: la madre entre los rayos" (Pascuala: Mother among Thunder); "Maruch: la abuela entre las veredas" (Maruch: Grandmother of the Roads); and "Makal: la hija de los tambores" (Makal: Daughter of the Drums). The accompanying description to each protagonist characterizes the poetic voices' human condition and her role in ensuring the survival of her family and the Indigenous group.

An ill-fated human crisis witnessed around the world, the massacre resulted in the slaughter, fragmentation, and displacement of family members, including men, across the southeast Mexican region. In very graphic terms, several kinetic images—metonyms—show the efforts made by each protagonist (Xunka, Pascuala, Maruch, and Makal) to undertake a painful and challenging journey in order to reunite with her Indigenous community and reaffirm the ancient preference for life. At the center of this resistance against the hegemonic metropolis and its national allies, the reader finds a grandfather, Caneck, who is the source of inspiration for the struggle of each protagonist, as well for Indigenous men, against the military attack and the resultant suffering. In the first two sections, Xunka and Pascuala relate the violence suffered at the hands of soldiers who carried out the massacre: burning Indigenous *naguas* or dresses, missing or dead women, an interrogated mother, a dead Xunka, a semi-buried Pascuala, enumerated victims, Zapatistas in mourning, and blood streams without borders. From a regenerative lens, these two sections also contain signs of hope: a call for resistance, liberty's arrival, vigilant voices, and a future victory.

In turn, the next two sections by Maruch and Makal affirm Indigenous survival over the centuries and a path to overcome the violent, inhumane effects of the massacre. Struggle metonyms and regenerative symbols emerge, such as a rebellious nature, the inspiring grandfather Caneck, an omnipotent sun, a dreamed morning, a girl-woman, cosmic weavings, and a renewing journey. In comparison to the cosmic and romantic imagery in *Rebozos of Love*, the images in *Tejedoras de rayos* are specific, concrete, and humane, and even show a Whitmanesque cosmicism. From the section entitled

"Makal: Daughter of Drums," the following image, which foregrounds the future, positions Makal's matrilineal worldview:

> Madre Grande, tú me enseñaste todo. Cómo envolver el vestido, cómo tejer,
>   cómo rezan las Pasiones por cuarenta días
> antes del *K'in nebal*, el festival de las nubes.
> Abuela Maruch, somos tejidos del universo ronco y fugaz sobre tu pecho.
> Tus duras manos tan lejos de mí, suben y bajan en la noche.

> Madre Grande, you taught me everything. How to wrap the dress, how to
>   weave, how to pray the *Pasiones* for forty days
> before the *K'in nebal*, the Festival of the Clouds.
> Grandmother Maruch, we are the weaving of the universe rough and fleeting
>   on your bosom. Your hard hands
> so far from me, rise and fall in the night.

(61; my translation)

As an integral part of a now substantial production by Herrera in 2000, *Tejedoras de rayos* represents the final break from an early idealized Chicano/a neo-indigenism that, as Michael Dowdy observes, was sustained under the influence of the poet Alurista (74–78).

Herrera's repeated pilgrimages into Indigenous México, as illustrated by *Night Train to Tuxtla* and *Mayan Drifter: Chicano Poet in the Lowlands of America*, led him to finally understand his own cultural limitations, particularly since he has always been, and is, a resident of the metropolis. His past idealizations of Indigenous Mexicans, which served as a rhetorical means for combating a marginalized and exploited Chicano/a—or ethnic—status in the United States, does not decisively benefit the Indigenous people of Chiapas, Mexico, who themselves experienced the Acteal massacre.

Among other things, *Tejedoras de rayos* stands out as an exercise of self-criticism. That is, Herrera realizes he nonetheless represents, in part, a neo-liberal United States. By symbolically recreating the Acteal massacre—in presenting an Indigenous rebellion and the resistance of four female Indigenous protagonists—Herrera still risks indulging in a form of cultural tourism associated with hegemonic power. Writing such an emotionally raw book, Herrera struggles to find the line between personal accommodation and the commodification of his art. However, *Tejedoras de rayos* has become recognized as an expression of solidarity—the global side of Herrera's pan-ethnic resistance—with a Mexican Indigenous community. The content surely aligns itself with the poetic practice he undertook back in the late 1970s when he lived in La Misión.

## *Los Vampiros de Whittier Boulevard*: An Engaged and Broad Dialogue with Mexico

Readers of Herrera's poetry would wait nine more years for his next Spanish-language book: *Los vampiros de Whittier Boulevard* (2009; The Vampires of Whittier Boulevard). In this anthology, he finally achieves a dialogue with Mexico, the homeland of his immigrant parents about which he had extensively written in English for Chicanos/as as well as mainstream America. Previously, only the three poems had been published for Mexican readership— "Quetzalcóatl," "Muchacha guinda," and "Cielo rojo." These three poems were included in the anthology *Chicanos: antología histórica y literaria* (Chicanos: Historical and Literary Anthology), edited by Tino Villanueva and published by Fondo de Cultura Económica in Mexico City in 1980.[14] The three poems offered the Mexican reader a reductive view of Herrera's poetic trajectory.

Selected by Mexican nationals Regina Lira and Gabriela Jáuregui, translated by Santiago Román, and published in Mexico City by Avra Ediciones, *Los vampiros de Whittier Boulevard* contains selected poems from thirteen collections previously published by Herrera: *Rebozos of Love* (1974), *Exiles of Desire* (1983), *Akrílica* (1989), *Facegames* (1987), *Night Train to Tuxtla* (1994), *The Dark Root of a Thousand Embraces: Dialogues* (1994), *Thunderweavers/Tejedoras de rayos* (2000), *Love after the Riots* (1996), *Border-Crosser with a Lamborghini Dream* (1999), *Notebooks of a Chile Verde Smuggler* (2002), *Lotería Cards and Fortune Poems: A Book of Lives* (1999), *187 Reasons Why Mexicanos Can't Cross the Border: Undocuments, 1971–2007* (2007), and *Half of the World in Light: New and Selected Poems* (2008).[15] In contrast, the anthology *Los vampiros de Whittier Boulevard* (2009) is Whitmanesque in nature: the Chicano poet reconfigures himself for a Mexican readership. The anthology contains six poems from *Exiles of Desire* that codified Herrera's world view of local and global pan-ethnic relations, also implying resistance: "Fotopoema de la Moratoria Chicana de 1980 / L.A." (Photo-Poem of the Chicano Moratorium of 1980 / L.A.) illustrates the 1970 Chicano Moratorium as his model of resistance in social acts; "¿Estás en esta nueva onda amerikana?" ("Are You Doing that New Amerikan Thing?") expresses the local side of his world view; and "Manifesto de Mission District"

(Mission Street Manifesto) recalls the global side: ". . . detengan al hombre neutrón al sueño nuclear a la línea asesina / al amo de alienación al imperio acicalado al traje de muerte / y levántense y levántense libres" (. . . [S]top the neutron man the nuclear dream the assassination line / the alienation master the well-groomed empire the death suit / and rise and rise libre libre [free free]; 109).

In line with Herrera's world view of a local and global pan-ethnic perspective, oftentimes implying resistance, poems from certain books feature the local, such as in *The Dark Root of a Thousand Embraces* and *Love after the Riot*. Poems from other collections feature the global like *Tejedoras de rayos*. And some books feature both the local and the global as in *Exiles of Desire, Akrílica, Facegames*, and *Night Train to Tuxtla*. Like these four, the two anthologies in English also do the same: *187 Reasons Why Mexicanos Can't Cross the Border: Undocuments, 1971–2007*, and *Half of the World in Light: New and Selected Poems*.[16] For specifics on the achieved dialogue with Mexico, we call attention to the interpretations already offered in this essay of three poetry books in Spanish: *Rebozos of Love, Akrílica*, and *Tejedoras de rayos*. Such interpretations include the poet's search for a new poetic language and the perils of accommodation and commodification.

Taken as a whole, the anthology in Spanish titled *Los vampiros de Whittier Boulevard* reveals thirty-five years of poetic production by Herrera. Partly rooted in southwest Mexican culture, he covers many themes, both local and global social acts from the 1970s to the 2000s (among them, Chicano neo-indigenism), shared experience with Central American and South American immigrants, barrio marginalization, ethnic interaction with Anglo-Americans, pilgrimages to Indigenous regions in Chiapas, Zapatista rebellion and resistance, Mexican American popular culture, family migration into the American Southwest, multi-ethnic protests against the vicious beating of Rodney King by the Los Angeles police, and continued Mexican (im)migration into the American Southwest as well as the rest of the United States. Once again, local resistance against a hegemonic society is synonymous with an activist Chicano/a lifestyle that engages in solidarity and struggles carried out by other American ethnic groups. Other themes are part of a global resistance, such as pilgrimages to Indigenous areas in Chiapas, the Zapatista rebellion, and continued (im)migration. In addition, the anthology *Los vampiros de Whittier Boulevard* contains a new poem, "Hustle the Fissure," that is global in intent and projection as it deals with the then recent 9/11 terrorist attack in New York. In fact, the theme poem, "Los vampiros de Whittier Boulevard," closes the anthology by expressing again local and global concerns, invoking centuries, geographies, historical and intellectual figures, as well as a concrete dialogue with the *other*:

De Cádiz a la colonia del Niño Perdido a Gregory Corso
¿Me recuerdas?
Bastardo-contra-sí mismo Tragándote aquí en medio de ti sí tú
*The outsider is the perfect insider* escribió
Isaac Rosenfeld en los '40 Subcomandante Marcos en los '90 Envuelto en
    luna verdosa un Cantinflas Nietzsche ladeado Aquí y en ningún lado
Hermanas esqueletos y los Otros muchos Otros en calcetines sangrientos y
    Kalashnikovs
Faldas de Tenejapa banderillas 750 millones de Xs marchando
Líneas trapezoidales Siqueiros Cuauhtémoc transgéneros.

From Cádiz to La Colonia del Niño Perdido to Gregory Corso
Remember me?
Bastard-against-itself
Swallowing you here in the middle of you yes you
*The outsider is the perfect insider* wrote
Isaac Rosenfeld in the 40's Subcomandante Marcos in the 90's A greenish
    moon-draped Cantinflas Nietzsche askew
Here and no where
Skeleton sisters and Others so many Others in bloody socks and Kalashnikovs
Tenejapa skirts banderillas 750 million Xs marching Trapezoid lines Sique-
    iros transgender Cuauhtémocs.

(254–255; translation by Santiago Román)

## *La fábrica* (*Notes on the Assemblage*): In Dialogue with Spain

While the anthology *Los vampiros de Whittier Boulevard* quantitatively augments and poetically advances the dialogue between Herrera and Mexico, *La fábrica* (2018), which is the translation of *Notes on the Assemblage* (2015), initiates for the first time a dialogue between the Chicano poet and Spain, extending geographically Herrera's local and global worldview. In *Notes on the Assemblage*, the title poem "Notes on the Assemblage," with its references to the plastic arts, is reminiscent of the book *Akrílica* and suggests that this new collection was also written with the intention of almost literally "painting" a community for the reader:

> utilice cartulinas blancas y negras y moteadas
>
> utilice cartulinas rasgadas raspadas y perforadas
>
> utilice papel pelado
> utilice cartón / empapado y
> comprimido
>
> use black & gray & speckled white construction paper
>
> use stripped scraped & perforated construction paper
>
> use bare paper
> use cardboard / wet &
> mashed.
>
> (30, 29)

As part of Michael Dowdy's socio-literary paradigm, involving molotovs and subtleties (61–63), this foregrounds the search for still another new poetic language. Thus, *Notes on the Assemblage* allegorizes the art of writing poems as an achievement that, in spite of a conscious diction and new rhetorical strategies, may not necessarily symbolize a utopia. Herrera tends to confirm in his writings what Dowdy argues: the possibility of accommodation and/or commodification in a neoliberal society—two social dynamics that separate the poet from social allies.

However, in an overall semantic shift for the reader in Spain, Herrera chooses through the translation to realign *La fábrica* by moving the second poem in the collection—"La fábrica de jabón" or "The Soap Factory"—to the beginning of the manuscript. In this way, he repositions his book. Echoing Charlie Chaplin's *Modern Times*,[17] Herrera also relates, within a tragic-comedy tone, a U.S. neoliberal society consisting of labor exploitation, imprisoned workers, and mandatory consumerism. Finding himself in such an ominous condition, an immigrant worker named Martínez experiences this dystopian reality while making soap as observed by his fellow worker Schwartz:

Pero está hecho por ti—y por mí

y por cada uno de nosotros
es por eso que estamos encerrados en esta lúgubre
Alcatraz de estiércol en esta despreciable cola
vestidos con esas tontas telas de plastilina
en estos funky pantalones de campo y sombreros de payasos tontos
estas tapas de McDonald's sobrantes y estas
camisetas anchas de fútbol de los Cowboys de perdedor

(La fábrica, 66)

But it is made by you—and me

and by each and everyone of us
that's why we are locked up in this dingy
Alcatraz of manure on this candy ass line-up
dressed up in these silly putty gowns
in these funk plaid overalls and dunce clown hats
these McDonald's leftover caps and these
loose Cowboy's loser football jerseys

(Assemblage, 65)

Like the poet who reads from a stage before an audience, Martínez and his fellow workers cannot escape a tragicomic life inside a *lúgubre* (dingy) factory of *estiércol* (manure), evoking the United States in the 2010s, at that time still experiencing the repercussions of the Great Recession. Therefore, for the Spanish reader, this allegory extends over the entire collection and its varied yet specific social acts within the context of global and pan-ethnic solidarity. In fact, the first part, titled "Ayotzinapa," deplores the disappearance of forty-three students in Mexico under unknown circumstances and, in parallel form, exposes police violence against Afro-Americans in the U.S. (via choke-hold deaths, deadly shootings). The repression of Afro-Americans by police receives further attention in two later poems. In part seven, the poem "Somos notablemente ruidosos no enmascarados" (We Are Remarkably Loud Not Masked) focuses on Afro-Americans assassinated or lynched by racist mobs or individuals. Among the dead youth noted, we find Jesse Washington, Trayvon Martin, and Eric Garner. *La fábrica*'s epilogue, "Poema por poema" (Poem by Poem) details the massacre of nine Afro-Americans who were praying inside a Black church in South Carolina. Those two poems, via the social acts symbolized, reinforce the solidarity between Chicanos and Afro-Americans as part of local resistance. In part six, the poem "Autobús de frontera" ("Borderbus") presents the journey of an undocumented Honduran immigrant across the American Southwest under the danger of being deported by the Border Patrol. At the same time, in "Are You Doing the New Amerikan Thing?," Herrera also considers the human condition of Anglo-Americans in two elegies in part four titled "Duros ganchos" (Hard Hooks). "Duros ganchos que te doblan las rodillas" (Hard Hooks that Fold You Down on Your Knees) eulogizes the death the poet Jack Gilbert, a friend of Allen Ginsberg, and "Hey Phil" recalls the poet Phil Levine, from Detroit, Poet Laureate of the United States from 2011 to 2012. Both elegies highlight interpersonal relations and human solidarity between Herrera and members of mainstream culture.

In an effort to expand and particularize his view of global resistance, some poems in *La fábrica* present social acts that take place outside of the Americas.[18] In part five, titled "Autobus de frontera" (Borderbus), the poem "Me llamo Kenji Goto," (I am Kenji Goto) refers to two journalists, Kenji Goto and Haruwa Yukawa, killed in Syria on January 2015. In "Pero yo fui el único que lo vio (las secuelas de los drones)" (But I Was the One That Saw It [Drone Aftermath]), criticism emerges regarding the use of drones as weapons of war abroad under the Obama administration. From part seven, two poems center social acts that refer to Eastern thought, specifically Buddhism: "Risueño dragón" (Smiling Dragon) and "Sábado noche en el cine budista" (Saturday Nite at the Buddhist Cinema). As part of *La fábrica*, these four poems reflect a further development in Herrera's long-held world view. As in the United States with *Notes on the Assemblage*, in Spain *La fábrica* repeatedly reinforces the notion that, even when using a tragicomic tone, Herrera has remained faithful to an agenda of local and global pan-ethnic resistance. He has pivoted from that position during the years he lived in La Misión, continuing to practice it from then until today.

## *El Crossover*: A Linguistically Enriching Dialogue with the Afro-American Community

Herrera's translation into Spanish of the novel in verse, *Crossover* (2014) by the poet Kwame Alexander, is an unexpected part of his oeuvre and opens up a new realm of his overall production. Like the original, *El Crossover* (2019) is innovatively structured into four quarters and one overtime, simulating a basketball game. The plot unfolds a moving competition between two twin brothers, Josh Bell and Jordan Bell, who compete against each other with the goal of seeing who will succeed and win more honors. In their efforts, they seek the approval of their father, a former professional basketball player. That passionate brotherly contest intensifies when a new, attractive girl registers in their high school. Because Herrera has only completed one translation into Chicano Spanish of a work in Afro-American English, we cannot apply the same criteria to this work as in the others. His language search is limited to reproducing semantically the original content into Chicano Spanish. This alone does not expand his literary expression in the Spanish of the U.S.-Southwest, but it does serve to further illustrate his linguistic dexterity.

In his translation, Herrera opens up a new linguistic space in Chicano/a literature at the level of morphology and semantics. The reader, in turn, finds in the novel *El Crossover* such words and idiomatic expressions—often playful puns—such as *dunkelicioso* or dunkenlicious; *driblar* or to dribble; *la mera leche* or real milk; *okey* or okay; *la onda del juego* or the game's flow; *todo ese jazz-jazz* or all that jazz-jazz; *retontón* or really dumb; *ese crossover perrón nasty* or that dog crossover nasty; *el cha-cha-cha slide* (same meaning); *bastante perro* or quite a dog; *rete-sorry* or real sorry; *un salto fadeaway* or fadeway jump; *hottie* (a phonetic borrowing); *cutie* (a phonetic borrowing); *pulquérrima* or pulque rhymes; *rapero* or rapper; *en la house* or in the house, *pívot de Croacia* or Croatian pivot; *porfa* or please; *wiri-wiri* or speaking nonsense, *flossiar* or to floss; *el más chido crossover-doble* or the coolest double crossover; and *nada little de ese muchacho* or nothing little about that boy.

In this way, Herrera's groundbreaking translation enriches Chicano/a literary registers much like other previous Chicano/a writers who have used the Spanish language in their creative writing: Miguel Méndez in *Peregrinos de Aztlán* (1974; *Pilgrims of Aztlán*) and *Los muertos también cuentan* (1995; *The Dead Also Tell Stories*), Margarita Cota-Cárdenas in *Puppet: A Chicano Novella* (1985); and Saúl Cuevas in *Barrioztlán* (1999).[19] Chicano/a authors who write in the Spanish language have at their disposal an expanded Spanish language that includes Afro-American words and varied English idiomatic expressions.

## Conclusion

Despite having published some twenty-two books of poetry and being named the Poet Laureate of California (2012–2014) and Poet Laureate of the United States (2015–2017), Juan Felipe Herrera is relatively unknown in the world among readers in Spanish both inside and outside the United States.[20] He began his career as a poet in 1974 with *Rebozos of Love*, of which eighty percent is written in Spanish. He continued writing poetry in Spanish until he published *Akrílica* (1989), which he had already begun writing in early 1977 before he entered Stanford University and began living in La Misión. But his geographical and cultural experience of a predominantly Latino/a community near a multi-ethnic San Francisco undoubtedly led him to write mainly in English. Consequently, he incorporated English into his poetic repertoire with *Exiles of Desire* (1983) and did not publish again a book in Spanish until 2000 with *Tejedoras de rayos*.

However, one can argue that, from 2000 forward, Herrera consciously decided to increase and diversify his dialogue with the Spanish-speaking world. Perhaps the Acteal massacre in 1997 impacted this personal decision, focused more on dialoguing in Spanish with his parents' native country. To achieve such a necessarily broad and complex Chicano-Mexicano dialogue, nine years later he published the anthology *Los vampiros de Whittier Boulevard* (2009), which is a compilation of poems taken from thirteen works published previously in the U.S. Another nine years later he engaged in a dialogue with Spain via the collection *La fábrica* (2018), a self-translation of *Notes on the Assemblage* (2015). Lastly, he diversified his own voice in Spanish by translating an award-winning novel in verse, *El Crossover* (2019; *Crossover*) by the Afro-American poet Kwame Alexander, in which Herrera expands and enriches Chicano Spanish at the morphological and semantic levels. This ensures and verifies that he has a qualified voice in the Spanish-speaking world inside and outside the U.S.

The six collections, as shown by our six brief analyses, demonstrate the work and mastery of not only one of the linguistic registers (Spanish) that make up contemporary Chicano/a literature, but also shed light on the other four: English, Spanglish, Caló, and translation. The six poetry books in Spanish manifest Juan Felipe Herrera's worldview that features local and global pan-ethnic foci with elements of resistance against hegemonic society. Such a worldview was originally brought to the forefront via their respective interviews in 1985 by the German critic Wolfgang Binder and reinforced in 2006 by Fredrick Luis Aldama and in 2018 by Alan Soldofsky.

# Notes

1. During those three-four years he met and befriended a young Alurista. Thus, Herrera begins his personal, cultural, and literary interactions with the Chicano poet who would become widely popular across the Southwest from 1969 to the early 1980s.
2. While at college, Herrera published poems in the magazine *Inside the East Side* that was housed in the Chicano Mexicano barrio named East Los Angeles (ELA).
3. To an extent, Herrera was already familiar with the Bay Area. In 1958, at ten years old, he lived in San Francisco and was enrolled in Bryant Elementary School, where he witnessed Beatniks often listening to blues and jazz sounds in the streets of the city.
4. Among the various projects that Herrera organized during the years he lived in the Mission District, are the magazines *Citybender* (1977–1981) and *Trapeze* (1980–1981). In addition, in line with his new sociocultural environment, he joined several literary associations such as Poetashumanos and the Union of Chicano and Latino Writers (UEECL). The union brought together poets from San Francisco, Redwood City, Menlo Park, and Oakland. As a relevant note, these two associations complemented the Indigenist group Servants of the Tree of Life under which Herrera had collaborated with Alurista in San Diego.
5. Herrera points to the emergence in the United States of a new generation of young poets whom he designates as "digital natives" because they use digital social media to write and disseminate their poems. Herrera conducts multiple poetry workshops and is constantly organizing one gathering after another to give the new generation an awareness of the art of writing and understanding poetry As a member of an older generation, he advises them to resist all narratives grounded in hegemonic power. That is, he is passing on the poetry torch.
6. Such a voice would evolve and mature in three subsequent poetry collections: *Night Train to Tuxtla: New Poems and Stories* (1994), *Mayan Drifter: A Chicano Poet in the Lowlands of America* (1997), and *Tejedoras de rayos* (2000).
7. At the level of form, Herrera experiments in *Rebozos of Love* with free verse, haiku, neologisms, metaphors constructed with juxtaposed nouns, and concrete poetry. Around seventy-four untitled poems and no page numbers make up the collection.
8. Of the two primary translators, Stephen Kessler had translated into the English language poetry by Pablo Neruda and Luis Cernuda. The other primary translator was Sesshu Foster. However, their translations were reviewed by Dolores Bravo, Magaly Fernández, and Juan Felipe Herrera himself. See Herrera's *Akrílica*, pp. ii.

9. The collection *Akrílica* shows a plastic influence from the Galería de la Raza in San Francisco as well as from several Chicano/a and Latino/a painters such as René Yáñez.
10. See the poems "Quentino," "Minerales en las piernas," "La 24 y el otoño," and "Es la tierra."
11. In the English translation, the four poems are titled: "Quentino," "Quentino's Journal: Fragments," "Concerning the Anti-teatro of Quentino's Journal," and "Paragraphs from Quentino's Journal."
12. In order of appearance in *Akrílica*, the three other poems are: "Boulevard Exilio," "La 24 y el otoño," and "Es la tierra."
13. Similar to *Rebozos of Love* (1974), two of the books feature each a new spiritual pilgrimage into Chiapas: *Night Train to Tuxtla* (1994) and *Mayan Drifter: Chicano Poet in the Lowlands of America* (1997).
14. In 1986, Herrera is surprisingly mentioned as a minor Chicano poet in the critical book *La literatura chicana* by Charles M. Tatum, which was published in Mexico City. On page 218, Tatum states: "El libro de Juan Felipe Herrera, *Rebozos of Love* (1974) nos recuerda la invocación de Alurista dedicada a la Amerindia. El poeta aboga por la reintegración del chicano con sus tradiciones culturales indígenas. Herrera ensaya libremente con neologismos, combinaciones originales del inglés y el español, con caligramas." (Juan Felipe Herrera's book, *Rebozos of Love* [1974] reminds us of Alurista's invocation dedicated to Amerindia. The poet advocates the reintegration of the Chicano with their Indigenous cultural traditions. Herrera rehearses freely with neologisms, original combinations of English and Spanish, with calligrams.)
15. *Los vampiros* also extends Herrera's dialogue with Mexico beyond the extensive, six-page narrative poem "Para siempre, Maga," published in *Akrílica* in 1989, which offers a critique of a Chicano writer who, as a cultural tourist, ventures into the border city of Tijuana, seeking a Chicano cultural rebirth in the middle of an extremely poor, marginalized, and exploited society. The critique comes via the lips of a Tijuana resident, named Maga, who dismisses his interest in the people there: "Te burlas, te imaginas, pero nunca te das cuenta de lo que/ realmente sucede." ("Para siempre, Maga;" 158 [You mock, you imagine, but you never realize what/ is really happening]).
16. The last two collections are in themselves based on previously published works.
17. The phrase "Modern Times" refers to Charlie Chaplin's 1936 comedy film, whose title is *Modern Times*, where the protagonist, a metalworker, survives under a modern industrialized society during the Great Depression.
18. In 2013, Herrera published the poetry collection *Senegal Taxi*, which expands his poetic space into Africa. Similar to covering the 1997 Acteal massacre in *Tejedoras de rayos*, the book *Senegal Taxi* dramatizes in great detail a massacre that took place in Darfur, Sudan, on August 2004, during a genocidal war.
19. The practice of translating Chicano/a novels into Spanish is very diverse and varies. The novel *Loving Pedro Infante* (2001) by Denise Chávez has been trans-

lated into two Spanish languages: Spanish of the U.S. Southwest and Mexican Spanish. *Borderlands / La Frontera: The New Mestiza* (1987) by Gloria Anzaldúa has been translated into two Spanish languages: Mexican Spanish and Spanish from Spain.

20. Aside from the six books of poetry discussed above, which were authored by Herrera, he has also published some 10 books for children and adolescents: among them, *El canto de las palomas* (1995; *Calling the Doves*) and *Desplumado* (2004; *Featherless*). Of these books, five have been translated into the Spanish language. However, these works warrant a separate study. They attempt to address a young Spanish-speaking audience.

## Works Cited

Acosta, Teresa Paloma. "Chicano Literary Renaissance." Texas State Historical Association, Handbook of Texas, accessed July 9, 2021. https://www.tshaonline.org/handbook/entries/chicano-literary-renaissance.

Aldama, Frederick Luis. "[Interview:] Juan Felipe Herrera." In *Spilling the Beans in Chicanolandia: Conversations with Chicano Writers and Artists*, 129–42. Austin: University of Texas Press, 2006.

Alexander, Kwane. *El Crossover*. Translated by Juan Felipe Herrera. Boston: Houghton Mifflin Harcourt, 2019.

Binder, Wolfgang. "Juan Felipe Herrera: San Francisco, California, October 6, 1981." In *Partial Autobiographies: Interviews with Twenty Chicano Poets*, 95–108. Erlangen: Palm and Enke, 1985.

Cota-Cárdenas, Margarita. *Puppet: A Chicano Novella*. Austin: Relámpago Books Press, 1985.

Cuevas, Saúl. *Barrioztlán*. Sonora, México: Editorial Orvis Press, 1999.

Dowdy, Michael. "Molotovs and Subtleties: Juan Felipe Herrera's Post-Movement *Norteamérica*." *Broken Souths: Latina/o Poetic Responses to Neoliberalism and Globalization*, 61–90. Tucson: University of Arizona Press, 2013.

Flores, Lauro H. "Juan Felipe Herrera (27 December 1948–)." *Dictionary of Literary Biography: Chicano Writers, Second Series*. Vol. 22, edited by Francisco A. Lomelí and Carl R. Shirley, 137–45. Detroit, Mich.: Gale Research, 1992.

Hernández, Cassy. "Opinion: As Centro Cultural de la Raza Turns 50, Our Movement is Flourishing." *The San Diego Union-Tribune*, July 8, 2021. https://www.sandiegouniontribune.com/opinion/commentary/story/2021-07-08/centro-cultural-de-la-raza-balboa-park-anniversary.

Herrera, Juan Felipe. *Akrílica*. Translated by Stephen Kessler, Sesshu Foster, Dolores Bravo, Magaly Fernández, and Juan Felipe Herrera. Santa Cruz, Calif.: Alcatraz Editions, 1989.

Herrera, Juan Felipe. *Exiles of Desire*. Fresno, Calif.: Lalo Press Publications, 1983.

Herrera, Juan Felipe. *La fábrica*. Translated by Nieves García Prados. Madrid: Valparaíso Ediciones, 2018.

Herrera, Juan Felipe. *Rebozos of Love / We Have Woven / Sudor de Pueblos / on Our Back*. San Diego, Calif.: Toltecas en Aztlán Publications, 1974.

Herrera, Juan Felipe. *Tejedoras de rayos/Thunderweavers*. Tucson: University of Arizona Press, 2000.

Herrera, Juan Felipe. *Los vampiros de Whittier Boulevard*. Translated by Santiago Román. México, D.F.: Avra Ediciones, 2009.

Lyotard, Jean-François. *The Postmodern Condition: A Report on Knowledge*, 9th printing. Translated by Geoff Bennington and Brian Massumi. Minneapolis: University of Minnesota Press, 1993.

Méndez M., Miguel. *Peregrinos de Aztlán*. Tucson, Ariz.: Editorial Peregrinos, 1974.

Méndez M., Miguel. *Los muertos también cuentan*. México: Universidad Autónoma de Ciudad Juárez, 1995.

Soldofsky, Alan. "A Border-Crosser's Heteroglossia: Interview with Juan Felipe Herrera, Twenty-First Poet Laureate of the United States." *MELUS* 43, no. 2 (2018) 196–226.

# PART II

## *On Camaraderie and Poetics*

Other Authors Reflect on Juan Felipe Herrera's
Impact on Chicano/a Literature

With Larry King. At Larry King Studios. Burbank, Ca. 2017. Photo by Alma Herrera.

## CHAPTER 8

# A Rascuache Prayer
### Reflections on Juan Felipe Herrera, My Homeboy Laureate[1]

LUIS ALBERTO URREA

come with me: I will be writing—

—JUAN FELIPE HERRERA, *EVERY DAY WE GET MORE ILLEGAL*

## 1.

I don't know if he is a boxer. But I can tell from his poems that he must be a dancer. That footwork is devilish. I sit back and try to chart the juxtapositions that come like bracing kicks all the way down his pages, as in "Roll Under the Waves" in *Every Day We Get More Illegal*:

> . . . there are memories trailing us empty orange and hot pink bottles of medicine left behind buried next to a saguaro. . . .
>
> (21)

I recently watched a Texas hurricane blow down part of Trump's border wall. I was amazed, as ever, by the imagery of the border: a hurricane in the desert, waves of rain and land clouds writhing and speeding like ghosts out of the wasteland, and that allegedly unbreachable steel boondoggle itself become wobbly as rubber as it collapsed.

Like the seekers it was built to deny.
During a plague year.

That vision could have been a stanza in *Every Day We Get More Illegal* (2020), the slender, ferocious, tender new volume by Herrera, the first Chicano poet laureate of the United States.

Ostensibly, the notes that became the poems in this depth charge were inspired by his duties as America's *poeta*, from 2015 to 2017, and by his travels around the country bearing witness to the many people he encountered. I can imagine the nights he spent in hotel rooms with the confessions of the day still echoing in his ears. Yeah, he was writing.

Herrera prophesies the wall's death scene in his book. He doesn't need violent winds to knock down the illusion of the border—he does this with the puffs of breath from all the people he conspires to give voice to in his songs. He's a canny and political writer. He echoes A. R. Ammons in the colons he sometimes deploys and Emily Dickinson, perhaps, in his dashes. He's a warrior troubadour; he knows the territory. He's got the lyric down. But the homie also knows car horns and laughter and accordion music and weeping. He is not afraid to scream like James Brown, whisper like Ko Un, rage at the abuser, and comfort the afflicted.

And he uses what voice he pulls from the wind, as in the poem titled "[3]" in *Every Day Wet Get More Illegal*:

underneath the code of the wall things are always

in motion

while we wait to cross. (16)

# 2.

Herrera and I come from the same barrio in San Diego. That simple fact has been endlessly mythic and mysterious to me. With his deadly playfulness, he might have coined a word for this feeling: *mythterious*.

If you came from that sunburned place, with those ancient pachucos and wizardly grandmothers, you'd know the kind of trickster with the smart kids constructed out of the polyglot threads of two crazy languages crashing like Chevy Trokas. Wordplay and thought-play dance all through Herrera's books, and both are unapologetic, seldom explained: if you don't (*can't*) get it, you won't. There is some precedent for this, which I will talk about in a minute.

Code-switching? Yes. Culture-switching, though? Is that a term? It is now. And not just "Latina/o/x." The dance is deep: street culture, Spanish, Spanglish, scholarly culture, poverty culture, Catholicism, shamanism, progressive poli-

**FIGURE 8.1** *Dance Hall, Bar, and Lowrider* (1995). Art by Nicholas Herrera. Courtesy Smithsonian American Art Museum, Gift of Chuck and Jan Rosenak and museum purchase through the Luisita L. and Franz H. Denghausen Endowment.

tics, literacy, anger sharp enough to turn unexpectedly and slice. But in the end, I believe Herrera's driving force, certainly expressed in this book, is witness.

Just like those old-school *vatos* we grew up with who had seen it all and feared nothing they'd admit to.

I was a boy at the far end of National Avenue, the thoroughfare that ran from my hill to his flats. Logan Heights, our own East Berlin. Herrera was in Barrio Logan itself, to the west, epicenter of Chicano/a evolution in San Diego, mother of revolution, the future birthplace of Chicano Park. We have this word that should be in *POETRY* magazine: *rascuache*. It is as funky as you think it is, and most outsiders probably found all of Logan pretty *rascuache*. Wait—it actually was, now that I reflect on it.

At that time, in 1970, a controversial people's uprising turned a freeway overpass and a demolition-threatened neighborhood into a people's park. Folks simply occupied the land armed with paint and brushes and food and will and faced off against the cops. International tourists now flock to visit the murals: vibrant depictions of Che Guevara, César Chávez, and Frida Kahlo and scenes from Chicano culture and mythology. The murals, once thought of as savage defacements by a bunch of commie wetbacks, are now cherished and studied around the world. The armed forces arrayed against the barrio in those days were not restrained, yet there was no secret police paramilitary in unmarked vans. There wasn't an industrial complex of camps for children, addressed viscerally in Herrera's new book.

It was an uprising that conservatives in this age would call Antifa rioting, and it attracted secret police from the bored ranks of Border Patrol agents with little to do. That was Herrera's part of the barrio.

He came from the truly Mexican end of the street—good food (Las Cuatro Milpas[2]) and the anchor church, Our Lady of Guadalupe (I was baptized there, as was my daughter). I was not across the tracks but across Wabash, the busy crossroad that formed a vast crucifix of our home. Our church was St. Jude's (patron saint of lost causes, ahem). I cite again from "America We Talk About It" in *Every Day We Get More Illegal*:

. . . Are you listening. I had to
learn. I had to gain, pebble by pebble, seashell by seashell, the

courage to listen to my self . . .

(3)

## 3.

We didn't have the density of culture of that west end. We had a multiplicity of cultures crammed into a block of apartments and alleys. Now it's gentrified at both ends. My part of the barrio today has joggers in spandex. Our awful apartments now have Miami colors and handsome plantings. Herrera's part has art galleries and sophisticated eateries. Up in Logan Heights, we never had a library—until now. And Starbucks too.

Eight years older than I, Herrera was in a different universe entirely. Generations move fast. And though I didn't know him then, I seem to have followed him. We moved on. He went to San Diego High; I went to Clairemont High (where, interestingly enough, I was in the drama department with poet Tom Sleigh).

Herrera got an EEOP grant to UCLA; I got an EEOP grant to UCSD (economic opportunity indeed.) We both hung around the foundational *raza* poet Alurista and his literary journal *Maize*, as well as San Diego's Centro Cultural de la Raza. Yet I don't know if we ever met. If we did, I was no doubt intimidated, as I was by all the older poets in that scene. We got to know each other only later, well into our careers, when we shared laughs and teasing at random literary festivals around the country.

Alurista was our Marxist shaman agitator, a poet with a bullfighter's name. He was well-versed in Carlos Castaneda's mysticism and in the dialectic; he was the king of code-switching. Unsatisfied with English/Spanish riffs, he added Caló (Chicano slang), then Nahuatl words.

Then, apparently feeling his work was still too accessible, he replaced the Nahuatl words with glyphs. A stanza might go from English to *vato* slang to a picture of a rabbit.

I am certain Herrera was playing close attention. I know I was. We all were in that small volcano of Southern California poets.

## 4.

Herrera's people were farmworkers. He saw what would have been exotic to me: the San Joaquin Valley, Salinas. Man, all I knew was Tijuana.

My dad was a cannery worker, then a bakery truck driver, then a bowling alley attendant.

Herrera's family lived in tents as they struggled to feed America.

See this poem, "Touch the Earth (once again)" in *Every Day We Get More Illegal*, one of the searing set pieces in his new collection, with its litany of "This is what we do" kicking off the lines as if in a Catholic prayer during Mass:

This is what we do:

this is what the cotton truck driver does:
this is what the tobacco leaf roller does:
this is what the washer-woman & the laundry worker does:
this is what the grape & artichoke worker does:

Until it reaches its amen moment:

how they touch the earth—for you[.] (20)

Lately, much has been made in literary circles about the failure of American publishing to see "minority" or "ethnic" writers as anything more than minstrels of their own suffering.

Mexicans? Must be some wall-climbing at midnight, eh? Where're the drug fiends and the gangbangers? Where's the mournfully beautiful hot lover girlfriend? All questions I have been asked by publishers. I suspect one of Herrera's weapons in this literary battle (along with our patented anger) is a clear drive toward witness. And within this witness, there is a vast reservoir of funk and humor and jokes and rock music.

Friends, the barrio is funny. My apartment held exactly three of us: Mom, Dad, and me—if you don't count the turtle and the guinea pig. Our mailbox must have been magical, though, because it received mail for at least ten other Urreas. It was always jammed with letters and government checks, so tight you couldn't shut the door. These other Urreas listed our address as their permanent residence, though they all lived in Tijuana. Even the mailman accosted my mother to ask how the hell many people lived in our apartment.

You can be *raza* and funny, *raza* and sad, *raza* and well-read, *raza* and spiritual, *raza* and trivial, *raza* and scholarly, *raza* and literate. You might have never had a *pistola* in your hand.

You might have read a lot of books, even if it took a couple of buses to get from Logan Heights to the library downtown. Herrera drops the names Elias

Canetti and Octavio Paz in his book, Ko Un and Basho. He throws down in polyglot riffs, using Spanish and English, yes, but you'll see a bit of Nahuatl float by as well.

## 5.

Were we unlikely writers to come from the barrio? Perhaps. But we weren't the only ones. I am by far not the only one from Tijuana either. Nor is Herrera the only one to come from the fields. We are legion. And none of us wants to be any version of a stereotype, noble savage, or cartoon. Tell you what, though—if we feel cartoony, we'll apply our own ink.

## 6.

Make no mistake: there are few cartoons in Herrera's latest works.

I first became aware of him when his third book, *Exiles of Desire*, was published in 1983. I myself was in exile, teaching Expos at Harvard, feeling as far from my roots as possible, trying to find a new voice, helping the poet Tino Villanueva launch a Chicano literary journal, and having coffee with Martín Espada. And Herrera's book dropped. It was like nothing I had read before; it was like everything I had read. It was my language and my milieu doing things I had not imagined doing. It was heavily influenced by the Bay Area; it had wafts of Beat energy while maintaining Indigenous prayers and themes of diaspora and displacement. I was measuring my own lines against his. My own themes and fevers. You stalk the voice when you're young; you parse the edges of the world the new poet walks. We were from Logan and Southern *Califas*—our names had the same syllabic count. Our last names were a weak slant rhyme. We were angry about the same things. But I was 10 years away from publishing my first book.

Now we see each other at literary events and sign books for each other. "You're so fancy, carnal," he says. "You came from the Heights."

Ha, ha, *rascuaches* at work. His second book, *Exiles of Desire* (1983) said:

Writing is richman's work, therefore richman's history. Lately, the unrich are growing accustomed to the forbidden pleasures of writing[.] (23)

A call to arms for a new history.

# 7.

"[B]order Fever 105.7 Degrees" in *Every Day We Get More Illegal* is the killer in this new book. There is no answer. There is no argument. It is carrying water into the Devil's Highway for a lost wanderer. It is tearing down the doors of a virulent detention center. It is a father's cry for a stranger's child. Its rage is beautiful. Its love is wounding. I think it is my favorite of his poems. I will try to be mature and not copy him now that we're both graybeards. Dedicated to Jakelin Amei Rosemary, he writes, "7 years old from Guatemala, with a fever of 105.7, who died in captivity . . ." (50). The poem continues:

> why do you cry
> those are not screams you hear across this cage
> it is                           a symphony—the border guard says
>
>                                                            (50)

It is not long. It is not a screed. It is a memorial Mass. And it ends:

> on the custody floor
> 105.7 degrees
>
> where do I go where did they go
> where do I go to breathe no more[.]
>
>                                                            (50)

This is not the end of the book. This is the singer taking a breath so he can make it to the end.

And we must say Amen.

## Notes

1. Originally published in *Poetry Foundation* in September 14, 2020. https://www.poetryfoundation.org/articles/154196/a-rascuache-prayer.
2. A long-standing, popular, folksy, family-run Mexican restaurant near downtown San Diego.

## Works Cited

Herrera, Juan Felipe. *Every Day We Get More Illegal*. San Francisco, Calif.: City Lights Books, 2020.

Herrera, Juan Felipe. *Exiles of Desire*. Fresno, Calif.: Lalo Press Publications, 1983.

# CHAPTER 9

# Gravy Donuts, 24/7

## A Personal Reading of Juan Felipe Herrera

TOM LUTZ

Juan Felipe Herrera and I were on our way back from the water park in Davenport, Iowa, with our assortment of children, an hour's drive straight down Interstate 80, in the summer of 1988. Of all the theme parks, the water ones are the most exhausting. The big straight slides like ski jumps, the curving spiral tubes, the wave machines and circus rides, combined with the fried food and sugar blasts—sugar drinks, sugar cones, sugar cotton, sugar bars—frazzle you over the hours, and on the ride home, the kids were a bit morose, a little whiny. Juan Felipe decided that we should get some gravy donuts, that we should all be on the lookout for gravy donuts, try to find the gravy donut store. Nobody asked what a gravy donut was, everyone just quietly giggled as he went on a gravy donut riff for twenty minutes. I could almost taste them. On either side of us was nothing but corn and soybean fields, the occasional woodlot or farmstead—for twenty miles at a time not even a gas station—but we all repeated, after Juan Felipe, "I bet up that road there are some gravy donuts. That looks like Gravy Donut Avenue." We ate imaginary donuts and digested our day. "We will need," he said, "to rustle up some horses—twelve horses—and cilantro."

That was when I first realized—though I would see it again and again over the years—that Juan Felipe was a 24-hour poet, an open-all-night poet, a man who, I like to say, never speaks in prose—a person whose spoken words are spoken word, who rarely stops smelting reality into language, who rarely stops conceiving new worlds, rarely takes a break from enhancing life with words, rarely stops producing pleasure through recorded and unrecorded speech.

Is it strange to write about a poet by telling random anecdotes? I think not. Besides, Herrera is a most autobiographical of poets: not just in the more obvious memoiristic poems and pieces like *Mayan Drifter* (1997), "Shawashté" (*Giraffe on Fire*, 2002), "Autobiography of a Chicano Teen Poet" and other poems in *Facegames* (1987), the diary entries of *Love After the Riots* (1996) and *Notebooks of a Chile Verde Smuggler* (2002), or the "Aztlán Chronicles" in *187 Reasons Mexicanos Can't Cross the Border* (2007), but everywhere, ubiquitously. His first young adult novel for Scholastic, *Downtown Boy* (2005), is at least partially autobiographical, as are, of course, the poems about family, and the many autobiographical moments that blossom within so much of the other writing. In a postscript to another book for young readers, *Laughing Out Loud, I Fly* (2015), he writes about discovering, as a seventeen-year-old in a San Francisco bookstore, a small book of poetry by Pablo Picasso, and how alive the words were that danced off the page, so alive that he smelled the pears and oranges; he felt the smooth almonds on Picasso's table, and the artist's childhood friend, Mesalina, even ran up and tugged at his shirt.

This, he realized, is what he wanted his poems to do: to bring the real into the eyes and mouths and hands of his readers, and this is what he offers young audiences—representation, but more than that, significance; and more than that, something so real it seems sensorial and palpable. In the end, he offers them pears and almonds.

A section of *Laughing Out Loud, I Fly* can stand as a manifesto:

> Laughing out loud, I fly, toward the good things, to catch Mamá Lucha on
> the sidewalk, after school, waiting for the green-striped bus,
> on the side of the neighborhood store, next to almonds, José's tiny wooden
> mule, the wiseboy from San Diego teeth split apart, like mine in the coppery afternoon[.] (5)

Like much of Juan Felipe's poetry for young readers, this is a poem that inhabits a child's perspective, but assumes that children need no more handholding to experience the sublime than adults do. It assumes, in fact, that they need even less—children are readier to laugh out loud at juxtaposition than adults are, and juxtaposition is the poet's tool, rather than the stuff that animates prose: narrative, sequence, causality, necessity, reason, and procedure. *Gravy. Donuts.* It is a juxtaposition that encourages narrative and frustrates narrative in equal measure. That makes meaning and laughs at meaning and multiplies meaning.

The young adult books, too, make no concessions, dumb nothing down. The speaker of *Skate Fate* (2011), the skater, adapting to his new foster home, often speaks like a skater: "Whatever you call it dude," he says, or "dunno," or

> hey waZup wait wait now now what wait did you say Aha wait my cell oh
>     well oH aha my cell wait oK OK ok now where was
> I wait hold Up i'll be there I am almost there[.] (53)

But here, too, pure poetry, with all its ontological alchemy, is given equal sovereignty:

> in brown & sepia music
> in blue nest nothingness absolute singular & cut to glass
> transformed into light & sky & void[.] (23)

Young adults, he knows, hear this. They hear "waZup" and they hear "blue nest nothingness," and they hear them without fear of contradiction. They hear them in apposition, in juxtaposition but also in combination—it is the province of both youth and poetry to accrete dream and reality, the conceptual and the concrete, the imagined and the unimagined. Youth and poetry play in a world of complex collage and layering, mixing given language and invented. We have multiple generations formed by hip-hop, after all, with its intense mixture of the sacred and profane, its multiple slangs and neologisms and lingos, its mashups and remixes and overdubs, its embrace of everyday speech as the basis, but not the limit, of its art. And like much of the poetry for adults Juan Felipe has written, the novels in verse *Downtown Boy* (2005) and *Cinnamon Girl: Letters Found Inside a Cereal Box* (2005) and the other works for children and young adults—all of it is euphorigenic; it wears its desire for rapture on its sleeve: "Laughing out loud, I fly, toward the good things" (5). There is no hiding, no fear of enchantment. An embrace of enchantment, for how does one fly without enchantment? If he wrote "I fly toward the good things," it might suggest a simple dead metaphor; "I fly, toward the good things" involves flying.

For years now, I have let his work wash over me: tonic, cleansing, a can opener for the heavens, and for darker realms. But sometimes I stop and try to discern how it works, how it enchants, how the magic is produced, how the trick works. The poetry comes in all shapes and sizes, all flavors and colors. Sometimes, as in "Black Tenor on Powell Street," from the early *Exiles of Desire* (1985), the lines are staccato, marching down the page:

Between the St. Francis And the palms

in the center
between bent mule drivers on the side

on the last cable car dreaming to the sky

you sang from the asphalt altar

in the room of sirens and statues. (6)

Each line makes its point, becomes a fulcrum to the next, and that line makes its point but pushes us forward, too. Ten years earlier, the poems in *Rebozos of Love / We Have Woven / Sudor de Pueblos / On Our Back* (1974), his first book, often use one-word or two-word lines in this way, in English, Spanish, and Spanglish:

| | |
|---|---|
| Quetzalcóatl | Quetzalcóatl |
| no sorrow | no sorrow |
| vida | life |
| brillando | shining |
| | |
| quetzalcóatl | quetzalcóatl |
| plumed heart | plumed heart |
| of struggle | of struggle |
| feliz | happy |
| laborando | working |
| transformando | transforming |
| dying constellations | dying constellations |

(70; my translation)

Sometimes these lines can be read like a sentence, as in "Black Tenor on Powell Street" in *Exiles of Desire*: "Between the St. Francis and the palms in the center, between bent mule drivers on the side on the last cable car dreaming to the sky, you sang from the asphalt altar in the room of sirens and statues" (6). But in "Quetzalcóatl," the lines do not follow syntactical logic, they insist, word by word (or phrase by phrase), on standing alone, on being considered as themselves (of struggle—happy—working—transforming—dying constellations), and later in the poem cycles of thought-action and raw crying "sangre" or blood, requiring us to let each do their own work, whatever that might be, and fit together as collage, not as syntax.

*Exiles of Desire* (1983) also has a number of short-line poems composed of few lines with more than seven or eight words, many with three, two, or one, as in "The Dreamboxer:"

With his hands the soft
ends of imagination cutting across
the other face blood opens its bell[.] (14)

But this poem opens and is punctuated with what reads like stage directions in paragraph form:

(He wakes up, rushes through clothes. He dresses. Leaving the apartment, leaving the gallery of silent morning rituals, he will penetrate the city; facing somewhere, some jovial coat, some nude statue, some quick mirage of shuffling ankles. He will follow the daily exercise of his existence.) (14)

The structure is as the structure does—each poem forms its form. I suppose this could be seen as a trivial statement: what poem does not form its own form? But upon reviewing the poetry from his first books to the present, I see a continual, evolving exploration of the relation of the poetic line to relational meaning. His masterpiece (I'll return to this poem later), "Saturday Night at the Buddhist Cinema" from *Notes on the Assemblage* (2015), achieves sublimity precisely through its deployment of the multiple relations of meaning to syntax, to collage, to apposition and juxtaposition, to narrative, to story, to discourse, to form. But if "Saturday Night" is the apotheosis, throughout his career he has kept these many different balls in the air, but as a shorthand, for now, I'll collapse all of them into the two categories: juxtaposition and narrative. In "Uno por uno" from *187 Reasons Mexicanos Can't Cross the Border: Undocuments, 1971-2007* (2007), for instance, the use of juxtaposition and narrative is apparent.

| | |
|---|---|
| uno por uno | one by one |
| dos por dos | two by two |
| eran treinta | they were thirty |
| eran cinco | they were five |
| eran eternos un esposo | they were eternal a husband |
| uno quería ser estudiante | one wanted to be a student |
| quería libros para estudiar | wanted books to study |
| quería lucir un traje azul de contador | wanted to sport a blue accountant suit |
| una quería una casita | one wanted a household |
| otra quizás aprender inglés | another wanted to learn English |
| uno por uno. | one by one. |
| (115) | (99–100) |

Within a single short line very complicated things can happen, and even here we can see his attention to collage interrupting syntax. For instance, in "eran eternos un esposo" (they were eternal, a husband) just above, what is the syntax of "they were eternal a husband"—not eternally a husband, but eternal a husband—and why are the subject and object not in agreement? "He was eternally a husband" is a simple idea. "They were eternal a husband" is not.

But just as often the poems employ long lines, comparable to the breathless breaths of Walt Whitman and Allen Ginsberg. The prose poems, of course, are built this way, like the sutras in *Notebooks of a Chile Verde Smuggler* (2002) or *Night Train to Tuxtla* (1994) or the "Aztlán Chronicles." Even the vertical poems can sound this way, while at other times the poems are formatted as classic long-line poems, like the poems in *Howl and Other Poems* by Ginsberg or *Leaves of Grass* by Whitman. And then, sometimes, they get super long, like this line from "Giraffe on Fire," canto 25:

He of the small mouth and large anus, he of the calling wire and the fast hand signs, as if he knew our songs, as if he knew our shuffle across the ashes and the crests where we take cane flutes for the winds and place bitter eucalyptus and rosemary for the Ceiba deity, as if he knew how to angle the hands and dip them into darkness, with weakness not strength, as if he knew the rose patterns of Chávez and the high thin voices of García's broken lyre made at San Juan Chamula and washed with pox, the nectar of the peasant students, as if he knew all this and the dark rings around our balché bowls in the circle of the night sweats and prayers, in front of the New Year God Pots, as if he knew this, he raises his hands in the shadow of Moya de Contreras, in the shadow of Valenciaga. . . . (*Giraffe on Fire*, 82)

Top that, Whitman! Take that, Ginsberg! This is the longest of long lines, the equivalent of saxophonist Rahsaan Roland Kirk's circular breathing, a line of endless, unbroken breath. It is impossible to not see some of the same processes of juxtaposition and collage at work, even as we read something else, something narratively more complex, syntactically more complex, and thus more complex in signification. Where the staccato poems ask us to slow down, to think through the relation of word to word and not just read for narrative, the incantatory effect of these long lines as well as this enchant-atory effect works like a mantra, a meditation, a guided meditation that encourages us to see what the Buddha suggested we might if we follow the Eightfold Path—it enables us to experience the collapse of the distinction between reality and illusion, between nirvana and samsara, between self and other, between signifier and signified, between poet and reader. It is the reason monks chant endless chants from France to Bhutan, from St. Petersburg to Bangkok—the song a mirror of the heart's beating, lyric in the center of the sentient being's breathing, language with the rhythm of the conscious breath.

We drove once in those years from Iowa City to the East Coast. I had some weird family in Connecticut, and he had relations in New York state—not at all odd, but complicated at the time. We were going straight through, a thousand miles, and we sailed past the water park in Davenport and across Illinois and Indiana and Ohio, and an hour or two over Ohio's eastern border, flying along that long, hilly, surprisingly straight highway through the Pennsylvania woods, and we stopped to gas up and take care of business. Getting back on the night road, quiet now in the darkness, ourselves quiet too after having talked for a dozen hours, absorbed by the strobe of headlights against the unbroken trees; we were solemn as we approached our duties. An hour later we saw big signs saying *Welcome to Ohio, the Buckeye State*. We were deflated, but also a bit kooky at 3:00 AM, realizing we had been going the wrong way through the summer night, hours of misdirection. We laughed, wept a little, laughed some more, and got another coffee as we turned around. "Ohio is so welcoming!" Juan Felipe said. "Ohio is always welcoming us! And now

Pennsylvania! It welcomes us again too!" At 7:00 or 8:00 AM we pulled up to his family's place.

The cross-country drive in America has a long history, and its representation in literature often involves discovery and wonder, but also often involves the return to our flight from family, and almost always offers a representation of the endless, restless diasporic churn of the American experience. Somehow, back before cell phones, I managed to pick him up on the way back. We were quiet again. The giddy fun of the ride out was gone. We had too much weight. In an interview recently, Juan Felipe talked about his family, about not knowing his half-siblings from his father's first family, and the interviewer, Andrew Winer, asked him if he felt anger about that. He said, "it was a hot coal." "You felt anger?" Winer asked again. "A little anger, and a hot coal, a little volcanic anger, and that little tiny hot coal" (2020). That night on Route 80, we drove home with our inner embers aglow, making sense of the twists and turns of family. "I come from a family of madmen and extravagant women" (1), he writes in "Crescent Moon on a Cat's Collar," a family narrative, both restrained and fabulist, from *Facegames* (1987), and I have some version of that myself. We were both still young men in those years, and better at having fun than dealing with demons.

Or at least some demons. *Akrílica* was published that year, 1989, and it has complex poems about a cousin in San Quentin, about the suicide of Lupe Vélez, about the war in El Salvador. The personal poems in this collection, such as "She Wants the Ring Like He Wants a Suit of Scars / But," which is also rendered in Spanish as "Ella quiere el anillo aquél quiere el traje de la cicatriz / pero," are hermetic, emotionally compelling but opaque, while the political poems are polemic and forceful, as in "24th & Autumn":

> the bodies of bright red oxygen who denounce the plague America the gangrene the Intervention the sores the CIA the pus of bayonets in El Salvador the mothers with daughters of seven and twenty Lenten years point at the Junta. . . . (99)

The distinction between the personal and the political is simply an analytic distinction (if not plain stupid), one that occurred to me because I kept seeing, as I reread in sequence, a difference between the nightmares of national and international violence (and dreams of local and national and international unity) and the personal dreamscapes. There is less of the playfulness—both at the level of image and structure and signification—in the political poems than in the poems of love and family and finding one's way, as might be expected. But beyond that, the darkness of what I am calling the political poems is, at times, as in "Your Throat Burns, Red," from *Giraffe on Fire* (2001), total, encompassing, brutal, unrelenting: "They burn her. / They execute her with rapid fire. / You wake up from the dead army rot / and you cry, sucker" (14). This kind of language employs a different representational matrix than "She wants a ring like he wants a suit of scars / but." (*Akrílica*, 71). That opening line asks us a number of questions—What is a suit of scars? Why does he want one? What is the relation of the ring to the suit? Why "but"? I suppose there are some questions we could ask about the passage describing "the plague America / the gangrene the Intervention the sores the CIA the pus of / bayonets in El Salvador. . . ." (*Akrílica*, 98) but the questions are less the point than the violence is—it is an indictment.

Juan Felipe and I both moved from the Bay Area to Iowa City in the late summer of 1988, me to start my first tenure-track job at the University of Iowa and him to do an MFA at the Iowa Writers Workshop. We had met only once in California, at La Peña in Berkeley, through José Cuéllar, aka Dr. Loco, ethnic studies scholar, anthropologist, musicologist, and bandleader, who had known him since the 1970s and knew we were both about to move to the Midwest. It was a loud and crazy night—I was playing in Dr. Loco's Original Corrido Boogie Band—so we didn't make much of a connection, but within a couple of weeks we had met again in Iowa, and Juan Felipe exercised one of his superpowers, which is to transform people immediately into old friends. We spent time at poetry readings, at music gigs, and hanging out in each other's kitchens and with our young kids. I supplied music for his readings, and he named our two-person "band" (Geoff Becker and me) *The Real World*. This was a year or two before the MTV show. Like a wizard, he turned the two of us into a band, and he made me, with a phrase, own the *real world*, pulled me out of my head and placed me—presto! laughing!—in front of *the real*. This, too, is what poets do.

*Night Train to Tuxtla* (1994) was the inaugural volume of University of Arizona Press's Camino del Sol series, that seminal line of books by Chicano/a authors. The title poem is one of his prose poems, a single long paragraph, narrative in a surreal mode. An excerpt from the middle reads:

Macedonio laughs. He's got his money wound in his socks. Glass socks, he mumbles, bought them at the San Antonio Bazaar. A man with a little green suitcase pulled them out, twisted them and lit one up with a match. Then, he stabbed it with a stiletto. Glass, he said. When do we get to Tuxtla? (56)

I'm reminded of Christian Marclay's *The Clock*, a twenty-four-hour-long film composed of thousands of clips from classic films, all with clocks or watches in them. As the film progresses, the clocks and watches click off the minutes in real time, minute by minute, and the quilt of movie moments somehow keep you on the edge of the seat. There is no narrative in a recognizable mode—that is, we don't follow plot points or character arcs, or act breaks, but we are following something story-like; we feel the tension and suspense of filmic narrative, and of course a clip from high noon arrives as the music swells. This is what it is like to be under the spell of Juan Felipe's narrative poems and narrative moments in lyric and other poems. We are given narrative situations, narrative lines, but not ever a simple story. The events in the paragraph here—Macedonio laughing, the man with the green suitcase, the glass socks, the mumble, the stabbing with a stiletto, the lighting on fire—lighting what, glass socks?—it all makes you wonder. What of it is happening, what is metaphor, what is mumbled, what thought, who is he talking to? None of it is simple, but it works, we get the tropes, we get the flavor, we get the noir attitudes, the tense cool, we get, finally, a complex image, and that is the payoff: not a tale with a beginning middle and end, no moral to the story, but an intricate objective correlative.

Take this moment from a later poem in *Night Train to Tuxtla*, where I and my guitarist friend Geoff Becker seem to have a sort of two-headed cameo, "Iowa Blues Bar Spiritual":

ladies night, smoky gauze balcony, whispering. Tommy Becker makes up
    words to "La Bamba"—request by Hard Jackson,

mechanic on the left side of Paulie, oldies dancer, glowing with everything
    inside of her, shattered remembrances, healed

in lavender nail polish, the jagged fingernail tapping. So play it hard above
    this floor, this velvet desert. I want

the Titian ochre yeast of winter, keyboard man, fix your eyes on my eyes and
tell me, handsome, how long will I live? (120)

It's a noir novel boiled down like a French sauce to its demi-glace essence.
And like the California noir writers, the worlds get mixed—the oldies dancer
with chipped nails who wants the Titian ochre yeast of winter—mixed until
we can taste what they have in common, taste the human being transcending castes and classes, taste the pure salt of dread and desire, the narrative
elements juxtaposed until the body is reduced to spirit, until the body is released to spirit, until, as the epigraph to "Night Train" (by his constant muse
Margarita Luna Robles) has it, we find the *"black clouds blending with the
white ones"* (55; italics in original). The "story" comes to its inevitable end for
the blues bar dancers, "jangling gold popcorn, chord makers / opal-eyed Su-
zie in a flannel shirt; we beckon the spark, the flaring / this lost body to live"
(120). Again, the story works, but the story is not just a story. It is primarily
there to activate the poem's more knotty and thorny work.

Francisco Lomelí in his foreword ("Juan Felipe Herrera: Trajectory and
Metamorphosis of a Chicano Poet Laureate") to Herrera's *Half the World
in Light: New and Selected Poems* (2008) is undoubtedly right to insist on
Juan Felipe's force, his influence, as a cultural nationalist, or as Rigoberto
González put it in the *Los Angeles Review of Books*: "He has remained clear-
eyed and committed to his vision: chronicling the historical, cultural and
political landscape of his Chicano consciousness" ("Global Voice and Vision," n.p.). True, and many of the essays in this volume address this. Even
titles can make such consciousness clear: "Aztlán Chronicles," for instance,
or "Norteamérica, I Am Your Scar." But Lomelí and González know this is
only part of the story. His many poems about Gaza and Afghanistan and
Syria, his many poems about unity—all the political moments put together
produce a portrait of a humanist, a sum, as Lomelí also notes, of many parts,
an amalgamator of social realms and global arts, and not just the literary
arts—philosophical, visual, theoretical, social scientific (he was, after all,
an anthropology doctoral student), musical, cinematic, theatrical, and, and,
and—that *and, and, and* is the key; like his multitudinous influences, his art
is additive, supplementary, containing multitudes, as Whitman says.

The poem that will be remembered as his greatest work is "Saturday
Night at the Buddhist Cinema" from *Notes on the Assemblage*. Like Walt

Whitman's "Song of Myself" or Emily Dickinson's "Because I Could Not Stop for Death" or Allen Ginsberg's "Howl" or Wordsworth's "Ode to Immortality" or Pablo Neruda's "Heights of Machu Picchu," this poem will be the definitive Juan Felipe Herrera poem—unless the definitive poem is not yet written. There are of course any number of other contenders: "This is My Last Report" from the new poems section of *Half of the World in Light* is pure genius—it would take an essay of its own to dissect—and so is the astounding "Come with Me" in *Every Day We Get More Illegal*, one of the unity poems, which finds yet another way to bring Spanish and English together. Or the twenty-eight-canto "Giraffe on Fire," a great encyclopedia of a poem.

But comparisons are odious or even controversial. Let's just say that in "Saturday Night at the Buddhist Cinema" (*Notes on the Assemblage*), I find all of Juan Felipe's tool kit fully employed, that is, we find all his strengths in full swing. The title itself is a funny, gravy-donut mash-up, Americana in the age of mechanical reproduction, dharma on the big screen. It opens with the circus garishness of "elephants / in cabaret dress reddish and cadmium blue/ & dolphins" (89) and then, whisk, pulls us out of the world of surreal imagery with the sudden appearance, within parentheses, of a somewhat timorous narrator, afraid he is interrupting, who then interrupts himself, addressing someone—us?—"remember the Castro theatre off of market?" (89) he asks, and then appears to be talking to someone who had been at the Castro with him, "maybe / 1992 during the Rodney King revolt" (89). When he and whoever he is talking to were there, maybe they saw Visconti's *Rocco & His Brothers.* This is something else we haven't mentioned: Juan Felipe's RPM, his References Per Minute, that is, those references (films, authors, places, myths, books, and more) create a collage, a cultural matrix that places us and the speakers of the poems in a dense web of signification and experience and aesthetic context. But we are only there, watching Visconti, for a moment, because we slide between worlds again, in the space of a word, or in the space between words, actually, and now "the dolphin was working this out somehow tweeting / blinking his tiny saucy eyes" (89) while the narrator sits "in the third row as usual" (89).

Then a stoic war horse is "pinned / with a hideous medal by the War Provosts" (89), waiting patiently for someone to take her home. This odd sense of longing—the longing of a fictitious horse to be taken home (where?) and freed from unwanted attention. This longing is as characteristic a feeling in Juan Felipe's works as any, as is the vague dread provoked by the "War Provosts"—the who? This is precisely how these poems work: of course there were war provosts, and of course there was a horse, and along with the horse a cow, eventually a pig, and remember the elephant? The world is a constant surprise and yet everything new is somehow expected and if not appreciated—nobody can appreciate war provosts—, accepted, because this, too is the nature of the phenomenal world. "The cow was there / in a Mexican Pancho Villa outfit" (89) and this is funny, returning us to the circus atmosphere we started with, but it also adds a revolutionary gloss to the reference matrix. All of this happens fast in the poem, at the speed of reading, and the cow is not the end of the line, or the stanza: it was there, dressed as Pancho Villa, "spraying everyone with snowflakes" (89) and we swap out worlds again, wondering where we are—snowflakes?—and the narrator, now our friend, adds a kicker. Here it is, starting with the cow:

the cow was there

in a Mexican Pancho Villa outfit
        spraying everyone with snowflakes & you you     should have seen us.

           (89)

"You should have seen us" is such an invitation to everyday intimacy, and a relaxed, unguarded way to treat not just the passing show, but us, his formally ordained auditors, as companions on this road—colloquial, palsy, complicit. You (we) should also have seen, the narrator tells us, the pig, the

pig in a wig of flames
in pinkish pajamas & a cigar doing a Fatty Arbuckle schtick he even ordered
    18 eggs over easy with 18 sides of sourdough cranberry sauce sardines & a
    side of pastrami

           (89)

What can we say about this barrage of pleasure? "Cranberry sauce sardines" (89) is a gravy donuts combo, except more so, and this kind of joyous catalogue is like Whitman on shrooms, as the riot of signifying continues. After the pig hangs off a ledge of the St. Francis Hotel yodeling to "a Gloria Swanson Look-alike in a cashmere robe" (89), the narrator confides:

(it was hilarious it was\
what we all dreamed of yes that was it          it
was what we all dreamed of) the chicken in kimono pirouetted with piquant
    harpsichord arpeggios
*Sonata in E Major* by Domenico Scarlatti. . . .

(89–90)

And we are just halfway through the poem. Among the things that fascinate me about this poem is the way, once I am done reading it, that I reinterpret the title, or the title reinterprets the poem, because in what way is this Buddhist cinema? What is Buddhist about this cinema? I'm not saying I have an answer to this question, but the narrator gets an enigmatic answer. "Where's the exit?" he asks Ava Gardner in a "emeraldine scaly dress," and she responds: "This *is* the exit" (90).

On one of our first nights in Iowa City we went out to a little basement bar that hosted a Monday night blues jam. I would spend most of my Monday nights at that jam for the next dozen years, as it migrated from bar to bar around town, and since there was no regular keyboardist, it was easy to become the house player. But this night we were new, we knew no one, and the guy who ran it had some very strange, chip-on-the-shoulder energy. In fact, I'd come to know him well over that decade-plus and never come to like him. He was the kind of bandleader who gave other soloists two sets of changes and played over eight or ten sets himself. Every song.

But as I say, that night we knew nobody. The bar was a small shotgun room with booths along one side and standing room on the other, a raised platform at the far end that I assumed covered some plumbing—it wasn't a real stage, one booth deep, the table of which held up some of the amps and speakers, the drum set barely squeezed in. We ordered the drink of choice at that time, a two-dollar pitcher of PBR, and listened to the local talent, which was quite good. The crowd became as rowdy as two-dollar-a-pitcher beer can make a crowd, and the applause for each solo and each song was raucous and good natured. We entered the spirit of the thing completely, cheering and whooping it up, and it seemed to me at the time that Juan Felipe's enthusiasm—and anyone who knows him has basked in the bighearted warmth of that enthusiasm—was part of what gave the night such a festive vibe. Somebody in the crowd was whooping loud, with a loud "HEY!" every few minutes. Each time he did, we would whoop in response. After we'd been doing this for a while, another musician leaned over and said, "Guys, guys, be cool, okay? He can't help it."

It turned out that it wasn't somebody cheering the band along, it was a guy with Tourette's, a sax player I'd later play with regularly, and when we turned around to see, sure enough, yes, it was Saul with a tic, not a passionate fan cheering. Chastened, we realized we had been unintentionally obnoxious. I don't know why I wanted to tell that story. But the poems sometimes do that, too, turn on a dime from jubilation to dejection. Life.

We felt terrible, for the same reason we were jubilant—we were experiencing the communal exuberance of song, and then we found we were breaking the rule of community, however accidentally. Although in his years as Poet Laureate of California and Poet Laureate of the United States, Juan Felipe's dedication to building community was given a bully pulpit and a bright spotlight, it has always been at the center of his vision and practice, from the early days of Alurista's *floricanto* on. And at the center of his Buddhist thought and his community activism is the concept of unity. His poem in 2020 in *The New York Times*, for instance, uses its first line as a title, "—i want to speak of unity . . ." in *Every Day We Get More Illegal* (2020):

> —i want to speak of unity that indescribable thing we have been speaking of
>> since '67 when I first stepped into with a cardboard box luggage piece I
>> was distracted by you your dances askew & somersaults the kind you see
> at shopping centers
> & automobile super sale events—the horns & bayonets most of all
> I wanted to pierce the density the elixirs of everything. . . .

(53)

And then there are many other occasions where he implores and invokes for larger plans, such as in "(A m e r I n d I a)," from the beginning of that first book, *Rebozos of Love* (1974):

| | |
|---|---|
| one heart rise | one heart rise |
| rasa rise | rasa [*sic*: raza or people] rise |
| la primavera to flow | spring to flow |
| and churn our destiny | and churn our destiny |
| cultivando | cultivating |
| laborando | toiling |

| | |
|---|---|
| one heart nation | one heart nation |
| liberando | liberating |
| one heart cosmos[.] | one heart cosmos[.] |
| (67–68) | (67–68) |

Yes, politics, Buddhism, unity. That is one summation of his work. But it leaves too much out. Humor, politics, Buddhism, noir, beat, unity, enchantment. The humor for me is key. "The Soap Factory," in *Notes on the Assemblage* (2015), for instance, starts "Soup, soup, soup, soup, / All we do is make soup here" (64); I find this very funny, funny like the chicken pirouetting in a kimono in a theatre in the Castro. Is this just me? I don't think so—the fourth repetition of soup is funny, the slight exasperation of the second line ("all we do!") is funny. The meta-function of the line, as a description of poetic method, is funny.

And of course, my reading of the poetry is inflected by my time with the poet. Juan Felipe and I have spent a fair amount of our relationship laughing with each other, and it may be that I inflect the poems with my sense of his conversation, but that is not all. When we first met, I was working for Culture Class, which billed itself at the time as "The Only Chicano Comedy Troupe in the Universe!" This was the big Culture Clash, not just Richard Montoya, Ric Salinas, and Herbert Sigüenza, but also José Antonio Burciaga, Marga Gómez, and Mónica Palacios. And that gig—I was their Paul Schaeffer, running the band on the side of the stage—was a crash course in Chicano humor. I was also playing with José Cuéllar, as I mentioned, who like Juan Felipe could move from life-and-death commentary to ebullient humor in a flash in his conversation and in his stage persona. As in the case of the Borscht Belt comics, their comedy was insider art for some of the audience and outsider art for others. But even more often the humor is based in pure joy of juxtaposition—"gravy donuts"—and the absurdity of human desire. It is Zen humor. "*Where's the Tuna*?" people shout at the Buddhist cinema. "*We want the Tuna*? / *We want the Tuna*! / What about the Tuna?" (90; italics in the original) Where, indeed?

I once got an email from Juan Felipe, replying to one I sent setting up a faculty meeting at UC Riverside. It read:

As long as you bring the sardines and bread rolls. I'll get the celery sodas.

A two-line poem, making the first line into a sentence, rather than a clause, makes it much funnier. "As long as you bring the sardines and bread rolls." Period. Funny. "Bread rolls." Funny. "Sardines"—the funniest fish. "Celery sodas." Funny. And these two short lines, all by their little selves, popped me out of the ridiculous mundane bureaucratic nonsense of everyday life and into the realm of reawakened sensual experience, into the realm of thought, into, in other words, the realm of poetry.

Gravy donuts.

Juan Felipe Herrera has taught me much over these thirty-some years, some of which is not just the matter, the stuff of this essay, but its structure. He explains what I mean by this in "A Percentage Will Survive," in *Half of the World in Light*:

> All this lacks definition (on purpose),
>
> it is my nature to lack proportion,
> volume, figure, intelligible historicity, time and its spatial quadrants,
>     remember—rubble, that is all I truly have—and you.

(288)

It's an odd place to end, a poem about nuclear war, about the Nomenclature and ideology like a bit between the teeth. But of course, it is much more complicated than that. It is also about poetry remaking the world. For that, he knows, we will need a lot of horses. And cilantro.

## Works Cited

Ginsberg, Allen. *Howl and Other Poems*. San Francisco, Calif.: City Lights Books, 1956.

González, Rigoberto. "Juan Felipe's Herrera's Global Voice and Vision." *Los Angeles Review of Books*. September 23, 2015.

Herrera, Juan Felipe. *187 Reasons Mexicanos Can't Cross the Border: Undocuments 1971–2007*. San Francisco: City Lights Books, 2007.

Herrera, Juan Felipe. *Akrílica*. Santa Cruz, Calif.: Alcatraz Editions, 1989.

Herrera, Juan Felipe. *Cinnamon Girl: Letters Found Inside a Cereal Box*. New York: HarperCollins Publisher, 2005.

Herrera, Juan Felipe. *Downtown Boy*. New York: Scholastic Press, 2005.

Herrera, Juan Felipe. *Every Day We Get More Illegal*. San Francisco: City Lights Books, 2020.

Herrera, Juan Felipe. *Exiles of Desire*. Houston, Texas: Arte Público Press, 1985.

Herrera, Juan Felipe. *Facegames*. Berkeley, Calif.: As Is/ So & So Press, 1987.

Herrera, Juan Felipe. *Giraffe on Fire*. Tucson: University of Arizona Press, 2002.

Herrera, Juan Felipe. *Half the World in Light: New and Selected Poems*. Tucson: University of Arizona Press, 2008.

Herrera, Juan Felipe. "i want to speak of unity," *New York Times Magazine*, August 12, 2020. https://www.nytimes.com/2020/08/06/magazine/poem-i-want-to-speak-of-unity.html.

Herrera, Juan Felipe. *Laughing Out Loud, I Fly*. New York: Joanna Cotler Books/ HarperCollins Publishers, 1998.

Herrera, Juan Felipe. *Love After the Riots*. Willimantic, Conn.: Curbstone Press, 1996.

Herrera, Juan Felipe. *Mayan Drifter: Chicano Poet in the Lowlands*. Philadelphia: Temple University Press, 1997.

Herrera, Juan Felipe. *Night Train to Tuxtla*. Tucson: University of Arizona Press, 1994.

Herrera, Juan Felipe. *Notebooks of a Chile Verde Smuggler*. Tucson: University of Arizona Press, 2002.

Herrera, Juan Felipe. *Notes on the Assemblage*. San Francisco: City Lights Books, 2015.

Herrera, Juan Felipe. *Rebozos of Love / We Have Woven / Sudor de Pueblos / On Our Back*. San Diego, Calif.: Tolteca Publications, 1974.

Herrera, Juan Felipe. *Skate Fate*. Rayo, N.Y.: HarperCollins Publishers, 2011.

Lomelí, Francisco A. "Foreword / Juan Felipe Herrera: Trajectory and Metamorphosis of a Chicano Poet Laureate." In *Half of the World in Light: New and Selected Poems*, xv-xxiv. Tucson: University of Arizona, 2008.

Marclay, Christian. *The Clock*. London: White Cube, 2010.

Whitman, Walt. *Leaves of Grass*. N.p.: Walt Whitman, 1855.

Winer, Andrew. "Juan Felipe Herrera & Andrew Winer, an Interview." *Parallel Stories Lecture*, Santa Barbara Museum of Art, March 8, 2020. https://www.youtube.com /watch?v=NjEhexC5914&t=1203s.

CHAPTER 10

# Weaving, Drifting, Assembling
## Memoria(s) from a Migrant's Notebook of Travel

SANTIAGO VAQUERA-VÁSQUEZ

"A shared word is always new"

— EDMOND JABÈS

## Rolling to Albuquerque in a Chicano Mini

In his poem, "Rolling to Taos in an Aztec Mustang," Juan Felipe Herrera writes about a trip from San Diego to Austin and then to Taos with a troupe of Aztec dancers. It's *un* trip across the Southwest, but it's also *un* trip across an early part of the Chicano movement as the poem is about a road trip to Austin for the Second Floricanto Festival at the University of Texas at Austin in 1975. The poet writes about meeting a troupe of Aztec dancers in Tijuana, taking them across to San Diego and then driving east in a Mustang to Austin. From there, they return west, stopping in Taos, New Mexico for a performance.

This poem—for me as a young scholar who secretly dreamed of being a writer—outlined perfectly what the Chicano/a movement was about: movement, physical movement, different kinds of movement, and more. As a young Chicano who had traveled up and down California his whole life, the poem captured the spirit of a community in *movimiento*.

At the end of the term when I moved from Iowa to New Mexico in 2010, I packed up my car and drove west with a quick detour first to Virginia. My road trip across the country was in some ways a mirror of an earlier one that I had taken almost a decade earlier when my then-wife and I left the Southwest to teach at Penn State. In our departure, we had packed up our lives in California

Mamá Lucha dressed as gypsy. Segundo Barrio/Second Ward, El Paso, Texas, 1936. B&W photo by Beto Quintana, Uncle.

and Texas for a new one. In my return to the Southwest, I was gathering my life in the Midwest and Mid-Atlantic for a homecoming. Instead of California, I was headed to New Mexico in my Mini Cooper. After thirteen years, I was moving back to the region of the country where I was born, the Southwest.

There I was: rolling into Albuquerque, not in a Mustang full of Aztec dancers, but in a Mini full of ghosts, some of them Aztec. There were my travel notebooks, my hard drives full of photos—Aztec dancers in San Diego and Mexico City, folk dancers in Turkey, street life in cities around the world—and the last of my books to teach courses on Chicano/a pop culture.

Inspired by the fragmentary, assembled structure of much of Juan Felipe Herrera's work, this essay is a series of jump cut reflections/notes/discharges on reading him during my traveling life. For a poet whose work is literally always on the move, this seems the best way to reflect on his poetry and its influence on my life as a reader and writer. Herrera's poetry is often an invitation to a dialogue. About border crossing. About connections. About joining together in song or in prayer. About gathering places and histories. About a shared world. About words placed into sentences assembled into verse.

A common theme in Herrera's poetic imagery is that of communion that is born out of practices of "weaving," "binding," "drifting," or "assemblage" since his first book, *Rebozos of Love / We Have Woven / Sudor de Pueblos / On Our Back* (1974) through his most recent, *Every Day We Get More Illegal* (2020). These words can also be read as acts of migration, from one object to another, one country to another, one community to another, and all speak to communion, to sharing, to coming together, and to a poetics of wandering. But not a wandering lost, rather, a wandering that is all about gathering. The woven strands that run through his poetry contribute a vast rebozo (shawl) of love. Through a reading of these strands, this essay reflects both on poetic fragments that float through the poet's work, with an eye towards a union with a reader, and this writer's introspections on reading Herrera. These notes that I present here are reflections, reactions, notes scribbled in the margins of my notebooks, assembling a map of a traveling life where meditations, pondering, musing, and ruminations take over our psyche.[1]

## Weaving a Rebozo of Love

Over a nearly fifty-year publishing career, Herrera's poetry and prose traverses the history of Chicano/a literature and multiple generations of poetry. From *Rebozos of Love* with poems like "Let Us Gather in a Flourishing Way,"

"En el Cosmos of Our Entrañas," "Amerindia" or "Vamos a cantar" to his most recent book, *Every Day We Get More Illegal* with poems such as "Touch the Earth (Once Again)," "I Want to Speak of Unity," and "Come with Me," the overall sense that one perceives is one of communion, a coming together, a weaving of communities and voice. In sum, his body of work is a vast rebozo of love, solidarity, rapport, consonances, and unity.

It is in this assembled nature of Herrera's poetics that Luis Alberto Urrea defines as *rascuache*.[2] For him, the word describes a style, a scene, a funkiness. As a form of subaltern knowledge, rascuache is marked by its flow and transformative ability. Tomás Ybarra-Frausto defines rascuache as "an underground perspective view from *los de abajo*, an attitude rooted in resourcefulness and adaptability, yet mindful of stance and style" (160). For Alicia Gaspar de Alba, rascuache is an oppositional praxis of resistance to hegemonic standards in the art world. Therein resides its popular pleasure, for in subverting dominant ideologies in "[turning] ruling paradigms upside down [. . .][this] witty, irreverent and impertinent posture that recodes and moves outside established boundaries' both evades power and empowers itself" (12).

In Urrea's, Ybarra-Frausto's, and Gaspar de Alba's formulations, the constant is versatility—perhaps survivalist—in the face of structures of power that would seek to marginalize communities. It can also be said that it is a strategy in migrant aesthetics as I will expand on later.

Herrera's poetry straddles various generations of Chicano/a cultural production, from the *movimiento* writing of the early 1970's through the more recent post-Aztlán cultural production of the early twenty-first century. At the same time, his work has continued to remain as pertinent to the political and social time in which he writes. As Francisco A. Lomelí rightly states,

> Herrera now stands at the apex of his long career of stylistic experimentations, epic introspections, and constant innovations, thanks in great part to his deep sense of versatility and immediacy. He has not stood still, bringing into play elements of activism from the Chicano Movement as a performer, poet, novelist, writer of children's books, teacher, cartoonist, photographer, chronicler, scriptwriter, and muralist—all integral to these writings across the genre spectrum. (November 14, 2020; n.p.)

The key here to reading Herrera's work is versatility and immediacy. Herrera's lyrical prowess owes much to rhythm and movement, in fact music and the act of singing are keywords in his work that flows effortlessly from English to Spanish to Nahuatl to Spanglish, and everything in between.

# Memoria(s) From a Migrant's Notebook of Travel: Salamanca

At the beginning of 2003, I arrived in Salamanca, Spain, to direct a semester long study abroad program for my university at the same time that I had two writing projects to complete. One was to transform a book of short stories into a novel. The other was to complete a long essay on the work of Herrera that I had been contracted to write. I took a few of his books—including *Akrílika* and *Night Train to Tuxtla*—a couple of novels by Latin American and Chicano writers, and a few slim volumes on philosophy and post-structuralist theory. I also had stacks of photocopies. These were some of the things I brought with me on my move across the Atlantic, items that could all fit into two medium sized suitcases.

In that long essay on Herrera, I began to further develop my thoughts on what I had called "wandering writing." Where before I had focused on the representation of place in northern Mexican border writing, with Herrera I was now focused on writing as a wandering act. But not a wandering lost; rather, a drifting. A movement across a page in a search for a connection with the reader. I began to think of his books as all constitutive of one larger book, one that was fragmented in style and assembled in scope. One that had multiple points of entry and exit. A rhizome. But also, a book. In taking the time to read a book, we are participating in a type of ethical practice: we are bound to the author via the book, and to the world of the book.

Through this process, we become responsible for the book. This responsibility we can see as ethical, but an ethics not as moral code but rather as a system of responsibility constructed dialogically. Moving outward from the book, we can consider Herrera's work in general as a dialogic body of poetry in communion with the Other who is the reader.

## Weaving: Poet from the Middle World

Herrera's work can be read as dispatches from the Middle World. His poems, a gathering of voices from that region in between, a borderlands, a liminal space. The South African poet, Breyten Breytenbach, to whom I owe this term, defines the Middle World as a world between the first and the third, a liminal space where "truths no longer fit snugly and certainties do not overlap" (135). It is a space conditioned by migration and wandering. While we also have similar terms in Chicano/a cultural studies—most often Nepantla and borderlands as referenced by Chicana writers and scholars Pat Mora and Gloria Anzaldúa—I prefer Breytenbach's model for speaking about mass movements across global borders. For him, the Middle World is a world between nations and populated by migrants. Its citizens—"uncitizens" as he calls them—are in constant migration. He further emphasizes that though the Middle World is everywhere, "belonging and not belonging," it is not "of the Center [. . .] since it is by definition and vocation peripheral; it is *other*, living in the margins, the live edges" (136).[3]

Herrera is indeed a barrio poet from this vantage point because the voices that populate his work are not only from the Americas, they are also from Africa, the Middle East, Europe, and Asia. While he often writes about the Chicano/a and Latino/a experience, in expanding his perspective to a global community of migrants, he notes how all our stories are bound together: we are all deserving of representation in a world that wants to keep our communities separate.

His work represents an iteration that our barrio and migrant stories are also those of other communities—the world in one.

The community that he invokes is woven together by history, culture, and language. For example, in the poem "Crescent Moon on a Cat's Collar" from *Facegames* is where the poet convokes a gathering of family history by declaring that his is a family of "madmen and extravagant women." (16). The poet then recounts various members of his family from Mexico and ends by declaiming that due to this family history, all are his enemies,

keep away from my eyes and especially
from the rhythms swelling up through my feet and out of the opal triumph of
my voice. (17)

The recollections, like his pocket full of "ancient coins," are his constant companions. They are the specters of the past that he carries as he moves, zigzagging across borders, as he weaves various strands of community into one assembled rebozo of history.

## Memoria(s) From a Migrant's Notebook of Travel: Cologne

Lecturing before an audience at the Global South Studies Center at the University of Cologne, Germany, I jokingly proposed to talk about the "unbearable lightness of being fronterizo." I had been re-reading Milan Kundera's *The Unbearable Lightness of Being* and I had begun to reflect on the author's ideas. In Kundera's rejection of Nietzsche's concept of eternal return, he espouses the idea of recognizing that life only leads to a sense of lightness: implying freedom. In particular, freedom from the burden of history. With the audience, I mused about the idea of being fronterizo as somehow implying a similar type of lightness: to be in the in-between is to be free of the constraints of the world, in particular the demands of Mexico and the United States, and that one must presumably choose one or the other. The lightness of being in the in-between is unbearable because it is a heavy burden deciding to choose both at the same time. I offer the work of Herrera as being an example of this, a weaving of national identities to forge something new, a synthesis, an assemblage.[4]

## Towards a Migratory Aesthetic

My first readings of Herrera were as a young reader hungry for lyrical distillations on the Chicano experience. As a fellow *Californiano*, I found in his book *Akrílica* a work that spoke to my own interests in artistic practices using collage, mixing of genres—prose poems like "Para siempre, Maga" (Forever Maga) alongside more formal poems like "Es la Tierra" (Earth Chorus)—and linguistic play as an intoxicating mix. In that book overflowing with love and life and lines like "Quién tendrá la fiebre del cielo" (I wonder who has heaven fever) from "Jesús McDonald" (Jesus McDonald) or "Ayer ahorqué el future" (Yesterday I strangled the future) from "Ayer / Five Tones Out of Time" (Yesterday / Five Tones Out of Time), I found writing that stayed with me.[5] The language was beautiful and terrible as it spoke of communion, border crossing, hope, and desire. "Language is substance," Ammiel Alcalay writes, "the very thread and texture of historical material" (47). And yet, at the same time that it is bound to history, language is also insubstantial, unbound, full of ghosts. This is what I found in *Akrílica*, a collection of poems bound to material history but also to the immaterial. That book led me to his others and eventually to a rented flat in Salamanca where I considered the paths and detours that led me there.

In my notes on wandering writing, I viewed it as a strategy for liberation, a mode for becoming, and a writing stylistics. Though I didn't call it that, I thought of it as an oppositional praxis, one that could be used to put into question forms of power; not in a head-on way, but more slyly, at an angle. Wandering embraces hybridity, mixedness, and blending. A wandering writing, as seen in the poetry of Herrera, can often lead to a space of becoming. For Gilles Deleuze and Félix Guattari, "becoming is like the machine: present in a different way in every assemblage, passing from one to the other, opening one onto the other, outside any fixed order or determined sequence" (347). Becoming is a process of assembling, moving from state to state: it is a gathering in a flourishing way that can lead to liberation.[6]

As a type of oppositional praxis—a type of decolonial *pensamiento fronterizo*, or border thinking—wandering writing can also serve as a strategy for a migratory aesthetic. For Mieke Bal, who coined the term, "Migratory Aesthetics" is

> a non-concept, a ground for experimentation that opens up possible relations with "the migratory," rather than pinpointing such relations. As a provisional circumscription of the modifier, let me call it a feature, or a quality of the world in which mobility is not the exception but on its way to becoming the standard, the means rather than the minority. (23)

Bal further argues that the force of the concept lies in its "condition of sentient engagement" (23), implying that the aesthetic comes not simply from the modifier "migratory" but from an experience that arises in the approach to a work.[7] In some ways, it is an *assembled* experience that arises in the relationship between reader (viewer), writer (artist), and text (work of art). In reading Herrera's work, an experience of the aleatory, or the migratory, is embedded within the flow of the poetry that often opens outward to connect to a larger sense of community.

It is in this sense of a migrant aesthetics that I read Herrera, and other Chicanos/as, that is, as writers practicing a *nomadic* process. From their nomadic, or wandering, perspective, they create with an eye towards intersectional/oppositional migratory flows in a virtual space *beyond* history, in a space of continual becoming. As Deleuze and Guattari write, "History is always written from the sedentary point of view and in the name of a unitary State apparatus, at least a possible one, even when the topic is nomads. What is lacking is a Nomadology, the opposite of a history" (23). In their conception, the nomad stands outside the sedentary and the fixed and is therefore dynamic, versatile (adaptive), and *deterritorializing.*

## A Calling Forth

At times a kaleidoscopic mixing of imagery, at times an invocation, Herrera's poetry is often a gathering. For example, the opening of "Ipal Nemohuani":[8]

> Ipal Nemohuani raíz de la vida
> tú eres el cantor[.] (77)

This poem from *Rebozos of Love* is a declaration for a poetics that will flow across multiple languages and topics over the next few decades. From Aztec/ Maya indigenist themes of the early Chicano movement, through the urban barrio poetics of the 1980's and 1990's to a trans-American and Global South move, Herrera's poetry keeps on flowing, ever expanding to encompass the vast diversity of communities in constant *movimiento.* We can trace this transition through poems such as "Quetzalcóatl No Sorrow" (*Rebozos of Love*), "Exiles" (*Exiles of Desire*), "Foreign Inhabitant" (*Facegames*), "Exile Boulevard" (*Akrílika*), *Memoria(s): From an Exile's Notebook of the Future,* and "Border Bus" (*Notes on the Assemblage*). In this move from the regional to the global, we note how Herrera refers to communities in movement, marginalized, nomadic, exiled: communities who are deterritorialized, unhomed. His poetic work serves as a calling forth of all those who are on a journey, but also it offers a path for finding communion as in the poem "Limpia for Walking into Clear Campos" in *187 Reasons Mexicanos Can't Cross the Border* (2007):

> I drop my burdens
> from my body that holds them
> . . . . . . . . . . . . . . . .
> As I walk, I drop my burdens.
>
> (126)

The poem is a litany, a prayer against solitude and burden. Of the eighty-six verses that make up the text, thirty-eight simply say, "I drop my burdens." The poem begins as a set of instructions for walking on an icy path that then leads into a song about dropping burdens. In this process of moving across a winter landscape, a deep connection with the interior self is sought. With each step, a burden is dropped, and a sense of lightness is attained. And in this lightness, solitude is pushed away in favor of a communion with the self. The poem concludes with a blurring of the self and the landscape: "As I walk, I melt with the snow" (126).

Edmond Jabès writes, "the world is exiled in the name. Within it there is the book of the world" (1991, 79). Writing, then, is a form of finding a way through exile. And it is an act that must continue, for as Jabès also writes, "writing does not mean stopping at the goal, but always going beyond" (79). In the vast book/production that is the work of Herrera, we see how his poetry is always moving beyond, in a way, gathering the voices of those who are deterritorialized to guide them, hopefully, towards a reterritorialization.

## Memoria(s) From a Migrant's Notebook of Travel: Barcelona

In Barcelona, I watched as Guillermo Gómez-Peña delivered a searing performance on border crossing. Shifting from Spanish to English to Catalan to Spanglish, to Ingleñol, and Catañol, I witnessed the power of migration and deterritorialization flowing through the multi-voiced performance of the former border *brujo* now Mexorcist unburdening himself before our very eyes. It was a riveting performance and when I saw it again a few years later in Chicago, I remained captivated. But what struck me then, and strikes me still, is the depth of solitude that comes out in the performance. As Jabès points out, "in every word of solitude there is the solitude of a word unspread" ("Margins," 12). I would offer a slightly different version: that in every word of solitude there is the solitude of a world unspread, closed, unable to loosen itself. Gómez-Peña's performance was a migrant's lament, a push against solitude, so that in loosening the self via a process of "Mexorcism" the solitude of the world can be, hopefully, transformed.

Similarly, Herrera has poems that are migrant laments that push against solitude in search for light.

# Drifting Across a Page, Drifting Across Borders

Like "weaving," "drifting" is another word that often appears in Herrera's work, most obviously in his book *Mayan Drifter*. What does it mean to drift? To wander. To meander. In this act of wandering, a wandering that often crosses borders, once again we are reminded that the aesthetic of Herrera's poetry is not one that is centered on the self as being in control, or one that is focused on a determined path towards enlightenment or creation. The importance is the dance, the weaving in and out, the need to move forward, even in the face of resistance.

In fall 2013 through the summer of 2014 there were several anti-immigration protests that took place in the Southwest. In one, three buses containing primarily Central American migrants who had been detained in south Texas were stopped by protesters in Southern California. The buses were on the way to the Murrieta Border Patrol Station where the undocumented immigrants were going to be processed. The protesters managed to block the buses and forced them to retreat. The buses drove to San Diego county where the immigrants were processed.[9]

Herrera's poem "Borderbus" in *Notes on the Assemblage* (2015) appears to be inspired by events such as this one. In it, two women converse on a bus traveling in the borderlands. One speaks in Spanish, referring to the other as "hermana" (sister), while the other tries to get her to speak English. As the poem progresses, we learn that the two are undocumented, the one who speaks Spanish is from Honduras, while we never learn where the other is from. The woman who speaks in Spanish keeps asking where they are going, while the other asks her to speak English. Finally, she says she knows where they are going:

Where we always go
To some detention center to some fingerprinting hall or cube Some warehouse warehouse after warehouse[.]

(59)

The Honduran doesn't understand, they have already been picked up, what else could the border guards want, she wonders. The other woman doesn't seem to care. She is already familiar with the process of being stuck in the Middle World borderlands space. The woman tells her companion just to tell the border guards that she came from "nowhere."

And we crossed the border from nowhere

And now you and me and everybody else here is

On a bus to nowhere you got it?

(60)

Soon after this exchange, the bus is stopped by protesters. The Honduran woman then begins to tell her story to her companion. She relates how she has traveled for forty-seven days from her country, across Mexico on the train, and the deserts in the Southwest. She tells of hunger and thirst, of being picked up in Brownsville and then transported to California. "[P]ero todavía no entramos y todavía el bordo / está por delante . . ." (but still we're not inside and still the border / lies ahead of us; 61), she declares.

The other woman does not understand. She just wants the Honduran to speak English. But the woman continues telling her story. Gangs killed her son and broke her father's legs. She had to leave her country and cross into the borderlands in her search for freedom. But the freedom she seeks is one that lies beyond border constraints.

The border bus is a liminal space in the Middle World. The Honduran acknowledges that she has crossed the border into the U.S., but for her, she has still not arrived. In the moment that she evokes her past, she brings forth her ghosts, the people that she carries in her memory. They are her border burden.

The bus, stuck in the borderlands, remains in limbo, in that Middle World. Here, the Honduran woman finds her moment of truth: she is crossing a border that is more than a wall, more than a river, more than a desert crossing. It is in that space of nowhere, of being in between, that she finds revelation. Those on the bus are from nowhere, treated as nothing: "No somos nada y venimos de la nada [. . .]" (We are nothing and we come from nothing; 63)—people without a place or a history—by the political systems that forced them to flee their countries and by those who do not want them to arrive; they are, at the same time, from everywhere. To be nothing is to be everything, the Honduran declares. And because of this, they will triumph. It is in her drifting state that the woman can speak her life and connect her story to a larger story of migration.

## Memoria(s) From a Migrant's Notebook of Travel: Erzurum

In Erzurum, Turkey, for a conference at Atatürk University, I gave a talk on Chicano/a punk and rascuache aesthetics. I focused on the use of cut and paste, collage, and other strategies of assemblage, such as Spanglish, as forms of deconstruction, ways to decolonize forms of power. I also made references to tangential strategies, narratives that cut across others to offer sideways glances that can also undermine power.[10] Though my focus was on punk rock, I included some samples from Herrera's poem "Notes on Other Chicana and Chicano Inventions" from *Notebooks of a Chile Verde Smuggler*, a packed-full poem of clever Chicano wordplays and contributions to popular culture: "Phrases like / You better wash those dishes Juan, / or I'll give you a wamazzo" (111).

During my travels through Turkey, sitting in my train cabin, watching the passing Turkish landscape, and reflecting on the conversations I had in Erzurum with a professor and graduate student interested in Chicano literature, I realized then that there is a growing interest not only in our literature but our culture too. Chicano writers like Herrera had been working for years to contextualize their work into a larger transnational story. After all, our stories are part of everyone's story.

## Specters in the Borderlands

The work that I teach most in my courses in cultura fronteriza (border culture) is Herrera's "Para siempre, Maga" (Forever, Maga) from *Akrílica*.[11] The poem, a prose poem, distills a number of themes present in his poetry: reading, history—in particular Chicano history—connections, and border crossing. The narrator, Steve, frequents the same bookstore in Tijuana to visit with Maga, even though he knows that it annoys her and her boss, the owner. Steve tells her stories of border crossers, asks for books from Joaquín Mortiz, Seix Barral, or from Tijuana's Centro Cultural de la Raza, and writes poetry for her. Steve performs his "Mexican" identity for her by speaking on Mexican themes. Maga responds with scorn. She laughs at "Esteves'" poetry that are "instantes concretos de tus profundas debilidades" (concrete instances of your profound weaknesses; 158, 159) and at his concern for the poor in Mexico,

> . . . ¿Qué te importan los ilegales?
> ¿Qué sabes tú de los polleros y su gula? ¿Acaso conoces a las putas y sus escenarios de esclavitud?

> What do you care about the illegals?
> What do you know about the coyotes and their greed? You're telling me you learned something about the whores and their slave situation?
>
> (158, 159)[12]

Her harshest criticism is aimed at his Chicano identity:

> Vienes de San Diego con tu ristra Chicana; bola de pochos altaneros. Y com-
> pran libros de Miguel León Portilla, Garibay y Octavio Paz.
> Los compran como compran el pan *La Tapatía*. Idólatras. A poco crees que
> a Don Octavio Paz le importa lo que le llamas
> "El movimiento chicano?" Fanfarronadas.
>
> (159)

> You come from San Diego with your Chicano line; bunch of arrogant *po-
> chos*.[13] And you buy books by Miguel León Portilla, Garibay and Octavio
> Paz. You buy them like you buy bread from *La Tapatía*.
> Idolizers. You don't think Mister Octavio Paz gives a damn about what you
> call "The Chicano Movement," do you? Rantings.
>
> (161)

With this, the text attacks a Chicanismo built upon an illusory nostalgia, a misreading of pre-Columbian Mexican myths that fails to consider current Mexican border culture. But her arguments fall on deaf ears when another voice enters the bookstore, a woman looking for her husband, Steve, whom she finds reading a magazine. This woman speaks to him as a child in condescending tones. She exposes Steve as a dreamer fantasizing over a picture of a Spanish actress, Magdalena Murillo.

However, this also does not faze him. Steve is too far gone into the fantasy. He promises to take her to the border, to show her:

> Te enseñaré las transparentes multitudes marchando hacia sus cajas sagradas
> de perfectos deseos y perfectas memorias.
> . . . . . . . . . . .
> Al final estaremos juntos. Ven amor. Quedaremos escritos en la cumbre de
> algún precipicio que nadie divisará: uno sobre el otro, como una
> X mayúscula sobre la tierra del Sur. Brillante. Para siempre.
> Para siempre, Maga.
>
> (162, 164)

> I'll show you the transparent multitudes marching toward their sacred cof-
> fins of perfect dreams and perfect desires.
> . . . . . . . . . . .

We'll be together at last. Come, my love. We'll remain inscribed on the face
of a cliff that no one will be able to make out:
one over the other, like a capital X above the land to the South. Brilliant.
Forever.

Forever, Maga.

(163, 165)

By attacking Steve's sense of identity, both Maga and his wife cause him to retreat and cross a border. The promise of "Para siempre, Maga" is the promise of the border as a safety zone. Once the couple crosses it, they will be together. The image of the cross (X) takes significance in the story; not only will Steve and Maga cross a border but they will also "cross" it out. But the border space that Herrera invokes is not the United States or Mexico, it is an amalgamation of the two, the intersection between Mexican and American. We see the reclamation of an identity that lies in an inward journey between Mexican and American, a Middle World space that is also a spectral site of becoming.

The conclusion of "Para siempre, Maga" implies a liberating moment: a step beyond into a borderless future where Steve is free from the burden of not being Mexican enough and Maga is lifted from the constraints of her performed existence. And this freedom comes from crossing—and crossing out—the border.

Border writing clearly situates itself on the periphery. Borders separate, but they also carry with them the desire for another, be it language, culture, or identity. Border writing presents a space that is neither here nor there, a region of possibility far from the ordered center which is attracted by another center. Borders present a fault line between two or more cultures, a seam that bears with it the desire for another.[14]

Writers living in border situations work from this liminal space—an area where referential codes mix and clash—deterritorializing language and culture and reterritoriatilizing them into a new identity in search of "one that is more than two." This in-between, liminal space is threatening to the first two. For as people who inhabit border regions map out a place for themselves in one space, they are at the same time influenced by another, undermining the homogeneous identity at the center. These border selves, decentered, are akin to secret agents, undermining one national identity through influences from another. Secret agents threaten the security of a homogeneous group because we don't know who they are. They infiltrate, undermine, and subvert power structures. Steve calls for new zones, a retreat into a region that is Other, a Middle World.

Much of Herrera's work disarticulates the hegemonic images that the centers of power attempt to impose on the region while offering a representation of a diverse community, rearticulating another map, one that arises from the community. Or, to use an example from Levinas, Herrera's poetry responds to that which is said by the centers of power with a saying that comes from *los de abajo* (the underdogs). Steve in "Para siempre, Maga" seeks an alternative code of conduct to what is expected: by setting foot into his dreamworld, he is separated from the world, but also free of its demands. And, yet, this freedom is an almost unbearable burden—how does one find liberation in the in-between while also remaining connected?

## Approaching Assemblages

Aside from weaving and drifting, a third key term in the Chicano writer's poetics is assembling. As an artistic practice, assemblage is the process of gathering different, often unrelated, objects together into a new object. As an aesthetic, it can often have a rascuache flair. As a working-class aesthetic, it is also a type of *pensamiento fronterizo* utilized by the Chicano community to resist hegemonic forms of power. An assemblage participates in this play of power, often functioning as a type of destabilizing machine.

Herrera's poetry, as true assemblage, zigs and zags, and at times bounces from one verse to the next without a logical connection: rather than progression, the effect is of an assembled accumulation. We find this in a poem like "187 Reasons Why Mexicanos Can't Cross the Border." The work is a list of 187 verses offering reasons why *mexicanos* can't cross:

> CAN'T CROSS because we've been doing it for over five hundred years
>     already. CAN'T CROSS because it's too easy to say "I am from here."
> CAN'T CROSS because Latin American petrochemical juice flows first.
>
>                                                                     (4–7)[15]

The accumulation of reasons—some heartbreaking, some tragic, some ironic and playful—gives this poem a sense of urgency as the context in which the text was written during the debates around Proposition 187 in California. The proposition, also called the Save Our State ballot initiative, was voted on in 1994. One of the many nativist propositions targeting California's Latino population in the 1990s, Proposition 187 was aimed at denying services—including health and education—to undocumented communities. The passage of the proposition galvanized the Latino community who rightfully saw it as a xenophobic attack on ethnic groups in the state.[16] Considered an "Emergency Performance Poem" by Herrera, the poem aims to energize a community traumatized by more than a hundred years of racist attacks and discrimination.

The fact that the poem is presented as a "list" is indeed telling. In an interview with *Spiegel*, Umberto Eco states,

> The list is the origin of culture. It's part of the history of art and literature. What does culture want? To make infinity comprehensible. It also wants to create order—not always, but often. And how, as a human being, does one face infinity? How does one attempt to grasp the incomprehensible? Through lists, through catalogs, through collections in museums and through encyclopedias and dictionaries. (*Spiegel*, n.p.)

In looking at the "lists" by Herrera—"187 Reasons" is one in a series of poems that includes "21 Rational Reasons Republicans Can't Jump," "Mexican Differences, Mexican Similarities," "Don't Worry, Baby," "Notes on Other Chicana and Chicano Inventions," among others—we might argue that his work is about taming the chaos of infinity. "We like lists," Eco declares, "because we don't want to die." (Beryer and Norris, n.p.)

A list is also a form of assemblage, a gathering of elements that work together to create something else.[17] In this case, this list of 187 reasons is not simply an enumeration, but a strategy for destabilizing a discourse of control that places Mexicans in the category of Other / Not Native / Illegal. As the poem works nomadically, it eludes control through an often humorous, sideways glance.

Several of Herrera's poetic list poems are assemblages of verses connected by a topic. They are not so much enumerations, but rather poetic strategies of survival as sideways moves to subvert discourses of control and domination, catalogs of resistance.[18] As assemblages, they establish connections with hegemony by undermining that connection, as we see in "187 Reasons Why Mexicanos Can't Cross the Border." The poem takes the admonition "Mexicanos can't cross the border" and turns it on its head through reasons like "because Nahuatl, Mayan & Chicano will spread to Canada" (8), "because we're destined to have the 'Go Back to Mexico' blues" (36), or "because for us the universe is one big barrio" (66). These often-humorous reasons are juxtaposed with others that are much darker in tone, such as "because it's better to be rootless, unconscious & rapeable" (35) or "because our starvation & squalor isn't as glamorous as Somalia's" (106). By zigzagging across the line between humor and tragedy, the poem works to raise urgency in the listener/reader about the need to fight back at laws that would attempt to force the Mexican and Mexican American community back into the shadows. The assumption is that by denying history and agency, people are easier to control.

## Memoria(s) From a Migrant's Notebook of Travel: Chios

On a trip to the Greek island of Chios, ten miles across the Aegean sea from the Turkish coastal city of Çesme, I take a walk to explore the castle of Chios. Here I look over the parapet and see on the beach a refugee camp organized by the United Nations High Commissioner for Refugees—housing what appears to be a few hundred Syrian migrants. Watching children playing on the beach, while adults milled around the tents, makes me recall my childhood visiting migrant camps in central California. While we never lived in one, my paternal grandparents did upon their arrival. The homes in the camp were plywood constructions, poorly insulated against the winter chill and the summer heat. I remember playing with other kids who lived in the camp while our parents sat outside my grandparent's home and talked.

Seeing this scene of Syrian migration on the shores of Europe, I am reminded again that the sea is a vast border, the Aegean and the Mediterranean seas are also crossing points through the Middle World. Though some migrants cross borders by bus or by walking across deserts, others do it by rubber raft or wooden boat. The migrant, the exile, and the border crosser launch themselves into the uncertainty of this Middle World in the hopes of finding connection, place, communion.

## A Foreigner Bearing a Bundle of Ghosts

In 1993, almost thirty years before the Syrian civil war sent millions of migrants through Turkey on a hopeful journey to Europe, Herrera published a limited-edition chapbook, *Memoria(s) from an Exile's Notebook of the Fu-*

*ture.* The poem was later incorporated into his 1994 collection, *Night Train to Tuxtla.* This collection, his sixth—without counting chapbooks—marks another step in the evolution of Herrera's poetry. Where in the earlier books he wove a connection to Chicano-Mexicano history, in *Night Train to Tuxtla* he continues to add to that history by advancing the hemispheric consciousness of *Akrílica* with a transnational thread in poems like "Memoria(s) From an Exile's Notebook of the Future" and "Letter to the Hungry Students of Berlin." In weaving the transnational into his poetic rebozo, he is binding it not just onto the history of Mexicano/Mexican American/Latin American/Chicano migration, but also adding all of that to a transnational border-crossing story. In this intertwining of a hemispheric American migration to migration stories in other parts of the world, the poem evokes a greater space beyond the Americas to a Global South.

Although *Memoria(s) From an Exile's Notebook of the Future* was written in the context of the 1991 Gulf War and the First Palestinian Intifada, while living in Turkey in 2016, I couldn't help but recall that poem as I wandered into Syrian neighborhoods in Istanbul. The poem is an assemblage placed as a counter to colonialism and to the silence that it imposes upon communities it aims to control. Unlike the type of list poems that populate Herrera's other works, this one offers a catalog of reflections, *memorias,* on wandering, exile, and trauma. In this long poem of 355 verses, the poet chronicles a journey from the Near East, the Eastern Mediterranean, to the United States. The tone of much of Herrera's work is often humorous, or full of wonder, but in this poem, as in "Borderbus," the tone borders on despair, loss, and the overwhelming sense of a journey that has no destination. It becomes a migrant's lament against the solitude of the world: a pushing back against silence through wandering, for as Jabès reminds us, "the beginning of action is passage, wandering." (1993, 160).[19]

The poem begins with an anonymous poetic voice declaring having taken a long journey, "carrying what was given / in sand and pouches / with all my familiars . . ." (5–7). The poetic voice moves from their country bearing the memory of the family's past. In this wandering, they are also gathering artefacts, objects that are added to the expanding *memorias* that fill the notebook. The movement of this diasporic poetic narrator roughly covers the Levant in the Eastern Mediterranean.

Intersecting the poetic *memorias* of wandering are brief images that reflect some of the trauma that the exiled poetic voice carries: "the sliced sugar-can / in the yard, left / with the imprint of six interrogators" (23), "this dead / contract on the shoulders to the skull fields, / to the circular concrete, three columns of army jeeps" (37), "an isolated unit, one last smoke, / tear gas in the coffee cans, / the eyes full of love and a newspaper stabbed / in the mouth, a knife in the shape of a tunnel" (91). In examples such as these there is violence, imprisonment, and torture: memories of a land and a community traumatized by history. These moments haunt the poetic voice and are part of the burden they carry as they wander from country to country. In their nomadism, they also bring in Spanish—"waiting for *mojo* [a garnish of parsley, onion and lemon], inside / the *brujería* [witchcraft], the dance-top falling" (113–114)—and make references to Mexico and Spain—"this Jewish Olmec face" (164), "a heat from a lagoon in Galicia" (177)—bringing those histories to bear on this exile's life. The poem traces a movement across the contemporary Levant, but also calls out to a longer history of migration of a Jewish diaspora, Sephardic and *Mizrahim*, in its references to Spain, Morocco, and other countries in the Middle East. As the writer and cultural critic Ammiel Alcalay observes in his essay "Finding a Language for the Memories of the Future": "The places that haunt, the moments that steal back into consciousness when you least expect them, make up a counter life, like the earliest memories that are so much a part of the way we act we can no longer remember them" (49).

The variety of references to place in the poem are the ghosts, the spectral traces of place and history that create this counter life, or, more precisely, a counter history, to illustrate a history of migration. In *Memoria(s) From an Exile's Notebook of the Future*, the poetic voice wanders from a past in the Levant into a present with his ghosts carrying him into the future. The title of the poem alludes to a temporal collapse where the past (*memorias*) and the future (notebook of the future) is an ongoing present. This sense of an ongoing present speaks to the transnational or a nomadic sense of time. This feeling of a "timeless" time is also noted in "Borderbus" where the passengers of the bus are separated in a space between borders and seemingly outside of time.

Dalia Kandiyoti has written in *Migrant Sites: America, Place, and Diaspora Literatures* (2009): "displaced subjects carry with them the narratives of their originary places, stories of eviction from place often constitute the core of their cultural and literary identities" (4). As we read these fragmented *memorias*, a picture begins to develop of the poet's wandering. Though "Home" is never defined, we can say that the poet has a home; it is in the objects they carry, the memories they write. Home is in the multiple places where they have passed. Their home is in routes, not roots. And because of this, they are in exile everywhere; they will always be foreign.

# Memoria(s) From a Migrant's Notebook of Travel: Conclusion

Gilles Deleuze and Félix Guattari have said that

> all history is really the history of perception, and what we make history with is the matter of a becoming, not the subject matter of a story. Becoming is like the machine: present in a different way in every assemblage, passing from one to the other, opening one onto the other, outside any fixed order or determined sequence. (347)

If we take this idea of history as a process of becoming, the poetics of Herrera is a poetry of becoming as it is imbued with a collective history of the Chicano community and its connections to a global history of migration and diaspora. The power of his poetry lies in its push towards liberation as a movement of people coming together to respond to systems of oppression. It is the social assemblage that will undermine colonizing power structures.

Juan Felipe Herrera's poetry has moved over the course of more than fifty years. It is a Chicano movement in and of itself, a poetry of *movimiento*. In a way, his poetry is a work of nomadology, a vast tapestry (rebozo) that incorporates threads of many colors. This nomadic project bears witness to another history, one often erased, hidden, or forgotten; one grounded in migration and exile and transnationalism. As a Chicano writer, Herrera's poetry grooves with the movement of a community that is always in transition, seeking a space for understanding in a country that has historically misunderstood them. The poetry flows with the community which he also connects to a larger, transnational community of border crossers. It is in this embrace of others that Herrera's humanity comes through.

These are all entries in my notebook of travel, dispatches from the borderlands. Thinking about all of that and remembering how my marked-up copies of Juan Felipe Herrera's books have journeyed with me, I look around at my writing space, the books, the notes, the things that I usually have close to me. And then I look at my place here in New Mexico, and I think, *Home, my home is here.*

# Notes

1. The type of conceptual reading that I undertake here is one that blends memoir with critical commentary through a process of intersecting modes of writing, objective and personal. It is a writing practice that is both a reading and reflection on poetic work that is situated on movement, and the movement of a reader. Each memoir section, "Memoria(s) from a Migrant's Notebook of Travel," is intended to intersect with the surrounding sections, offering another angle to enter the conceptual framework. In essence, this is an entangling of genres that comments on—while also being—a practice of migrant aesthetics.

2. Throughout this essay I will be employing the concept of "assemblage" in a way that echoes Deleuze and Guattari's formulation of the concept *agencement*, which has been translated into English as "assemblage." As Manuel DeLanda notes, "The word in English fails to capture the meaning of the original *agencement*, a term that refers to the action of matching or fitting together a set of components (*agencer*), as well as to the result of such an action: an ensemble of parts that mesh together well. The English word used as translation captures only the second of these meanings, creating the impression that the concept refers to a product not a process" (1). In my reading of Herrera's poetics, I suggest that his poetry is an assemblage that implies both a structure—the poem—and a liberatory process for undermining structures of power.

3. For Breytenbach, those who are from there are "defined by what they are not, or no longer, and so much by what they oppose or even reject [. . .] To be of the Middle World is to have broken away from the parochial, to have left 'home' for good (or for worse) whilst carrying all of it with you, and to have arrived on foreign shores (at the onset you thought of it as 'destination', but not for long), feeling at ease there without ever being 'at home'" (143). We must recognize too, that Breytenbach speaks to various levels of middle worldness: from the trauma of exile to the economies of migration to the tragedy of being a refugee to the possibilities of being an expatriate. The Middle World posits a counter-narrative to the flows of power that would attempt to control, to place limits.

4. "Being Chicano," Ricardo Sánchez reminds us, "is not just projecting certain Mexican cultural norms—for we are neither Mexican nor American (in the gringo sense of being Amerikan). We are not a fragmented people lost in bilingualism—for we have fused dual worlds of language / culture / historicity / experience into a very real and operative linguistic / cultural view of the universe [. . .]" (19).

5. A confession. Part of the book is structured like an art exhibit—each poem in the section "Gallery" references a painting technique, "Eclipse / Watercolor 41 x 80 / San Francisco," "Mexican World Mural / 5 X 25"—and when I sat down

in Salamanca to envision my collection of stories as a novel, I decided to structure the book as a series of paintings that would lead to a different story. I later realized that I was influenced by *Akrílica*.

6. The notion of liberation has a deep root in Chicano literature. In the 1970's, the poet Ricardo Sánchez argued that Chicano liberation would be found through a process of *entelequia*. For him, this philosophical term that refers to the realization of potential, was an apt metaphor for understanding the Chicano experience. Francisco Lomelí rightly observes a connection between Sánchez' concept of *entelequia* and Gloria Anzaldúa's conceptualization of mestizaje ("Whirlwind," x). For a more extended review of this idea, see Vaquera-Vásquez 2019.

7. Bal notes, "the world as we knew it, art as we knew it, the limits and concepts and distinctions by which we lived, were all transformed by the brief sensation of losing clarity [. . . .] The sentient encounter that is the aesthetic event became migratory in this sense: detached from the self-evident certainty of who and where we are, and tumbling inside the experience of someone else caught in a state of mobility which curiously imprisons him" (28).

8. According to the Online Nahuatl dictionary—https://nahuatl.uoregon.edu/content/ipalnemohuani—"Ipal Nemohuani," often transcribed as "Ipalnemohuani" is a reference to a Creator God, and means "he through whom one lives."

9. https://www.kpbs.org/news/2014/jul/01/protestors-turn-back-bus-migrant-children-murrieta/.

10. Doris Sommer refers to this sideways glance as "wiggle room," a "move from the waist (or hip) not forward or backward, but sideways" (5).

11. As a collection, *Akrílica*, is very interesting for its form, but also for the fact that Herrera writes all the poems in Spanish. The English versions of the poems are all translations by a team of writers: Stephen Kessler and Sesshu Foster are the principal translators, but they are also assisted by Dolores Bravo, Magaly Fernández, and Juan Felipe Herrera.

12. As the book is a bilingual edition, the Spanish original is on one page and the translation is on the facing page.

13. An acculturated Mexican.

14. "The relationship with the other is not an idyllic and harmonious relationship of communion," Levinas writes, "or a sympathy through which we put ourselves in the other's place; we recognize the other as resembling us, but exterior to us; the relationship with the other is a relationship with a Mystery" (43).

15. Originally published as a chapbook with Borderwolf Press in 1994, the version cited here is included in Guillermo Gómez-Peña's, *Temple of Confessions: Mexican Beasts and Living Santos* from 1996. In 2007, the poem was remixed for Herrera's subsequent book, *187 Reasons Mexicanos Can't Cross the Border: Undocuments, 1971–2007*.

16. The responses included several important examples of activist art, including works by Lalo Alcaraz and the faux documentary, *A Day Without a Mexican*.

Though the initiative passed, it was delayed by the courts and eventually found unconstitutional by a federal court in 1997.

17. As Eco notes, "The list becomes a way of reshuffling the world, almost putting into practice Tesauro's method of accumulating properties in order to bring out new relationships between disparate things, and in any case to cast doubt on those accepted by common sense" (*Lists* 187). In this way, we can see how a list can be an assemblage. With regards to unity in a list as assemblage, Deleuze and Parnet note, that an assemblage's "only unity is that of a co-functioning: it is a symbiosis, a 'sympathy'. It is never filiations which are important, but alliances, alloys . . ." (69).

18. Regarding poetic lists, Eco points out: "poetic lists are *open*, and in some way presuppose a final *etcetera*. They aim at suggesting an infinity of persons, objects, events, for two reasons: (1) the writer is aware that the quantity of things is too vast to be recorded; (2) the writer takes pleasure—sometimes a purely auditory pleasure—in ceaseless enumeration." (*Lists*, 122–123)

19. In reading this piece, I am also reminded of Palestinian poet Mahmoud Darwish's poem, "Those Who Pass Between Fleeting Worlds." Both speak of wandering, border crossing, and the need for memory.

## Works Cited

Alcalay, Ammiel. "Finding a Language for the Memories of the Future." *Shofar: An Interdisciplinary Journal of Jewish Studies* 14, no. 1 (Fall 1995): 45–52.

Anzaldúa, Gloria. *Borderlands/la Frontera: A New Mestiza*. San Francisco, Calif.: Aunt Lute Books, 1987.

Bal, Mieke. "Lost in Space, Lost in the Library." In *Essays in Migratory Aesthetics: Cultural Practices Between Migration and Art-Making*, edited by Catherine Lord and Sam Durrant, 23–36. Amsterdam: Rodopi, 2007.

Beyer, Susanne, and Lothar Gorris. "Spiegel Interview with Umberto Eco: 'We Like Lists Because We Don't Want to Die.'" SPIEGEL International, November 11, 2009. https://www.spiegel.de/international/zeitgeist/spiegel-interview-with-umberto -eco-we-like-lists-because-we-don-t-want-to-die-a-659577.html.

Breytenbach, Breyten. *Notes from the Middle World*. Chicago: Haymarket Books, 2009.

Darwish, Mahmoud. "Those Who Pass Between Fleeting Words." *Middle East Report and Information Project* 154, (September/October 1988). https://merip.org/1988 /09/those-who-pass-between-fleeting-words/.

DeLanda, Manuel. *Assemblage Theory*. Edinburgh: Edinburgh University Press, 2016.

Deleuze, Gilles, and Félix Guattari. *A Thousand Plateaus: Capitalism and Schizophrenia*. Translated by Brian Massumi. Minneapolis: University of Minnesota Press, 1994.

Deleuze, Gilles, and Claire Parnet. *Dialogues II*. New York: Columbia University Press, 2002.

Eco, Umberto. "My Lists." In *Confessions of a Young Novelist*, 121–204. Cambridge, Mass.: Harvard University Press, 2011.

Gaspar de Alba, Alicia. "A Theoretical Introduction: Alter-Native Ethnography, a lo rasquache." In *Chicano Art Inside/Outside the Master's House: Cultural Politics and the CARA Exhibition*, 1–30. Austin: University of Texas Press, 2021. https://doi.org/10.7560/728011-003.

Herrera, Juan Felipe. *187 Reasons Mexicanos Can't Cross the Border: Undocuments, 1971–2007*. Tucson: University of Arizona Press, 2007.

Herrera, Juan Felipe. *187 Reasons Why Mexicanos Can't Cross the Border: An Emergency Poem*. Fresno, Calif.: Borderwolf Press, 1995.

Herrera, Juan Felipe. *Akrílica*. Santa Cruz, Calif.: Alcatraz Editions, 1989.

Herrera, Juan Felipe. *Facegames*. San Francisco, Calif.: As Is/So & So Press, 1987.

Herrera, Juan Felipe. *Memoria(s) from an Exile's Notebook of the Future*. Santa Monica, Calif.: Santa Monica College Press, 1993.

Herrera, Juan Felipe. *Notes on the Assemblage*. San Francisco: City Lights Books, 2015.

Herrera, Juan Felipe. *Night Train to Tuxtla*. Tucson: University of Arizona Press, 1994.

Herrera, Juan Felipe. *Notebooks of a Chile Verde Smuggler*. Tucson: University of Arizona Press, 2002.

Herrera, Juan Felipe. *Rebozos of Love / We Have Woven / Sudor de Pueblos / On Our Back*. San Diego, Calif.: Toltecas en Aztlán, 1974.

Jabès, Edmond. *A Foreigner Carrying in the Crook of His Arm a Tiny Book*. Translated by Rosemarie Waldrop. Middletown, Conn.: Wesleyan University Press, 1993.

Jabès, Edmond. *The Book of Margins*. Translated by Rosemarie Waldrop. Chicago: University of Chicago Press, 1993.

Jabès, Edmond. "Test and Book." In *From the Book to the Book: An Edmond Jabès Reader*, translated by Rosemarie Waldrop, 79–82. Hanover, N.H.: Wesleyan University Press, 1991.

Kandiyoti, Dalia. *Migrant Sites: America, Place, and Diaspora Literatures*. Hanover, N.C.: Dartmouth College Press, 2009.

Kundera, Milan. *The Unbearable Lightness of Being*. Toronto: 68 Publishers, 1984.

Levinas, Emmanuel. "Time and the Other." In *The Levinas Reader*, edited by Seán Hand, 37–58. Oxford: Basil Blackwell, 1989.

Lomelí, Francisco A. "Foreword: Ricardo Sánchez: A Whirlwind Uncontained." In *Chicano Timespace: The Poetry and Politics of Ricardo Sánchez* by Miguel R. López, vii-xi. College Station: Texas A&M Press, 2001.

Lomelí, Francisco A. "Juan Felipe Herrera: A Poet in Movement." *Los Angeles Review of Books*, November 14, 2020, https://lareviewofbooks.org/article/juan-felipe-herrera-a-poet-in-movement/.

López, Miguel R. *Chicano Timespace: The Poetry and Politics of Ricardo Sánchez*. College Station: Texas A&M Press, 2001.

Mora, Pat. *Nepantla: Essays from the Land in the Middle*. Albuquerque: University of New Mexico Press, 2008.

Sánchez, Ricardo. *Hechizospells*. Los Angeles: Chicano Studies Center, University of California, 1976.

Sánchez, Ricardo. "It Is Urgent." In *Canto y grito mi liberación: The Liberation of a Chicano Mind*, 131. New York: Anchor Books, 1973.

Sommer, Doris. "Introduction: Wiggle Room." In *Cultural Agency in the Americas*. Edited by Doris Sommer, 1–28. Durham, N.C.: Duke University Press, 2006.

Urrea, Luis Alberto. "A Rascuache Prayer: Reflections on Juan Felipe Herrera, My Homeboy Laureate." *Poetry Foundation, Prose*, September 14, 2020, https://www.poetryfoundation.org/articles/154196/a-rascuache-prayer.

Vaquera-Vásquez, Santiago. "The Unbearable Lightness of Being Fronterizo." *Ex-Centric Narratives: Journal of Anglophone Literature, Culture, and Media*, no. 3 (2019): 136–150.

Ybarra-Frausto, Tomás. "Rasquachismo: A Chicano Sensibility." In *Chicano Art: Resistance and Affirmation, 1965–1985*, edited by Richard Griswold del Castillo, Teresa McKenna and Yvonne Yarbo-Bejarano, 55–162. Los Angeles: Wright Art Gallery, University of California, 1991.

# PART III

## The Child-Poet Within Me

Toward an Analysis of Juan Felipe Herrera's Children and Young Adult Literary Production

"Rainbow Dog," color pencil drawing by six-year-old Kaili Kauka.

# CHAPTER 11

# Juan Felipe Herrera's Illustrated Books for Young Readers
## Chicano Children's Literature con Cilantro

MANUEL M. MARTÍN-RODRÍGUEZ

Though best known in most literary circles for his daring poetic and narrative work for older readers, Juan Felipe Herrera is also a prolific and innovative author of illustrated books for children. In this area, he belongs to the pioneering group of writers initially associated with the now defunct Children's Book Press, whose catalog was later absorbed by Lee & Low, which has revived Children's Book Press as one of its current imprints. The works of that group were characterized, among other things, by their commitment to bilingualism and to social justice, as well as by the exploration of collective and self-identity. Many Children's Book Press authors, including Herrera, added to those features an element of imaginative playfulness that I have tried to capture in my subtitle. While earlier children's literature had featured references to food, culture, and music in largely descriptive and, at times, stereotypical terms, Herrera—among others—disrupted predictable images and concepts (including food and music) by infusing them with new, imprecise meanings whose affective charge was unmistakable for his target audience. *Super Cilantro Girl/La superniña del cilantro* (2003) and *Calling the Doves/El canto de las palomas* (1995) are superb examples of that critical playfulness that stimulates the reader's imagination without heavily over determining or dictating how to read culture.

In this chapter, I will analyze Herrera's illustrated children's books published to date to better delineate his poetics as a combination of memory, allusion, humor (with some touches of the absurd), a commitment to environmental and social justice, a vindication of difference, as well as the metaliterary aspects that celebrate both the roles of the author and of the reader as essential for literary communication. Though these traits are visible in all of his books, and though I intend to treat his oeuvre in a holistic manner, I will emphasize memory and autobiography in my discussion of *Calling the Doves/El canto de las palomas* (1995), *The Upside Down Boy/El niño de cabeza* (2000), *Grandma and Me at the Flea/Los meros remateros* (2002), and *Imagine* (2018); humor and zaniness in *The Upside Down Boy*; environmental and social justice in *Super Cilantro Girl/La superniña de cilantro* (2003) and in *Coralito's Bay/Bahía de Coralito* (2004); difference (including the portrayal of different abilities, an area in which Herrera's children's literature is truly foundational) in *Featherless/Desplumado* (2004); and the metaliterary dimension in *Grandma and Me at the Flea* and in *Super Cilantro Girl*.

To better appreciate Herrera's original contributions to the genre of the illustrated children's book, it is important to begin with a brief consideration of the immediate context in which his children's books were published. As late as 1981, in "Chicano Culture and Children's Literature," Sylvia Cavazos Peña lamented the scarcity of relevant materials in that field, as well as the problems that plagued most of the available books at the time. According to Peña,

> if we are trying to determine the cultural relevancy of literature for Chicano children we will have as hard a time in finding suitable materials in English as in Spanish. For even though many works are representative of universal cultural values and cannot be ignored, the sad fact is that very few materials have been written by Chicanos or about Chicanos. And in many of those, Chicanos and Mexicans are quite often stereotyped or presented in a condescending manner. (31)

Though Peña acknowledged the pioneering work of authors like Ernesto Galarza as exceptions to that norm, she was correct in her assessment of a bleak panorama in which Mexicans and Chicanos/as were portrayed as rural simpletons or as incompetent human beings unable to take care of themselves and/or to solve their own problems. Four years later, in 1985, Gerald A. Reséndez in "Chicano Children's Literature" elaborated on that type of portrayal by discussing the racial undertones of what he termed the "white savior fiction," a dominant plot tool by which Mexican and Mexican American characters were rescued from whatever predicament in which they found themselves by the swift, knowledgeable intervention of an Anglo-American character (108).

As a result, and as I have explored elsewhere, the modern aspects of Mexican life and the participation of Chicanos/as in contemporary life in the United States were all but replaced by a narrative insistence on depicting a backward population that seemed to live outside of historical time, and for whose children the main aspiration appeared to be that of owning a *burro* of their own (Martín-Rodríguez, "Chicano/a Children's Literature," 23).[1] Such a master narrative, which served as an obvious justification of interventionism, provided the allegorical support for numerous plots in children's books of the first six decades of the twentieth century, and the trend continued—to a lesser degree—until the explosion of multicultural children's literature started to revert that course in the final decades of the twentieth century (even though stereotypes persist in both literature and film).

Also characteristic of those mainstream children's books on Mexicans and Chicanos/as was a reductionist approach to the representation of space. Geographical precision tended to be replaced by a generic identification in which the main referent, Mexico, stood as an almost empty signifier meant to represent any and all of that country's extremely diverse regions, as if details and differences were not meaningful or relevant. What readers could see in the illustrations in those books, and what they could read about in those texts, was often a fuzzy image of Mexican spaces, almost a fabricated theatrical background, best explained through Julianne Burton's film-analysis insights—in "Don (Juanito) Duck and the Imperial-Patriarchal Unconscious: Disney Studios, the Good Neighbor Policy, and the Packaging of Latin America"—on Disney's *The Three Caballeros*, an early 1940s animated movie set in several Latin American countries, including Mexico. According to Burton, in that film "personality assumes precedence over geography and literal depictions of place give way to more mythic geographies animated by imagination and desire" (27). The power of the heterological gaze that Burton observes in that film also applies to most children's books dealing with Mexico and Mexicans, and it serves a similar purpose as the allegory of colonization mentioned above.[2] As I suggest below, Herrera's decolonial approach to children's literature quite decisively challenges that particular understanding of (human) geography by insisting on a sort of topographical precision that identifies migratory routes, community enclaves, and even socially-significant spaces for community gatherings. His spaces are not *Mexican* in a predetermined or essentialist sense; rather, they *become* Mexican as people of Mexican origin claim them as workplaces, places of residence, or spaces for amusement, cultural performances, or any other types of social interaction.

Such a nuanced approach to identity and culture was instrumental in contributing to develop what we could call the second wave in the history of Children's Book Press. Founded in 1975 with a grant from the Department of Education, Children's Book Press became the first publisher to focus on multicultural books for young readers ("Children's Book Press History," n.p.). But its first publications focused mostly on legends and on other folkloric material, which gave its products a distinct bent towards the past and a certain quasi-anthropological feel. By the 1990s, however, authors like Francisco X. Alarcón and Herrera succeeded in publishing books more directly connected to the present and specifically to life in the multicultural United States. As Alarcón explained in an interview with Frederick L. Aldama, his reasons for authoring books for children included a sense of giving back to the community, countering prevailing ethnocentric messages, celebrating and promoting bilingualism, and providing Latino/a children with opportunities to see themselves in literature (Aldama, 44). These are all aspects that apply to the body of work that Herrera published with Children's Book Press and beyond, as I will analyze below.

In the works for children by Herrera, one of the main strategies for providing Chicano/a young readers with opportunities to see themselves in print involves a consistent autobiographical discourse. By presenting his own personal story for the reader's consideration, he vindicates the literary significance of lives that are often deemed unremarkable and socially insignificant in dominant discourses. At the same time, by reflecting on his life as a child and by telling the story of growing up in the midst of the farmworker migratory cycles that many other families of Mexican origin have also experienced, Herrera appeals to that common bond for recognition and empathy. Present in many of his books, the autobiographical bent is especially foregrounded in the quartet of books formed by *Calling the Doves/El canto de las palomas*,

*The Upside Down Boy/El niño de cabeza, Grandma and Me at the Flea/Los meros remateros*, and *Imagine/Imagina*.[3] The first three of these titles form a trilogy of sorts, covering pre-school early childhood (*Calling the Doves*), the experience of entering the educational system (*The Upside Down Boy*), and the joys of immersing oneself in family and community during weekends (*Grandma and Me*). *Imagine*, published eighteen years after the release of *Grandma and Me*, may be seen as a coda to Herrera's autobiographical project, since it is written as a comprehensive reflection on his childhood from the perspective of having served as the 21st United States poet laureate from 2015 to 2017, and because it sums up the other three autobiographical books, all this while inviting young readers to envision what their own lives could be in the future.

Given the mainstream literary context outlined above, this strategy of narrating one's own life also serves as an effective corrective to typecasting and stereotyping. Herrera is not interested in telling the story of *a Mexican* or *a Mexican American* but, rather, he wants to tell *his own* story as a member of a specific family and of a set of communities. In this, he joins the efforts of other Chicano/a authors who have embarked on what Norma E. Cantú termed *autobioethnography* (xi), a writing process that begins in the particular (the author's personal life story) to broaden into the collective (the story of the author's family and community). Writing from the inside of that experience, from the particular to the general, serves as an oppositional response to the kind of pre-established conceptions and expectations that abounded in mainstream books written from the opposite angle, i.e., from the general (telling the story of a Mexican) to the particular (telling the story of, say, Paco), a heterological endeavor inevitably fraught with problems.

Of equal importance in the case of Herrera is the fact that he tells his auto-bioethnographic stories in a style that combines realistic detail with poetic ambiguity. Social realism has served minority and protest literatures well by allowing authors to describe the harsh conditions of life for the disenfranchised, among other aspects, and Herrera could have easily opted to write in that vein, as many Chicano/a authors have done.[4] But Herrera, like Alarcón, privileges the power of images to engage the readers in an active, participatory manner. Through unexpected, yet powerful images, Herrera manages to transform the ugly, the unseeming, into scenarios of creativity and new possibilities, thus turning disenfranchisement into empowerment. A prime example of this technique is found in *Calling the Doves*. In telling the story of his homeless family, which at one point in the story travels from crop to crop, sleeping in a tent pitched in the fields, the narrator reminisces on the day his father decided to build "a one-room house / on top of an abandoned car" (11). He devotes two stanzas to that episode. The first is descriptive, realistic, and the lines just quoted continue: "He hammered two-by-fours and plywood / onto the old Ford chassis and dipped / his brush into buckets of white paint" (11). The second stanza, however, embraces the rasquache creativity of the father, transforming his labor into a less practically- and more artistically-oriented endeavor:[5] "From the distance, my house was / a short loaf of bread on wheels" (11). By thus transforming the empirical world through ideation, Herrera's narrator shows the reader the way to convert life (no matter how destitute) into art, poverty into wealth. In that latter sense, the final lines of the second stanza further expand on the alimentary metaphor of the house as a loaf of bread by describing the nurturing aspect of its interior: "Inside it was a warm cave of conversations. / Mexican songs and auctions blared / from a box radio on the wall" (11). The symbolic womb (actually referred to as a cave) is pregnant with communicative love and with the supplement of the voices of secondary-orality cultural products.[6] In their apparent deprivation, the family actually lives a rich spiritual and cultural life, an element further explained by the (somewhat enigmatic) title of the book, which will be analyzed next.

Prior to reading this book, it is difficult to guess what its title may refer to. Readers encounter the first reference to calling the doves on page fourteen, when Juanito's father stops working to take a lunch break:

> He would put his hands up to his mouth
> and whistle deeply as if he had a tiny clarinet
> inside the palms of his hands.
> . . . . . . . . . . . . . . . . . .
> Sooner or later a real dove would fly in
> and perch itself on a nearby tree.
>
> (14)

At this point, an at-face-value type of reading would suggest that the title phrase just refers to a leisure activity meant to alleviate the burdens of physical labor. Herrera's careful phrasing, however, prepares readers for a much richer interpretation that unfolds from this point on up to the end of the book. Essential, in that regard, is the expressive phrase "as if," which suggests the transcendental possibility of—once again—turning lack into surplus; though the father owns no *real* musical instrument, he compensates for that absence through resourcefulness and skill, and thus the *imaginary* clarinet ends up attracting a *real* dove.

More importantly, the paternal act of calling the doves allows Juanito to reminisce on the following page about his mother's own artistic talents:

Sometimes my mother would surprise us at dinner
by reciting poetry.

. . . . . . . . . . . . .

she would rise to her feet
with her hands up as if asking for rain.

Rhyming words would pour out of her mouth
and for a moment the world would stop spinning.

(16)

By repeating the conjunction "as if," Herrera invokes—once again—Juanito's (and the reader's) analogical powers, but he constructs these two scenes in a sort of structural chiasmus, in which the imaginary clarinet sounds attract a real dove while the real poetry recitation brings down an imaginary downpour of rain. Two ideas emerge as essential from these two key episodes. In the first place, Herrera's readers are allowed to appreciate the fact that art and artistic abilities are not the patrimony of the upper classes, and that humble workers (both male and female) may indeed produce art in multiple ways. In addition, Herrera offers his young readers an implicit explanation of how to produce art in writing by starting with a firm grip on reality (the fields, the tractor work, the cooking) and then by using the power of images and imagination to create an artistic (an "as if") version of the universe. Such a strategy allows him to compare the truck with a loaf of bread, as already mentioned, the *campesinos* in the fields with tropical birds (4), the tent in which the family sleeps with a giant tortilla (6), the sky with a spoon (8), et cetera, throughout the book. By the end of the story, when the family moves to the city so that Juanito might get a school education, young Juanito foretells his future as an author (Herrera) while further clarifying the meaning of the title of this book: "I knew / one day I would follow my own road. / I would let my voice fly the way my mother recited poems, / the way my father called the doves" (30). By turning his biographical experiences into literature, he fully fulfills Juanito's prediction/promise. He continues the family tradition of transcending and transforming life into art, thereby grounding this activity on family traditions and ethics, while making sure that his transition into print culture does not alienate him from his past.

*The Upside Down Boy* further develops the story of young Juanito as he enters the world of schooling. This book explores key issues for many Latino/a children, such as the transition from a life in Spanish at home to one that is lived mostly in English in schools and city streets. In addition, the transition from a rural life to an urban environment is also explored effectively.

That latter contrast is first presented as Juanito walks to school with his father for the first time: "People speed by alone in their fancy melting cars. / In the valleys, campesinos sang '*Buenos días*, Juanito'" (7). The group image of the *campesinos*, and their uplifting communicative interaction with the child (which makes their words sound like a song) mitigate somehow the initial impression of these other "people" and their solipsistic, silent lives in their fast cars. A number of other key elements make this contrast most poignant, including the alternation between English and Spanish (people/ *campesinos*); the rootedness of the *campesinos* (in the valleys in which they physically stand and labor) versus the uprootedness of the people, whose feet do not touch the ground as they speed by as almost disembodied presences; as well as the enigmatic image of the melting cars, a potential reference to the distortion produced by speed or, perhaps, a more learned allusion to the surrealistic style of Salvador Dalí and his famous melting clocks, often interpreted as a critique of materialism and of a modern world regulated by schedules.

In the poignant exploration of those two worlds in *The Upside Down Boy*, Herrera takes advantage of linguistic differences to further stimulate young readers' imaginations through images and humor. When Juanito first learns the English-language word "recess," he points out that it "Sounds like '*reses*'—like the word for cattle" (13) in Spanish, a bilingual pun beautifully captured in Elizabeth Gómez's accompanying illustration. By gently addressing this potentially traumatic moment in a child's life, the author shows his readers a less-threatening side of language, one in which misunderstanding and lack of understanding are indeed challenges but not unsurmountable barriers. Juanito's ability to pun on the word "recess" and his overall creative approach to mastering a foreign language can make young (and old) readers laugh, teach them coping strategies and, to a certain extent, serve as a form of bibliotherapy, empowering readers to address potential traumas and negative experiences.[7] Moreover, Juanito's bilingual pun evidences yet again a critique of the alleged *lack* that allows dominant discourses to see children, immigrants, foreigners, etc., as *less than*: rather than focusing on Juanito's failure to understand the English language, Herrera chooses to stress his overall linguistic abilities.

For this and other reasons, in *The Upside Down Boy*, Herrera presents creativity and imagination as resilient human skills and as coping mechanisms that Juanito uses effectively to make sense of his present without forgetting the past. Once he learns the alphabet in school, he takes advantage of a finger-painting exercise to write his name with seven chile figures twisted and bent to form the different letters. In describing the process, more importantly, Juanito offers the readers several images that skillfully bring together his past and present worlds. First, he considers the chalkboard: "I see a row / of alphabet letters and addition numbers. If I learn them / will they grow like seeds?" (10). Next, he ponders "If I learn the English words / will my voice reach the ceiling, weave through it / like grape vines?" (10) And then, as mentioned earlier, he writes his name with chile-shaped letters and he draws "crazy tomato cars and cucumber sombreros" (10). Though entering school is often presented as walking into an entirely foreign world in which minority children find themselves lost, Juanito's analogical powers manage to reterritorialize the unknown space of the school through the familiar images of his *campesino* childhood: the row of letters and numbers suggest the *surcos* (rows) in the fields, or the straight lines in vineyards, and the unfamiliar world of the city and its cars is rendered familiar by their transformation into tomato cars. In a symbolic manner, through images and shapes, Juanito manages to blend and bring the *campesino* past into his urban present, thus refusing to see them as entirely incompatible. In this manner, he reduces his outside world into his own.

The process of reterritorialization continues as Juanito brings his drawings home to be praised and celebrated by his family. But this is not an instance of facile oppositional cultural critique in which home and family are presented as positive versus the more hostile world of streets and schools. Instead, Herrera blurs the boundaries of those two worlds by elaborating on the experiences of Juanito's parents with schooling and learning. While none of them could enjoy the full experience of formal education, the reader learns that Juanito's mother won a spelling contest while she was in third grade and that his father devised a rasquache method for learning English by paying coworkers to teach him words (23).

This is a most important aspect for the reader to keep in mind (especially for the reader familiar with *Calling the Doves*) in order to make sense of the last part of *The Upside Down Boy*. Juanito is praised in school for his beautiful voice when he sings in class, and the first poem he writes earns him an A. A quick reading of this section might lead us to interpret this as a paean to his school success, as if that were an element that could separate him from his family and from his *campesino* past. Yet, as the reader might remember from *Calling the Doves*, Juanito's introduction to poetry occurred in the fields by listening to his mother recite verses, and his early exposure to the world of music included listening to his father calling the doves "as if he had a tiny clarinet / inside the palms of his hands" (*Calling the Doves*, 14). In that sense, the ending of *The Upside Down Boy* may be read as the first step in accomplishing the goal of becoming an author, foretold at the end of *Calling the Doves*. Using a harmonica gifted to him by his father (notice, once again, the effort to connect the worlds of home and school), Juanito directs a choir of students as they sing poems during a school open house event while his teacher (Mrs. Sampson) wears "a chile sombrero" (31). This symbolic reversal of roles leaves Juanito in a professorial position at the end of the story, while his teacher dons a hat that—in a different context—could have easily been a stereotypical image of Mexicans.

The third book in Herrera's autobiographical trilogy takes place a few years later in Juanito's life. He is now in the care of his grandmother, as his parents have traveled north for the apple picking season (*Grandma*, 6). To cover Juanito's expenses while they are gone, his parents have left behind gently used clothes that Juanito and his grandmother take to the flea market to sell. If the first two books of the trilogy explored mostly family and school, in this third autobiographical installment Herrera focuses on community. The flea market becomes a microcosm of the community in which Juanito learns of the many ties binding people together. As he run errands to different stands for his grandmother, other sellers offer Juanito gifts for her, in compensation and thanks for services she has rendered or is rendering them (rubbing down injured body parts, writing a letter to a landlord, sharing a recipe to be used during a *quinceañera* party, etc.). Bartering, more than selling, describes the economy of this flea market in which old alliances are reaffirmed and new ones developed. The mood is both festive and hopeful, as mutual aid and support are reaffirmed page after page.

In such a context, at least as far as children's literature is concerned, there is always a risk of turning the young protagonist(s) and, by extension, the young readers, into spectators of an adult world of which they are not yet a meaningful part of. Herrera circumvents that danger by turning Juanito's artistic productivity into a desirable communal good. As his grandmother trades a shawl for a flowerpot with a female customer, she adds a couple of gifts to the trade: several spools of thread

> and this little book
> of my grandson's poems.
> He gave them to me when I returned
> from the hospital last year.
> They always give me hope.
>
> (29)

In this momentous ending, Juanito ceases to be a passive boy and an observer to realize that he is also a participant in and a contributor to the community's holistic well-being. His goal to become an author has now crystallized into a reality, and Juanito's empowerment is almost complete.

By incrementing Juanito's degree of agency as he grows up in the three books discussed so far, Herrera decisively contests the traditional representation of Mexican-origin boys in mainstream children's literature as helpless and clueless simpletons in need of a white savior that could solve their problems, as exemplified by the character Pedro in Marjorie Flack and Karl Larsson's homonymous book titled *Pedro* (see endnote 2). In the same vein, his treatment of geographical and social spaces also contrasts sharply with previous trends in children's literature and entertainment. Spaces in Herrera's books are not charged with pre-established meanings as signifiers for vague or general referents such as "Mexico" or "a Mexican town" that lend themselves to stereotyping. On the contrary, Herrera is painstakingly precise in his geographical mappings, identifying by name towns like Delano, Salinas, Parlier (*Calling*, 23) and El Paso (*Upside Down*, 23) or larger areas like the San Joaquín Valley (*Upside Down*, 17) that are informed by both a personal and a collective history of migration and agricultural work. Even his treatment of spaces associated with leisure and bartering results in profound changes in the depiction of Mexican-origin communities. While in *Pedro*, to continue using this example for contrast, the market is geared toward an economy of subordination that serves the tourist/foreign consumer, Herrera's flea market is an organic community space in which mutual support, bartering, and sharing goods and information strengthen the community rather than making it dependent on the powerful outsider. The flea market offers no crafts and curios for the wealthy foreigner but, rather, reusable goods and shareable knowledge to strengthen the internal bonds that form community.

Herrera's autobiographical trilogy is complemented, as mentioned, by *Imagine*, a book written in a rhythmic, almost choral style by having the text in each page begin with the conjunction "if" and by ending each page with the gentle invitation "imagine." This consistent interplay of anaphora and epistrophe, rather than making the text repetitive, creates a musicality that lends itself very well to a sort of call-and-response reading, of the kind Herrera uses often in his public performances. The word "imagine," printed in a slightly larger font than the others, easily becomes the cue for the young reader's *response* to the text introduced by each of the previous conditional sentences.

Older readers who have that kind of cultural capital might be able to connect Herrera's *Imagine* to Rudyard Kipling's famous poem "If," an earlier example of anaphoric, inspirational literary discourse. But what in Kipling's poem reads as general wisdom, Herrera translates into situated knowledge (the life of farmworkers, linguistic difference, etc.), and Kipling's quasi-Biblical redemptive promise at the end ("Yours is the Earth and everything that's in it / And—which is more—you'll be a Man, my son!," 646) remains an unfulfilled (to be determined by the reader) destiny in Herrera's book: "imagine what you could do" (n. p.). True to his commitment to stimulating the reader's own ideational power, Herrera leaves the ending of his book open as an invitation to his readers to metaphorically write their own books/ lives. As such, *Imagine* is not an inspirational book because it tells the story of someone's success, of a potential role model, but rather because it expresses confidence in everybody's ability to construct their own pathways toward the future.

Beyond the autobiographical, Herrera has also written powerful stories with fictional protagonists to deal more directly with some of the most pressing social issues affecting Mexican-origin people (and others) in the United

Herrera's Illustrated Books for Young Readers **253**

States. A most successful, well-known book in that regard is *Super Cilantro Girl*. In it, Herrera deals with the difficult subject of a parent's deportation. As he often does in his books for children, Herrera contextualizes his somewhat fantastic story in a preface page in which he offers a brief historical understanding of the U.S.-Mexico border. Noting that people could freely cross the border until 1924, as his own family did, Herrera then asks the central question shaping *Super Cilantro Girl*: "What about families kept apart by borders?" (2), a non-rhetorical question that, if anything, has taken even greater currency since *Super Cilantro Girl* was published in 2003.[8]

Though grounded in history and in social trends, Herrera's consideration of family separation at the border takes a figurative shape as the notion of the hero is introduced in the preface: "Maybe, I dreamed—and still dream—there is a way to bring families back together. It will take a heroic effort from someone like *El Santo* or the star of this story, but it can be done" (2). By grounding the hero figure in a Mexican popular culture framework (through the reference to the *lucha libre* fighter Rodolfo Guzmán Huerta, known as El Santo), Herrera seems to suggest from the start that solving this particular problem would require a decisive action from within, not the intervention of the white savior that so commonly appeared in earlier books for children, as discussed throughout this chapter. This is indeed what occurs when Esmeralda Sinfronteras (literally, "Borderless Emerald"), the book's protagonist, undergoes a physical and mental transformation that can be read on a multiplicity of levels.

At the most immediate level, Esmeralda's metamorphosis resonates with the plight of many transnational families in the United States: her mother has been detained at the border on her return trip from a visit to Mexico, which creates understandable anxieties for the girl, even if her grandmother assures her there is nothing to fear, since Esmeralda's mother is a citizen of the United States. For some reason not spelled out in the story, however, the authorities say she needs a green card. The fact that Esmeralda *does fear* for her mother, despite those reassurances, harks back to a history of mistreatment of Mexican individuals and families at the international border with Mexico, as well as to well documented instances in which U.S. citizens of Mexican origin were deported to Mexico despite their legal status (Moloney, 92).

As a result, the story then takes an allegorical turn that straddles the boundaries of the superhero genre of popular culture, allegory, surrealism, and intertextual allusion. Perhaps as a side effect of holding a bunch of cilantro she picked from their garden before talking to her grandmother, Esmeralda's hands (first) and her entire body (eventually) begin turning green progressively. While at school, she also grows taller (shortly after being called Esmeralta—tall Esmer—by a nurse who mispronounces her name), and her hair becomes a green tangle of vine-like hair. Unable to fit in her house anymore, Esmeralda borrows a shawl from her mother, crafts a green mask to cover her face and, as Super Cilantro Girl, flies to the border, where she rescues her mother from a holding cell, and they both fly back home. To stall the border patrol cars and helicopters in their pursuit, Super Cilantro Girl touches a tree that, thanks to her superpowers, creates a growth spurt of nature all around. As a result, the border physically disappears, and their pursuers stop to "smell the green aromas" (26) and enjoy the beauty of their new surroundings. Upon arriving home, Esmeralda falls asleep on top of the roof of her house, only to awake in her own bed the following morning as a regular-sized, brown skinned girl whose mother is waiting for her in the living room with a bouquet of calla lilies. The suggestion that it was all a dream occurs only at the end of the book.[9] Consequently, before getting to its conclusion, the readers must deal both with the traumatic, common real-life occurrence of family separation and with the figurative, surrealistic elements of the tale before reaching the happy ending.

Needless to say, characters who grow to giant size and vegetation that shoots off likewise are not uncommon in traditional children's tales, as in the case of "Jack and the Beanstalk."

What is worth analyzing in this case are the ways in which Herrera characterizes people, objects, and natural elements with polysemic significations that are not only culturally grounded, but also enticing for the reader's imagination to engage in an active process of sense-making and ideation. For example, the fact that the beanstalks in Jack's story are green plays no significant role in that tale, in which the magic power of the seeds and the height of the stalks are the most relevant aspects. But Esmeralda's name, her turning green, and her superhero name are all but crying for the reader's interpretive, culturally-informed powers. From early on, in fact, Herrera plays with words designing colors in an almost pictorial manner, alerting his readers that *green* is in itself a polysemic term: it can describe the color of the permanent resident card and the color of cilantro, but while the latter is natural, endowed with positive symbolism, the former is artificial and ominous to a certain extent (at least in this context of border-crossing enforcement).

Green is also the color of the precious stone emerald, the meaning of the protagonist's name in Spanish; and green is a dominant color in vegetation, which contrasts with the drab "grey walls of wire and steel between the United States and Mexico" (22). But green is also the color of the uniforms of the border patrol.

As the book advances, it appears as if Herrera would want his readers to be able to differentiate positive connotations of "green" from those that are tainted by a threatening undertone. To that end, he resorts to a curious use of adjectivization by repeating the word *green* when he wants to accentuate the more uplifting references to that color. As she worries about her mother, Esmeralda "holds the green-green cilantro leaves, shaped like hearts with wings, and presses them gently between her hands" (6). Later, when Esmeralda transforms herself into Super Cilantro Girl, "she picks a fresh bouquet of cilantro from her mother's garden and whispers to the green-green leaves" (20). And, later, during the pursuit scene described above, this is how she devises a plan to stop the officers: "We'll make everything so green-green, the border will disappear!" (26).[10] The effects are immediate, and vegetation grows beyond control all around the border area. The outcome is both utopic and heartening: the officers stop the chase, they get out of their vehicles to smell "the green aromas" (26), and they even learn some Spanish to proclaim "*¡Qué bonito!*" (26; How pretty!; emphasis in the original). The scene is beautifully captured in one of Honorio Robledo Tapia's best illustrations for this book, a two-page spread with a wealth of natural images in multiple shades of green and other different colors.

In describing the scene of the pursuit and of the bountiful growth of plants and trees touched by Esmeralda, I have refrained (on purpose) from using the word *magical*. While the association of some Latino/a literature with magical realism has become somewhat of a cliché since—at least—the 1990s,[11] a more operative term in this context might be *tropicalization*, a notion that has fascinated Herrera since the 1980s (Ruiz, 130). In "Riffs on Mission District Raza Writers," published in 1998 (five years before *Super Cilantro Girl*), Herrera muses on a tall palm tree in the middle of San Francisco's Mission district (a predominantly Latino/a urban area at the time), and he proposes that "the palm tree is the radical image, the voice and language that heightens and colors the new vision, the new Latino aesthetic mission—a *tropicalization* of our lives. A new poetics of political, cultural, and literary 'greenness' emerges with the works of the Pocho-Che poets, underscored by Víctor Hernández-Cruz's own book, *Tropicalization* [*sic*]" (219; emphasis in the original).

Political, cultural, and literary greenness are indeed at the heart of *Super Cilantro Girl* in which Herrera substitutes the palm tree for the cilantro bunch to extend his reflections on what he terms the "*tropicalization of our lives.*" Applied to the political discourse on the border, tropicalized greenness is summarized in the already quoted exclamation, "We'll make everything so green-green, the border will disappear!" (26). The cultural aspects of greenness, in turn, permeate *Super Cilantro Girl* through the rendering of traditionally-valued practices (gardening, pottery making), through the playful wishing not upon a star but upon a cilantro bunch, as well as through oblique references to Mexican art that (older) readers may be able to appreciate, as in the calla lilies that her mother brings back from Mexico, greatly popularized in the paintings of Diego Rivera in association with Indigeneity and with the female body—two aspects that resonate with Esmeralda's story as well.

As for the concept of "literary greenness," Herrera's contribution is remarkably complex for a children's book, and while in "Riffs on Mission District Raza Writers" the author references Víctor Hernández-Cruz, I propose that *Super Cilantro Girl*'s main intertextual referent is actually Federico García Lorca's poem "Romance sonámbulo" (sleepwalk romance), not only because of its famous opening line, "Verde que te quiero verde" (29; Green, how I want you green)[12] but because of several other elements worth highlighting. Before proceeding, though, it is worth noting that Herrera has acknowledged to have read Lorca since (at least) the late 1980s and early 1990s (Aldama, 138), so that my claim does not sound unnecessarily contrived or farfetched. Moreover, beyond specific points of connection between both texts that I will discuss below, it is far more important to highlight the overall inspirational presence in Herrera's work of Lorca's surrealistic and enigmatic images, as well as Lorca's penchant for singing about the marginalized, darker-skinned gypsies in Spain, donning them with a literary dignity that social practices of exclusion denied them at the time.

Still, there are some specific literary resources shared between "Romance sonámbulo" and *Super Cilantro Girl* that are worth exploring in detail. Esmeralda's turning green can be said to echo the description of the female gypsy character in Lorca's poem: "Con la sombra en la cintura / ella sueña en su baranda, / verde carne, pelo verde, / con ojos de fría plata" (29; With the shade around her waist / she dreams on her balcony / green flesh, her

Herrera's Illustrated Books for Young Readers **257**

hair green, / with eyes of cold silver). Both texts also share a penchant for the rhetorical use of synesthesia, in which sensorial impressions are described by associating stimuli with senses different from the ones that would normally perceive them. In Herrera's book, as mentioned, the border patrol officers stop chasing Super Cilantro Girl "to smell the green aromas" (27), thus donning the color green (normally perceived through sight) with olfactory properties that colors do not have. Lorca used the same rhetorical device in the first half of the line, "Verde viento. Verdes ramas" (29; Green wind. Green branches), perhaps in a slightly more enigmatic manner, but suggesting metonymically that—by blowing around tree branches—the wind could somehow pick up the color of their leaves. A third connection might be seen in the way in which both texts are constructed around the juxtaposition of confining rules and spaces, on the one hand, and of symbols that appear to promise freedom from those restrictive elements, on the other. In Lorca, the presence of Spain's military police (the *guardia civil*) and the somewhat oppressive space of the house where the gypsy woman awaits her lover are constantly challenged by the images of the ship and the horse ("El barco sobre la mar / y el caballo en la montaña"; The ship out on the sea / and the horse on the mountain; 29), both suggestive of unrestricted movement. In *Super Cilantro Girl*, that symbolic function is played by a small bird with a crooked beak that appears at three key moments: first, as Esmeralda awakens from her first night worrying about her mother (and thus, the bird may symbolize the dawning of a new state of affairs or the promise of a future solution—or, as K. E. Bundy suggests, it could be understood as a "nomadic subject that could function as both her guardian in the spirit world and a witness on the material plane" [142]); later, when "Esmeralda flies through the clouds to the border with *her* bird" (21, my emphasis); and, finally, at the end of the book when "a bird with a crooked beak pecks at the glass, then flies high over the green-green cilantro patch, free and *sin fronteras* [borderless]" (31, emphasis in original). As such, Herrera's bird is more explicitly positive than Lorca's horse and ship, and its crooked beak may be symbolic of the downtrodden's empowering capabilities and sense of agency (a theme that Herrera further develops in *Featherless*, as discussed below). This "imperfect" bird is nonetheless resilient and quite able to surmount obstacles and disregard borders and artificial boundaries. More recently, other Chicano/a authors, such as Francisco X. Alarcón (e.g. *Borderless Butterflies*, 2014), have embraced the monarch butterfly as a comparable symbol, based on that insect's migratory routes across borders, but Herrera's clever touch of donning the humble bird with a crooked beak is pregnant with relevant connotations not found in those other images, especially since Chicanos/as have had to confront a history of mischaracterization for lacking wholeness or as suffering from some sort of identitarian decadence, often described as "no longer true Mexicans," "pochos," or "not American enough."

In any case, what interests me of this intertextual connection with Lorca's "Romance sonámbulo" is not so much to speculate on the possibility of specific literary influences but, rather, the ways in which Herrera tropicalizes Lorca's imagery and themes to tell the story of Esmeralda. Whatever Herrera draws from Lorca, he uses it to construct that original poetics of political, cultural and literary 'greenness' that he defined as "a *tropicalization* of our lives" ("Riffs," 219), which may further explain my subtitle "Chicano Children's Literature con Cilantro" as an acknowledgment of such a tropicalization of children's literature. *Super Cilantro Girl* offers young and adult readers a perfect example of how to rethink and rewrite the politics of borders and immigration, cultural affirmation, and literary empowerment by effecting a Latino/a-centric radical rethinking of self, family, community, and power. If *el duende* (fairy or genie) can be said to define Lorca's poetics,[13] *cilantro* accomplishes the same for Herrera's tropicalized vision.[14]

Published in 2004, *Featherless/Desplumado* is also centered on the topics of resilience, empowerment, and agency. Its main protagonist is Tomasito, a young boy born with spina bifida who has recently moved from Mendota, California, to Fresno, also in California. Tomasito feels out of place in his new school, finding it difficult to make friends, especially when everybody appears to be interested only in finding out why he is in a wheelchair. To cheer him up, Tomasito's father brings him a pet bird that serves as a sort of objective correlative in the story: the little bird is featherless and it has a misshapen leg. As Tomasito's father explains, "He was born a little different, like you were" (4). As the book progresses, Tomasito moves from a position of mild self-hatred and despair through a process that involves making a friend (Marlena), getting into the school soccer team (the Fresno Flyers) as a substitute player, and realizing that he can be both different from the other children and part of a team with them. The story ends after Tomasito scores a header and his team wins a soccer game. As a member of the Fresno Flyers, Tomasito takes a hint from Marlena's words of encouragement (full of easy-to-decode symbolism), and he understands that his wheelchair can be the wings that he needs to "fly" as a Flyer, and that his head work can make him a valuable team player. Back home, Tomasito shares the newly gained insights with both his pet bird and the readers: "You can be a flyer too, Desplumado, / There is more than one way to fly!" (30).

In addition to these positive messages about the differently abled, without a doubt the most important aspect of this book, *Featherless* is also worth discussing in light of some of the main characteristics of Herrera's children's books poetics. Though this story is not autobiographical, it does share with Herrera's trilogy a preference for geographical precision rather than relying on larger markers of place, nation, or even ethnicity (e.g. Mexico, Aztlán, and the like). Through references to Fresno and Mendota, and by noting that Tomasito's father works at the Pinedale Motel, Herrera situates this story in a meaningful spatial context which resonates with Chicano/a and Latino/a social history (even if the town names may not be familiar to readers outside of the San Joaquín Valley) while remaining story-specific, not metonymically apt to construct any kind of broader narratives.

In *Featherless*, moreover, Herrera continues to shun the tradition of the white savior (prolonged in both literature and film until the present),[15] opting instead to underscore the notions of agency, problem solving, and community empowerment. Tomasito's father, his friend Marlena, and Coach Gordolobo—each of them in their own ways—are enablers to Tomasito's adaptation success story, but they do not solve his problems for him. Partly for that reason, Herrera also offers an important image of caring parenthood and non-toxic masculinity by making Tomasito's father his main caretaker and advisor in a most gentle, non-authoritarian or condescending manner.[16]

Tomasito's accomplishments are also kept at a reasonable scale in the story. There are no Hollywood-like miracles allowing him to walk at the end, as there are no significant changes in his condition. What the story chronicles is a process of understanding that different people are differently abled and, thus, Tomasito's main achievement is not joining the team or scoring a goal but, rather, overcoming a state of mind that made him see his body in a negative way.

Needless to say, readers may be able to extrapolate that lesson to other contexts that the story does not address (language barriers, class disadvantages, and the like), thus adapting *Featherless* to personal circumstances. But as one of the early Latino/a children's books on disability, *Featherless* remains a milestone in Herrera's career and in Latino/a children's literature.

The final book to be discussed in this chapter can also be read as a Chicano/a-centric intervention or commentary on broader social and environmental issues. Though perhaps not his most well-known children's book, *Coralito's Bay* nonetheless embodies much of the essence of Herrera's approach to poetic storytelling for young readers. The book centers on an asthmatic boy named Coralito, as he embarks on a dream-induced adventure through the Monterey Bay National Marine Sanctuary.[17] During his dream journey, as well as during the opening and closing frames of the story (in which Coralito interacts with his parents while awake) Herrera paints a vivid, thought-provoking picture of the physical, geographical, and mental environment of Coralito, well complemented by Lena Shiffman's detailed illustrations.

One of the signature elements of Herrera's poetic style present in *Coralito's Bay* involves the playful cultural reterritorialization achieved by donning comparisons with referents directly associated with Chicano/a everyday reality and language. As Coralito dreams that he travels under the ocean in a submarine troca (the Chicano/a linguistic adaptation of the word *truck*), the levers that control the vessel are said to be churros (6), and a cluster of algae seen outside are described as looking like enchilada sauce (22); corals, in turn, are compared to red nopales (22; an edible cactus). By bringing external reality and nature literally home, Herrera not only delimits the ideal reader for the book (one that can understand and relish these words and comparisons), but he also effects a decisive control of perspective and point of view. He grounds the cognitive ability to comprehend and describe reality on a distinct Chicano/a epistemological knowledge base, one that is not separated from the space of home and family but, rather, infused and inspired by those funds of knowledge that Chicano/a children may acquire as they interact with domestic rituals and practices.[18]

To a certain extent, strategies like this have been a staple in children's entertainment. For example, in the 1940s films that Disney made under the auspices of the Good Neighbor policy about Latin America, a South American human and physical landscape that the studio perceived as utterly foreign to the United States viewer was rendered understandable by comparing that external reality to home-based referents. In that manner, the Argentinean gaucho was described as a South American cowboy, and Brazil's carnival was interpreted for the Disney audiences as a mixture of Mardi Gras in New Orleans and New Year's Eve celebrations in New York.

But there are key differences between Herrera's use of this strategy and the Disney approach that are worth highlighting. The Disney films reified and simplified culture and cultural practices in order to render them familiar, and they did so by turning the Other into an object of contemplation and analysis, thus maintaining a hierarchical control of the gaze. Herrera, on the other hand, literally places the perennial Other in the driver's seat, allowing him to interpret domestic (not foreign) realities and landscapes through analogical thinking that validates and celebrates culture. By thus controlling the gaze, Coralito's cognitive processes turn analogical thinking and comparison into a counterhegemonic strategy.

Moreover, once the strategy has been sufficiently employed so as to make the reader comfortable with it (thus lending itself to the reader's own additional ideation or to activities in which a young reader may be encouraged by an adult to come up with similar comparisons based on the text and/or the illustrations), Herrera gives it an additional twist by invoking legends and tales with which many Chicano/a children can be expected to be familiar, such as the story of La Llorona: "'What's that? *La Llorona* has come to get me? The Weeping Woman Ghost?' It was a hydromedusa, a see-through jelly head in the shape of a misty parachute with stringy tentacles and red eye-spots that dangle in the dark" (30).

The rhetorical power of this move might be best perceived by analyzing how the appearance of the hydromedusa results in a double imagistic process, supplemented by a factual description of the creature. All in all, in just three lines of text, Herrera offers young readers a sampling of three discursive strategies and of what they contribute to sense-making and other cognitive processes. Working backwards from the end of the quote, we encounter the kind of referential discourse most typical of scientific description ("with stringy tentacles and red eye-spots that dangle in the dark"), a metaphorical, non-culturally-grounded analogical discourse ("in the shape of a misty parachute"), and the mythopoethical discourse of folk beliefs ("What's that? *La Llorona* has come to get me?"). Though practical for the analysis, it should be apparent that reversing the order of those discursive modalities and reading the quote backwards make it lose most of its poetic power, even though the rearranged text starts with factual perception and then moves on to non-factual cognition. What makes the quoted text so impressive in its original order is that it moves the reader from the most deeply-felt, visceral reaction (connected to the ancestral beliefs learned from the community) to an intermediate state in which Coralito's mind is still working by analogy (but no longer through ancestral culture), and finally to a matter-of-fact contemplation of the physical appearance of the creature. In doing so, Herrera refuses to privilege scientific discourse (perhaps even questioning its alleged detachment and neutrality), giving primacy instead to poetic (imagistic) and culturally-based epistemes.

A comparable strategy serves Herrera to delve into serious environmental and social matters that, while they may appear peripheral to some readers, are nonetheless central to the story of Coralito as a geographically-grounded, socially-situated tale. Upon encountering a blue whale, for example, Coralito compares the whale's migratory patterns to his own: "I migrate too, from crop to crop, just like you" (20). Referring, most likely, to an experience lived in the past (Coralito's mother works at a restaurant in the present of the story) or to a practice to which the family returns in a cyclical manner, Coralito's words bring reality home, implicitly stressing how language and cognition are always culturally and socially grounded. A descriptive, scientific assertion such as "blue whales are a migratory species" would not have the same affective or even conceptual meaning for an upper-class child as it would for the child of migrant, farm working parents. Seemingly aware of the difference, the Monterey Bay National Marine Sanctuary made the connection explicit on the Dedication page of the book: "Dedicated to the many migrant families living on the central coast of California.—MBNMS" (3).

Some readers may be puzzled by this dedication, initially unable to find what connects migrant families to a marine sanctuary. Quite subtly, but quite effectively, Herrera supplies a first clue on pages twenty-four through twenty-seven. In those pages, Coralito encounters a wave of dark water "traveling out from the land" (24), which he is quick to interpret thanks to those home-based funds of knowledge that shape his cognitive abilities:

> Coralito knew the black water was from polluted storm water being flushed from city streets and the fields where his parents worked. "*Es el aceite*, it's the oil from cars, and the tired soil from farm lands," his father had said. "It can run into the ocean and cause harm," mamá had told him. (27)

The powerful ecological and conservationist message implicit in this quote is further expanded when Coralito wakes up hungry from his dream and is offered a tostada with ceviche: "Sea food tostadas? Yes, I am hungry mamá.

But, we must not eat too many sea animals! We must not harm them by polluting our waters!" (33).

Still, the connection between the book's ecocritical message and the migrant families to which it is dedicated may require additional scrutiny. The reader knows from the beginning of the story that Coralito suffers from asthma (4). Readers from migrant families and those otherwise informed about that type of lifestyle would know that most migrant families in California have followed the crops at one time or another, as Coralito himself suggests is the case with his own family on page twenty. The mention of "the tired soil from farm lands" (24) all but spells out the environmental and human-health consequences of the pervasive use of pesticides in California's agricultural fields. As Hernández, Parrón, and Alarcón explain in "Pesticides and Asthma," "pesticide aerosols or gases, like other respiratory irritants, can lead to asthma through interaction with functional irritant receptors in the airway and promoting neurogenic inflammation" (90). In that light, Coralito's efforts to prevent the black water from reaching the depths of the ocean (27) symbolically act to protect marine life from the ills that have affected him personally. This is reinforced by the analogy between the coral's branches and the human lungs when Coralito addresses the ocean creature:

"Red nopales? Red cactus? Wait! That's coral. Pink and purple. Looks like short forests, like tender lungs—like mine!" The hydrocoral branches were crusty, with little holes where tiny polyps lived. They were open, almost like saying, "Thanks for coming, Coralito. *Gracias.*" Coralito opened his arms too. "My name is Coralito, like you! I want my lungs to say thanks too. But there is too much itchy dust in the air," Coralito said to his coral friends growing on the rocky reefs. "Is there itchy dust in the waters too?" he asked. (24)

Coralito's encounter with the blue whale, therefore, takes on an added meaning as the migrant of the oceans and the migrant of the land become aware of the interconnectedness of their plight and of the need to preserve the ecological balance. Without making this association, the message in the final lines of the book might sound contrived or farfetched, but once the reader connects the dots it becomes a logical ending to the story: "Yes, mamá. The *santuario* is out there. And it is in here too. El *santuario* is inside all of us—an ocean of miracles and *amor*" (34).

Taken as a whole, Juan Felipe Herrera's illustrated books for children constitute a significant creative body whose literary and social value rests on a number of parameters explored throughout this chapter. At a historical juncture in which the very notion of Latino/a childhood underwent a radical redefinition, as explored in endnote 8, his books provide a set of uplifting narratives for young readers with which they can negotiate complicated personal and societal issues as they reflect on Herrera's characters and on their experiences. This does not mean that Herrera's books provide a sugarcoated representation of the Chicano/a experience; on the contrary, what the author offers his young readers is a nuanced depiction of complex situations that require his characters to empower themselves through personal transformation, social engagement, and an acute sense of agency, which contrasts with earlier characterizations of Mexican-origin children in literature.

In addition, Juan Felipe Herrera's illustrated books for children stand out for their treatment of language and imagery in a playful, inspirational manner. Metaphors, similes, puns, and a multitude of other rhetorical and discursive figures appear in these books to share with their readers the joyful realization that, much as one's life does not have to be socially predetermined, neither is language reduced to its denotative, referential nature. By constantly stimulating the imagination of his young readers, Herrera not only tells stories in his books, but he also converts them into a poetic laboratory in which children can learn how words and discourse shape (rather than just describe) the world.

## Notes

1. For additional details on literature about Mexicans and Chicanos/as during that period, see Martín-Rodríguez "Chicano/a Children's Literature," especially the section "*A Burro of One's Own*: Mexican and Mexican American Children in Anglo American and Mainstream Literature" (19–24).

2. For the reader unfamiliar with those earlier books, a quick summary of Marjorie Flack and Karl Larsson's *Pedro*, will serve to better appreciate this difference. The book summary on the inner flap of *Pedro*'s first edition summarizes plot and setting as follows: "It was on a gay fiesta day when the whole family came to the city from the small village to sell their pottery in the market place, that Pedro met the rich señorita and a new life began for this little Mexican boy" (n. p.). The book itself identifies the village as Naranja, "a sleepy, quiet little place" (13), and the city as Taxco. Pedro is promised a few pesos of his own if sales go well, and he considers the possibility of buying a burro (in Spanish in the book)

with the money (12). At the market, both the text and Larsson's illustrations make it clear that the wares are traditional crafts intended for American tourist buyers. Pedro sells a jug to "a beautiful lady," an American residing in Taxco (24). Eventually, the lady hires him for a few days, during which an awestruck Pedro marvels at such things as lamps and showers, thinking them miraculous. Once he takes a shower, he looks "like a different boy . . . one worthy to be a mozo to the beautiful señorita!" (53). After saving an American boy from being hurt by a bull at a *charreada*, Pedro is offered an informal scholarship to go to school with that boy and live part of the year in Taxco with the American family. Since this book deals with family, poverty, and schooling, I believe it serves as a perfect point of comparison with Herrera's autobiographical books, and I will make additional references to it in the body of this chapter.

3.  Of these titles, *Imagine* and *Imagina* are the only ones that were published as two separate books, rather than as an en-face bilingual book, as is the case with the others.

4.  Even in the field of Chicano/a children's literature, Gloria E. Anzaldúa's *Friends from the Other Side* could serve as an example in that regard.

5.  As conceptualized by T. Ybarra-Frausto, the term "rasquache" has come to signify an alternative aesthetic rooted in Chicano/a creativity, often predicated in making do with whatever materials are available. See Ybarra-Frausto, *passim*.

6.  Walter J. Ong coined the term "secondary orality" to differentiate the technological oral/aural (television, film, the radio and other similar media) from the traditional oral culture which entails a set of norms and values, as well as an agonistic participative atmosphere that secondary orality no longer possesses (108).

7.  Bibliotherapy refers to "the use of any kind of literature by a skilled adult or other interested person in an effort to normalize a child's grief reactions to loss, support constructive coping, reduce feelings of isolation, and reinforce creativity and problem solving" (Berns 234). According to Gomm, the benefits of "using a bibliotherapeutic approach to support immigrant children include providing a safe distance for children to discuss their challenges, reducing isolation [. . .] and fostering expression and conversation" (6).

8.  The Trump presidency (2017–2021) implemented severe family-separation policies which resulted in large numbers of children detained and kept in cages in detention centers near the U.S.-Mexico border while their parents and/or other relatives were deported. On October 21, 2020, *The New York Times* reported that the parents of 545 children separated at the border could not be found (Dickerson).

9.  For an intertextual analysis of this dream state through the lens of Lewis Carroll, see Bundy, 137–138. As Bundy effectively argues in connection with *Super Cilantro Girl*, "Rather than the dismissive and clichéd, 'It was all just a dream,' the seemingly impossible performance of heroism or magic in the dream state can leak into a material reality and assert agency for children living in a world dictated by adults" (138).

10. On that same page, the adjectivization technique is applied to the color brown as well when Esmeralda "touches a brown-brown tree" (26), making it grow beyond control.
11. For more on how the U. S. book industry has used this label in connection with Latino/a literature, see Martín-Rodríguez, *Life*, chapter 4.
12. All Lorca translations (except for the title of the poem, which he leaves in Spanish) are by William Bryant Logan, available at https://poets.org/poem/romance-sonambulo.
13. A difficult term to describe precisely, Lorca borrowed the word "duende" from the world of *flamenco* music, in which it designates authenticity and inspiration. In an essay on the concept, Lorca defined "duende" as "the spirit of the earth" ("Play and Theory of Duende," 57–58), which resonates quite aptly with the thematics of *Super Cilantro Girl*.
14. Herrera's engagement with the poetic symbolism of cilantro continued immediately after *Super Cilantro Girl* with the editing of the 1995 anthology "Cilantro Facials." Though the anthology was not published as such, there are several manuscripts of it preserved in private collections and in Herrera's archives at Stanford University. Those archives also contain materials such as "Cilantro Man," presented as a show by Teatro Zapata in 1995.
15. As seen, for example in the 2015 film *McFarland, USA*, directed by Niki Caro and also set in California's Central Valley.
16. The presence of strong father figures in several of Herrera's illustrated books sharply contrasts with the critical interest that the figure of the absent father in Herrera's *Downtown Boy* has attracted. Serrato first reflected on the "examples of masculinity" and the impact that images of fathers might have on young Chicano readers (154–155) from a Critical Masculinity Studies point of view, and Rodríguez, more recently, sees the topic as "an opportunity to also understand the systemic oppressions that make it difficult for fathers to parent" (92).
17. This book was commissioned by the Monterey Bay Museum (private email from the author, dated January 22, 2021).
18. The term "funds of knowledge" was popularized by Norma González, Luis C. Moll, and Cathy Amanti, in their edited 2005 book of that title. Their "Preface" defines the term as follows: "The concept of *funds of knowledge* [. . .] is based on a simple premise: People are competent, they have knowledge, and their life experiences have given them that knowledge" (n.p.).

## Works Cited

Aldama, Frederick Luis. "Francisco X. Alarcón." In *Spilling the Beans on Chicanolandia: Conversations with Writers and Artists*, 37–51. Austin: University of Texas Press, 2006.

Anzaldúa, Gloria E. *Friends from the Other Side/Amigos del otro lado*. San Francisco, Calif.: Children's Book Press, 1993.

Berns, Carol F. "Bibliotherapy: Using Books to Help Bereaved Children." *Omega: Journal of Death & Dying*, 48, no. 4 (2004): 321–36.

Bundy, Katherine Elizabeth. "Was It All a Dream? Chicana/o Children and Mestiza Consciousness in *Super Cilantro Girl* (2003) and 'Tata's Gift' (2014)." In *Voices of Resistance: Interdisciplinary Approaches to Chican@ Children's Literature*, edited by Laura Alamillo, Larissa M. Mercado-López, and Cristina Herrera, 151–62. Lanham, Md.: Rowman and Littlefield, 2017.

Burton, Julianne. "Don (Juanito) Duck and the Imperial-Patriarchal Unconscious: Disney Studios, the Good Neighbor Policy, and the Packaging of Latin America." In *Nationalisms and Sexualities*, edited by Andrew Parker, Mary Russo, Doris Sommer, and Patricia Yaeger, 21–41. New York: Routledge, 1992.

Cantú, Norma Elia. *Canícula: Snapshots of a Girlhood en la Frontera*. Albuquerque: University of New Mexico Press, 1995.

Caro, Niki, dir. *McFarland, USA* (film). Walt Disney Pictures-Mayhem Pictures, 2015.

"Children's Book Press History." www.leeandlow.com/imprints/children-s-book -press/articles/children-s-book-press-history. Accessed 26 March 2021.

Dickerson, Caitlin. "Parents of 545 Children Separated at the Border Cannot Be Found." *The New York Times*, October 21, 2020, www.nytimes.com/2020/10/21/ us/migrant-children-separated.html.

Ferguson, Norman, dir. *Three Caballeros, The* (film). Walt Disney Pictures, 1944.

Flack, Marjorie, and Karl Larsson. *Pedro*. New York: Macmillan, 1940.

García Lorca, Federico. "Play and Theory of Duende." Translated by Christopher Maurer. In *In Search of Duende*, 56–72. New York: New Directions, 2010.

García Lorca, Federico. "Romance sonámbulo." *Romancero gitano (1924–1927)*. 8th ed. Madrid: Espasa-Calpe, 1937.

Gomm, Robert J. "Content Analysis of 50 Picture Books for Latino Immigrant Children: Implications for Supportive Bibliotherapy." Educational Specialist in School Psychology Thesis, Brigham Young University, 2012.

González, Norma, Luis C. Moll, and Cathy Amanti, eds. *Funds of Knowledge: Theorizing Practices in Households, Communities, and Classrooms*. Mahwah, N.J.: Lawrence Earlbaum Associates, 2005.

Hernández, Antonio F., Tesifón Parrón, and Raquel Alarcón. "Pesticides and Asthma." *Current Opinion in Allergy and Clinical Immunology* 11, no. 2 (2011): 90–96.

Herrera, Juan Felipe. *Calling the Doves/El canto de las palomas*. San Francisco, Calif.: Children's Book Press, 1995.

Herrera, Juan Felipe. *Coralito's Bay/Bahía de coralito*. Monterey, CA: Monterey Bay Sanctuary Foundation, 2004.

Herrera, Juan Felipe. *Downtown Boy*. New York: Scholastic Press, 2005.

Herrera, Juan Felipe. *Featherless/Desplumado*. New York: Children's Book Press, 2004.

Herrera, Juan Felipe. *Grandma and Me at the Flea/Los meros meros remateros*. San Francisco, Calif.: Children's Book Press, 2002.

Herrera, Juan Felipe. *Imagina*. Somerville, Mass.: Candlewick Press, 2020.

Herrera, Juan Felipe. *Imagine*. Somerville, Mass.: Candlewick Press, 2018.

Herrera, Juan Felipe. "Riffs on Mission District Raza Writers." *Reclaiming San Francisco: History, Politics, Culture: A City Lights Anthology*, edited by James Brook, 217–230. San Francisco, Calif.: City Lights Books, 1998.

Herrera, Juan Felipe. *Super Cilantro Girl/La superniña del cilantro*. San Francisco, Calif.: Children's Book Press, 2003.

Herrera, Juan Felipe. *The Upside Down Boy/El niño de cabeza*. San Francisco, Calif.: Children's Book Press, 2000.

Kipling, Rudyard. "If." In *Rudyard Kipling's Verse: Inclusive Edition*. N.p.: Doubleday, Page & Co., 1919.

Martín-Rodríguez, Manuel M. "Chicano/a Children's Literature: A *Transaztlantic* Reader's History." *Journal of American Studies of Turkey*, no. 23 (2006): 15–35.

Martín-Rodríguez, Manuel M. *Life in Search of Readers: Reading (in) Chicano/a Literature*. Albuquerque: University of New Mexico Press, 2003.

Moloney, Deirdre M. *National Insecurities: Immigrants and U. S. Deportation Policy Since 1882*. Chapel Hill: University of North Carolina Press, 2012.

Ong, Walter J. *Orality and Literacy: The Technologizing of the Word*. London: Methuen, 1982.

Peña, Silvia C. "Chicano Culture and Children's Literature." In *Understanding the Chicano Experience Through Literature*, 28–37. Houston: Mexican American Studies, 1981.

Reséndez, Gerald A. "Chicano Children's Literature." In *Chicano Literature: A Reference Guide*, edited by Julio A. Martínez, and Francisco A. Lomelí, 107–21. Westport, Conn.: Greenwood Press, 1985.

Rodríguez, Sonia Alejandra. "'You Wanna Be a Chump/or a Champ?': Constructions of Masculinity, Absent Fathers, and Conocimiento in Juan Felipe Herrera's *Downtown Boy*." In *Voices of Resistance: Interdisciplinary Approaches to Chican@ Children's Literature*, edited by Laura Alamillo, Larissa M. Mercado-López, and Cristina Herrera, 91–104. Lanham, Md.: Rowman and Littlefield, 2017.

Ruiz, Tony. "Juan Felipe Herrera: 'Visión Tropical' in San Francisco's Mission District." *CEA Critic* 75 no. 2 (2013): 129–141.

Serrato, Phillip. "A Portrait of the Artist as a Muchachito: Juan Felipe Herrera's *Downtown Boy* as a Poetic Springboard into Critical Masculinity Studies." In *Voices of Resistance: Interdisciplinary Approaches to Chican@ Children's Literature*, edited by Laura Alamillo, Larissa M. Mercado-López, and Cristina Herrera, 61–76. Lanham, Md.: Rowman and Littlefield, 2017.

Ybarra-Frausto, Tomás. "Rasquachismo: A Chicano Sensibility." In *Chicano Art: Resistance and Affirmation, 1965–1985*, edited by Teresa McKenna, Yvonne Yarbro-Bejarano, and Richard Griswold del Castillo, 155–62. Los Angeles, Calif.: Wright Art Gallery, 1991.

## CHAPTER 12

# Girlhood and Writing as Sustenance in Juan Felipe Herrera's *Cinnamon Girl: Letters Found Inside a Cereal Box*

TREVOR BOFFONE AND CRISTINA HERRERA

In his foreword to the edited volume, *Voices of Resistance: Interdisciplinary Approaches to Chican@ Children's Literature*, Juan Felipe Herrera poses critical and necessary questions to readers and scholars about the visionary, often unacknowledged, depth of Chicano/a children's and young adult literature:

> How does the text, the actual words, the images blurring into phrase, and the gestures of the major characters inhabiting the books—how do they say things, mean things in and of themselves, and how are they (in some odd way) loosely threaded to all of us, pulling in, for, out, and against the larger grid of power? And—how do we speak of the writing about ourselves? (viii)

Herrera's rich postulations invoke the critical power of Chicano/a literature for young people, the way it demands from its readers, children and adults alike, a new way, a better way, of existing and being in this imperfect world. This chapter addresses the significance of this better way of existing through an analysis of his understudied verse novel, *Cinnamon Girl: Letters Found Inside a Cereal Box*. This central tenet found in Herrera's work, that is, an insistence on the power of art and love to heal a community's spirit, is crucial to our understanding of how this text deftly captures a young Latina's growth as she confronts the traumatic impact of living in a pre- and post-9/11 world.

With a career spanning over forty years, Juan Felipe Herrera is one of the most gifted writers of our generation. His poetry, stories, and texts for young audiences are known for their lyrical and often experimental, even whimsical, style. Recognized as the U.S. Poet Laureate (2015–17) and one of the most highly regarded Chicano poetic voices, Herrera should equally be known for being a prolific writer of children's and young adult literature. Yet, as Chicano/a and Latino/a children's literature scholars have noted, literature for youth readers has seldom been considered a "serious" endeavor, even when published by highly regarded writers, including Herrera, or when these works tackle significant themes such as gender, trauma, power, migration, or race.[1] Herrera's young adult literature, in particular, demonstrates the necessity of privileging the voices of youth, empowering them to articulate the pains of belonging, trauma, identity, and loss, especially when young people's voices are so often marginalized or simply ignored.

One such young adult work is Herrera's novel in verse, *Cinnamon Girl: Letters Found Inside a Cereal Box* (2005), a text that has received surprisingly little critical attention despite being one of the few Latino/a texts (and even fewer young adult texts) that uses the 9/11 timeframe as a thematic backdrop. Taking place in the months, days, and weeks prior to September 11, 2001, as well as in the aftermath of that national tragedy, Yolanda, also known as Canela/Cinnamon Girl (hereinafter referred to as Canela), explores issues such as belonging, mourning, and the meaning of resilience when she learns her beloved Uncle DJ is severely injured in the World Trade Center attack. With this traumatic event hitting close to home, Yolanda must make sense of this new environment of tragedy, mourning, and loss. As an adolescent Puerto Rican girl who must figure out what it means to come of age during a time that would eventually become known simply as "9/11," Herrera's novel demonstrates how young adult literature is an important platform in which to explore this period of time that is seldom viewed from the perspective of young people. In literature scholar Marta Caminero-Santangelo's examination of literary and journalistic accounts of undocumented border crossing, "Narrating the Non-Nation: Literary Journalism and 'Illegal' Border Crossings," she notes that "in the wake of 9/11, titles linking immigration to threats to America's national security and even survival have proliferated" (158). Herrera's *Cinnamon Girl*, like the texts examined by Caminero-Santangelo, shares a concern with the 9/11 and post-9/11 context of hyper surveillance, policing, and racialization of Brown people in a landscape reeling from the traumas of a terrorist attack.[2] However, *Cinnamon Girl's* classification as a young adult text challenges our understanding of what it means to live within the urban setting of New York City, the major site of the 9/11 attack, most notably through the text's narrative structure as a verse novel but also by its use of a young female, Latina voice.

This chapter addresses such concerns raised above through an analysis of Herrera's young adult novel, *Cinnamon Girl: Letters Found Inside a Cereal Box*, which utilizes a young female protagonist voice in a post-9/11 world and features Herrera's signature genre-pushing elements, such as verse and epistolary formats. While Herrera is known for his explorations of genre, we examine *Cinnamon Girl* within a context of experimental forms in Latino/a letters, especially its occurrence within Latino/a young adult literature. To do this, we argue that the novel positions the protagonist as a creator and holder of knowledge who uses writing as her tool to convey the traumas of her uncle's injury in the World Trade Center attack and her subsequent feelings of loss, confusion, and displacement. In this way, writing enables the protagonist to communicate with her injured uncle and to convey the traumas of living in the aftermath of the 9/11 terrorist attack. As such, although her writing is an intimate act shared between herself and her uncle, it speaks to the larger anxieties that the New York Latino community faces in times of crisis. With this chapter, we also underscore the need for scholars to consider the inclusion of children's and young adult literature as legitimate sites of inquiry into discussions of race, power, belonging, trauma, and gender. Importantly, we highlight Herrera's innovative contributions to the young adult literature canon, Canela's own counter narrative that refuses invisibility as a speaking subject who chronicles what it means to come of age after 9/11.

## Genre and Young Adult Literature

While Herrera is known for his explorations of genre, we examine *Cinnamon Girl* within a context of experimental forms in Latino/a letters, especially its occurrence within Latino/a young adult literature. Latino/a young adult (YA) literature, that is, literature that is written for and marketed to teenagers and young adults roughly between the ages of thirteen and nineteen, has grown as a vibrant body of work with a great deal of texts written in verse format, most notably by important Latino/a writers, such as Elizabeth Acevedo, Margarita Engle, and David Bowles, for example. We note the importance of Herrera's use of a common form in children's and young adult literature, the verse narrative, seen, for example, in his well-known text for young readers, *Downtown Boy*, published the same year as *Cinnamon Girl*. Yet, significantly, *Cinnamon Girl* has not garnered nearly as much scholarly attention as *Downtown Boy*, though the texts share much in common, namely their use of the verse structure and their thematic concerns with gender, although to be clear, one text is narrated by a young Chicano while the other speaker is a Puerto Rican teenage girl.[3] With these texts, Herrera is one of the many Latino children's and young adult writers who utilize the verse form to document trauma, pain, and the confusing period of life known as adolescence. As children's literature Mike Cadden explains, verse novels have their origin in epic tales that "combine poetic convention with story" ("Rhetorical Technique," 130). Because verse novels resist rigid generic categories, blurring the lines between poetry and prose, Herrera's frequent use of this genre is not surprising, given that adolescence is itself a complicated period of life that is often considered to be somewhere between childhood and adulthood. The "inbetweenness" of verse novels (should we read them as poetry? as novels?) directly connects to the inbetweenness of young adulthood (are young adults really adults? are they children? who decides?).

In her analysis of Chicana young adult (YA) writer Guadalupe García McCall's Pura Belpré Award-winning verse novel, *Under the Mesquite* (2011), Cristina Herrera maintains that the protagonist's "voice, hardships, and struggles are elevated through García McCall's employment of this genre that privileges the protagonist's point of view as a budding writer who struggles to make a place for herself" (196), not unlike Juan Felipe Herrera's protagonist in *Cinnamon Girl*, who comes of age during a particularly dark period in American history. "The verse novel form, which itself defies generic classifications, is the ideal structure for a text that narrates a young Tejana's emerging voice," she adds, alluding to the narrative intimacy that the verse form creates (C. Herrera, 203). As a genre that utilizes both novelistic and poetic elements, texts like *Cinnamon Girl* deliberately blur the boundaries between prose and verse to provide added nuances to speech and voice patterns, encouraging readers to say the words aloud, much as we would read a poem. In one moment early in the text, for instance, Canela examines herself in the mirror and attempts to "wiggle / my red plumpy tongue" (30), inviting readers to do the same. As readers, we speak alongside Canela, the verse structure encouraging a beautiful symmetry between speaker (Canela) and reader (us) that may be unavailable to us in traditional prose novels.

Herrera's wide use of the verse novel raises several key questions; indeed, we must also ask why the verse form is so common in Latino/a YA literature. In addition to McCall's *Under the Mesquite* and Herrera's works, Elizabeth Acevedo's debut novel, *The Poet X* (2018) as well as her most recent text, *Clap When You Land* (2020), are written in verse. Why verse? What can novels in verse do that non-verse novels cannot? Similar to poetry, which can structurally be fragmented, loose, and in free form, verse novels also highlight the important relationship between form and content. Pieces are missing and not always linear. Much like Canela's experience, which appears fragmented and unusual, due to the traumas of living and surviving a catastrophic event, the reader must piece together the days and months leading to 9/11 and Uncle DJ's subsequent recovery. According to Cadden, the verse structure centers "a focus on the rhythms of the character's spoken voice that does ask the reader to 'hear' the speaker" ("The Verse Novel," 22). As we read a verse text aloud, the combination of our own voice speaking the words forces us to listen to the nuances, rhyme patterns, tone, and speed of the text, allowing us to almost literally hear the protagonist. That is, there is an "orality" component to merge reading and sound. By *hearing* the protagonist, the writer establishes a more intimate relationship between reader and narrator/protagonist, merging the sound of our voice reading the text aloud with the words that are intended to be spoken by the protagonist. Children's literature scholar, Karen Coats, further insists that when we examine verse novels, we owe particular attention to structure: "metaphor and poetic form merit reconsideration in light of special issues related to the embodiment of the implied audience of middle grade (MG) and young adult (YA) verse narratives" (147). She further elaborates on why verse novels are a fitting form used by writers of youth literature:

> In the process of creating a setting and a character or set of characters, the poetry in a MG or YA verse novel often works to directly allegorize embodiment, not through a verbal metaphor that requires interpretation or even through a direct expression of a psychological state or physical action. Instead, embodied experience is given visual form through spatial arrange-

ment, or expressed sonically through distinctive rhythms, with font styles acting as stage directions for oral interpretation. (147–48)

Throughout *Cinnamon Girl*, we see Coats' argument bear out, namely in how Herrera effectively connects form to Canela's own embodiment and conflicted thoughts, for example, in a moment in the text when Canela is chased off by school bullies:

Then gray smoke no sound as
I fall.

(142)

The gray smoke, an allusion to both the Ground Zero dust particles that sicken her uncle and kill countless other victims, is projected onto Canela's body as she, too, falls. The ashes that inevitably form after smoke are visualized in Herrera's one-word lines, and we likewise see the stacked lines practically resembling a standing body who then falls to the ground. In the case of *Cinnamon Girl*, the verse structure makes starkly evident the fragmentation of Canela's voice as she struggles to speak aloud and articulate her anguish. Given that "the most prominent feature of the verse novel is voice" (Alexander, 282), the complexities of coming of age during 9/11 are more powerfully conveyed through this form. Although speaking of *Downtown Boy*, Phillip Serrato's assessment may equally apply to *Cinnamon Girl* because an experimental form that is "Written in a freer form of verse" allows "words—and, thus, thoughts and emotions—[to] uninhibitedly spill over the page" (72). Words themselves may appear to resemble the emotions they are conveying, with elements like unusual line breaks, fused sentences, and shortened stanzas that communicate disjuncture, confusion, and chaos. The verse form, then, is especially useful for articulating the traumas of profound loss, and it is not surprising that in the YA novels referenced above, the protagonists in them suffer from the death of family members, self-doubt, and have a desire to give voice to the overwhelming emotions that result from loss.

## What's Inside the Cereal Box: Writing as Nourishment

In addition to its relationship to a growing body of Latino/a young adult novels in verse, *Cinnamon Girl* falls within a tradition of Latino/a writers writing about young girls coming-of-age. Germinal works such as Sandra Cisneros' *The House on Mango Street* (1984), Josefina López's *Real Women Have Curves* (1990), Michele Serros' *Chicana Falsa* (1993), Jasminne Mendez's *Island of Dreams* (2013), Isabel Quintero's *Gabi, A Girl in Pieces* (2014), and Erika L. Sánchez's *I Am Not Your Perfect Mexican Daughter* (2017), to name a few, situate young Latinas as writers. And, most pertinent to this chapter, these texts explicitly represent young Latinas as writers. As a result, these women quite literally write themselves into the narrative, essentially pushing against rigid notions of girlhood that have been inflicted upon them by patriarchal forces. Moreover, these writers also challenge rigid notions of genre. As Gloria Anzaldúa writes, Latino/a cultural norms, specifically the Chicano/a community, "expect women to show greater acceptance of and commitment to, the value system than men. [. . .] If a woman rebels, she is a *mujer mala*. If a woman doesn't renounce herself in favor of the male, she is selfish. If a woman remains a virgin until she marries, she is a woman" (17). This is precisely the reality that the protagonists of the aforementioned texts push against and defy. Writing, therefore, is just one tool that Latina girls can deploy to challenge the cultural expectations that these young women face.

Writing has often been a source of empowerment for Latinas, something that is also reflected in the scholarly record with notable interventions made by Gloria Anzaldúa, Cherríe Moraga, Alvina Quintana, and Tey Diana Rebolledo.[4] For example, in "Women: Prisoners of the Word," Alvina Quintana sees writing as a tool for women to demystify themselves and question the conventional gender roles that have historically been placed on young Latinas. According to Quintana, writing "provides the stage for a multiplicity of voices, experiences, issues which speak to the subordination of women to ideology and thus replaces the oversimplistic stereotypes so often used to categorize and define women" (209). In this way, Canela's narrative in *Cinnamon Girl* can stand apart from Esperanza's in *The House on Mango Street* and Ana's in *Real Women Have Curves*. While Esperanza and Ana may use writing as a way to dream about escaping their current circumstances and neighborhoods, Canela's writing demonstrates that she has no intentions of leaving her community. That said, the collective writing of these three protagonists forges a counter-narrative that presents the plurality of Latina girlhood. Although there are certainly experiences that these young women share, their stories stand alone and do not need the approval of anyone. As writers like Cisneros, López, and Herrera reveal, there is no singular way to be a Latina teen. In the case of *Cinnamon Girl*, Herrera positions the protagonist Canela, the titular cinnamon girl, as a creator and holder of knowledge who uses writing as her tool to convey the traumas of her uncle's injury in the World Trade Center and her subsequent feelings of loss, confusion, and displacement. For Canela, writing is necessary specially to work through trauma, as she confides to her friend,

> across the curb outside school and run by my building up, up, floor after
> > floor until we are out of breath
> on the rufeh. The sky wrinkled and droopy with ash.
>
> This is where
> you will help me collect voices, Rezzy.
>
> (40–41)

Although the sky is "wrinkled and droopy with ash," a visually stunning description of Ground Zero and broader New York City skyline, Canela is fueled with a poetic calling at this sight. Art written for the victims of the attack, which includes DJ, is cathartic, as it is the only thing that can convey the anguish of the survivors, a call to arms to speak of traumas rather than allow language, like ash, to simply fall and bury under debris and rubbish. Accordingly, writing becomes a form of sustenance to communicate with her Uncle DJ while also speaking to the traumas of living in the aftermath of the 9/11 terrorist attack.

While in *Chicana Falsa*, Michele Serros longs for a desk of her own from which she can take on the power of the pen, Canela finds solace in the most unlikely of places—an empty cereal box that her father gave her. Although the significant role of the cereal box is apparent from the book's subtitle, *letters from inside a cereal box*, on multiple occasions throughout the novel, Herrera signals the import of Canela's cereal box. At the beginning of the novel, Canela reveals:

> It's jes' a cereal box,
> with my writing and some letters inside.
>
> (5)

As this passage reveals, Canela does not always recognize the power of the cereal box and, specifically, having a space of her own to house her words.

She often downplays it; she doesn't see its relevance or importance. To her, it's "jes' a cereal box" and it might as well "jes' be her writing." That's it. As such, it would be easy for the casual reader to dismiss the cereal box altogether, perhaps even questioning why Herrera would include this seemingly bizarre character detail. But, as Canela's journey underscores, there is so much more to not just her writing, but specifically to *where* her writing lives. Since its advent in the late 19th century, cereal has become synonymous with breakfast—the "most important meal of the day." This is to say that Herrera's use of the cereal box is not casual. Rather, the benefits of cereal parallel the myriad ways that Canela's cereal box feeds the community spiritually. Take, for example, the aforementioned passage from the novel in which Canela entreats Rezzy to help her collect voices from the rooftop. Seeing the dust and ashes from ground zero as a sight of destruction and chaos, Canela attempts to transplant trauma into the creation of art, nourishing victims and survivors alike with the power of poetry. Like cereal, which is packaged neatly inside a box, with contents that will nourish the consumer, Canela's words will feed the community spiritually and potentially heal her traumatized family and injured uncle.

Given the nourishing qualities of Canela's cereal box, her decision to continually return to the cereal box is clear. She believes that her letters and poems can quite literally heal her uncle both physically and spiritually. Much as medicine and liquids are pumped into patients through an IV, Canela's words function in a similar manner, the poetry offering a healing salve for DJ even beyond the confines of consciousness. Herrera writes,

> Pull them out in little bundles tied together with red strings. Untie one and read it.
> Maybe uncle DJ will hear me and wake up, I tell Rezzy. Maybe, she says. Jes' maybe.
>
> (5)

Later, while Uncle DJ is still in a coma, Canela bears witness to her Tía Gladys, DJ's wife, trying to comfort him. Despite their bonds as spouses, however, she is missing a key ingredient. In this world, Canela's writing is what nourishes him and provides a beacon of hope that things will, in fact, get better despite how grim the present situation may appear. That is, her writing is what comforts him during the worst moment of his life. In telling Rezzy, "Maybe uncle DJ will hear me and wake up," Canela reflects the unwavering loyalty that poetry, and more specifically her poetry, can and will awaken and heal her poisoned uncle. Poetry need not be something to which only awake and breathing people can benefit; here, Herrera posits that art can transcend the boundaries of life and near-death. Seeing Tía Gladys struggle to comfort Uncle DJ, Canela reaches into her backpack, grabs her cereal box, pulls out a poem, and reads it to him:

Night's when i listen to uncle DJ's songs From his tenement
    rooftop—RadioSabor
Porto'rican Oldies, he would say.

(56–57)

Canela's poem immediately conjures the sounds of Celia Cruz and the images of Tía Gladys dancing to the salsa beats while the family enjoys what was then just an average night on their New York rooftop, but is now something they would long to have again. In other instances, she takes out some of the letters so that she can "pretend uncle DJ is talking to me" (17), revealing how writing and exchanging letters is a shared bond between the two and is something that, in this family, only they experience. As much as her words comfort her uncle, despite his being in a coma, his words also comfort her and help reassure her that things will be okay.

Things will get better. Canela's poetry demonstrates the novel's unwavering belief in the power of art to heal and bridge community during times of turmoil. Her uncle will heal and so will the New York community in the aftermath of the 9/11 terrorist attacks. They simply need faith, time, and, perhaps most importantly, they need community and communication.

Despite being a young teen, Canela is a powerful figure in this community, something that her writing enables, despite operating out of her cereal box. In addition to her and her uncle sharing a bond through her words, others in her community also find solace and nourishment through her writing, demonstrating the power of writing as a lifeline for the community. In other words, this is the power of writing, both poetry and prose, again revealing communication as a vital lifeline. For example, her best friend Rezzy enjoys hearing Canela read the letters out loud. While talking about fashion and experimenting with makeup like any regular pair of young girls might do after school, Rezzy abruptly changes the subject to the letters. Herrera writes,

Read me some more of your letters, Yo, Rezzy peeks into my backpack. Your
letters, wula!

(33)

In her letter, she tells Uncle DJ to thank Tía Gladys for a book of poems
written by canonical Puerto Rican poet Julia de Burgos. Although Canela
admits that she "doesn't understand them, weird," she is grateful for this gift
(33). On the cusp of her thirteenth birthday, Canela now has the guidance of
Julia de Burgos to help teach her about the art of writing poetry. Although
Canela does not necessarily need this book to solidify her role as a writer
and her relationship to writing, it does, nevertheless, position her within a
lineage of Puerto Rican women's literature. To be sure, Canela has not yet
reached the stature of Burgos, but the novel insists on recognizing Canela as
an emerging artist and community voice with cultural role models to whom
she can aspire to be one day. As Canela's journey uncovers, her work is just
as vital as someone with the legendary stature that de Burgos holds. Writing,
then, becomes a way for Canela to grow into her role as a leader and poetic
healer in this community.

As Canela knows, the act of writing a Latina experience serves as an
empowering act for young girls. It becomes, then, a space to develop her
voice as a Latina, which engages her in an act of decolonizing herself from
the male-centered narrative that she finds herself in, simply by being born
into a Puerto Rican family. Canela's process begins with a blank piece of
paper. In "'The Blank Page' and the Issues of Female Creativity," Susan Gubar establishes the blank page as a fundamental metaphor for the issues of
female creativity. According to Tey Diana Rebolledo, Gubar "argues that
women who have been silenced and limited in their creative endeavors experience their own bodies as the only available medium of their art" (147).
Canela's letters and poems, therefore, offer an ideal platform for her nascent creativity and her *latinidad* to materialize. In a similar vein, Sandra
Gilbert and Susan Gubar in "Infection in the Sentence: The Woman Writer
and the Anxiety of Authorship," propose that because male writers have
defined women in accordance with monolithic stereotypes, it is necessary
for female writers to define themselves as women against rigid definitions,
essentially demonstrating the multiplicity of female experience and identity
(24). In Canela's community, young girls are not viewed as writers, which
makes her relationship with Uncle DJ even more noteworthy as it demon-

strates the intergenerational bonds that writing can enable. While the pair find themselves separated by distance (when Canela and her family temporarily move to Iowa) and by Uncle DJ's injury, writing offers a site for Canela to find grit and sustenance. And, perhaps most important, writing is a way for her to process the emotionally volatile aftermath of a violent attack. Herrera writes,

> Why do you write? Why
>
> do you keep these old letters?
> Rezzy asks me. I say nothing.
>
> Write to hold back my tears. Write
>
> with my hard eyes open wide in the hospital room flickering with candles,
>     yellow, green,
> Red-red.
>
> (10)

Canela's use of writing as a backdrop to her coming-of-age experience recalls Hélène Cixous's groundbreaking essay "The Laugh of the Medusa" in which she calls for women to reexamine the tradition by which they have been and continue being defined. Cixous encourages women to insert themselves into the narrative, quite literally rewriting a more inclusive version of history and the dominant discourses that have sought to silence young women such as Canela.

According to Cixous,

> Women must write themselves: must write about women and bring women to writing, from which they have been driven away as violently as from their bodies—for the same reasons, by the same law, with the same fatal goal. Woman must put herself into the text—as into the world and into history—by her own movement. The future must no longer be determined by the past. (347)

In this fashion, Cixous calls for women to reconsider the tradition and sociocultural elements by which they are characterized. Only through writing and inserting female expression will the prospect of rewriting history materialize. Canela's writing as seen in *Cinnamon Girl* manifests this belief. Canela uses letters and poetry as tools to liberate both herself and the collective plight of her community after the chaos and uncertainty of 9/11.

Significantly, however, Cixous's theory does not engage in the particularities of what it means to be a woman of color who writes, let alone a *teenage* girl of color who writes. Scholar Adrianna Santos posits that "there is a particular need to tell authentic stories of Chicano/a and Latino/o teenagers as *writers* because of the specific social conditions that silence their narrative. This is not a new concept in Chicanx/Latinx literature" (46; original italics). By embedding herself into the narrative, women writers, such as Canela, can rupture patriarchal notions of Latino/a identity and situate young Latinas as leaders who hold the power to imagine a new version of New York's Latino/a community, one that is definitively a herstory (Cixous, 350). Not surprisingly, Latina writing is empowering and allows Canela to take on a higher level of agency, something that enables authentic change. Canela's coming-of-age journey in *Cinnamon Girl* is no different. Writing helps her develop her own voice and, as a result, enables her to recognize the agency that she has always had, but perhaps did not know how to manifest. For example, Canela scribbles a note to her father, saying that she is going "to help the others so uncle DJ can live. Don't worry. Going to do it my way" (J. F. Herrera 64). By doing things her way, that is, with the power of the pen, Canela takes on a leadership role and finds agency in her writing. To that end, writing is not only communal but empowering.

## Being Latina in a Post-9/11 World

One of the few young adult texts that examines the post-9/11 landscape from a distinct adolescent Latina perspective, *Cinnamon Girl* traces Canela's process of voicing the pain and trauma that will shape her young life. In particular, her own family's survival of this act of violence forces Canela to confront what it means to be a young girl of color within a climate of hyper surveillance, racial resentment, and increased Islamophobia, the latter with which her friend, Rezzy, and her family are targeted:

Rezzy glances at me from the crowd—she's still wearing

my black tights and denim jacket. We are not terrorists, uncle Rummi

Says, ducking the photographers, Now I go back to Kuwait, no business, no
life here no more.
Everything lost. All lost.

(126)

Uncle Rummi's mournful lament, "Everything lost. All lost," connects with Canela's own feelings of loss, confusion, and despair. Like Rezzy's uncle, whose business is torched in a likely hate crime, Canela feels the suffocation and chaos surrounding her, and she is unable to make sense of an act of violence that targets her friend's family and almost kills her beloved uncle.

However, in giving voice to members of the Muslim community, Herrera's text forges alliances between immigrant communities that are all potential targets of racialized acts of violence. The irony, of course, is that as Puerto Ricans, Canela's family are not immigrants but U.S. citizens; yet, as Canela comes to realize, citizenship, or in the case of Rezzy's family, business ownership, means little within a landscape that marks all Brown people as suspect, as "illegals" or "terrorists." For example, a study conducted by sociologists from University of Texas in 2016 found that "following the al-Qaeda-led terrorist attacks on Sept. 11, 2001, the fear of another attack, coupled with Islamophobia, streamlined immigration agendas with anti-terrorism rhetoric, policies, and institutional efforts, racializing Latinos in a new way" ("9/11," n.p.). While Canela may not fully grasp the extent of what Rezzy's family and many Muslims endured in this anti-Muslim climate, her race, phenotype, and gender are always potential markers of "outsiderness," particularly during a time in which "patriotism" was (and is) narrowly defined as loyalty to (white) America.

As a teenager who witnesses the attack on her hometown and her friend's subsequent departure from a city that is now hostile to its Muslim residents, Canela offers up a symbolic act of healing, her *manda* (Spanish for a promise made), returning the Ground Zero dust particles she gathers to the site of the attack. Sonia Alejandra Rodríguez argues that Herrera's children's and young adult literature, which she defines as "conocimiento narratives," can engage children to "process the violence they witness and the experience at home, in their communities, and as subjects of the US nation, and to transform that knowledge into one that can shift their realities" (93). In gathering and collecting the dust, which compiles the particles of the buildings, debris, and even human remains, Canela invokes her own burial ceremony, reminiscent of the Biblical passage, "ashes to ashes, dust to dust." Poetry becomes scripture:

> After the towers went down,
> so many words came rushing out of me more than ever before.
>
> (24)

Both the act of writing poetry and fulfilling her *manda* create the means by which Canela can perform healing (w)rites to articulate her coming-of-age as a 9/11 teen. The poetry that "came rushing out of me" signals the need to search from within, to uncover what is buried beneath the surface, in this case, the words that Canela will need to pay homage to her community of survivors.

To "process the violence" of this new landscape, as Rodríguez suggests, Canela must articulate the events that will transform her life and the lives of those inhabiting New York City. In her attempt to make peace with this tragedy, when Canela collects the dust and ashes of her city to return to Ground Zero, she is viciously attacked by classmates, releasing the anguish and self-imposed guilt she has over her inability to fulfill this *manda* she has made for to herself:

> *I thought, I thought,*
> *I could save all the voices, uncle DJ.*
> *But I couldn't. Just couldn't. I am so sorry, uncle DJ. All I have is what's inside*
> *my backpack. Nothin' but dust . . .*
>
> *Why did you have to go and deliver roses!*
>
> (143–44; italics in original)

Canela's feelings of failure and inadequacy erupt, along with the despair she has virtually kept to herself over Uncle DJ's routine roses delivery that makes him an unwitting victim of the World Trade Center attack. Although she believes that she "just couldn't" save the voices, we suggest that she *does* save these voices, and in speaking of her pain, finds hers. Canela reduces the act of healing and spirituality as merely being "all I have is what's inside my backpack," much as she describes her poetry being "jes' words," and in doing such, we are reminded of how the voices of youth are seldom considered, much less fundamental, to understanding national tragedies like 9/11.

But in centering Canela's voice as she digs up the dirt, excavating her own words in the process, Herrera's novel insists that young voices like Canela's matter. Canela moves from being an observer to an actor, from passivity to praxis, thus transforming into a person of moral accountability and social conscience.

## Conclusion

In our co-edited volume, *Nerds, Goths, Geeks, and Freaks: Outsiders in Chicanx and Latinx Young Adult Literature,* we laid the groundwork for a typology of Latino/a teenagers that encompasses the various identities that young people take on as an act of resistance and autonomy. We centered these so-called "outsiders" to explore the strategies that Latino/a teens take to expand ways of creating and performing latinidad. Some of these teens are ChicaNerds and LatiNerds who find solace in books and reading. Some are otherworldly Latinos/as with magical powers that must protect their communities. Some are urban Latinos/as teens who push against the predominant cholo/a stereotype. And others are young Puerto Rican girls whose cereal boxes may as well be their own personal branch of the New York Public Library.

Regardless of the strategies they employ, "As outsiders, these Latinx youth must take back their own narrative," an act that responds to Chicana theorist Emma Pérez's concept of the "Decolonial Imaginary" (Boffone and Herrera, 7). Pérez calls for Latinos/as, and specifically Latinas, to "revise our history and reinscribe it with the new" (127). This is precisely the cultural work that Canela engages in throughout Juan Felipe Herrera's *Cinnamon Girl: Letters Found Inside a Cereal Box.* Just like the young Latinas in *The House on Mango Street, Real Women Have Curves,* and *I Am Not Your Perfect Mexican Daughter, Cinnamon Girl*'s Canela theorizes her identity as a writer "to forge new paths for Latinx youth to follow in ways that harmonize notions of being different and fitting in" (Boffone and Herrera 8). For Canela the Cinnamon Girl, her new path is to take up the power of the pen and write herself into existence while broadening the stories of other marginalized groups within the story. Subsequently, her journey as a writer grants her the agency she needs to provide *ánimo* (encouragement) to her friends and relatives in the wake of the World Trade Center terrorist attacks. Her writing—that is, her outsiderness—facilitates a healing process that recognizes the pain and trauma that 9/11 has inflicted upon the New York community while also comforting her literary muse, Uncle DJ, as he recovers in the hospital following the attack. Juan Felipe Herrera's groundbreaking young adult novel illustrates that, by embracing her outsiderness and accepting her love of writing, Canela can use her creativity to adapt and thrive in a post-9/11 world that further subjugates communities of color. While the mainstream may potentially view the letters and poems in Canela's cereal box as insignificant, as Uncle DJ, Rezzy, and other members of the Cinnamon Girl's community understand, writing is indeed shown to be a powerful act. There is power in words. The power to bring people together. The power to heal. The power to expose just how much we need to pay attention to the voices of young Latinas.

## Notes

1.  For more on the systemic devaluing of Latino/a children's and young adult literature, see Trevor Boffone and Cristina Herrera, *Nerds, Goths, Geeks, and Freaks: Outsiders in Chicanx and Latinx Young Adult Literature*, Cristina Herrera, *ChicaNerds in Chicana Young Adult Literature: Brown and Nerdy*, and Gabriela Baeza Ventura, "Latino Literature for Children and the Lack of Diversity."
2.  Among others, Caminero-Santangelo addresses Luis Alberto Urrea's *The Devil's Highway* and Sonia Nazario's *Enrique's Journey*.
3.  For more on *Downtown Boy*, see Phillip Serrato and Sonia Alejandra Rodríguez.
4.  For more on the role of Latina writing, see Gloria Anzaldúa, "How to tame a Wild Tongue" from *Borderlands/La Frontera*; Cherríe Moraga, *A Xicana Codex of Changing Consciousness: Writings 2000–2010*; Alvina Quintana, "Women: Prisoners of the Word;" and Tey Diana Rebolledo, *Women Singing in the Snow: A Cultural Analysis of Chicana Literature*.

## Works Cited

"9/11 Merged U.S. Immigration and Terrorism Efforts at Latinos' Expense, Study Finds." American Sociological Association, press release, August 20, 2016, https://www.asanet.org/press-center/press-releases/911-merged-us-immigration-and-terrorism-efforts-latinos-expense-study-finds.

Acevedo, Elizabeth. *Clap When You Land*. New York: HarperTeen, 2020.

Acevedo, Elizabeth. *The Poet X*. New York: HarperTeen, 2018.

Alexander, Joy. "The Verse-Novel: A New Genre." *Children's Literature in Education*, 36, no. 3 (2005): 269–83.

Anzaldúa, Gloria. *Borderlands/La Frontera: The New Mestiza*. San Francisco, Calif.: Aunt Lute Books, 1987.

Baeza Ventura, Gabriela. "Latino Literature for Children and the Lack of Diversity." In *(Re)Mapping the Latina/o Literature Landscape: New Works and New Directions*, edited by Cristina Herrera and Larissa M. Mercado-López, 241–54. New York: Palgrave Macmillan, 2016.

Boffone, Trevor and Cristina Herrera. "Introduction: Weirding Out Latinx America." In *Nerds, Goths, Geeks, and Freaks: Outsiders in Chicanx and Latinx Young Adult Literature*, edited by Trevor Boffone and Cristina Herrera, 3–11. Jackson: University Press of Mississippi, 2020.

Cadden, Mike. "Rhetorical Technique in the Young Adult Verse Novel." *The Lion and the Unicorn* 42, no. 2 (April 2018): 129–44.

Cadden, Mike. "The Verse Novel and the Question of Genre." *ALAN Review* 39, no. 1 (Fall 2011): 21–27.

Caminero-Santangelo, Marta. "Narrating the Non-Nation: Literary Journalism and 'Illegal' Border Crossings." *Arizona Quarterly: A Journal of American Literature, Culture, and Theory* 68, no. 3 (Fall 2012): 157–76.

Cisneros, Sandra. *The House on Mango Street*. New York: Vintage Books, 1991.

Cixous, Hélène. "The Laugh of the Medusa." In *Feminisms: An Anthology of Literary Theory and Criticism*, edited by Diane Herndl and Robyn R. Warhol, 347–62. New Brunswick, N.J.: Rutgers University Press, 1997.

Coats, Karen. "Form as Metaphor in Middle Grade and Young Adult Verse Novels." *The Lion and the Unicorn* 42, no. 2 (April 2018): 145–61.

Gilbert, Sandra M., and Susan Gubar. "Infection in the Sentence: The Woman Writer and the Anxiety of Authorship." In *Feminisms: An Anthology of Literary Theory and Criticism*, edited by Diane Herndl and Robyn R. Warhol, 21–32. New Brunswick, N.J.: Rutgers University Press, 1997.

Gubar, Susan. "'The Blank Page' and the Issues of Female Creativity." *Critical Inquiry* 8, no. 2 (Winter 1981): 243–63.

Herrera, Cristina. *ChicaNerds in Chicana Young Adult Literature: Brown and Nerdy*. New York: Routledge, 2020.

Herrera, Cristina. "Seeking Refuge *Under the Mesquite*: Nature Imagery in Guadalupe García McCall's Verse Novel." *Children's Literature Association Quarterly* 44, no. 2 (Summer 2019): 194–209.

Herrera, Juan Felipe. *Cinnamon Girl: Letters Found Inside a Cereal Box*. New York: HarperTeen, 2005.

Herrera, Juan Felipe. *Downtown Boy*. New York: Scholastic Press, 2005.

Herrera, Juan Felipe. "Enthralling: Notes." In *Voices of Resistance: Interdisciplinary Approaches to Chican@ Children's Literature*, edited by Laura Alamillo, Larissa M. Mercado-Lopez, and Cristina Herrera, vii-viii. Lanham, Md.: Rowman and Littlefield, 2017.

López, Josefina. *Real Women Have Curves*. Woodstock, Ill.: Dramatic Publishing, 1990.

Méndez, Jasminne. *Island of Dreams*. Moonpark, Calif.: Floricanto Press, 2013.

Moraga, Cherríe. *A Xicana Codex of Changing Consciousness: Writings 2000–2010*. Durham, N.C.: Duke University Press, 2011.

Nazario, Sonia. *Enrique's Journey: The Story of a Boy's Dangerous Odyssey to Reunite with His Mother*, rev. ed. New York: Random House, 2014.

Pérez, Emma. *The Decolonial Imaginary: Writing Chicanas Into History*. Bloomington: Indiana University Press, 1999.

Quintana, Alvina E. "Women: Prisoners of the Word." In *Chicana Voices: Intersections of Class, Race, and Gender*, edited by Teresa Córdova, 208–19. Albuquerque: University of New Mexico Press, 1993.

Quintero, Isabel. *Gabi, a Girl in Pieces*. El Paso, Texas: Cinco Puntos Press, 2014.

Rebolledo, Tey Diana. *Women Singing in the Snow: A Cultural Analysis of Chicana Literature*. Tucson: University of Arizona Press, 1995.

Rodríguez, Sonia Alejandra. "'You Wanna Be a Chump/or a Champ?': Constructions of Masculinity, Absent Fathers, and Conocimiento in Juan Felipe Herrera's *Downtown Boy*." In *Voices of Resistance: Interdisciplinary Approaches to Chican@ Children's Literature*, edited by Laura Alamillo, Larissa M. Mercado-López, and Cristina Herrera, 91–104. Lanham, Md.: Rowman and Littlefield, 2017.

Sánchez, Erika L. *I Am Not Your Perfect Mexican Daughter*. New York: Penguin Random House, 2017.

Santos, Adrianna. "Broken Open: Writing, Healing, and Affirmation in Isabel Quintero's *Gabi, A Girl in Pieces* and Erika L. Sánchez's *I Am Not Your Perfect Mexican Daughter*." In *Nerds, Goths, Geeks, and Freaks: Outsiders in Chicanx and Latinx Young Adult Literature*, edited by Trevor Boffone and Cristina Herrera, 45–59. Jackson: University Press of Mississippi, 2020.

Serrato, Phillip. "A Portrait of the Artist as a Muchachito: Juan Felipe Herrera's *Downtown Boy as a Poetic Springboard into Critical Masculinity Studies*." In *Voices of Resistance: Interdisciplinary Approaches to Chican@ Children's Literature*, edited by Laura Alamillo, Larissa M. Mercado-López, and Cristina Herrera, 61–76. Lanham, Md.: Rowman and Littlefield, 2017.

Serros, Michele. *Chicana Falsa: And Other Stories of Death, Identity, & Oxnard*. Valencia, Calif.: Lalo Press, 1993.

Urrea, Luis Alberto. *The Devil's Highway: A True Story*. New York: Little, Brown and Company, 2004.

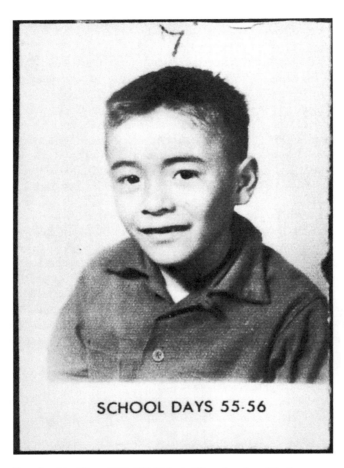

Young Boy School Photo, B&W—1955–56, Central Elementary, Escondido, Ca.

## CHAPTER 13

# Juan Felipe Herrera's Children's Picture Books

## An Affirmation of Chicano/a Identity through Visual Literacy and Bilingualism

MARINA BERNARDO FLÓREZ AND
CARMEN GONZÁLEZ RAMOS

## Chicano/a Children's Literature, Picture Books, and the Representation of Identity

Chicano/a children's literature was born in the wake of the *movimiento chicano*, an integral part of the civil rights movement of the 1960s and especially the 1970s. In the 1990s, as a part of the rising trend of multiculturalism and as a cultural product and a reflection of power relations, Chicano/a children's literature strove to provide an authentic and accurate representation of Chicano/a identity. The representation of Mexican Americans in children's literature until then had been based on cultural homogeneity, historical distortion, and stereotypes.

Since the 1990s, renowned Chicano/a writers such as Rudolfo A. Anaya, Juan Felipe Herrera, Sandra Cisneros, Gloria Anzaldúa, and Pat Mora, among others, started imagining the self in their books for children, legitimizing Chicano/a's intercultural identities through the reconstruction of the relationship between the Chicano/a community and the acts of reading and writing.

Chicano/a authors then and now share a common goal: to provide Chicano/a children with positive representations of their culture and identity through authentic, quality books that reflect their intercultural and interlingual experience. Rather than reinforcing stereotypes or promoting simplistic views of multiculturalism, Juan Felipe Herrera's picture books provide an opportunity to empower children and encourage young readers to celebrate the diverse cultural heritage of the United States.

The purpose of this study is to analyze a number of picture books authored by Herrera and illustrated by different artists in order to highlight the elements which allow him to provide Chicano/a children with positive representations of their culture and identity. Our approach is based on the interdependence of two signifying systems—text and illustrations—characteristic of picture books, a genre in itself within children's literature in which the relationship between the two codes, the visual and the verbal, changes the meaning of both, thus gaining meaning through more than the mere sum of its parts (Nodelman, 1988). In our approach we underline the importance of visual literacy in the development of children's identity and self-perception, as well as the use of language for giving voice and visibility to subjects who have been effectively silenced in mainstream Anglo culture.

The picture books selected for our analysis are divided into two groups, the first group including three autobiographical picture books: *Calling the Doves/El canto de las palomas* (1995), *The Upside Down Boy/El niño de cabeza* (2000), and *Imagine* (2018). The second group of picture books involves *Grandma and Me at the Flea/Los meros meros remateros* (2002), *Super Cilantro Girl/La superniña del cilantro* (2003), and *Featherless/Desplumado* (2004). In the analysis of the first group which we call the "trilogy of autobiographical cuentos," we focus on the autobiographical elements that Latino/a and Chicano/a children can identify with both visually and verbally when reading these picture books, thus validating cultural memory, community and environment. In the second group, titled "superheroines and superheroes blurring borders and overcoming limitations," we concentrate on *Grandma and Me at the Flea*, *Super Cilantro Girl*, and *Featherless* where the main characters empower themselves and show young readers how to overcome limitations and thereby affirm their identities by blurring borders, both real and metaphorical ones.

Picture book scholars such as Perry Nodelman, David Lewis, and Maria Nikolajeva are the main sources we refer to in our theoretical framework for our analysis of the visual and verbal codes. Although we include the illustrations considered pivotal for our study, we use description as part of the analysis of illustrations because, according to David Lewis, despite the fact that description is considered to be a lower kind of approach than argument or analysis, in describing something, we favor certain choices of vocabulary depending on the particular perspective from which we look at the object being described, on how we see the images we describe, and, ultimately, on how we understand that image (Lewis, 2).

We also take into consideration the work of Joseph Schwarz, Jacque Roethler, as well as Paulo Freire and Donaldo Macedo to refer to the development of children's identity and literature. In addition, the work by Peter Felten, Kathleen Ellen O'Neil, Lee Galda and Kathy G. Short, as well as Cyndi Giorgis, Nancy J. Johnson, Annamarie Bonomo, Shrissie Colbert, Angela Conner, Gloria Kauffman, and Dottie Kulesza has provided us with the central notions to develop the concept of visual literacy. During our analysis of the picture books selected for this study, we also refer to the work of Bettina Kümmerling-Meibauer, Esmeralda Santiago, Tiffany Ana López, Yuyi Morales, Laura Barbas-Rhoden, Renata Morresi, Laura Alamillo, Sonia A. Rodríguez, Carolina Fernández Rodríguez, and Katherine E. Bundy.

Personal interviews conducted with Herrera serve as an essential instrument to extrapolate from the literary content and context. The importance of interviews is paramount because they are considered another dimension of writing, as Ana Louise Keating explains in *Interviews/Entrevistas with Gloria Anzaldúa* (2000). Furthermore, in his introduction to *Spilling the Beans in Chicanolandia: Conversations with Writers and Artists* (2006), Frederick Luis Aldama notes that "the interview then becomes an improvised conversation between the interviewer and the author [. . . .] This process allows one to probe deeply into the author's work, learn of his or her points of view about it, and learn the circumstances in which he or she has written and produced it" (11–12).

## Visual Literacy and Identity Formation

Nodelman (1999) and Joseph Schwarcz (1991) are among the scholars who link the reading of picture books to the development of children's identity or schemata, their mental structure, patterns of thought and behavior. In his studies on identity formation in children from ethnic minorities, Jaque Roethler in "Reading in Color: Children's Book Illustrations and Identity Formation for Black Children in the United States" warns of the dangers of negative representations of minorities as well as the absence of representation, claiming that they "undermine self-perception, which is at the very root of the child's thinking, and it may have far-reaching and detrimental effects" (98). Using Freire and Macedo's metaphor in *Literacy: Reading the Word and the World* (1987), as we learn to read the words, we also learn to read the world, and our place in it. They point out that the way we read "is inextricably linked to forms of pedagogy that can function either to silence and marginalize students or to legitimate their voices in an effort to empower them as critical and active citizens" (19).

But we also learn to read the world through our understanding of visual images thanks our ability to construct meaning from those images. According to Peter Felten in his article "Visual Literacy" (2008), the term refers to the ability to understand, produce, and use culturally significant images, objects, and visible actions. In fact, the concept of literacy itself has been rethought in the past century in order to be more inclusive of the various modalities which the emergence of new technologies have led to blend: not only images and written and spoken texts, but also gestures, symbols, and sound, as Anne Bamford points out in "The Visual Literacy White Paper" (2013). Images have been central to our lives and, for thousands of years, they have been created by humans to convey meaning and knowledge to tell stories. However, it is now in the twenty-first century that the so-called "pictorial turn" has taken place when new technologies have made images central to communication and to making meaning (Felten, 60). Notwithstanding the fact that in their daily lives children are surrounded by visual images which they need to use and interpret, this does not mean that they naturally have visual literacy skills, especially if we consider that in terms of visual cognition and perception, seeing is not a simple process of passive reception because it also involves active construction of meaning. As Felten contends, "If the *physical* act of seeing involves active construction, then the *intellectual* act of interpreting what is seen must require a critical viewer" (61). Thus, children must learn to analyze and think critically about the significance of what they are seeing. If writing is essential to reach textual literacy, then, in terms of visual design, the capacity to manipulate and make meaning with images is a central component of visual literacy (61). As in textual literacy, learning the skills to become visually literate requires training and practice by mastering the syntax and semantics of visual language in order to recognize, produce and employ those two together. However, schools have traditionally considered textual literacy as the only source of knowledge, and academic training is still very much focused on verbal texts. It is of utmost importance that readers from a young age learn the key elements of visual art, the so-called visual grammar (O'Neil, 2011), that is, a set of techniques with which they can recognize emotions and atmospheres. Among the elements employed by artists/illustrators to create effects are the use of color, line, shape, size and style. It is this way in which the artist combines the previous elements in order to express feelings or describe qualities, and composition, the placement of characters and other elements within a picture to establish their relationship (Nikolajeva and Scott, 2006).

In picture books, meaning is the result of the interplay of the two codes, the visual and the verbal, neither of which would make sense when experienced independently of the other (Salisbury and Styles, 2012), challenging the boundaries between word and image. This complex literary genre offers a unique opportunity for children by becoming mentor texts as Galda and Short state in their study "Visual Literacy: Exploring Art and Illustration in Children's Books" (1993). This is particularly key for emergent and novice readers in order to develop visual literacy, given that drawing is an essential part of the writing process, and also because young readers can go back to the illustrations in picture books "to explore, reflect, and critique those images" (506). This synergy of the two media conveys a complex and meaningful story to young readers, whose ability to read pictures as well as text allows them to comprehend picture books fully. Illustrations enable readers to understand, interpret, and respond to the story since they play a critical role in developing literary elements such as setting, plot, and character through the use of the various elements of lines, color, perspective, composition, design and others. In the case of characters as the driving force of the story—especially critical in creating literary meaning—illustrations in picture books not only convey external features, such as appearance, gender, and age, but also internal facets as poses, gestures, and facial expressions which reveal emotions and attitudes (Nikolajeva and Scott, 86). Visual literacy not only allows young readers to understand, recognize, and critically interpret the aforementioned elements to gain full comprehension of the picture book story, but it also enhances the reader's aesthetic experience. The combination of an engaging story and well-crafted and creatively conceived illustrations stimulates aesthetic thinking to create meaning in the transaction with the reader (Giorgis *et al*, 146).

As mentioned before, visual literacy is important in the development of children's identity and self-perception because pictorial language stems from the culture in which the artist lives and works and is used to convey meaning to members of that culture. Illustrations and text carry deeper and subtler connotations portrayed through choice of terms, color, tone, media, or style (O'Neill 2011, 215). As Herrera stated in a personal interview from February 2021, "a Latino/a children's book, by its very nature, provides stories, terms, images and cultural melodies when it is read, ways of speaking, and family interrelationships" (Bernardo, 2021). These "cultural melodies" accompany children in their understanding of the thoughts, feelings, and actions communicated by the picture book as they create connections between these terms and images and their own vital experience. In this way, "Latinx children's picture books are multi-books in one. Identity, then, is five-fold: child's relationship with the story, mother, family and larger group—and self" (Bernardo 2021).

## Herrera's Trilogy of Autobiographical Cuentos: *Calling the Doves*, *The Upside Down Boy* and *Imagine*

Many Latino/a authors have expressed concerns about feeling invisible and nonexistent as children due to the lack of children's books reflecting their lives early on. Esmeralda Santiago has confessed that she was one "who could not find [her]self in the literature" (133), or Tiffany Ana López has also claimed that she was the "child who was always searching for herself within the pages of a book" (17). In "Splendid Treasures of *Mi Corazón*," Yuyi Morales talks about her discovery of Latino/a children's books in the US, and how they made her proud of her culture, her language, her accent, her beauty: "a body of books that took pride and honor in what it means to be bilingual, to speak Spanish or Spanglish, to have an accent, to be multicolored, [. . .] to have an *abuelita*, to be a *niño* or a *niña*" (x). Issues of identity and representation, so pervasive in Chicano/a literature, are essential in its children's literature as well.

Herrera claims that "these stories have been denied, separated, banned or simply unavailable to the Latinx children" (Bernardo 2021), and his bilingual picture books aim to empower them and legitimize their intercultural identity. Based on events from the author's own life, rather than mere descriptive, recapitulative, and retrospective accounts, these stories actively reconstruct autobiographical landmarks, many of them representative of the Chicano/a experience. Bettina Kümmerling-Meibauer, in "Remembering the Past in Words and Pictures: How Autobiographical Stories Become Picturebooks," considers that the author of autobiographical picture books functions as an auto-ethnographer (210), linking personal experience to a wider perspective of cultural memory. Countering the Anglo perspective based on the traditionally individualistic Bildungsroman, identity negotiation and construction in Herrera's *cuentos* take place within the community and the environment.

For example, *Calling the Doves*, published in 1995, is a poignant portrayal of the lives of migrant workers seen through the eyes of Juanito, or Herrera as a young boy. Winner of the Ezra Jack Keats award among others, the picture book presents itself as a first-person narrative, and the authenticity of the autobiography is reinforced by paratextual passages in dust jackets, the dedication, the foreword, and the copyright page. The dedication opens the story with a double spread containing the portraits of both his mother and father and a narrative poem which sets the intention for the whole picture book, in essence a tribute to his parents and the author's upbringing in the Valley:

My mother and father were farmworkers, and I grew up travelling with them through the mountains and valleys of California.

This book is dedicated to my mother Lucha and my father Felipe, who loved the open sky and the earth when it is tender.
They taught me that inside every word there can be kindness. (2–3)

*Calling the Doves* would be one of the bilingual stories that, according to Laura Barbas-Rhoden in "Toward an Inclusive Eco-Cosmopolitanism: Bilingual Children's Literature in the United States" (2011), "seek[s] to shape values and identities in ways that directly contest dominant ideologies in US consumer culture, [. . .] stories that reclaim landscapes for humble workers" (365). Through Herrera's evocative text and Elly Simmons' vibrant illustrations, we witness different scenes of life on the road, much as if we were browsing through an old family album or scrapbook. In fact, Herrera provided Simmons with family photos as an inspiration for her illustrations, which, in the author's opinion, "proved to be extremely beneficial for the rendition of the book" (Bernardo 2021). The book's formal typography and arrangement of elements, with the text in English and Spanish on the verso and the corresponding illustration on the recto, adds to this impression. There are only two exceptions to this composition. First, the double spread depicting the makeshift trailer his father built (10–11), where the text is included over the panels of the trailer and the illustration contains texts echoing the "conversations, Mexican songs and auctions blared from a box radio" (11), mentioned in the text. Another example would be the one depicting the family's cyclic migration following the different harvests. The pictures of the different seasons and crops frame the text with huge grapes and melons alternating with a setting sun in six stages in the sky, creating a pattern which cinematically parallels cyclical time in nature.

Mixing colored pencils, casein, and acrylic paints on rag paper, Simmons obtains an opaque, thick finish with vivid details, reminiscent of hazy childhood memories, that allow us to see how "campesinos dotted the land like tropical birds" (4), or a dirt patio became "a sand-colored theater" (12) where Juanito learned to sing. Sleeping under the stars, howling with wolves, playing with turkeys, or attending an improvised fiesta, "a home-made city of brown faces with smiles and music" (28), Juanito grows in connection with nature. With a rich palette that combines intense warm and cool colors with curved and organic lines, irregular shapes, and the melting of natural and manufactured objects, the enchanting illustrations represent the sustainability and communion with the environment of migrant life. According to Barbas-Rhoden, this "idyllic portrayal [. . .] does not erase the markers of poverty and marginalization—such as homelessness or hardship—but rather envelops these in poetry that emphasizes the familial love and natural sense of beauty his parents taught him" (372).

Lucha and Felipe stay at the center of each and every scene, as nurturers and healers, as loving parents, but also as an example of creativity. Over dinner, her mother would recite poetry: "Rhyming words would pour out of her mouth and for a moment the world would stop spinning" (16), while his father would play the harmonica and tell stories, or make bird calls, "whistl[ing] deeply as if he had a tiny clarinet inside the palms of his hands" (14), thus providing young Juanito an early aesthetic formation. When he is eight years old, his parents decide it is time to settle down so that Juanito can go to school. And as they leave their migrant life and the story comes to an end, Herrera acknowledges both his growing up in the Valley and his parents' teachings as the origin of his poetic voice:

**FIGURE 13.1** *Calling the Doves/El canto de las palomas* (1995) by Juan Felipe Herrera and illustrated by Elly Simmons, 4–5. Courtesy of Lee & Low Books.

I had gathered the landscapes
of the Valley close to my heart
. . . . . . . . . . . . . . . . . .
As the cities came into view, I knew
one day I would follow my own road.
I would let my voice fly away the way my mother recited poems,
the way my father called the doves.

(Calling the Doves / El canto de las palomas, 32)

Herrera's autobiographical *cuento* offers poignant vignettes about growing up in the Valley by emphasizing creativity, communion with nature and family love, and counteracting negative stereotypes about migrant life. Text and illustrations work together to allow the youngest readers in their process of acquiring visual literacy to identify with Juanito's childhood, and value the elements which make their own families unique.

The second picture book in this biographical trilogy by Herrera is *The Upside Down Boy* (2000), which continues the story in *Calling the Doves* as Juanito, the alter ego of the author, starts school and becomes accustomed to his new life in the city. Illustrator Elizabeth Gómez's palette of bright, saturated colors gives shape to this new world full of "fancy melting cars"

(7) where "the city streets aren't soft with flowers" and "buildings don't have faces" (28). The story revolves around Juanito's main challenge adjusting to this new environment, going to school, and his "feelings of displacement, represented on the cover by the physical suspension of Juanito, who floats upside down over a baseball field" (89).

Juanito does not speak English, and he feels "funny," and even fears his "tongue will turn into a rock" (7). One of the most powerful scenes shows how Juanito steps into school with his burrito de papas. He asks "¿Dónde estoy?," (Where am I?) but his "question in Spanish fades" (8). It's a strange alien world, and Juanito is alone, unable to speak the language in an almost claustrophobic environment where kids laugh at him and even inanimate objects seem to be hostile, as the "locked fences," "the thick door that slams behind [him]," or "the clock that clicks and aims its strange arrows at [him]" (8). The illustration adds to this oppressive feeling, showing a close up of Juanito's sad countenance facing the readers, with a classroom full of children looking back at him from their desks (fig. 13.2). Even the brown bag he is carrying, which we know contains his burrito de papas, flags him as different.

In *Growing up Chicana*, López recalls how taking a tortilla to school set her apart, and exposes the absence of certain foods, icons of cultural identity, in children's books: "I read of children taking their sandwiches to school, yet never in my childhood reading experiences did I read about a child taking a tortilla" (18). Language, environment, and even food add to Juanito's sense of estrangement, embodied in his being or at least feeling upside down. On a double page spread in which Juanito literally flies upside down over the school, he verbalizes his feeling of displacement: "When I jump up / everyone sits. / When I sit / all the kids swing through the air. / My feet float through the clouds / when all I want is to touch the earth. / I am the upside down boy" (14).

In an interview with Jerry Griswold, Herrera talks about those first days at school as full of "ruptures, estrangements, even imprisonments" (Griswold 2019). He states: "They seemed at odds with the other 'sentidos' or feelings I remember from my childhood: stars at night, the howling of coyotes, dew on the grass in the morning" (Griswold). In another interview with Alan Soldofsky, Herrera recalls being punished for speaking Spanish until he "shut down when he was reprimanded and spanked" (207). But thanks to his third grade teacher, Mrs. Sampson, whom the picture book is dedicated to, he starts to find his voice. She asks him to sing in front of the class and tells him

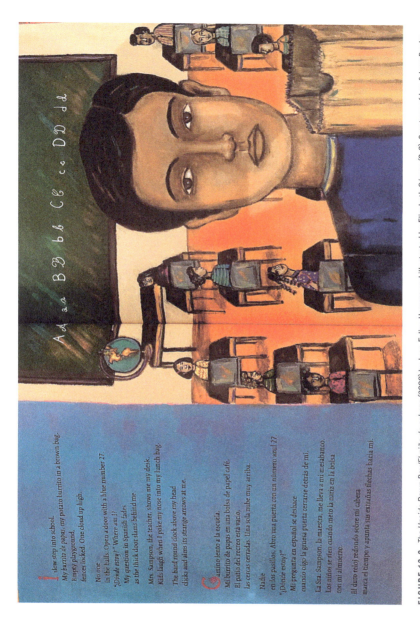

**FIGURE 13.2** *The Upside Down Boy/El niño de cabeza* (2000) by Juan Felipe Herrera and illustrated by Elizabeth Gómez (8–9). Courtesy of Lee & Low Books.

he has a beautiful voice, and for Herrera "that just swept away all the other stuff, swept it out of [his] mind, out of [his] body" (207–8).

Singing in front of the class marks a turning point in Juanito's development at school, from being "frozen" (18) and shut down to progressively adapting to his new life by creatively combining his cultural background and the school's environment in his first experiments with art, music, and poetry. In Renata Morresi's words, "Juanito is able to reconcile the different dimensions with a creative gesture of creolization" (89). Finger painting at school, Juanito makes "wild suns," "crazy tomato cars and cucumber sombreros," and writes his "name with seven chiles" (10). At home, his paintings are much appreciated as the "spicy sun" reminds his father of "hot summer days in the San Joaquin Valley," and the "flying tomatoes" are, in her mother's opinion, "ready for salsa" (17). When asked by Mrs. Simpson to write a poem, his family becomes the focus: "Papi Felipe with a moustache of words. / Mama Lucha with strawberries in her hair. / I see magic salsa in my house and everywhere!" (24). According to Morresi, the poem "beautifully symbolizes how rural origins, the family world, and native language meet the city neighborhood, the school world, and the new language" (90). Eventually, we see Juanito's success at school, as he gets an A on his poem, and on Open House Day, in front of his family, he performs as El Maestro Juanito, the choir conductor. Using his father's harmonica, and opening with "Uno . . . dos . . . and three!" (31), Juanito completes the first stage of a process of acculturation which counters stories of assimilation based on rupture with the parents' culture. His initial sense of displacement, of being upside down, and his difference, become a powerful site for identity formation and creative fulfilment, a development that underlines the importance of making these stories available for Latino/a students.

In a personal interview with Herrera, he recalls his visit to an elementary school in St. Petersberg, Florida:

> There was rice and beans, guacamole and chips being served. The students had painted a mural of one of the book's scenes—*The Upside Down Boy/El niño de cabeza*.
>
> Imagine the fusion of all these elements as I read and as they called back certain phrases. (Bernardo, n.p.)

For the classroom of mostly Latino/a children, the experience was really emotional: "[w]hen an author walks in with a bilingual book with a relatable story, and is read in a relatable voice, then the room explodes." It is really essential to provide Chicano/a and Latino/a children with bilingual books such as *Calling the Doves* and *The Upside Down Boy* which they can find "relatable" and which validate visually and verbally these children's cultural knowledge. Both books contain texts in English and Spanish. The English text characteristically includes Spanish words, especially from those semantic fields expressing emotional closeness such as family, food or the environment. In his own words, Herrera likes "to liberate the words," "to have micro-liberations" (Soldofsky, 217). In a very delicate balance that allows both the monolingual and bilingual readers to enjoy the *cuentos* (short stories), Herrera uses loanwords such as *fiesta* or *campesinos* (farmworkers), incorporated into the mainstream lexicon to varying degrees, and translates or explains the words when the meaning may not be inferred by context or illustrations, while at the same time avoiding double talk in the characters dialogue with translations that would result in redundancy for bilingual children.

In an interview with Griswold, Herrera claims to write in English first, then translate to Spanish, then back to English, so it "keeps going back and forth." Monolingual children have access to one of the stories "but for kids who know both English and Spanish, the result is stereo [. . .], more than bilingual, the experience is interlingual" (n.p.).

Published in 2018, *Imagine* is an illustrated poem which widens the scope of both *Calling the Doves* and *The Upside Down Boy* while we follow the main character's journey as a migrant workers' son who becomes poet laureate of the U.S., mirroring Herrera's biography. Dreamlike pen and foam monoprint illustrations by Lauren Castillo are utilized in this story, first depicting the boy's life in nature, playing with flowers in the fields, tadpoles in creeks, and sleeping under the stars. Presented in the first person, but always addressing the reader directly, the boy tells us of his life in the valley, echoing the story in *Calling the Doves*, always moving with the harvests: "If I jumped up high / into my papi's army truck / and left our village of farmworkers / and waved adios / to my amiguitos, / imagine" (5–6). The poem moves from a natural setting to urban concrete, as we follow the child to the city and witness his struggles at school. In a scene which reminds us of the one in *The Upside Down Boy*, the boy stands at the door of the classroom, separated from all the other students: "If I opened / my classroom's wooden door / not knowing how to read / or / speak in English, / imagine." (15–16; figure 13.3).

**FIGURE 13.3** *Imagine* (2018) by Juan Felipe Herrera and illustrated by Lauren Castillo (15–16). Courtesy of Candlewick Press.

The parallelism of the conditional structures used in every sentence and the repetition of the evocative imperative "imagine" on each double page spread provides a calming rhythm to the experience when read aloud, while these elements prompt us to turn page after page. The parallelism of using the same conditional structure for all the lines of the poem and the reiteration of the invitation to "imagine" propel the narrative forward. A creative use of white space adds to the quiet, powerful rhythm by creating harmony and balance, thus giving the picture book a cinematic montage quality. This leads the reader to better capture various autobiographical events in the poem. We see the child practicing with English words, turning words into stories, poems, and songs, and subsequently a book of poems as he becomes a young man. The asymmetrical composition of spreads adds dynamism, and this sense of movement is aided by diagonal compositions that push the story forward.

On a double page spread, we can see the boy in the top left hand corner of the verso from whom flows a stream of words zigzagging to his other self in the bottom right hand corner of the recto, physically gathering selected words from the flow to create such narratives (figure 13.4). Similar compositions show an older child with his notebook of poems walking along a path meandering through both pages, or the youth playing the guitar on the verso with his music and lyrics literally flying to the other side where the young man sits at a table while incorporating them into a book. These

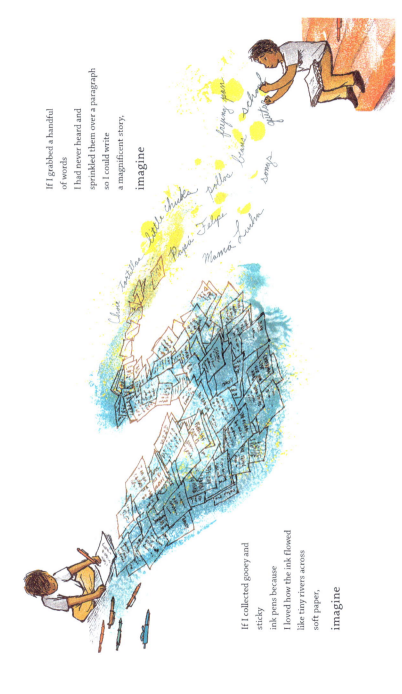

FIGURE 13.4 *Imagine* (2018) by Juan Felipe Herrera and illustrated by Lauren Castillo (19-20). Courtesy of Candlewick Press.

dynamic illustrations, interspersed in a variety of other spreads with varied compositions, keep a steady rhythm and the reader engaged, and, in most cases, inspired.

The picture book ends with Herrera giving his speech as poet laureate of the U.S., finally coming back to an empty landscape with the final line of the poem that at last completes the conditional "imagine what you could do" (29–30). Full of optimism and hope, *Imagine* makes the readers believe in the opportunity of improvement for self or social circumstances. At the same time, this metaliterary approach focuses on the character as a reader. That way, the writer invites children to relate to his own experiences, encouraging them to envision all the possibilities that may await them.

## Superheroines and Superheroes Blurring Borders and Overcoming Limitations: *Grandma and Me at the Flea, Super Cilantro Girl* and *Featherless*

The main characters in Herrera's picture books which we analyze in this section represent superheroines and superheroes who empower Chicano/a and Latino/a children to claim their identity by blurring linguistic and political borders.

In *Grandma and Me at the Flea*, published in 2002, Juanito (we assume, Herrera's child self or alter ego) tells us about spending his Sunday at the *remate*, the flea market, where his grandma Esperanza takes him in her van to sell secondhand clothes. We learn from the very beginning of the story that Juanito's parents are farmworkers in the north during the apple season, and that this is a happy and special occasion for the child: grandma and he prepare all the secondhand clothes to sell at the flea market, and they sing while driving to the *remate*. There he will spend his Sunday going round the booths to run errands for his grandma with his friends Danny and Floribey. The colorful illustrations by Anita De Lucio-Brock, clearly influenced by Mexican folk techniques in the use of bright colors, for instance, depict people and objects in detail while they take the reader from the zarape booth to the music tent, passing from the scary woman who sells cowboy boots to the chile tent, to the belt-man, then to the toy booth, and finally to the jewelry-man.

By running his grandma's errands, Juanito realizes how the *remate* is a community in which everybody helps one another, exchanging objects,

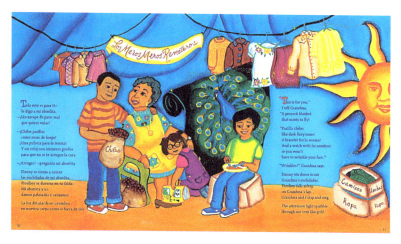

FIGURE 13.5 *Grandma and Me at the Flea/Los Meros Meros Remateros* (2002) by Juan Felipe Herrera and illustrated by Anita De Lucio-Brock, 30–31. Courtesy of Lee & Low Books.

but especially exchanging hope, symbolized by Grandma Esperanza's name ("hope" in Spanish). Juanito's centrality in the picture book is represented both visually, appearing on each double page spread, and verbally, when he tells his story in the first-person singular, thus sharing his point of view with the reader. Nevertheless, it is grandma Esperanza as the heroine who represents generosity and empathy not only by exchanging products with the other members of the community in the flea market, but also by giving them hope. That is the case towards the end of the picture book when she trades with a woman Juanito's little book of poems for her flowerpot, thereby explaining: "He gave them to me when I returned from the hospital last year. They always give me hope" (29). She reminds her grandson: "A true *rematero* is kind and generous, Juanito" (29).

The special relationship between child protagonists and their grandmothers is present and central in various Chicano/a picture books, such as Francisco Alarcón and Maya González's picture books of poems devoted to the seasons: *Laughing Tomatoes and Other Spring Poems/Jitomates risueños y otros poemas de primavera* (1997), *From the Bellybutton of the Moon and Other Summer Poems/Del ombligo de la luna y otros poemas de verano* (1998), *Angels Ride Bikes and Other Fall Poems/Los ángeles andan en bicicleta y otros poemas de otoño* (1999), *Iguanas in the Snow and Other Winter Poems/Iguanas en la nieve y otros poemas de invierno* (2001). Published between 1997 and 2001, Alarcón's grandmother's centrality is represented both visually and verbally as the storyteller whose stories in Nahuatl captivated Alarcón as a child. Maya González also illustrated Amada I. Pérez's picture book, *Nana's Big Surprise* (2007), in which Nana, the protagonist's elder Spanish-speaking grandmother, visits the family after her husband's passing. The presence of the protagonists' grandmothers in these stories allow for the use of translanguaging in the English version of the written text, such as in the case of *Grandma and Me at the Flea* where Herrera includes words in Mexican Spanish which are culturally loaded in order to promote and validate the language Chicano/a children acquire in their homes and in their interactions with family and community members (Alamillo, 160). Some of these words are references to Mexican culture such as Cantinflas, the famous Mexican comedian, *mariachis*, and *quinceañera*, and most of them refer to the culinary arts of Mexican food: *nopalitos, burritos, chile rayado, chile pasilla, mole, chile colorado, piquín, tamales*, as well as to everyday objects of *rebozos, zarapes, telenovelas*. The objects and products in the booths, traditional of Mexican-Chicano/a culture, are depicted in the borderless illustrations[1] with their names written in Spanish: *verdura, fruta, ropa nueva y usada, rebozos, camisas, botas*, etc. (figure 13.5). The special relationship between grandmothers and children through language and culture brings to light the interdependence between generations, family, and community. Grandmothers become agents of influence and change in the lives of their grandchildren by using translanguaging in their exchanges, thus blurring the linguistic borders imposed by restrictive language policies in schools (Alamillo, 152).

It is in *Super Cilantro Girl* (2003) where Herrera and illustrator Honorio Robledo Tapia present a superheroine, visually representing an uplifting image in this picture book cover as Super Cilantro girl flies through the sky, one arm raised like Superman. She is depicted as a superheroine wearing a green mask, gloves, bright green tights, boots, and a shiny yellow shirt. Her hair and eyes are bright green, and she is carrying a woman in her shirt front pocket. She is accompanied by a bird, shown flying on the back cover as Super Cilantro Girl's alter ego. The story tells us about Esmeralda Sinfronteras (meaning "borderless" or "without borders"), a girl whose mother has been stopped at the border in Tijuana because authorities say that she needs a green card to enter into the United States. However, as Esperanza's grandmother reassuringly remarks: "She's a citizen, Esme. Everything will be OK" (5). At bedtime, holding the green cilantro leaves she has taken from her mother's garden she makes a wish: "I hope mamá comes home soon" (6). In the morning, a bird taps on Esmeralda's window, presented as an instrumental part of Esmeralda's transformation into Super Cilantro Girl: her hands first turn green, then her teeth, her eyes, her hair, until finally she becomes so tall that she cannot go into her own house. When she sees her mother is not at home, she decides to rescue her from the detention center at the border and bring her back. Subsequently, she makes a green mask, wears Abuelita's starry shawl as a cape, puts on her best green tights, and finally slips on her favorite gold hightop sneakers. Herrera's story is full of symbolism as translated visually by Robledo Tapia in his illustrations: to begin with, the girl's name, Esmeralda Sinfronteras, carries the meaning of the green color ("esmeralda" means "emerald," a green gem) which predominates in the pictures throughout the book, and which is associated with both cilantro, one of the herbs most used in traditional Mexican cooking, and the plant which helps the protagonist turn into a superheroine. Green is also the color of the permanent resident card which allows immigrants to live and work permanently in the United States, thus representing a symbol of otherness as Sonia Rodríguez points out in her study "Conocimiento Narratives: Creative Acts and Healing in Latinx Children's and Young Adult Literature" (13).

With the help of the fresh bouquet of cilantro from her mother's garden, Esmeralda, now transformed into the Super Cilantro Girl, flies to the border accompanied by the mysterious bird (figure 13.6) until she gets to the gray walls of wire and steel that mark the separation between the U.S. and Mexico. She takes her mother into her shirt pocket and flies back home where Esmeralda falls asleep, later waking up in the morning and finding her mother there. The story closes when the bird flies "free and *sin fronteras*" (31).

Since the girl's last name, Sinfronteras, translates as "without borders" in English, this conveys a clear message of the girl's ability to overcome physical and psychological borders, that is, suggesting the separation between mother and immigrant children face when trying to cross into the United States. Green is the color of the peritexts and the endpapers, the front endpapers used by Herrera to explain how his family crossed *la frontera* in Tijuana many times to go to the doctor or to the movies to see superhero films. His mother needed to show her green card because when she crossed from Mexico to the United States, there was already a border: "But what about families kept apart by borders? I wondered. Maybe, I dreamed—and still

**FIGURE 13.6** *Super Cilantro Girl/La Superniña del Cilantro* (2003) by Juan Felipe Herrera and illustrated by Honorio Robledo Tapia (20–21). Courtesy of Lee & Low Books.

dream—there is a way to bring families together. It will take a heroic effort from someone like *El Santo* or the star of this story, but it can be done" (2–3). The fact that Esmeralda's mother is a citizen and does not need a green card to enter the country, but is stopped at the border, makes it clear that she is stopped because it is assumed she is undocumented due to her Mexican features.

In her article "Latina Super-heroines: Hot Tamales in Tights vs. Women Warriors, Wrestlers and Guerrilla Fighters of La Raza," Carolina Fernández Rodríguez argues that the political intent of the story in *Super Cilantro Girl* resides in the attempt to empower young Chicanas by helping them understand the plight of grown-ups as confronted with the difficulties of living undocumented in the United States without green cards or families separated by the Mexico-U.S. border (121). Nevertheless, Katherine Elizabeth Bundy's reading of Super Cilantro Girl's story in "Was It All a Dream? Chicana/o Children and Mestiza Consciousness in *Super Cilantro Girl* (2003) and *Tata's Gift* (2014)" is framed within Gloria Anzaldúa's concept of *mestiza consciousness* in *Borderlands/La Frontera: The New Mestiza* (1987), given that its dream state construes Esmeralda's transformation into a superheroine in her sleep—a call-to-action to transcend "binary limitations that the hybrid subject such as the mestiza or the chicano/a embodies and performs as border identities" (139). The *mestiza* dream state, here represented verbally and visually by the bird, is the moment when identity negotiation takes place. According to Bundy, in Chicano/a children's and juvenile literature specifically, dreams function as "a space for expressing desires for the future" and become a source to "help resolve problems in the child's waking life" (138). The symbolism of Esmeralda Sinfronteras' name gains full meaning when Super Cilantro Girl's powers make the border disappear: "We'll make everything so green-green, the border will disappear!" (26), while cilantro grows everywhere, and makes the officers all of a sudden speak Spanish.

Esmeralda Sinfronteras becomes the image of the *mestiza*/Chicana/ hybrid subject who blurs cultural and linguistic borders, thanks to her active imagination and her agency, symbolized by her transformation into a superheroine.

Overcoming obstacles and blurring the limitations for differently-abled children is what Tomasito, the hero in *Featherless* (2004), does. Unlike Super Cilantro Girl, Tomasito does not transform into a superhero with a cape and superpowers, but rather, he overcomes the limits imposed by his physical condition: born with spina bifida, he is in a wheelchair and he dreams of playing soccer in his new school team. From the very beginning, we see Tomasito in his wheelchair thanks to Ernesto Cuevas, Jr.'s brilliant illustrations, including the boy's expression on his face conveying sadness. The story opens when the boy's father surprises him with a little pet, a featherless little bird with a tiny curled up leg with a bell hanging from his neck. "If he doesn't have feathers, he can't fly!" (4), states Tomasito as he looks closely at the bird in the cage. The parallelism between the boy and the little bird, now named Desplumado, is clearly represented both verbally and visually. When Tomasito's father says that Desplumado was born different, like the boy was, the borderless illustration shows a close-up image of the boy's face looking at the bird in the cage. However, the illustration makes the reader feel as if they were inside the cage with the bird, and it is the boy who seems to be in the cage, his face seen behind the cage bars (fig. 13.7).

Tomasito seems to feel trapped, not only because he is in a wheelchair, but also because he is a newcomer at school: "We just moved here. Back in Mendota, I knew everyone. Now everybody asks me all over again why I'm in a wheelchair" (7). Being differently-abled and a newcomer makes Tomasito feel as an outsider in the community where his father and his school friend Marlena are the ones who encourage him to overcome the obstacles he faces on a daily basis. It is Marlena, who also dreams of playing soccer,

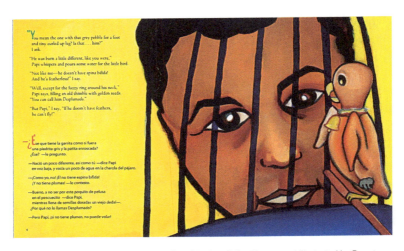

**FIGURE 13.7** *Featherless/Desplumado* (2004) by Juan Felipe Herrera and illustrated by Ernesto Cuevas, Jr., 4–5. Courtesy of Lee & Low Books.

who tells the boy to use his wings to play if he cannot use his legs. Again, it is in the dream state that the turning point in the story takes place. As in *Super Cilantro Girl*, it is when sleeping in his room that Tomasito, always accompanied by Desplumado in his cage, imagines that he is training and finally playing with the school soccer team, the Fresno Flyers, waking up next morning with the sensation of floating and flying with the little bird. But when he wakes up, he is falling off his bed. Trying to stand up, he tells his father that he wants Desplumado to fly, and his father realizes that the boy is actually talking about himself: "You mean, *you* want to fly, *hijo*" (26). The words *you* and *hijo* are emphasized in italics both in the English and Spanish texts. The story closes when Tomasito finally plays with his team and the crowd cheers him on. His teammates gather around him after he scores a goal with a *cabeza*, or headshot, becoming the hero of the soccer match. The last double page spread shows a close-up of Tomasito holding Desplumado in his hands, finally freeing the little bird from his cage, stroking the bird's head and saying "You can be a flyer too, Desplumado. There's more than one way to fly!" (30). Herrera's expressive prose interplays with Cuevas' brilliant colorful illustrations to tell Tomasito's story of achievement with the help of his father and Marlena. The predominant colors throughout the picture book are yellows, oranges, and greens that represent daytime and dark blues and mauves that set the tone for the nighttime, especially in the double page spread in which the boy wakes up after dreaming he is flying free with Desplumado. The borderless image shows Tomasito falling off his bed, the written text reading "Up, up . . . Then crackity-crack goes my back— Boom-boom crash!" (24–25), as the boy tries to stand up and the little bird looks at him from his cage on the right edge of the illustration.

Although the story centers around Tomasito's blurring the limitations he needs to face for being differently-abled, Marlena is also an example of blurring the limitations marked, in her case, by traditional and restrictive gender roles. She loves playing soccer and is not only a member of the soccer school team, but she also gives Tomasito encouragement when he dreams of playing with the Fresno Flyers: "Be a flyer!," she says to Tomasito, "Use your wings!" (12–13). The double page spread of this scene shows Tomasito and Marlena on the soccer field on the recto side at the front of the illustration, emphasizing their centrality in the story. She is wearing the team uniform while the other players in the team are celebrating and cheering at the back and at the center of the image. Thus, playing in the school soccer team allows both Tomasito and Marlena to overcome the restrictions implied by being differently-abled (in the case of Tomasito) and imposed by traditional gender roles (in the case of Marlena) consequently providing them with a sense of belonging.

In the back endpapers[2] both Herrera and Cuevas tell us about the importance of community for them: Cuevas's love for the arts is rooted in his experiences in the fields with his parents. Born in Texas, his paintings express his love and deep understanding for the Chicano/a culture. For this Chicano/a artist art is an exploration of self and a vehicle to express one's voice while developing community. On his part, in the back endpapers, Herrera includes a short text entitled *Everyone asks Tomasito* where he explains what spina bifida is and how it can affect children's lives. He reminds the reader that Latino/a women have the highest risk of spina bifida pregnancies, and includes the link of the Spina Bifida Association of America to find further information.

## Picture Books: Redrawing Boundaries within Children's Literature

After analyzing Herrera's autobiographical *cuentos* and the three picture books in which the author and illustrators blur the limitations imposed on the Latino/a and Chicano/a communities, we witness how these picture books provide Chicano/a children with positive representations of their culture.

*Imagine, Calling the Doves,* and *The Upside Down Boy* are autobiographical picture books which allow children to follow young Herrera's inspiring trajectory. Both his poetic texts and the illustrations of his artistic partners highlight essential aspects of Chicano/a children's lives and let the readers develop their visual literacy by immersing themselves in a dreamlike, lyrical world full of empowering experiences, creativity, and imagination. As we have seen in such autobiographical *cuentos*—actually a form of narrative poetry—his picture books become powerful tools for various ends: empowering Latino/a children, legitimizing their intercultural identity, and establishing how identity negotiation and production in these *cuentos* take place within the community and the environment. By emphasizing the important role of family and community, and by transforming the world by means of creativity and imagination, Herrera's stories for children empower younger readers to overcome the oppressive feelings of displacement and non-belonging.

The picture books in the second group—*Grandma and Me at the Flea, Super Cilantro Girl,* and *Featherless*—expose young Latino/a and Chicano/a readers to culturally significant images and symbols (the *remate, cilantro,* and the green card, the school soccer team, among others) to which they can relate to enhance self-perception and construct their identities. As we pointed out in the case of *Grandma and Me at the Flea,* the presence of the protagonist's grandmothers and the use of translanguaging in both the verbal and the visual codes are a significant tool to validate the language of interaction with family and community. Through fantasy and the dream-like state, the stories of self-empowerment in *Super Cilantro Girl* and *Featherless* give voice and visibility to identities which have been silenced and socially erased due to ethnicity, disability, or gender.

We have also noted how the picture book offers two voices or codes: the verbal and the pictorial, which can mostly empower young readers and subliminally validate their cultural knowledge by redrawing boundaries and by creating a sense of interactivity within the different ways of coordinating pictures and text. Readers are required to bring their own answers and their own resolutions and interpretations to the works, as Frederick Luis Aldama has observed in *Spilling the Beans in Chicanolandia: Conversations with*

*Writers and Artists* (259). This tends to engender a special collaborative relationship between children and adults, the visual representations allowing for a more balanced power dynamic between less experienced child readers and adults.

Throughout our study we have also emphasized how cultural knowledge can help young readers understand the visual code used by artists in order to achieve better comprehension of the thoughts, feelings, and actions communicated by them through the images they create. This is especially applicable for Chicano/a and Latino/a children whose identity has too often been silenced or misrepresented, so that they see themselves for the first time in the books they encounter. The stories in the picture books created by Juan Felipe Herrera and the different artists/illustrators together use their respective art to support their community while empowering children to become critical and active citizens by linking their personal experience to a wider perspective of cultural memory while developing visual literacy.

## Notes

1. Borderless illustrations or illustrations which bleed onto the edges extend to the edge of the page without frames or borders, thus enhancing identification with the characters and, according to Nikolajeva and Scott's analysis, conveying a sense of a hidden viewer whose perspective is very close to the image (Nikolajeva and Scott 95).
2. In picture book terminology, "endpapers" refers to those first (front endpapers) and last pages (back endpapers) which provide important information about the book both in terms of text and illustration.

## Works Cited

Alamillo, Laura, Larissa M. Mercado-López, and Cristina Herrera, eds. *Voices of Resistance. Interdisciplinary Approaches to Chican@ Children's Literature.* Lanham, Md.: Rowman and Littlefield, 2018.

Alarcón, Francisco X. *Laughing Tomatoes and Other Spring Poems/ Jitomates Risueños y Otros Poemas de Primavera.* Illustrated by Maya González. San Francisco, Calif.: Children's Book Press, 1997.

Alarcón, Francisco X. *From the Bellybutton of the Moon and Other Summer Poems/ Del ombligo de la luna y otros poemas de verano.* Illustrated by Maya González. San Francisco, Calif.: Children's Book Press, 1998.

Alarcón, Francisco X. *Angels Ride Bikes and Other Fall Poems/Los ángeles andan en bicicleta y otros poemas de otoño.* Illustrated by Maya G. González. Children's Book Press, 1999.

Alarcón, Francisco X. *Iguanas in the Snow and Other Winter Poems/Iguanas en la nieve y otros poemas de invierno*. Illustrated by Maya González. San Francisco, Calif.: Children's Book Press, 2001.

Aldama, Frederick Luis. *Spilling the Beans in Chicanolandia: Conversations with Writers and Artists*. Austin: University of Texas Press, 2006.

Anzaldúa, Gloria. *Borderlands/La Frontera. The New Mestiza*, 4th ed. San Francisco, Calif.: Aunt Lute Books, 2012.

Anzaldúa, Gloria. *Interviews/Entrevistas*. Edited by Ana Louise Keating. New York: Routledge, 2000.

Bamford, Anne. "The Visual Literacy White Paper." Commissioned by Adobe Systems Pty Lmd, Australia, 2013. Retrieved from https://aperture.org/wp-content/uploads/2013/05/visual-literacy-wp.pdf.

Barbas-Rhoden, Laura. "Toward an Inclusive Eco-Cosmopolitanism: Bilingual Children's Literature in the United States." *Interdisciplinary Studies in Literature and Environment* 18, no. 2 (2011): 359–376.

Bernardo Flórez, Marina. Personal interview with Juan Felipe Herrera, February 21, 2021.

Bundy, Katherine E. "Was It All a Dream? Chicana/o Children and Mestiza Consciousness in *Super Cilantro Girl* (2003) and *Tata's Gift* (2014)." In *Voices of Resistance. Interdisciplinary Approaches to Chican@ Children's Literature*, 151–162. Edited by Laura Alamillo, Larissa M. Mercado-López, and Cristina Herrera. Lanham, Md.: Rowman and Littlefield, 2018.

Campbell Naidoo, Jamie, ed. *Celebrating Cuentos. Promoting Latino Children's Literature and Literacy in Classrooms and Libraries*. Santa Barbara, Calif.: Libraries Unlimited, 2011.

Crossetto, Alice, Rajinder Garcha, and Mark Horan. *Disabilities and Disorders in Literature for Youth*. Lanham, Md.: Scarecrow, 2009.

Felten, Peter. "Visual Literacy." *Change: The Magazine of Higher Learning*, 40, no. 6 (2008): 60–64.

Fernández Rodríguez, Carolina. "Latina Super-heroines: Hot Tamales in Tights vs. Women Warriors, Wrestlers and Guerrilla Fighters of La Raza." *Complutense Journal of English Studies* 23 (2015): 115–136.

Freire, Paulo, and Donaldo Macedo. *Literacy: Reading the Word and the World*. London: Routledge, 1987.

Galda, Lee and Kathy G. Short. "Visual literacy: Exploring Art and Illustration in Children's Books." *The Reading Teacher* 46, no. 6 (1993): 506–516.

Giorgis, Cyndi, Nancy J. Johnson, Annamarie Bonomo, Shrissie Colbert, Angela Conner, Gloria Kauffman, and Dottie Kulesza. "Children's Books: Visual Literacy." *The Reading Teacher* 53, no. 2. (1999): 146–153.

Griswold, Jerry. "An Interview with Juan Felipe Herrera: An interview with the first Latino Poet Laureate of the United States about his Books for Kids." *Medium*, Oct. 24, 2019, medium.com/@jerrygriswold/juan-felipe-herrera-93f371a88afe. Retrieved from http://archive.parentschoice.org/article.

Herrera, Juan Felipe. *Calling the Doves/El canto de las palomas.* Illustrated by Elly Simmons. San Francisco, Calif.: Children's Book Press, 1995.

Herrera, Juan Felipe. *Featherless/Desplumado.* Illustrated by Ernesto Cuevas, Jr. New York: Children's Book Press, 2004.

Herrera, Juan Felipe. *Grandma and Me at the Flea/Los meros meros remateros.* Illustrated by Anita DeLucio-Brock. San Francisco, Calif.: Children's Book Press, 2002.

Herrera, Juan Felipe. *Imagine.* Illustrated by Lauren Castillo. Somerville, Mass.: Candlewick Press, 2018.

Herrera, Juan Felipe. *Super Cilantro Girl/La superniña del cilantro.* Illustrated by Honorio Robledo Tapia. San Francisco, Calif.: Children's Book Press, 2003.

Herrera, Juan Felipe. *The Upside Down Boy/El niño de cabeza.* Illustrated by Elizabeth Gómez. San Francisco, Calif.: Children's Book Press, 2000.

Kümmerling-Meibauer, Bettina. "Remembering the Past in Words and Pictures: How Autobiographical Stories Become Picturebooks." In *New Directions in Picturebook Research.* Edited by Teresa Colomer, Bettina Kümmerling-Meibauer, Cecilia Silva-Díaz, 205–215. New York: Routledge, 2009.

Lewis, David. *Reading Contemporary Picturebook: Picturing Text.* London: Routledge, 2001.

López, Tiffany Ana. *Growing up Chicana/o.* New York: Avon, 1995.

Morales, Yuyi. "Splendid Treasures of *Mi Corazón.*" In *Celebrating Cuentos: Promoting Latino Children's Literature and Literacy in Classrooms and Libraries.* Edited by Jamie Campbell Naidoo, ix-xi. Santa Barbara, Calif.: ABC-CLIO, 2011.

Morresi, Renata. "Borders, *Pachangas,* and Chicano/a Children's Picture Books." In *Space and Place in Children's Literature: 1789 to the Present.* Edited by Maria Sachiko Cecire, Hannah Field, Kavita Mudan Finn, and Malini Rov, 75–94. London: Routledge, 2016.

Nikolajeva, Maria, and Carol Scott. *How Picturebooks Work.* New York: Routledge, 2006.

Nodelman, Perry. *Words about Pictures.* Athens: University of Georgia Press, 1988.

Nodelman, Perry. "Decoding the Images: How Picture Books Work." In *Understanding Children's Literature.* Edited by Peter Hunt, 128–39. Routledge, 1999.

O'Neil, Kathleen Ellen. "Developing Visual Literacy for Greater Comprehension." *The Reading Teacher* 65, no. 3 (November 2011): 214–223.

Pérez, Amada I. *Nana's Big Surprise/Nana, ¡Qué sorpresa!* Illustrated by Maya González. San Francisco, Calif.: Children's Book Press, 2007.

Prior, Lori Ann, Angeli Willson, and Miriam Martínez. "Visual Literacy as a Pathway to Character Understanding." *The Reading Teacher* 66, no. 3 (2012): 195–206.

Rodríguez, Sonia A. "Conocimiento Narratives: Creative Acts and Healing in Latinx Children's and Young Adult Literature." *Children's Literature* 47 (2019): 9–29.

Roethler, Jacque. "Reading in Color: Children's Book Illustrations and Identity Formation for Black Children in the United States." *African American Review* 32, no. 1 (Spring 1998): 95–105.

Salisbury, Martin, and Morag Styles. *Children's Picturebooks: The Art of Visual Storytelling.* London: Laurence King Publishing, 2012.

Santiago, Esmeralda. "A Puerto Rican Existentialist in Brooklyn: An Interview with Esmeralda Santiago." In *Latina Self-Portraits: Interviews with Contemporary Women Writers.* Edited by Bridget Kevane and Juanita Heredia, 130–140. Albuquerque: New Mexico University Press, 2000.

Schwarcz, Joseph H., and Chava Schwarcz. *The Picture Book Comes of Age: Looking at Childhood through the Art of Illustration.* Chicago: American Library Association, 1991.

Soldofsky, Alan. "A Border-Crosser's Heteroglosssia: Interview with Juan Felipe Herrera, Twenty-First Poet Laureate of the United States." *MELUS: Multi-Ethnic Literature of the U.S.* 43, no. 2 (Summer 2018): 196–226.

Vardell, Sylvia M. *Poetry People: A Practical Guide to Children's Poets.* Westport, Conn: Libraries Unlimited, 2007.

Villarreal, Alicia, Sylvia Minton, and Miriam Martínez. "Making Meaning Through Visual Art in Picture Books." *The Reading Teacher* 69, no. 3 (2015): 265–275.

# PART IV

*Mapping the Sojourn of a Maverick*

**FIGURE 14.1** At Library of Congress, with Dr. James Billington (RIP), Head Librarian, Library of Congress. Selected me as Poet Laureate. Photo by Shawn Miller. 2015

CHAPTER 14

# The Poet, the Playwright, and the Citizen

## An Interview with U.S. Poet Laureate Juan Felipe Herrera

FRANCISCO A. LOMELÍ AND OSIRIS ANÍBAL GÓMEZ

## Part I: Interview a la Brava

**Can you describe for us how your initial inspiration to write poetry took place: when, how, where, what kind of expression emerged or the type of experimentations you explored? What was the context of your writing space? (FAL)**

Poetry came to me, and I moved into its quarters little by little. Traveling in my father's '40s Army truck pulling our handmade trailer, gazing at the green fields, slanting telephone poles, the cable swinging low and the rainy road ahead, the orange, red, and yellow land, alfalfa, corn and bursting fruit orchards. All this and more—Greyhound depot life, barrio scenes and aromas of the Wonder bread factory next to the railroad tracks and the tiny Coronet Pedro Infante Cinema in Logan Heights barrio, San Diego. Our tiny trailer and its three steps into ranchitos and mountains. And, most magical, the stories of my mother about life in a Mexico City orphanage during the Mexican Revolution, or about leaving Colonia Niño Perdido near Tepito and heading to Juárez, Chihuahua, and finally making to El Segundo Barrio in El Paso, Texas. And she recited poems and sang *corridos* (ballads), played word games, threw riddles in the air so I could catch them and decipher them— little did I know that she was preparing me to be a poet and a man on stage with endless audiences. Every member of my extended family became, in short time, a character in my ongoing novel or poem that I sketched, expanded, revised in my imagination.

Imagine this world cast on the road, in deserts, side-of-the-road micro-villages, city-outskirts, mountain tops, and open country. Each scene, each mound of earth, each bus stop and apple-pie ten-minute pause on the winding road—all this was crucial and necessary in my formation as a poet and artist. And—it was all kindled by my mother's storytelling and passionate voice and life.

Later, as I moved on through middle and high school, in San Diego, my teachers presented key materials that later would further enrich my sense of poetry, writing, and my levels of aesthetic intensity. I chose a high level. After delving into the Italian Renaissance, the impressionists, expressionism, and surrealism, I leaned toward Salvador Dalí, Georges Braque, Pablo Picasso, René Magritte, and, later, Henri Matisse and Andy Warhol, Peter Max, and Jasper Johns. In terms of writers, I chose Herman Hesse, Franz Kafka, Thomas Mann, Jiddu Krishnamurti, Antonin Artaud, Paul Sartre, and Federico García Lorca. All this fascinated me.

Abstraction, big mind, wild images, a sense of emergency, and stiletto-sharp investigations into reality. By my senior year, I admired installations and assemblages as well as experimental theatre. In my senior art studio class, I constructed a giant wooden panel made of two by fours, painted white enamel with a rubber baby nailed and crucified, painted black. My concept was racism. This project created quite a stir in school. With my books on hand, I was prepared for q&a—*The Autobiography of Malcom X* and a sociology paperback. This sounds quite astute, yet I was walking on thin ice. My choices were magnificent, however, I was not aware of how much I loved art and writing. I was ahead of myself and lacked mentors outside of school.

Experimental theater took a hold of me as paged through Artaud. I didn't have an art studio—I lived with my mother in a tiny apartment a few blocks from San Diego High. My father had passed away when I was in tenth grade. I ambled here and there. All I had was my love for the arts, drawing, and for writing—with nowhere to go. So, I wrote a tiny experimental play series that I called, "Liquid Theatre," after Artaud's *Theatre of the Double*. And his use of trance language—another most attractive approach. Themes inspired by *Mann's Transposition of Two Heads* were mesmerizing, phrases and images from Hesse's Steppenwolf were also magnetic to the point that I started to write poems in square shapes wherein lived the words in caps and an "electric rat." Krishnamurti provided the format of discussion followed by short, story-like paragraphs. This was also very appealing to me. By August, 1967, I left for UCLA, where I would create Chicano Teatro, and multi-form performance with El Teatro Tolteca—incorporating modern dance, slide show, and poetry as the main characters. My workspace was anywhere. These influences and experiments would continue throughout my life.

**As poet, writer, actor, maestro, photographer, playwright, you embody the complete intellectual and artistic figure in pursuit of naming and knowing the intangible. What is this journey like? Do you feel that your investigations and art practice bring you closer to understanding the problems of our present human condition? (OAG)**

One art piece or scene or painting, sculpture, or performance leads to a wider field of art. Every move into art and letters provides inspiration and an inner exhilarating conversation to explore, discover, and create. I had everything I needed just by looking at a biography book cover on Toulouse Lautrec in the San Diego Public Library on "E" Street. This gave me incredible energy to draw, write, and think as an artist, an investigator of color and mediums and the lovely, odd, bare-bone life of a painter. This was true when I attended concerts at UCLA in the late sixties. After seeing East Coast experimental theatres such as Café La Mama and the Open Theatre, I was ready to build my own groups. The same was true for a concert by the Maurice Bejart Twentieth Century Ballet—I wanted to construct similar choreographies with our ragtag Chicano *teatro*—Teatro Chichimeca and Teatro Tolteca. Such is the journey. Since I knew jazz bass player, Roberto Miranda, Congero, Billy Loo, and modern dance artist, Maruka, I called on them to form a poetry jazz ensemble and readings on campus and in Santa Monica. Art is always looking for art, this is the key, and this is the life. Since I was a poet, I blended my writing and voice with these experiments. For me, experiment and multi-art is the medium. It is collective and each artist provides pathways to new work and new vistas. All this involves travel and performance, conversations, observation, learning, challenges, art spaces, and art galleries where more is available, and these are the music and poetry audiences. It is not just the art, it is the *people as one*, that is, the audience, the community. All this is part of the art, the poem and the ever-blossoming and expanding ideas and new directions for the work at hand. Of course, all this requires a nomadic lifestyle, intense concentration, and abandonment of day-to-day concerns and family, or at least absences. Life is on the road, in gyms, buses, and cars or in old convents, sleeping on concrete with many and brushing your teeth on a tiny faucet, waiting in line.

Unfortunately, there comes a moment when you must choose a medium—painting, sculpture, collage, theatre, playwriting, jazz, or poetry. As you know, I chose poetry. This has other requirements—a desk, a typewriter (or desktop), paper, journals, fountain pens, and soft-lead pencils. And isolation. The only person you talk to is yourself. The menu—peanut butter sandwiches, or burritos, yogurt, bananas, mixed nuts, apples, and water. Any food calling for more attention is going to steal your time for the poem or phrase sizzling in your head. You literally have to run and dive into the work, or else it disappears. Once in a while you visit your mother, once in a while you turn around and visit your partner in the next room, and once in a while you pick up the phone and say hello to your children. When you do visit, at any moment you may dash to the corner or rest room and madly scribble something on a shred of paper you picked up somewhere. Your world comes together when you read your work; for a brief moment, in front of an audience, you appear as a regular poet, a human being. You ask, does all this bring me closer to understanding the problems of the human condition? You begin to reflect on the questions you pose. The ones wiggling on paper. Sometimes they light up if you give them time. Remember, time? When I give them time, all this I have been doing for more than half a century, reveals something very simple—it was about love. It was about assembling a moment of true community. What love? The things you wrote about, the thing you were after, the things you gave to thousands, with every cell and second you had in your hands and offered with your voice. The words that you sang out, the ones that lasted for a handful of minutes and a few seconds and left you the way flowers go, just a few hours. A ceremonial poet is a poet that offers her voice and poem as a bouquet of flowers, something that will fade in short time, like life itself, in the plenum of infinite vastness. It is called *in xóchitl in cuícatl*, Flower-Song. The poet as the singer, the Cuícatl, sings out the way a flower bursts out its tiny life with its allotted joy.

**Many critics have pointed out that your essence as an avant-garde poet comes from deploying and rethinking poetic devices rooted in oral traditions. Yet, we believe your ceremonial voice comes from your ability**

The Poet, the Playwright, and the Citizen **323**

**to capture and decipher the diglossia within the Chicano experience and the search for *a homeland*. Therefore, what does it mean to be a ceremonial being? A foot soldier of *la palabra*? (OAG)**

My imagination comes from my mother Lucha's daily storytelling, ideas, proverbs, riddles, and songs from the Mexican Revolution during years spent in an orphanage in Mexico City and in la colonia del El Niño Perdido, at the margins of Tepito. The many very frank conversations with my mother also guided me to speak from deep sources.

Her love for performance in tiny living spaces, whether in a trailer or one- or two-room apartments, offered me the desire and possibility of being on stage or merely making up stories that involved two or three characters. As time passed, I noticed that every member of my family, my uncles Fernando Guzmán-Guevara, Roberto Quintana, and Vicente Quintana, were all unique figures, brave seekers of new horizons, and some were artists in their own right, regardless, they were all brimming with the stories of their life journeys. My uncle Fernando had the analytic skills of a lawyer, his unrealized career. In California, his office was the laundry and steaming machines that he opened and filled. Uncle Chente was a rebel artist, he painted in whatever material he could find, working in acrylics, oils, and also was adept at sculpture—all self-taught. Tío Roberto was one of the first post-Revolution poets of the borderlands of Juárez, Chihuahua, [and] El Paso, Texas. He flourished in radio XEJ and was known throughout Juárez/El Paso, both cities—a radio man, a writer, an actor, and an organizer of cultural events in El Paso. Later, in the '50s, he was the first to organize annual "Días del Grito" (The Cry of Independence) in the Civic Center of San Francisco, Scottish Hall, with poets, dancers, and musicians. My uncles were from another time, yet, what they taught me was key—art at all costs, self-made and self-propelled, [and to be] callers and builders of community. My family was my first school, my first creative workshop, my borderlands art degree, my poetry and community MFA (Mexican Family Art). I must say that my love for the "avant-garde" probably comes from the daring vision of my family to make a new life on the land, the stage, canvas, stone, and the microphone. It was a brave drive, a hearth fire that kept each one of my family members going, doing, creating, presenting. I see that now, I feel it. As I have said earlier, once I became aware of the various art movements from the Renaissance to pop art, everything came together. I knew where to seek Picasso, Dalí, and Jean Cocteau. Georgia O'Keeffe and Hart Crane, no one mentioned until decades later. It took a while to add these major American artists and writers to my palette. Put all this together and you'll get a sense of my "avant-garde" sources. The "ceremonial" aspects emerged in the later sixties and early seventies with the publication of my first book in 1974, *Rebozos of Love / We Have Woven / Sudor de Pueblos / On Our Back.* Although it could be seen as a collection of poems, it really is one poem. Recently, I discovered, as I mentioned earlier, that it is a *floricanto,* a flower-song or in the words of the Mexica prince of Texcoco and poet, Nezahualcóyotl, it is a *in xóchitl in cuícatl,* a singing flower, an *offering and celebration* more than a ceremony—a philosophical root source for Latinx poets of the twenty-first century. In order to have a notion of homeland you have to have a set of root sources. An experimental notion of homeland was central to all social movements during the 70s. For the Chicanx artists, mostly, homeland was a continental sphere with its apex in the Southwest or as Alurista and Luis Valdez (and anthropologists) called it, "Aztlán." It was more of a galvanizing symbolic medium than a sacred social source. Being a poet involves opening as many levels as possible and doors of awareness of culture, art, history, physics, and philosophy. And most important, the suffering of all peoples. The homeland changes with every global crisis. Sooner or later, the poet adopts the world. I see myself as a human being calling for humanity—that is my home.

**Who might be the ten key persons of influence to which you can attribute a direct intellectual or poetic genealogy at different/key points of your life? Please explain each one briefly & what they contributed to your formation. (FAL)**
My mother, Lucha Quintana Herrera Martínez, no doubt, was my principal influence in how I thought about life, how I perceived it, how I delighted in its multi-form offerings—the sky, the land, the ocean, nature and its animals and its peoples. Not to mention, ever-expanding curiosity and love for surprise and discovery: all essential ingredients for an artist. Most of all, the constant, never-ending questions that have to do with things beyond the absurd, that is, consumerism, materialism, leisure culture and power. To reiterate—my three uncles: Roberto, Vicente, and Eugenio Quintana—each of them were pioneers, the actor and radio personality, the bohemian painter and the seer. All essential in my life.

And teachers from third grade to high school: Mrs. Lelya Sampson, who gave me my life's key—"You have a beautiful voice—," in third grade, she told me at Lowell Elementary in Logan Heights Barrio, San Diego. Mr. Robert Hayden, who believed in my playwriting potential in sixth grade at Patrick Henry Elementary, San Francisco, Mr. Shuster in seventh grade at Roosevelt Junior High in San Diego who presented the great composers, Ludwig van Beethoven, Wolfgang Amadeus Mozart, Jean Sibelius, Felix Mendelssohn, and Johann Sebastian Bach. To this day I listen to the work of these virtuosos. In ninth grade at Roosevelt Jr. High, Mr. Warner taught us how to write a power sentence and the richness of vocabulary—to this day, I apply his teachings. In tenth grade, Mr. Frank Petrich was essential: he taught me about the painting movements since the Renaissance to the pop art of Andy Warhol, and Mrs. Steiger, the following year, in studio art, in 1966, believed in my controversial installation on race and told me while I was presenting it, "I am right behind you." And there is Mr. Whightman in English Lit that taught us Sartre, and in his summer school "great books" class, he presented us with the great philosophers, in particular, Arthur Schopenhauer's *The World as Will and Idea*. All this stimulated me and began to set the tone for the underpinnings of my poetics. And finally, Mr. Ezra Harrison-Maxwell, my choir teacher from tenth to twelfth grade. Here, I learned to sing in a collective setting, be on stage and also present the choir to the audience. Once Mr. Maxwell told me, "You have a good voice, John-John, but you are only using one third of it!" Most of my life has been dedicated to encouraging students and communities to value their inner self, their true voice.

I have been blessed, fortunate, and lucky in having so many beautiful, well-prepared, and caring teachers. Each one of them contributed to my dedication to art, voice, metaphysics, the questions of existence, ontology, religion, self-realization, and community.

In the world of poetry, I was fortunate once again—in 1962, my father had us move to 11th and "D" Street, a deserted place two blocks from Broadway. Next door lived ninth grader, Alurista, one of the pioneers of what came to be known as Chicano poetry. This is how we met and continued as friends, poets and artists until 1974.

Painters have always been major figures for me.

Picasso—For his insatiable hunger for painting, his milieu of artists and friends, his outspoken intensity, his various phases and uses of diverse mediums, his life as an artist. Dalí—I have always loved, his inner burning desire to paint, to be a radical, to draw from the jagged shapes of his early environments on Cadaques, and later, his installations, his sofa in the shape of

Mae West's lips, not to mention his association with García Lorca and Luis Buñuel. I love all these artists and have since high school.

Vincent Van Gogh—in a similar manner, I am highly moved by his thick art, his brutal landscapes and his dark renditions of "The Potato Eaters." Gauguin and his relationship with Van Gogh made me think on their collision as friends and their different palettes and journeys. The life of artists at that time was thrilling, rough-cut, as their life conditions and their personal visions of their art and world. Matisse—simply for his paper cut-outs and his creative use of materials when he no longer could paint with a brush or sculpture. I love every phase of his development. And his studios—his room at Regina Hotel in Nice, France, I find exhilarating for its window view of the beach. Not to mention his sculpture and his mastery of the proportions of the human body and his way of applying almost imperceptible distortions which add a radical sensitivity. Magritte was most interesting to me because of his play with image and word, how he reversed signifiers from the signified and, of course, his painting of things, like a room with a giant shaving brush and comb. Artaud—again, a most fiery personality and a man in search of language and mind, his plays, his acting in the Alfred Jarry theatre, his face and his brutal letters to editors. Most of all, I was intrigued by his concepts of theatre and his ritual poetry influenced by the heightened practices of the Tarahumara of Chihuahua. His inner-invented languages. Max Beckmann—a fierce force, exiled from Germany during Hitler's rule. He said to his art students in NYC, "if you don't use the color black in your work, it is not art." This was quite a powerful message for me. How does the poet transpose this to the written word: deep honesty and revelation, fearless truth. Frida Kahlo, of course, for her genius, bravery, self-portraits, her borderlands visions and her definitions of Mexico and surgical gender self-examinations, self-presentations, fearlessness, her story, her relationship with Diego. Her moment in time in Mexico and the USA. She was the force of the twentieth century.

Beyond these influences—I must say that the postwar Polish poets of the Holocaust have inspired me with their non-ornamental writing ethics. Direct, succinct, naked talk, impossible talk about things and events that are ungraspable—the horrific massacres of millions, the Jews. Our brothers, our sisters. This has moved me to write "things-as-it-is" poems, the many in the one, noir, just say it. Three of the poets that I love: Tadeusz Rozevicz, Wislava Szymborska and Zbigniew Herbert. Of course, there is Cezlaw Milosz, who is most responsible for bringing out their work in his anthology, *Provinces.*

**You offer a vast & eclectic array of philosophers/writers/artists that you cite as instrumental in your synthesis of ideas, concepts, and motivation. How did you pick and choose them? (FAL)**

Philosophy and art have been central for me since I was at San Diego High (1964–67). Part of it had to do with taking a "Great Books" philosophy summer school class with Prof. David Whitman. I was also in his English Lit class in senior year. He was a free thinker, eccentric and a magnificent teacher. Schopenhauer was key, as I mentioned earlier. In English Lit, during the year, he read the Peanuts cartoon strip every morning while wearing dark glasses. At times he gave us a choice for essays. On the chalkboard he would ask us to choose, (1) write the essay as assigned, (2) write about a tree, or (3) discuss the existential dilemma of Roquentin in *Nausea* by Sartre (as assigned). I veered between the tree and Roquentin. The other factor that tilted me toward philosophy was hanging out with Alurista and his cousin, Hugo Repetto, fresh from Mexico City and Hugo's girlfriend, Jeanne Landale, sister of Tommy Landale, who was one of my school buddies. Those three were always talking about Sartre and Simone de Beauvoir and Freud's notion of psychoanalysis. If you saw me with them, you would not notice since I did not speak up or lead any conversation. I was most comfortable being a listener, an expert listener. On the other hand, my crew, my age, talked about guitars and made jokes and I drew cartoons per request. Back to the philosophers—there was something that truly attracted me to the big thinkers, most of them existentialists, which was in vogue at the time—I mean going back as far as Schopenhauer to Nietzsche and then leaping to Sartre. *Thus Spake Zarathustra* was quite a book. I carried it through the halls on occasion. Its poetry and tone moved me.

My mother, Lucha, was always a natural philosopher, and asked the big questions about freedom, hunger, and liberation. And, of course, the '60s were made of pure, undiluted questions, pondering and experimental thought, globally and nationally, picking at the nerves of revolution, identity, war and peace, violence, homeland, body, magic and what was called at that time, "self-realization." It was raining philosophy and I was thirsty. Ever since then, I have followed up given my interests in power and culture and religion. Here is one of the keys: philosophy is concerned with a meta-reality, not the typical day-to-day life, or as Schopenhauer says, we all have a "a metaphysical need." To notice the way power, ideology, and beliefs are manipulated and the consequences peoples suffer is the responsibility of peoples that hold humanity close to their heart. Lately, I choose to listen to the online videos of the Dalai Lama.

He speaks of ahimsa/nonviolence, karuna/compassion, the misperception of reality, climate change, world-identity, humanity, and our interdependence. What will happen without dealing with these things?

**Most readers of your work are keenly aware of your working-class background & how your parents' experience as migrant workers shaped you. To what do you attribute that strong impact or influence if you sought a space of intellectual independence where you could transcend your social class and your family background? What compels you to return to the same fountains of origin for a worldview that makes itself manifest throughout your work? (FAL)**

As you know, a larger, deeper, more "authentic" motion of self-reflection, self-re-creation and self-realization (again, terms that were popular in the '60s and '70s) came to their apogee in the '60s—a time when I was in middle and high school and when I entered UCLA and was immersed in one way or another in the multiple social, pop-cultural, and cultural movements of the West Coast, the Southwest, the nation, Latin America, and with the world at large. All these forces were braided—of power, culture and the transformative call for new identities. Think of the Women's Movement, Chicano, Black, Gay, Native, Asian, South Asian self-reconstruction. And note that all of these movements had attached music, curriculum, nascent publications, vernaculars, arts, newspapers, radio stations, clubs, performance, and cultural centers—as well as a charismatic leadership, with many followers. In such a whirlpool of investigation and community, I discovered and experimented with the key notion of the times—Chicano identity. For this, I read Native American stories, Aztec history, and Mesoamerican archaeology (remember, I was an Anthro major). One of the most attractive books for me was Jerome Rothenberg's book, used in my Anthro 101 class, *Technicians of the Sacred: A Range of Poetries from Africa, America, Asia, Europe, and Oceania*. Here, I had the texts of sacred songs, materials attached to drawings, life-cycle chants, voices capable of changing life and bodies of young writers. These expressive materials contributed to new claims for a newfound identity.

Also, I noticed that the Chicano *movimiento* was claiming "Indian" identities, without direct knowledge of such elements, perhaps here and there, but not in full contact. When my anthro professor Dr. Nicholson (in my Aztec and Mayan Culture class) announced that there were only 500 Lacandón Mayan Indians left in Chiapas, I was shocked. "We have to go!" I said to my classmate, Manuel. "Why?" he said. "Because we have to save them!" I said. Idealistic and imperial, yet I believed in touching base with sisters and brothers I had never met, in what I considered my homeland. This was not verbiage or a banner of "pride." I was on a mission—it involved rescue, danger, culture, power, knowledge, and a search for a new idea and interconnection of self, nation, and poetry, that feverish thing we had inside of our brown bodies, unseen, unheard, unknown.

In 1970, I assembled a group, Renacimiento, Revival, Aztlán Collective. To keep this anecdote short—we journeyed to the last two Lacandón Mayan villages of Chiapas, Najá and Lacanjá Chan Sayab. I met with the elders, listened to their stories, noticed their living conditions as best as I could, and as a team, we did the same. Identity, as you can guess, took a backseat. What we found was beautiful and also a peoples pushed to the edges of the rainforest, exploited by the lumber, chicle, and floral industries, as well as the fauna. It was nothing new to the Lacandón. It was new to me.

I realized I could not change the forces of class and power. The notion of identity was not worthy. The significance lay in the ways power worked in Mexico and how it was directed toward the Native peoples, at the hands of the *Ladino* (mixed between Indigenous and European). Subcomandante Marcos later would address these disparities. Identity became a condition of class and power. As time went on, I revisited the same villages in '92, and later wrote about the massacres of Acteal, Chiapas. I was never a nationalist. The thrown-around term, "nationalism," was never defined, discussed—it was mentioned here and there, perhaps similar in manner to the term "Azltán," however Aztlán had two key proponents, Alurista and Luis Valdez, two major figures in the late '60s and most of the '70s. Adelaida del Castillo from UCLA, Betita Martínez from Nuevo Mexico and Chicana women's collectives in San Diego, I believe, took another track regarding the Meso-American cultural and historical relationships with Latino/a identity—Malintzin Tenepal, being of major interest. My *indigenismo* was born in moments of being in between worlds. In between the abyss of powerlessness and the mountain peak of commitment.

**How would you distinguish and differentiate from your early intuited *indigenismo* from your cultural nationalism days in the 1970s to the**

**more transnational *indigenismo* you have talked about in the last four decades? (FAL)**

1832 "B" street was my last address in San Diego and my mother's. Not far from this little apartment, almost on the edge of 12th Street, a major thoroughfare, and few blocks down where Alurista lived—it's a long story. We had known each other, and lived together on occasion, since 1962. This was 1966, senior year. I was about to leave for UCLA and my mother back to San Francisco, which is another story too. In any case, often I would bop to Alurista's hut. We chatted about Jazz, played congas and guitar, I would draw my new art approaches, multi-style pen drawings. One day, Alurista blurted out, "Juan Felipe, from this day on, I am calling myself a Chicano." "A Chicano?" I said. I had heard the term before at a UCSD panel. It was rarely uttered. I had also been chair of the "Human Relations Student Club" at San Diego High, a political group that was quite aware of the civil rights movement. Alurista had been the chair a few years before me. By now, he had returned from Chapman College and lived on "B." These were the years when he was an outstanding visual artist. Back to the point: by 1968, at UCLA, I was a full-fledged member of UMAS that morphed into MEChA (Movimiento Estudiantil de Chicanos de Aztlán—Chicano Student Movement of Aztlán). These are organizational moments that were imbued with an expanding consciousness, action, investigation, and the creation of a large network of students, faculty, community leaders, protests, and state-wide networks and actions. Remember, the most important elements had to do with writing, the development of a collective consciousness, a new language and set of symbols. The more these things were energized the more the *movimiento* evolved and attracted students, literature, followers, and the arts. I was involved at various levels—poet, teatrista, playwright, speaker, and group organizer (*teatro*, group journeys, and spoken word jazz ensembles). All these elements galvanized my participation, shaped my vision, and expanded my thinking in the *movimiento*.

Chicano verse was not a "craft," nor was it "poetry" or "literature." Believe it or not.

We must keep in mind that we invented something new. Something that did not exist before the '60s. It was *floricanto*. In its true sense—as Nezahualcóyotl, Mexica poet and philosopher of Texcoco, Mexico, of the late 1400s, demonstrates in his poetry—it was closer to a communal celebration, an offering and a notice of our brief relationship in the vastness of life. It was

The Poet, the Playwright, and the Citizen **331**

not a "literary product," as Henry Lewis Morgan, grandfather of anthropology, in his groundbreaking work, *Ancient Society* of 1877, would have us acknowledge, the key pivot from "savages and barbarians" to "civilization." We were operating from an ancestral, meso-hemispheric plane. It was a collective, ecstatic source experience.

**You have self-translated many of your writings, one book in particular is *Tejedoras de rayos/Thunder Weavers* (2000). What does a bilingual edition allow you to accomplish? Would you say there's a shift in perspectives when you switch between your two worlds?**

¿Existen dos Juan Felipe Herrera? [Are there two Juan Felipe Herreras?] (OAG)

When we reclaim all of our languages—Spanish, Nahuatl, Caló, and many more, Mixteco, Zapoteco, Huichol, Mayan, for example, we open the doors to millions. We empower our embrace of humanity. It is that simple. This gesture was present from 1969, when Alurista had his first draft of *Floricanto*, to finally culminate in his first book *Floricanto en Aztlán* in 1971. And it continues with new generations of writers and thinkers, mostly women, I would say. As writers we need to test the publishers. Read the recent young adult novels by Aída Salazar and Meg Medina, Margarita Engle and Elizabeth Acevedo—and there it is. The big bilingual and trilingual writing wave is gaining height day to day. Each language is a new music, happiness blossoms in the audience—too long our tongue has been split in half. There is more a shift in *melody and feel* than in perspective when I write in more than one language; the magic takes on a new flow—sound, assonance, long line rhythms, pop icons, vernacular, symbolic village/town/city/border bundles and word streams. You will need new hydraulic brakes. Three words will mess you up. Try it. Three new bilingual terms will liberate someone in the audience.

**Writing about injustice, pain, violence, outrage, diaspora, and uncertainty is a form of community. Your work is clearly one of many intents at building a sense of belonging, so what is your personal understanding of *community* in your creative process? (OAG)**

One of the incredible gifts of the Chicana, Chicano *movimiento*, now Latino/a, was that it was propelled by kindness, more than what we used to call our general mission, *concientización* (consciousness raising), that is, to bring about a new consciousness, a historical, cultural, and political sense of our predicament, to recognize the levers of power through time, and their effect on our sense of being—in America and in the Americas. We truly were after *Tierra y Libertad* [Land and Liberty]. Chicano Park, in Logan Heights barrio, San Diego, is a prime example. This was the mission of the visual artists, the poets and writers, the singers, songwriters, and musicians, educators, sociologists, and historians, and of course, the most potent, *teatros*. We saw ourselves as sisters and brothers; we met often and on the road. We went on journeys—Guillermo Aranda, one of our great muralists, voyages to Mexico City to study the murals of Diego Rivera, José Clemente Orozco and David Alfaro Siqueiros and returned to apply his findings with the *movimiento's* vision in mind. The *teatro* women, that journeyed to Mexico City for the 5th TENAZ Teatro Festival in 1974, held in Tlatelolco, including *teatros* from Chile, Peru, Colombia, Central America, and the USA (to name a few), had similar concerns. What I am saying is that the notion of community was vast, collective, and was replenished with every new event, journey, and crisis. What I am doing these days is continuing the task of community, with others. We may not use the same terms, yet we expand and refigure the same vision. Through the years, five decades now, this changes. My focus is humanity. Seven point eight billion human beings. All of us, all living beings. We speak of borders, and yet, sometimes, we forget the larger orb of peoples suffering, acutely, incredibly.

We must rethink our grasp of this planet. This is our community, and it can only be embraced with kindness and compassion. Ideology and its cousins had their function more than half a century ago. Now is the time for a planetary embrace and an aesthetics with the same radius. Recently NASA invited me to write words of kindness and wisdom (I say this at the risk of arrogance) for generations two million years from now. This poem will be engraved with other writings on a plaque, a component within the uncrewed, robotic, interplanetary spacecraft, Lucy, headed to the sun. Before being pulled by the sun's forces it will have finished a number of investigations of the seven Trojans, asteroids, with materials relating to the sun's origins. The key is that the craft will be spotted by astrophysicists on Earth two million years from now and its materials made public for a future generation. Perhaps we can answer questions such as these—Who were we? What happened on Earth in 2020? Was kindness possible?

## The Poet, the Playwright, and the Citizen 333

*Every Day We Get More Illegal* (2020) is the intriguing title of your latest
book which we believe truthfully depicts the current social and political
climate not only here in the U.S. but all over the world. Could you elaborate on how touring the U.S. for the past four years helped you come
up with this title? What faces, voices, and images contributed to this
powerful title? (OAG)

In two years of being on the road across America, on television and radio,
and reading to thousands of people in various spaces, from small bookstores,
gardens, members-only clubs to immense auditoriums, I noticed hunger
for something new, hunger for discussions and poems on climate change,
enthusiasm for Latinx poems and stories, and parents curious and smiling
in full-immersion bilingual schools, military-dress students at attention in
class, families wondering what I was saying, working class students upset
that I "only wrote for my people," and teachers saddened that their students
were stepping out because ICE was conducting sweeps in their city and
they had taken on day jobs to support the family and thereby not leave their
parents endangered at work. I noticed students and schools in small towns
framed outside of the main and lucrative city, Brown faces in the back of the
signing table wanted to say something, somehow, in this odd thing called a
"poetry reading." I noticed Brown women who were dealing with the migrant
violence at play and were surviving. On a visit to a class in Jackson Hole, Wyoming, I sat down and listened to a student's poem, a tenth grader, perhaps.
He uttered that "Half of me was still in Mexico." He remembered his dog,
his rooster, half of his rough-cut world. And yet, he was writing poetry and
reading it out loud. To be summarized as an illegal being is to be cut in half.
One half visible, illegal the other invisible something. Are we invisible? If it
was not for teachers encouraging our youth to speak out their experience,
their migrant lives, their border shock, their stories of crossing the impossible fire line, their family words, who would we be? In many ways, those two
years, those thousands of peoples coming together in tight and wide spaces,
those moments were not about poetry, they were about liberation. And it
did seem like a new policy, a newfangled requirement, a new kind of test, an
additional mile, a new crew of border guards, a new map of border stations
was installed. Every day. It appeared to be an easy maneuver to make these
things take place. No one seemed to complain. The wheels of injustice turned
silently and expensively, but not for the migrant. I had to write about it, one

way or another. Otherwise, my life would be meaningless. My poetry would be just poetry. It would not be an offering of kindness, it would not be an acknowledgment and cry of so many lives throne and tossed into cages and pressed into bank notes for someone ready to profit from the innocent, for example, the shelter industry. The practice of a poet is to practice noticing the world and most of all noticing the suffering all around. For a moment, we can breathe, say hello, smile and show our faces, Brown, studious, anxious, concerned and painted with wisdom. Every day.

I thank all my teachers in trailers, classrooms, streets, apartments, fields, and kind audiences.

*12-27-20*

# Part II

**You have been intimately involved in poetry slam sessions in San Francisco and the Bay Area since the 1980s and 1990s that confirm your status as a performance poet. Some of the other key figures were Francisco X. Alarcón, Lucha Corpi, and others. How did you become engaged in such a medium/format and how did it fulfill your desire for expression? How did you benefit from this experience and how long did it last?**

**Did your writing change in any significant way after that, and how did performance impact or change your writings? (FAL)**

There were various scenes—the most important was the Movimiento Voz del Pueblo (Movement Voice of the People)—this is where you stand on a platform, makeshift, or local site such as a community center. *Campesino* stages in small worker towns were more mobile and open-air.

Here is where you had to shout, communicate, be direct, and establish an immediate and deep relationship with the audience. The San Diego Centro cultural scene as a Chicano experimental platform where I wrote "Papaya," in one run, for example, on an electric typewriter at El Centro Cultural de la Raza in San Diego. This poem turned out to be my first spoken word piece that lasted decades in its popularity. Not much later I overlaid it with percussion, forming a band—TROKA (formed with F. X. Alarcón) with two congas and a set of timbales [kettledrum]. The musicians were John and Abel Martínez on conga (brothers of Víctor Martínez) and Félix Contreras on timbales. The poem was written in 1974, the band through the '80s and '90s. The band started in the late '70s. In the late '70s and early '80s, being

FIGURE 14.2 Juan Felipe Herrera drawing, an original work—"Automatika Series" at the Prints and Photographs Division, Library of Congress, DC, 2016. Photo by Shawn Miller.

at Stanford, I hung out in San Francisco cafés and reading spaces, the Co-Misery Café, for example. This is where, in the evening, I listened to a young man riff out an endless, one boppin' phrase poem, with extreme energy and close up to the scattered audience, in low light. This definitely inspired me to jam the phrases and to add tons of power to the piece as a whole, "Mission Street Manifesto" is an outcome of that reading. At this time, the term "slam" was not used, or "spoken word," we were all just finding ways to "say it." The writing has to change the rhythms and the sound, velocity, and accents. I used an expanded, modified sonnet form, iambic pentameter, with eighteen syllable lines, in one long and thick stanza, first read at the Grand Piano Café in Haight Ashbury. As you know, performance has been the central key to what started as Chicano and Chicana poetry. We did not start with readings. We started with rallies and protests. All my poems, in one way or another, are performance.

**Much of your writing is characterized by nomadic elements (constant moving, noticing those who are going from one place to another, transformations) on the part of the poetic voices/narrators, the subjects, many themes and the stories you tell. Why has this become a basic staple of your poetry and what does it say about your ceaseless pursuit of a poetic footing? (FAL)**
The movement is a natural process. It has to do with the artist's need to always change, create, modify, experiment, challenge, remake, invent, and always find new ground and be open to global influences. My approach is not singular. Each moment is unique. Change is at the heart of all things.

**Some of us believe you have been the "best kept secret" of Chicano literature, as you are barely now receiving your due. Before being the recipient of the poet laureate award of California (2012–2014) and subsequently the poet laureate award of the U.S. (2015–2017), you had moved within many circles but you also slowly defied such circles by expanding your vision, your concerns, and your explorations. How have such awards impacted your inspirations, your direction, and your goals? As you look in the rearview mirror, how would you assess or describe your trajectory from your humble beginnings to your consistent experimentations and thematic revelries? (FAL)**
Practitioners of poetry and the arts work in the dark in a sense, at the margin. Sometimes awards and recognitions arrive at the table, yes. Each step is a lesson along the way. Writing, as private as it seems, is also a collective and total action. Everyone and everything are part of it, that is, the writing, the moment, the context, the audience, the environment, nature, and city, the space itself.

It is one big reverberating sphere, like our native poetics to this day. My trajectory has been a life path. Every day since 1961, I have considered poetry and since 1966, I have written it, and as time passed, I began to add stages, music, *teatro*, backdrops, modern dance, collective voices, lights, bands, school audiences, radio, television, video, and Zoom. And international connections and exchanges. It has been a most personal, incredible, natural,

The Poet, the Playwright, and the Citizen  **337**

collective life. I have learned from my audiences, students, teachers, and most of all my mother, Lucha, and father, Felipe Emilio—humanity.

**With the extensive experience you now have in the world of poetry with new books, a myriad of public presentations, and even Zoom sessions, how has poetry changed around you as a medium of expression and how have you tried to change it? Has your relationship changed with/toward your writings? (FAL)**

Yes, poetry has changed, just as the eighteenth century Spanish poets [were] influenced by Luis de Góngora and then moved on to more "realistic" poetry by the end the century. As you know, we started in the late '60s, let's say for the moment, with a bilingual and native Mexica and urban, rural poetics of the Southwest. This is rare in the twenty-first century. We write mostly in English and mostly, more formally, given the increased rate of Latinx in academic MFA creative writing workshops. Very few include bilingual work, public political voicing. Once again, more openness is taking place as we speak. I go about my business keeping a focus on our migrant border realities. And I also have enjoyed pouring in a heavy dose of line, phrase, and stanza work since the '90s. On occasion I notice that, as a whole, we continue to produce work centered on our stories, our ancestors, our communities, and our social response to our historical experience in the USA. I enjoy new treks across the page and out of the page—I appreciate new ventures into drawing the poem, moving out of the "workshop poem," making circular mandala poems on Covid-19, for example, and the "infinite poem." This structure uses just one core line. It adds words vertically to each word in the singular horizontal core line, it almost looks like a butterfly. The poem of "civilization" is most restricting. The true poem is made to blast out of your chest.

**Do you think there was a new consciousness, a new awakening, a new reckoning about writing in general at the turn of the twenty-first century? How would you describe it for poetry, specifically from your personal perspective? Do you sense any fundamental changes in poetics with the turn of a new century or do you see it as a continuum? If pivotal changes did occur, what might they be; if it is a continuum, how does it continue to be so? (FAL)**

We began to get our manuscripts into the hands of big publishers, like Aída Salazar, to receive national awards, like Liz Acevedo, form national

Latinx poetry cadres, like Cantomundo, to enter into MFA's and to strut down the halls with our folios—and to form solid small presses linked to universities, much like Carmen Giménez-Smith's Naomi Press at Virginia Tech. As it must be, we did lose our raw, collective, hands-on, open-air poetics along with our garage-made newspapers and mags. We got what we wanted that we never wanted. One of the fundamental changes has to do with the terms and the core of the poem. I'd have to read more recent poems to tell you. Hybrid aesthetics are major at this time—the classical poem is dissolving, the one that has its singular and recognizable integrity. Current materials are crossed over with erasure, other art forms, cross-outs, ripped areas, internet media, voice-over, images, multi-formats, invasive voices, and anti-logic.

**In *Border-Crosser with a Lamborghini Dream*, the idea is uttered that language escapes you and then epistemology insinuates what a "punk half panther" is. From there, a manifesto of ambiguity emerges surrounding "blood" in various forms ("abandoned blood," "blood on the wheel," "say blood man," "chicken blood townships," "Aztec blood sample," "last blood words," etc.). Then why does the book end in a circular fashion: "we press into our little knotted wombs / wonder about our ends, then, our beginnings"? How does this encapsulate or capture the essence of the whole book? (FAL)**

The blood poems are from the impulse for a "Blood Affabet," that is, an alphabet with each letter delving into the ontological layers of Being given that blood is the most precious substance of a human being, life. This notion had to do with reflections on Mexica rituals, symbols, and culture. It also had to do with power and viruses. The poems that survived the initial draft are in this book. Various concepts came to me during the writing of *Border-Crosser*. So, I attempted a number of projects that became the full text— there is no monumental lens, only fractures, complete and in fragments.

**How different is Juan Felipe Herrera, the writer of today, and Juan Felipe Herrera from fifty, forty, thirty years ago? What constitutes the major changes and shifts where we can pinpoint those various degrees of evolution? What books (either yours as poetic experiments or others' books) have shaped or transformed you altogether into a new poetic**

voice? Or have the metamorphosis and/or metagenesis been more subtle? Please explain through one or two books as examples. (FAL)

Each book is a unique life moment. The Bay Area yielded *Exiles of Desire* and *Akrílica*, two of my favorite books—those were years of protest and wars, U.S. involvement in Central America, El Salvador, Guatemala, and Nicaragua, for example. I shape the books as I change. It is a matter of reflecting on our experience within a larger experience taking place, a fusion of ideas, language, the suffering of the people, peace, and war—reverberating together. Yet, the meanings must be extracted, the rise and fall of power and the radical sweeping change must be grasped, the stories, voices, cruelties, landscapes, yearnings and screams must be heard, seen, touched, and tasted. The fleeing of peoples must be chronicled, saved, lit, and propelled to the public at large. The Juan Felipe today is the Juan Felipe back then just beginning. It has taken more than half a century for me to assemble the instruments, terms, places, and locate the peoples, sit with them. Most of all to meet the core of things, drop the boosters of influence. What is that core?

Kindness, compassion. The rest was always extra.

**Looking back at 1992–1997, the time period that birthed *Mayan Drifter*, how much has your understanding and practice of Chicano indigenism changed since making that life changing trip to the Selva Lacandona? Do you believe poetry can make possible a realistic, non-romanticized, and decolonized encounter between Chicano/a poets and Indigenous communities? (OAG)**

As you know, my trek to Indigenous Mexico (which is all of Mexico, as Judith Friedlander said in her groundbreaking book of 1973, *Being Indian in Hueyapan*) began in 1970. In short, I organized a team of UCLA student-friends to trek to three cultural arenas. From the first encountered by Cortez, the Totonacas of Veracruz, the massacred, the Maya-Tzotzil-Tzeltal and the most pushed out of the region, the Lacandón Maya, to the last encountered, the Huichol of Nayarit, Jalisco and Zacatecas. We filmed, taped, used various still cameras and sat down and conversed with the peoples. Twenty-four years later I returned to the Lacandón. I felt I needed to offer what little I had from the initial voyage—a VHS cassette of the "rush print" of 1200 feet of B&W film. Silly, yet true. That is the full scope. The "decolonized encounter" is a dialogue, not note-taking, not filming, not collecting. It is face-to-face, in whatever manner things take place. As key sociocultural anthropologist Clifford Geertz said in the early 1970, it is a reflexive "thick description" that includes the visitor. More recently, in *Economies of Abandonment*, Elizabeth A. Povinelli speaks of entering "radical spaces." Perhaps this takes place and comes to be with a poetics of dialogue. The key is to acquire and enter the insight that the meeting is all inclusive—from all points, a 380-degree immersion and synthesis of consciousness.

**Beyond the political and historic transcendence of Indigenous discourse as an element of Chicano/a identities, why do you believe searching, understanding, and perhaps even reconnecting with Indigenous history is such an important trope in Chicano literature? Furthermore, would you say that such aesthetic explorations run the risk of forcing the idea that all Chicanos/as have a direct connection to living Indigenous communities, a concept that could translate to the appropriation of Indigenous voices in resistance? (OAG)**

It is beyond a trope. We are human beings considering being an integral part of humanity, in particular, a Native community that is part and parcel of who we are—just do a little DNA research and you'll see. Reconnecting is also about the breaking the borders of colonialism, usurpation, and servitude. Further, these Native Mesoamerican groups hold the manuscripts where ancient systems of precepts abide—sources that will enhance our triturated, occupied belief systems. We cannot escape our relationships with our Native peoples. It all began with an overwhelming wave of wanting to do something about the limited number of five hundred Lacandón Mayas left on the "regions of refuge" that Mexican anthropologist, Aguirre-Beltrán, mentioned in his groundbreaking book by the same title. I wanted to see our peoples face-to face. It all had to do with the ongoing notion of "identity" we were all espousing—Native, Mexican, European, Latinx—an exhilarating concept, yet, without grounded human relationships of knowledge. Most of all, it was about activist compassion.

The notion of appropriation is a useful one. However, it assumes there is a static cultural space and historical moment. It can never be grasped since everything is in rapid change as we speak. Of course, if our focus is on material culture and superficial collections of stories, then we have a problem. Our relationship must be centered on our common dynamic humanity.

*Laughing Out Loud, I Fly*, a homage to Pablo Picasso's *Hunk of Skin*, and in many ways, an exploration of your childhood, is a beautiful testimony of your bilingual poetic force. Compared to your other bilingual books, it seems that in *Laughing Out Loud, I Fly* the musicality of your verse reaches new frontiers, in terms of your own work, in the Spanish version. Could you talk about how the poetic process and reconstruction of an infantile voice and memory is deeply rooted to the reclaiming of the so-called mother tongue? Do you consider Spanish your mother tongue? Or, *¿quizá tienes dos o tres madres?* [Or perhaps you have two or three mothers?] (OAG)

Good questions. I wrote the entire text at my brother-in-law's kitchen table in San José during Thanksgiving. About a three-hour sitting. Picasso has always been a great mystery and inspiration for me since 1969–71 when I spent a year with my cousins in the Mission District—the "beatnik years." My cousin Tito, older than me, has ink prints of Picasso's work on the wall in addition to his jazz album covers. Later at San Diego High I followed up with his art. Of course, in San Francisco, during the late seventies I purchased *Trozo de piel* (Hunk of Skin), his 1958 poetry collection. It was an incredible, intense inspirational moment. I noticed his unique way of writing a poem and how he wove his own childhood into the poems. As you know, Picasso was a collage and hybrid media master since the early twentieth century. I was so moved that I had to write a book in the same manner—something made of things, diverse elements, colors, materials, and flashes of a childhood story. I brought in my early days, and I even added a few referents to Picasso's story, and I invented many things. It indeed was a "hunk of skin." It was more like a table of things arranged by the eye, tongue, and hand. I recommend it. It took three hours because a poem is a sudden flash of a world you have not seen before on the verge of being born. I had to write before it disappeared.

Good question—Spanish. Mamá Lucha taught me to read in Spanish from a primer she purchased at our Macy's—the Goodwill. Letters, tiny stories with morals, like the one about planting trees. One tree uncared for, the other cared for—one grew tall, the other was broken and crooked. I wanted to be that tall tree. My other languages are barrio Spanish, Chuko talk, *campesino* dialect, El Paso border dialect, Mexico City riffs—and, formal school English, poetry workshop talk, jazz ensemble English, Chicano, Latino/a poet talk.

**When speaking of bilingual poetry collections, readers and critics always wonder and study which version of the poem is the original. I don't personally believe bilingual poets can determine either poem as the original. In a way, saying there's a first poem could imply then that the second one is a translation. In your poetics, even in collections like *Rebozos of Love* (written predominantly in Spanish), it is very clear that you continuously translate concepts from the English to Spanish and vice versa. This is an effect that unveils an aspect of your poetic process which I would say is always a linguistic, intellectual, oral, and aesthetic negotiation between two worlds; one that shows that a real body of knowledge can live inside another one, thus creating a new poetic language where we can see how poets/readers truly can transverse across linguistic systems through poetry. Could you elaborate on the bilingual creative process as a simultaneous non-binary craft? (OAG)**

It all has to do with the burst of the unconscious-conscious word—a necessary process. It is nearly impossible if a poem is solely a rational project. Where would you go to collect the images, the flow, the melody, the floating memory-pictures, the textures, and the sudden "leaping" that poet Robert Bly wrote about in his *Leaping Poetry* volume of the early '70s? Creating with two or more languages in a poem intensifies this process, like two derailing train cars jumping into each other's tracks all the way home. The availability of a wider and more complex set of musical instruments is at hand. In *Akrílica* of the '80s, I introduced Portuguese, French, and German, in addition to the Spanish and English. In the world the oceans of language are vast. We must become world poets. When I want to have a certain melodic feel, flow, a dynamic vocab palette and music in the poem—I write in Spanish. For the poem of the day, I write in English. Lately, I have been getting back to bilingual experiments. It is easy to abandon Spanish since power is always at the edge of the table—publishers, editors, audiences, literary charters—however, all this under rapid change. Good thing. What does this dual process, if such thing is possible, allow you to challenge about written and spoken language? It is always a melding of thought, thought-fragments, conversation, ideas, radical experiments, documents, and events at hand. A new language erupts from this geyser.

**You possess a great wealth of linguistic registers that embellish your poetic voice; however, this plethora of voices has allowed you also to**

The Poet, the Playwright, and the Citizen **343**

move across genres, confronting issues related to childhood and youth. You speak from and with children's and teenage voices that contribute greatly to Chicano letters, and this allows academics and readers to appreciate your commitment to American society. What do your children's books and *literatura juvenil* [young adult literature] say about your literary project overall? (OAG)

In a sense, El Movimiento Chicano of the late '60s and early '70s was oriented toward addressing all of the sectors in our communities. It was also a collective effort of kindness. Our charge was to dedicate our lives to social change and to uplift our people's expressive abilities in order to rethink, write, educate, and fulfill our human vision of unity and harmony. To accomplish that we had to diversify our work and our audiences. Writing children's literature is one tier of many available to a writer. For me, it has opened hundreds of audiences, forums, conferences, stages across the United States, Mexico, Latin America, China, Italy, Spain, Africa, and even the Canary Islands. I am humbled and thankful to all. What have you learned from writing these genres? Simplicity, kindness, depth, and structure. Without these elements writing for youth is impossible. We all know that simplicity is a must. Complex, convoluted, elevated stories and vocab will not bring the story to light. Without kindness there is no reason to write a children's book. Here the goal is to relate to the experience of children and youth, to contribute a precept, a challenge that must be overcome as in the incredible book of many prizes, *The Poet X* by Elizabeth Acevedo. And, there must be depth, these books have to truly get to an emotional core, a life insight. Finally, structure, the nemesis to all poets. A poem is free to roam, even if it has a metrical system. A young adult novel will be bland, boring and blah without a carefully built main character and lacking a careful flow of rise, fall, crises, rise-again, fail, resolution, and reversal, surprise in the novel's architecture. The poem, at this time, is exploding in a vortex of intense experiment. Anthony Cody's recent *Borderland Apocrypha* is a genre-changing text.

**Explain when you reached the conclusion that "I am a poet." It must have been either a slow process or a sudden life-changing point and watershed moment in your life. What motivated that realization? How & when did it happen? Did you foresee a certain plan, a particular agenda, a point of departure, a launching point, a decisive moment of**

**commitment? How did your world change at that very moment of no return? (FAL)**

It all is gradual, yet with key stages. In 1961, in San Francisco at Patrick Henry Elementary School, I decided to memorize a poem and read it out loud in the cafeteria, in place of my report on the Bay of Fundy, in Nova Scotia. Things didn't work out because I thought I had to wear a tux. Yet, the initial impulse was blinking this red light. In middle school, Roosevelt Junior High, San Diego, I decided in seventh grade that I was not going to join band (as much as I loved it).

Instead, I was going to the class I feared. The fear was the key. I joined choir to be called on to stand up in front of everyone and sing, follow the piano, sing the song. Soon enough, I would get to the stage and the curtains would open and there I was in a barbershop quartet, a choir, and later with a traveling group of madrigals. I took time. Later at UCLA, I formed a jazz poetry ensemble and blasted poems from the steps of Royce Hall Quad. I challenged myself at the free speech grassy mound on Kerkhoff Plaza. I hollered so my trembling voice would go undetected. I created Chicano, hybrid (dance, music, images) street *teatros*. Little by little, my poet's wings took flight. Then there is the participation in making newspapers, magazines, chapbooks, posters, broadsides, pamphlets of poetry for the people. Learning, writing, speaking, printing, performing, alone and collectively, all this always in motion. Then one day you turn around and you glimpse at yourself, somehow, you notice, you just might be a poet. Five decades later, it does not matter. The heart, the people, the Earth, matter.

**Your first book, *Rebozos of Love / We Have Woven / Sudor de Pueblos / On Our Back* (1974), marks a key juncture in your early stage as a lyrical poet, heavily invested in cultural nationalism of Amerindia and verses in the form of calligrams. How did both trends (philosophical and in terms of technique) become blended essentially into one? (FAL)**

As you know, a tepid nationalism was at the core of the Chicano movement and its various tributaries such as poetry, muralism, *teatro*, dance, and music. It was not a full-blown nationalism with uniforms, ritual artifacts, and charters. Yes, it did show up in various "softer" forms such as ballet folklórico, murals, newspapers, posters, and poetry. You are right, I did take notice of Alurista's concepts of Amerindia, Aztlán, and his global aspirations—Africa and Asia. I met him in seventh grade, throughout middle school. We lived about ten feet from each other on 11th and "D" Street in downtown San Diego. We lived together for a short period of time in my tiny apartment with my parents when we moved a few blocks away. Also, I visited him often in Tijuana, Colonia del Rubí, a rather recent development of rough-cut brick houses in the hills.

The idea of Amerindia was a provocative one—redefining the Western Hemisphere as our Native cultural source. For me, it was about harmony and unity. I preferred unity over an exploitative system of border work, separation, and suffering. *Rebozos* rises from these sentiments. The technique served itself. I did not think of a technique. It all came from one phrase, "Let us gather in a flourishing way." All I did was follow the trail of such a call. Indeed, the poem became a call, a single chant that made the book. Unity, harmony, Amerindia, the Earth and the cosmos.

**In addition, your language choices are clearly grounded on the oral aspects of Spanglish as complemented by numerous neologisms. In a sense, the book represents not only a breaking-out point but a poetic manifesto, paralleling what Alurista had introduced in *Floricanto en Aztlán* (1971) with his code-switching and free-flowing verses. In a way, the book has no real beginning and no end, but rather, a circular structure echoing Octavio Paz's *Piedra de sol* (1958), suggesting at times a cosmic spirituality. Alurista [to the point that some of the hand-written parts mirror his writing style] and Paz seem to have influenced you to express a new aesthetic via two distinct points of inspiration. Comment on all this. (FAL)**

Like I said earlier, Alurista was quite an influential force, for thousands. He had the right idea, a grand unity and reclaiming our "Chicano talk," even though this bilingualism had been already in motion set by Raúl Salinas in the late '50s and José Montoya in the '60s. Even Bob Dylan, in the '70s, waxed bilingual in his experimental novel, *Tarantula*, recalling his travels to Mexico. Paz is another key figure. As we know, *Piedra de sol* by Octavio Paz was written in the '50s, the text, a mesh of Mexica, national Mexican culture and time-space affinity wheels in counter-action. A magnificent project. I had not immersed myself in Paz. My interests were visual art, folk songs, philosophy, India, Lorca, Sartre, and surrealism.

**After *Rebozos of Love* you seem to have experienced a hiatus, meanwhile experimenting with theater and photography while also traveling to Mexico to see the Indigenous peoples firsthand. While initially your approach seemed more anthropological, it quickly evolved and took on a whole new form. (FAL)**

Anthropology was my major at UCLA and at Stanford. It gave me a set of flexible frames where I could consider cultural experience, cultures, peoples, "ways of life," and endangered groups, flora, and fauna—and a global view of people and their lives in various world arenas. Like it or not, anthropological perspectives to this day are useful and most interesting. In short, I learned to think of human beings and not just a slow-moving magma of people swishing in and out unknown places for unknown reasons. I became more concerned with Native peoples in Chiapas, Veracruz, and Nayarit, not just the "Aztecs," even though the Huichol speak an Uto-Aztecan branch of Nahuatl and whose musical instrument, el tepo drum, is quite similar to the Mexica drum.

**In the late 1970s and early 1980s you seemed to leave behind your newly formed Chicano identity to confront a Mexican Indian past you had not come to terms with. What was that like? How would you describe that process of *concientización* that allowed you to penetrate this parallel world that had up to that point usually been described by others from a removed, exotic point of view? How would you describe this newly found mind-set and how did it prepare you for your next stage (in part writing travel books or testimonial travels)? Give examples of books and possibly poems. (FAL)**

Once you realize you are just talking and not taking action, you choose to take action. This is why I organized a group in 1970, as an undergrad, to film and record Native groups in Mexico (Totonacas, Lacandón Mayas, and Huichol). They all had different experiences with the Spanish invasion and occupation. And this is why I revisited the Lacandones in 1993 and why I wrote *Mayan Drifter* and *Thunderweavers*. You either are going to act and write or just write or just ignore it all. I gave it my best.

It is good to travel. It is also daring. You'll eventually find you can make way and let the road open before you and that people will welcome you sooner or later—you must bring gifts, if you want gifts to be given to you. When I traveled I changed. I was not longer the same guy. I had met up with larger human reality. The beauty of the people, the few crumbs upon which they subsist, the incredible generosity, the arduous life, work, and a banana and one large hard corn tortilla for dinner. Not everyone is the same, of course. I met pioneers, like Chan K'in the last of the Lacandón To'ohils, teachers and leader of their pueblo. And Gertrude Blom, a pioneering European woman that (with her archeologist husband Franz) in the fifties founded a Lacandón Maya cultural center in San Cristóbal de las Casas. I met her in 1970 and in 1992.

Both passed away a year later. The book that includes these travels is *Mayan Drifter* written in 1993–97. The next stage had to be a more human one, a more inclusive one, a more reflective one. After decades of writing, thinking, reading, traveling, poetry stops being poetry. It becomes you and you become it. Humanity appears.

**One notable influence on the Chicano movement and its literary production, particularly in their performative elements and dress, was the hippie movement, something that has been either overlooked or conveniently ignored. Yet, some of the exotic qualities of returning to nature, indulgence in drugs, the philosophy of love, and a thirst for a politics of either free spirit or egalitarianism all led toward the idealization of our Indigenous past and a relatability to our working-class origins—often farmworker background. Please discuss further as an open-ended question. (FAL)**

The story of the movement was not the hippie, it was a thick tornado of global, philosophical, artistic, and musical influences. For the Chicano poet of the '60s it was a new beginning. You had to put down your small-town life and pick up your kundalini and begin to cultivate your third eye. Truly. Our day-to-day culture was no longer valid or reliable. We had to look deeper. Our radius was now tied to the cosmos, and it was now carved into deep Asian belief systems. We could now choose between East and West. I chose East. It wasn't "nature," it was you. It wasn't non-sense, it made sense. It was not war and materialism. It was based on Nonviolence, Compassion, Kindness, Peace of Mind and Altruism. It matched how I was brought up as a farm worker child. The Indigenous idealism you mention gave way and we had to take on a new path. By the early '80s I began to unravel notions of exile, surveillance, appropriation, power, and migration. I took this up in *Exiles of Desire* in 1983. During the same time, living in San Francisco, a city of high migrant influx from Central America, and becoming close friends with another poet-pioneer, Francisco X. Alarcón, I became exposed to new literary materials and visceral social change at the same time. These elements gave life to *Akrílica*, the most experimental text I have, one that I dedicated almost every hour of the day. Víctor Martínez was also another poet, great thinker, that highly influenced me during this decade—a key decade in Chicano literature. Francisco and Víctor were voracious readers of Chinese classics, philosophy, Latin American literature and American and European poetry. From Lu Chi to Herbert Zbigniew to Julio Cortázar and back. Perhaps this was my most fecund literary environment and most intense personal and artistic growth period. I thank Víctor and Francisco (RIP) for all their ever-close, warm-hearted friendship and brilliant, genius minds.

**Spanglish has been a hallmark and signature of your writing style. You obviously come from a bilingual background at home, school, and in your social interactions, but when did this mode of expression take on a greater or central importance in your writings? (FAL)**
It heated up in eleventh grade. By then I had been captivated by Antonin Artaud, the fierce, French, experimental poet and actor in the experimental Alfred Jarry theatre. What was most incredible was his journey to visit the Tarahumara in Chihuahua, Mexico, and to partake in their peyote ceremonies. After these ordeals and visits he returned to France and began to write in ritual, hallucinogenic terms. This was most exhilarating for me as a young artist and poet. As you know, Bob Dylan made a similar gesture after visiting Juárez, Chihuahua. *Tarantula*, his travel novel about the journey, had bilingual phrases here and there. All this was parallel to Alurista's influence. We lived together in San Diego and in Tijuana, sporadic encounters. We delved into art and discussions. Not to mention the civil rights movement, which had been boiling since the early sixties and its rethinking of language, culture, and power. Ideal for a new kind of Chicano poetics. In my senior year I wrote a small collection titled *Liquid Theatre*, modeled after Artaud. The language was invented, abbreviated, in fountain pen ink. Between 1964–67, it all came together.

**One can initially detect Alurista's influence, but your background is similar to his, so your Spanglish is determined more by what discourses of language you have consciously chosen. As a whole, you resort to Span-**

glish frequently, sometimes to even underscore an image or incident, but what is it that determines your syntactical logic and how do you negotiate that in terms of style? (FAL)

What I write is more akin to the moment, the impulse, and the materials that I want to display on the page. On occasion I reintroduce terms from our own language. Not long ago I wrote "California Brown," for one of John Freeman's publications. I was very interested in the use of Caló, an abandoned dialect in our now "professional" MFA and book making, prize-winning poetics. I wanted to bring it back, one of our expressive origins. The negotiation is freedom.

As a tactical strategy, how do you choose or regulate the "right" language for a poem (or in prose)? The issue of order in the structure and theme come together by what means? You frequently indulge or move from one genre, or a set of word combinations that resemble one genre, but you often leap without a moment's notice onto another genre. How does that process work and how are you able to seamlessly cross from a realm of one genre to another at the same time you keep a certain kind of "order" in mind? For example, in *Love after the Riots*, you reveal hints at how you view your style: "A living, clear, style with subterfuge" (51) or "Sanskrit grammar" (38) or "a tropical tongue (10)." (FAL)

Once again—a writer has many languages/worlds at hand. Millions of instruments and entrances into the work. Ritual language, as in Jorge Guillén's work, hybrid page performance as in the recent work of Anthony Cody, use of Nahuatl as Anzaldúa's early stellar contributions and most recent material by Aída Salazar. Then we have the work evidenced by Naomi Press's Akrílica series. We are now tapping a forceful whorl of linguistic experimentation in our writing. In "Love after the Riots," I viewed Fellini's film, *La Dolce Vita*, while writing non-stop for the length of the movie, then I spliced sections, fragments and added timeslots. You see, it is also the external media and environment that highly influences the writer and poem. It is a reflexive writing process that delivers something most unique; Picasso used old baskets to sculpt a goat.

Your conscious choice to write children's literature did not take place until you were well established as a poet fully committed to Chicano/a thematics and an overwhelming ethnic vanguard expression. The year

**1995 marks another landmark when you began to explore children's and young adult literature. What propelled that aspiration/inspiration in the middle of such landmark works, such as *Night Train to Tuxtla* (1994), *187 Reasons Why Mexicanos Can't Cross the Border* (1995), and *Love after the Riots* (1996), when you explored social and cultural issues that included transnationalism, indigenism and movements? (FAL)**

Harriet Rohmer, publisher of San Francisco's Children's Book Press, called me and invited me to write a children's book. After various cruddy attempts, she said, "send me your poems." This gave her an idea how I write. "Send me your story," she said. "My story?" I said. "Yes, she said." "Ok," I said wondering what I was going to write. I wrote *Calling the Doves*, winning the Ezra Jack Keats award in NYC. Happiness drenched me. I was so glad because I included my mother and father's story. That was a great gift to them and to the parents of so many farm worker children across the nation. Children's books are lovely, they are highly welcomed by Latinx teachers, children, and parents! Children's lit is a magical land. Filled with happiness, truth, warmth, smiles, and harmony!

**Much of your writings contain elements of chronicling a people's presence but with a particular angle on or preference for a testimonial lens. Some of this also offers elements of travel literature where the poetic voices are moving from one topic or issue to another with the objective of revealing glimpses into people's lives as they grapple with surroundings or their social circumstances. What motivates that kind of perspective on a consistent basis? (FAL)**

I want to tell people's stories, in particular their suffering and their transcendence through terrible obstacles. They do not have access to media the way we do in this country. We can offer a channel of exposure, knowledge and concern, action. It does not matter what people may say about these attempts. Writing is not for writers, it is for the people.

**Other works, such as *Akrílica*, represent a series of canvases and photographic images along with testimonial slices of people's lives as if to complement their existence with intra-historical renditions. Extensive experimentation and word plays here flourish into a rich collection that produces a watershed in both Chicano and American poetry for its freshness and originality. The poems function much like a harbinger of**

The Poet, the Playwright, and the Citizen **351**

**new vistas and voices that by 1989 had jelled into something totally new. What can you reveal about that stage of your writings that marked a new direction and a new language? (FAL)**
I had already written *Exiles of Desire* in 1983 (Lalo Press and University of Houston reprint) which was a concerted effort to move on from *Rebozos*, that is, from Aztlán poetics. I wanted something more conceptual, with half a glass of Cortázar, two cups of García Márquez, and a tablespoon of Carlos Fuentes and César Vallejo. I wanted to apply some of their fiction techniques and the dismantling of terms in my poems. Not to mention the desire to upset the typical architecture of the poem. Alarcón, being a Latin Americanist, always was working on one book or another, so I questioned him, shared my inclinations for drama, art, and performance. It was most beneficial. Then, there is the joy of uncovering a new field of poetics, styles, speakers and voice. The *Akrílica* had a slow start, in 1977. Little by little it took flight. By 1978, I was working away full-time on the book. I finished its core by 1983. Went on to other projects, *Facegames*, for example, 1987 (As Is/So & So Press, Oakland). Indeed, it was a new stage.

**Did this book mark a fundamental change in your writing? It seems that it did due to the degree of experimentation and poetic modalities. It seems to indicate and pivot a new discovery of poetics. Explain. (FAL)**
Yes, it did. It was a pivot, however, like I mentioned, I did not follow its advice. I jumped to other scenes. Before *Akrilíca*, there was a decade of experimentation, art scenes, poet relationships and world events that led up to it. After its production, I started over.

It was when I moved on to the Iowa's Writer's Workshop in 1988 and treaded new literary arenas. The American poetry scene—Levertov, Hugo, Graham, Stern as well as giants like Attila Jozef and Gombrowicz. Because I continued to explore new scenes, I left *Akrílica* intact. As a matter of fact, it will come out again this Fall of '21 with a new translation by a new generation of poets. It will also include some of my photography and drawings. Good ol' *Akrílica*. I thank Stephen Kessler of Alcatraz Editions in Santa Cruz for publishing such a high-quality book and Cecilia Brunazzi, who lived across from my apartment on Capp Street, San Francisco, for designing the cover.

**Many readers and critics make a big deal about how poets resort to theory(ies) in order to move their literary agenda into new facets and lin-**

**guistic terrains. What is your opinion of such a statement and how true is it? (FAL)**

Theory is always exciting. More inspiring is to reflect on big minds like Einstein, Foucault, and Gombrowicz and also to notice the lives and art of great painters and sculptors such as William Kentridge, Alexander Calder, Matisse for example. Theory is always looking for a page, it erupts from a little corner somewhere in the city and then it grabs you. Just like Anzaldúa's borderlands theory, material culture of Marxism, language, poetry, and on it goes. Theory can serve as a mind stew to dip into, however, for me, it is better to enjoy art as it is being made in a café.

***Rebozos of Love / We Have Woven / Sudor de Pueblos / On Our Back*** **(1974) is perhaps one of your principal books where you evoke the ceremonial element of the art of** *in xóchitl in cuícatl.* **Every chant in that book affirms your profound knowledge and respect for the Mesoamerican literary legacy present in collections such as the** *Cantares Mexicanos, Romances de los Señores de la Nueva España,* **among others. Besides the influence of such literary traditions, what contemporary live Indigenous voices and experiences are you in contact with? How can** *flor y canto* **be renovated, enriched, and transformed in places outside of Nahua communities and in other languages, for example, among emerging Chicano and Latino poets in the U.S.? (OAG)**

Good question. The Chicano literary movement of the 1960s and 1970s was a radical step regarding our Native roots. Yet, it weakened. By the 1990s, to this day it has been revived mostly at the hand of women undergrads, grads, and scholars. What may be missing is the probability that the poems of the early Nahua poets, like Nezahualcóyotl, are more than poems. They provide various philosophical precepts on metaphysics, ontology, and ethics. In the heat of unearthing our cultural inheritance we focused on monuments, deities carved on stone, symbols and rituals, and left the books, text and writing behind—the embedded teachings.

**In** *Mayan Drifter: Chicano Poet in the Lowlands of America* **(1997), you conclude the "American Prelude(s)" by writing: "My goals the culture and critics ask. To go into America as I go into myself, I respond. I have a particular historical and psychic possibility, given my place as a Chi-**

The Poet, the Playwright, and the Citizen **353**

cano. It is a life and cultural riddle that I have at hand, an American poetics of and for the twenty-first century [. . .] I say, 'I want to write America.'" In many ways, this is the backbone of your newest book *Every Day We Get More Illegal* (2020), a collection of poems where you continue to push the limits of poetics, language, and otherness. What lessons from your journey into the Selva Lacandona have allowed you to fulfil in your ongoing trajectory into the real America? (OAG)

"America" changes every second. As we can see these days—in the USA, there are two Americas, one is extremist, the other, the abandoned one. The journey to Maya country and Native Mexico contained a figure larger than America. It was humanity. When we enter Native country, we notice the sediment and strata of colonialism, servitude—power, most of all. Power, takeover, and war continues to rage as we speak—throughout the globe. The lens must be global. My lessons were the suffering of the people and yes, resilience.

**"Luz [light] tone bright brillos [shining]," "sprout spring primaveras [springs]," "hatchbacks doblados [folded]," "renacimiento rebirth to cosechas ricas [rich harvests]," "glowing new mañanitas today," "the fountain of rainbows entre tus miradas [between your gazes]." These are just a few examples of what I call the "butterfly verse," a poetic device deeply rooted in a bilingual-bicultural worldview. It's not just code-switching. It's the deployment of two cognitive spaces, and multiplicity of imagery grounded in the masterful knowledge of your two native tongues: English and Spanish. The "butterfly verse" allows you to conjoin words in Spanish and English with similar meanings but sustained by images of varying visual force. I wonder if this aspect of your poetry somewhat exemplifies or sums up the reconciliation of your Chicano experience? Or better yet, the pursuit of an expressive, literary, and cultural symmetry, much like the image of the mariposa? (OAG)**

This style of writing is joyful. It has all the beauties available to a poet, from rhyme to register, to phrase, to syntax, and on. Yet, all this is compounded into a multidimensional orb by the intersections and transpositions of two languages and a variety of dialects. It simply is what language can do when you liberate it and allow other languages to enter into its usual private domain—it provides an undiscovered stone that opens into a treasure. This is possible in all cultures.

**We can say all artistic practices are a form of traveling, a cognitive and affective journey, and in this sense every single one of your books *es un camino* [is a path]. To quote Francisco A. Lomelí, you're a poet in movement, one whose craft is in deep dialogue with place and space. However, could you talk about how your many travels across the U.S.—as poet laureate—and all over Latin America have informed, shaped, and transformed your vision as a poet throughout the years? (OAG)**

Poetry became my life. A life of delving deeper and deeper into questions, cultures, earth, and cosmos. Most of all, the ultimate goal of a human being—compassion, harmony with everyone and everything. The walls came down, the fences burned. All that was left is love. Another point is that being in a cadre of writers, for example, in the Bay Area, most of the time with Francisco X. Alarcón and Víctor Martínez, I came upon many writers, from Jorge Amado, Nicanor Parra, Cuban writers (on our cultural, scholarly journey to Cuba in 1979), Julio Cortázar, Manuel Puig, Jorge Luis Borges, Pablo Neruda, María Luisa Bombal, Martin Heidegger, Lu Chi, and more. Then as I mentioned earlier, the most dynamic sources of discovery take place in the readings across the city cafés, studios, galleries, and artist spaces. This is where poets are testing new poems, styles, voicing, media hybrids, and audiences. We also have leading poets in various locations of the area, such as Jack Hirschman in North Beach, Alejandro Murguía, Lucha Corpi, Cecilia Güidos, Roberto Vargas and Jorge Herrera, Jorge Argueta in the Mission District and Janice Mirikitani, Nelly Wong, Alfredo Arteaga, the Tenderloin, Genny Lim in Chinatown, Devorah Major in Western Edition, Steve Abbot in the Haight, Will Alexander—this is a short list. All these poets were an incredible, inspirational furnace. Not to mention the bookstores themselves—at City Lights in North Beach. I bumped into books by Lawrence Ferlinghetti, Robert Desnos, of course, Allen Ginsberg, Gregory Corso, Jack Kerouac, and Aloys P. Kaufmann. At Bookworks in the Mission we had the readings and books and each other. The Galería de La Raza was always cookin' and so was the East Bay, with another wave of key writers, Ishmael Reed, David Henderson, Avotja—founders of *Umbra* magazine. As I mentioned, the late '70s through the '80s were boiling with poetry, peoples' magazines, poets, muralists, painters, migrantes poetas, bookstores, and activismo. My travels across the USA as a laureate were ongoing every week, almost, of 2015–17. I met high school youth, middle and elementary, migrant youth, parents, children and teachers from all grades. The audiences were magnificent whether I was in Silver City in the mountains of Southern New Mexico or up in Connecticut, or midway in Minnesota or on the East coast in NYC or Florida. It was such joy to perform together with special needs youth and elders, reading poetry and a play on the challenges of having an overseer managing your freedom. Youth wanted me to read poems on climate change, city college teachers wanted me to know about recent ICE sweeps that resulted in their students dropping out so they could find employment to sustain their families since their undocumented parents had to leave their jobs. On various occasions, I arrived right after a tragedy (Parkland) or a death of a student. In these cases, I already had prepared a poem—these were some of the most moving work I did on the road. So much so, that in Skidmore College, in Saratoga Springs, where a student had died the day before my arrival, the parents of that student, Wilhelm Gold, made a plaque of my poem and placed it on his grave.

This is what poetry does. This is what I came for since the beginning.

**What about your travels to Indigenous communities in Mexico and Central America? (OAG)**

Yes, I stared at reality. Riding in Combis, stuffed Volkswagens, it was a good thing, not a bad thing, I traveled also in a 1970 pickup truck in 1970. On my return in 1993, in San Cristóbal de Las Casas, I saw Gertrude Blom for the last time, in her 90s, barely able to walk and talk. I had met this magnificent pioneering woman in 1970 when I came with the Renacimiento Revival Aztlán Collective, the group I invited to come with me to film, take photos, and record interviews, and meet peoples and move through the terrain. The truth has not changed, I learned. Once we arrived in Najá and Lacanjá Chan Sayab in the northeast edge of Chiapas (by Cessna), we sat down and listened to Pepe Chan Bol tell us the stories of exploitation by the lumber industry of precious woods, and on—the decay of flora and fauna by the florist industry of the United States, the chicle trees, poachers, and the rape of women. As you can see this was not the rosy Aztlán dream. Wherever I went, I noticed the uneven power relationships of the Ladino (Mexican national) and the "Indio." I saw the deep cultures of Tzotzil-Tzeltal peoples and their history everywhere I traveled. The Maya had not been conquered, [but] overrun. Near the city center we visited small pueblos like Joigelito and sat in the community church and outside we joined in on the Sunday celebrations. Each one of these sites was a new entrance into the real story—power, empowerment, and powerlessness. Huichol country, mountain villages and town shanties and ceremonies of El Palo Volador provided new lenses as well. It was a matter of sacred ceremonies in the midst of industrial suction and urban materialism. What we had left behind centuries ago still had a beating heart. And who we were was up for grabs—lost, soulless brown bodies, oscillating without a source, unable to thread back our precepts of wisdom.

**It's been twenty-one years since the publishing of *Tejedoras de rayos/Thuderweavers*, and still the EZLN remains vigilant and resisting, and the painful memories of Acteal are still an open wound in the collective. We believe that *Tejedoras de rayos* is about hope, Indigenous consciousness, and a call to action. Could you reflect on your objectives and state of mind when you wrote this book? (OAG)**

Since I had been in the same region in 1970 and '93, I had to do something. As you can see, the Native lives at the whim of those in power. In this case, a brutal massacre. My three tools at hand were writing, poetry, voice—and my imagination and memory. The most powerful force at my disposal was compassion—my inner powers ready to launch me to do something about it all, so people would no longer suffer. That is the goal. So, I wrote *Tejedoras*. The art of a *tejedora*, a weaver, is a most incredible expressive form in every Mayan village. It literally interlocks history, sacred stories, and the notion of interconnecting with the universe as it may continue. I wanted to tell the story of three *tejedoras*. This was the task of this poetry project. In Huichol country, among countless small miracles, I met up with my goal—to find a new poetics and poetry. However, I deviated and lost my focus filming and taking part in the villages' rituals of the celebration of the First Corn harvest. Much later I found the answer regarding a Native poetics vs American poetry culture. In short, Native poetics is everything at once, from Earth root to cosmos, from speaker to healer to listener to the blood of a sacrificed chicken. For us, it is merely a skill, a form, a product, a career, an aesthetic choice, a political manifesto and maneuver—a questionable step from being a "savage," "barbarian," on the bridge of "progress," toward "civilization," as Louis Henry Morgan, the "father of anthropology," wrote in his groundbreaking book, *Ancient Society*, in 1877.

The Poet, the Playwright, and the Citizen **357**

**Could you elaborate on how poetry can help those of us who don't live in such a community understand Indigenous communities who fight for their human rights on a daily basis? (OAG)**

Expand your consciousness. Connect with humanity. See things as they are. Accept, learn, change, give to others, take a leap, make an offering of your life in the vastness of the peoples throughout the Earth. The only "difference" is your perception. The various meanings attached to the term and notion of "Difference" have to do with sustaining power. I am interested, as we all are, with liberation, peace, and compassion for all—7.8 billion human beings.

*August 8, 2021*

# Part III

**It appears that movement is a constant in your writings that manifests itself in multiple ways. At times it resembles a sense of restlessness in your style and the rapid-fire verses. Other times it is intimately related to the overall experience of migrating or immigration status. What might be the origins of such an ever-present theme or subject? Can you relate how much you moved with your family and to what destinations and what indelible marks that left in your psyche? (FAL)**

All is movement. What is moving, perhaps, is my excitement to write the poem—a life, my joy in what I have in mind—not a theme or a precise subject, rather a wave of inspiration and energy, images, ideas, a place to land the poem. And I know that I only have seconds or a minute to put it down on paper or on the screen. Rainbows only a moment, then gone. The movement is of deep, quick-subtle thought.

As far as my familia on the move, a typical *campesino* family of the 1940s–60s, a family without resources. And a family that loved to move and see new sights, work in new places. Life can be rich for a migrant family, rich in adventure, new paths, challenges and ideas. Fowler, Escondido, Ramona, Milpitas, San Diego, San Francisco—and within each city. My memories are mostly of the open air, the wide horizons, ranchitos, forests, turkey ranches, mountains, lakes, *campesinos* having fiestas in the mountains, at night.

Deep scenes: 1955—Lincoln Rd. Outskirts of Escondido, Ca. My father, Felipe, worked the ranchito owned by Mr. López and his little familia—when the Border Patrol pulled away my little friends out of their house, the Ló-pezes never to be seen again. With my father, I planted corn, and also fed the animals—pigs, chickens; watered the plants—onions and pumpkins, bell peppers and the corn stalks.

Most memorable are the lives of Mexicanos on the road, in the mountains, on the sides of the dusty highways, never in the city.

**In your two more recent books, *Borderbus* and *Every Day We Get More Illegal*, you place the issues, dilemmas, and controversies surrounding immigration in center stage, whereas in the past you brought it up with regularity but it usually did not figure as the main focus. What accounts for the change of immigration becoming the hub and core of your recent writings? (FAL)**

I have sharpened my view on subject matter—*los migrantes*, the ones that suffer. It is an increasing condition of violence. I have experimented with poetry, *teatro*, and art for decades. I have changed the text into a more conversational and direct form and a first-person voice. In this way the reader inhabits the person, the people rarely seen face-to-face. To this day, migrants are the most brutalized, quietly, viciously. I must speak, I must write. Otherwise, I am merely a jester of terms and symbols.

**Did the backdrop of the Trump presidency spark or contribute to some kind of urgency to address it more directly? (FAL)**

Yes it did. We became political pawns, chess pieces, a gambling game for the desire for power. The border is a wound, as Anzaldúa said, it is also a marketplace of narratives for American meaning and a purification station whereby America attempts to guard a fading luster, its history.

**You frequently allude to your participation in theatrical performances in your career, especially during your formative years. However, it is rarely a subject covered by critics. Can you explain why this might be and the role this form of art plays in your overall approach to writing? (FAL)**

You are correct. In 1968, as I strolled Dolores Park in the Mission District (I lived four blocks or so from the area), I noticed a small stage being constructed. When I arrived, I read it: Teatro Campesino.

The youth on the stage performed, "No le saco nada a la escuela." I was so moved that when I returned to my mother's tiny apartment #2 at 2044 Mission Street, I told her "I saw a *teatro*, the Teatro Campesino! When I get back to UCLA, I am going to start one!" And I did: "El Teatro Chichimeca, then El Teatro Tolteca." At Stanford, 1980, TROCA [Trabajadores Organizados por la Cultura y el Arte or Organized Workers for Culture and Art] Rhythm & Sign Ensemble (with Francisco X Alarcón, and percussionists, Abel and John Martínez, Félix Contreras). When I arrived to work at CSU-Fresno State in 1990, I began the Teatro Zapata. Later, in 2004 or so, at UC Riverside, I created the Verbal Coliseum, an open-air multiform volunteer poetry group, available to the public. Just recently, due to the need for farmworkers to have more access to Covid-19 vaccines, I started the Teatro Familia Feliz and performed at the Madera, California, flea market. I called on my Teatro Zapata students, twenty years older. They were great. *Teatro* allows the writer to create dynamic platforms for a new kind of poetics. With Teatro Tolteca there was no storyline or characters as we know them, there were figures in movement, images on screens, modern dance steps, live jazz, and Lynne Romero's poem as the fluid text, "Speak Forth Fire Mouth." On my table I have a sketch of "Fractal States," in similar fashion. Here the subject is the continuity of the ongoing patterns of violence, separation, division, and the call for unity and kindness through time.

I have no idea what's on the critics' table. The 1960s were a cauldron of experimental theatre, music, dance, installation, photography, film, drama, painting, Indian and Native thought and word art, poetry. I was interested in all those fields. My various 1950s–1960s trips to San Francisco with my mother gave me direct contact with the arts, music, and poetry. Calder, Brubeck, Trader, Horace Silver, Thelonius Monk and Mongo Santamaría. Later, North Beach, Haight Ashbury, and the Mission District. Not to mention Tijuana and Mexico. I wondered in every zone and noticed, heard what was going on. Later, in the 1970s, 1980s, 1990s to the present, I actively participated in each area with poet friends and artists.

**In reviewing your trajectory as a writer, it appears you first wrote as an act of urgency to define your subject in relation to your community, then you devoted various books to the exploration of topics that allowed you to discover and address issues in a wide variety of social contexts (including abroad), plus you dedicated yourself to numerous experimental works (*Akrílica, Giraffe on Fire, Lotería Cards and Fortune Poems, Night Train to Tuxtla, Notebooks of a Chile Verde Smuggler, Senegal Taxi, Cin-***

*namon Girl: Letters Found Inside a Cereal Box, 187 Reasons Mexicanos Can't Cross the Border,* **and** *Borderbus,* **etc.), but more recently your writings seem to be laying out a series of crumbs to lead the reader to the promised land of conscience. Do you agree, disagree, or is there more (or less) to this? (FAL)**

I am always exploring. Things are always being discovered, new words, new scientific inroads, new language and text palettes, new music, new terms, new world struggles, new crises—new ways of seeing the world. New philosophies. New cultural tensions. New nests of and for violence. New erosion of what once was taken for granted—even conscience. After five decades of writing and noticing things, I have become more aware that the core most important is kindness. This will require a different way of thinking, writing, and offering of the art, the poem. More direct, non-ornamental, that is, not constructed with the usual genre-required ingredients such as phrase, line, stanza, caesura, image, meter, and a variety of tropes.

**After a career of around fifty years, what are some of the life lessons you have learned from the process of writing in general and also your extensive involvement in the arts (*teatro,* film, photography, etc.)? You have learned to compose ideas and sentiments via verse and prose but if you could tell the next generation of writers what there is to learn and what to apply to personal interests and inclinations, what would this be? What might be the essence of Juan Felipe Herrera as an individual and a writer? What has made you tick and, ultimately, how would you define yourself? (FAL)**

After many readings, writing, audiences, collaborations, travels, reading, visits across the USA, Mexico, Spain, Native communities, correctional facilities, prisons, classrooms, stages, from the fields to universities, forests, and mountains—I learned that poetry is life, an offering and celebration of life in a world of impermanence. Also, that the journey of a poet is one of giving, not boasting, a road of kindness, a road of truth, it is you, it is one of standing up and offering your voice and every atom of your being. The audience has come to you and now you have to come to the audience, there is no middle ground.

The second lesson is that every poem you write is a discovery of reality. The more you write, reflect, learn, read, you must cultivate it to get to the next poem, to the next realization, the next wider horizon and deeper awareness. The poet everyday must get closer to humanity, reality, with deeper and more inclusive values. It does not matter how you write. It does not matter if your language is simple, basic. What matters is that you are embracing the moment, humanity, with your breath, your ink.

Next Generation: I see the role of a poet to be one of kindness, always finding new ways to cultivate it—writing and kindness: all audiences, all peoples, all living things. At this moment, we must address violence, war, disarmament, global solidarity, climate change, division, and hate. The time is over for nostalgia, identity exclusiveness, cultural debates—we must address unity, planetary identity, all people, all things, all beings.

My Essence: As simple as I can.

What makes me tick: My love for reflection, curiosity of all things, people, Earth, animals, plants, peace, creative expression, the brilliance of happiness and compassion.

Defining myself: No definition. At best, son of Lucha Quintana Herrera and Felipe Emilio Herrera who led simple lives, who were kind and giving, who owned nothing more than a few letters, scarves, a tiny address book, a hat, and a hammer.

*December 20, 2021*

# Addendum: *Rewind*

**How do I identify myself?**
In the late sixties, perhaps since senior year at San DIego, I began to think about being a Chicano. Alurista one day at his apartment on "B" Street stated, "From this day on, I am a Chicano." It must have been late 1966, or '67 when I left to UCLA. I lived two blocks up on "B" Street, half a block from 12th. It was a call to be part of the new Chicano *movimiento*.

It was a heartfelt collective identity, more than a perceived social ethnic one. As time went by and as the *movimiento* changed and branched out into multiple channels of social and gender identities. This wider spectrum of sociopolitical-cultural identities allowed for more choices and orientations. Recently, we are Latinx. I am more inclined toward a "humanity" identity. It embraces all 7.9 billion human beings—there are no divisions, separations, and sectors. DNA demonstrates this. Given my DNA, I have Native roots, like we all do, and Mongolian ancestors, and other roots. DNA & social change and most of all personal choice and vision influence the ID title we take, pronounce, and create. We need unity in these times. Think on it.

My advice for new gen writers:

Writing is a deep act of kindness—it is an act for others, simply. Also, it is a link to all past writers and thinkers. It is a circle. Do not think about writing—just write. As you write, words appear and each one will encourage you toward the next word. Sometimes a phrase or word, or a handful of words will energize you to write immediately. Picasso found a straw basket once and made a goat plaster sculpture out of it. Write freely. You must free your mind. Cszelaw Milosz calls for "Freedom of Thought" in his incredible book of the '40s, *The Captive Mind*, referring to Hitlerism and Stalinism. You must reflect on this—*do you want freedom of thought?* If yes, then write your thoughts and express yourself and speak of the world around you and in you.

Writing a poem is more than technique and devices and workshops. They are good things, your cohort is a great thing. However, most of all it is up to you to fully allow your mind to be free, your thoughts to be shared, and your heart to be warm—for others. Writing is also art. Writing is something like painting, you create images, portraits, murals, photos, figures, and characters, and you make them speak too. It can turn into a musical score and a theatre drama. The great Spanish poet Federico García Lorca accomplished all these things—poetry, music, and theatre. Poetry, remember, also takes you to an audience. It is more than words on paper or on the screen. Before you know it, you are standing on a stage, in farm working fields or on a university platform or in front of elementary school students, teachers, and parents. You'll be on YouTube, Zoom, and on. What do you want to say to the people? You become a speaker. Or do you want to be silent?

This happens little by little and it can also happen now. Choose now. Also choose your words, your ideas. We need peace, we need community, we need encouragement, we need hope. This is where you come in. This is where your kindness writes, speaks, and pours itself onto the world.

*Dec. 24, 2021*

# CHAPTER 15

# Juan Felipe Herrera

## Notes on the Formation of an Artist

RENATO ROSALDO

Juan Felipe Herrera became widely known when he served two terms as the poet laureate of the United States (2015–2017). He is the first and only Latino to have been named to that prestigious position, but his life and works are not as well-known as they deserve to be. It appears that the bias that has hampered the recognition of Latino/a poets in general has blocked the public discussion of Juan Felipe's life and works. It is in that spirit that I feel an urgent need to contribute a brief essay to the discussion of his life and artistic accomplishments.

Juan Felipe Herrera, who was the twenty-first poet laureate of the United States, was born on December 27, 1948, in Fowler, California, near Fresno. When reflecting on his trajectory as a poet Juan Felipe attributed much of his early development to his parents, particularly his mother. His parents followed and harvested crops in the San Joaquin Valley. His father drove a 1940s Army truck and a homemade trailer, taking Juan Felipe as a child on the road, past agricultural fields bursting with crops ready for his family to harvest. This education of the young poet was supplemented by "Greyhound depot life, barrio scenes, and the tiny Coronet Pedro Infante cinema in Logan Heights barrio, San Diego" (Lomelí and Gómez, December 27, 2020). When he was a child, his mother told what for him were magical stories about her life in a Mexico City orphanage during the Mexican Revolution (1910–

1920), plus stories about her journey from Colonia Niño Perdido near Tepito, Mexico City, to Juárez, Chihuahua, and eventually to El Segundo Barrio in El Paso, Texas. With her only child, her son, Juan Felipe, she recited poems, sang *corridos* (ballads), played word games, challenged him with riddles, as if preparing him for life as a poet and a performer on stage, doing *teatro* (theater), spoken word, and stand-up comedy. His father died when Juan Felipe was in tenth grade.

During middle school and high school in San Diego (1964–69), Juan Felipe's teachers gave him readings that enriched his understanding of poetry, writing, and art from the Renaissance through impressionism and expressionism to surrealism. The works and lives of painters captured his imagination, particularly Dalí, Braque, Picasso, Magritte, Matisse, and Warhol. He says, for example, that Picasso was a role model: "his insatiable hunger for painting, his milieu of artists and friends, his outspoken intensity, his various phases and uses of diverse mediums, his life as an artist" (Lomelí and Gómez, December 27, 2020). Writers he cites as crucial that he read during his high school years include Hesse, Kafka, Mann, Krishnamurti, Artaud, Sartre, and Lorca. His reading was wide and eclectic. For example, he read the postwar Polish poets of the Holocaust who wrote in accord with "non-ornamental" ethics. They included Tadeusz Rosevicz, Wislava Szymborska, Zbigniew Herbert, and Cezlaw Milosz.

These readings I find remarkable when I compare them with what I was given at Tucson High School (1955–59). At 18 years of age, Juan Felipe was the right man in the right place at the right time. Yet he says at the time he had not fully grasped how much he was in the thrall of art and writing. He gravitated to art that was experimental and avant-garde. It was primarily his teachers rather than members of the wider world of art who served as Juan Felipe's mentors. A splendid teacher of his was named David Whitman. Fundamental for Whitman were Schopenhauer, Nietzsche, and Sartre. Juan Felipe was most attracted by what he called "abstraction, big mind, wild images, a sense of emergency" (Lomelí and Gómez, December 20, 2020). He not only read but also wrote. During high school Juan Felipe wrote a small experimental play series which he named "Liquid Theater" after Artaud's "Theater of the Double."

Juan Felipe looked to his uncles (his mother's brothers) as well as to his parents as models for his artistic accomplishments. His uncle Vicente Quintana was an artist who painted in acrylics and oils, and was skilled as a sculptor. Another uncle, Roberto Quintana, was a poet who broadcast on Radio XEJ and was well known in the borderlands of Juárez and El Paso. Historians would do well to study virtuosos in radio during the 1930s and before to understand the early formation of Chicano culture. Uncle Roberto at times performed with the famous Mexican comic, Tintán. His uncle Roberto's lasting lesson to Juan Felipe was "art at all costs, self-made, and self-propelled" (Lomelí and Gómez, December 20, 2020). His uncles and parents were his first school, his first creative workshop, his borderlands art degree, and his poetry and community MFA (Mexican Family Art). He says his love of the avant-garde "probably came from the daring vision of my family to make a new life on the land, the stage, canvas, stone and the microphone" (Lomelí and Gómez, December 20, 2020).

Fellow writer Luis Alberto Urrea recalls his years of middle school and high school in San Diego and says, "Herrera and I come from the same barrio in San Diego" (Urrea, 2). "Eight years older than I, Herrera was in a different universe entirely. We both hung around the foundational *raza* poet Alurista and his literary journal *Maize*, as well as San Diego's Centro Cultural de la Raza" (Urrea, 4–5). Most probably influenced by Alurista, Juan Felipe dedicated himself to working in the tradition of Nezahualcóyotl (fasting coyote), the ruler-poet prince of Texcoco during the 1400s who practiced *flor y canto* (flower-song), which was about offering and celebration rather than being (as in the Anglo-American tradition), poetry that was created through the use of craft and that aspired to be literature. Herrera and Urrea lived in a cultural hot spot of Southern California with remarkable institutions, polyglot wordplay, gifted high school teachers, and accomplished poets who came together in parks and at readings where they nourished one another's work in the tradition of *flor y canto*, which became, as Juan Felipe said, a "root source" through which young poets could merge ritual and art in "a communal celebration, an offering" (Lomelí and Gómez, December 20, 2020) and be able to value their inner selves and speak in their true voices. Juan Felipe then deeply shaped Chicano poetry which in turn shaped him, becoming a major influence on his work. Thus he came to see himself as working in the tradition of *flor y canto*, even while still in high school, and for years after.

In August 1969 Juan Felipe left for UCLA where he had received an Education Opportunity Program (EOP) scholarship and where he became an anthropology major. At UCLA he attended concerts and saw such East Coast experimental theaters as Café La Mama and the Open Theater. These East

Coast experimental theaters led him to attempt new choreographies with his Chicano *teatro*: Teatro Chichimeca and Teatro Tolteca. Juan Felipe helped form a poetry jazz ensemble. He blended his writing with such experiments. Experiment and multi-art were his artistic centers of gravity. He also immersed himself in the social and cultural movements of the day. He lists the movements that most shaped him, "the women's movement, Chicano, Black, gay, Native, Asian, South Asian self-reconstruction" (Lomelí and Gómez, December 20, 2020). He noticed that the Chicano movement was claiming Indigenous identities without having had direct contact with native communities. He took his perception to heart and set off with other aspiring Chicanos for two Maya villages of the Selva Lacandona, Chiapas, Mexico. He put himself in direct touch with the native people he saw as brothers and sisters. Such was the depth of his artistic and political commitment.

In 1977 he went to Stanford to study in its cultural anthropology PhD program. As he progressed toward his PhD, he earned, as was part of the program, an MA in anthropology.

Characteristically modest, Juan Felipe did not call attention to his own erudition. During his period in the PhD program I was Juan Felipe's academic advisor. I found him to be an outstanding student among his peers. In our program he completed all the requirements for the PhD in good standing: the courses, the exams, and all the other requirements, except the dissertation. This occurs so often in PhD programs it is known by an informal title: ABD (All But Dissertation). He continued writing poetry at a prodigious rate during the PhD program. In retrospect he found that his poetry, like that of Nezahualcóyotl, was about moments of love, moments of true community. His works were offerings, flower-songs. I remember how in those years he often came by my office with fellow poet, Francisco X. Alarcón, to say that they had started a new poetry magazine (*Vórtice* and *Metamorfosis* are two I recall). He would ask me to write a poem for his new magazine. I would say I didn't know where to begin. He would reply that he'd read my prose and knew I could write poetry. Juan Felipe lived in San Francisco's Mission District where he co-founded the Mission Cultural Center and his work became internationalist, informed by Latin American and African national liberation struggles, as it was shaped in particular by the art and politics of Nicaragua's Sandinista revolution. It was also deeply shaped by an educational trip a group of us, his fellow students and teachers, "cultural workers," made to Cuba in the summer of 1979. He wears his knowledge lightly, enjoys acting like a guy who just walked in off the street, but his knowledge from travel and study is at the core of his verse, much as he tries to hide it under a bushel basket.

At Stanford, under President Donald Kennedy, the University actively recruited faculty and students. The student dorm headed by poet and visual artist Tony Burciaga and Cecilia Burciaga became a center for the arts and mounted many a Flor y Canto event. Many years later, when I began writing poetry, I called Juan Felipe and told him what I was writing. He drove from Fresno to see me the next day and read and commented on my poems. I was deeply grateful for his generous sense of community.

In 1988 Juan Felipe completed an MFA at the Iowa Writers' Workshop. After his MFA he became chair of Chicano and Latin American Studies at California State University, Fresno. In 2005 Juan Felipe was appointed to the Tomás Rivera Endowed Chair in Creative Writing at the University of California, Riverside. In 2008 he received The National Book Critics Circle Award for his book of selected poems, *Half the World in Light: New and Selected Poems*. He held the position at Riverside until 2012 when Governor Jerry Brown named him poet laureate of California. He was also elected chancellor of the Academy of American Poets, a post in which he served 2011–2016. He was appointed by the Library of Congress to be United States Poet Laureate (2015–2017). The rest is history.

## Works Cited

Lomelí, Francisco A., and Osiris Aníbal Gómez. "The Poet, the Playwright, the Citizen and the Maverick: An Interview with U.S. Poet Laureate Juan Felipe Herrera." In *Juan Felipe Herrera: Migrant, Activist, Poet Laureate*, edited by Francisco Lomelí and Osiris Aníbel Gómez, 319–362. Tucson: University of Arizona Press, 2023.

Soldofsky, Alan. "A Border-Crosser's Heteroglossia: Interview with Juan Felipe Herrera, Twenty-First Poet Laureate of the United States." *MELUS* 43, no. 2 (Summer 2018): 196–226.

Urrea, Luis Alberto. "A Rascuache Prayer: Reflections on Juan Felipe Herrera, My Homeboy Laureate." *Poetry Foundation, Prose*, September 14, 2020. https://www.poetryfoundation.org/articles/154196/a-rascuache-prayer.

# CHAPTER 16

# Bibliography by and on Juan Felipe Herrera 2022[1]

DONALDO W. URIOSTE

## Poetry (Chronological)

*Rebozos of Love / We Have Woven / Sudor de Pueblos / On Our Back.* San Diego, Calif.: Toltecas en Aztlán, 1974. Republished as *Rebozos of Love: Floricanto 1970–1974.* McAllen, Texas: FlowerSong Press, 2021.

*Mission Street Manifesto: For All Varrios.* San Francisco: Lalo Press Publications, 1983.

*Exiles of Desire.* Fresno, Calif.: Lalo Press Publications, 1983. Reprint, Houston, Texas: Arte Público Press, 1985.

*A Night in Tunisia: Newtexts.* Co-published with Margarita Luna Robles. Stanford, Calif.: Diseños Literarios, 1985.

*Facegames.* San Francisco, Calif.: As Is/So & So Press, 1987.

*Zenjose: Scenarios.* San José, Calif.: printed by the author, 1988.

*Akrílica.* Translations by Stephen Kessler & Sesshu Foster; with Dolores Bravo, and Magaly Fernández, Santa Cruz, CA: Alcatraz Editions, 1989. Edited by Farid Matuk, Carmen Giménez and Anthony Cody. Revised and expanded edition, Notre Dame: Noemi Press, Inc., 2022.

*Memoria(s) from an Exile's Notebook of the Future.* Santa Monica, Calif.: Santa Monica College Press, 1993.

*The Roots of a Thousand Embraces: Dialogues.* San Francisco, Calif.: Manic D Press, 1994. Reprint, San Francisco, Calif.: Manic D Press, 2016.

*Night Train to Tuxtla.* Camino del Sol Series. Tucson: University of Arizona Press, 1994.

*187 Reasons Why Mexicanos Can't Cross the Border: An Emergency Poem.* Fresno, Calif.: Borderwolf Press, 1995.

*Love after the Riots.* Willimantic, Conn.: Curbstone Press, 1996.

*Border-Crosser with a Lamborghini Dream.* Camino del Sol Series. Tucson: University of Arizona Press, 1999.

*Lotería Cards and Fortune Poems: A Book of Lives.* Linocut illustrations by Artemio Rodríguez. San Francisco, Calif.: City Lights Books 1999.

*Thunderweavers/Tejedoras de Rayos.* Camino del Sol Series. Tucson: University of Arizona Press, 2000.

*Giraffe on Fire.* Camino del Sol Series. Tucson: University of Arizona Press, 2001.

*Notebooks of a Chile Verde Smuggler.* Camino del Sol Series. Tucson: University of Arizona Press, 2002.

*187 Reasons Mexicanos Can't Cross the Border: Undocuments, 1971–2007.* San Francisco, Calif.: City Lights Books, 2007.

*Half the World in Light: New and Selected Poems.* Camino del Sol Series. Tucson: The University of Arizona Press, 2008.

*Los vampiros de Whittier Boulevard.* Translation of *Vampires of Whittier Boulevard* into Spanish by Santiago Román. Mexico City: Avra Ediciones, 2009.

*Senegal Taxi.* Camino del Sol Series. Tucson: University of Arizona Press, 2013.

*Notes on the Assemblage.* San Francisco: City Lights Publishers, 2015.

*La fábrica / Notes on the Assemblage.* Edited and translated by Nieves García Prados. Granada, Spain: Valparaíso Ediciones, 2018.

*Jabberwalking.* Somerville, Mass.: Candlewick Press, 2018.

*Borderbus.* Prints by Felicia Rice with an introduction by Carmen Giménez Smith. Chicanx/Latinx Series. Santa Cruz, Calif.: Moving Parts Press, 2019.

*Every Day We Get More Illegal.* San Francisco, Calif.: City Lights Publishers, 2020.

# Children's Literature

*Calling the Doves/Canto a Las Palomas.* Illustrated by Elly Simmons. San Francisco, Calif.: Children's Book Press, 1995.

*Cilantro Girl/La Superniña del Cilantro.* Illustrated by Honorio Robleda-Tapia. San Francisco, Calif.: Children's Book Press, 2003.

*Coralito's Bay/La Bahía de Coralito.* Illustrated by Lena Shiffman. Monterey, Calif.: Monterey Bay Sanctuary Foundation, 2004.

*Featherless/Desplumado.* Illustrated by Ernesto Cuevas, Jr. San Francisco, Calif.: Children's Book Press, 2004.

*Grandma & Me at the Flea/Los Meros Meros Remateros.* Illustrated by Anita Lucio-Brock. San Francisco, Calif.: Children's Book Press, 2002.

*Imagine.* Illustrated by Lauren Castillo. Somerville, Mass: Candlewick Press, 2018.

*Laughing Out Loud, I Fly: Poems in English and Spanish.* Illustrated by Karen Barbour. New York: HarperCollins-Joanna Cotler Books, 1998.

*The Upside Down Boy/El Niño de Cabeza.* Illustrated by Elizabeth Gómez. San Francisco, Calif.: Children's Book Press, 2000.
*Cerca/Close.* Illustrated by Blanca Gómez. Somerville, Mass.: Candlewick Press, 2019.
*Lejos/Far.* Illustrated by Blanca Gómez. Somerville, Mass.: Candlewick Press, 2019.

## Young Adult Fiction

*CrashBoomLove: A Novel in Verse.* Albuquerque: University of New Mexico Press, 1999.
*Cinnamon Girl: Letters Found Inside a Cereal Box.* New York: HarperCollins–Joanna Cotler Books, 2005.
*Downtown Boy.* New York: Scholastic Press, 2005.
*Skatefate.* New York: HarperCollins; Rayo, 2011.

## Nonfiction

*Mayan Drifter: Chicano Poet in the Lowlands of America.* Philadelphia: Temple University Press, 1997.
*Portraits of Hispanic American Heroes.* Illustrated by Raúl Colón. New York: Dial-Penguin, 2014.
*Magnifying the People's Voice: A Laureate's Journey Across America.* With Cindy Urrutia. Fresno, Calif.: Press at California State University, Fresno, 2017.
Ed. *Elotes con Sangre: The Journey Home, Photographs and "Nierikas" (Yarn Paintings) of the Land of Wixáritari, First Peoples, the Huichol Nation of Mexico, 1970.* Fresno, Calif.: The Press at California State University, Fresno, 2016.

## Miscellaneous Writings by Juan Felipe Herrera

"ABC." In *Open a World of Possible: Real Stories about the Joy and Power of Reading,* edited by Lois Bridges, 122–123. New York: Scholastic, 2014. [Story, Memoir]
"About the Author." In *Border-Crosser with a Lamborghini Dream.* Camino del Sol Series. Tucson: University of Arizona Press, 1999. [Prose]
"A Certain Man." In *From the Belly of the Shark: A New Anthology of Native Americans; Poems by Chicanos, Eskimos, Hawaiians, Indian, Puerto Ricans in the U.S.A., with Related Poems by Others,* edited by Walter Lowenfels, 101. New York: Vintage Books, 1973. [Poetry]
"A Poem Review of the Elephant Man." *The Threepenny Review,* no. 12 (1983): 16. [Poetry]
"After All," "We Are Made," "House Is Empty Now," and "A Crack Inside My Breast." In *Poems for a Small Planet: Contemporary American Nature Poetry,* edited by Robert Pack and Jay Parini, 90–92. Hanover, N.H.: University Press of New England, 1993. [Poetry]

"Alligator," and "Loss, Revival and Retribution (Neon Desert Collage)." *The American Poetry Review* 21, no. 6 (1992): 45. [Poetry]

"American Summations." *What the World Hears: California Poets in the Schools 2009 Statewide Anthology*, edited by Michael McLaughlin, Alexa Mergen, and Giovanni Singleton, 164–165. San Francisco: California Poets in the Schools, 2009. [Poetry]

"Anthropomorphic Cabinet," and "Border-Crosser with a Lamborghini Dream." *Compost: A Journal of Art, Literature, and Ideas*, no. 8 (Winter 1996–97): 172–174, 182–184. [Poetry]

"Antiteatro y poemas," "Emelio / Walking the Waterfront," "B Street Second Floor / Mural 14 x14," "La Puerta en el mar," "Dudo las luces," "5x25 Mundo mexicano mural," "Portrait of Woman in Long Black Dress / Aurelia," "La furia de las abejas," and "El caos debajo de los botones / acrílica en azul 30x30." In *Cenzontle: Chicano Short Stories and Poetry; Irvine, 1978–1979*, edited by Orlando Ramírez, Art Godínez, Helena María Viramontes, 74–93. Irvine: Department of Spanish and Portuguese, University of California, Irvine, 1979. [Poetry and theater]

"Antiteatro y poemas, 1978–79," "Memoir: Checker-Piece, 1984–85." In *The Chicano/Latino Literary Prize: An Anthology of Prize-Winning Fiction, Poetry, and Drama*, edited by Stephanie Fetta, 25–30, 101–104. Houston: Arte Público Press, 2008. [Poetry & Memoir]

"Anzaldúa Lives On: Poetry, Transformations and Flashes into the Serpent Eye." Introduction to *Imaniman: Poets Writing in the Anzalduan Borderlands*, edited by Ire'ne Lara Silva and Dan Vera, 5–8. San Francisco, Calif.: Aunt Lute Books, 2017. [Introduction]

"Aphrodisiacal Dinner Jacket," "Anthropomorphic Cabinet," and "From Love after the Riots, 3:07 AM." In *El Coro: A Chorus of Latino and Latina Poetry*, edited by Martín Espada, *The Massachusetts Review* 36, no. 4 (Winter 1995/96): 619–620. [Poetry]

"Are You Doing that American Thing?." In *Literatura Chicana 1965–1995: An Anthology in Spanish, English, and Caló*, edited by Manuel de Jesús Hernández-Gutiérrez and David William Foster, 254–256. New York: Garland Publishing, 1997. [Poetry]

"Arizona Green." *The Progressive Magazin* 75, no. 7 (July 2011): 38. [Poetry]

"Arizona Green (Manifesto #1070)." *Zyzzyva* 26 no. 2 (Fall 2010): 89–91. Reprinted in *Poetry of Resistance: Voices for Social Justice*, edited by Francisco X. Alarcón and Odilia Galván Rodríguez, 93–94. Tucson: University of Arizona Press, 2016. [Poetry]

"Auburn" *Bloomsbury Review* 14, no. 3 (1993): 32. [Poetry]

"Auburn." In *Poetry in Motion from Coast to Coast: 120 Poems from Subways and Buses*, edited by Elise Paschen and Brett Fletcher Lauer, 79. New York: W.W. Norton, 2002. [Poetry]

"Ayotzinapa." *The Progressive Magazine* 80, no. 8 (September 2016): 45. [Poetry]

"Basho & Mandela." *The New Yorker* 96, no. 26 (September 7, 2020): 63. [Poetry]

"Behind the Storm This Life," "Ripped Mandibles It Is About This War," "My Mother Meanders When She Sees Me Skipping Across Avenues," and "The Shrapnel That Is What the Palette Knife Is Pushing Moving Stripping." In *Bear Flag Republic: Prose Poems and Poetics from California*, edited by Christopher Buckley and Gary Young, 198–199. Santa Cruz, Calif.: Greenhouse Review Press/Alcatraz Editions, 2008. [Poetry]

"Binoculars (Manhattan, Circa 1943)," "Iowa Blues Bar Spiritual," and "Norteamérica, I Am Your Scar." *New England Review* 13, no. 3/4 (April 1991): 242–249. [Poetry]

"Blood on the Wheel." In *The Poem Is You: 60 Contemporary American Poems and How to Read Them*, by Stephanie Burt, 192–195, 195–199. Cambridge, Mass.: The Belknap Press of Harvard University Press, 2016. [Poetry & critical comment]

"Blowfish: An Autobiography." In *New Chicano Writing Volume 1*, edited by Charles M. Tatum, 119–141. Tucson: University of Arizona Press, 1992. [Poetry and Prose]

"Book Review of *Farewell to the Coast* by Alejandro Murguía." *Metamorfosis: The Journal of Northwest Chicano Art and Culture* 3, no. 2 (1980–1981): 108. [Book Review]

"Border Crosser with a Lamborghini Dream," "Pick Up Your Severed Head & Let Me Get on, Baby," "Selena in Corpus Christi Lacquer Red," and "Outside Tibet: Word on Ice." *The Americas Review* 24, no. 3–4 (1996): 47–49, 144–147. [Poetry and Prose]

*Border-Crosser with A Lamborghini Dream*: "Blood Night Café," and "Selena in Corpus Christi Lacquer Red;" *Giraffe on Fire*: "Ofelia in Manhattan, Circa 1943;" *Notebooks of a Chile Verde Smuggler*: "Immigrant Fortune Teller Machine," "Fuzzy Equations," and "Letanía para José Antonio Burciaga." In *Camino del Sol: Fifteen Years of Latina and Latino Writing*, edited by Rigoberto González, 63–77. Tucson: University of Arizona Press, 2010. [Poetry]

"The Boy of Seventeen," "Water Girl," "Earth Chorus," "These Words Are Synonymous, Now," and "Pyramid of Supplications." In *After Aztlán: Latino Poets of the Nineties*, edited by Ray González, 101–110. Boston: D.R. Godine, 1992. [Poetry]

"California Brown," In *Freeman's California: The Best New Writing on California*, edited by John Freeman, 145–148. New York: Grove Press, 2019. [Poetry]

"The Califas Movimiento: 1964–1984." *Poetry Flash* 20, no. 20 (1985): n.p. [Poetry]

"Candy & Toys," "Verde que te quiero," and "Slic Ric Salinas Rapping on 24th," *Literatura de las Fronteras/Border Literature: Memoria del Encuentro de Literatura de las Fronteras (Tijuana, Junio/Julio 1988)*, edited by José Manuel Di-Bella, Rogelio Reyes, Gabriel Trujillo Muñoz, and Harry Polkinhorn, 77–78. Mexicali, B.C.: Instituto de Cultura de Baja California; San Diego: San Diego State University Institute for Regional Studies of the Californias, 1989. [Poetry]

"Cantos." *Bilingual Review/La Revista Bilingüe* 2, no. 1–2 (1975): 176–178. [Poetry]

"The Cassettes," "Notes on Other Chicana and Chicano Inventions," "Rodney King, the Black Christ of Los Angeles and All Our White Sins—May 1, 1992," "Zoot Suit on a Bed of Spanish Rice," "Milagros & Angels," and "Mariachi Drag Star." In *Currents from the Dancing River: Contemporary Latino Fiction, Nonfiction, and Poetry*, edited by Ray González, 121–136. New York: Harcourt Brace, 1994. [Poetry & Prose]

"Chantlove." *El Tecolote: Revista Literaria de El Tecolote* 40, no. 15 (July/August, 2010) 3. [Poetry]

"Chicano Literature 100." *University of Arizona Poetry Calendar*, (Fall 1993). [Poetry]

"Cien años de don Luis Leal." In *Cien años de lealtad en honor a Luis Leal, vol. II*, edited by Sara Poot Herrera, Francisco A. Lomelí, and María Herrera-Sobek, 1447–1448. Santa Barbara: University of California Santa Barbara; Mexico City: Universidad Nacional Autónoma de México, 2007. [Poetry]

"The Colored Trickster and the Frida Painter: On the Utterance of Multiculturalism in Our Own Land." In *Multi-America: Essays on Cultural Wars and Cultural Peace*, edited by Ishmael Reed, 102–109. New York: Penguin Books, 1998. [Essay/Memoir/Drama]

"Days of Invasion." In *Mirrors Beneath the Earth: Short Fiction by Chicano Writers*, edited by Ray González, 99–112. Willimantic, Conn: Curbstone Press, 1992. [Short Story]

"Days of Invasion." In *Under the 5th Sun: Latino Literature from California*, edited by Rick Heide, 376–382. Santa Clara, Calif.: Santa Clara University; Berkeley: Heyday Books, 2002. [Short Story]

"De timbales y cascabeles." *Aztlán: Chicano Journal of the Social Sciences and the Arts* 1, no. 2 (1970): vi–vii. [Poetry]

"Diana García, When Living Was a Labor Camp." In *Reading U. S. Latina Writers: Remapping American Literature*, edited by Alvina E. Quintana, 103–112. New York: Palgrave Macmillan, 2003. [Review]

"Earth Chorus." In *From Totems to Hip-Hop: Poetry Across the Americas, 1900–2002*, edited by Ishmael Reed, 30–32. New York: Thunder's Mouth Press, 2003. [Poetry]

"Ejotes con mayonesa," Bisbee Poetry Festival Calendar (1993): 22. [Poetry]

"& ese muro." Translation of "& That Wall" by Francisco A. Lomelí, *Ventana Abierta: Revista Latina de Literatura, Arte y Cultura*, 12, no. 39–42 (2015–2017): 25–26.

"Eight Poems: 'It Van Begin with Clouds,' 'We Were Approaching Wabash Street,' 'Ourselves,' 'Rain Dogs,' '[Untitled # 6],' 'Dear Prudence,' ''Vimeo # 9,' and 'Spattered on the Wall'." In *Angels of the Americlypse: An Anthology of New Latin@ Writing*, edited by Carmen Giménez Smith and John Chávez, 91–97. Denver, Colo.: Counterpath Press, 2014. [Poetry]

"Ese vato de atolle." In *Mr. Spic Goes to Washington* by Ilán Stavans, 80–81. Berkeley, Calif.: Soft Skull Press, 2008. [Poetry]

"Es la tierra" / "Earth Chorus." In *Chicanas y Chicanos en Diálogo*, Series Quarry West, 26. edited by Francisco X. Alarcón and Lorna Dee Cervantes, translation by Stephen Kessler & Sesshu Foster, 107–110. Santa Cruz: University of California, Santa, Cruz, 1989. [Poetry]

"Exiles." In *Made in Aztlán*, edited by Philip Brookman and Guillermo Gómez-Peña, 70. San Diego, Calif.: Centro Cultural de la Raza, 1986. [Poetry]

"Exiles," "Inside the Jacket," "Cimabue, Goya, Beginnings," and "El secreto de mis brazos/The Secret of My Arms." In *How Much Earth: An Anthology of Fresno Poets*, edited by Christopher Buckley, David Oliveira, and M.L. Williams, 63–66. Berkeley: Roundhouse Press, 2001. [Poetry]

"Exiles," and "Days of Invasion." In *Under the 5th Sun: Latino Literature from California*, edited by Rick Heide, 43–44, 376–382. Santa Clara, CA: Santa Clara University; Berkeley, Calif.: Heyday Books, 2002. [Poetry]

"Exiles." In *Lengua Fresca: Latinos Writing on the Edge*, edited by Harold Augenbraum and Ilán Stavans, 45–46. Boston: Houghton Mifflin, 2006. [Poetry]

"Exiles." In *California Poetry: From the Gold Rush to the Present*, edited by Dana Gioia, Chryss Yost, and Jack Hicks, 285–287. Santa Clara, Calif.: Santa Clara University; Berkeley, Calif.: Heyday Books, 2003. [Poetry]

"Exiles," "Literary Asylums," and "Quentino," In *The Norton Anthology of Latino Literature*, edited by Ilán Stavans, Edna Acosta-Belén, Harold Augenbraum, María Herrera-Sobek, Rolando Hinojosa and Gustavo Pérez Firmat, 1684–1686. New York: Norton, 2010. [Poetry, Prose]

"Exiles," and "Inside the Jacket." In *Mexican American Literature: A Portable Anthology*, edited by Dagoberto Gilb and Ricardo Angel Gilb, 201–204. Boston: Bedford/St. Martin's 2016. [Poetry]

"The Experiment." In *Poems for Political Disaster: A Chapbook*, edited by Timothy Donnelly, B.K. Fischer, Stefania Heim, and Matt Lord, 61–62. Cambridge, Mass.: Boston Review, 2017. [Poetry]

"Febrero," "At the Moon Cafe," and "Evaluación." *Maize* 1, no. 3 (1978): 52–54. [Poetry]

"Federico García Lorca & The Angels of Celery." *Los Angeles Review of Books* 14 (2017): n.p. [Poetry]

"Federico García Lorca & The Angels of Celery/Federico García Lorca & gli angeli del sedano," "The Fruit Fly & Its Yeast, Its Protein Function/La drosofila & il suo lievito, la sua funzione proteica," "Ochre Yellow Green Stone Huichol Campo/Ocra giallo verde pietra accampamento Huichol," and "187 Reasons Mexicanos Can't Cross the Border (Remix)/187 motivi per cui i messicani non possono attraversare il confine, (remix)." Italian Translations by Erminio Corti. *Ácoma: Rivista internazionale di studi nordamericani*, no. 19 (Fall/Winter 2020): 90–106. [Poetry]

"Ferlinghetti on the North Side of San Francisco," "La 24 y el otoño," and "Black Tenor on Powell Street," "Cerco Blanco," "The Balloon Man," and "Fighting City Hall: On Being a Chicano Filmmaker." *Metamorfosis: The Journal of Northwest Chicano Art and Culture* 3, no. 2 (1980–1981): 35–37, 77–82. [Poetry and Memoir]

"Floating Cities & Coughing Radiators." *LA Weekly* (November 1993): 22–23. [Review]

"Foodstuffs They Never Told Us About," "Machofilia," "Ever Split Your Pantalones While Trying to Look Chingón?," and "Don't Worry Baby." *Luna: A Journal of Poetry and Translation* 4, no. 4 (2000): 86–96. [Poetry and Narration]

Bibliography by and on Juan Felipe Herrera 2022 **375**

"For the Ones Who Put Their Names on the Wall." In *Tales of Two Americas: Stories of Inequality in a Divided Nation*, edited by John Freeman, 69. New York: Penguin Books, 2017. [Poetry]

"Foreign Inhabitant," "Story & King Blvd: Teenage Totems," and "Velvet Baroque/Act." In *An Ear to the Ground: An Anthology of Contemporary American Poetry*, edited by Marie Harris and Kathleen Agüero, 122–124. Athens: University of Georgia Press, 1989. [Poetry]

"Foreword: Crazy Coyote with Gimmicky Legs: Mosaikintro." In *Mosaic Voices: A Spectrum of Central Valley Poets*, edited by Dorina K. Lazo, 7. Fresno, Calif.: Poppy Lane Publishing, 2002. [Forward]

"Foreword: Enthralling Notes." In *Voices of Resistance: Interdisciplinary Approaches to Chican@ Children's Literature*, edited by Laura Alamillo, Larissa M. Mercado-López, and Cristina Herrera, vii–viii. Lanham, Md.: Rowman and Littlefield, 2017. [Forward]

"Fore-word Flow." In *Skin Tax: Poems* by Tim Z. Hernández, ix–xii. Berkeley, Calif.: Heyday Publications, 2005. [Foreword]

"Foreword: Mission Muralizations: 1943–2016." In *The Mission* by Dick Evans, ix–xv. Berkeley, Calif.: Heyday; San Francisco, Calif.: Precita Eyes Muralists Association, 2017. [Forward]

"Foreword." In *Latinx Poetics: Essays on the Art of Poetry*, edited by Rubén Quesada, 6–8. Albuquerque: University of New Mexico Press, 2022. [Forward]

"Foreword." In *Poems for Political Disaster: A Chapbook*, edited by Timothy Donnelly, B.K. Fischer, Stefania Heim, and Matt Lord, i–ii. Cambridge, Mass.: Boston Review, 2017. [Forward]

"Foreword." In *Sueño: New Poems* by Lorna Dee Cervantes, ix. San Antonio, Texas: Wings Press, 2013. [Forward]

"Foreword: TecoPoetas from La Misión Will and Shall Continue." In *Poetry in Flight/ Poesía en Vuelo: Anthology in Celebration of El Tecolote*, edited by Francisco X. Alarcón, Eva Martínez, Nina Serrano, and Harold Terezon, 10–11. San Francisco, Calif.: Acción Latina, 2017. [Forward]

"Foreword: They Carry Butterflies in Their Hands." In *Poetry of Resistance: Voices for Social Justice*, edited by Francisco X. Alarcón and Odilia Galván Rodríguez, xi. Tucson: University of Arizona Press, 2016. [Forward]

"Foreword to the New Edition: Life in Motion." In *Snake Poems: An Aztec Invocation* by Francisco X. Alarcón, edited by Odilia Galván Rodríguez, translated by David Bowles and Xánath Caraza, xi–xvi. Camino del Sol Series. Tucson: University of Arizona Press, 2019. [Forward]

"The Four Quarters of the Heart: A Photographic Portfolio by San Francisco Photographer María Pineda." *Metamorfosis: The Journal of Northwest Chicano Art and Culture* 3, no. 2 (1980/1981): 66–74. [Photography Review]

"Frida's Aria: Towards an Aesthetics of the Dispossessed in the Twenty-First Century." In *Without Discovery, A Native Response to Columbus*, edited by Ray González,

205–221. Seattle: Broken Moon Press, 1992. Reprinted in *Tamaqua*, Pan American Issue 4, no. 1 (Spring 1993): 187–215. [Essay]

"From Word to World: Reflections on the Ezra Jack Keats Award." *Journal of Children's Literature* 26, no. 1 (2000): 54–59. [Essay]

"Fuselage Installation." *The American Poetry Review* 20, no. 1 (January/February 1991): 48. [Poetry]

"Fuselage Installation (1991)," "The Weaning of Furniture-Nutrition (1995)," and "Hallucinogenic Bullfighter (1995)." In *The Body Electric: America's Best Poetry from the American Poetry Review*, edited by Stephen Berg, David Bonnano, and Arthur Vogelsang, 253–255. New York: W. W. Norton & Company, 2000. [Poetry]

"Future Boy." In *Voices in First Person: Reflections on Latino Identity*, edited by Lori Marie Carlson, 52–53. New York: Atheneum Books for Young Readers, 2008. [Poetry]

"Los Galácticos de Aztlán Norte." *Huizache: The Magazine of Latino Literature*, no. 1 (2011): n.p. [Poetry]

"Glamourous Treacheries." *High Plains Review* (Spring 1992): 100. [Poetry]

"Gráfika." In *Nueva narrativa chicana*, edited by Oscar U. Somoza, 94–102. Mexico City: Editorial Diógenes, S.A., 1983. [Poetry & Prose]

"Guadalupe María," "Si yo soy rascuachi." In *Festival Flor y Canto II: An Anthology of Chicano Literature from the Festival Held March 12–16, 1975, Austin, Texas*, edited by Arnold C. Vento, Alurista, and José Flores Peregrino, 93–94. Albuquerque, N.M.: Pajarito Publications; Austin: Center for Mexican American Studies, University of Texas, Austin, 1979 [Poetry]

"Güernika—Pana(ma)," and "Northamérica, I am Your Scar." In *Borderlands Literature: Towards an Integrated Perspective/Encuentro Internacional de la Literatura de la Frontera*, edited by Harry Polkinhorn, José Manuel Di Bella, and Rogelio Reyes, 137–144. San Diego: Institute for Regional Studies of the Californias, San Diego State University; Mexicali, B.C.: XIII Ayuntamiento de Mexicali, 1990.

"Güernika—Pana(ma)." *Ergo!: The Bumbershoot Literary Magazine*, no. 7 (1992): 65–67. [Poetry]

"Güernika—Pana(ma)," "Anti-Cover #6: Mother Jones," "Anti-Cover #7: Christopher Unborn," "Anti-Cover #8: The Forthcoming Noriega Account," "Anti-Cover #11: Three Latino Publishers in the United States," and "Anti-Cover #18: Sor Juana Inez de la Cruz." *Puerto del Sol* 27, no. 1 (1992): 101–109. [Poetry]

"El herido," "El viejo," "El diablo," "La trampa," "El hijo pródigo," and "La serpiente." *Fourteen Hills: The San Francisco State University Review* 5, no. 2 (1999): 111–16. [Poetry]

"How Much Earth, 2001." In *Naming the Lost: The Fresno Poets: Interviews and Essays*, edited by Christopher Buckley, 392. Nacogdoches, Texas: Stephen F. Austin State University Press, 2021. [Short Essay]

"How to Make World Unity Salsa" / "Salsa piccante dell'unità mondiale: ricotta," Translated by Pina Piccolo, *Sagarana: Rivista Letteraria Trimestrale*, no. 36 (July 2009): n.p. [Poetry]

Bibliography by and on Juan Felipe Herrera 2022 **377**

"How to Live with a Feminista and (Still) Be Macho: Notes Unabridged." In *Muy Macho: Latino Men Confront Their Manhood*, edited by Ray González, 51–56. New York: Anchor Books; Doubleday, 1996. Reprinted in *Sudden Fiction Latino: Short-Short Stories from the United States and Latin America*, edited by Robert Shapard, James Thomas, and Ray González, 166–170. New York: W.W. Norton, 2010. [Essay]

"Hunting Passion." *The Reader Magazine*, Redlands, Calif. (Fall 2007): 10–12, 15, 20. Reprinted, *The Reader Magazine*, local e-edition, May 3, 2012.

"I, Citalli 'La Loca' Cienfuegos: Sutra on the Category Makers." *POG*, no. 2 (Spring 2001): 56. [Poetry]

"In 1960" and "There Are Impressionists on Logan Street." *Revista Chicano-Riqueña* 6, no. 3 (1978): 31. [Poetry]

"In the Cannery the Porpoise Soul," "Mar 3," "At the Moon Café," "Gallery of Time," and "Let Me Talk of the Years." In *Calafia: The California Poetry*, edited by Ishmael Reed, 144–148. Berkeley, Calif.: Y'Bird, 1979. [Poetry]

"In the Late Summer of 1990 . . ." In *First Light: A Festschrift for Philip Levine on His 85th Birthday*, edited by Christopher Buckley, 41. Fresno, Calif: Press at California State University, Fresno; Santa Cruz, Calif.: Greenhouse Review Press, 2013. [Section Introduction].

"Inside the Jacket," "Cimabue, Goya, Beginnings," "El secreto de mis brazos," and "Exiles." In *How Much Earth: The Fresno Poets*, edited by Christopher Buckley, David Oliveira and M.L. Williams, 63–66. Berkeley, Calif.: Roundhouse Press, 2001. [Poetry]

Et al. "Inside the Notebooks." *Poets & Writers Magazine* 50, no.1 (January/February 2021): 42–43. [Prose]

"Into the Abyss: Foreword." In *Poems for Political Disaster*, edited by Timothy Donnelly, B.K. Fischer, Stefania Heim, and Matt Lord, 5–6. Cambridge, Mass.: Boston Review, 2017.

"Introduction." In *No Golden Gate for Us* by Francisco X. Alarcón, v–vi. Santa Fe, N.M.: Pennywhistle Press, 1993. [Prose]

"Iowa Blues Bar Spiritual." In *The Best American Poetry, 1992*, edited by Charles Simic, 99–100. New York: Charles Scribner's Sons, 1992. Reprinted in *New England Review* 15, no. 1 (January 1993): 138–40. Reprinted in *Real Things: An Anthology of Popular Culture in American Poetry*, edited by Jim Elledge and Susan Swartwout, 113. Bloomington: Indiana University Press, 1998. [Poetry]

"I Want to Speak of Unity." *The New York Times Magazine*, New York Times, (August 9, 2020): MM10. [Poetry]

"Jets," and "Juntos Nosotros, Pablo: The Literary Mission, 1973–1988." *Quarry West: A Journal of Literature & the Arts*, no. 25 (1988): 29–30, 52–54. [Poetry]

"Juan Felipe Herrera: On the Poetry of Federico García Lorca." In *The Books That Changed My Life: Reflections By 100 Authors, Actors, Musicians, and Other Remarkable People*, edited by Bethanne Kelly Patrick, 108–10. New York: Regan Arts, 2016. [Essay]

"Last Call: How to Make a Chile Verde Smuggler." *The Massachusetts Review* 40, no. 4 (Winter 1999): 567. [Poetry]

"The Last Lords of the Border: A Hip-Hop Day of the Dead." In *Migrant Deaths in the Arizona Desert: La Vida No Vale Nada*, edited by Raquel Rubio-Goldsmith, Celestino Fernández, Jessie K. Finch, Araceli Masterson-Algar, 254–60. Tucson: The University of Arizona Press, 2016. [Performance]

"Last Thursday." *Chelsea Review* (2000): 23. [Poetry]

UNO ["Let Us Gather in a Flourishing Way"], DOS ["Rebozos of Love"], TRES ["Hace muchos años huichol"], CUATRO ["Chapulines Fly"], CINCO ["Sky"], SEIS ["Calavera del sol"], SIETE ["Mujer de sol ¿Por qué estás triste?"], OCHO ["Sunrise Butterfly"], NUEVE ["Come tu frijol carnal y nala"], DIEZ ["Vamos a cantar"], ONCE ["Dawning Luz"], DOCE ["Corazón de venado"], and TRECE ["Los grillos tocan sus acordiones"]. In *Festival de Flor y Canto: An Anthology of Chicano Literature*, edited by Alurista, F.A. Cervantes, Juan Gómez-Quiñones, Mary Anna Pacheco, and Gustavo Segade, 94–102. Los Angeles: University of Southern California Press, 1976. [Poetry]

"Let Us Gather in a Flourishing Way," "Quetzalcoatl No Sorrow," and "Libélula." *Arquitrave* 7, no. 40 (December 2008): 10–16. [Poetry]

"Letter to Sudan: Last White Male Rhino on Earth." In *Love Can Be: A Literary Collection about Our Animals*, edited by Louisa McCune and Teresa Miller, 78–80. Oklahoma City: University of Oklahoma Press, 2018. [Poetry]

"Loss, Revival and Retribution (Neon Desert Landscape)" and "Alligator." *American Poetry Review* 21, no 6 (November/December 1992): 45. [Poetry]

"Love the Victim More Than You Love His Killer," "One Is for Maáx, One Is for Jabalí," and "Advanced Graffiti." *Oxygen Magazine*, no. 6 (1993): n.p. [Poetry]

"Lucha Is Short for Light." In *Our Mother's Spirits: On the Death of Mothers and the Grief of Men*, edited by Bob Blauner, 249–258. New York: HarperCollins/Regan-Books, 1997. Reprinted in 1999. [Essay/Memoir]

"Machofilia," and "Dangerous Phases in Amorous Encounters." *Chelsea* 70–71, (2001): 262–265. [Poetry]

"M.O.C.O.S.: ('Mexicans or Chicanos or Something')." *The Threepenny Review*, no. 57 (1994): 29. [Memoir]

"Memoir: Checker-Piece." In *Best New Chicano Literature 1989*, edited by Julian Palley, 83–87. Tempe, Ariz.: Bilingual Press/Editorial Bilingüe, 1989. Reprinted in *The Chicano/Latino Literary Prize: An Anthology of Prize-Winning Fiction, Poetry, and Drama*, edited by Stephanie Fetta, 101–105. Houston, Texas: Arte Público Press, 2008. [Short story]

"Memoria(s) from an Exile's Notebook of the Future." *Luzitania (For/Za Sarajevo)*, no. 5, edited by Martim Avillez, and Ammiel Alcalay, n.p. New York: Lusitania Press, 1993. [Poetry]

"Memory iii." *In the Grove (Pákatelas: An Homage to Andrés Montoya)*, guest edited by Daniel Chacón (Spring 2008): 152. [Elegy]

Bibliography by and on Juan Felipe Herrera 2022 **379**

"Mexican World Mural, 5 x 25." In *Conspire: To Breathe Together*, edited by Merle Bachman, John Benson, Kate Brandt, Christine Carraher, Philip M. Klasky, Charlie Halloran, and Cynthia Wolterding, 29. San Francisco, Calif.: Fire in the Lake, 1985 [Poetry]

"Mind Core." *Poetry (Chicago)* 208, no. 5 (September 2016): 454–55. [Poetry]

"Mission Street Manifesto: Circa 1959–1982 (Raza Writing in the Mission District-San Francisco.)," *The Guadalupe Review* 1, no. 1 (October 1991):175–216. [Essay]

"¿Mujer de sol por qué estás triste?," "Radio Couples," "Suicide in Hollywood / Lupe Vélez (Circa, 1923) / Serigrafía de una actriz mexicana," "La Puerta en el mar," "Dudo las luces," and "El cuarto amarillo." In *La voz urgente: antología de literatura chicana en español*, edited by Manuel M. Martín-Rodríguez, 175–85. Madrid: Editorial Fundamentos, 1995.

"Muscatine County Fair at West Liberty, Iowa." and "Saudi Journal." *River Styx*, no. 36 (1992): 3–10. [Poetry]

"My Rice Queens," and "Jute-Boy at the Naturalization Derby." *The Iowa Review* 26, no. 2 (Summer 1996): 99–100. [Poetry]

"Night Painters." *Forward* 8, no. 1 (1988): 114–115. [Poetry]

"Nina de Agua," and "That Today Is / for Chente / San Quentin." *Miquiztli: A Journal of Arte, Poesía, Cuento, y Canto* (1978): 9, 22. [Poetry]

"9:40 pm," and "3:35 am." In *Poetry Like Bread: Poets of The Political Imagination from Curbstone Press*, edited by Martín Espada, 142–143. Willimantic, Conn.: Curbstone Press, 1994. [Poetry]

"19 Powkroskaya Street," "The Women Tell Their Stories," and "Enter the Void." *BOMB Magazine*, no. 98 (2007): 102–103. [Poetry]

"99 the Road." In *Highway 99: A Literary Journey through California's Great Central Valley*, edited by Stan Yogi, Gayle Mac, and Patricia Wakida, 373–74. Revised and updated edition. Berkeley, Calif.: Great Valley Books/Heyday Books, 2007. [Poetry]

"Nonifesta: On Writing Around Writing." In *Angels of the Americlypse: An Anthology of New Latin@ Writing*, edited by Carmen Giménez Smith and John Chávez, 99–102. Denver, Colo.: Counterpath Press, 2014. [Essay]

"Norteamérica, I Am Your Scar." *New England Review* 13, no. 3–4 (1991): 246–49. Reprinted in *New Visions of Aztlán* 1, no. 1 (April 1990): 19–20. [Poetry]

"On the Day of the Dead, Mr. Emptiness Sings of Love." *New England Review* 14 no. 4 (October 1992): 216–17. [Poetry]

"One by One: Running Poem." *Camino Real: Estudios de las Hispanidades Norteamericanas* 1, no. 0 (2009): 17–29. [Poetry]

"1/7/90:2," "11/23/90:2," "12/20/90:3" "The Soldier's Bluish Mane." *The Guadalupe Review*, no. 1 (October 1991): 105–10. [Poetry]

"1/7/90:2," and "11/20/90:3." *A Measured Response* (1993): 98–101. [Poetry]

"187 Reasons Why Mexicanos Can't Cross the Border: An Emergency Performance Poem." In *Temple of Confessions: Mexican Beasts and Living Santos*, edited by

Guillermo Gómez-Peña and Roberto Sifuentes, 102–10. New York: PowerHouse Books, 1996. [Poetry]

"187 Reasons Why Mexicanos Can't Cross the Border (remix)." In *Chicano and Chicana Art: a Critical Anthology*, edited by Jennifer A. González, C. Ondine Chavoya, Chon Noriega, 406–409. Durham, N.C.: Duke University Press, 2019. [Poetry]

"Para siempre, Maga." In *Cuentos Chicanos: A Short Story Anthology*, 2nd edition, edited by Rudolfo A. Anaya and Antonio Márquez. 100–105. Albuquerque: University of New Mexico Press, 1984. [Short Story]

"Pelle scura di California." Italian Translation of "California Brown" by Damiano Abeni, In *Freeman's California*, Italian Edition, edited by John Freeman. Florence: Edizioni Black Coffee, 2020, n.p. [Poetry]

"Photograph with Tony, Francisco & Jorge Outside Brava Theatre, San Francisco, 9/15/12, Poem," and "The More You (Hotel Realization Poem #1. 9/22/13, Washington D.C.)." In *Fightin' Words: 25 Years of Provocative Poetry and Prose from "The Blue Collar PEN*," edited by Judith Cody, Kim McMillon and Claire Ortalda, 66–67. Oakland, Calif.: PEN Oakland; Berkeley, Calif.: Heyday, 2014. [Poetry]

"Photo-Poem of the Chicano Moratorium 1980 / L.A." *Revista Chicano-Riqueña* 10, no. 3 (1982): 5–9. Reprinted in *The American Poetry Review* 14, no. 4 (1985): 32–33. [Poetry]

"Photo-Poem of the Chicano Moratorium 1980 / L.A.," "Outside Tibet: Word on Ice," and "Selena in Corpus Christi Lacquer Red." In *The Floating Borderlands: Twenty-Five Years of U.S. Hispanic Literature*, edited by Lauro Flores, 106–113. Seattle: University of Washington Press, 1998. [Poetry & Prose]

"La plazita." *The Bloomsbury Review* 27, no. 2 (March/April 2007): 7. [Poetry]

"Poem by Poem." In *Bullets into Bells: Poets & Citizens Respond to Gun Violence*, edited by Brian Clements, Alexandra Teague, and Dean Rader, 81–82. Boston: Beacon Press, 2017. [Poetry]

"Poema para Cecilio," In *Cantos al Sexto Sol: An Anthology of Aztlanahuac Writings*, edited by Cecilio García-Camarillo, Roberto Rodríguez, Patrisia Gonzales, xvii–xviii. San Antonio, Texas: Wings Press, 2002. [Poetry]

"The Poetry of America," "Atavistic: Traces After the Rain," "Future Martyr of Supersonic Waves," and "The Dream of Christopher Columbus." *Luna: A Journal of Poetry and Translation* 1, no. 1 (1998): 54–60. [Poetry]

"The Poetry of America," "Future Martyr of Supersonic Waves," "Resurrection of the Flesh," "The Yellow Room," "When He Believed Himself to Be a Young Girl Lifting the Skin of the Water," "Portrait of Woman on Long Black Dress / Aurelia," "The Dream of Christopher Columbus," "Mexican World Mural 5x25," "Cherry Bowl with Blue Revolver: Neo-American Landscape," and "Atavistic: Traces after the Rain." In *Touching the Fire: Fifteen Poets of Today's Latino Renaissance*, edited by Ray González, 215–36. New York: Anchor Books/Doubleday, 1998. [Poetry]

"The Poetry of America" and "What Are Poets For?" *The Bloomsbury Review* 15, no.1 (January/February 1995): 11, 15. [Poetry]

"The Poetry of America/Poesía de América," "The Dream of Christopher Columbus/ El sueño de Cristóbal Colón," "The Anthropomorphic Cabinet/El gabinete antropomórfico," "Foreign Inhabitant/Habitante extranjero," and "Aphrodisiac Dinner Jacket/El esmoquin afrodisiaco." In *Usos de la imaginación: poesía de l@s latin@s en EE.UU.*, edited by Lisa Rose Bradford and Fabián Osvaldo Iriarte, 117–139. Mar del Plata, Argentina: Eudem, 2009. [Poetry]

"Portrait of a Nation as a Ten-year-Old Chicano." In *Rediscovering America: The Making of Multicultural America, 1900–2000*, edited by Carla Blank, 217–20. New York: Three Rivers Press, 2003. [Biographical Essay]

"Portrait/Nude #30 / 4 x 6," "Portrait/Nude #9 / 7 x 11," "Arc," "Saguaro," "The Boy of Seventeen," and "Reversible Lovers." In *Under the Pomegranate Tree: The Best New Latino Erotica*, edited by Ray González, 91–94, 263–72. New York: Washington Square Press, 1996. [Poetry]

"Quetzalcóatl." *Hispamérica* 2, no. 6 (1974): 107. Reprinted in *A través de la frontera*, edited by Salvador Leal, 220–221. Mexico City: Centro de Estudios Económicos y Sociales del Tercer Mundo, Instituto de Investigaciones Estéticas, U.N.A.M., 1983. [Poetry]

"Quetzalcóatl," "Muchacha guinda," and "Cielo rojo." In *Chicanos: Antología histórica y literaria*, edited by Tino Villanueva, 296–299. Mexico City: Fondo de Cultura Económica, 1980. [Poetry]

"Radiante(s)." *Poetry, Chicago: Poetry Foundation* 207, no. 6 (March 2016): 596–97.

"Radio Couples," "El muchacho de diecisiete," "Informe poético: sobre sirvientas / hacia un modelo de ser hispanik urbano en EE.UU.," and "Suicide in Hollywood / Lupe Vélez (circ. 1923) / serigrafía de una actriz mexicana." In *Palabra nueva: Poesía chicana*, edited by Ricardo Aguilar, Armando Armengol, and Sergio D. Elizondo, 21–26. El Paso: Texas Western Press, University of Texas at El Paso, Dos Pasos Editores, 1985. [Poetry]

"Reflections on the Ezra Jack Keats Award: From Words to World," *Library Journal for Children's Books* (Spring 2000): 51–56. [Essay]

"Review of *How Much Earth, 2001*," "Review of *Bear Flag Republic*," and "Review of *First Light: A Festschrift for Philip Levine on His 85th Birthday*." In *Naming the Lost: The Fresno Poets, Interviews and Essays*, edited by Christopher Buckley, 392–95. Nacogdoches, Texas: Stephen F. Austin State University Press, 2021. [Prose]

"Riffs on Mission District Raza Writers." In *Reclaiming San Francisco: History, Politics, Culture: A City Lights Anthology*, edited by James Brook, Chris Carlsson, and Nancy J. Peters, 217–30. San Francisco, Calif.: City Lights, 1998. [Essay]

"Rudolfo Anaya por la tierra roja." *Camino Real: Estudios de las Hispanidades*, Número especial dedicado a Rudolfo A. Anaya (January 2022): 205. [Poetry]

"Saturday Night at the Buddhist Cinema." *American Poet* 42 (Spring 2012): 50–52. Reprinted by *Los Angeles Review of Books* (Winter 2015): 60. [Poetry]

"Sensemayá (Song for the Killing of a Snake)." Translation of "Sensemayá (Canto para matar a una culebra)" by Nicolás Guillen. In *Resistencia: Poems of Protest and*

*Revolution*, edited by Mark Eisner & Tina Escaja, with an introduction by Julia Alvarez, 17. Portland, Ore.: Tin House, 2020. [Poetry translation]

"Set 23. *Grandma and Me at the Flea* by Juan Felipe Herrera," and "Set 38. *The Upside Down Boy* by Juan Felipe Herrera." In *Learning from Latino Role Models: Inspire Students through Biographies, Instructional Activities, and Creative Assignments* by David Campos, 141–146, 223–228. Lanham, Md.: Rowman & Littlefield, 2016. [Instructional resources]

"Shawashté." *New England Review* 14, no. 4 (October 1992): 218–20. [Poetry]

"Social Distancing." *American Poet*, no. 59 (Fall/Winter 2020): 66. [Poetry]

"Son dos días para un jinete (América)." *Mester* 7, no. 1 (1978): 19. [Poetry]

"Southern California Nocturne (Circa 1964)" and "The Sea During Springtime." In *Paper Dance: 55 Latino Poets*, edited by Víctor Hernández Cruz, Leroy V. Quintana, and Virgil Suárez, 87–93. New York: Persea Books, 1994. [Poetry].

"Stars of Juárez: Notes from the Musical [Essay]," "The Audition [Drama]," "Cutting Pockets in El Paso, Texas [Poetry]," "¡Vamos a Bailongo! [Drama]" and "It's My Revolution [Poetry]," *Huizache: The Magazine of Latino Literature*, no. 3 (2013): 70–79.

"Suicide in Hollywood / Lupe Vélez-Serigradia de una Actriz Mexicana (Circa 1923)." *Red Trapeze: A Monthly Monopoem Magazine* 1, no. 3 (March 1980): n.p. [Poetry]

"The Sweet Vortex of the Singers." In *The Wind Shifts: New Latino Poetry*, edited by Francisco Aragón, xiii–xvii. Tucson: The University of Arizona Press, 2007. [Foreword]

"Taking a Bath in Aztlán," In *Cantos al Sexto Sol: An Anthology of Aztlanahuac Writings*, edited by Cecilio García-Camarillo, Roberto Rodríguez, Patrisia Gonzales, 223–24. San Antonio: Wings Press, 2002. [Memoir]

"Tatarema." *Mid-American Review* 12, no. 1 (Fall 1991): 61–65. [Poetry]

"This Was Iowa." *Iowa Journal of Literary Studies* 11, no. 1 (1991): 65–70. [Poetry]

"Tutu sol." *Revista Canaria de Estudios Ingleses*, no. 8l (November 2020): 269–71. [Short story]

"Two Tacos al Pastoral, Por Favor," and "Public Obsidian: Transamerican Talks, Sutras and Journals." *The Americas Review* 25, Valedictorian Issue (1999): 48–76. [Mixed genres]

"2015–2017: Juan Felipe Herrera [1948-]: 'Fulgencio salió de Oaxaca hacia El Norte,' 'Entrar el vacío,' 'Mitad mexicano,' 'Borderbus,' and 'El soldado en la habitación vacía." In *Antología de poetas laureados estadounidenses (1937–2018)*, edited and translated by Luis Alberto Ambroggio, 513–31. Madrid: Vaso Roto Ediciones, 2019. [Poetry]

"Train Notes." Introduction to *Night Train to Tuxtla*, ix–xiii. Camino del Sol Series. Tucson: The University of Arizona Press, 1994. [Introduction]

"Unarchived Messages." *Chicano/Latina Poets: A Special APR Supplement, The American Poetry Review* 40, no. 5 (2011): 23. [Introduction]

"Uno," "Black Tenor on Powell Street," "Jagged Anise," "The Waiters," and "Radio Couples." In *Contemporary Chicano Poetry: An Anthology*, edited by Wolfgang Binder, 85–93. Erlangen, Germany: Verlag Palm & Enke, 1986. [Poetry]

Bibliography by and on Juan Felipe Herrera 2022 **383**

"Velvet Howl." In *The Wind Shifts: New Latino Poetry*, edited by Francisco Aragón, 3–8. Tucson: University of Arizona Press, 2007. [Foreword]

"Veracruceando = Veracruzing." In *Literatura de la Frontera México-Norteamericana: Cuentos = U.S./Mexican Border Literature: Short Stories*, edited by José Manuel Di-Bella, Rogelio Reyes, Gabriel Trujillo Muñoz, and Harry Polkinhorn, 57–71. Mexicali: Universidad Autónoma de Baja California; Calexico, Calif.: San Diego State University, 1989. [Short story]

"Veracruzing: A Chicano Travelogue." *Five Fingers Review*, no. 4 (1986): 9–14. [Short story]

"Voor Altijd, Maga." Dutch translation of "Para Siempre, Maga," in *De Avonturen Van De Chicano Kid En Andere Verhalen*, edited by Hub Hermans, 87–94. Houten, Netherlands: Novib/Het Weredvenster, 1990. [Short story]

"We Are Remarkably Loud Not Masked." *The Progressive Magazine* 79, no. 7–8 (July/August 2015): 58.

"We are Remarkably Loud Not Masked." In *What Saves Us: Poems of Empathy and Outrage in the Age of Trump*, edited by Martín Espada, 88–89. Evanston, Ill.: Curbstone Books/Northwestern University Press, 2019. [Poetry]

"The Weaning of Furniture-Nutrition," "When He Believed Himself to Be a Young Girl Lifting the Skin of the Water," "The Concert or the Red Piano or the Red Orchestra," "Metamorphosis of Auschwitz," and "Hallucinogenic Bullfighter." *The American Poetry Review* 24, no. 4 (July/August 1995): 3–5. [Poetry]

"Writing Kindness," Introduction to *Twenty Poems: In Memoriam*, edited by Edward Vidaurre, Katie Hoerth, José V. Chapa, and Daniel García Ordaz, 3–4. McAllen, Texas: El Zarape Press, 2014. [Introduction]

"You Throw a Stone." *The New York Times Magazine*, (March 6, 2016): 19(L). [Poetry]

"Zoot Suit on a Bed of Spanish Rice." *Argonaut: New Series*, no 1 (January 1993): 193–97. [Short story]

## Sound Recordings

"For the Ones Who Put Their Names on the Wall." In *Tales of Two Americas: Stories of Inequality in a Divided Nation*, edited by John Freeman, read by Corey M. Snow and Teri Schnaubelt. Old Saybrook, Conn.: Tantor Audio, 2017. Compact disc audiobook.

*Half of the World in Light: New and Selected Poems*. Tucson: University of Arizona Press, 2008. Compact disc audiobook.

"Introduction to 'Papaya.'" *Palabra: A Sampling of Contemporary Latino Writers*, a videorecording by Benjamín Alire Sáenz & Rosemary Catacalos. San Francisco, Calif.: The Poetry Center and American Poetry Archives, SFSU, 1993. VHS.

*JabberWalking*. Read by the author. Grand Haven, Mich.: Candlewick on Brilliance Audio, 2018. Compact disc audiobook.

"Logan Heights and the World." *Poetry On Record: 98 Poets Read Their Work, 1888–2006*, compiled and produced by Rebekah Presson Mosby, disc 4. Los Angeles,

Calif.: Shout Factory; New York: Sony BMG Music Entertainment, 2006. Compact disc audiobook.

*Notes on the Assemblage.* Read by the author, Cambridge, Mass.: Audible Studios, 2017. Audible audio ed.

*Portraits of Hispanic American Heroes.* Read by Luis Moreno, Prince Frederick, Md.: Recorded Books, 2015. Compact disc audiobook.

*Poet Laureate Juan Felipe Herrera Reads from His Work* [*Half of The World in Light: New and Selected Poems, Senegal Taxi, and Notes on the Assemblage*]. With the Archive of Hispanic Literature on Tape (Library of Congress). Recorded September 11, 2015. Online audio. http://hdl.loc.gov/loc.mbrsrs/ahlot.2016686193.

"Poem by Poem." With Benjamin Boone, as heard on *The Poets are Gathering*, produced and edited by Benjamin Boone. Recorded by Maximus Media, Fresno, Calif.: Recorded July 17, 2017. Online audio file. https://benjaminboone.bandcamp .com/track/poem-by-poem-feat-juan-felipe-herrera-17, https://soundcloud.com /benjaminboone/poem-by-poem-feat-juan-felipe.

"The Poets are Gathering." With Benjamin Boone, as heard on *The Poets are Gathering*, produced and edited by Benjamin Boone. Recorded by Maximus Media, Fresno, Calif., July 17, 2017, uploaded to YouTube, 3 November 2020. Video; online audio. https://www.youtube.com/watch?v=5WGWKlnmMAI, https://sound cloud.com/benjaminboone/the-poets-are-gathering-feat.

"Papaya." With The Troka Rhythm and Sign Ensemble. YouTube video, uploaded April 18, 2013. https://www.youtube.com/watch?v=vyV-sZMo8yQ.

## Translation

Alexander, Kwame. *The Crossover: A Basketball Novel.* Translated by Juan Felipe Herrera as *El crossover*. Boston; New York: Houghton Mifflin Harcourt, 2019.

## Juan Felipe Herrera Writings Online

"@ the Crossroads—A Sudden American Poem." *Poem-a-Day*, Academy of American Poets, July 10, 2016. Reprinted in *From the Catbird Seat: Poetry and Literature at the Library of Congress*, July 11, 2016. [Poetry] https://poets.org/poem/cross roads-sudden-american-poem, https://blogs.loc.gov/catbird/2016/07/the-cross roads-a-sudden-american-poem-by-21st-poet-laureate-juan-felipe-herrera/.

"A Certain Man." PEN America, July 27, 2009. [Poetry] https://pen.org/a-certain -man/.

"All the Thoughts at a Football Game." Poets.org, 2015. https://poets.org/poem/all -thoughts-football-game.

"California Poetry: 'Almost Livin', Almost Dyin'." *State Lines. San Francisco Chronicle*, March 9, 2017. [Poetry] https://www.sfchronicle.com/books/article/State-Lines -California-poetry-Almost-10987367.php.

"Almost Livin', Almost Dyin'." Poetry Foundation, n.d. [Poetry] https://www.poetry
foundation.org/poems/91750/almost-livin39-almost-dyin39-, https://soundcloud
.com/mevalemaiz/juan-felipe-herrera-almost-living-almost-dying [Audio].

"Video Poem: U.S. Poet Laureate Juan Felipe Herrera Live from D.C.!." *Hola Cultura*,
Chicanos/Literature, September 17, 2015. [Poetry] https://holacultura.com/video
-poem-u-s-poet-laureate-juan-felipe-herrera-live-from-d-c/.

"America, We Talk About It." *Literary Hub* (blog). September 22, 2020. [Poetry]
https://lithub.com/america-we-talk-about-it/.

"And If the Man with the Choke-hold." *Los Angeles Review of Books*, December 6,
2014. [Poetry] https://lareviewofbooks.org/article/man-choke-hold/.

"El Ángel de la Guarda (The Guardian Angel)." *J'S THEATER Blogspot*, April 5, 2011.
https://jstheater.blogspot.com/2011/04/poem-juan-felipe-herrera.html.

"Anthropoetry." Review of *The Day of Shelly's Death: The Poetry and Ethnography
of Grief* by Renato Rosaldo. *Los Angeles Review of Books*, March 7, 2014. [Book
review] https://lareviewofbooks.org/article/anthropoetry/.

"Aquí y allá." Translated into Spanish as "Here and There," by Carlos Alcorta, *Literatura y arte*, WordPress.com, April 18, 2015. [Poetry] https://carlosalcorta.word
press.com/2015/04/18/juan-felipe-herrera-aqui-y-alla/.

"Are You Doing That New Amerikan Thing?/¿Estás en esa nueva onda amerikana?"
*Peregrinos y sus letras*, n.d. [Poetry] http://www.peregrinosysusletras.net/juan
-felipe-herrera1.html.

"Arizona Green (Manifesto #1070)." *On-Line Poetry Festival: Responses to Arizona.*
In "Online Poetry Festival: Responses to Arizona," *La Bloga, The World's Longest-
Established Chicana Chicano, Latina Latino Literary Blog*, May 11, 2010. [Poetry]
https://labloga.blogspot.com/2010/05/guests-roberto-cantu-jose-antonio.html.

"[Arizón maricopa tempe tu tierra roja]," "Photo-Poem of the Chicano Moratorium
1980 / L.A.: Photo I. Pilgrimage," "Fotopoema de la Moratoria Chicana de 1980 /
L.A.: Foto I. Peregrinación, (Translation by Santiago Román)," "Ode to the Industrial Village of the World," and "The Poets are Gathering." *Peregrinos y sus letras*
(blog), August 18, 2021. [Poetry] http://www.peregrinosysusletras.net/escritora
-invitadoa.

"Ayotzinapa." *The Progressive Magazine: A Voice for Peace, Social Justice, and the
Common Good*, September 22, 2016. Reprinted in *San Francisco Art Quarterly:
LXAQ*, no. 2 (February 27, 2017): n.p. [Poetry] https://progressive.org/magazine
/ayotzinapa/, https://www.sfaq.us/2017/02/notes-on-the-assemblage/.

"Ayotzinapa/Ayotzinapa," "Don't Worry Baby/No te preocupes, baby." Translated
by Lauro Flores. *Peregrinos y sus letras*, September 8, 2021. [Poetry] http://www
.peregrinosysusletras.net/juan-felipe-herrera.

"Basho & Mandela." *The New Yorker*, audio, September 7, 2020. [Poetry] https://www
.newyorker.com/magazine/2020/09/07/basho-and-mandela.

"Bay Bridge Inauguration Poem: For All Bridge Dreamers, Bridge Builders & Bridge
Crossers." *UCR Today*, September 2, 2013. Reprinted *UCR: The Magazine of UC*

*Riverside*, Spring 2014. [Poetry] https://ucrtoday.ucr.edu/17253, https://magazine archive.ucr.edu/998.

"Blood Gang Call." Iowa City/Johnson County Senior Center Technology and Video. YouTube video uploaded May 24, 2016. [Poetry] https://www.youtube.com/watch ?v=B9mR7a_P5gY.

"Blood on the Wheel." Poetry Foundation, n.d. [Poetry] https://www.poetryfoun dation.org/poems/55752/blood-on-the-wheel.

"Borderbus." Poetry Foundation, n.d. [Poetry] https://www.poetryfoundation.org /poems/91751/borderbus.

"Borderbus." *Dissident Voices: The Poetry of Resistance*, May 5, 2017. [Poetry] https:// dissidentpoetry.wordpress.com/2017/05/05/borderbus/.

"Borderbus." *IBERO: Revista de la Universidad Iberoamericana* 50 (1 June 1, 2017): 62. [Poetry] http://revistas.ibero.mx/ibero/articulo_detalle.php?id_volumen=36 &id_articulo=637&id_seccion=667&active=1&pagina=53.

"Borderbus," "So Poetry Became My Thing," and "We Weren't Poor, We Were Pioneers." SoundCloud audio, June 4, 2017. [Poetry & stories] https://soundcloud .com/gemini-ink/sets/juan-felipe-herrera-autograph-series.

"Borderless in El Paso, Texas," "Sin fronteras en El Paso, Texas," "We Won't Forget Dayton, Ohio," and "No olvidaremos a Dayton, Ohio." Translated into Spanish by Lauro Flores. *Los Angeles Review of Books* (blog), August 4, 2019. [Poetry] https:// blog.lareviewofbooks.org/poetry/borderless-el-paso-texas/.

"Breathe We." *Poem-a-Day*, Academy of American Poets, September 14, 2020. [Poetry] https://poets.org/poem/breathe-we.

"Floricanto for Francisco. Pushcart Floricanto. [Canto for Francisco X. Alarcón]." *Bloga: The World's Longest-Established Chicana Chicano, Latina Latino Literary Blog*, February 2, 2016. [Poetry] https://labloga.blogspot.com/2016/02/floricanto -for-francisco-pushcart.html.

"Corazón Papaya." Translated and set to music by Jorge Luján. YouTube video uploaded September 18, 2018. [Audio] https://www.youtube.com/watch?v=zE5ygk MqTBo.

"Distant Migrants." Library of Congress, Don Quixote and Pablo Neruda Collections, January 2016. [Poetry] https://www.loc.gov/item/poetry-00000282/don-quixote -pablo-neruda-collections/.

"Dolphinating." *Poem-a-Day*, Academy of American Poets, March 11, 2014. [Poetry] https://poets.org/poem/dolphinating.

"Each Book Is a Story." *From the Catbird Seat: Poetry & Literature at the Library of Congress* (blog), December 14, 2016. https://blogs.loc.gov/catbird/2016/12/the -poet-laureate-meets-the-librarian-of-congress/.

"Enter the Void." Poetry Foundation, n.d. [Poetry] https://www.poetryfoundation.org /poems/58274/enter-the-void.

"A conversation with Juan Felipe Herrera [including the poem, 'Enuf']." *On the Seawall*, November 3, 2020. [Poetry] https://www.ronslate.com/a-conversation-with -juan-felipe-herrera/.

"Every Day We Get More Illegal." Poets.org, n.d. [Poem & audio] https://poets.org/poem/everyday-we-get-more-illegal.

"Every Day We Get More Illegal," Incredible Bridges: Poets Creating Community, Academy of American Poets. Recorded March 30 2016, uploaded April 12, 2016. YouTube video. [Poetry] https://www.youtube.com/watch?v=5-zkbugz6E.

"Exiles." Poetry Foundation, n.d. [Poetry] https://www.poetryfoundation.org/poems/58270/exiles-56d23c7eba08b.

"Five Directions to My House." Poets.org, 2008. [Poetry] https://poets.org/poem/five-directions-my-house.

"Five Directions to My House" [March 11, 2014], "Tomorrow I Leave to El Paso" [March 2014], "Let Me Tell You What a Poem Brings" [April 14, 2015], and "In Search for an Umbrella in NYC" [April 24, 2015]. *Poem Hunter.com*. [Poetry] https://www.poemhunter.com/juan-felipe-herrera/poems/.

Et al. "You Can Sum Up a Poem with One Sentence, Marvin Bell Said," in "For Marvin Bell." *Los Angeles Review of Books*, October 3, 2020. [Elegy] https://lareviewofbooks.org/article/for-marvin-bell/.

"Federico García Lorca & The Angels of Celery," "The Fruit Fly & Its Yeast, Its Protein Function," and "Ochre Yellow Green Stone Huichol Campo." *SUBNIVEAN*, no. 1 (Fall 2020): n.p. [Poetry] https://www.subnivean.org/juan-felipe-herrera-lorca-angels.

"Five Poems: 'Notes on the Assemblage,' 'The Experiment,' 'Green House,' 'Even the Gun Does Not Want to Be a Gun,' and 'White Dove—Found Outside Don Teriyaki's.'" *Boston Review: A Political and Literary Forum*, April 5, 2015. [Poetry] http://bostonreview.net/poetry/national-poetry-month-2015-juan-felipe-herrera-five-poems.

"For Jayne Cortez, R.I.P." *Los Angeles Review of Books*, January 5, 2013. [Elegy] https://lareviewofbooks.org/article/for-jayne-cortez-r-i-p/.

"Grafik." Poetry Foundation, n.d. [Poetry] https://www.poetryfoundation.org/poems/52287/grafik.

"Half-Mexican" and "Five Directions to My House." In "Interviews and Poems: Fresno's Juan Felipe Herrera Named U.S. Poet Laureate," by Ezra David Romero. *NPR For Central California*, FM89, audio, June 10, 2015. [Poetry] https://www.kvpr.org/post/interview-and-poems-fresnos-juan-felipe-herrera-named-us-poet-laureate.

"Half-Mexican." *Dissident Voices: The Poetry of Resistance*, May 16, 2017. https://dissidentpoetry.wordpress.com/2017/05/16/half-mexican/.

"Here and There." *Poem-a-Day*, The Academy of American Poets, April 14, 2015. [Poetry] https://poets.org/poem/here-and-there.

"Hey Phil." *Los Angeles Review of Books*, February 17, 2015. [Elegy] https://lareviewofbooks.org/article/hey-phil/.

"Hey Phil." Academy of American Poets, SoundCloud audio, 2016. https://soundcloud.com/poets-org/juan-felipe-herrera-hey-phil.

"Jack Gilbert, 1925–2012." *Los Angeles Review of Books*, November 14, 2012. [Elegy] https://lareviewofbooks.org/article/jack-gilbert-1925-2012/.

"I Am Merely Posing for a Photograph." Poetry Foundation, n.d. [Poetry] https://www
.poetryfoundation.org/poems/52285/i-am-merely-posing-for-a-photograph,
https://blueflowerarts.com/artist/juan-felipe-herrera/.

"I Forget the Date." Poetry Foundation, n.d. [Poetry] https://www.poetryfoundation
.org/poems/58273/i-forget-the-date.

"I'll Take a Bullet for You." *The Los Angeles Times*, December 24, 2015. [Poetry]
https://www.latimes.com/local/lanow/la-me-ln-poet-laureate-san-bernardino
-massacre-20151224-story.html.

"Imagine What You Could Do," and "Poem by Poem." *CapRadio, Insight, Arts and
Lifestyle*, audio, July 1, 2015. [Poetry] https://www.capradio.org/news/insight/2015
/07/01/insight-070115c/.

"In Search of an Umbrella in NYC." Poets.org, 2014. [Poetry] https://poets.org/poem
/search-umbrella-nyc.

"In the Cannery the Porpoise Soul." Poetry Foundation, n.d. [Poetry] https://www
.poetryfoundation.org/poems/52282/in-the-cannery-the-porpoise-soul.

"Into the Abyss: An Introduction to Poems for Political Disaster" *Boston Review: A
Political and Literary Forum*, January 19, 2017. [Foreword] http://bostonreview
.net/poetry/juan-felipe-herrera-abyss.

"Inside the Jacket." Entertainment & Arts, *The Los Angeles Times*, May 21, 2012. [Po-
etry] https://www.latimes.com/entertainment/arts/la-xpm-2012-may-21-la-me
-poet-laureate-poem-20120521-story.html.

"Iowa Blues Bar Spiritual." Poetry Foundation, n.d. [Poetry] https://www.poetry
foundation.org/poems/52306/iowa-blues-bar-spiritual.

"I Want to Speak of Unity." *The Today News*, August 6, 2020. Reprinted in The *New
York Times Magazine*, August 9, 2020. [Poetry] https://thetodaynews.com.pk
/latest/poem-i-want-to-speak-of-unity/, https://www.nytimes.com/2020/08/06
/magazine/poem-i-want-to-speak-of-unity.html.

"I Will Lov U 4Ever, Orlando." *The Takeway*, NY Public Radio, WNYC Studios, audio, 17 June 2016. [Poetry] https://www.wnycstudios.org/podcasts/takeaway
/segments/us-poet-laureate-juan-felipe-herrera-reflects-year-mass-shootings.

"Jackrabbits, Green Onions & Witches Stew." Poets.org, 2014. [Poetry] https://poets
.org/poem/jackrabbits-green-onions-witches-stew.

"Jackrabbits, Green Onions and Witches Stew." In "Juan Felipe Herrera: Dear
Poet." Poets.org, Academy of American Poets, video, January 20, 2015. [Poetry]
https://poets.org/text/video-juan-felipe-herrera-reads-jackrabbits-green-onions
-witches-stew.

"El Jardín: Rare Books" and "My Mother's Tiny Old Red Address Book." Library
of Congress, Sylvester & Orphanos Publishers Archives, January 2016. [Prose
and poetry] https://www.loc.gov/item/poetry-00000286/sylvester-orphanos
-publishers-archives/.

"Joanna Ramos I Promise." Arts and Culture, *UCR Today*, May 20, 2013; Reprinted
*Long Beach Press Telegram*, News, May 21, 2013. [Poetry] https://ucrtoday.ucr
.edu/14998.

"Juan Felipe Herrera lee algunos poemas de su más reciente libro *Notes on the Assemblage*: ['Fulgencio salió de Oaxaca hacia El Norte,' 'En la media medianoche,' 'Ayotzinapa,' 'Poema por poema,' 'Y si el hombre con el choke-hold,' 'Tasmano,' and 'Borderbus']." *Democracy Now!*, video, October 16, 2015. [Poetry] https://www.democracynow.org/es/2015/10/16/el_poeta_juan_felipe_herrera_lee.

"Juan Felipe Herrera lee algunos poemas de su más reciente libro *Notes on the Assemblage*." *Democracy Now! en Español*, SoundCloud audio, October 16, 2015. [Poetry] https://soundcloud.com/democracynowes/juan-felipe-herrera-lee-algunos-poemas-de-su-mas-reciente-libro-notes-on-the-assemblage.

"Juan Felipe Herrera on raulsalinas." *La Bloga: The World's Longest-Established Chicana Chicano, Latina Latino Literary Blog*, February 28, 2008. [Eulogy] https://labloga.blogspot.com/2008/02/juan-felipe-herrera-on-raulsalinas.html.

"Juan Felipe Herrera Reads from *Half of the World in Light: New and Selected Poems*." PEN America. The 2009 Beyond Margins Celebration, SoundCloud audio, October 26, 2012. [Poetry] https://soundcloud.com/penamerican/juan-felipe-herrera-reads-from.

"Juan Felipe Herrera Reads from *Half of the World in Light: New and Selected Poems*" ["Los chapulines verdes vuelan," "Children of Space," and "La Palma,"]. PEN America. The 2009 PEN Beyond Margins Celebration, video, December 7, 2009. Uploaded to YouTube December 18, 2009. [Poetry] https://www.youtube.com/watch?v=3QXh7Bq4Oa4.

"Juan Felipe Herrera, Select Poems: 'Let Us Gather in a Flourishing Way,' 'Quentino,' and 'Mud Drawing #15. Abdullah, the Village Boy with One Eye.'" Smith College, The Boutelle-Day Poetry Center. Visiting poets, Fall 2015. https://www.smith.edu/academics/poetry-center/juan-felipe-herrera.

"Let Me Tell You What a Poem Brings." Poetry Foundation, n.d. Reprinted in *The Two-Way*, NPR, June 10, 2015. [Poetry] https://www.poetryfoundation.org/poems/52286/let-me-tell-you-what-a-poem-brings, https://www.npr.org/sections/thetwo-way/2015/06/10/412909814/juan-felipe-herrera-named-u-s-poet-laureate.

"Let Me Tell You What a Poem Brings." *Audio Poem of the Day*, Poetry Foundation, audio, June 17, 2015. [Poetry] https://www.poetryfoundation.org/podcasts/77093/let-me-tell-you-what-a-poem-brings, https://www.poemhunter.com/poem/let-me-tell-you-what-a-poem-brings/.

"Let Us Gather in a Flourishing Way." *Rural Assembly Everywhere*, YouTube video, November 2, 2020. https://www.youtube.com/watch?v=ij6cUo61N7c.

"[Let Us Gather in a Flourishing Way]." Poetry Foundation, audio, n.d. [Poetry] https://www.poetryfoundation.org/poems/52283/let-us-gather-in-a-flourishing-way, https://www.poetryfoundation.org/play/77094, https://soundcloud.com/search?q=Juan%20Felipe%20Herrera.

"[Let Us Gather in a Flourishing Way]." Past Guests, *Lannan Center for Poetics and Social Practice* (blog), n.d. [Poetry] https://lannan.georgetown.edu/past-guests/juan-felipe-herrera/.

"Little Ones We Carry You." Arts and Culture, *UCR Today*, December 17, 2012. [Elegy] https://ucrtoday.ucr.edu/10847.

"Little Wall Big Wall" and "The Fruit Fly & Its Yeast, Its Protein Function." *Santa Clara Magazine*, April 20, 2017. [Poetry] https://magazine.scu.edu/magazines /spring-2017/well-versed/.

"Luz." Feature, *The Cortland Review*, Winter 2009. [Poetry] https://archive.cortland review.org/features/09/winter/herrera.php#1.

"María de la Luz Knows How to Walk." *Poem-a-Day*, The Academy of American Poets, audio, March 20, 2017. [Poetry] https://poets.org/poem/maria-de-la-luz -knows-how-walk.

"Mexican Differences Mexican Similarities" [excerpt], "Everyday We Get More Illegal," and "Exiles." In "Indigo Kalliope: 2nd Tuesday: Every Day We Get More Illegal," *Daily Kos*, March 8, 2016. [Poetry] https://www.dailykos.com/stories/2016/3 /8/1495861/-Indigo-Kalliope-2nd-Tuesday-Everyday-We-Get-More-Illegal.

"Mind Core." *Poetry Magazine*, Poetry Foundation, September 2016. [Poetry] https:// www.poetryfoundation.org/poetrymagazine/poems/90282/mind-core.

"Mud Drawing # 9: The Kalashnikov AK-47" [Juan Felipe Herrera Reads from *Senegal Taxi Mud Drawings*]. The UC Riverside Culver Center of the Arts, May 4, 2012. Uploaded to YouTube, video, May 15, 2012. [Poetry] https://www.youtube.com /watch?v=uUy9K3Cjx5A.

"My Mother's Name Lucha." Poets.org, 2012. [Poetry] https://poets.org/poem/my -mothers-name-lucha.

"New Gardens." Library of Congress, Poetry and Literature, Commentator's Poem, n.d. [Poetry] https://www.loc.gov/programs/poetry-and-literature/audio-recordings /poetry-of-america/item/poetry-00000277/juan-felipe-herrera-denise-levertov/.

"Nohemi—a Song for Paris." Poets.org, 2015. [Elegy] https://poets.org/poem/nohemi -song-paris, https://blogs.loc.gov/catbird/2015/11/nohemia-song-for-paris/.

"Ode for Howard Zinn." *The Progressive Magazine: A Voice for Peace, Social Justice, and the Common Good*, February 16, 2010. [Poetry] https://progressive.org /dispatches/ode-howard-zinn/.

"187 Reasons Mexicanos Can't Cross the Border, excerpt." Poetry at the Ruskin. Uploaded by Poetry.LA, video, November 19, 2007. [Poetry] https://www.youtube .com/watch?v=W8Ben-1n5zQ&t=47s.

"187 Reasons Mexicanos Can't Cross the Border (Remix)." *La Bloga: The World's Longest-Established Chicana Chicano, Latina Latino Literary Blog*, November 29, 2007. [Poetry] https://labloga.blogspot.com/2007/11/187-reasons-mexicanos -cant-cross-border.html.

"187 Reasons Why Mexicanos Can't Cross the Border: A Reading." The Emily Dickinson Lecture, Penn State University, video, October 19, 2016. [Poetry] https:// www.youtube.com/watch?v=hO5tvz3GvrE&t=121s.

"Open" and "You Just Don't Talk About It." *Literal Magazine, Latin American Voices/ Voces Latinoamericanas*, October 20, 2020. [Poetry] https://literalmagazine.com /juan-felipe-herrera/.

Bibliography by and on Juan Felipe Herrera 2022   **391**

"Papers No Papers." *Poets and Dreamers*, September 8, 2018. [Poetry] http://www
.poetsanddreamers.com/poetrymore.

"Peeling Chile Green with My Sister Sara, Brazito, New Mexico, 2014." *ShareAmerica*, Bureau of Global Public Affairs, U.S. Department of State, September 1,
2016. [Poetry] https://share.america.gov/poets-labor-day-tribute-to-those-who
-work/.

"Perched on Nothingness." *Los Angeles Review of Books*, April 30, 2012. [Poetry]
https://lareviewofbooks.org/article/perched-on-nothingness/.

"Poem by Poem." Poetry Foundation, audio, n.d. [Poetry] https://www.poetryfoun
dation.org/poems/147303/poem-by-poem.

"Poem by Poem." Academy of American Poets, SoundCloud audio, 2017. https://
soundcloud.com/poets-org/juan-felipe-herrera-poem-by-poem.

"Poem for the Librarian." Library of Congress, video, 15 November 15, 2016. [Poetry]
https://www.loc.gov/item/webcast-7574/.

"A Poetry Reading." *VOCA*, University of Arizona Poetry Center, audio, September 15, 1993. [Poetry] https://voca.arizona.edu/readings-list/191.

"Poetry Reading: 'Watering Cebolla While My Father Burns Leña,' 'Machofilia(s),'
'I, Citlalli "La Loca" Cienfuegos: Sutra on the Ninth Sun,' 'Let Us Gather in a
Flourishing Way,' and 'Arizón maricopa tempe tu tierra roja.'" *VOCA*, University
of Arizona Poetry Center, video, March 14, 2009. [Poetry] https://voca.arizona
.edu/readings-list/191.

"Punk Half Panther." Poetry Foundation, n.d. [Poetry] https://www.poetryfoundation
.org/poems/54461/punk-half-panther.

"Radiante(s)." Poetry Foundation, n.d. [Poetry] https://www.poetryfoundation.org
/poetrymagazine/poems/58862/radiante-s.

"Roll under the Waves." *Weekly Poem on Trump Presidency, Love's Executive Order*,
June 15, 2018. [Poetry] https://www.lovesexecutiveorder.com/juan-felipe-herrera.

"Salsa piccante dell'unità mondiale: ricetta." Italian translation of "How to Make
World Unity Salsa" by Pina Piccolo, *Sagarana*, no. 36, (July 2009): n.p. [Poetry]
http://www.sagarana.net/rivista/numero36/poesia15.html.

"Saturday Night at the Buddhist Cinema." Poets. org, 2013. [Poetry] https://poets.org
/poem/saturday-night-buddhist-cinema.

"Selected Poems by Juan Felipe Herrera ['Half Mexican,' '5 Directions to My House,'
and 'Blood on the Wheel' (an excerpt)]." Books, *The New York Times*, June 10,
2015. [Poetry] https://www.nytimes.com/2015/06/10/books/selected-poems-by
-juan-felipe-herrera.html.

"Social Distancing." Poets.org, audio, 2020. [Poetry] https://poets.org/poem/social
-distancing.

"Son dos días para un jinete (América)." *Mester* 7, no. 1 (1978): 19. https://escholarship
.org/uc/item/910261vx?.

"Song Out Here." Poets.org, 2014. [Poetry] https://poets.org/poem/song-out-here.

"Song Out Here." Academy of American Poets, SoundCloud audio, 2017. https://
soundcloud.com/poets-org/juan-felipe-herrera-song-out-here-with-intro.

"Still Here I (the Deported Father Said)." *Poets and Dreamers*, September 9, 2018. [Poetry] http://www.poetsanddreamers.com/poetry.

"They Fought Back (Field Notes): A Poem in Honor of Anthropologist Roberto Alvarez." *Anthropology News*, Association of Latina and Latino Anthropologists, June 20, 2019. https://anthrobookforum.americananthro.org/index.php/2019/06/19/they-fought-back/.

"This Is My Last Report." Poetry Foundation, n.d. [Poetry] https://www.poetryfoundation.org/poems/58275/this-is-my-last-report.

"Thought Poem for Víctor Martínez (Undelivered)." *Poem-a-Day*, Academy of American Poets, audio, July 15, 2016. [Poetry] https://poets.org/poem/thought-poem-victor-martinez-undelivered, https://soundcloud.com/search?q=Juan%20Felipe%20Herrera.

"Tomorrow I leave to El Paso, Texas." Poets.org, 2010. [Poetry] https://poets.org/poem/tomorrow-i-leave-el-paso-texa.

"Touch the Earth (Once Again)." *Poetry Daily*, September 16, 2020. [Poetry] https://poems.com/poem/touch-the-earth-once-again/.

"Tragedy and Flowering/Tragedia y florecimiento" and "Fill Yourself with Joy." News, University of California, April 15, 2014. [Poetry] https://www.universityofcalifornia.edu/news/remembering-lives-lost.

"Tragedy and Flowering/Tragedia y florecimiento," "Fill Yourself with Joy," "The Runner," and "Little Ones We Carry You." Creating Poetry in Solidarity, *UCR: The Magazine of UC Riverside*, Spring 2014. [Poetry] https://magazinearchive.ucr.edu/998.

"You Can't Put Muhammad Ali in a Poem." Bay Area Book Festival, Berkeley. Recorded June 2016, uploaded to YouTube, June 28, 2016. https://www.youtube.com/watch?v=lM3HgIFhDvU.

"Walking Together (again)." *The Current*, UC Santa Barbara, May 27, 2014. [Poetry] https://www.news.ucsb.edu/2014/014196/walking-together-again.

"Wanda Coleman, 1946–2013." *Los Angeles Review of Books*, November, 23 2013. [Eulogy] https://lareviewofbooks.org/article/wanda-coleman-1946-2013/.

"War Voyeurs." Poetry Foundation, n.d. [Poetry] https://www.poetryfoundation.org/poems/52284/war-voyeurs.

"Water Water Water Wind Water." Poetry Foundation, n.d. [Poetry] https://www.poetryfoundation.org/poems/58271/water-water-water-wind-water.

"We Are Remarkably Loud Not Masked." *The Progressive Magazine: A Voice for Peace, Social Justice, and the Common Good*, July 1, 2015. Reprinted in Poetry Foundation, n.d. [Poetry] https://progressive.org/magazine/we-are-remarkably-loud-not-masked/, https://www.poetryfoundation.org/poems/91749/we-are-remarkably-loud-not-masked.

"Web Extra: Juan Felipe Herrera Reads 'Poem by Poem.'" PBS.org, Chicago Tonite, video, May 2, 2017. [Poetry] https://www.pbs.org/video/web-extra-juan-felipe-herrera-reads-poem-poem-fwkoba/.

"Where I Used to Walk." *Los Angeles Review of Books*, July 17, 2016. [Poetry] https://lareviewofbooks.org/article/used-to-walk-juan-felipe-herrera/.

"'Where We Find Ourselves:' Juan Felipe Herrera's Poem on the Shooting at UCLA." *Los Angeles Times*, June 3, 2016. [Poetry] https://www.latimes.com/books/la-ca-jc-juan-felipe-herrera-poem-20160602-snap-story.html.

"Ya tocan las flautas." In "Don Luis Leal ¡Presente!; Al Amigo LEAL, Homenaje de once escritores," *La Bloga: The World's Longest-Established Chicana Chicano, Latina Latino Literary Blog*, February 2, 2010. [Elegy] https://labloga.blogspot.com/2010/02/don-luis-leal-presente.html.

"You & I Belong in This Kitchen." Poets.org, 2012. [Poetry] https://poets.org/poem/you-i-belong-kitchen.

"You Can't Put Muhammad Ali in a Poem." *Los Angeles Review of Books*, June 4, 2016. [Poetry] https://lareviewofbooks.org/article/cant-put-muhammad-ali-poem/.

"You Can't Put Muhammad Ali in a Poem." In "Juan Felipe Herrera: Dear Poet 2017," Academy of American Poets, YouTube video, January 10, 2017. [Poetry] https://www.youtube.com/watch?v=R84YCmfMfXM.

"You Throw a Stone." *New York Times Magazine*, March 6. 2016. [Poetry] https://www.nytimes.com/interactive/2016/03/06/magazine/juan-felipe-herrera-you-throw-a-stone.html.

"Readings by Juan Felipe Herrera and Cristina García." With Cristina García. The 2011 Lannan Spring Literary Sympsium and Festival: Writing Dangerously in Immigrant America, Georgetown University, video, April 6, 2011. [Poetry] https://vimeo.com/22905416.

Et al. "Your Literacy Blanket Poem." Library of Congress, video, November 11, 2020. [Poetry] https://www.loc.gov/item/webcast-9509/.

# Critical Works on Juan Felipe Herrera
## Books

Gagne, Tammy. *Juan Felipe Herrera: From Migrant to Poet Laureate.* Unsung Heroes of Hispanic Heritage Series. Hallandale, Fla: Mitchell Lane Publishers, 2021.

## Articles, Chapters, and Critical Annotations

Alarcón, Francisco X. "*Los vampiros de Whittier Boulevard* o la metapoética chicana comprometida desmistificadora de Juan Felipe Herrera." *Letras Latinas Blog*, December 23, 2009. http://letraslatinasblog.blogspot.com/2009/12/francisco-x-alarcon-on-juan-felipe.html.

Anonymous. "Juan Felipe Herrera, (b. 1948): 'Exiles,' 'Literary Asylums,' 'Quentino.'" In *The Norton Anthology of Latino Literature*, edited by Ilán Stavans, Edna Acosta-Belén, Harold Augenbraum, María Herrera-Sobek, Rolando Hinojosa and Gustavo Pérez Firmat, 1684–1689. New York: W.W. Norton, 2010.

Aragón, Francisco. "JUAN FELIPE HERRERA in the House: JFH Testimonio on the Occasion of a Laureateship." *Letras Latinas Blog*, Institute for Latino Studies, University of Notre Dame, June 10, 1915. http://letraslatinasblog.blogspot.com/2015/06/juan-felipe-herrera-in-house.html.

Aragón, Francisco. "JFH Testimonio on the Occasion of a Laureateship." *La Bloga: The World's Longest-Established Chicana Chicano, Latina Latino Literary Blog*, June 19, 2015. https://labloga.blogspot.com/2015/06/juan-felipe-herrera-week-continues-on.html.

Aragón, Francisco. "This is Personal: A Testimoio of Juan Felipe Herrera." *Blog on the Hyphen*. April 23, 2017. https://latinx.wordpress.com/2017/04/23/this-is-personal-a-testimonio-of-juan-felipe-herrera/.

Backlund, Anya. "Juan Felipe Herrera: United States Poet Laureate (2015–2017); Mexican American Performer & Activist; National Book Critic Circle Award Winner." Blue Flower Arts: A Literary Speakers Agency, n.d. https://blueflowerarts.com/artist/juan-felipe-herrera/.

Baldwin, Emma. "'El Ángel de La Guarda' by Juan Felipe Herrera." Poem Analysis, n.d. https://poemanalysis.com/juan-felipe-herrera/el-angel-de-la-guarda/.

Blood, Katherine "Ingenuity and Homage: Poetic Lotería by Artemio Rodríguez." *On Paper: Journal of the Washington Print Club* 1, no. 2 (Fall 2016): 23–24. Reprinted in *From the Catbird Seat: Poetry and Literature Blog at the Library of Congress*, December 12, 2016. https://blogs.loc.gov/catbird/2016/12/ingenuity-and-homage-poetic-lotera-by-artemio-rodrguez/.

Borja, Lalo. "Juan Felipe Herrera." *Arquitrave* 7, no. 40 (December 2008): 3–9.

Brammer, Ethriam. "Herrera, Juan Felipe (b. 1948–)." In *Encyclopedia of Hispanic-American Literature*, edited by Luz Elena Ramírez, 150–52. New York: Facts on File, 2008. Reprinted 2013.

Britannica Kids. "Juan Felipe Herrera." Articles, n.d. [Annotation] https://kids.britannica.com/kids/article/Juan-Felipe-Herrera/633367.

Buckley, Christopher. "Juan Felipe Herrera." In *Naming the Lost: The Fresno Poets Interviews and Essays*, edited by Christopher Buckley, 392. Nacogdoches, Texas: Stephen F. Austin State University Press, 2021.

Bundy, Katherine Elizabeth. "Was It All a Dream? Chicana/o Children and Mestiza Consciousness in *Super Cilantro Girl* (2003) and 'Tata's Gift' (2014)." In *Voices of Resistance: Interdisciplinary Approaches to Chican@ Children's Literature*, edited by Laura Alamillo, Larissa M. Mercado-López, and Cristina Herrera, 151–162. Lanham, Md.: Rowman and Littlefield, 2017.

Burt, Stephanie. "Juan Felipe Herrera: Undocumentary." *Close Calls with Nonsense: Reading New Poetry*, 91–94. Minneapolis, Minn.: Graywolf, 2009.

Burt, Stephanie. "Juan Felipe Herrera: 'Blood on the Wheel;' Tracing the Many Conflicting Meanings of the Word 'Blood.'" Poem Guide, Poetry Foundation, September 25 2012. http://www.poetryfoundation.org/learning/guide/244636#guide.

Cárdenas, Brenda. "Secret Rubble Juggler." In *Angels of the Americlypse: An Anthology New Latin@ Writing*, edited by Carmen Giménez Smith and John Chávez, 87–90. Denver, Colo: Counterpath Press, 2014.

Carter, Cassandra. "Herrera's Poetic Revolution." *Green Mountains Review* 29, no. 2 (2017): 135–38.

Cavallari, Héctor Mario. "La muerte y el deseo: notas sobre la poesía de Juan Felipe Herrera." *La Palabra: Revista de Literatura Chicana* 4–5, no. 1–2 (1982): 97–106.

Cengage Learning Gale. "Overview: 'Everyday We Get More Illegal." In *Poetry for Students*, edited by Kristen A. Dorsch, no 57, Farmington Hills, Mich.: Gale, 2018.

Corti, Erminio. "Elementi della tradizione culturale mesoamericana nella poesia del Renacimiento Chicano." *Quaderni del Dipartimento di Lingue e Letterature Neolatine dell'Università di Bergamo* (2001): 139–170.

Corti, Erminio. "El sol lo cargo en mi bolsa: il lungo viaggio di Juan Felipe Herrera." Introduction to the Poetry of Juan Felipe Herrera. *Ácoma: Rivista Internazionale di Studi Nordamericani*, no. 19 (Fall/Winter 2020): 85–89.

Cresci, Karen Lorraine. "La vida sin fronteras de Juan Felipe Herrera." *Huellas de Estados Unidos: Estudios, Perspectivas y Debates desde América Latina*, no. 9 (October 19, 2015): 110–126. Reprinted in *Boletín SAAS* (Spanish Association for American Studies), no. 14, (2015): n.p. http://www.saasweb.org/OtherImages/BOLET%C3%8DN%20SAAS-2015.pdf.

Cruz, Víctor Hernández. Introduction to *Facegames* by Juan Felipe Herrera, i–ii. Berkeley: As Is/So & So, 1987.

Cummins, Amy. "Education in Children's Picture Books Portraying Mexican American Immigrants and Written by Mexican American Authors." *The Dragon Lode* 33, no. 2 (2015): 82–90.

Day, Frances Ann. "Juan Felipe Herrera." In *Latina and Latino Voices in Literature for Children and Teenagers*, 181–182. Portsmouth, N.H.: Heinemann, 1997.

Day, Frances Ann. "Juan Felipe Herrera." In *Latina and Latino Voices in Literature: Lives and Works, Updated and Expanded*, 185. Westport, Conn.: Greenwood Press, 2003.

Dean, Tim. "'A Way to Attain a Life without Boundaries:' The Poetry of Juan Felipe Herrera." *IPRH Blog: Illinois Program for Research in the Humanities*, The University of Illinois at Urbana-Champaign, April 22, 2016. https://iprh.wordpress.com/2016/04/22/a-way-to-attain-a-life-without-boundaries-the-poetry-of-juan-felipe-herrera/.

Dorsch, Kristen A., ed. *A Study Guide for Juan Felipe Herrera's "Every Day We Get More Illegal."* Vol. 7 of *Poetry for Students*. Farmington Hills, Mich.: Gale, 2018.

Dowdy, Michael. "Molotovs and Subtleties: Juan Felipe Herrera's Post-Movement Norteamérica." In *Broken Souths: Latina/o Poetic Responses to Neoliberalism and Globalization*, 61–90. Tucson: University of Arizona Press, 2013.

Duplan, Anais. "'Poetry and Environmental Justice: Let Us Gather in A Flourishing Way' by Juan Felipe Herrera." Poetry Society of America, n.d. https://poetrysociety.org/features/poetry-environmental-justice/on-the-importance-of-psychomagic-gathering-and-poetry.

Flores, Lauro H. "Auto/referencialidad y subversión: observaciones (con)textuales sobre la poesía de Juan Felipe Herrera." *Crítica: A Journal of Critical Essays* 2, no. 2 (1990): 172–81.

Flores, Lauro H. "Juan Felipe Herrera (27 December 1948—)." In *Dictionary of Literary Biography*. Vol 122, *Chicano Writers: Second Series*, edited by Francisco A. Lomelí and Carl R. Shirley, 137–145. Detroit: Gale Research, 1992.

Gagnon, Milan. "Reclaiming the Sleepless Volcano: How Celebrated Chicano Poet Juan Felipe Herrera Found His Voice," Poetry Foundation, February 25, 2009. https://www.poetryfoundation.org/articles/69238/reclaiming-the-sleepless -volcano.

*Gale Literature: Contemporary Authors.* "Juan Felipe Herrera." Gale, 2016.

García, Edgar. "A Migrant's Lotería: Risk, Fortune, Fate, and Probability in the Border-lands of Juan Felipe Herrera and Artemio Rodríguez's *Lotería Cards and Fortune Poems." Modern Philology: Critical and Historical Studies in Literature, Medieval Through Contemporary* 118, no. 2 (November 2020): 252–76.

García, Rupert. Introduction to *Lotería Cards and Fortune Poems: A Book of Lives* by Juan Felipe Herrera, ix–x. San Francisco, Calif.: City Lights Books, 1999.

González, Rigoberto. "Juan Felipe Herrera's Global Voice and Vision." *Los Angeles Review of Books*, September 23, 2015. Reprinted in *Pivotal Voices, Era of Transition: Toward a 21st Century Poetics*, 170–82. Ann Arbor: University of Michigan Press, 2017. https://lareviewofbooks.org/article/juan-felipe-herreras-global-voice -and-vision/.

Gross, Anisse. "U.S. Poet Laureate Juan Felipe Herrera Signs with Candlewick." Book News, *Publisher's Weekly*, September 29, 2015. https://www.publishers weekly.com/pw/by-topic/childrens/childrens-book-news/article/68199-u-s-poet -laureate-juan-felipe-herrera-signs-with-candlewick.html.

Hart, James D., Wendy Martin, and Danielle Hinrichs, eds. "Herrera, Juan Felipe (1948–): Celebrated American Poet." In *Concise Oxford Companion to American Literature*, 2nd Edition, 32. Oxford: Oxford University Press, 2021.

Hernández-G., Manuel de Jesús. "Juan Felipe Herrera: una cara en español de resistencia local y global pan-étnica," Escritor/a Invitado/a, *Peregrinos y sus letras blog*, April 7 2021. http://www.peregrinosysusletras.net/escritora-invitadoa/juan-felipe -herrera-una-cara-en-espanol-de-resistencia-local-panetnica-y-globalizada.

Hoffert, Barbara. "Juan Felipe Herrera Named Poet Laureate." *Library Journal* 140, no. 12 (July 2015): 22.

Hoffert, Barbara. "Poet Laureate Herrera." *Library Journal* 140, no. 14 (September 2015): 102.

Hoover, Joseph. "Just Verse [*Notes on the Assemblage*]." *America* 214, no. 14 (April 2016): 34–46. Printed online as "Looking for Justice in Poetry: America's Spring Poetry Review," *America: The Jesuit Review*, April 25, 2016. https://www.america magazine.org/issue/just-verse.

Kanellos, Nicolás. "Juan Felipe Herrera (1948–)." In *Hispanic Literature of the United States: A Comprehensive Reference*, 106. Westport, Conn.: Greenwood Press, 2003.

Kanellos, Nicolás, and Cristelia Pérez. "Juan Felipe Herrera (1948–)." In *The Greenwood Encyclopedia of Latino Literature, Vol. 2: G–P*, 562–63. Westport, Conn.: Greenwood Press, 2008.

Kessler, Steffen. "Aviso: Forewarned." *187 Reasons Mexicanos Can't Cross the Border: Undocuments 1971–2007* by Juan Felipe Herrera, 17–19. San Francisco, Calif.: City Lights, 2007. [Foreword]

Laínez, René Colato. "Living to Tell the Story: The Authentic Latino Immigrant Experience in Picture Books (Part 5), *The Upside Down Boy/El niño de cabeza* by Juan Felipe Herrera." *La Bloga: The World's Longest-Established Chicana Chicano, Latina Latino Literary Blog*, May 12, 2007. https://labloga.blogspot.com/2007/05/living-to-tell-story-authentic-latino.html.

Latimer, Clay. "Juan Felipe Herrera: From Migrant Son to Acclaimed Poet." *The Hispanic Outlook in Higher Education* 21, nol. 20 (August 2011): 24–25.

Lomelí, Francisco A. "Foreword / Juan Felipe Herrera: Trajectory and Metamorphosis of a Chicano Poet Laureate." In *Half of the World in Light: New and Selected Poems* by Juan Felipe Herrera, xv–xxiv. Tucson: University of Arizona Press, 2008.

Martínez, David Tomás. "A Personal Laureate: Reflections on Juan Felipe Herrera's Appointment as Poet Laureate of the United States." *Los Angeles Review of Books*, July 14, 2015. https://lareviewofbooks.org/article/a-personal-laureate-reflections-on-juan-felipe-herreras-appointment-as-poet-laureate-of-the-united-states.

Martínez Wood, Jamie. "Herrera, Juan Felipe (1948–): Poet, Children's Book Writer, Young Adult Writer, Educator." *Latino Writers and Journalists*, 109–111. New York: Facts on File, 2007.

Martín-Rodríguez, Manuel M. "Juan Felipe Herrera (1948–)." In La voz urgente: antología de literatura chicana en español, 175–176. Madrid: Editorial Fundamentos, 1995.

Miranda, Deborah. "40 Years of Activist Poetry: Juan Felipe Herrera." *Chican@ Literature: A Mosaic, a Weaving, a Puzzle*, March 6, 2011. http://literaturamosaic.blogspot.com/2011/03/40-years-of-activist-poetry-juan-felipe.html.

Morresi, Renata, "'Let's Have a Pachanga!:' comunità e rappresentazione nei libri per l'infanzia chicana." Àcoma: Rivista internazionale di Studi Nordamericani 17, no. 39 (Spring 2010): 87–100.

My Poetic Life. "Juan Felipe Herrera." Poets, biography, n.d. https://mypoeticside.com/poets/juan-felipe-herrera-poems.

Nikolis, Anastasia. "Chronicling National Poetry Month, vol. 4: Poet Laureate Juan Felipe Herrera's Closing Events." *From the Catbird Seat: Poetry and Literature Blog at the Library of Congress*, April 24, 2017. https://blogs.loc.gov/catbird/2017/04/chronicling-national-poetry-month-vol-iv-poet-laureate-juan-felipe-herreras-closing-events/.

Oliver-Rotger, María Antònia. "Travel, Autoethnography, and Oppositional Consciousness in Juan Felipe Herrera's *Mayan Drifter*." In *Imagined Transnationalism in U.S. Latino/a Literature, Culture, and Identity*, edited by Kevin Concannon, Francisco A. Lomelí, and Marc Priewe, 171–99. New York: Palgrave Macmillan, 2009. https://doi.org/10.1057/9780230103320_11.

Pisarz-Ramírez, Gabriele. "Reimagining America: Postnational Perspectives in Chicano Border Discourses." In *E Pluribus Unum? National and Transnational Identities in the Americas/Identidades nacionales y transnacionales en las Américas*, edited by Sebastian Thies and Josef Raab, 277–90. Berlin: LIT Verlag; Tempe, Ariz.: Bilingual Press/Editorial Bilingüe, 2008.

Poetry International Archives. "Juan Felipe Herrera (United States, 1948)." June 26, 2017. https://www.poetryinternational.org/pi/poet/28355/Juan-Felipe-Herrera /en/tile.

Reid, Rob. "Herrera, Juan Felipe, *Crashboomlove*: A Novel in Verse." *Reid's Read-Alouds 2: Modern-Day Classics from C.S. Lewis to Lemony Snicket*, 47. Chicago: American Library Association, 2011. [Curriculum resource]

Rodríguez, Andrés. "Contemporary Chicano Poetry: The Work of Michael Sierra, Juan Felipe Herrera, and Luis J. Rodríguez." *Bilingual Review/La Revista Bilingüe* 21, no 3, (September/December 1996): 203–218.

Rodríguez, Sonia Alejandra. "'You Wanna Be a Chump/or a Champ?': Constructions of Masculinity, Absent Fathers, and Conocimiento in Juan Felipe Herrera's *Downtown Boy*." In *Voices of Resistance: Interdisciplinary Approaches to Chican@ Children's Literature*, edited by Laura Alamillo, Larissa M. Mercado-López, and Cristina Herrera, 91–104. Lanham, Md.: Rowman and Littlefield, 2017.

Rodríguez, Sonia Alejandra. "Conocimiento Narratives: Creative Acts and Healing in Latinx Children's and Young Adult Literature." *Children's Literature: Annual of The Children's Literature Association and The Modern Language Association Division on Children's Literature* 47 (2019): 9–29.

Rodríguez-Valls, Fernando, and María Capdevila. "¿Qué voces escuchas? Aproximación a la lectura de cuentos a través de los ojos de los héroes silenciosos." *Bilingual Review/La Revista Bilingüe* 33, no. 5 (May 2017): 63–75. https://bilingual review.utsa.edu/index.php/br/article/view/292/280.

Ryan, Bryan, ed. "Herrera, Juan Felipe (1948–)." *Hispanic Writers: A Selection of Sketches from Contemporary Authors*, 254. Detroit: Gale Research, 1991.

Ruiz, Tony. "Juan Felipe Herrera: 'Vision Tropical' in San Francisco's Mission District." *CEA Critic: An Official Journal of the College English Association* 75, no. 2 (July 2013): 129–141.

Serrato, Phillip. "A Portrait of the Artist as a Muchachito: Juan Felipe Herrera's *Downtown Boy* as a Poetic Springboard into Critical Masculinity Studies." In *Voices of Resistance: Interdisciplinary Approaches to Chican@ Children's Literature*, edited by Laura Alamillo, Larissa M. Mercado-López, and Cristina Herrera, 61–76. Lanham, Md.: Rowman & Littlefield, 2018.

Sonksen, Mike. "Juan Felipe Herrera: Poet Laureate of Aztlán and America." *KCET, History and Society*, June 12, 2015. https://www.kcet.org/history-society/juan -felipe-herrera-poet-laureate-of-aztlan-and-america.

Trigonakis, Elke Sturm. "Global Playing in Poetry: The Texts of Juan Felipe Herrera and José F. A. Oliver as a New Weltliteratur." In *Transcultural Localisms: Responding to Ethnicity in a Globalized World*, edited by Yiorgos Kalogeras, Eleftheria Arapoglou, and Linda Manney, 27–46. Heidelberg, Germany: Universitätsverlag Winter, 2006.

Urrea, Luis Alberto. "Rascuache Prayer: Reflections on Juan Felipe Herrera, My Homeboy Laureate." *Poetry Foundation*, September 14, 2020. https://www.poetry foundation.org/articles/154196/a-rascuache-prayer.

Vaquera-Vásquez, Santiago R. "Juan Felipe Herrera (1948–)." In *Latino and Latina Writers I: Introductory Essays, Chicano and Chicana Authors*, edited by Alan West-Durán, María Herrera-Sobek, and César A. Salgado, 281–298. Scribner Writers Series. New York: Scribner's, 2004.

Voigt, Benjamin. "Juan Felipe Herrera 101: A Look at the Poetry and Politics of the U.S. Poet Laureate." Poetry Foundation, August 3, 2015. https://www.poetryfoun dation.org/articles/70252/juan-felipe-herrera-101.

Vourvoulias, Sabrina. "Juan Felipe Herrera (1948—), U.S. Poet Laureate." *Nuestra América: 30 Inspiring Latinas/Latinos Who Have Shaped the United States* by Sabrina Vourvoulias, 55–57. Philadelphia: RP Kids, 2020.

Wegner, John. "Under the Neon Worm: Ideological Consciousness and Code Switching in Juan Felipe Herrera's *Border-Crosser with a Lamborghini Dream*." *Western American Literature* 41, no. 4 (Winter 2007): 373–91. https://www.researchgate.net /publication/283248989_Under_The_Neon_Worm_Ideological_Consciousness _and_Code_Switching_in_Juan_Felipe_Herrera's_Border-Crosser_with_a _Lamborghini_Dream.

Yeung, Heather. "Herrera, Juan Felipe (1948–)." *The Oxford Companion to Modern Poetry*, edited by Jeremy Noel-Tod and Ian Hamilton, 1494. Oxford: Oxford University Press, 2014; 2022.

# Interviews

Aldama, Fredrick Luis. "Juan Felipe Herrera." In *Spilling the Beans in Chicanolandia: Conversations with Writers and Artists*, 129–142. Austin: University of Texas Press, 2006.

Alvarado, Lisa. "Interview with Juan Felipe Herrera." *La Bloga: The World's Longest-Established Chicana Chicano, Latina Latino Literary Blog*, February 21, 2008. https://labloga.blogspot.com/2008/02/interview-with-juan-felipe-herrera.html.

Athitakis, Mark. "The Populist Poet: Our Interview with U.S. Poet Laureate J.F.H." *Fine Books & Collections* 14, no. 1 (Winter 2016): 26–29.

Binder, Wolfgang. "Juan Felipe Herrera." In *Partial Autobiographies: Interviews with Twenty Chicano Poets*, 95–108. Erlangen, Germany: Verlag Palm and Enke Erlangen, 1985.

Blakley, Matt. "'To Find Our Larger Self:' An Interview with Juan Felipe Herrera by Robert Casper." *From the Catbird Seat: Poetry and Literature Blog at the Library of Congress*, July 12 2016. https://blogs.loc.gov/catbird/2016/07/to-find-our-larger -self-an-interview-with-juan-felipe-herrera/.

Boyd, Krys, host. "A Talk with Juan Felipe Herrera." *Think Radio Program*, KERA, audio, May 12, 2016. https://think.kera.org/2016/05/12/a-talk-with-juan-felipe -herrera/.

Boodhoo, Niala, host. "U.S. Poet Laureate [Juan Felipe Herrera], & a Beautiful Planet in IMAX." *The 21st Show*, Illinois Public Media, audio, April 29 2016. https://will .illinois.edu/player/audio/the-21st-u.s.-poet-laureate-a-beautiful-planet-in-imax.

Brandeis, Gayle. "A Conversation with California Poet Laureate Juan Felipe Herrera." *Artbound*, KCET, audio, July 8, 2012. https://www.kcet.org/shows/artbound/a-conversation-with-california-poet-laureate-juan-felipe-herrera.

Brown, Jeffery. "Juan Felipe Herrera's Winding Path to Poetry." *PBS NewsHour with Jeffrey Brown*, YouTube video, June 10 2015. https://www.youtube.com/watch?v=iykpWev3NLY.

Caine, Paul. "Poet Laureate on the Power of Poetry and Working with CPS." Interview & Poetry Reading, *Chicago Tonight*, WTTW News, May 2 2017. https://news.wttw.com/2017/05/02/poet-laureate-power-poetry-and-working-cps.

Carrera, Cristina. "A Conversation with Juan Felipe Herrera, Author of *Every Day We Get More Illegal*." *My America: Immigrant and Refugee Writers Today*, American Writers Museum, video, September 30, 2020. https://www.youtube.com/watch?v=DrFjQe37Fus.

Casper, Robert. "Juan Felipe Herrera and Robert Pinsky Live Q&A: 2020 National Book Festival." *Poetry & Prose Stage*, Library of Congress, video, September 26, 2020. https://www.loc.gov/item/webcast-9578/.

Cavaliere, Grace. "Juan Felipe Herrera: The 21st Poet Laureate of the United States." *The Poet and the Poem*, The Library of Congress, audio. September 2015. https://www.gracecavalieri.com/poetLaureates/JuanFilipeHerrera.html.

Cavaliere, Grace. "The Poet and the Poem from The Library of Congress: Juan Felipe Herrera, 21st U.S. Poet Laureate." *Paterson Literary Review* no. 45 (2017): 279–288.

Chacón, Daniel and Benjamín Alire Saenz. "Words on a Wire: Interview with Juan Felipe Herrera." *Words on a Wire*, KTEP-El Paso, podcast audio, October 1, 2011. https://www.podomatic.com/podcasts/wordsonawirehttp://www.ktep.org/.

Chacón, Daniel. "Words on a Wire; Writers Talking to Writers: Juan Felipe Herrera." *Words on a Wire*, KTEP-Chicago, podcast audio, October 14, 2012. https://www.ktep.org/post/words-wire-juan-felipe-herrera.

Chacón, Daniel and Tim Hernández. "Words on a Wire; Writers Talking to Writers: Juan Felipe Herrera." *Words on A Wire*, KTEP-El Paso, podcast audio, February 21, 2016. https://www.ktep.org/post/words-wire-juan-felipe-herrera-2.

Collopy, Trisha. "This Giant Classroom That Is America: A Conversation with Juan Felipe Herrera." *NCTE Council Chronicle* 26, no. 3 (March 2017): 14–17. https://library.ncte.org/journals/CC/issues/v26-3/29032.

Colorín Colorado. "Meet the Authors: Juan Felipe Herrera." ¡Colorín Colorado!, video, April 27, 2017. https://www.colorincolorado.org/videos/meet-authors/juan-felipe-herrera.

Dees, Jenn. "The Pen Ten: An Interview with Juan Felipe Herrera." PEN America, September 24, 2020. https://pen.org/the-pen-ten-juan-felipe-herrera/.

De Greff, Dana. "Poet Laureate Juan Felipe Herrera on First Miami Book Fair Visit: 'Looking Forward to Meeting the Local Poets.'" Interviews, *Miami New Times*, November 13, 2015. https://www.miaminewtimes.com/arts/poet-laureate-juan-felipe-herrera-on-first-miami-book-fair-visit-looking-forward-to-meeting-the-local-poets-8043458.

Dodge Poetry. "Ask a Poet: Juan Felipe Herrera." *The Dodge Blog*, September 2, 2016. https://blog.grdodge.org/2016/09/02/ask-a-poet-juan-felipe-herrera/.

DiGrappa, Emy. "Juan Felipe Herrera: His Poetry Forces Us to Confront Society and Its Paradoxes—Interview." *What's your Why?*, Wyoming Humanities, SoundCloud audio, 2017. https://soundcloud.com/thinkwy/juan-felipe-herrera-his-poetry-forces-us-to-confront-society-and-its-paradoxes.

Elman, Raymond. "A Conversation with U.S. Poet Laureate Juan Felipe Herrera." Interviews, *Inspicio*, video, November 18, 2018. http://inspicio.fiu.edu/interviews/juan-felipe-herrera/.

Elum, Angela. "Juan Felipe Herrera: Interview." *New Letters*, audio, 2016. https://www.newletters.org/on_the_air_shows/juan-felipe-herrera-3/.

Fahle, Rich. "Juan Felipe Hererra Interview." *Book View Now*, PBS.org, video, 1 April 2016. https://www.pbs.org/video/book-view-now-juan-felipe-hererra-interview-2016-awp-conf-book-fair/.

Fahle, Rich (host), and Kwame Alexander (guest host). "Interview with Juan Felipe Herrera *on Portraits of Hispanic American Heroes*." *Book View Now*, PBS.org, YouTube video uploaded September 6 2015. https://www.youtube.com/watch?v=lGqT6lxZsMc.

Faith & Leadership Staff. "Juan Felipe Herrera: Do Not Let Yourself Think You Cannot Contribute." Arts & Culture, *Faith & Leadership*, February 21, 2017. https://faithandleadership.com/juan-felipe-herrera-do-not-let-yourself-think-you-cannot-contribute.

Farrell, Della. "Juan Felipe Herrera's Latest Is a 'Blue-Cheesy' Triumph of Poetry & Storytelling." *School Library Journal*, March 27, 2018. https://www.slj.com/?detailStory=juan-felipe-herreras-latest-blue-cheesy-triumph-poetry-storytelling.

Fenster, Josephine. "Squaring Off: Speaking for the Children . . . and the Ak-47; California Poet Laureate Juan Felipe Herrera Channels the Many Voices of Africa." *Zócalo: Public Square*, March 28, 2013. https://www.zocalopublicsquare.org/2013/03/28/speaking-for-the-children-and-the-ak-47/books/squaring-off/.

Feraca, Jean. "Juan Felipe Herrera, Radio Interview." *Here on Earth*, Wisconsin Public Radio, YouTube audio, April 8, 2008. https://www.youtube.com/watch?v=UYczOv1qiQg.

Foster, Sesshu. "From Logan to the Mission: Riding North through Chicano Literary History with Juan Felipe Herrera." *The Americas Review: A Review of Hispanic Literature and Art of the USA* 17, no. 3–4 (1989): 68–87.

Francisco, Ariel. "Interview with Juan Felipe Herrera." *Gulf Stream Magazine: South Florida's Literary Current*, online issue no. 14, November 2015. https://gulfstreamlitmag.com/archives/online-archives/current-issue-4/features/interview-with-juan-felipe-herrera/.

García Echeverría, Olga, et al. "Interview with Juan Felipe Herrera." *Latino Book Review*, July 8, 2017. https://www.latinobookreview.com/interview-with-juan-felipe-herrera.html.

García-Navarro, Lulu, host. "Juan Felipe Herrera Paints Portrait of America in New Poetry Collection." *Weekend Edition Sunday*, NPR, audio, September 27, 2020.

https://www.npr.org/2020/09/27/917424893/juan-felipe-herrera-paints-portrait-of-america-in-new-poetry-collection.

García Prados, Nieves. "Entrevista a Juan Felipe Herrera." *Poéticas: Revista de Estudios Literarios* 4, no. 9 (June 2019): 97–103.

Garza, Oscar. "An Evening with Juan Felipe Herrera." ZPS Podcast, *Zócalo Public Square*, audio, July 18, 2012. https://soundcloud.com/zocalopublicsquare/an-evening-with-juan-felipe-herrera.

Goodman, Amy. "First Latino U.S. Poet Laureate Juan Felipe Herrera on Migrant Farmworkers, the Border and Ayotzinapa." *Democracy Now!: Independent Global News*, KCET, video, October 9, 2015. https://www.democracynow.org/2015/10/9/first_latino_us_poet_laureate_juan.

Goodman, Amy. "A Conversation with First Latino U.S. Poet Laureate Juan Felipe Herrera (Part 2)." *KCET, Democracy Now!: Independent Global News*, video, October 12, 2015. https://www.democracynow.org/2015/10/12/a_conversation_with_first_latino_us.

González, Ray. "Poetry Marauder: An Interview with Juan Felipe Herrera." *The Bloomsbury Review* 20, no. 2 (March/April 2000): 19–20.

Green, Timothy. "From a Conversation with Juan Felipe Herrera." *Rattle* no. 44 (Summer 2014). https://www.rattle.com/from-a-conversation-with-juan-felipe-herrera.

Griswold, Jerry. "An Interview with Juan Felipe Herrera." *Children's Media and Choice Reviews, Play Blog*, Parent's Choice, n.d. http://archive.parentschoice.org/article.cfm?art_id=295&the_page=editorials.

Griswold, Jerry. "Juan Felipe Herrera: An Interview with The First Latino Poet Laureate of the United States about His Books for Kids." *Parents' Choice*, May 2007. Remastered, October 23, 2019. https://medium.com/@jerrygriswold/juan-felipe-herrera-93f371a88afe.

Guerrero, Jean. "Juan Felipe Herrera Discusses Border Walls and The Power of Words." KPBS: San Diego Public Radio & TV, YouTube video, January 26, 2017. https://www.youtube.com/watch?v=jBoV1lNsScY.

Herrera, Juan Felipe. "Poetry Career / Young Minds Dreaming." Ask an Author Series Interview, KnowItAll.org, South Carolina State Library, video, 2019. https://www.knowitall.org/video/juan-felipe-herrera-poetry-career-young-minds-dreaming.

Hinojosa, María. "From Chicano Punk to Poet Laureate: Juan Felipe Herrera." *LatinoUSA*, NPR.org, audio, January 8, 2016. https://soundcloud.com/latinousa/from-chicano-punk-to-poet-laureate-juan-felipe-herrera.

Hockenberry, John. "U.S. Poet Laureate Juan Felipe Herrera on a Year of Gun Violence." *The Takeaway*, WNYC Studios, audio, June 17, 2016. https://www.wnycstudios.org/podcasts/takeaway/segments/us-poet-laureate-juan-felipe-herrera-reflects-year-mass-shootings.

Hsieh, H. Philip. "Juan Felipe Herrera." In *Poets about Poetry: Interviews with Contemporary American Poets*, 96–107. Fremont, CA: EGW Publishing Inc., 2016.

Keckeisen, Kevin. "Interview with Juan Felipe Hererra." Features, *The Highlander*, University of California, Riverside, May 8, 2012. https://www.highlandernews.org /3405/interview-with-juan-felipe/.

King, Larry. "Interview: U.S. Poet Laureate Juan Felipe Herrera Shares His Words of Power & Passion." *PoliticKING, Larry King Now*. Recorded July 21, 2015, uploaded to YouTube July 23, 2015. http://www.ora.tv/politicking/2015/7/21/poet-laureate -juan-felipe-herrera-joins-larry-king-politicking-0_14phl5b52oeb. https://www .youtube.com/watch?v=1Xk0op1AjHY&t=109s.

Kraske, Steve, host. "Former 'Lost Star' Is Now U.S. Poet Laureate." *Up to Date*, KCUR 89.3, audio, May 27, 2017. https://www.kcur.org/show/up-to-date/2016-05-27 /former-lost-star-is-now-u-s-poet-laureate#stream/0.

Laínez, René Colato. "Juan Felipe Herrera Interview on Authenticity." *La Bloga: The World's Longest-Established Chicana Chicano, Latina Latino Literary Blog*, February 10, 2007. https://labloga.blogspot.com/2007/02/juan-felipe-herrera-inter view-on.html.

Lau, David. "We Must Act but How? A Conversation with Juan Felipe Herrera (Part 1 of 3)" *Harriet*, Poetry Foundation, April 30, 2014. https://www.poetryfoundation .org/harriet/2014/04/we-must-act-but-how-a-conversation-with-juan-felipe -herrera-part-1-of-3.

Lau, David. "We Must Act but How? A Conversation with Juan Felipe Herrera (Part 2 of 3)." *Harriet*, Poetry Foundation, May 2, 2014. https://www.poetryfoundation .org/harriet/2014/05/we-must-act-but-how-a-conversation-with-juan-felipe -herrera-part-2-of-3.

Lau, David. "We Must Act but How? A Conversation with Juan Felipe Herrera (Part 3 of 3)." *Harriet*, Poetry Foundation, May 4, 2014. https://www.poetryfoundation .org/harriet/2014/05/we-must-act-but-how-a-conversation-with-juan-felipe -herrera-part-3-of-3.

Linn, Sarah. "U.S. Poet Laureate Juan Felipe Herrera on Poetry, Progress and his California Roots." *Artbound*, KCET, September 14, 2015. https://www.kcet.org /shows/artbound/us-poet-laureate-juan-felipe-herrera-on-poetry-progress-and -his-california-roots.

López-Maldonado, Luis. "Letras Latinas Exclusive: An Interview with Juan Felipe Herrera." *Letras Latinas Blog*, Institute for Latino Studies, University of Notre Dame, September 26, 2016. https://letraslatinasblog.blogspot.com/search?q=%22 Letras+Latinas+Exclusive%3A+an+interview+with+Juan+Felipe+Herrera%22.

López-Maldonado, Luis. "Oral History Interview with U.S. Poet Laureate Juan Felipe Herrera." *Letras Latinas Blog*, Institute for Latino Studies, University of Notre Dame, video. Recorded October 6, 2016, uploaded to YouTube October 11, 2016. https://www.youtube.com/watch?v=l-U29FazGQA.

López-Maldonado, Luis. "Juan Felipe Herrera in Conversation with Luis López-Maldonado." *Notre Dame Review*, no. 44 (Summer/Fall 2017): 73–77.

Matuk, Farid. "Interview with Juan Felipe Herrera." *Akrílica*, Revised and Expanded edition, 32–39. Notre Dame: Noemi Press, Inc., 2022.

Medrano, Michael Luis. "Learning to Not Write: An Interview with Juan Felipe Herrera." *Dislocate: A Minnesota Journal of Writing & Art*, July 2004, 12–17.

Montagne, Renee, host. "Poet Laureate's Migrant Childhood Was Like 'Living in Literature Every Day.'" *Morning Edition*, NPR.org, audio, September 15, 2015. https://www.npr.org/transcripts/438630601.

Nilsen, David. "A Conversation with Juan Felipe Herrera." *On the Seawall: A Community Gallery for New Writing and Commentary*, November 3, 2020. https://www.ronslate.com/a-conversation-with-juan-felipe-herrera/.

North, Bonnie, host. "United States Poet Laureate Juan Felipe Herrera: Writing and Reinvention." *Lake Effect Show*, WUWM 89.710, audio, June 2016. https://www.wuwm.com/post/united-states-poet-laureate-juan-felipe-herrera-writing-and-reinvention#stream/0.

Olivas, Daniel. "Three Questions for Juan Felipe Herrera Regarding His New Book, *Portraits of Hispanic American Heroes*: Daniel Olivas Interviews Juan Felipe Herrera." *Los Angeles Review of Books*, December 4, 2014. https://lareviewofbooks.org/article/three-questions-juan-felipe-herrera-regarding-new-book-portraits-hispanic-american-heroes.

Oller, Denisse. "Interview with Juan Felipe Herrera." The Joseph A. Unanue Latino Institute, Seton Hall University, video, uploaded to YouTube July 21, 2016. https://www.youtube.com/watch?v=QR3i7VcRt_4.

Opinion Contributor. "Juan Felipe Herrera, the First Latino to Be U.S. Poet Laureate, Is Master of Many Forms." *The Bangor Daily News*, June 11, 2015. https://bangordailynews.com/2015/06/11/living/juan-felipe-herrera-the-first-latino-to-be-us-poet-laureate-is-master-of-many-forms/.

Osorio, Nathan Xavier. "Poetry Is Built for Compassion: An Interview with Juan Felipe Herrera." The Humanities Institute, UC Santa Cruz, February 27, 2019. https://thi.ucsc.edu/poetry-built-compassion-interview-juan-felipe-herrera/.

*Poets & Writers Magazine*. "Ten Questions for Juan Felipe Herrera: Author of *Everyday We Get More Illegal*." 50 & Forward, September 22, 2020. https://www.pw.org/content/ten_questions_for_juan_felipe_herrera.

Presson, Rebekah. "Juan Felipe Herrera Interview." *New Letters on the Air*, Poetry, University of Missouri-Kansas City, audio, 1992. https://www.newletters.org/on_the_air_shows/juan-felipe-herrera-2/.

Raskin, Jonah. "Interview with U.S. Poet Laureate Juan Felipe Herrera." *San Antonio Express News*, September 11, 2015, 1–2. Posted Online in *SFGATE: News & Media Website*, September 11, 2015. https://www.sfgate.com/books/article/Interview-with-U-S-poet-laureate-Juan-Felipe-6498519.php.

Reed, Josephine. "Juan Felipe Herrera: U.S. Poet Laureate and NEA Literature Fellow." NEA Podcast, The National Endowment for the Arts, audio, September 17, 2015. https://www.arts.gov/stories/podcast/juan-felipe-herrera#transcript.

Rogers, Pamela. "Full Interview with Poet Juan Felipe Herrera." *Buttons & Figs podcast*, audio, May 11, 2020. https://soundcloud.com/buttonsandfigs/extra-extra-full-interview-with-poet-juan-felipe-herrera.

Romero, Ezra David. "Interview and Poems: Fresno's Juan Felipe Herrera Named U.S. Poet Laureate." KVPR: Valley Public Radio, audio, June 10, 2015. https://www.kvpr.org/post/interview-and-poems-fresnos-juan-felipe-herrera-named-us-poet-laureate#stream/0.

Romero, Ezra David. "U.S. Poet Laureate Juan Felipe Herrera's Second Term to Focus on Youth, Fresno." Valley Public Radio: FM89, NPR for Central California, Valley Edition, audio, August 2, 2016. https://www.kvpr.org/post/us-poet-laureate-juan-felipe-herreras-second-term-focus-youth-fresno#stream/0.

Ruyak, Beth. "A Conversation with U.S. Poet Laureate Juan Felipe Herrera." *Insight*, CapRadio, audio, July 1, 2015. https://www.capradio.org/news/insight/2015/07/01/insight-070115c/.

Salas, Crystal AC. "Walking in Empty: A Conversation with Poet Juan Felipe Herrera." *World Literature Today: Your Passport to Great Reading*, April 13, 2021. https://www.worldliteraturetoday.org/blog/interviews/walking-empty-conversation-poet-juan-felipe-herrera-crystal-ac-salas.

Samano, Miguel. "Q&A with Poet Laureate Juan Felipe Herrera." *The Stanford Daily*, March 2017. https://www.stanforddaily.com/2017/03/09/qa-with-poet-laureate-juan-felipe-herrera/.

Serenity and CMG Street Team. "Interview With Juan Felipe Herrera the Poet Laureate." *What's Up KC?*, YouTube video, May 29, 2016. https://www.youtube.com/watch?v=_Lhzx66WTnA.

Soldofsky, Alan. "A Border-Crosser's Heteroglossia: Interview with Juan Felipe Herrera; Twenty-First Poet Laureate of the United States." *MELUS: The Journal of the Society for the Study of the Multi-Ethnic Literature of the United States* 43, no. 2 (June 2018): 196–226.

Torres, Michael and Christopher Buckley. "Torches Lighting the Way: An Interview with Juan Felipe Herrera." *The Normal School: A Literary Magazine*, May 20, 2020. https://www.thenormalschool.com/blog/torches-lighting-the-way-interview. Repeated in *Naming the Lost: the Fresno Poets: Interviews and Essays*, edited by Christopher Buckley, 393–400. Nacogdoches, Texas: Stephen F. Austin State University Press, 2021.

Villarreal, Vanessa Angélica. "*Every Day We Get More Illegal*: A Virtual Conversation with Vanessa Angélica Villarreal & Former U.S. Poet Laureate Juan Felipe Herrera." *The Word: A Storytelling Sanctuary*, video, October 3, 2020. https://www.youtube.com/watch?v=Y_w90PMWo8c.

Wasser, Fred. "Juan Felipe Herrera: A Poet without Borders." KNPR: Nevada Public Radio, audio, September 25, 2015. https://knpr.org/knpr/2015-09/juan-felipe-herrera-poet-without-borders?

Wetherington, Laura. "Audio Interview with Juan Felipe Herrera." Sierra Nevada College Poetry Center, SoundCloud audio, March 29, 2014. https://soundcloud.com/sierranevadacollege/juan-felipe-herrera.

White, Jenn. "U.S. Poet Laureate Juan Felipe Herrera Wraps Up Project with Chicago Students." *Morning Shift*, WBEZ: Chicago's NPR News Source, audio, April 28,

2017. https://www.wbez.org/stories/us-poet-laureate-juan-felipe-herrera-wraps -up-project-with-chicago-students/cc6db18f-84db-4882-ad17-d40b407cdbcf.

Winer, Andrew. "Juan Felipe Herrera & Andrew Winer, an Interview." *Parallel Stories Lecture*, Santa Barbara Museum of Art, video, March 8, 2020. https://www .youtube.com/watch?v=NjEhexC5914&t=1203s.

Young, Robin. "U.S. Poet Laureate Juan Felipe Herrera Celebrates MLK Day." *Here and Now*, WBUR: Boston's NPR News Station, audio, January 18, 2016. https:// www.wbur.org/hereandnow/2016/01/18/juan-felipe-herrera-mlk-day.

Zaragoza, Diana. "El poeta chicano que denuncia las injusticias contra los migrantes." El *Universal: Noticias de México y el Mundo,* December 2009. http://www .eluniversal.com.mx/cultura/61728.html.

*Zócalo Public Square.* "United States Poet Laureate Emeritus Juan Felipe Herrera: 'I Was a Mariachi Embryo.'" In the Green Room, May 7, 2020. https://www.zocalo publicsquare.org/2020/05/07/united-states-poet-laureate-emeritus-juan-felipe -herrera/personalities/in-the-green-room/.

# Book Reviews

Abos, Elena. Review of *The Upside Down Boy/El niño de cabeza*, by Juan Felipe Herrera. *The Horn Book Magazine* 76, no. 5 (September 2000): 595.

*American Poets: The Journal of The Academy of American Poets.* Unsigned review of *Half the World in Light: New and Selected Poems*, by Juan Felipe Herrera. N.d. https://poets.org/book/half-world-light-new-and-selected-poems.

*American Poets: The Journal of the Academy of American Poets.* Unsigned review of *Senegal Taxi,* by Juan Felipe Herrera. no. 44 (Spring 2013). Republished on *Poets. Org,* February 19, 2014. https://poets.org/text/juan-felipe-herrera-senegal-taxi.

Ashmore, Ann Mulloy. Review of *Calling the Doves/El canto de las palomas*, by Juan Felipe Herrera. *Book Links* 18, no. 6 (2009): 46.

Ayres, Annie. Review of *Calling the Doves: El canto de las palomas*, by Juan Felipe Herrera. *Booklist* 92, no. 9–10 (January 1996): 823.

Báez, Diego. Review of *Every Day We Get More Illegal*, by Juan Felipe Herrera. *Booklist* 116, no. 22 (August 2020): 17.

Baird, Robert P. Review of *Half of the World in Light*, by Juan Felipe Herrera. *Digital Emunction,* April 2009. http://robertpbaird.com/wpcontent/uploads/2012/09/DE -JuanFelipe-Herrera-review.pdf.

Bandre, Patricia, et al. "Well Versed: Twenty-Eight Titles to Celebrate in April and throughout the Year." Review of *JabberWalking*, by Juan Felipe Herrera. *School Library Journal* 65, no. 3 (2019): 42.

Broussard, Kelli. Review of *Skate Fate*, by Juan Felipe Herrera. *Library Media Connection* 29, no. 5 (2011): 72.

Berman, Barbara. "What We Need: Juan Felipe Herrera, Maw Shein Win, and John Freeman." Reviews of *Every Day We Get More Illegal, Storage Unit for the Spirit Horse,* and *The Park. The Rumpus,* October 30, 2020. https://therumpus.net/2020 /10/juan-felipe-herrera-maw-shein-win-and-john-freeman/.

Berman, Barbara. Review of *Notes on the Assemblage*, by Juan Felipe Herrera. *The Rumpus*, October 2015. https://therumpus.net/2015/10/02/notes-on-the-assemblage-by-juan-felipe-herrera/.

Bird, Elizabeth. Review of *JabberWalking*, by Juan Felipe Herrera. *School Library Journal*, 29 August 2018. https://blogs.slj.com/afuse8production/2018/08/29/review-of-the-day-jabberwalking-by-juan-felipe-herrera/.

*Blog on the Hyphen*. "Latino Book Review's List for 2017 Outstanding Latino Authors." Includes unsigned review of *Notes on the Assemblage*, by Juan Felipe Herrera. December 20, 2017. https://latinx.wordpress.com/2017/12/20/latino-book-reviews-list-for-2017-outstanding-latino-authors/.

*BookDragon: Books for the Diverse Reader*. Unsigned review of *Portraits of Hispanic American Heroes*, by Juan Felipe Herrera. Smithsonian Asian Pacific American Center. September 25, 2014. http://smithsonianapa.org/bookdragon/portraits-of-hispanic-american-heroes-by-juan-felipe-herrera-illustrated-by-raul-colon/.

*Booklist*. Unsigned review of *CrashBoomLove: A Novel in Verse*, by Juan Felipe Herrera. Vol. 97, no. 14 (March 2001): 1384.

*Booklist*. Unsigned review of *Grandma and Me at the Flea/Los Meros Meros Remateros*, by Juan Felipe Herrera. Vol. 98, no. 22 (August 2002): 1979.

*Booklist*. Unsigned review of *Laughing Out Loud, I Fly/A Carcajadas yo vuelo*, by Juan Felipe Herrera. Vol. 96, no. 14 (March 15, 2000): 1342.

Bradburn, Frances. Review of *CrashBoomLove*, by Juan Felipe Herrera. *Booklist*, no. 11 (February 2000): 1018.

Budin, Miriam Lang. Review of *Cinnamon Girl: Letters Found inside a Cereal Box*, by Juan Felipe Herrera. *School Library Journal* 51, no. 11 (November, 2005): 137.

*Bulletin of the Center for Children's Books*. Unsigned review of *Calling the Doves*, by Juan Felipe Herrera. Vol. 49 (December 1995): 129.

*Bulletin of the Center for Children's Books*. Unsigned review of *The Upside Down Boy*, by Juan Felipe Herrera. Vol. 53 (April 2000): 282.

Burt, Stephen. "Punk Half Panther." Review of *187 Reasons Mexicanos Can't Cross the Border: Undocuments 1971–2007* & *Half of the World in Light: New and Selected Poems*, by Juan Felipe Herrera. *The New York Times Book Review*, (August 10, 2008): 20(L). https://www.nytimes.com/2008/08/10/books/review/Burt2-t.html?pagewanted=print&r=0.

Camargo, Rosie. Review of *Lejos/Far*, by Juan Felipe Herrera. *Booklist* 115, no. 22 (August 2019): 69.

Campbell Carlson, Patricia. Review of *Imagine*, by Juan Felipe Herrera. *Spirituality Practice: Resource for Spiritual Journeys*, n.d. https://www.spiritualityandpractice.com/book-reviews/view/28635/imagine.

Cárdenas, María and Beverly Slapin. Review of *Imagine/Imagina*, by Juan Felipe Herrera. *De Colores: The Raza Experience in Books for Children*, May 4, 2020. http://decoloresreviews.blogspot.com/2020/05/imagine-imagina.html.

Cauchy, H. Shaw. Review of *Thunderweavers/Tejedoras de Rayos*, by Juan Felipe Herrera. *Foreword Reviews*, March/April 2000. https://www.forewordreviews.com/reviews/buddhists-talk-about-jesus-christians-talk-about-the-buddha/.

Cerro, Dornel. Review of *Portraits of Hispanic American Heroes*, by Juan Felipe Herrera. *Goodreadswithronna* (blog), October 8, 2014. https://www.goodreadswith ronna.com/2014/10/08/portraits-of-hispanic-american-heroes-by-juan-felipe -herrera/.

Chaudhri, Amina. Review of *Imagine*, by Juan Felipe Herrera: Own Voices for Young Readers. *Booklist* no. 9–10 (January 2019): S35–36.

Chávez, Denise. Review of *Every Day We Get More Illegal*, by Juan Felipe Herrera. *The American Booksellers Association*, The November 2020 Indie Next List Preview, September 29, 2020. https://www.bookweb.org/news/november-2020-indie-next -list-preview-578322.

Chen, Sandie Angulo. "Celebrate Cinco de Mayo with Inspiring Picture Book." Review of *Portraits of Hispanic American Heroes*, by Juan Felipe Herrera. *South Florida Sun Sentinel*, May 4, 2015. https://www.sun-sentinel.com/entertainment/sfp -book-review-portraits-of-hispanic-american-heroes-celebrate-cinco-de-mayo -with-inspiring-picture-boo-20150504-story.html.

Coats, Karen. Review of *SkateFate*, by Juan Felipe Herrera. *Bulletin of the Center for Children's Books* 64, no. 7 (March 2011): 331.

Cruz, Víctor. Review of *Love after the Riots*, by Juan Felipe Herrera. *Harvard Review*, no. 11 (1996): 175–176.

Dar, Mahnaz, et al. "Best books 2013." [Includes Review of *Senegal Taxi*, by Juan Felipe Herrera]. *Library Journal* 138, no. 20 (December 2013): 26–28.

Díaz, Shelley. Review of *Portraits of Hispanic American Heroes*, by Juan Felipe Herrera. *School Library Journal* 60, no. 11 (November 2014): 134.

DiGirolomo, Kate, et al. "Best Books 2015." Includes review of *Notes on the Assemblage*, by Juan Felipe Herrera. *Library Journal* 140, no. 20 (December 2015): 30–40.

Donahue, Alice. "¡Mira Look!" Review of *Portraits of Hispanic American Heroes*, by Juan Felipe Herrera. *Vamos a Leer: Teaching Latin America Through Literacy* blog, September 2016. https://teachinglatinamericathroughliterature.wordpress.com /2016/09/19/mira-look-portraits-of-hispanic-american-heroes/.

Drake, Monica. "Lotería." Review of *Lotería Cards and Fortune Poems: A Book of Lives*, by Juan Felipe Herrera. *The Portland Mercury*, February 22, 2001. https:// www.portlandmercury.com/portland/loteria/Content?oid=24025.

Durán-Cerda, Dolores M. Review of *Thunderweavers/Tejedoras de Rayos*, by Juan Felipe Herrera. *Arizona Journal of Hispanic Cultural Studies*, no. 4 (2000): 300–301.

Encarnación, Mónica. Review of *Lejos/Far*, by Juan Felipe Herrera. *Common Sense Media*. September 17, 2019. https://www.commonsensemedia.org/book-reviews /lejos-far.

Engberg, Gillian. Review of *Grandma and Me at the Flea/Los Meros Meros Remateros*, by Juan Felipe Herrera. *Booklist* 98, no. 15 (April 2002): 1333.

Engberg, Gillian. Review of *Downtown Boy*, by Juan Felipe Herrera. *Booklist* 102, no. 8 (December 2005): 45.

Fagerberg, Jerard. Review of *SkateFate*, by Juan Felipe Herrera. *The Baltimore Sun*, March 2, 2011. https://www.baltimoresun.com/citypaper/bcp-cms-1-1112209 -migrated-story-cp-20110302-books-20110302-story.html.

Finn, Ashleigh. Review of *SkateFate*, by Juan Felipe Herrera. *The Horn Book Guide* 22, no. 2 (Fall 2011): 384.

Fogliano, Julie. Review of *JabberWalking*, by Juan Felipe Herrera. *The New York Times Book Review* (April 22, 2018): 22(L). Posted online: April 13, 2018. https://www.nytimes.com/2018/04/13/books/review/kwame-alexander-rebound.html.

Freeman, John. "The Best New Books to Read This Summer." Includes review of *Every Day We Get More Illegal: Poems*, by Juan Felipe Herrera. *Literary Hub*, May 26, 2020. https://lithub.com/your-2020-summer-books-preview/.

Gardner, Jan. Review of *Notes on the Assemblage*, by Juan Felipe Herrera. The Discovery, *The Boston Globe*, September 19, 2015. https://www.bostonglobe.com/arts/books/2015/09/19/discovery-notes-assemblage-juan-felipe-herrera/sP1ODiIsswpkGKYom9TZpN/story.html.

Gatto, A. Review of *Exiles of Desire: Poetry*, by Juan Felipe Herrera. *Avance: The New Latin Entertainment Magazine* 2, no. 1 (January/February 1984): 40–41.

Gilbert, Greg. Review of *Every Day We Get More Illegal*, by Juan Felipe Herrera. *Cholla Needles Arts & Literary Library*, October 4, 2020. https://www.chollaneedles.com/2020/10/review-every-day-we-get-more-illegal-by.html.

Gonzales, Grace Cornell. Review of *Calling the Doves/El canto de las palomas*, by Juan Felipe Herrera. *De Colores: The Raza Experience in Books for Children*, February 28, 2014. http://decoloresreviews.blogspot.com/2014/02/calling-doves-el-canto-de-las-palomas.html.

Gonzales, Grace Cornell. Review of *Super Cilantro Girl/La superniña del cilantro*, by Juan Felipe Herrera. *De Colores: The Raza Experience in Books for Children*, June 2013. http://decoloresreviews.blogspot.com/2013/06/super-cilantro-girl-la-supernina-del.html.

Gonzales, Grace Cornell. Review of *Upside Down Boy/El niño de cabeza*, by Juan Felipe Herrera. *De Colores: The Raza Experience in Books for Children*, October 2013. http://decoloresreviews.blogspot.com/2013/10/upside-down-boy-el-nino-de-cabeza.html.

González, Rigoberto. "Activist Poetry That Won't Make You Run the Other Way: Rigoberto González on Juan Felipe Herrera." [Review and discussion of *187 Reasons Mexicanos Can't Cross the Border: Undocuments 1971–2001*]. *Poetry off The Shelf: The Poetry Reader*. Poetry Foundation, audio, March 10, 2008. https://www.poetryfoundation.org/podcasts/74949/activist-poetry-that-wont-make-you-run-the-other-way.

Gordon, Suzanne. Review of *Downtown Boy*, by Juan Felipe Herrera. *School Library Journal* 52, no. 1 (January 1, 2006): 133.

Gotera, Vince. Review of *Half of the World in Light: New and Selected Poems*, by Juan Felipe Herrera. *The North American Review* 293, no. 5 (September/October 2008): 44.

Goykadosh, Brachah. Review of *Notes on the Assemblage*, by Juan Felipe Herrera. *Boston Review: A Political and Literary Forum* 41, no. 1 (January/February 2016): 68. Posted online: February 4, 2016. https://bostonreview.net/poetry/microreviews-february-16.

Guenter, Scot. Review of *Thunderweavers/Tejedoras de rayos*, by Juan Felipe Herrera. *Studies in American Indian Literatures* 14, no. 4 (2002): 54–57.

Hinojosa-Cisneros, Carolina. Review of *JabberWalking*, by Juan Felipe Herrera. *Latinxs in Kid Lit: Exploring the World of Latinx YA, MG and Children's Literatures*, June 2018. https://latinosinkidlit.com/2018/06/14/book-review-jabberwalking-by-juan-felipe-herrera/.

Hoffert, Barbara. "Best Poetry of 2008." Includes a review of *Half of the World in Light: New and Selected Poems*, by Juan Felipe Herrera. *Library Journal* 134, no. 7 (April 15, 2009): 95–96.

Hoffert, Barbara. Review of *Senegal Taxi*, by Juan Felipe Herrera. *Library Journal* 138, no. 7 (April 15, 2013): 82–83.

Hoffert, Barbara. "Poet Laureate Herrera." Review of *Notes on the Assemblage*. *Library Journal* 140, no. 14 (September 2015): 102. https://www.libraryjournal.com/review/notes-on-the-assemblage.

Hoffert, Barbara, Fred Muratori, and Annalisa Pešek. "Best Poetry of 2020." Includes a review of *Every Day We Get More Illegal*, by Juan Felipe Herrera. *Library Journal*, November 30, 2020. https://www.libraryjournal.com/?detailStory=best-books-of-2020-poetry.

Hommel, Maggie. Review of *Downtown Boy*, by Juan Felipe Herrera. *The Bulletin of the Center for Children's Books* 59, no. 6 (February 2006): 267.

HP0312_RPEMS. Review of *Skate Fate*, by Juan Felipe Herrera. *LitPick: A Reading and Writing Initiative That Connects Authors with Readers*, n.d. https://litpick.com/review/skate-fate-review-hp0312rpems.

Huston, Karla. Review of *Every Day We Get More Illegal*, by Juan Felipe Herrera. *Library Journal* 145, no. 9 (September 2020): 73. Posted online: September 1, 2020. https://www.libraryjournal.com/?reviewDetail=every-day-we-get-more-illegal.

*Iowa Magazine: For University of Iowa Alumni and Friends*. Unsigned review of *Every Day We Get More Illegal*, by Juan Felipe Herrera. Winter 2020/2021, 44.

Jackson, Cathy. "Akrilica Shows Poet's Vision." The Daily Iowan (June 19, 1989): 1 & 7.

Kaszuba Locke, J. A. Review of *Cinnamon Girl: Letters Found Inside a Cereal Box*, by Juan Felipe Herrera. *Bookloons Reviews*, n.d. http://www.bookloons.com/cgi-bin/Review.asp?bookid=4515.

*Kirkus Reviews*. Unsigned review of *Cerca/Close*, by Juan Felipe Herrera. Vol. 87, no. 24 (December 2019): 169–170. Posted Online: November 24, 2019. https://www.kirkusreviews.com/book-reviews/juan-felipe-herrera/cerca-close/.

*Kirkus Reviews*. Unsigned review of *Cinnamon Girl: Letters Found Inside a Cereal Box*, by Juan Felipe Herrera. Vol. 73, no. 14 (July 2005): 791. Posted Online: May 20, 2010. https://www.kirkusreviews.com/book-reviews/juan-felipe-herrera/cinnamon-girl/.

*Kirkus Reviews*. Unsigned review of *Downtown Boy*, by Juan Felipe Herrera. Vol. 73, no. 20 (October 2005): 1139. Posted Online: May 20, 2010. https://www.kirkusreviews.com/book-reviews/juan-felipe-herrera/downtown-boy/.

*Kirkus Reviews.* Unsigned review of *Featherless/Desplumado,* by Juan Felipe Herrera. Vol. 72, no. 13 (July 2004): 630. Posted online: May 20, 2010. https://www.kirkus reviews.com/book-reviews/juan-felipe-herrera/featherlessdesplumado/.

*Kirkus Reviews.* Unsigned review of *Imagine,* by Juan Felipe Herrera. Vol. 85, no. 18 (September 2018): 89. Posted online: August 27, 2018. https://www.kirkusreviews .com/book-reviews/juan-felipe-herrera/imagine-herrera/.

*Kirkus Reviews.* Unsigned review of *JabberWalking* by Juan Felipe Herrera. Vol. 86, no. 2 (January 15, 2018): 105. Posted online: December 11, 2017. https://www .kirkusreviews.com/book-reviews/juan-felipe-herrera/jabberwalking/.

*Kirkus Reviews.* Unsigned review of *Laughing Out Loud, I Fly: Poems in English and Spanish,* by Juan Felipe Herrera. Vol. 66, no. 10 (May 15, 1998): 738. Posted Online: May 20, 2010. https://www.kirkusreviews.com/book-reviews/juan-felipe-herrera /laughing-out-loud-i-fly/.

*Kirkus Reviews.* Unsigned review of *Portraits of Hispanic American Heroes* by Juan Felipe Herrera. May 15, 2015. Posted online: May 2, 2015. https://www.kirkus reviews.com/book-reviews/juan-felipe-herrera/portraits-of-hispanic-american -heroes/.

*Kirkus Reviews.* Unsigned review of *Skatefate,* by Juan Felipe Herrera. Vol. 79, no. 4 (February 2011): 313. Posted online: February 10, 2011. https://www.kirkusreviews .com/book-reviews/juan-felipe-herrera/skatefate/.

Kirsch, Jonathan. "A Haunting Collection of Los Angeles Still Lives." Review of *Sins of the City: The Real Los Angeles Noir* by Jim Heimann and *Lotería Cards and Fortune Poems: A Book of Lives,* by Juan Felipe Herrera. West Words, *The Los Angeles Times,* November 1999. https://www.latimes.com/archives/la-xpm-1999 -nov-03-cl-29152-story.html.

Kline, Julie. Review of *Featherless/Desplumado,* by Juan Felipe Herrera. *Booklist* 101, no. 2 (September 2004): 250.

Kogiashvili-Amar, Hiam. Review of *SkateFate,* by Juan Felipe Herrera. *Journal of Adolescent & Adult Literacy* 54, no. 8 (2011): 633–634.

Kun, Josh. "A Line in the Sand" Review of *Hyperborder: The Contemporary U.S.-Mexico Border and Its Future,* by Fernando Romero and *187 Reasons Mexicanos Can't Cross the Border: Undocuments 1971–2007,* by Juan Felipe Herrera. *The Los Angeles Times,* February 17, 2008. https://www.latimes.com/archives/la-xpm -2008-feb-17-bk-kun17-story.html.

*Latino Book Review.* Unsigned review of *Borderbus,* by Juan Felipe Herrera, with prints by Felicia Rice. August 6, 2019. https://www.latinobookreview.com/borderbus— -poem-by-juan-felipe-herrera-prints-by-felicia-rice-latino-book-review.html.

Lempke, Susan Dove. Review of *Imagine,* by Juan Felipe Herrera. *The Horn Book Magazine* 94, no. 6 (November/December 2018): 61–62.

Lempke, Susan Dove. Review of *JabberWalking,* by Juan Felipe Herrera. *The Horn Book Magazine* 94, no. 3, Special Issue: Making a Difference (May/June 2018): 145.

Lempke, Susan Dove. Review of *JabberWalking,* by Juan Felipe Herrera. *The Horn Book Guide to Children's and Young Adult Books* 29, no. 2 (Fall 2018): 186.

*Library Media Connection.* Unsigned review of *Calling the Doves,* by Juan Felipe Herrera. No. 21 (2003): 41.

*Library Media Connection.* Unsigned review of *Grandma and Me at the Flea/Los Meros Meros Remateros,* by Juan Felipe Herrera. No. 21 (2003): 40.

*Library Media Connection.* Unsigned review of *The Upside Down Boy,* by Juan Felipe Herrera. Vol. 21 (2003): 41.

Llera, Katie. Review of *Portraits of Hispanic American Heroes,* by Juan Felipe Herrera. *School Library Journal* 62, no. 6 (2016): 59.

Lomelí, Francisco A. "Juan Felipe Herrera: A Poet in Movement." Review of *Every Day We Get More Illegal. Los Angeles Review of Books,* November 14, 2020. https://la reviewofbooks.org/?p=315556&post_type=article&preview=1&_ppp=e41b49088.

Lomelí, Francisco A., and Donaldo W. Urioste. Review of *Rebozos of Love / We Have Woven / Sudor de Pueblos / On Our Back,* by Juan Felipe Herrera. In *Chicano Perspectives in Literature: A Critical and Annotated Bibliography,* 26–27. Albuquerque: Pajarito Publications, 1976.

Luis-Brown, David. Review of *Love After the Riots* and *Mayan Drifter: Chicano Poet in the Lowlands of America,* by Juan Felipe Herrera. *The Americas Review* 25, Valedictorian Issue (1999): 245–248.

Lund, Elizabeth. Best Poetry Collections of 2015: Review of *Notes on the Assemblage,* by Juan Felipe Herrera. Arts & Entertainment, *The Washington Post,* November 18, 2015. https://www.washingtonpost.com/entertainment/books/best-poetry-collections-of -2015/2015/11/18/400e8fe2-7902-11e5-b9c1-f03c48c96ac2_story.html.

Lund, Elizabeth. "A New Collection from the Poet Laureate and Other Best-Poetry Books." Includes review of *Notes on the Assemblage,* by Juan Felipe Herrera. *The Washington Post,* August 18, 2015. https://www.washingtonpost.com/entertain ment/books/a-new-collection-from-the-poet-laureate-and-other-best-poetry -books/2015/08/18/d15acf90-3f66-11e5-8d45-d815146f81fa_story.html.

McDonald, Sheri, and Sally Rasch. Review of *Grandma and Me at the Flea/Los Meros Meros Remateros,* by Juan Felipe Herrera. *Book Links* 15, no. 4 (2006): 33.

McHenry, Eric. Review of *Notes on the Assemblage,* by Juan Felipe Herrera. *The New York Times Book Review,* December 27, 2015, 26(L). https://www.nytimes.com /2015/12/27/books/review/poetry.html.

McKee, Louis. Review of *187 Reasons Mexicanos Can't Cross the Border,* by Juan Felipe Herrera. Spoken Word 1971–2007. *Library Journal* 133, no. 9 (May 2008): 101–102.

Menge, Dawn. Review of *Imagine,* by Juan Felipe Herrera. *Children's Bookwatch,* February 2019, n.p.

Morey, Lisa. Review of *Portraits of Hispanic American Heroes,* by Juan Felipe Herrera. *Kiss the Book: Reviews for School Librarians* (blog), February 17, 2015. https:// kissthebook.blogspot.com/2015/02/portraits-of-hispanic-american-heroes.html ?m=0.

mngiadmin. Review of *Portraits of Hispanic American Heroes,* by Juan Felipe Herrera. *NextGen, YourHub.com,* books, September 2, 2015.

Mujica, Bárbara. Review of *Tejedoras de Rayos/Thunderweavers*, by Juan Felipe Herrera. *Américas* 52, no. 3 (May 2000): 63.

Naffis-Sahely, André. On the Border: An Elder Guardian of Literature in The U.S. Review of *Every Day We Get More Illegal*, by Juan Felipe Herrera. *TLS: The Times Literary Supplement*, no. 6152, February 26, 2021. https://www.the-tls.co.uk/articles/every-day-we-get-more-illegal-juan-felipe-herrera-review-andre-naffis-sahely/.

Nash, Susan Smith. Review of *Giraffe on Fire*, by Juan Felipe Herrera. *World Literature Today* 76, no. 1 (2002) 162–163.

Nash, Susan Smith. Review of *Mayan Drifter: Chicano Poet in the Lowlands of America*, by Juan Felipe Herrera. *World Literature Today* 72, no. 4 (1998): 846.

Nelson, Cyns. Review of *The Upside-Down Boy*, by Juan Felipe Herrera. *Bloomsbury Review* 20, no. 2 (March/April 2000): 20.

*New York Times Book Review*. "100 Notable Books of 2008." Unsigned review of *Half of The World in Light: New and Selected Poems*, by Juan Felipe Herrera. December 2008, 9(L).

*New York Times Book Review*. "Editors' Choice Recent Books of Particular Interest." Includes unsigned review of *Half of the World in Light: New and Selected Poems*, by Juan Felipe Herrera. August 17, 2008, 22(L).

Nye, Naomi Shihab. Review of *Every Day We Get More Illegal*, by Juan Felipe Herrera. *The New York Times Magazine* (August 9, 2020): 10(L).

Olszewski, Lawrence. Review of *Notebooks of a Chile Verde Smuggler*, by Juan Felipe Herrera. *Library Journal* 127, no. 13 (August 2002): 101.

Olszewski, Lawrence. Review of *Love after the Riots*, by Juan Felipe Herrera. *Library Journal* 121, no. 6 (April 1996): 84.

Ontiveros, Roberto. Review of *Every Day We Get More Illegal*, by Juan Felipe Herrera. Arts, *The Austin Chronicle*, September 25, 2020. https://www.austinchronicle.com/arts/2020-09-25/every-day-we-get-more-illegal-by-juan-felipe-herrera/.

Ontiveros, Roberto. "U.S. Poet Laureate Juan Felipe Herrera to Speak at Palo Alto Wednesday [Review of *Notes on the Assemblage*]." ArtSlut Blog, *San Antonio Current*, November 4, 2015. https://www.sacurrent.com/ArtSlut/archives/2015/11/04/us-poet-laureate-juan-felipe-herrera-to-speak-at-palo-alto-wednesday.

Owen, Maryann. Review of *Imagine*, by Juan Felipe Herrera. *Booklist* 115, no. 2 (September 2018): 51.

Padilla, Gerald A. Review of *Laughing Out Loud, I Fly*, by Juan Felipe Herrera. *Latino Book Review*, November 30, 2016. https://www.latinobookreview.com/juan-felipe-herrera.html.

Pérez, Andrés and Daniel Alejandro González. Review of *Imagine*, by Juan Felipe Herrera. *NABE Perspectives* 44, no. 1 (2020): 26–27.

Portillo Alvarado, Gabriela. "America Are You Listening: Gabriela Portillo Alvarado Reviews Three Poetry Titles on Immigration, Trauma, Racism, and America." Review of *The Book of Dirt*, by Nicole Santalucia; *Adelante*, by Jessica Guzman, and *Every Day We Get More Illegal*, by Juan Felipe Herrera. *Jacket2 Capsule Reviews*, September 10, 2020. https://jacket2.org/commentary/america-are-you-listening.

*Publishers Weekly Reviews.* "The ABCs of Identity: Inclusive Volumes Seek to Inspire, Educate, and Entertain Youngest Readers." Unsigned review of *Lejos/Far* by Juan Felipe Herrera. Vol. 266, no. 37 (September 16, 2019): 75–77.

*Publishers Weekly Reviews.* Unsigned review of *Border-Crosser with a Lamborghini Dream,* by Juan Felipe Herrera. Vol. 246, no. 4 (January 1999): 91. Posted Online: January 4, 1999. https://www.publishersweekly.com/978-0-8165-1932-3.

*Publishers Weekly Reviews.* Unsigned review of *Cinnamon Girl: Letters Found Inside a Cereal Box,* by Juan Felipe Herrera. Vol. 252, no. 36 (September 2005): 70. https://www.publishersweekly.com/978-0-06-057984-5.

*Publishers Weekly Reviews.* Unsigned review of *CrashBoomLove: A Novel in Verse,* by Juan Felipe Herrera. Vol. 246, no. 40 (October 1999): 67.

*Publishers Weekly Reviews.* Unsigned review of *Every Day We Get More Illegal,* by Juan Felipe Herrera. Vol. 267, no. 38 (September 2020): 65. Posted online: September 16, 2020. https://www.publishersweekly.com/9780872868281.

*Publishers Weekly Reviews.* Unsigned review of *Grandma and Me at the Flea/Los Meros Meros Remateros,* by Juan Felipe Herrera. Vol. 249, no. 6 (February 2002): 189. Posted online: February 1, 2002. https://www.publishersweekly.com/9780 892391714.

*Publishers Weekly Reviews.* Unsigned review of *Imagine,* by Juan Felipe Herrera. Vol. 265, no. 32 (August 2018): 70. Republished *Publishers Weekly Reviews* 265, no. 49 (November 2018): 105. Posted online: August 6, 2018. https://www.publishersweekly.com/978-0-7636-9052-6.

*Publishers Weekly Reviews.* Unsigned review of *JabberWalking* by Juan Felipe Herrera. Vol. 265, no. 1 (January 2018): 59.

*Publishers Weekly Reviews.* Unsigned review of *JabberWalking* by Juan Felipe Herrera. Vol. 265, no. 49 (November 2018): 96. Posted online: January 1, 2018. https://www.publishersweekly.com/978-1-5362-0140-6.

*Publishers Weekly Reviews.* Unsigned review of *Laughing out Loud, I Fly,* by Juan Felipe Herrera. Vol. 245, no. 22 (June 1, 1998): 65.

*Publishers Weekly Reviews.* Unsigned review of *Lejos/Far,* by Juan Felipe Herrera. Vol. 266, no. 48 (November 27, 2019): 14. Posted online: September 11, 2019. https://www.publishersweekly.com/9780763690632.

*Publishers Weekly Reviews.* Unsigned review of *Love after the Riots,* by Juan Felipe Herrera. Vol. 243, no. 12 (March 18, 1996): 67.

*Publishers Weekly Reviews.* Unsigned review of *Mayan Drifter: Chicano Poet in the Lowlands of America,* by Juan Felipe Herrera. Vol. 244, no. 1 (January 6, 1997): 57. Posted online: January 27, 1997. https://www.publishersweekly.com/978-1-56639-481-9.

*Publishers Weekly Reviews.* Unsigned review of *Night Train to Tuxtla,* by Juan Felipe Herrera. Vol. 241, no. 30 (July 25, 1994): 44. Posted online: August 1, 1994. https://www.publishersweekly.com/9780816514595.

*Publishers Weekly Reviews.* Unsigned review of *Notebooks of a Chile Verde Smuggler* by Juan Felipe Herrera. Vol. 249, no. 29 (July 22, 2002): 171. Posted online: July 22, 2002. https://www.publishersweekly.com/978-0-8165-2215-6.

*Publishers Weekly Reviews.* Unsigned review of *Notes on the Assemblage* by Juan Felipe Herrera. January 4, 2016. https://www.publishersweekly.com/9780872866973.

*Publishers Weekly Reviews.* Unsigned review of *Portraits of Hispanic American Heroes*, by Juan Felipe Herrera. August 4, 2014. https://www.publishersweekly.com/978-0-8037-3809-6.

*Publishers Weekly Reviews.* Unsigned review of *Senegal Taxi*, by Juan Felipe Herrera. Vol. 260, no. 8 (February 2013). Posted online: March 1, 2013. https://www.publishersweekly.com/978-0-8165-3015-1.

*Publishers Weekly Reviews.* Unsigned review of *Thunderweavers/Tejedoras de Rayos*, by Juan Felipe Herrera. Vol. 247, no. 10 (March 2000): 107. Posted online: February 1, 2000. https://www.publishersweekly.com/978-0-8165-1986-6.

Purpura, Lia. Review of *Border Crosser with a Lamborghini Dream*, by Juan Felipe Herrera. *The Antioch Review* 58, no. 3 (Summer 2000): 380–381.

Quintana, Paula. Review of *Super Cilantro Girl/La Superniña del Cilantro*, by Juan Felipe Herrera. *Childhood Education* 81, no. 1 (2004): 46.

Quiroa, Ruth. Review of *Lejos/Far* and *Cerca/Close*, by Juan Felipe Herrera. *SLJ: School Library Journal*, September 20, 2019. https://www.slj.com/?reviewDetail=lejos-far-cerca-close.

Ratner, Rochelle. Review of *Border-Crosser with a Lamborghini Dream*, by Juan Felipe Herrera. *Library Journal* 124, no. 1 (January 1999): 103.

Ratner, Rochelle. Review of *Night Train to Tuxtla*: *New Poems and Stories*, by Juan Felipe Herrera. *Library Journal* 119, no. 13 (August 1994): 86.

Rebolini, Arianna and Tomi Obaro. "29 Books We Couldn't Put Down This Year: From Stunning Poetry and Illuminating Nonfiction to Heart-Wrenching Novels." Includes review of *Every Day We Get More Illegal*, by Juan Felipe Herrera. *BuzzFeed News*, December 11, 2020. https://www.buzzfeednews.com/article/arianna rebolini/best-books-2020-recommendations.

Redburn, Maria. Review of *Calling the Doves/El canto de las palomas*, by Juan Felipe Herrera. *School Library Journal* 41, no. 12 (December 1995): 97.

Reissman, Rose. Jabber Walking: Scribble, Color, Talk, and Write Poetry on the Go with Poet Laureate, Felipe Herrera! Review of *Jabberwalking*, by Juan Felipe Herrera. *Literacy Special Interest Blog*, January 24, 2019. http://literacyspecialinterest.blogspot.com/2019/01/jabber-walking-scribble-color-talk-and.html.

*Rhapsody in Books* (blog). Unsigned review of *Portraits of Hispanic American Heroes*, by Juan Felipe Herrera. June 16, 2018. https://rhapsodyinbooks.wordpress.com/2018/06/16/kid-lit-review-of-portraits-of-hispanic-american-heroes-by-juan-felipe-herrera/.

Rochman, Hazel. Review of *Cinnamon Girl: Letters Found Inside a Cereal Box*, by Juan Felipe Herrera. *Booklist* 101, no. 22 (August 2005): 1966.

Rochman, Hazel. Review of *SkateFate*, by Juan Felipe Herrera. *Booklist*, vol. 107, no. 21 (July 1, 2011): 56.

Ross, Alison. "Poet Laureate Juan Felipe Herrera Sings 'Every Day We Get More Illegal.'" Review of *Every Day We Get More Illegal*. *Pop Matters*, December 1, 2020. https://www.popmatters.com/juan-felipe-herrera-2649095395.html.

Rua-Larsen, Marybeth. Review of *Notes on the Assemblage*, by Juan Felipe Herrera. In *Magill's Literary Annual 2016*, edited by Gabriela Toth, Kendal Spires, and Matthew Akre, 432–436. Ipswich, MA: Salem Press, 2016.

Saecker, Tasha. Review of *Imagine*, by Juan Felipe Herrera. *Waking Brain Cells* (blog), October 25, 2018. https://wakingbraincells.com/2018/10/25/review-imagine-by-juan-felipe-herrera/.

Sánchez, Greg. Review of *Night Train to Tuxtla*, by Juan Felipe Herrera. *World Literature Today: A Literary Quarterly of the University of Oklahoma* 69, no. 3 (1995): 589.

Scheuer, Mary Ann. "Celebrating Latina Activists during Women's History Month." Review of *Portraits of Hispanic American Heroes*, by Juan Felipe Herrera. *Great Kid Books* blog, March 13, 2017. http://greatkidbooks.blogspot.com/2017/03/hispanic-american-heroes.html.

*School Library Journal*. Unsigned review of *CrashBoomLove: A Novel in Verse*, by Juan Felipe Herrera. Vol. 46, no. 8 (2000): 37.

Sifuentes, Roberto. Review of *Rebozos of Love / We Have Woven / Sudor de Pueblos / on Our Back*, by Juan Felipe Herrera. *Aztlán: A Journal of Chicano Studies* 6, no.1 (Spring 1975): 128.

Simmers, Tim. Review of *Every Day We Get More Illegal*, by Juan Felipe Herrera. *Fresno Community Alliance*, May 3, 2021, Updated August 7, 2021. https://fresnoalliance.com/every-day-we-get-more-illegal/.

Sinofsky, Esther. Review of *Cinnamon Girl: Letters Found inside a Cereal Box*, by Juan Felipe Herrera. *Library Media Connection* 24, no. 7 (2006): 67–68.

Slapin, Beverly. Review of *Featherless: Story/Desplumado: Cuento*, by Juan Felipe Herrera. *De Colores: The Raza Experience in Books for Children*, October 3, 2013. https://decoloresreviews.blogspot.com/search/label/Juan%20Felipe%20Herrera.

Smith, Maggie Mason. Review of *Imagine*, by Juan Felipe Herrera. *School Library Journal* 64, no. 10 (2018): 93.

*Smithsonian*. Unsigned review of *Calling the Doves*, by Juan Felipe Herrera. Vol. 26, no. 8 (November 1995): 170.

Stevenson, Deborah. Review of *Jabberwalking*, by Juan Felipe Herrera. *The Bulletin of the Center for Children's Books* 71, no. 7 (March 2018): 292.

Stevenson, Deborah. Review of *Imagine*, by Juan Felipe Herrera. *The Bulletin of the Center for Children's Books* 72, no. 4 (December 2018): 167.

Stone, Jonathan. Review of *Borderbus*, by Juan Felipe Herrera, with prints by Felicia Rice. *Parenthesis*, no. 37 (2019): 42–43.

Sutter, Herman. Review of *CrashBoomLove: A Novel in Verse*, by Juan Felipe Herrera. *School Library Journal* 46, no. 3 (2000): 238.

*Teacher Librarian*. "The Best, Notable & Recommended for 2001" Unsigned review of *Crashboomlove: A Novel in Verse* by Juan Felipe Herrera. Vol. 28, no. 4 (2001): 9.

Teicher, Craig Morgan. "From Mexico Kidnappings to Eric Garner, Herrera Writes Poetry of the Moment." Review of Herrera's *Notes on the Assemblage*. NPR Book Reviews, September 16, 2015. https://www.npr.org/2015/09/16/437287870/from-mexico-kidnappings-to-eric-garner-hererra-writes-poetry-of-the-moment.

Teicher, Craig Morgan. "Guns, God and a Reggae Beat: A 2013 Poetry Preview of *Senegal Taxi* by Juan Felipe Herrera." NPR Book Reviews, January 7, 2013. https://www.npr.org/2013/01/07/168535270/guns-god-and-a-reggae-beat-a-2013-poetry-preview.

*The Five Owls.* Unsigned review of *Calling the Doves*, by Juan Felipe Herrera. No. 10 (1996): 59.

*The Horn Book Guide.* Unsigned review of *Calling the Doves*, by Juan Felipe Herrera. No. 7 (1996): 99.

*The Horn Book Guide.* Unsigned review of *Grandma and the Flea/Los Meros Meros Remateros*, by Juan Felipe Herrera. No. 13 (2002): 331.

*The Horn Book Guide.* Unsigned review of *Laughing Out Loud, I Fly*, by Juan Felipe Herrera. No. 9 (1998): 370.

*The Horn Book Magazine.* Unsigned review of *The Upside Down Boy*, by Juan Felipe Herrera. Vol. 76, no. 5 (September 2000): 595.

*The Reading Teacher.* Unsigned review of *Calling the Doves*, by Juan Felipe Herrera. No. 50 (1996): 244.

Treviño, Rose Zertuche. Review of *Calling the Doves / El canto de las Palomas*, by Juan Felipe Herrera. *School Library* Journal 42, no. 2 (February 1996): 128.

Ulin, David L. "The Better Angels of His Nature: In *Every Day We Get More Illegal*, Juan Felipe Herrera Doubles Down on Hope." *Alta: California Book Club*, November 16, 2020. https://www.altaonline.com/books/poetry/a34670441/juan-felipe-herrera-every-day-we-get-more-illegal/.

Valle, Emilio. Review of *Night Train to Tuxtla*, by Juan Felipe Herrera. *World Literature Today* 69, no. 3 (1995): 227–229.

Wall, Catherine E. Review of *Lotería Cards and Fortune Poems: A Book of Lives*, by Juan Felipe Herrera. *World Literature Today* 75, no. 1 (2001): 120.

Ward, Rebecca. Review of *The Upside Down Boy / El Niño de Cabeza*, by Juan Felipe Herrera. *Book Links* 18, no. 6 (July 1, 2009): 48.

Welton, Ann. Review of *Featherless/Desplumado*, by Juan Felipe Herrera. *School Library Journal* 50, no. 9 (1 September 2004): 196.

Welton, Ann. Review of *Grandma and Me at the Flea/Los Meros Meros Remateros*, by Juan Felipe Herrera. *School Library Journal* 48, no. 6 (June 1, 2002): 128.

Welton, Ann. Review of *Super Cilantro Girl: Letters Found Inside a Cereal Box*, by Juan Felipe Herrera. *School Library Journal* 49, no. 12 (December 1, 2003): 143.

Welton, Ann. Review of *The Upside Down Boy/El Niño de Cabeza*, by Juan Felipe Herrera. *School Library Journal* vol. 46, no. 3 (2000): 225.

Weisman, Kay. Review of *JabberWalking*, by Juan Felipe Herrera. Booklist 114, no. 11 (February 1, 2018): 42.

Westmoore, Jean. Review of *Imagine*, by Juan Felipe Herrera; and *Sweep* by Jonathan Auxier. *The Buffalo News*, November 30, 2018. https://buffalonews.com/entertainment/books/books-in-brief-imagine-by-juan-felipe-herrera-sweep-by-jonathan-auxier/article_32af6d23-9de1-5b80-a328-3070597721a0.html.

Whalin, Kathleen. Review of *Laughing Out Loud, I Fly*, by Juan Felipe Herrera. *School Library Journal* 144, no. 5 (May 1998): 156.

Wildhood, Megan. "Esperanza: In *Every Day We Get More Illegal,* Former U.S. Poet Laureate Juan Felipe Herrera Imparts Hope through Poetry." *Real Change: Seattle's Award-Winning Street Newspaper,* July 1, 2020. https://www.realchangenews.org/2020/07/01/esperanza.

Williamson, Hilary. Review of *Jabberwalking,* by Juan Felipe Herrera. Teens, *Bookloons Reviews,* n.d. http://www.bookloons.com/cgi-bin/Review.asp?bookid=19812.

Wilson, JJ Amaworo. Review of *Notes on the Assemblage,* by Juan Felipe Herrera. October 2016. Republished in *Southwest Festival of the Written Word,* October 28, 2016. https://jjawilson.wordpress.com/2016/10/24/notes-on-the-assemblage-by-juan -felipe-herrera/. https://swwordfiesta.org/review-of-notes-on-the-assemblage/.

*World Literature Today.* Unsigned review of *Night Train to Tuxtla,* by Juan Felipe Herrera. Vol. 69, no. 3 (1995): 589.

Zelinsky, Paul O. "Picture Books about Dreams and Dreamers of All Kinds." Review of *Imagine,* by Juan Felipe Herrera. Children's Books, *The New York Times Book Review,* September 16, 2018, 26(L). https://www.nytimes.com/2018/09/14/books /review/il-sung-na-dreamer-morales-raul-colon-imagine-herrera-castillo.html.

Zuffa, Rachel. Review of *Jabberwalking,* by Juan Felipe Herrera. *School Library Journal* 64, no. 4 (2018): 155. Posted online: April 5, 2018. https://www.slj.com/?detail Story=jabberwalking-juan-felipe-herrera-slj-review.

Zvirin, Stephanie. Review of *Cinnamon Girl: Letters Found inside a Cereal Box,* by Juan Felipe Herrera. *Booklist* 102, no. 21 (July 2006): 50.

# Juan Felipe Herrera's National Projects During His Two Terms as Poet Laureate of The United States

Byrne, Maura, Anne Holmes, and Peter Armenti. "About Juan Felipe Herrera at the Library of Congress." Juan Felipe Herrera, U.S. Poet Laureate: A Resource Guide, *LOC Research Guides,* 2020. https://guides.loc.gov/poet-laureate-juan-felipe -herrera/activities-at-the-library#s-lib-ctab-23011177-0.

# 1st Year Projects: 2015-2016
## Project 1: *La Casa de Colores*

Herrera, Juan Felipe. "La Casa de Colores: Poet Laureate Project." Poetry & Literature Program, Library of Congress, 2015. https://www.loc.gov/programs/poetry-and -literature/poet-laureate/poet-laureate-projects/la-casa-de-colores/.

### PART 1: *LA FAMILIA*

Herrera, Juan Felipe. "La Familia: 'Family Words and Story Poems.'" Part 1, La Casa de Colores Project, Poetry & Literature Program, Library of Congress, September 15–October 14, 2015. https://www.loc.gov/programs/poetry-and-literature /poet-laureate/poet-laureate-projects/la-casa-de-colores/.

Herrera, Juan Felipe. "La Familia: 'Migrants: Portraits and Friendships.'" Part 2, La Casa de Colores Project, Poetry & Literature Program, Library of Congress, October 15–November 14 2015. https://www.loc.gov/programs/poetry-and-literature/poet-laureate/poet-laureate-projects/la-casa-de-colores/la-familia/item/poetry-00000187/migrants-portraits-and-friendships/.

Herrera, Juan Felipe. "La Familia: 'Language Weavers.'" Part 3, La Casa de Colores Project, Poetry & Literature Program, Library of Congress, November15–December 14, 2015. https://www.loc.gov/programs/poetry-and-literature/poet-laureate/poet-laureate-projects/la-casa-de-colores/la-familia/item/poetry-00000190/language-weavers/.

Herrera, Juan Felipe. "La Familia: 'Let Me Tell You What Peace Can Bring.'" Part 4, La Casa de Colores Project, Poetry & Literature Program, Library of Congress, December 15, 2015–January 14, 2016. https://www.loc.gov/programs/poetry-and-literature/poet-laureate/poet-laureate-projects/la-casa-de-colores/la-familia/item/poetry-00000192/let-me-tell-you-what-peace-can-bring/.

Herrera, Juan Felipe. "La Familia: 'Thank-You Poems to Our Vets.'" Part 5, La Casa de Colores Project, Poetry & Literature Program, Library of Congress, January 15–February 14, 2016. https://www.loc.gov/programs/poetry-and-literature/poet-laureate/poet-laureate-projects/la-casa-de-colores/la-familia/item/poetry-00000194/thank-you-poems-to-our-vets/.

Herrera, Juan Felipe. "La Familia: 'My Democracy.'" Part 6, La Casa de Colores Project, Poetry & Literature Program, Library of Congress, February 15–March 14, 2016. https://www.loc.gov/programs/poetry-and-literature/poet-laureate/poet-laureate-projects/la-casa-de-colores/la-familia/item/poetry-00000196/my-democracy/.

Herrera, Juan Felipe. "La Familia: 'World Unity Tortillas.'" Part 7, La Casa de Colores Project, Poetry & Literature Program, Library of Congress, March 15–April 14, 2016. https://www.loc.gov/programs/poetry-and-literature/poet-laureate/poet-laureate-projects/la-casa-de-colores/la-familia/item/poetry-00000198/world-unity-tortillas/.

PART 2: *EL JARDÍN* (THE GARDEN)

Herrera, Juan Felipe. "El Jardín (The Garden)." La Casa de Colores Project, Poetry & Literature Program, Library of Congress, 2015–2016. https://www.loc.gov/programs/poetry-and-literature/poet-laureate/poet-laureate-projects/la-casa-de-colores/el-jardin/.

Herrera, Juan Felipe, and Cathy Kerst. "El Jardín: Poet Laureate Juan Felipe Herrera Discusses the WPA California Folk Music Project Collection." La Casa de Colores Project, Poetry & Literature Program, Library of Congress, September 9, 2015. Video. https://www.loc.gov/item/webcast-6845/.

Herrera, Juan Felipe, and Catalina Gómez. "El Jardín: Poet Laureate Juan Felipe Herrera on the Huexotzinco Codex." La Casa de Colores Project, Poetry & Literature

Program, Library of Congress, September 8, 2015. Video. https://www.loc.gov/item/webcast-7139/.

Herrera, Juan Felipe, and Georgette Dorn. "El Jardín: Poet Laureate Juan Felipe Herrera on Rare Cuban Treasures from the Ediciones Vigía Collection." La Casa de Colores Project, Poetry & Literature Program, Library of Congress, January 21, 2016. Video. https://www.loc.gov/item/webcast-7266/.

Herrera, Juan Felipe, and Juan Manuel Pérez. "El Jardín: Poet Laureate Juan Felipe Herrera on the Don Quixote & Pablo Neruda Collections." La Casa de Colores Project, Poetry & Literature Program, Library of Congress, January 21, 2016. Video. https://www.loc.gov/item/poetry-00000282/don-quixote-pablo-neruda-collections/.

Herrera, Juan Felipe, and Juan Manuel Pérez. "El Jardín: Poet Laureate Juan Felipe Herrera on the Don Quixote." La Casa de Colores Project, Poetry & Literature Program, Library of Congress, January 21, 2016. Video. https://www.loc.gov/item/webcast-7243/.

Herrera, Juan Felipe, and Katherine Blood. "El Jardín: The Mission Gráfica / La Raza, San Quentin Arts, and Elizabeth Catlett Collections." La Casa de Colores Project, Poetry & Literature Program, Library of Congress, September 11, 2015. Video. https://www.loc.gov/item/webcast-7315/.

Herrera, Juan Felipe, and Katherine Blood. "El Jardín: Lincoln Campaign Poster & Prayer Rug for America." La Casa de Colores Project, Poetry & Literature Program, Library of Congress, September 11, 2015. Video. https://www.loc.gov/item/webcast-7044/.

Herrera, Juan Felipe, and Katherine Blood. "El Jardín: Asamblea de Artistas Revolucionarios de Oaxaca: Juan Felipe Herrera's 'Automatika' Series." La Casa de Colores Project, Poetry & Literature Program, Library of Congress, September 11, 2016. Video. https://www.loc.gov/item/webcast-7388/.

Herrera, Juan Felipe, and Margaret Kruesi. "El Jardín: Poet Laureate Juan Felipe Herrera Discusses Literatura de Cordel." La Casa de Colores Project, Poetry & Literature Program, Library of Congress, September 9, 2015. Video. https://www.loc.gov/item/webcast-6921/.

Herrera, Juan Felipe, and Mark Manivong. "El Jardín: Poet Laureate Juan Felipe Herrera Discusses Sylvester & Orphanos Publishers Archives." La Casa de Colores Project, Poetry & Literature Program, Library of Congress, January 20, 2016. Video. https://www.loc.gov/item/webcast-7172/.

Herrera, Juan Felipe, and Nathan Dorn. "El Jardín: Poet Laureate Juan Felipe Herrera on the Hispanic Law Collection." La Casa de Colores Project, Poetry & Literature Program, Library of Congress, January 19, 2016. Video. https://www.loc.gov/item/webcast-7222/.

Herrera, Juan Felipe, and Todd Harvey. "El Jardín: Juan Felipe Herrera Discusses Alan Lomax & Woody Guthrie, Folk Song Pioneer." La Casa de Colores Project, Poetry & Literature Program, Library of Congress, September 9, 2015. Video. https://www.loc.gov/item/webcast-6957/.

## 2nd Year Projects: 2016-2017

Library of Congress. "U.S. Poet Laureate Juan Felipe Herrera Launches His Second-Term Projects." News from the Library of Congress, Library of Congress, October 6, 2016. https://www.loc.gov/item/prn-16-179/u-s-poet-laureate-juan-felipe -herrera-launches-his-second-term-projects/2016-10-06/.

### Project 1: *The Technicolor Adventures of Catalina Neon*

Herrera, Juan Felipe. "The Technicolor Adventures of Catalina Neon." With illustrations by Juana Medina. Read.gov, The Library of Congress, 2016–2017. http:// www.read.gov/catalinaneon/index.html.

Herrera, Juan Felipe. "[Chapter 1:] Meet Catalina Neon and Her Doggy, Tortilla" With illustrations by Juana Medina. Read.gov, The Library of Congress, 2016– 2017, 4–9. http://www.read.gov/catalinaneon/Book/#page/4/mode/2up. [Text] http://stream.media.loc.gov/poetry/catalinaneon/Catalina_Neon_Chapter1.mp3. [Audio]

Herrera, Juan Felipe. "[Chapter 2:] Galactic Poetry Cosmic Library." With illustrations by Juana Medina. Read.gov, The Library of Congress, 2016–2017, 10–17. http:// www.read.gov/catalinaneon/Book/#page/10/mode/2up. [Text] http://stream .media.loc.gov/poetry/catalinaneon/Catalina_Neon_Chapter2.mp3. [Audio]

Herrera, Juan Felipe. "[Chapter 3:] Enter the Neon." With illustrations by Juana Medina. Read.gov, The Library of Congress, 2016–2017, 18–25. http://www.read .gov/catalinaneon/Book/#page/19/mode/1up. [Text] http://stream.media.loc.gov /poetry/catalinaneon/Catalina_Neon_Chapter3.mp3. [Audio]

Herrera, Juan Felipe. "[Chapter 4:] Behind the Door: Detrás de la Puerta." With illustrations by Juana Medina. Read.gov, The Library of Congress, 2016–2017, 26–33. http://www.read.gov/catalinaneon/Book/#page/18/mode/1up. [Text] http://stream .media.loc.gov/poetry/catalinaneon/Catalina_Neon_Chapter4.mp3. [Audio]

Herrera, Juan Felipe. "[Chapter 5:] We're Real Cool." With illustrations by Juana Medina. Read.gov, The Library of Congress, 2016–2017, 34–41. http://www.read .gov/catalinaneon/Book/#page/34/mode/1up. [Text] http://stream.media.loc.gov /poetry/catalinaneon/Catalina_Neon_Chapter5.mp3. [Audio]

Herrera, Juan Felipe. "[Epilogue:] Ride Out from Poetry Planeta." With illustrations by Juana Medina. Read.gov, The Library of Congress, 2016–2017, 42–47. http:// www.read.gov/catalinaneon/Book/#page/42/mode/1up. [Text] http://stream .media.loc.gov/poetry/catalinaneon/Catalina_Neon_Chapter6.mp3. [Audio]

### Project 2: *Wordstreet Champions and Brave Builders of the Dream*

Caine, Paul. "Poet Laureate on the Power of Poetry and Working with CPS." Chicago Tonight, Arts & Entertainment, WTTW, video, May 2, 2017. https://news.wttw .com/2017/05/02/poet-laureate-power-poetry-and-working-cps.

Casper, Rob. "Wordstreet Champions and Brave Builders of the Dream." *From the Catbird Seat: Poetry and Literature Blog,* The Library of Congress, February 27, 2017. https://blogs.loc.gov/catbird/2017/02/wordstreet-champions-and-brave -builders-of-the-dream/.

Poetry Foundation. "United States Poet Laureate Works on Yearlong Project with Chicago Public Schools: Juan Felipe Herrera Works with CPS Teachers to Reimagine How Poetry Is Taught." Press Release, November 9, 2016. https://www.poetry foundation.org/foundation/press/91329/united-states-poet-laureate-works-on -yearlong-project-with-chicago-public-schools-.

Juan Felpe Herrera. "Wordstreet Champions and Brave Builders of the Dream." *The Library of Congress, Poetry and Literature,* n.d. http://maint.loc.gov/poetry/word street/.

White, Jenn. "U.S. Poet Laureate Juan Felipe Herrera Wraps Up Project with Chicago Students." Morning Shift, WBEZ91.5 Chicago, April 28, 2017. [Audio Interview] https://www.wbez.org/stories/us-poet-laureate-juan-felipe-herrera-wraps-up -project-with-chicago-students/cc6db18f-84db-4882-ad17-d40b407cdbcf.

### Project 3: The Creation of a West Coast Office: *The Laureate Lab Visual Wordist Studio.*

Kohlruss, Craig. "Juan Felipe Herrera Takes You on a Tour of Fresno State's Laureate Lab." Theatre & Arts, Entertainment, *The Fresno Bee,* February 6, 2018. https:// www.fresnobee.com/entertainment/performing-arts/article145722344.html.

Uribes, Tom. "Laureate Lab: Spaces for Creativity: 4 Poet Laureates at Open House." Laureate Labs, *Fresno State News,* May 8, 2017. http://www.fresnostatenews.com /2017/05/08/laureate-lab-spaces-for-creativity-4-poet-laureates-at-open-house/.

## Juan Felipe Herrera's Projects During His Two-Year Term as Poet Laureate of California

### Project 1: The Most Incredible & Biggest Poem on Unity in The World

Bose, Lilledeshan. "Juan Felipe Herrera Launches 'The Most Incredible and Biggest and Most Amazing Poem on Unity in the World: California Poet Laureate Juan Felipe Herrera Kicks off 2-year Collaborative Project; Calls It a 'Rolling Wave of Poetry.'" Arts & Culture, *UCR Today,* Arts & Culture, June 27, 2012. https://ucr today.ucr.edu/7462.

Bose, Lilledeshan. "A Traveling Poetry Handshake: California Poet Laureate Juan Felipe Herrera Looks Back at Five of the Best Moments of His Tenure." *UCR: The Magazine of UC Riverside,* Spring 2014. https://magazinearchive.ucr.edu/998.

Fitzwater, Caitlin. "California Poet Laureate Juan Felipe Herrera Calls for Participation in the Unity Project." News, The California Arts Council, n.d. https://arts.ca .gov/press_release/california-poet-laureate-juan-felipe-herrera-calls-for-partici pation-in-the-unity-project/.

Herrera, Juan Felipe, Project Director, et al. "The Most Incredible & Biggest Poem on Unity in the World: A California Poet Laureate Project." N.p. [PDF] https://gluckprogram.ucr.edu/sites/g/files/rcwecm731/files/2018-08/CW11_UnityPoem JFHerrera.pdf.

Miller, Bettye. "Unity Poem Project Submissions Deadline is July 1: California Poet Laureate Juan Felipe Herrera Will Present 'The Most Incredible & Biggest Poem on Unity in the World' at California Unity Poem Fiesta Oct. 9." Arts & Culture, *UCR Today*, April 15, 2014. https://ucrtoday.ucr.edu/21642.

Shukis, Shane. "Poetry Then, Poetry Now: A Poet Laureate and His Legacy." Arts & Culture, *UCR Today*, March 24, 2015. https://ucrtoday.ucr.edu/27950.

## Project 2: "I Promise Joanna/Yo Te Prometo Joanna"— Anti-Bullying State-Wide Campaign for 5th Graders

Herrera, Juan Felipe. "CA Poet Laureate Juan Felipe Herrera's Anti-Bullying Poetry Project." *California Humanities* (blog), May 9, 2013. https://calhum.org/ca-poet -laureate-juan-felipe-herreras-anti-bullying-poetry-project/.

Miller, Bettye. "California Poet Laureate Launches Bullying-Awareness Project: UC Riverside's Juan Felipe Herrera and Gluck Fellows Program of The Arts Use Poetry to Empower Children." Poetry, Arts & Culture, *UCR Today*, May 20, 2013. https://ucrtoday.ucr.edu/14998.

*Harriet.* "i-Promise Joanna: California Poet Laureate Launches Anti-Bullying Effort." Poetry News, Poetry Foundation, June 6, 2013. https://www.poetryfoundation .org/harriet/2013/06/i-promise-joanna-california-poet-laureate-launches-anti -bullying-effort.

*Long Beach Press Telegram.* "State Poet Laureate Juan Felipe Herrera Fights Bullying." News, May 21, 2013; updated September 1, 2017. https://www.presstelegram.com /2013/05/21/state-poet-laureate-juan-felipe-herrera-fights-bullying/.

*Social Work Today.* "California Poet Laureate Launches Bullying-Awareness Project." News, June 3, 2013. https://www.socialworktoday.com/news/dn_060313.shtml.

## Project 3: Creating Poetry in Solidarity: Poems for Newton, Conn., after the mass shooting at Sandy Hook Elementary School; poems for Boston after the bombing at the Boston Marathon; Hawak Kamay: poems to the Philippines after a super-typhoon decimated the island of Leyte

Herrera, Juan Felipe, and Marisa Urrutia Gedney, eds. "The Most Incredible and Biggest Poem on Unity in the World." *La Bloga: The World's Longest-Established Chicana Chicano, Latina Latino Literary Blog*, December 23, 2012. https://labloga .blogspot.com/2012/12/the-most-incredible-and-biggest-poem-on.html.

Highlander Staff. "Helping Hands for Haiyan." Features, *The Highlander: University of California, Riverside*, November 26, 2013. https://www.highlandernews.org /11438/helping-hands-for-haiyan/.

Lovekin, Kris. "Holding Hands with the Storm Tossed of the Philippines: A New Poetry Project from UC Riverside Professor Juan Felipe Herrera Aims to Provide Comfort for Storm Victims and Their Far-Flung Relatives." Inside UCR, Arts & Culture, *UCR Today*, November 14, 2013. https://ucrtoday.ucr.edu/19136.

Mayorga, Dean. "California Poet Laureate Starts Unity Poem for Newtown Victims." *The Highlander*, University of California, Riverside, January 8, 2013. https://www.highlandernews.org/6285/california-poet-laureate-starts-unity-poem-for-newtown-victims/.

Miller, Bettye. "California Poet Laureate Launches Poem for Newtown, CT: Unity Poetry Wall Project by UC Riverside's Juan Felipe Herrera Invites Americans to Express Their Thoughts about the Dec. 14 Mass Shooting." Inside UCR, *UCR Today*, December 17, 2012. https://ucrtoday.ucr.edu/10847.

Miller, Bettye. "Poems for Boston: California Poet Laureate and UC Riverside Poetry Students Offer Verses of Condolence and Hope in Wake of Boston Marathon Bombing." Poetry, Arts & Culture, Inside UCR, *UCR Today*, April 18, 2013. https://ucrtoday.ucr.edu/13814.

Miller, Bettye. "Remembering Lives Lost." News, *University of California*, April 15, 2014. https://www.universityofcalifornia.edu/news/remembering-lives-lost.

Muckenfuss, Mark. "UCR: Poet Laureate's Class Sends Verses to Boston." Local News, *The Press-Enterprise*, April 17, 2013. https://www.pe.com/2013/04/17/ucr-poet-laureate8217s-class-sends-verses-to-boston/.

Sipin, Melissa R. "Books: Typhoon Yolanda and The Art of Call-And-Response." *Hyphen: Asian America Unabridged* (blog), June 26, 2014. https://hyphenmagazine.com/blog/2014/6/26/books-typhoon-yolanda-and-art-call-and-response.

## Project 4: "Stars of Juárez: Cuca & Eva": A Documentary Musical

Chacón, Daniel. "Words on a Wire. Juan Felipe Herrera." *Words on a Wire*, KTEP-El Paso, Texas, October 14, 2012. [Audio Interview] https://www.ktep.org/post/words-wire-juan-felipe-herrera.

Lau, David. "We Must Act But How? A Conversation with Juan Felipe Herrera (Part 1 of 3)." Featured Blogger, *Harriet*, Poetry Foundation, April 30, 2014. https://www.poetryfoundation.org/harriet/2014/04/we-must-act-but-how-a-conversation-with-juan-felipe-herrera-part-1-of-3.

Shukis, Shane. "New Performance-Poem by Juan Felipe Herrera Reimagines the Juárez Border Arts Renaissance of the 1930s." *UCR Today*, October 19, 2012. https://ucrtoday.ucr.edu/9641.

# Additional Online Resources

Akpan, Uwem, Juan Felipe Herrera, and Lily Hoang. "Readings, Crossing Over: The 2009 Beyond Margins Celebration." Crossing Over: The 2009 Beyond Margins Celebration, PEN America, video, October 26, 2012. https://pen.org/multimedia/crossing-over-the-2009-beyond-margins-celebration-3/.

Alvarado, Lisa. "Juan Felipe Herrera Continues to Amaze." *La Bloga: The World's Longest-Established Chicana Chicano, Latina Latino Literary Blog*, June 19, 2008. https://labloga.blogspot.com/2008/06/juan-felipe-herrera-continues-to-amaze.html.

Alvarado, Lisa. "Juan Felipe Hererra—Más y Más." *La Bloga: The World's Longest-Established Chicana Chicano, Latina Latino Literary Blog*, 20 November 2008. https://labloga.blogspot.com/2008/11/juan-felipe-hererra-ms-y-ms.html.

Alvarado, Lisa. "Spoken Word, Borders and Juan Felipe Herrera." *La Bloga: The World's Longest-Established Chicana Chicano, Latina Latino Literary Blog*, November 29, 2007. https://labloga.blogspot.com/2007/11/187-reasons-mexicanos-cant-cross-border.html.

Arellano, Gustavo, Angie Cruz, Carolina Ebeid, Rigoberto González, Juan Felipe Herrera, David Tomás Martínez, and Carmen Giménez Smith. "The Cinnamon Tsunami Is Here: A Latin@ Writers' Roundtable." *Gulf Coast: A Journal of Literature and Fine Arts* 25, no. 2 (Summer/Fall 2013): 120–138. http://gulfcoastmag.org/journal/25.2/the-cinnamon-tsunami-is-here/.

Argueta, Jorge. "Poet, Writer Recognizes Friend as New U.S. Poet Laureate." Commentary, *El Tecolote*, June 22, 2015. https://eltecolote.org/content/en/poet-writer-recognizes-friend-as-new-u-s-poet-laureate/.

The Aspen Institute. "Aspen Words Presents Juan Felipe Herrera at Winter Words 2016." *Winter Words Author Series*, video, 2016; uploaded to YouTube January 25, 2016. https://www.youtube.com/watch?v=xABtoYDOZaA&feature=emb_title.

Ayuso, Silvia. "'Un medio mexicano': El nuevo poeta de Estados Unidos; La Biblioteca del Congreso elige al hispano Juan Felipe Herrera como nuevo poeta laureado del país." Cultura, *El País América*, June 11, 2015. https://elpais.com/cultura/2015/06/10/actualidad/1433954525_757612.html.

Biala, Arlene, Diana García, and Juan Felipe Herrera. "Poetry Reading Celebrating 'One Life: Dolores Huerta.'" Poetry & Literature Center, Library of Congress, video, March 8, 2016. https://www.loc.gov/item/webcast-7372/.

Bancroft, Colette. "Hear the Voice of U.S. Poet Laureate Juan Felipe Herrera in St. Petersburg on Monday." Books, *Tampa Bay Times*, March 17, 2016. https://www.tampabay.com/features/books/hear-the-voice-of-us-poet-laureate-juan-felipe-herrera-in-st-petersburg-on/2269743/.

Barba, Wendy. "New U.S. Poet Laureate Juan Felipe Herrera, the Chicano's Literary Rock Star." MitúVoice, Things That Matter, *Mitú*, June 11, 2015. https://wearemitu.com/mitu-voice/fun-facts-poet-laureate-juan-felipe-herrera/.

Blakley, Matt. "@ the Crossroads-A Sudden American Poem by 21st Poet Laureate Juan Felipe Herrera." *From the Catbird Seat: Poetry & Literature at the Library of Congress Blog*, July 11, 2016. https://blogs.loc.gov/catbird/2016/07/the-crossroads-a-sudden-american-poem-by-21st-poet-laureate-juan-felipe-herrera/.

Bose, Lilledeshan. "A Traveling Poetry Handshake: California Poet Laureate Juan Felipe Herrera Looks Back at Five of the Best Moments of His Tenure." *UCR: The Magazine of UC Riverside* 9, no. 2 (Spring 2014): n.p. https://magazinearchive.ucr.edu/998.

Boston Review Editors. "Boston Review's Top 20 Poems of 2015 [Five Poems by Juan Felipe Herrera]." Arts in Society, *Boston Review: A Political and Literary Forum,* December 16, 2015. http://bostonreview.net/blog/top-poems-2015.

Bridges, Analese. "Poet Laureate Juan Felipe Herrera Brings an Activist Voice to Poetry." Arts, *Duke Today,* November 18, 2016. https://today.duke.edu/2016/11/poet-laureate-juan-felipe-herrera-brings-activist-voice-poetry.

Brown, Jeffrey. "How One Poet Is Helping Chicago Students Find Their Voice through Verse." *PBS NewsHour,* PBS.org, video, May 30, 2017. https://www.pbs.org/news hour/show/one-poet-helping-chicago-students-find-voice-verse.

Brooks, Katherine. "Our Poet Laureate Is Trying to Find America's Voice in a Crowd-sourced Poem." Cuture & Arts, *Huff Post,* March 30, 2016. https://www.huffpost .com/entry/juan-felipe-herrera-poem_n_56f97a99e4b014d3fe23af02.

Caraza, Xánath. "Juan Felipe Herrera in Kansas City, MO [Photos]." *La Bloga: The World's Longest-Established Chicana Chicano, Latina Latino Literary Blog,* May 30, 2016. https://labloga.blogspot.com/2016/05/juan-felipe-herrera-in-kansas-city -mo.html.

Casper, Rob. "Catching Up on the Laureate." *From the Catbird Seat: Poetry and Literature Blog at the Library of Congress,* September 30, 2015. https://blogs.loc.gov /catbird/2015/09/catching-up-on-the-laureate/.

Casper, Rob. "Meet Our New Poet Laureate—Online." *From the Catbird Seat: Poetry and Literature Blog at the Library of Congress,* June 12, 2015. https://blogs.loc.gov /catbird/2015/06/meet-our-new-poet-laureate-online/.

Casper, Rob. "The Poet Laureate Joins an AFC Workshop on Corridos." *From the Catbird Seat: Poetry & Literature at the Library of Congress Blog,* October 28, 2015. https://blogs.loc.gov/catbird/2015/10/the-poet-laureate-joins-an-afc-work shop-on-corridos/.

Casper, Rob. "The Poet Laureate Meets the Librarian of Congress." *From the Catbird Seat: Poetry & Literature at the Library of Congress Blog,* December 14, 2016. https://blogs.loc.gov/catbird/2016/12/the-poet-laureate-meets-the-librarian-of -congress/.

Charles, Ron. "Juan Felipe Herrera Becomes First Mexican American U.S. Poet Laureate." *The Washington Post,* June 10, 2015. https://www.washingtonpost.com /entertainment/books/juan-felipe-herrera-becomes-first-hispanic-american -us-poet-laureate/2015/06/09/12de51b8-0eb0-11e5-adec-e82f8395c032_story .html.

Children's Museum of Atlanta. "*Imagine* by Juan Felipe Herrera." Tiny Club: *Imagine,* video, October 5, 2020. https://childrensmuseumatlanta.org/blog/tiny-club -imagine/, https://www.youtube.com/watch?v=6LN-6axuRv4.

City Lights Booksellers & Publishers. "*Everyday We Get More Illegal*: Juan Felipe Herrera with Jericho Brown." LitQuake: San Francisco's Literary Festival, video, October 11, 2020. https://www.youtube.com/watch?v=hK-Om4bO9mk&feature=youtu.be.

City of Riverside, "Artist's Corner—Juan Felipe Herrera: 2012–2014 California Poet Laureate; His Journey in the Art of Poetry," YouTube video, uploaded July 13, 2012. https://www.youtube.com/watch?v=qYHcCvotXMs.

Colin, Chris. "The Poet in Chief Tries to Capture the National Mood in an Epic, Crowdsourced Poem." *The California Sunday Magazine*, February 4, 2016. https://story.californiasunday.com/poet-laureate-juan-felipe-herrera.

Contreras, Félix. "Guest DJ: California Poet Laureate Juan Felipe Herrera." *Alt Latino*, NPR.org, April 18, 2013. https://www.npr.org/sections/altlatino/2013/04/18/177629103/guest-dj-with-california-poet-laureate-juan-felipe-herrera.

Cornish, Audie. "New U.S. Poet Laureate Hopes to Invite All Communities to Express Themselves." *All Things Considered*, NPR, audio, June 10, 2015. https://www.npr.org/2015/06/10/413455586/new-u-s-poet-laureate-hopes-to-invite-all-communities-to-express-themselves.

Copley, Rich. "Former U.S. Poet Laureate Opens Conference by Turning the Immigrant Story Around." *The Presbyterian Outlook*, February 8, 2019. https://pres-outlook.org/2019/02/former-u-s-poet-laureate-opens-conference-by-turning-the-immigrant-story-around/.

Crapo, Trish. "'Imagine, Even the Ghosts Were Trying to Get Away'; U.S. Poet Laureate Juan Felipe Herrera Reads at Smith College." *Greenfield Recorder*, December 16, 2015. https://www.recorder.com/Archives/2015/12/Books-Crapo-Poets-Herrera-GR-120515.

Daly, Meg. "The People's Poet: U.S. Poet Laureate Juan Felipe Herrera Crosses Borders and Generations." *Planet Jackson Hole*, April 18, 2017. https://archive.planetjh.com/2017/04/18/feature-the-peoples-poet/.

Dean, Michelle. "U.S. Poet Laureate Juan Felipe Herrera: 'Poetry is One of the Most Beautiful Ways of Participating.'" Poetry, *The Guardian*, Jun 16, 2015. https://www.theguardian.com/books/2015/jun/16/juan-felipe-herrera-poetry-is-one-of-the-most-beautiful-ways-of-participating.

De León. Kevin. "Senator de León Congratulates Juan Felipe Herrera, Nation's First Latino Poet Laureate." California State Senate, July 6, 2015. Video. https://www.youtube.com/watch?v=Cdhk8-jkFCQ.

Delgado, Martha. "Juan Felipe Herrera Writes Poem about the UCLA Shooting." *The Highlander*, UC Riverside, June 20, 2016. https://www.highlandernews.org/24819/juan-felipe-herrera-writes-poem-ucla-shooting/.

Dwyer, Colin. "Juan Felipe Herrera Named U.S. Poet Laureate." *The Two-Way*, NPR.org, audio, June 10, 2015. https://www.npr.org/sections/thetwo-way/2015/06/10/412909814/juan-felipe-herrera-named-u-s-poet-laureate.

*Excélsior California*. "Juan Felipe Herrera, primer hispano en ser nombrado Poeta Laureado California." Especiales, March 29, 2012, updated October 10, 2017. https://www.excelsiorcalifornia.com/2012/03/29/juan-felipe-herrera-primer-hispano-en-ser-nombrado-poeta-laureado-california/.

Escamilla, Rachelle. "Legacy of Poetry Day 2016 with Juan Felipe Herrera." *Out of Our Minds Poetry Radio Show*, KKUP Cupertino, SoundCloud audio, May 5, 2016. https://soundcloud.com/rachelle-escamilla/legacy-of-poetry-day-2016-on-kkup.

Espinoza, Alex. "Juan Felipe Herrera, U.S. Poet Laureate, on Eating Too Many Chilaquiles and Returning to L.A." *Los Angeles Times*, March 31, 2016. https://www.latimes.com/books/jacketcopy/la-ca-jc-juan-felipe-herrera-20160403-story.html.

Florido, Adrián. "Juan Felipe Herrera on Poetry in Tough Times." *NPR.org*, Books, 12 April 2017. https://www.npr.org/2017/04/12/523466543/juan-felipe-herrera -on-poetry-in-tough-times.

Florido, Adrián, and Juan Felipe Herrera. "Francisco Alarcón, Whose Poetry Explored Chicano Life in the U.S., Dies." *All Things Considered*, NPR, audio, January 20, 2016. https://www.wbez.org/stories/francisco-alarcon-whose-poetry -explored-chicano-life-in-the-us-dies/1c8d753f-4752-4ead-904b-3576ad638541.

Fresno Poets' Association. "Fresno Poets Archive 08: Juan Felipe Herrera and Margarita Luna Robles: An Evening of Multimedia Performance Poetry." Video, November 1, 1990, uploaded to YouTube October 10 2017. https://www.youtube.com /watch?v=xEoFDoK3R9A.

García, Marcela. "New U.S. Poet Laureate Juan Felipe Herrera an Affirmation of Latino Identity." *Boston Globe*, June 11, 2015. https://www.bostonglobe.com /opinion/2015/06/11/new-poet-laureate-juan-felipe-herrera-affirmation-latino -identity/r5PWFOaI2DwZu9U2T5UpcM/story.html.

García, Mario T. "Poet's Honor Spotlights Latinos." *National Catholic Reporter* 51, no. 19 (July 3, 2015): 31. Posted online as "Powerful Latino Poet Chosen as U.S. Poet Laureate," June, 17, 2015. https://www.ncronline.org/blogs/ncr-today /powerful-latino-poet-chosen-us-poet-laureate.

Garner, Dwight. "Juan Felipe Herrera, Poet Laureate with a Working-Class Voice Meant to Be Spoken." Critic's Notebook, *The New York Times*, June 10, 2015. https://www.nytimes.com/2015/06/10/books/juan-felipe-herrera-poet-laureate -with-a-working-class-voice-meant-to-be-spoken.html.

González, Martha, Juan Felipe Herrera, Hugo Morales, Louie Pérez, Rafael Pérez-Torres, and Quetzal. "Speak the People / the Spark / el Poema: Celebrating Juan Felipe Herrera," *Library of Congress*, video, April 26, 2017. https://www.loc.gov /item/webcast-7908/.

Gordon, Larry. "A Totally Californian Poet Laureate." Entertainment & Arts, *The Los Angeles Times*, May 20, 2012. https://www.latimes.com/entertainment/arts/la -xpm-2012-may-20-la-me-poet-laureate-20120521-story.html.

Grech, Aaron. "Juan Felipe Herrera Named U.S. Poet Laureate." *The Highlander*, University of California, Riverside, June 23, 2015. https://www.highlandernews.org /20246/juan-felipe-herrera-named-u-s-poet-laureate/.

Hamilton, Matt. "After San Bernardino Massacre, U.S. Poet Laureate Writes in Hope." *The Los Angeles Times*, California, December 24, 2015. https://www.latimes.com /local/lanow/la-me-ln-poet-laureate-san-bernardino-massacre-20151224-story .html.

*Harriet* staff. "Juan Felipe Herrera Appointed Poet Laureate of California." *Harriet*, Poetry News, Poetry Foundation, March 23, 2012. https://www.poetryfoundation .org/harriet/2012/03/juan-felipe-herrera-appointed-poet-laureate-of-california.

*Harriet* staff. "Juan Felipe Herrera Named U.S. Poet Laureate." *Harriet*, Poetry Foundation, June 10, 2015. https://www.poetryfoundation.org/harriet/2015/06/juan -felipe-herrera-named-us-poet-laureate-.

Harriet staff. "Juan Felipe Herrera Profiled at University of Notre Dame Website." *Harriet*, Poetry Foundation, October 4, 2016. https://www.poetryfoundation.org/harriet/2016/10/juan-felipe-herrera-profiled-at-university-of-notre-dame-website.

Harriet staff. "Juan Felipe Herrera Reviews *The Day of Shelly's Death: The Poetry and Ethnography of Grief*, Renato Rosaldo's First Collection of *Antropoesía*." *Harriet*, Poetry Foundation, March 17, 2014. https://www.poetryfoundation.org/harriet/2014/03/juan-felipe-herrera-reviews-the-day-of-shellys-death-the-poetry-and-ethnography-of-grief-renato-rosaldos-first-collection-of-antropoesia-.

Haven, Cynthia. "Lightning-Bolt Laureate: For Juan Felipe Herrera, Poetry Is Action. In Full Color." *Stanford Magazine*, September/October 2016. https://stanfordmag.org/contents/lightning-bolt-laureate.

Heim, Joe. "Juan Felipe Herrera, U.S. Poet Laureate." *The Washington Post*, March 5, 2017, n.p.

Herrera, Juan Felipe. "3 Words That Can Make Someone's Day." *The Oprah Winfrey Network Show*, video, September 30, 2015. https://www.youtube.com/watch?v=yzr9IKZnUAA.

Herrera, Juan Felipe. "21st Poet Laureate Inaugural Reading." Library of Congress, video, September 15, 2015. www.loc.gov/item/webcast-6840.

Herrera, Juan Felipe. "The Art of Revision." Poets. org, Academy of American Poets, 2014, uploaded to YouTube, June 8, 2015. https://www.youtube.com/watch?v=Loa0s-2DlFw.

Herrera, Juan Felipe. "Be a Friend to Yourself." *The Oprah Winfrey Network Show*, video, January 27, 2016. https://www.youtube.com/watch?v=zB67pxWS9KY&t=14s.

Herrera, Juan Felipe. "Bilingual Children's Books / Young Minds Dreaming. (Readings from *Calling the Doves* and *The Upside Down Boy*)." Ask an Author Series, *KnowItAll*, South Carolina State Library, video, 2019. https://www.knowitall.org/video/juan-felipe-herrera-bilingual-childrens-books-young-minds-dreaming.

Herrera, Juan Felipe. "California's Poet Laureate Juan Felipe Herrera [Presents Recent Works]." ANR Statewide Conference, UCTV, Ontario, Calif., April 9, 2013, uploaded to YouTube November 18, 2013. https://www.uctv.tv/shows/Californias-Poet-Laureate-Juan-Felipe-Herrera-25742.

Herrera, Juan Felipe. "Do Not Let Yourself Think You Cannot Contribute." Literature, Arts & Culture, *Faith and Leadership*, February 21, 2017 https://faithandleadership.com/juan-felipe-herrera-do-not-let-yourself-think-you-cannot-contribute.

Herrera, Juan Felipe. "A Father's Day Tale." UCTV, video, 5 August 2013. https://www.uctv.tv/shows/A-Fathers-Day-Tale-by-Juan-Felipe-Herrera-25525.

Herrera, Juan Felipe. "How to Thrive When You're Feeling Stalled." *#OWNSHOW* (*The Oprah Winfrey Network Show*), video, 22 September 2015. https://www.youtube.com/watch?v=m5bQBnBkTgk.

Herrera, Juan Felipe. "Jabberwalking with Juan Felipe Herrera." *Bay Area Book Festival*, video, 28 April 2018. https://www.baybookfest.org/session/jabberwalking-with-juan-felipe-herrera/.

Herrera, Juan Felipe. "Juan Felipe Herrera Celebrates DIA (El día de los niños / el día de los libros [Day of the Child / Day of the Book]), with His Book *Portraits of Hispanic American Heroes.*" *LOC's Young Readers Center & the Center for the Book*, 27 April 2016, video uploaded to YouTube, 7 July 2017. https://www.youtube.com/watch?v=HkfCPziSW2U.

Herrera, Juan Felipe. "Juan Felipe Herrera: 2013 National Book Festival." *Library of Congress*, Final Readings, video, 22 September 2013. [Poetry & Prose] https://www.loc.gov/item/webcast-6076/.

Herrera, Juan Felipe. "Juan Felipe Herrera: 2015 National Book Festival: A Discussion of *Portraits of Hispanic American Heroes.*" *Library of Congress*, video, 5 September 2015. https://www.loc.gov/item/webcast-6977/.

Herrera, Juan Felipe. "Juan Felipe Herrera: 2017 National Book Festival: A Discussion of Poetry and His Poetic Creativity." *Library of Congress*, video, 2 September 2017. https://www.loc.gov/item/webcast-8052/.

Herrera, Juan Felipe. "Juan Felipe Herrera: 2020 National Book Festival Launches *Every Day We Get More Illegal.*" Poetry & Prose, Library of Congress, video, September 26, 2020. https://www.youtube.com/watch?v=cBSjO5dP76E.

Herrera, Juan Felipe. "Juan Felipe Herrera on the Poet's Civic Duty Today." Poets.org, Academy of American Poets, video, September 13, 2015. https://poets.org/text/video-juan-felipe-herrera-poets-civic-duty-today.

Herrera, Juan Felipe. "Juan Felipe Herrera: Poetry Reading." William H. Hickok Reading Series, *New Letters on the Air*, University of Missouri-Kansas City, audio, 2016. https://www.newletters.org/on_the_air_shows/juan-felipe-herrera/, https://www.newletters.org/on_the_air_shows/juan-felipe-herrera-3/.

Herrera, Juan Felipe. "Juan Felipe Herrera Reads from His Works." *Festival de Flor y Canto de Aztlán*, University of Southern California, Los Angeles, YouTube video, November 1973. https://www.youtube.com/watch?v=cK0ilQrpk50.

Herrera, Juan Felipe. "Juan Felipe Herrera Reads and Discusses Denise Levertov's 'Making Peace.'" Poetry of America, Poetry & Literature, Library of Congress, audio, n.d. https://www.loc.gov/programs/poetry-and-literature/audio-recordings/poetry-of-america/item/poetry-00000277/juan-felipe-herrera-denise-levertov/.

Herrera, Juan Felipe. "Juan Felipe Herrera Sings and Reads from His Poems." *Festival de Flor y Canto*, University of Southern California, September 2010. Uploaded to YouTube June 10, 2015. https://www.youtube.com/watch?v=7aIEC3clkPs.

Herrera, Juan Felipe. "Juan Felipe Herrera: una visión local y global de resistencia pan-étnica." Reading and interview with Manuel de Jesús Hernández, Graciela Rodríguez Silva, and Daniel Vargas, *Festival Internacional de Literatura*, Sonora, November 4, 2021. Video. https://www.facebook.com/watch/?v=1452391685146673, https://www.facebook.com/FestivalInternacionaldeLiteraturaSonora/videos/1452391685146673.

Herrera, Juan Felipe. "Juan Felipe Herrera Poet Laureate Visits New Mexico: Offers Words of Praise To Students and Community Poets." Recorded December 7,

2015, uploaded to YouTube February 9, 2016. https://www.youtube.com/watch?v
=Py8DnlQqd7A.

Herrera, Juan Felipe. "Juan Felipe Herrera Visits Riverside City College: Personal Life Stories and Poetry Reading." *Riverside City College*, video, May 22, 2012. Uploaded to YouTube May 30, 2012. https://www.youtube.com/watch?v=BRl2vWvv8ow.

Herrera, Juan Felipe. "Keynote Address: Inauguration of Timothy P. White." University of California, Riverside, March 17, 2009. Video. https://www.youtube.com /watch?v=GssQoeUkzTU.

Herrera, Juan Felipe. "Literacy Talk: Denzil Mohammed, Immigrant Learning Center [Juan Felipe Herrera Interviews Denzil Mohammed]." Library of Congress, November 11, 2020. Video. https://www.loc.gov/item/webcast-9501/.

Herrera, Juan Felipe. "The Making of an American Poet: California Poet Laureate Juan Felipe Herrera on Inspiration, Revision, and What It Means to Be a Mexican-American Writer." *The Takeaway, Zócalo Public Square*, video, June 18, 2012. Video. https://www.zocalopublicsquare.org/category/events/video-archive/?post Id=33339.

Herrera, Juan Felipe. "The Natural History of Chicano Literature: A Performance Lecture." UCTV, University of California, Riverside, January 31, 2008. Video. https:// www.youtube.com/watch?v=g7ZLhIjURFw&t=396s.

Herrera, Juan Felipe. *Guide to Juan Felipe Herrera Papers*. Online Archive of California (OAC), Processed by Bill O'Hanlon and Malgorzata Schafer, Department of Special Collections and University Archives, Stanford University, 2003, republished 2019. https://oac.cdlib.org/findaid/ark:/13030/kt4g5005kj/.

Herrera, Juan Felipe. "Poet Laureate Juan Felipe Herrera Closes His Term." Library of Congress, April 13, 2016. Video. https://www.loc.gov/item/webcast-7394/.

Herrera, Juan Felipe. "The Powerful Quality You Already Possess." *The Oprah Winfrey Network Show*, October 9, 2015. Video. http://www.oprah.com/own-show/juan -felipe-herrera-the-powerful-quality-you-already-possess#ixzz6esYatSU6.

Herrera, Juan Felipe. "The Real Reason behind Loneliness." *The Oprah Winfrey Network Show*, September 22, 2015. Video. https://www.youtube.com/watch?v=Qlm pkLKN3ws.

Herrera, Juan Felipe. "Today Is a New Day; 2017 Commencement Speech: Santa Clara University." June 19, 2017. Video. https://www.youtube.com/watch?v=ffPDX111 kas&t=417s.

Herrera, Juan Felipe. "What to Do When You're Overwhelmed." *The Oprah Winfrey Network Show*, September 24, 2015. Video. https://www.youtube.com/watch?v= 5OcoIoE3iBg&index=5295&list=ULpA2xbbrn-HU.

Herrera, Juan Felipe. "U.S. Poet Laureate Juan Felipe Herrera on a Year of Gun Violence" *The Takeway*, NY Public Radio, WNYC Studios, audio, June 17, 2016. https://www.wnycstudios.org/podcasts/takeaway/segments/us-poet-laureate -juan-felipe-herrera-reflects-year-mass-shootings.

Herrera, Juan Felipe. "*We Live in a Different Home Now.*" *The Poetry of Home, The Washington Post* & Library of Congress, April 23, 2020. Video. https://www.wash

ingtonpost.com/video/entertainment/the-poetry-of-home/juan-felipe-herrera
-we-live-in-a-different-home-now/2020/04/23/3c3d9e94-9c5a-4842-9d35-648f
8f08292e_video.html?

Herrera, Juan Felipe, et al. "The Smudge and the Scrawl: Inside the Writer's Note-book." *Poets & Writers Magazine* 49, no. 1 (January/February 2021): 30–47. https://www.pw.org/content/januaryfebruary_2021.

Herrera, Juan Felipe, Marisa Urrutia Gedney, and Freddy López. "El Planeta-From Plankton to Afghanistan: A Poetry Reading." *Los Angeles Public Library, ALOUD Podcast*, audio, 20 June 2013. https://www.lapl.org/books-emedia/podcasts/aloud /el-planeta%E2%80%94-plankton-afghanistan-poetry-reading.

Herrera, Juan Felipe, and Tom Lutz. "U.S. Poet Laureate Juan Felipe Herrera: The Further Adventures of Mr. Cilantro Man [A Conversation]." Aloud podcast, *Los Angeles Public Library*, audio, April 20, 2016. https://www.lapl.org/books-emedia /podcasts/aloud/us-poet-laureate-juan-felipe-herrera-further-adventures.

Higgins, Jim. "10 Reasons to See U.S. Poet Laureate Juan Felipe Herrera at UWM." Entertainment, *The Milwaukee Journal Sentinel*, February 6, 2016. https://archive .jsonline.com/entertainment/books/10-reasons-to-see-us-poet-laureate-juan -felipe-herrera-at-uwm-b99673565z1-370289461.html/.

Holmes, Anne. "Chronicling National Poetry Month, Vol. 4: Poet Laureate Juan Fe-lipe Herrera's Closing Events." *From the Catbird Seat: Poetry & Literature at the Library of Congress Blog*, April 24, 2017. https://blogs.loc.gov/catbird/2017/04 /chronicling-national-poetry-month-vol-iv-poet-laureate-juan-felipe-herreras -closing-events/.

Holmes, Anne. "Hooray for Juan Felipe!" *From the Catbird Seat: Poetry & Literature at the Library of Congress Blog*, June 2, 2017. https://blogs.loc.gov/catbird/2017 /06/hooray-for-juan-felipe/.

Holmes, Anne. "New Podcast Episode: Juan Felipe Herrera and the National Book Fes-tival Youth Poetry Slam." *From the Catbird Seat: Poetry and Literature at the Library of Congress Blog*, May 31, 2018. https://blogs.loc.gov/catbird/2018/05/new-podcast -episode-juan-felipe-herrera-and-the-national-book-festival-youth-poetry-slam/.

Holmes, Anne. "Oh What a Night!: 'Speak the People / the Spark / el Poema." *From the Catbird Seat: Poetry & Literature at the Library of Congress Blog*, May 11, 2017. https://blogs.loc.gov/catbird/2017/05/oh-what-a-night-speak-the-people the-sparkel-poema/.

Holmes, Anne. "Poet Laureate Visits Library's Asian Division." *From the Catbird Seat: Poetry & Literature at the Library of Congress Blog*, January 3, 2017. https://blogs .loc.gov/catbird/2017/01/poet-laureate-visits-librarys-asian-division/.

*IBERO.* "Juan Felipe Herrera: Despertar la conciencia a través de la poesía." La llama inextinguible, *México ante la era Trump*, vol. 50 (June 1, 2017): 53–58. http:// revistas.ibero.mx/ibero/articulo_detalle.php?id_volumen=36&id_articulo=637& id_seccion=667&active=1&pagina=53.

Jeremias, Sofia. "Poet Laureate Juan Felipe Herrera Speaks on Immigration." Cath-olic Institute for Lasallian Social Action, Saint Mary's College of California, No-

vember 23, 2015. https://www.stmarys-ca.edu/poet-laureate-juan-felipe-herrera
-speaks-on-immigration.

Kauffman, Gretel. "Meet the New U.S. Poet Laureate: Juan Felipe Herrera." *The Christian Science Monitor*, June 10, 2015. https://www.csmonitor.com/Books/2015 /0610/Meet-the-new-US-poet-laureate-Juan-Felipe-Herrera.

Kellogg, Carolyn. "Juan Felipe Herrera New U.S. Poet Laureate: 'Shout It from The Roof Tops.'" Books, *Los Angeles Times*, June 9, 2015. https://www.latimes.com /books/jacketcopy/la-et-jc-poet-laureate-herrera-20150610-story.html.

Kellogg, Carolyn. "Juan Felipe Herrera's Words of Wisdom: You. Have. A. Beautiful. Voice." Books, *The Los Angeles Times*, April 13, 2016. https://www.latimes.com /books/jacketcopy/la-et-jc-juan-felipe-herrera-la-times-book-prize-20160412 -story.html.

Kellogg, Carolyn. "L.A. Times Book Prizes Will Honor Juan Felipe Herrera, James Patterson; Finalists Announced." Books, *The Los Angeles Times*, February 23, 2016. https://www.latimes.com/books/la-et-jc-la-times-book-prize-finalists-20160222 -story.html.

Kellogg, Carolyn. "U.S. Poet Laureate Juan Felipe Herrera on the Art of Poetry." Books, *Los Angeles Times*, June 10, 2015. https://www.latimes.com/books/jacket copy/la-et-jc-poet-laureate-juan-felipe-herrera-the-art-of-poetry-20150610 -story.html.

Kessler, Stephen. "America's New 'Bard Without Borders.'" Opinion, *Santa Cruz Sentinel*, 19, 2015; Updated: September 11, 2018. https://www.santacruzsentinel.com /2015/06/19/stephen-kessler-americas-new-bard-without-borders/.

Kracmer, Chip. "Author Calls for Border Reforms." *The Badger Herald*, April 11, 2008. https://badgerherald.com/news/2008/04/11/author-calls-for-bor/.

Laínez, René Colato. "Juan Felipe Herrera: His Picture Books and Middle Grade/ Young Adult Books." *La Bloga: The World's Longest-Established Chicana Chicano, Latina Latino Literary Blog*, June 17, 2015. https://labloga.blogspot.com/2015/06 /juan-felipe-herrera-his-picture-books.html.

Lohse, Deborah. "You Are That New Day: U.S. Poet Laureate Delights Santa Clara University Class of 2017 with Poem, 'Today Is a New Day.'" News and Events, Santa Clara University, June 17, 2017. https://www.scu.edu/news-and-events /press-releases/2017/june-2017/you-are-that-new-day.html.

Lund, Elizabeth. "An 'Assemblage' to Hear Juan Felipe Herrera." *The Washington Post*, August 19, 2015, n.p.

Lynch, Rene. "Video: See How Juan Felipe Herrera Won the Crown of Poet Laureate." Books, *The Los Angeles Times*, June 10, 2015. Video. https://www.latimes.com /books/jacketcopy/la-et-jc-poet-laureate-juan-felipe-herrera-reading-poetry -20150610-htmlstory.html.

Mary Baldwin University. "Former Poet Laureate Juan Felipe Herrera Named 2019– 20 Doenges Artist." News, January 17, 2019. https://marybaldwin.edu/news /2019/01/17/former-poet-laureate-juan-felipe-herrera-named-2019-20-doenges -artist/.

Maureen, blog editor. "Monday Muse: New California Poet Laureate." *Writing Without Paper Blog*, March 26, 2012. https://writingwithoutpaper.blogspot.com/2012/03/monday-muse-new-california-poet.html.

McCrae, Fiona, moderator. "Juan Felipe Herrera & Tom Sleigh [Read from and Discuss Their Work]." Library of Congress, April 26, 2017. Video. https://www.loc.gov/item/webcast-7976/.

Mckinney, Cristóbal. "Former US Poet Laureate Reflects on His Writing and the Iowa Writers' Workshop: Juan Felipe Herrera Says the Workshop Was One of Three Main Phases of His Life." *Iowa Now, Writing Arts*, July 3, 2017. https://now.uiowa.edu/2017/07/former-us-poet-laureate-reflects-his-writing-and-iowa-writers-workshop.

Miller, Bettye. "California Poet Laureate Celebrates Bay Bridge: Juan Felipe Herrera Will Read an Original Poem During Chain-Cutting Ceremony On San Francisco-Oakland Bay Bridge." Poetry, Arts and Culture, *UCR Today*, August 28, 2013. https://ucrtoday.ucr.edu/17253.

Miller, Bettye. "Culver Center Hosts California Poet Laureate: Juan Felipe Herrera Will Present His First Public Reading on May 4 of New Work Since His Appointment by Gov. Jerry Brown." Poetry, Arts and Culture, *UCR Today*, April 26, 2012. https://ucrtoday.ucr.edu/5548.

Miller, Bettye. "Juan Felipe Herrera Named California Poet Laureate: The Award-Winning UC Riverside Poetry Professor Is Known for Chronicling the Lives of Mexican Americans." *UCR/Today, Arts & Culture*, Poetry, 21 March 2012. https://ucrtoday.ucr.edu/4265.

Miller, Bettye. "Remembering Lives Lost." News, University of California, April 15, 2014. https://www.universityofcalifornia.edu/news/remembering-lives-lost.

Mochari, Ilan. "7 Surprisingly Practical Lessons from America's New Poet Laureate." Lead, *Inc.*, June 10, 2015. https://www.inc.com/ilan-mochari/poet-laureate-juan-felipe-herrera.html.

Moore, Francesca. "A Night with Former U.S. Poet Laureate Juan Felipe Herrera." Arts and Culture, May 24, 2018. https://triton.news/2018/05/night-former-us-poet-laureate-juan-felipe-herrera/.

Morrissey, Kate. "Poet Laureate Celebrates Dual Immigrant, Migrant Identity." Immigration, *The San Diego Union-Tribune*, January 24, 2017. https://www.sandiegouniontribune.com/news/immigration/sd-me-poet-laureate-20170124-story.html.

Munslow, Julia. "U.S. Poet Laureate Decries Trump Wall." Arts and Entertainment, *The Emory Wheel*, February 22, 2017. https://emorywheel.com/u-s-poet-laureate-decries-trump-wall/.

O'Gara, Nick. "U.S. Poet Laureate Explores Positive Poetics with Tucson Students: A Performance from Juan Felipe Herrera at Davis Bilingual; and a Special Message in Spanish from the Poet." *Arizona Spotlight*, aArizona Public Media, NPR.org, audio, March 24, 2017. https://radio.azpm.org/p/radio-azspot-splash/2017/3/24/108036-us-poet-laureate-explores-positive-poetics-with-tucson-students/.

## Bibliography by and on Juan Felipe Herrera 2022 435

Peña, Daniel. "Half the World More: Juan Felipe Herrera and the Centering of Chicana/o Letters." *Ploughshares at Emerson College* (blog), June 18, 2015. http://blog.pshares.org/index.php/half-the-world-more-juan-felipe-herrera-and-the-centering-of-chicanao-letters/.

Ramos, Manuel. "Murals, Poets, Books, Honors, New Theater—and SB1070. Juan Felipe Herrera Awarded Guggenheim Fellowship." *La Bloga: The World's Longest-Established Chicana Chicano, Latina Latino Literary Blog*, April 30, 2010. https://labloga.blogspot.com/2010/04/murals-poets-books-honors-new-theater.html.

Ramos, Manuel. "Librarian of Congress Appoints Juan Felipe Herrera Poet Laureate. Juan Felipe Herrera Named National Poet Laureate." *La Bloga: The World's Longest-Established Chicana Chicano, Latina Latino Literary Blog*, June 12, 2015. https://labloga.blogspot.com/2015/06/juan-felipe-herrera-named-national-poet.html.

Rappaport, Scott. "*Borderbus*: A Community Conversation about Migration, Art, and Social Justice," UCSC NewsCenter, February 26, 2019. https://news.ucsc.edu/2019/02/borderbus-alumna-rice.html.

Reyes, Barbara Jane. "My California: Three Questions for Our State's New Poet Laureate, Juan Felipe Herrera." Poetry News, *Harriet*, Poetry Foundation, April 27, 2012. https://www.poetryfoundation.org/harriet/2012/04/my-california-three-questions-for-our-states-new-poet-laureate-juan-felipe-herrera.

Rodríguez, Diana. "Juan Felipe Herrera: The Latino US Poet Laureate." *La Prensa San Diego, La Prensa América* 41, no. 4 (27 January 2017): n.p.

Rodríguez, R. Joseph. "Our U.S. Poet Laureate and Hispanic Heritage." *NCTE Blog*, National Council of Teachers of English, September 22, 2015. https://ncte.org/blog/2015/09/hispanic-heritage/.

Rogers, Pamela. "Jabber-Walking with Poet Juan Felipe Herrera." *Buttons & Figs podcast #51*, audio, May 8, 2020. http://buttonsandfigs.com/51-jabber-walking-with-poet-juan-felipe-herrera/, https://app.kidslisten.org/ep/Buttons-and-Figs-51-Jabber-Walking-with-poet-Juan-Felipe-Herrera.

Saldívar, Steve. "Former U.S. Poet Laureate Juan Felipe Herrera Wants Poetry to Be Joyous." Books, Entertainment & Arts, *The Los Angeles Times*, April 13, 2018. https://www.latimes.com/books/la-ca-jc-juan-felipe-herrera-20180413-story.html.

Samuels, Iris. "U.S. Poet Laureate Herrera Encourages Students to Speak Out on Social Issues." News, Princeton University, September 23, 2016. https://www.princeton.edu/news/2016/09/23/us-poet-laureate-herrera-encourages-students-speak-out-social-issues.

Savvas, Theo. "First Hispanic Poet Laureate Juan Felipe Herrera Signals a New Direction for U.S. Literature." Arts & Culture, *The Conversation, Arts & Culture*, June 23, 2015. https://theconversation.com/first-hispanic-poet-laureate-juan-felipe-herrera-signals-a-new-direction-for-us-literature-43659.

Schlesinger, Paul. "Words from Third Grade Teacher Inspires U.S. Poet Laureate." *The Collegian*, October 29, 2015. https://collegian.csufresno.edu/2015/10/words-from-third-grade-teacher-inspires-u-s-poet-laureate/#.YAaO2-hKj5Z.

Schuessler, Jennifer. "From Farm Fields to Poet Laureate." Books, *New York Times*, June 10, 2015. https://www.nytimes.com/2015/06/10/books/juan-felipe-herrera-of-california-to-be-next-poet-laureate.html.

Schuessler, Jennifer. "Juan Felipe Herrera." E-paper, Arts & Travel, *The Post and Courier*, June 13, 2015. Updated November 2, 2016. https://www.postandcourier.com/features/arts_and_travel/juan-felipe-herrera/article_13d63287-9251-5837-9dff-309563a99f89.html.

Schuessler, Jennifer. "Juan Felipe Herrera Named to Second Term as Poet Laureate." *ArtsBeat: New York Times Blog*, April 13, 2016. https://artsbeat.blogs.nytimes.com/2016/04/13/juan-felipe-herrera-named-to-second-term-as-poet-laureate/.

Sedano, Michael. "Juan Felipe Herrera Delivers Sayers Lecture at his Alma Mater." *La Bloga: The World's Longest-Established Chicana Chicano, Latina Latino Literary Blog*, May 23, 2017. https://labloga.blogspot.com/2017/05/juan-felipe-herrera-delivers-sayers.html.

Sedano, Michael. "Juan Felipe Herrera, United States Poet Laureate: A Photographic Celebration." *La Bloga: The World's Longest-Established Chicana Chicano, Latina Latino Literary Blog*, June 16, 2015. https://labloga.blogspot.com/search?q=Juan+Felipe+Herrera.

Stanford, Daphne. "Juan Felipe Herrera, Poet Laureate for the Masses." Our World, *Cultural Weekly*, November 4, 2015. https://www.culturalweekly.com/juan-felipe-herrera-poet-laureate-for-the-masses/#disqus_top.

Sturm, Nick. "U.S. Poet Laureate Juan Felipe Herrera Enchants Jubilant, Diverse Audience at Emory." *ARTS ATL*, February 27, 2017. https://www.artsatl.org/u-s-poet-laureate-juan-felipe-herrera-enchants-jubilant-diverse-audience-emory/.

Syed, Razi. "Local Writers Share Their Articles, Poetry and More at Lithop." Local News, *The Collegian*, April 24, 2016. https://collegian.csufresno.edu/2016/04/local-writers-share-their-articles-poetry-and-more-at-lithop/.

Takano, Mark (U.S. Representative). "Congratulations to Juan Felipe Herrera." *Congressional Record, House of Representatives* 161, no. 101 (23 June 2015): H548. www.congress.gov/congressional-record/2015/06/23/house-section/article/H4548-1.

Tejada-Flores, Rick. "Juan Felipe Herrera, California Poet Laureate." *Go Chanting, Libre!*, (documentary film) produced in 1984 by Ed Kissam and Rick Tejada-Flores for KRCB TV, uploaded to YouTube June 18, 2012. Video. https://www.youtube.com/watch?v=S6ZiUn-ItWg.

Tobar, Héctor. "California's Poet Laureate Likes to Turn the Tables." Books, *Los Angeles Times*, July 4, 2013. https://www.latimes.com/books/la-xpm-2013-jul-04-la-ca-jc-juan-felipe-herrera-20130707-story.html.

Tory, Caroline, guest blogger. "Juan Felipe Herrera's Long Road to United States Poet Laureate." *Aspen Words Literature Blog*, January 21, 2016. https://www.aspeninstitute.org/blog-posts/juan-felipe-herrera-s-long-road-united-states-poet-laureate/.

Trainer, Mark. "A Poet's Tribute to Those Who Work." *ShareAmerica*, Bureau of Global Public Affairs, U.S. Department of State, September 1, 2016. https://share .america.gov/poets-labor-day-tribute-to-those-who-work/.

Urschel, Donna. "Juan Felipe Herrera Named Poet Laureate for Second Term." News, Library of Congress, April 13, 2016. www.loc.gov/item/prn-16-068/.

Uribes, Tom. "New Exhibition Shows Poet Laureate Herrera's Indigenous Perspective." Academics, September 30, 2016. http://www.fresnostatenews.com/2016/09 /30/new-exhibition-shows-poet-laureate-herreras-indigenous-perspective/.

*The View Talk Show.* "National Hispanic Heritage Month: Juan Felipe Herrera." American Broadcasting Company, Uploaded to September 22, 2021. https://www .youtube.com/watch?v=c1obEr0mMF8&list=RDCMUCeH6qE4V7n5tVwP7Nkd rtJg&start_radio=1&rv=c1obEr0mMF8&t=50.

Vourvoulias, Sabrina "Juan Felipe Herrera Wants to Write an Epic American Poem . . . with You." *Al Día: Literature*, September 6, 2015. https://aldianews.com/articles /culture/literature/juan-felipe-herrera-wants-write-epic-american-poem-you /40457.

Walt Whitman Birthplace Association. "2020 Poet-in-Residence Juan Felipe Herrera." WWBA Poets-in-Residence Program, 2020. https://www.waltwhitman.org /poets-poetry/2020-poet-in-residence/.

White, Meera. "Poetry Is like Recess." Uncut, Arts, *Quintessential Kenyon: Student Life*, April 11, 2017. https://blogs.kenyon.edu/quintessential-kenyon-student-life -uncut/post/poetry-is-like-recess/.

Wilkens, John. "New Poet Laureate Found His Voice in SD." Books, *The San Diego Union-Tribune*, June 10, 2015. https://www.sandiegouniontribune.com/entertain ment/books/sdut-juan-felipe-herrera-poet-laureate-2015jun10-story.html.

Wilkens, John. "Poet Laureate's Defining Moment." People, *The San Diego Union-Tribune*, August 22, 2015. https://www.sandiegouniontribune.com/lifestyle/people /sdut-poet-laureate-teacher-2015aug22-story.html.

Wolf, Jessica. "Former Poet Laureate Juan Felipe Herrera Receives UCLA Medal: Alumnus Shares Stories of How Campus Shaped His Worldview and His Work." Arts & Culture, *UCLA Newsroom*, October 31, 2017. https://newsroom.ucla.edu /stories/former-poet-laureate-juan-felipe-herrera-receives-ucla-medal.

# Note

1. Many thanks to consultant Francisco A. Lomelí for his assistance in gathering and confirming bibliographical data.

# CONTRIBUTORS

**Trevor Boffone** is a lecturer in the Women's, Gender & Sexuality Studies Program at the University of Houston. He is the author of *Renegades: Digital Dance Cultures from Dubsmash to TikTok* and co-editor of *Encuentro: Latinx Performance for the New American Theater; Nerds, Goths, Geeks, and Freaks: Outsiders in Chicanx and Latinx Young Adult Literature; Shakespeare and Latinidad;* and *Seeking Common Ground: Latinx and Latin American Theatre and Performance.*

**Marina Bernardo-Flórez** is a recent PhD at ADHUC within the Department of Modern Languages and Literatures and English Studies, at the University of Barcelona. Graduated in English Studies at the University of Barcelona and in Translation and Interpreting at the Universitat Autònoma de Barcelona, and with an MA in Construction and Representation of Cultural Identities. She focuses her research on children's literature, identities, and border spaces.

**Manuel de Jesús Hernández-G.** is an associate professor of Spanish in the School of International Letters and Cultures at Arizona State University. His areas of expertise are Spanish, English, and Chicano and Latino studies. He has served and directed the track of Chicano Studies in Spanish at his university. He has published five books, directed 12 dissertations and 21 MA theses on Chicano/a and U.S. Latino/a literature and culture. He also received an important international award for his teaching and scholarship, having produced anthologies on Chicano/a literature.

**Whitney DeVos** is a recent PhD in Literature at the University of California at Santa Cruz. She specializes in hemispheric American literatures with a focus on race and nationalism. Her dissertation examines how documentary poetry theorizes the limitations of liberal democracy and its institutions, particularly citizenship, from the postwar period to NAFTA.

**Michael Dowdy** teaches poetry and Latinx literature at the University of South Carolina, where he is professor of English and core faculty in Comparative Literature. His books include *Broken Souths: Latina/o Poetic Responses to Neoliberalism and Globalization* and, as coeditor with Claudia Rankine, the critical anthology *Poetics of Social Engagement*.

**Osiris Aníbal Gómez** is an assistant professor in the Department of Spanish and Portuguese Studies at the University of Minnesota Twin Cities. His areas of expertise include contemporary Indigenous literatures of Mexico, Mexican literature, Chicano literature and translation studies. His work explores the condition, aesthetics, and social and political transformation possibilities of bilingual Indigenous and Chicanx writers. He is the lead editor of the collection *Caleidoscopio verbal: lenguas y literaturas originarias* with co-editors Sara Poot-Herrera and Francisco A. Lomelí, and Associate Editor at *Hispanic Issues* and *Hispanic Issues On Line*.

**Carmen González Ramos** is an independent scholar who research has focused on Chicana literature for twenty years. She is currently interested in Children's literature, a topic on which she has already published four articles: "No More Viejas Brujas," "Recipes for a Latina Identity," "Intercultural/ Interlingual Identity," and "Viva la Lucha," in which she has discussed *cuentos* by authors such as Gloria Anzaldúa, Pat Mora, and Yuyi Morales.

**Cristina Herrera** is Professor of Chicano and Latin American Studies at California State University, Fresno. She is author of two manuscripts, including *ChicaNerds in Chicana Young Adult Literature: Brown and Nerdy*, and co-editor of multiple volumes, such as *Nerds, Goths, Geeks, and Freaks: Outsiders in Chicanx/Latinx Young Adult Literature* and *Voices of Resistance: Interdisciplinary Approaches to Chican@ Children's Literature*.

**María Herrera-Sobek** is an emeritus professor of Chicana/o Studies at the University of California at Santa Barbara, and retired Vice Chancellor for Diversity, Equity and Inclusion. She specializes in theories and analyses of folklore, gender, culture, oral tradition, feminism, film, as well as ethnic construction. Her books include *The Bracero Experience, The Mexican Corrido: A Feminist Analysis, Northward Bound: The Mexican Immigrant Experience in Ballad and Song,* and *Chicano Folklore: A Handbook.*

**Francisco A. Lomelí** is an emeritus professor of Chicana/o Studies and Spanish & Portuguese Departments at the University of California at Santa Barbara. He has published extensively on both Latin American and Chicano/a literatures with an emphasis on the novel, Southwestern literary production, the U.S.-Mexico border and Spanglish. He has to his credit various award winning works such as *Chicano Literature: A Reference Guide* (co-editor Julio Martínez), *Handbook of Hispanic Cultures in the United States: Literature and Art* and *Aztlán: Essays on the Chicano Homeland* (2nd edition with co-editors Rudolfo Anaya and Enrique Lamadrid) along with *Defying the Inquisition in Colonial New Mexico: Miguel de Quintana's Life and Writings, The Writings of Eusebio Chacón* (co-editor Gabriel Meléndez), *Routledge Handbook of Chicana/o Studies* (co-editors Denise Segura and Elyette Benjamin-Labarthe), and *Human Rights in the Americas* (co-editors María Herrera-Sobek and Luz Angélica Kirschner). He is a member of the North American Academy of the Spanish Language.

**Tom Lutz** is Distinguished Professor in Creative Writing at University of California, Riverside and the author of *Aimlessness*, a philosophical investigation, the travel trilogy *At Home in the World* (*The Kindness of Strangers, The Monkey Learned Nothing,* and *Drinking Mare's Milk*), the novels *Born Slippy* and *Still Slippy,* the cultural histories *Doing Nothing* and *Crying,* the literary histories *Cosmopolitan Vistas* and *American Nervousness,* and the photographic essay, *Portraits: Moments of Intimacy on the Road.* His work has appeared in numerous important journals, *LA Times, Chicago Tribune, New York Times Magazine, New York Times* and dozens of other literary and academic journals and books. He is the editor of over twenty books and the founding editor and publisher of *Los Angeles Review of Books.*

**Manuel M. Martín-Rodríguez** is Professor of Literature and Founding Faculty at the University of California, Merced. He is the author of numerous articles, as well as several books, including *Life in Search of Readers: Reading (in) Chicano/a Literature, Cantos a Marte y das batalla a Apolo: cinco estudios sobre Gaspar de Villagrá, Gaspar de Villagrá: legista, soldado y poeta* and *P. Galindo: obras (in)complete de José Díaz*. He is also a member of the North American Academy of the Spanish Language.

**Marzia Milazzo** is an associate professor of English at the University of Johannesburg. Her first book, *Colorblind Tools: Global Technologies of Racial Power* traces the racial technology of colorblindness from the Americas to South Africa, and from the colonial to the contemporary era, to offer a global reflection on antiblackness and white supremacy. Her articles have appeared in, among other venues, *Journal of Commonwealth and Postcolonial Studies*, *Research in African Literatures, Journal of International and Intercultural Communication, Journal of Applied Philosophy* and *Current Writing*.

**Maria Antònia Oliver-Rotger** is an associate professor of humanities at Universitat Pompeu Fabra. She is the author of *Battlegrounds and Crossroads: Social and Imaginary Space in Writings by Chicanas*. Her essays on the testimonial, documentary, and auto-ethnographic aspects of Chican@ writings have appeared in *JAS, Signs, Interdisciplinary Literary Studies, Aztlán* and *Melus*. She is the editor of *Identity, Diaspora, and Return in American Literature*.

**Rafael Pérez-Torres**, a professor of literatures in English at UCLA, works at the intersections of Chicana/o literature and culture, gender and sexuality studies, postmodernity, globalization, and hemispheric studies. He has written numerous articles and authored three books: *Movements in Chicano Poetry: Against Myths, Against Margins, Mestizaje: Critical Uses of Race in Chicano Culture*, and *To Alcatraz, Death Row, and Back: Memories of an East L.A. Outlaw*.

**Renato Rosaldo**, an emeritus professor from Stanford University, has published five collections of poetry. His bilingual, Spanish-English, collection, *Rezo a la mujer araña*, won the American Book Award (2004). *Diego Luna's Insider Tips* won the Many Mountains Moving Press Book Prize Selected by Martín Espada. With Duke University Press he published *The Day of Shelly's Death* and *The Chasers*.

**Donaldo W. Urioste** is an emeritus professor of Spanish language and Hispanic literatures, and founding Director of the Institute for World Languages and Cultures at California State University at Monterey Bay. Prior to coming to CSUMB as a founding faculty member, he taught at Colorado College and at California Lutheran University, where he taught Spanish Language, Latin American, and Chicano literature and culture courses. He co-authored *Historical Dictionary of U.S. Latino Literature* with Francisco A. Lomelí and María Joaquina Villaseñor.

**Luis Alberto Urrea** is the author of eighteen books, including the nonfiction volumes *The Devil's Highway*, a finalist for the 2005 Pulitzer Prize for general nonfiction, and *Across the Wire*. His other awards include a Lannan Literary Award and an American Book Award. He has written other works, including *The Hummingbird's Daughter* (2005), *Queen of America* (2011), and *Into the Beautiful North* (2014), He teaches creative writing at the University of Illinois in Chicago.

**Santiago Vaquera-Vásquez** is an unrepentant border crosser, ex-dj, and Xicano writer. An associate professor of Creative Writing and Hispanic Southwest Literatures and Cultures at the University of New Mexico, he has also taught and lectured at universities across the United States, Latin America, and Europe. He has also held Fulbright Fellowships in Spain, Turkey, and Poland. His books include, *Luego el silencio* (2014), *One Day I'll Tell You the Things I've Seen* (2015), *En el Lost 'n' Found* (2016), and others. Widely published in Spanish, his literary work has appeared in anthologies and literary journals in Spain, Italy, Latin America, and the United States.

# INDEX

9/11 (terrorist attack), 270, 271, 276, 281, 283

*187 Reasons Mexicanos Can't Cross the Border: Undocuments, 1971–2007*, 10, 17–18, 30, 44n3, 53, 82, 148, 151, 152, 157n6, 173, 174, 196, 199, 221, 229, 350, 360

*187 Reasons Why Mexicanos Can't Cross the Border: An Emergency Poem*, 16, 157n4

Abbot, Steve, 354

*Abutebaris modo subjunctive denuo* (You've been misusing the subjunctive again), 54

Acevedo, Elizabeth, 272, 273. *See also Clap When You Land; The Poet X*

Acosta, Teresa Paloma, 166

*Across the Wire: Life and Hard Times on the Mexican Border*, 113n6. *See also* Urrea, Luis Alberto

Acteal, Chiapas, 170, 171, 329

admixtures, 15, 42

Africa/n, 217, 218

African American civil rights movement, 133

agglutinations, 14, 121, 125–27

Aguirre Beltrán, Gonzalo, 340

Ahmed, Sara, 61, 62, 66. *See also Stranger Encounters: Embodied Others in Post-Coloniality*

*Akrílica*, 15, 164, 168, 169, 174, 181n8, 182n9, 202, 203, 219, 231, 339, 342, 348, 350

*alabanzas* (chants), 150

Alamillo, Laura, 291

Alarcón, Francisco X., 13, 47, 163, 164, 244, 245, 257, 305, 334, 348, 351, 354, 366. *See also* children's literature; González, Maya

Alcaraz, Lalo, 235n16

Aldama, Frederick Luis, 162, 181, 312

Alegría, Fernando, 40, 164

Alfaro Siqueiros, David, 332

*Alturas de Macchu Picchu*, 147, 206. *See also* Neruda, Pablo

Alurista, 8, 13, 42n1, 66, 94, 121, 165, 170, 172, 181n1, 181n4, 182n14, 191, 209, 325, 331, 345, 348, 361. *See also Floricanto en Aztlán*

Amado, Jorge, 354

*The American Poetry Review*, 70, 71

Ammons, A. R., 188

*An Analytical Dictionary of Nahuatl*, 134. *See also* Karttunen, Frances

Anaya, Rudolfo A., 113n3, 289

*Angels of the Apocalypse*, 89n1. *See also* Chávez, John; Giménez Smith, Carmen

anti-Vietnam War, 133

"antropoesía" (anthropoetry), 5, 8, 136, 138, 139, 145, 156

## 446 Index

"antropolocos" (anthropologist plus 'loco'), 107. *See also* Blom, Gertrude

Anzaldúa, Gloria, 13, 28, 43n1, 95, 96, 113n5, 149, 265, 275, 285n4, 289, 291, 308, 349, 352, 358

Aranda, Guillermo, 332

Arau, Sergio, 151. *See also* "A Day Without a Mexican: Video Clip"

*The Archive and the Repertoire: Performing Cultural Memory in the Americas,* 139. *See also* Taylor, Diana

Arguedas, José María, 99

Argueta, Jorge, 354

Arias, Arturo, 157n3

Artaud, Antonin, 320, 348, 364

Arteaga, Alfred, 54, 73, 89n2. *See also Chicano Poetics: Heterotexts and Hybridities*

assemblage, 10, 57, 72; agglutinations, 14, 121, 125–27; amalgamation, 10, 11

Asturias, Miguel Angel, 99

autobiographical *cuentos* (short stories), 294, 297, 312

autobiographical writing, 250, 252. *See also* Juanito

*The Autobiography of Malcom X,* 320. *See also* X, Malcolm

"Automatika Series", 335

*The Aztecs,* 128. *See also* Fagan, Brian M.

Aztlán (Aztec mythic homeland), 128, 132, 259, 324, 329, 344, 355

Bach, Sebastian, 325

ballet folklórico, 344

Barbas-Rhoden, Laura, 291

*Barrioztlán,* 179. *See also* Cuevas, Saúl

Bashō, Matsuo, 13, 25, 33, 34

The Beats, 165

Beauvoir de, Simone, 327

Bernardo-Flórez, Marina, 5, 16, 289

Bethoven Van, Ludwig, 325

"Bibliography by and on Juan Felipe Herrera", 368–437. *See also* Urioste, Donaldo W.

bilingualism, 284

bilingual writing, 248, 249, 331, 337, 341, 342, 353. *See also* code-switching

Binder, Wolfgang, 162, 164, 165, 180

Blanchott, Maurice, 79. *See also The Writing of the Disaster*

Blom, Frans, 104, 107

Blom, Gertrude, 104, 107, 109. *See also* "antropolocos" (anthropologist plus 'loco')

*Bloodlines: Myth, Indigenism, and Chicana/o Literature,* 95, 113n5. *See also* Contreras, Sheila Marie

*Bloodroot,* 121. *See also* Villanueva, Alma

Boffone, Trevor, 5, 269; *Literaure,* 284, 285n1. *See also Nerds, Goths, Geeks, and Freaks: Outsiders in Chicanx and Latinx Literature*

Bolaño, Roberto, 80, 81

Bombal, María Luisa, 354

Bonnano, David, 70

Bonomo, Annamarie, 291

*El Boom Latinoamericano,* 164

*Borderbus,* 18, 19, 31, 358

*Border-Crosser with a Lamborghini Dream,* 16, 31, 88, 173, 338

*Borderlands / La Frontera: The New Mestiza,* 95, 96, 112, 183n19, 308. *See also* Anzaldúa, Gloria

Border Protection, Antiterrorism, and Illegal Immigration Control Act of 2005 (H.R. 4437), 151, 158n8

Borges, Jorge Luis, 354

Bowles, Davis, 272

Bravo, Dolores, 181n8

Breytenbach, Breyten, 217, 234n3

*Broken Souths: Latina/o Poetic Responses in Neoliberalism and Globalization,* 89n5. *See also* Dowdy, Michael

Bruce-Novoa, Juan, 113n4. *See also Chicano Authors: Inquiry by Interview*

Bundy, Katherine E., 257, 291

Burciaga, Cecilia, 367

Burciaga, José Antonio, 13, 28, 40, 66, 210, 367
Burt, Stephanie, 82
Butler, Judith, 43n2

Cadden, Mike, 272, 273
California, 323
*Calling the Doves / El canto de las palomas*, 16, 241, 242, 244, 245, 290, 297, 301, 312, 350
*caló* (Chicano slang), 93, 120, 121, 122–23, 129, 191, 331
*campesino* (farmworker), 124, 125, 146, 247, 249, 301, 334, 341, 357
Caminero-Santangelo, Marta, 270
Candlewick Press, 303
Canela (character), 272, 273, 274, 275, 277, 280, 282, 283, 284
Canetti, Elias, 62–64, 193. *See also Crowds and Power*
*cantos* (chants), 118, 119
Cantú, Norma E., 245. *See also* autobiographical writing
Cardenal, Ernesto, 147. *See also Los ovnis de oro: poemas indios*
Carroll, Lewis, 18
Castaneda, Carlos, 11, 191
Castellanos, Rosario, 99
Castillo, Ana, 10, 121. *See also My Father Was a Toltec*
Cavazos, Sylvia, 242
Central America, 223, 339, 348, 355
Centro Cultural de la Raza Toltecas en Aztlán, 152, 163, 191, 334, 365
Cernuda, Luis, 181n8
Cervantes, Lorna Dee, 66n1, 165
Chan K'in Nahá, Viejo, 94, 98, 100, 101, 103, 110, 111, 146
Chaplin, Charlie (Chaplinesque), 176, 182n17
Chávez, César, 13, 190
Chávez, Denise, 182n19. *See also Loving Pedro Infante*

Chávez, John, 89n1. *See also Angels of the Apocalypse*
Chiapas, 329, 346, 355
Chicano/a literature, 215, 225, 269, 281, 336, 340, 351
*Chicano Authors: Inquiry by Interview,* 113n4. *See also* Bruce-Novoa, Juan
Chicano Moratorium, 14, 141, 142
Chicano Movement (movimiento chicano), 13, 38, 39, 85, 93, 94, 140, 141, 144, 145, 153, 157n2, 213, 216, 233, 289, 328, 331, 343, 347, 361; Chicano Renaissance, 66, 93, 166; "postmovement poetics", 157, 233
Chicano Park, 190
*Chicano Poetics: Heterotexts and Hybridities,* 55, 73. *See also* Arteaga, Alfred
Chicano Renaissance, 66, 93, 166. *See also* Chicano Movement
*Chicanos: antología histórica y literaria,* 173. *See also* Villanueva, Tino
Chicano Walkouts (1968), 136
Children's Book Press, 241, 244
children's identity, 294
children's literature, 6, 8, 241, 243, 251, 256, 270, 289, 308, 341, 343, 349; children's literature: bibliographical list, 369–70. *See also* decolonial
*Cinnamon Girl: Letters Found inside a Cereal Box,* 16, 197, 268, 269, 270, 274, 276, 281, 360
Cisneros, Sandra, 275, 289. *See also The House on Mango Street*
*Citybender,* 18n4
City Lights Books, 33, 354
Ciudad Juárez, Chihuahua, 323, 348, 364
civil rights, 11, 13, 40
Cixous, Hélène, 280
*Clap When You Land,* 273
Clifford, James, 113n7. *See also Writing Culture: The Poetics and Politics of Ethnography*
Coatlicue (mother earth), 96

**448** Index

Coats, Karen, 274

code-switching, 121, 122, 223, 345; Afro-American words, 179; Chicano Spanish, 179, 341; Spanglish, 136, 181n19, 188, 294, 348

Cody, Anthony, 343, 349

Colbert, Shrissie, 291

Cold War, 76

colonialism, 353

colonization, 244

Colosio, Luis Donaldo, 148, 156

Columbus, Christopher, 109

community in writing, 218, 220, 221, 233, 244, 252, 261, 275, 277, 278, 279, 282, 283, 284, 285, 289, 312, 323, 331, 332, 340, 357, 362, 365

Conner, Angela, 291

Contreras, Sheila Marie, 95, 113n5. *See also Bloodlines: Myth, Indigenism, and Chicana/o Literature*

Corales *vs.* Bennett, 154, 155, 158n9

Coralito (character), 260, 261, 262, 263

*Coralito's Bay / Bahía de Coralito*, 242, 260

Corpi, Lucha, 334, 354

*corridos* (ballads), 7, 150

Corso, Gregory, 354

Cortázar, Julio, 351, 354

Cota-Cárdenas, Margarita, 179. *See also Puppet: A Chicano Novella*

*Country of Memory*, 49. *See also* Fishman, Charles

*CrashBoomLove: A Novel in Verse*, 16

crisis of representation, 103

critical works on Juan Felipe Herrera, 393–99

*El Crossover*, 178, 179

*Crowds and Power*, 62, 63. *See also* Canetti, Elias

Cuéllar, José (aka Dr. Loco), 203, 210. *See also* Dr. Loco's Original Corrido Boogie Band

Cuevas, Saúl, 179. *See also Barrioztlán*

Culler, Jonathan, 61, 66

cultural nationalism, 8, 95; Aztec and Mayan mythology, 95

Culture Clash, 13, 210

cummings, ee, 28

Dalai Lama, 13, 328

Dalí, Salvador, 13, 320, 323, 364

Darfur (Sudan), 9, 37, 38, 182n18

*Dark Root of a Thousand Embraces: Dialogues*, 173, 174

*The Day of Shelly's Death: The Poetry and Ethnography of Grief*, 138, 145, 156. *See also* Rosaldo, Renato

"A Day Without a Mexican: Video Clip", 151, 152, 153, 154, 155, 156. *See also* Arau, Sergio

decolonialism, 8, 26, 27, 43n1, 48; colonial/imperialist designs, 54, 56; colonizers and explorers, 112; Eurocentric assumptions, 96; fetishization, 101, 112; social justice, 132–33; *Stranger Encounters: Embodied Others in Post-Coloniality*, 61, 76

decolonial, 220, 244, 279

Decolonial Imaginary, 284

deconstruction, 53, 66

Dees, Jenn, 35, 44n5

DeLanda, Manuel, 234n2

Deleuze, Gilles and Félix Guattari, 220, 221, 233, 234n2

De Lucio-Brock, Anita, 304

Derrida, Jacques, 51, 52, 63, 65, 66n2, 67n2

*Desplumado / Featherless*, 183n20, 258, 259, 290, 309, 312

deterritorializing, 221, 222, 227. *See also* Deleuze, Gilles and Félix Guattari

DeVos, Whitney, 4, 136

Dickinson, Emily, 188

dictatorships, 77

Disney movies, 243, 260, 261

displacement, 300

Dobbs, Lou, 54; bigotry toward immigrants, 54, 67

Dorfman, Ariel, 80. *See also Heading South, Looking North: A Bilingual Journey*
Dowdy, Michael, 4, 69, 89, 89n5, 102, 145, 149, 155, 168, 172, 176. *See also Broken Souths: Latina/o Poetic Responses in Neoliberalism and Globalization*
*Downtown Boy*, 196, 197
Dr. Loco's Original Corrido Boogie Band, 203
Dufourmantelle, Anne, 51, 52, 63, 65

East Los Angeles, 181n2
Eco, Umberto, 229, 236n17
Ejército Zapatista de Liberación Nacional (Zapatista National Liberation Army or EZLN), 101, 102, 144, 145, 170, 174, 356
empowerment, 258, 290
*El encanto de las palomas / Calling the Doves*, 183n20, 295, 301
*Encuentro Femenil*, 141
Engle, Margarita, 272
English language usage, 223, 242, 296, 301, 310, 337, 341
*entextualization*, 147. *See also* McEnaney, Thomas
environmental imaginary, 117, 131–32, 300
*Erased Faces*, 112. *See also* Limón, Graciela
Espada, Martín, 73, 193
*Ethnopornography: Sexuality, Colonialism, and Archival Knowledge*, 106. *See also* Sigal, Pete; Torririci, Zeb; Whitehead, Neil
Evans-Pritchard, E.E., 105
*Every Day We Get More Illegal*, 18, 19, 27, 32, 48, 52, 53, 60, 65, 73, 75, 87, 88, 187, 188, 190, 192, 193, 206, 209, 215, 333, 358
*Exiles of Desire*, 14, 74, 78, 139, 141, 142, 157, 173, 174, 193, 197, 198, 199, 221, 339, 347

*La fábrica*, 175, 176, 177, 178. *See also Notes on the Assemblage*
*Facegames*, 15, 140, 196, 218, 221, 351
Fagan, Brian M., 128. *See also The Aztecs*
Felten, Peter, 291
Feminist movement, 132
Fernández, Magaly, 181n8
Fernández Rodríguez, Carolina, 291
Fishman, Charles, 49; *Country of Memory*, 49; *The Wal-Mart Effect*, 49
Flaherty, Robert, 137, 156. *See also Moana*
Flores, Gloria Amalia, 118
Flores, Tatiana, 158n7
*Floricanto en Aztlán*, 94, 121, 209, 345. *See also* Alurista
Floricanto Festivals, 8, 45, 212; "flower and song", 66n1
flower-Song (in xóchitl in cuícatl), 322, 324, 326, 352; *floricanto*, 330, 365
Floyd, George, 87
*Forms of a World: Contemporary Poetry and the Making of Globalization*, 74. *See also* Hunter, Walt
Foster, Sesshu, 181n8
Franco, Jean, 156
Freire, Paulo, 291
The Fresno Poets, 165
Fuentes, Carlos, 351
"funds of knowledge", 266n18. *See also* González, Norma

Galarza, Ernesto, 242
Galda, Lee, 291
Galdámez, Misael, 159n10
La Galería La Raza, 354
García, Edgar, 88
García Lorca, Federico, 13, 170, 256, 320, 345, 362, 364
García Márquez, Gabriel, 351
García McCall, Guadalupe, 272. *See also Under the Mesquite*
García, Rupert, 35
Gaspar de Alba, Alicia, 216

**450** Index

"genre jumping" or "genre leaping", 10. *See also* Castillo, Ana

George, E. Marcus, 113n8. *See also* Clifford, James; *Writing Culture: The Poetics and Politics of Ethnography*

Gibler, John, 83, 84, 85, 86, 88, 89n7. *See also I Couldn't Even Imagine That They Would Kill Us*

Giménez Smith, Carmen, 89. *See also Angels of the Apocalypse*

Ginsberg, Allen, 13, 201; "rapid simultaneities", 45, 178, 200

Giorgis, Cyndi, 291

*Giraffe on Fire*, 196, 201

global capitalist expansion, 41, 76

global pandemic, 87

Global South, 30, 38, 39, 44n4, 221

global "we", 69, 76, 77; public "we" poems, 72, 73; "we" in the archives, 74

Gogh Van, Vincent, 326

Gómez, Elizabeth, 248, 297

Gómez, Marga, 210

Gómez, Osiris Aníbal, 4, 5, 7, 19, 319, 364. *See also* "The Poet, the Playwright, and the Citizen. An Interview with U.S. Poet Laureate Juan Felipe Herrera"

Gómez-Peña, Guillermo, 222

González, Maya, 305

González, Norma, 266n18

González, Rachel V., 122. *See also caló*

González, Rigoberto, 205

González-Ramos, Carmen, 5, 16, 289

Grandin, Greg, 157n3

*Grandma and Me at the Flea / Los meros remateros*, 242, 245, 290, 304, 312

*Gravy Donuts*, 195–203. *See also* Lutz, Tom

Greenblatt, Stephen, 43n1

Grierson, John, 137, 156. *See also* Of Japanese Descent: An Interim Report

Griswold, Jerry, 298

*Growing up Chicana*, 298. *See also* López, Tiffany

Guevara Che, 11, 39, 190

Güidos, Cecilia, 354

*Half the World in Light: New and Selected Poems*, 17–18, 49, 70, 78, 81, 173, 174, 205, 206, 211, 267

*Handbook of Middle American Indians*, 134n3. *See also* Manning, Nash; Wauchope, Robert

*Heading South, Looking North: A Bilingual Journey*, 80. *See also* Dorfman, Ariel

Hegemony, 32, 54, 59, 73, 76, 181n5

Hendrix, Jimi, 29

Heredia, Juanita, 89n4. *See also Mapping South American Latina/o Literature in the United States*

Hernández Cruz, Víctor, 13, 15, 163, 165, 256

Hernández, Ellie, 157n1. *See also* "postmovement poetics"

Hernández-G, Manuel de Jesús, 5, 160, 162

*Heroes and Saints*, 131. *See also* Moraga, Cherríe

Herrera, Cristina, 5, 16, 269. *See also Nerds, Goths, Geeks, and Freaks: Outsiders in Chicanx and Latinx Literature*

Herrera, Jorge, 354

Herrera, Papá Felipe Emelio, 13, 47, 361

Herrera, Mamá Lucha, 13, 361. *See also* Quintana Herrera Martínez, Lucha

Herrera-Sobek, María, 5, 14, 117

"heteroglot interzone", 56. *See also* Arteaga, Alfred; *Chicano Poetics: Heterotexts and Hybridities*

Hirschman, Jack, 164

Hong, Cathy Park, 79

*The House on Mango Street*, 275. *See also* Cisneros, Sandra

*Howl and Other Poems*, 200. *See also* Ginsberg, Allen

Huerta, Dolores, 13

Hughes, Langston, 73
Huidobro, Vicente, 13
Huichols, 129
Huitzilopochtli (Aztec God of War), 122
humor, 13, 210; Chaplinesque and Cantinflas, 13, 210; Zen humor, 210
*The Hungry Woman: A Mexican Medea*, 96. *See also* Moraga, Cherríe
Hunter, Walt, 74. *See also Forms of a World: Contemporary Poetry and the Making of Globalization*

ICE (Immigration and Customs Enforcement), 33, 355
*I Couldn't Even Imagine That They Would Kill Us*, 83, 86. *See also* Gibler, John
illegal, 270, 333
illustrated children's books (or picture books), 242, 264, 290, 293, 302, 305, 311
*Imagina*, 265
*Imagine*, 242, 245, 252, 265, 290, 301, 304, 312
*Imperial Eyes: Travel Writing and Transculturation*, 97, 98, 103, 114n9. *See also* Pratt, Mary
Indigeneity, 8, 9, 12, 99, 113n2; Amerindian spirituality, 3, 14, 344; Aztec Amerindia, 40; Aztec and Mayan mythology, 95, 117; Chicano Indigenism, 90, 221; *indigenismo*, 329; Indigenous heritage, 118; the Indigenous Other, 90; Indigenous thought and influence, 128–31; *In Lak 'Ech* (you are my other I), 167; Mexica (Aztec), 122, 337, 338; neo-indigenism, 9, 170; neoliberal indigenism, 170
Instituto Nacional Indigenista (National Indigenist Institute), 104
intercultural, 289
interview with Juan Felipe Herrera by Francisco Lomelí and Osiris Gómez, 7, 19, 35, 319; interview by Alan

Soldofsky, 162, 165; interview by Frederick L. Aldama, 162; interview by Wolfgang Binder, 162, 165
*I, Rigoberta Menchú: An Indian Woman in Guatemala*, 99. *See also* Menchú, Rigoberta
islamophobia, 282
*Island of Dreams*, 275. *See also* Méndez, Jasminne
Islas, Arturo, 27

Jabès, Edmond, 222
*Jabberwalking*, 18, 31
jazz, 322, 341, 344, 359
Jewish diaspora, 232
Johansson Keraudren, Patrick, 125. *See also* agglutination
Jong-Un, Kim, 63
Juanito (character), 247, 248, 250, 251, 296, 298, 304
justice, 13, 38, 39, 51

Kafka, Franz, 320, 364
Kahlo, Frida, 13, 15, 43n1, 190
Kandiyoti, Dalia, 232. *See also Migrant Sites: America, Place, and Diaspora Literatures*
Karttunen, Frances, 134. *See also An Analytical Dictionary of Nahuatl*
Katzenberger, Elaine, 33
Kauffman, Gloria, 291
Kessler, Stepehen, 29, 181n8
Kosofsky Sedwick, Eve, 42n2
Ku Klux Klan, 60
Kulesza, Dottie, 291
Kümmerling-Meibauer, Bettina, 295
Kundera, Milan, 219

Lacandón región (Mexico) or Lacandones, 41, 90, 97, 100, 101, 102, 103, 104, 105, 106, 107, 109, 110, 111, 112, 144, 145, 329, 340, 366
Lamadrid, Enrique, 113n3

latina/o, 281
Latinidad, 279
Latorre, Guisela, 113n2
*Laughing Out Loud, I Fly*, 196, 341
Lee & Low Press, 241
*Leaves of Grass*, 165, 200. *See also* Whitman, Walt
Leqis, David, 290
Levinas, Emmanuel, 228
Levine, Phil, 178
Lévi-Strauss, Claude, 105
Library of Congress, 367
Lim, Genny, 354
Limón, Graciela, 112. *See also Erased Faces*
Liquid Theater, 364
*La literatura chicana*, 182n14. *See also* Tatum, Charles M.
La Llorona (legend), 261
Logan Heights (San Diego), 190, 191, 192, 193, 319, 325, 330, 341, 363
Lomelí, Francisco, 3, 4, 5, 7, 19, 33, 48, 93, 113, 200, 216, 319, 354, 364. *See also* "The Poet, the Playwright, and the Citizen. An Interview with U.S. Poet Laureate Juan Felipe Herrera"
López, Josefina, 275
López, Tiffany Ana, 291. *See also Growing Up Chicana*
*Lotería Cards and Fortune Poems: A Book of Lives*, 16, 27, 31, 32, 35, 36, 88, 173, 359
lotería game (Mexican bingo), 35; *patolli* game, 36
"lo transfronterizo" (transborder movement), 19
*Love After the Riots*, 16, 173, 174, 196, 349
*Loving Pedro Infante*, 182n19. *See also* Limón, Graciela
Luna Robles, Margarita, 13, 205
Luther King Jr., Reverend Martin, 67n5
Lutz, Tom, 5, 6, 195

Ma'ax, K'ayum, 92, 101, 102, 103, 105, 106, 108, 109, 111, 113, 144, 146, 148
Macedo, Donaldo, 291
*Maize* (literary journal), 191
Manifesto, 174
Manning, Nash, 134n3. *See also Handbook of Middle American Indians*
*Mapping South American Latina/o Literature in the United States*, 89n4. *See also* Heredia, Juanita
Marcha de la Reconquista (March of the Reconquest, 1970), 136
Marclay, Christian, 204
Marcos, Subcomandante, 98, 113n7
Martínez, Abel, 334, 359
Martínez, John, 334, 359
Martínez, Víctor, 40, 75, 334, 354
Martín-Rodríguez, Manuel, 5, 16, 241
maverick alchemist, 3, 11, 13, 20, 28; marauding rebel, 41
Maya (peoples and/or culture), 221, 339, 355
*Mayan Drifter: Chicano Poet in the Lowlands of America*, 16, 31, 53, 92–113, 136, 137, 144, 145, 147, 148, 150, 157n6, 172, 181n6, 182n13, 196, 223, 339, 346
McEnaney, Thomas, 147. *See also entextualization*
MEChA (Movimiento Estudiantil de Chicanos de Aztlán), 330
*Memoria(s) from an Exile's Notebook of the Future*, 15, 230, 232
Menchú, Rigoberta, 98, 99, 100, 103, 147, 148, 157n3. *See also I, Rigoberta Menchú: An Indian Woman in Guatemala*
Méndez, Jasminne, 275. *See also Island of Dreams*
Méndez, Miguel, 179. *See also Los muertos también cuentan; Peregrinos de Aztlán*
Mesoamerica, 340
*mestizaje* (racial mixture), 55, 308

*Metamorfosis* (magazine), 366
Mexica (Aztec), 122, 128, 328
Mexico, 219, 243, 251, 253
Mexico City, 323, 327, 364
miscellaneous writings by Juan Felipe
  Herrera, 370–83
Middle World, 223, 224, 227, 230
Mignolo, Walter, 44n4
*Migrant Sites: America, Place, and Diaspora Literatures*, 232
migration, 12, 13, 25, 30, 31, 32, 33, 232,
  233; exile *vs.* refugee, 80, 83; Lou
  Dobbs, 54; South American exiles, 78;
  "zero tolerance", 45, 51, 60
Milazzo, Marzia, 4, 90, 92
Miller, Hillis, 52, 110
Milosz, Csezlaw, 362, 364
Mission Cultural Center, 366
Mission District (La Misión), 9, 38, 39,
  40, 163, 164, 165, 169, 181n4, 255, 341,
  354, 358
"Mission Street Manifesto", 335
*Moana* (film) by Robert Flaherty, 137
*Modern Times*, 182n17. See also Chaplin,
  Charlie
*mojado*, 31. See also "wetback"
Montoya, Emanuel, 143
Mora, Adriana, 112
Mora, Pat, 289
Moraga, Cherríe, 95, 131, 275, 285n3. See
  also *Heroes and Saints; The Hungry
  Woman: A Mexican Medea*
Morales, Yuyi, 281
Morresi, Renata, 291
Mozart, Wolfgang Amadeus, 325
El Mozote massacre (El Salvador), 73
*Los muertos también cuentan* (*The Dead
  Also Tell Stories*), 179. See also Méndez, Miguel
multiculturalism, 289, 290
Muslims, 262, 282
*My Father Was a Toltec*, 121. See also
  Castillo, Ana

Nahuatl (Aztec language), 125, 126, 221,
  306, 331, 346. *See also* polysynthetic
  language
Naomi Press, 338
*The Narrow Road to the Deep North*, 33.
  *See also* Bashō, Matsuo
NASA, 332
*Nerds, Goths, Geeks, and Freaks: Outsiders in Chicanx and Latinx Literature*,
  284, 285n1. *See also* Herrera, Cristina
Neruda, Pablo, 13, 45, 147, 181n8, 206,
  354. *See also Alturas de Macchu
  Picchu*
*New Chronicle*, 98. *See also* Poma de
  Ayala, Guaman
*New Historicism and Cultural Materialism*, 42n1
Newsom, Gavin, 159n10
New York City, 326, 350
Nezahualcóyotl, 13, 134, 324, 331, 352,
  365
Nieto-Gómez, Anna María, 141
Nietzsche, Fedrick, 327, 364
*A Night in Tunisia: Newtexts*, 15
*Night Train to Tuxtla*, 10, 15, 30, 34, 70,
  72, 81, 172, 174, 181n6, 182n13, 200,
  203, 204, 217, 231, 350, 359
Nikolajeva, Maria, 290
*La noche de Tlatelolco*, 86. *See also* Poniatowska, Elena
Nodelman, Perry, 290
Noel, Urayoán, 143, 155
nomadic, 220, 322, 336
nonfiction, 370
North Atlantic Free Trade Agreement
  (NAFTA), 102, 148, 170
*Notebooks of a Chile Verde Smuggler*, 8, 9,
  10, 17, 31, 37, 173, 196, 200, 225
*Notes on the Assemblage* (also *La fábrica*),
  18, 19, 32, 57, 73, 75, 83, 85, 86, 175,
  176, 177, 178, 199, 200, 205, 206, 221,
  223
Nowak, Mark, 76. *See also Social Poetics*

Of Japanese Descent: An Interim Report, 137. *See also* Grierson, John

Oliver-Rotger, Maria Antònia, 4, 46, 97; "autoethnography", 97

O'Neil, Kathleen Ellen, 291

online writings by Juan Felipe Herrera, 384–93

Orozco, José Clemente, 332

*Our World Is Our Weapon*, 113n7. *See also* Marcos, Subcomandante

*Los ovnis de oro: poemas indios*, 147. *See also* Cardenal, Ernesto

pachuco (stylized Chicano youth), 11

Palacios, Mónica, 210

Palau, Karina Ruth-Esther, 107

panethnic Latino identity, 150, 162

Parra, Nicanor, 354

El Paso, Texas, 323, 365

Paz, Octavio, 193, 226, 344

PEN Interview with Juan Felipe Herrera, 35

*pensamiento fronterizo* (border thinking), 220, 228

*Pensamiento serpentino*, 94. *See also* Valdez, Luis

*Peregrinos de Aztlán*, 179. *See also* Méndez, Miguel

Pérez, Domino, 113n5

Pérez, Emma, 284. *See also* Decolonial Imaginary

Pérez-Torres, Rafael, 4, 11, 25, 33

Picasso, Pablo, 13, 320, 323, 341, 364

*Piedra de sol*, 345. *See also* Paz, Octavio

Piña Chan, Román, 128

Pinochet, Augusto, 80

Pisarz-Ramírez, Gabriele, 99, 102

*piscadores* (harvesters), 87

*El Plan Espiritual de Aztlán*, 95, 113n3

pochismos (Anglicized Spanish), 122–23; popular Spanish or "non-standard Spanish", 123, 296, 306, 341, 342. *See also* Spanglish

pocho (assimilated Chicano), 39

Pocho-Ché Collective, 39, 163

Poetashumanos (poet group), 181n4

poet laureate, 3, 6, 18, 60, 180, 209, 336; America's *poeta*, 188; "Poet Laureate Consultant in Poetry", 60, 69, 73, 83; "we" after the laureate years, 87

"The Poet, the Playwright, and the Citizen. An Interview with U.S. Poet Laureate Juan Felipe Herrera", 314. *See also* Lomelí, Francisco; Gómez, Osiris Aníbal

*The Poet X*, 343

poetics and hospitality, 48

poetry books by Juan Felipe Herrera, 368–69

*Poetry Foundation*, 194

poetry slams, 334, 335

polysynthetic language, 125. *See also* Nahuatl (Aztec language)

Poma de Ayala, Guaman, 98. *See also New Chronicle*

Poniatowska, Elena, 86. *See also La noche de Tlatelolco*

"post-Chicano Beatnik" or "post-Beatnik Chicano", 11, 13, 29

"post-movement poetics", 157, 233

Pratt, Mary, 97. *See also Imperial Eyes: Travel Writing and Transculturation*

PRI (Partido Revolucionario Institucional), 94, 104

projects as Poet Laureate of California, 422–24

projects as Poet Laureate of the United States, 418–22

proposition, 16, 53, 187, 228; Save Our State Initiative, 67n3, 82

Puig, Manuel, 354

*Puppet: A Chicano Novella*, 179. *See also* Cota-Cárdenas, Margarita

qualities of Juan Felipe Herrera: Amerindian spirituality, 14, 26, 45, 69, 167;

"assemblage", 217, 219, 229; Aztec dancer, 8; baroque excess, 28; barrio homie militant, 8; bohemian disposition, 9; border crosser, 8; Carlos Santana and Che Guevara wannabe, 11; cartoonist, 8; chronicler, 8, 9, 10; "cinematic montage", 302; documentary buff, 8; eclectic, 26; ethnographic gaze, 9, 90, 102, 103, 105, 111, 146; hallucinatory, 10, 25; memorialist, 9; meta-poet, 11; minimalist, 11, 14, 25, 28; mock technocratic language, 149; "mud drawings", 10, 37; muralist, 8; musician, 11; neo-indigenism, 9, 170; one-person vanguard, 10; people's poet, 12; performative cultural poetics, 42, 48, 75; performing artist, 11, 25, 26, 27, 28, 29, 38, 42, 43n2; photographer, 8; poetry in communion with the Other, 215, 230; pundit of creative writing, 8; "quicksilver poet", 11, 25; rasquache sensibility, 5, 9; revolutionary and counter-revolutionary thought, 38; ritualized movement of religious procession, 30, 31; shaman, 8, 11, 25, 26, 42, 47, 188; showman, 25, 26, 42; Southwest shuffle, 11, 15; stand-up comedian, 8, 25; storyteller, 45; street smarts, 9; sympathizer with the underdog, 12; trickster, 11, 47–48; tropicalist period (*See* Ruiz, Tony), 38, 40; video artist, 8; "wandering writing", 217; warrior troubadour, 188; "zigzagging across borders", 218, 230. *See also* Luis Alberto Urrea

Quetzalcóatl (Toltec god), 37, 99, 128, 166, 167

Quevedo, Francisco de, 28

Quiñónez, Naomi, 131

Quintana, Alvina, 275

Quintana Herrera Martínez, Lucha, 324, 327

Quintana, Roberto, 364

Quintana, Vicente, 364

Quintero, Isabel, 275

racism, 320

radio, 328

*ranchero* hats, 41

rasquache sensibility, 5, 9, 190, 193. *See also* Ybarra-Frausto, Tomás

raza (people), 192

Reagan era, 40

*Real Women Have Curves*, 275. *See also* López, Josefina

Rebolledo, Tey Diana, 275

*rebozo* (long Mexican scarf), 120

*Rebozos of Love / We Have Woven / Sudor de Pueblos / On Our Back*, 14, 93, 94, 112, 113n1, 117–34, 136, 163, 166, 167, 168, 169, 171, 173, 174, 181n7, 182n13, 182n14, 198, 209, 215, 221, 324, 342, 344

Reed, Ishmael, 164, 165

Renacimiento Revival Aztlán Collective, 355

representation (theorethical concept), 289, 291

Reséndez, Gerald A., 243

reterritorialization, 222, 249

reviews of books by Juan Felipe Herrera, 406–18

*la revolución*, 104

Rigoberta, Frida, 41

*The Rigoberta Menchú Controversy*, 157n3. *See also* Stoll, David

Rivera, Diego, 13, 332

Rivera Garza, Cristina, 79

Rodríguez, Artemio, 35, 88

Rodríguez, Sonia Alejandra, 282, 291

Roethler, Jacque, 291

"Rolling to Taos in an Aztec Mustang", 213

Román, Santiago, 173

*The Root of a Thousand Embraces: Dialogues*, 15

Rosaldo, Renato, 6, 13, 43n1, 138, 146, 151, 155, 156, 157n3. *See also The Day of Shelly's Death: The Poetry and Ethnography of Grief*
Rothenberg, Jerome, 328
Ruiz, Tony, 38, 39. *See also* "Visión Tropical"

Salazar, Aída, 337
Salazar, Rubén, 142, 156, 157n2
Saldaña Portillo, María Josephina, 96, 112
Sampson, Lucille, 11, 44n3
Sánchez, Érika L., 275
Sánchez, Ricardo, 28, 113n4, 234n4, 235n6
San Cristóbal de las Casas, 104, 105, 355
San Diego Public Library, 321
San Francisco, California, 323, 335, 341, 344
Santana, Carlos, 11, 13, 29
"Santa Niña, La", 36
Santiago, Esmeralda, 291, 294
Santo Niño de Atocha, 36
Sartre, Jan Paul, 320, 345, 364
Savci, Evren, 152
Schwarcz, Joseph, 291
*The Scream* (painting), 78
*Senegal Taxi*, 10, 18, 31, 37, 182n18, 359
Sensenbrenner Bill, 153, 159n10
Sephardic diaspora, 232
Serros, Michele, 275
*Servidores del arbol de la Vida* (Servers of the Tree of Life), 166
*The Shrunken Head of Pancho Villa*, 131. *See also* Valdez, Luis
Sigal, Pete, 106. *See also Ethnopornography: Sexuality, Colonialism, and Archival Knowledge*
Silver Dollar Café, 140
*Skate Fate*, 197
Slinn, E. Warwick, 43n2
social justice, 117

*Social Poetics*, 76, 77, 83, 85. *See also* Nowak, Mark
*soldaderas* (women soldiers), 120
Soldofsky, Alan, 92, 96, 97, 152, 156, 162, 165, 166
Soltero, Anthony, 153, 154, 155, 156, 158n9
sound recordings by Juan Felipe Herrera, 383, 384
Spanglish, 136, 181n19, 188, 294, 348
Stanford University's Special Collections, xi, 70, 74
Steinbeck, John, 13
Stoll, David, 157n3. *See also The Rigoberta Menchú Controversy*
storytelling, 320
*Stranger Encounters: Embodied Others in Post-Coloniality*, 61. *See also* Ahmed, Sara
stylistic elements in Juan Felipe Herrera: "aesthetics of chaos", 48, 66; "antropoesía" (anthropology and poetry), 5, 8; assemblage, 10; "autoethnography", 97, 245; biblical allusion to sin, 58; Chicano *Grapes of Wrath*, 7; clever intertextualities, 4; collages, 75; cosmic and bucolic world view, 166, 170; Derrida and Dufourmantelle, 52, 65; divergence in the parallelism between morality and the law, 59; *engage* art, 35; environmental imaginary, 117, 131, 132; epistemological and ontological underpinnings, 73; flair for the understatement, 10; grass-roots Chicano poetics, 10; haikus, 15; hospitality and rights, 47; humor in children's literature, 242; hybridized writings, 7, 10, 14, 15, 20, 39; idiosyncratic poetic vision, 74; improvisational poetics, 75; Indigenous thought and influence, 128–31; indocumentos / undocuments, 148, 149, 150; infantile poetic

voice, 343; linguistic rendezvous, 4; literary synthesizer, 11, 14; materiality of language, 8, 26, 30, 34, 37, 42, 43n2; "meta-ideologizing", 48, 53, 66; *mytherious*, 188; "new hot language", 40; poems of address, 60; poetic calligrapher, 5, 11, 182n14; poetic experimentations, 4, 8, 20, 30, 35, 42; "poetics of reconciliation" (*See* Dowdy, Michael); "post-movement poetics", 157n1 (*See also* Hernández, Ellie); polysemy and wordplay, 10; public "we" poetics, 85; remix, 13; repetition, 127–28; re-signifying language play, 47, 53, 57, 66; rhapsodist, 14; ruminations of anaphora and incantations, 8, 25, 57 challenging pure abstraction, 8, 50; satirical, 28; surrealist, 10, 28, 29, 85; "Tender Chaos", 46, 48; thematic introspections, 4; translanguaging, 312, 342; "unconditional hospitality", 51; "weaving", 215 (*See also* Vaquera-Vásquez, Santiago); word glyphs, 11, 191
Sufi mysticism, 13, 29
*Super Cilantro Girl / La superniña de cilantro*, 241, 242, 253, 255, 290, 306, 312
superheroine, 304, 305
surrealism, 253, 320, 345

Tafolla, Carmen, 66n1
Taínos, 110
Tatum, Charles M., 182n14. *See also La literatura chicana*
Taylor, Diana, 139. *See also The Archive and the Repertoire: Performing Cultural Memory in the Americas*
Teatro Campesino (Farmworker Theater), 13, 358. *See also* Valdez, Luis
Teatro Chichimeca, 366
Teatro Tolteca, 163, 321, 366

Teatro Zapata, 359
Texcoco, Lake, 37, 330
textual literacy, 292
Third World, 39, 40
*Thunderweavers / Tejedoras de rayos*, 94, 170, 171, 172, 173, 174, 181n6, 331, 356
Tijuana, Mexico, 225
Tlatelolco Plaza, 151
Tonatiuh (Lord of Creation), 167
Torririci, Zeb, 106. *See also Ethnopornography: Sexuality, Colonialism, and Archival Knowledge*
translating, 301, 342
translation, 340, 342
*Troka* (music band), 334
Tropicalization, 255, 257, 258
Trump, Donald, 63, 187, 265n8, 358

*Under the Feet of Jesus*, 131. *See also* Viramontes, Helena María
*Umbra* (magazine), 354
*The Unbearable Lightness of Being*, 219. *See also* Kundera, Milan
Under the Mesquite, 284. *See also* García McCall, Guadalupe
Union of Chicano and Latino Writers (UEECL), 181n4
Universidad Nacional Autónoma de México (UNAM), 105
*The Upside Down Boy / El niño de cabeza*, 242, 245, 248, 250, 251, 290, 297, 301, 312
Urioste, Donaldo W., 364. *See also* "Bibliography by and on Juan Felipe Herrera"
Urrea, Luis Alberto, 5, 6, 9, 113n6, 187, 216, 285n2, 365; "Rascuache", 216n2. *See also Across the Wire: Life and Hard Times on the Mexican Border*
U.S. conservatism, 40
U.S.-Mexico border, 253, 255, 265n8
Uto-Aztecan tribes, 129, 346

Valdez, Luis, 94, 122, 165, 324. *See
also Pensamiento serpentino; The
Shrunken Head of Pancho Villa;* Teatro
Campesino
Vallejo, César, 351
Valoshinov, Valintine N., 43n2
*Los vampiros de Whittier Boulevard*, 173,
174, 175, 182n15
Vaquera-Vásquez, Santiago, 5, 6, 10, 213
Vargas, Roberto, 163, 354
*Vato* slang (barrio dude), 191
Vélez, Lupe, 170
Villanueva, Alma, 121. *See also Bloodroot*
Villanueva, Tino, 66n1, 121, 173, 193. *See
also Chicanos: antología histórica y
literaria*
Viramontes, Helena María, 131. *See also
Under the Feet of Jesus*
"Visión Tropical", 39, 40. *See also* Ruiz, Tony
visual literacy, 291, 292, 294, 312
Vogelsang, Arthur, 70
*Voices of Resistance: Interdisciplinary
Approaches to Chican@ Children's
Literature*, 269
*Vórtice* (magazine), 366

*The Wal-mart Effect*, 49. *See also* Fishman,
Charles
Warhol, Andy, 320, 364
Wauchope, Robert, 134n3. *See also Hand-
book of Middle American Indians*

"wetback", 31. *See also mojado*
Whitehead, Neil, 106. *See also Ethnopor-
nography: Sexuality, Colonialism, and
Archival Knowledge*
Whitman, Walt, 162, 165, 200, 201. *See
also Leaves of Grass*
Whitmanian poetics, 73
*Writing Culture: The Poetics and Politics
of Ethnography*, 113n8. *See also* Clif-
ford, James; George, E. Marcus
*The Writing of the Disaster*, 79. *See also*
Blanchott, Maurice

X, Malcolm, 13
*XCP Cross Cultural Poetics*, 76, 77, 89n3

Yáñez, René, 182n9
Ybarra-Frausto, Tomás, 9, 216, 265n5
young adult fiction, 270, 271, 370

Zamora, Bernice, 66n1
Zapata, Emiliano, 170
Zedillo, Ernesto, 148, 170
Zen Buddhism, 29, 34, 201, 210
Zen humor, 210
*Zenjose: Scenarios*, 15
Zepeda-Millán, Chris, 157n5
Zeretsky, Eli, 61
Zeta-Acosta, Oscar, 13
Zócalo, 151